Agriculture
and Economic Survival

Agriculture and Economic Survival

The Role of Agriculture in Ecuador's Development

EDITED BY

Morris D. Whitaker and Dale Colyer

Westview Press
BOULDER • SAN FRANCISCO • OXFORD

Westview Special Studies in Social, Political, and Economic Development

This Westview softcover edition is printed on acid-free paper and bound in library-quality, coated covers that carry the highest rating of the National Association of State Textbook Administrators, in consultation with the Association of American Publishers and the Book Manufacturers' Institute.

Copyright © 1990 by Westview Press, Inc.

Published in 1990 in the United States of America by Westview Press, Inc., 5500 Central Avenue, Boulder, Colorado 80301, and in the United Kingdom by Westview Press, 36 Lonsdale Road, Summertown, Oxford OX2 7EW

Library of Congress Cataloging-in-Publication Data
Agriculture and economic survival : the role of agriculture in
  Ecuador's development / edited by Morris D. Whitaker and Dale
  Colyer.
    p. cm. — (Westview special studies in social, political, and
economic development)
  Includes bibliographical references and index.
  ISBN 0-8133-8118-5
  1. Agriculture—Economic aspects—Ecuador. 2. Agriculture and
state—Ecuador. I. Whitaker, Morris D. II. Colyer, Dale.
III. Series.
HD1887.A38   1990
338.1′09866—dc20
                                                              90-44808
                                                                   CIP

Printed and bound in the United States of America

The paper used in this publication meets the requirements
of the American National Standard for Permanence of Paper
for Printed Library Materials Z39.48-1984.

10   9   8   7   6   5   4   3   2   1

CONTENTS

viii

TABLES

FIGURES

PREFACE

The two editors served as agricultural policy advisors to the U.S. Agency for International Development Mission in Ecuador from 1984 to 1990 while on loan from and with the support of Utah State University and West Virginia University. This book is an outgrowth of their experiences. During those years the Agricultural Sector Reorientation Project and two policy analysis agencies were established: the Ministry of Agriculture's Policy Analysis Unit and the Agricultural Policy Institute (IDEA), a non-profit foundation. As part of the continuing policy analysis effort, work on a detailed study of Ecuador's agricultural sector began in February 1988 under the direction of the senior editor. A series of 21 working papers was prepared, revised and integrated into an agricultural sector assessment. This book is based on that report with approval of the Mission.

The working papers were built on a myriad of studies, many developed under the sector reorientation project, plus original analyses from secondary and primary data. There are numerous published and unpublished studies, reports, theses and documents about economic and agricultural development in Ecuador. The approach employed was to review and interpret these studies and to synthesize and incorporate their findings into the appraisal. The more important and germane studies are cited in the references; others are covered in an annotated bibliography by the co-editor.

This evaluation of Ecuador's agricultural sector addresses critical issues that must be faced if the country is to fully benefit from its superb agricultural potential. It investigates the role of agriculture in economic development, identifies constraints to progress and makes recommendations for faster growth and development. The conceptual foundation that undergirds the assessment comprises three interrelated elements: the induced innovation model of agricultural development, the pervasive effect of macroeconomic polices on agricultural growth, and the emergence of a new global economic order. Specific analyses and studies of the agricultural sector include: an overview of theoretical constructs; macroeconomic and sectoral policies; agricultural growth, trade and nutrition; renewable natural resources; population growth and the labor market; the production milieu and factor use; public irrigation projects; marketing; credit; social institutions and gender; public sector institutions; and the human capital and science base.

The conclusion is that the principal challenge facing Ecuador's economy is to make the transition from a low-productivity agriculture primarily dependent on natural resources to a highly productive sector based on science and investment in human capital. The specific analyses tend to reveal the same major constraints: discriminatory macroeconomic policies that subsidize industry, home goods and urban people at the expense of agriculture, tradeables and rural people; and major deficiencies in the human capital and science base resulting in low agricultural productivity. An outward-oriented growth strategy is proposed with two principal recommendations: (1) rationalize the inward-oriented macroeconomic policy matrix by reducing and eliminating trade barriers, reducing government expenditures and deficits, unfettering capital markets and unifying the exchange rate; and (2) greatly strengthen the science base for agriculture by making research autonomous; paying competitive salaries for scientists; greatly increasing research funding; consolidating extension services, technical high schools and university faculties; linking the various components of the science base both nationally and internationally; and improving rural education.

Ecuador is an Andean country and as such it shares many of the difficulties of its neighbors, Colombia and Peru. However, it has been able to avoid many of the problems those countries face with their intertwined guerilla movements and drug trafficking. With the discovery of oil in its eastern Amazonian area, Ecuador leaped from its status as one of the poorest South American countries to middle income status during the 1970s, but falling oil prices, natural disasters and the emergence of the international debt dilemma have produced economic crises in the 1980s.

The Ecuadorian economy has been stagnant for nearly a decade, with per capita output lower in 1989 than in 1980. The country is heavily dependent on petroleum exports but is expected to become a net importer of petroleum products shortly after 2000. As petroleum reserves become increasingly exhausted, dependence on agriculture as the principal economic sector will grow. But if agriculture is to make its maximum and sustained contributions to Ecuador's economy, the recommendations of this evaluation must be implemented expeditiously. Thus, one purpose of this book is to focus debate and discussion that will lead to the development of improved policies for agricultural development.

We are indebted to Mr. Frank Almaguer, Director of USAID/Ecuador, Mr. Richard Peters, Chief of the Office of Agriculture and Natural Resources and Ing. Nepatalí Bonifaz of IDEA for financial support as well as conceptual contributions to the effort. We also are grateful to Joe Goodwin, former agricultural officer in USAID/Ecuador, who helped conceptualize the sector reorientation project and the need for a sector assessment. The strong support of four successive Ecuadorian Ministers of Agriculture, Marcel Laniado de Wind, Marcos Espinel, Enrique Delgado and Mario Jalil, was crucial for carrying out essential policy analyses and dialogue.

We also are appreciative of the insights we gained about Ecuadorian agriculture from many discussions with Jorge Soria, IDEA; David Franklin and Grant Scobie, Sigma One Corporation; and Jaime Flores, José Orellana, Fernando Ortiz, Marco Peñaherrera and Scott Smith, of USAID. We also thank Ramiro Lopez and Alfonso Moscoso who contributed insights about the realities of farming in Ecuador. Important additional contributions were made by the following colleagues who reviewed drafts of the manuscript and provided access to data: Alfonso Mosquera, ANCO; Manuel Jaramillo, Catholic University; Victor Mendoza and Guillermo Ojeda, CEDEGE; Patricio Leon, Central Bank; Patricio Toledo, CLIRSEN; Nelson Toledo, DINAF; Manuel Durini, ENDESA; Jorge Chang, Francisco Muñoz, Tomas Dousdebes, Bolívar Navas and Jorge Uquillas, FUNDAGRO; Pablo de la Torre, IDEA; Carlos Criollo, INEC; Jorge Sotomayor, Arturo Orquera and César Sarmiento, INERHI; Juan Vega, INIAP; Carlos Basantes, MAG/Marketing; Mario Lalama, Mónica Acosta and Mauricio Cuesta, MAG/PAU; Franklin Maiguashca, Office of the President; Ralph Franklin, Rigoberto Stewart, Kelly Harrison and Lloyd Brown, Sigma One Corporation; Patricio Izurieta, Ricardo Izurieta, Galo Izurieta, Antonio Teran, Nícolas Guillen and Ignácio Pérez, the private agricultural sector; and William Goodman, Guillermo Jauaregui, Fausto Maldonado, Patricio Maldonado, Robert Mobray, David Nelson, and Bambi Arellano, USAID. We express appreciation to the large number of other people who provided information and contributed in other ways to this endeavor.

Finally, we express our heartfelt thanks to Cecilia Ortiz, who served as research assistant and computer specialist. This book could not have been completed without her highly professional work and loyal service. We also thank Teresa Santelí S. for similar dedicated assistance during the early phases of the sector assessment.

The findings, conclusions and recommendations plus any errors are the responsibility of the authors and do not necessarily represent the positions of the U.S. Agency for International Development or of the Government of Ecuador.

ACRONYMS

AIMA Wood Industry Association, Asociación de Industriales Madereros.

AFABA Feed Manufacturers Association, Asociación de Fabricantes de Alimentos Balanceados.

ANCO National Association of Sheep Growers, Asociación Nacional de Criadores de Ovejas.

APPY Association of Producers and Processors of Cassava, Asociación de Productores y Procesadores de Yuca.

ASA Agricultural Service Agency, Agencia de Servicios Agropecuarios.

BCE Central Bank of Ecuador, Banco Central del Ecuador.

BNF National Development Bank, Banco Nacional de Fomento.

CAF Andean Development Corporation, Corporación Andina de Fomento.

CAME Ecuadorian Agrarian Military Draft, Conscripción Agraria Militar Ecuatoriana.

CARE Cooperative for American Relief Everywhere, Cooperativa Americana para Ayuda Mundial.

CEA Center for Studies and Analysis, Centro de Estudios y Análisis.

CEAS Ecuadorian Center for Social Action, Centro Ecuatoriano de Acción Social.

CEDEGE Study Commission for the Development of the Guayas River Basin, Comisión de Estudios para el Desarrollo de la Cuenca del Río Guayas.

CEDIG Ecuadorian Center for Geographic Research, Centro Ecuatoriano de Investigación Geográfica.

CELADE Latin American Demographic Center, Centro Latinoamericano de Demografía.

CENDES Center for Industrial Development, Centro de Desarrollo Industrial.

CEPAL Economic Commission for Latin America, Comisión Económica para América Latina (U.N.).

CEPLAES Planning and Studies Center, Centro de Planificación y Estudios.

CESA Ecuadorian Center for Agricultural Services, Centro Ecuatoriano de Servicios Agrícolas.

CFN National Finance Corporation, Corporación Financiera Nacional.

CGIAR Consultative Group on International Agricultural Research, Grupo Consultivo para la Investigación Agrícola Internacional.

CIAT International Center for Tropical Agriculture, Centro Internacional de Agricultura Tropical (CGIAR).

CIM Interamerican Commission on Women, Comisión Interamericana de Mujeres (MAG).

CIP International Potato Center, Centro Internacional de la Papa (CGIAR).

CLIRSEN Center for the Survey of Natural Resources by Remote Sensing, Centro de Levantamientos Integrados de Recursos Naturales por Sensores Remotos.

CONACYT National Council on Science and Technology, Consejo Nacional de Ciencia y Tecnología.

CONADE National Development Council, Consejo Nacional de Desarrollo.

CONFCA National Council of Agricultural Science Faculties, Consejo Nacional de Facultades de Ciencias Agropecuarias.

CONUEP National Council of Universities and Polytechnic Schools, Consejo Nacional de Universidades y Escuelas Politécnicas.

CORDES Corporation for Development Studies, Corporación de Estudios para el Desarrollo.

CREA Center for the Economic Recovery of Azuay, Cañar and Morona-Santiago, Centro de Reconversión Económico del Azuay, Cañar y Morona Santiago (MAG).

CRM Center for the Rehabilitation of Manabi, Centro de Rehabilitación de Manabí (MAG).

CRS Catholic Relief Services, Servicios Católicos de Ayuda.

DAC Development Assistance Committee, Comité para la Ayuda al Desarrollo (OECD).

DINACONTES National Directorate for the Control of Narcotics, División Nacional Contra el Tráfico Ilícito de Estupefacientes.

DINAF National Forestry Directorate, Dirección Nacional Forestal (MAG).

EAP Economically Active Population, Población Economicamente Activa.

EMSEMILLAS National Seed Company, Empresa Mixta de Semillas.

EMBRAPA Brazilian Public Corporation for Agricultural Research, Empresa Brasileña de Investigación Agropecuaria.

ENAC National Agricultural Storage and Marketing Company, Empresa Nacional de Almacenamiento y Comercialización (MAG).

ENPROVIT National Company for Basic Products, Empresa Nacional de Productos Vitales (MAG).

FAO Food and Agriculture Organization, Organización para la Agricultura y la Alimentación (U.N.).

FENACOMI National Federation of Retail Merchants, Federación Nacional de Comerciantes Minoristas.

FERTISA Ecuadorian Fertilizer Company, Fertilizantes Ecuatorianos, Compañía de Empresa Mixta.

FIDA International Fund for Agricultural Development, Fondo Internacional de Desarrollo Agrícola.

FODERUMA Fund for Marginal Rural Development, Fondo de Desarrollo Rural Marginal (BCE).

FONARYD National Fund for Irrigation and Drainage, Fondo Nacional para Riego y Drenaje.

FUNDAGRO Foundation for Agricultural Development, Fundación para el Desarrollo Agropecuario.

GDP Gross Domestic Product, Producto Interno Bruto.

GOE Government of Ecuador, Gobierno del Ecuador.

GTZ Agency for Technical Cooperation, Sociedad para Cooperación Técnica (West Germany).

ICNND Interdepartmental Committee on Nutrition for National Defense, Comité Interdepartamental de Nutrición para la Defensa Nacional.

IDA International Development Association, Asociación Internacional para el Desarrollo (World Bank).

IDB Inter-American Development Bank, Banco Interamericano de Desarrollo.

IDEA Agricultural Policy Institute, Instituto de Estratégias Agropecuarias.

ICDR International Center for Development Research, Centro Internacional para la Investigación de Desarrollo (Canada).

IERAC Ecuadorian Institute for Agrarian Reform and Colonization, Instituto Ecuatoriano de Reforma Agraria y Colonización (MAG).

IETEL   Ecuadorian Institute of Telecommunications, Instituto Ecuatoriano de Telecomunicaciones.

IFPRI   International Food Policy Research Institute, Instituto de Investigación de Política Alimentaria Internacional (CGIAR).

IGM   Military Geographic Institute, Instituto Geográfico Militar.

IICA   Interamerican Institute for Agriculture Cooperation, Instituto Interamericano de Cooperación para la Agricultura (OAS).

IMF   International Monetary Fund, Fondo Monetario Internacional.

INAMHI   National Institute of Meteorology and Hydrology, Instituto Nacional de Metereología e Hidrología.

INCAP   Nutrition Institute of Central America and Panama, Instituto de Nutrición de Centro América y Panamá.

INCRAE   Institute for the Colonization of the Amazon Region, Instituto Nacional de Colonización de la Región Amazónica Ecuatoriana.

INEC National Institute of Statistics and Census, Instituto Nacional de Estadísticas y Censos.

INECEL   Ecuadorian Electrification Institute, Instituto Ecuatoriano de Electrificación.

INEM   National Employment Institute, Instituto Nacional de Empleo.

INERHI   Ecuadorian Institute of Water Resources, Instituto Ecuatoriano de Recursos Hidráulicos (MAG).

INIAP   National Institute of Agricultural Research, Instituto Nacional de Investigaciones Agropecuarias (MAG).

ININMS   National Institute for Nutritional Research and Social Medicine, Instituto Nacional de Investigación Nutricional y Medicina Social (MSP).

INNE   Ecuadorian National Institute of Nutrition, Instituto Nacional de Nutrición del Ecuador (predecessor of ININMS).

IRRI   International Rice Research Institute, Centro Internacional de Investigación del Arroz (CGIAR).

ISNAR   International Service for National Agricultural Research, Servicio Internacional para la Investigación Agrícola Nacional (CGIAR).

ISS   Institute of Social Studies, Instituto de Estudios Sociales (Holland).

JUNAPLA   National Planning Commission, Junta Nacional de Planificación (predecessor of CONADE).

MAG   Ministry of Agriculture, Ministerio de Agricultura y Ganadería.

MBS   Ministry of Social Welfare, Ministerio de Bienestar Social.

MEC   Ministry of Education and Culture, Ministerio de Educación y Cultura.

MICEI   Ministry of Industry, Commerce and Integration, Ministerio de Industrias, Comercio y Integración (predecessor of MICIP).

MICIP   Ministry of Industry and Commerce, Ministerio de Industrias, Comercio, Integración y Pesca.

MOP   Ministry of Public Works, Ministerio de Obras Públicas.

OAS   Organization of American States, Organización de Estados Americanos.

OECD   Organization for Economic Cooperation and Development, Organización para el Desarrollo y la Cooperación Economica.

ORSTOM   Office of Overseas Science and Technology Research, Office de Recherche Scientifique et Technique d'Outre-Mer (France).

PAU   Policy Analysis Unit, Unidad de Análisis de Políticas (MAG).

PETROECUADOR   Ecuador Petroleum Company, Petroleos del Ecuador (successor agency of CEPE).

PIP Product Research Program, Programa de Investigación en Producción (INIAP).

PREALC Regional Employment Program for Latin America and the Caribbean, Programa Regional del Empleo para América Latina y el Caribe (U.N.).

PREDESUR Regional Program for the Development of Southern Ecuador, Programa Regional para el Desarrollo del Sur (MAG).

PROFOGAN Livestock Development Project, Proyecto de Fomento Ganadero.

PRONAMEC National Program for Agricultural Mechanization, Programa Nacional de Mecanización Agrícola (MAG).

PRONAREG National Program for Agrarian Regionalization, Programa Nacional de Regionalización Agraria (MAG).

PROTECA Program for the Development of Agricultural Technology, Programa de Desarrollo Tecnológico Agropecuario (MAG).

PVO Private Voluntary Organization, Organización Privada Voluntaria.

REE Research, Education and Extension, Investigación, Educación y Extensión.

RRA Rapid Rural Appraisal, Investigación Rural Rápida.

RTTS Rural Technology Transfer System, Sistema para la Transferencia de Tecnología Rural (USAID).

SCIA Interamerican Cooperative Agricultural Service, Servicio Cooperativo Interamericano de Agricultura.

SEAN National System of Agricultural Statistics, Sistema Estadístico Agropecuario Nacional (INEC).

SEDRI Subsecretariat of Integrated Rural Development, Subsecretaría de Desarrollo Rural Integral (MBS).

TGC Tribunal of Constitutional Guarantees, Tribunal de Garantías Constitucionales.

TSE Supreme Electoral Tribunal, Tribunal Supremo Electoral.

UAPPY Union of Cassava Producer and Processor Associations, Unión de Asociaciones de Productores y Procesadores de Yuca.

UNDP U.N. Development Program, Programa de Desarrollo de las Naciones Unidas.

UNFPA U.N. Fund for Population Activities, Fondo para las Actividades Poblacionales de las Naciones Unidas.

USAID U.S. Agency for International Development, Agencia para el Desarrollo Internacional de los Estados Unidos.

USDA U.S. Department of Agriculture, Departamento de Agricultura de los Estados Unidos.

WFP World Food Program, Programa Mundial de Alimentos (U.N.).

WHO World Health Organization, Organización Mundial de la Salud.

ABOUT THE AUTHORS

Morris D. Whitaker is Professor of Economics and Director of International Programs at Utah State University (USU). He served as Agricultural Policy Advisor to USAID/Ecuador (1987-1990), was previously Director of International Programs at USU (1982-1987), was a member of the U.S. Presidential Task Force to Ecuador (1984), was Senior Advisor to the Director of the U.S. Agency for International Development (1981-1982) and Deputy Director of the Staff of the Board for International Food and Development (1980-1982), served as policy advisor to the Bolivian Ministry of Agriculture (1973-1976), and worked in Brazil with the Getulio Vargas Foundation (1967-1969). Dr. Whitaker has had numerous consulting assignments in Latin America, Asia, the Near East and Africa. He received his Ph.D. in Agricultural Economics from Purdue University in 1970.

Dale Colyer is Professor of Agricultural Economics, West Virginia University. He was Agricultural Policy Advisor to USAID/Ecuador (1984-1987), served as Director of the Division of Resource Management at West Virginia University (1978-1983), was on the faculty in agricultural economics at the University of Missouri (1963-1970), was a Fulbright Lecturer in Rosario, Argentina (1968), and was Research Assistant at the Federal Reserve Bank of Kansas City (1958-1960). Dr. Colyer has had short term consultancies in Ecuador, Benin and Brazil. He received his Ph.D. in Agricultural Economics from the University of Wisconsin in 1963.

Jaime Alzamora is Agricultural Economist and Research Associate, U.S. Agency for International Development, Ecuador. He received his M.Sc. from Virginia Polytechnic Institute in 1970.

Rae Lesser Blumberg is Associate Professor of Rural Sociology, University of California, San Diego. Her Ph.D. is from Northwestern University, 1970.

Duty Greene is Senior Policy Advisor, Ministry of Agriculture, Ecuador, and Agricultural Economist, Sigma One Corporation, Research Park Triangle, North Carolina. His Ph.D. is from the University of Minnesota, 1988.

Hugo Ramos is Agricultural Economist, Agricultural Policy Institute, Ecuador. His Ph.D. is from Michigan State University, 1989.

Harold Riley is Professor Emeritus of Agricultural Economics, Michigan State University. His Ph.D. is from Michigan State University, 1954.

Lindon Robison is Professor of Agricultural Economics, Michigan State University. His Ph.D. is from Texas A & M University, 1975.

Douglas Southgate is Associate Professor of Agricultural Economics, Ohio State University. His Ph.D. is from the University of Wisconsin, 1980.

David Tschirley is Agricultural Economist, Agricultural Policy Institute, Ecuador, and Assistant Professor of Agricultural Economics, Michigan State University. His Ph.D. is from Michigan State University, 1989.

1

AGRICULTURE

AND ECONOMIC GROWTH

Morris D. Whitaker

Economic growth and development in any modern society are concerned fundamentally and primarily with improving the well-being of people. One major objective is to increase the production of goods and services as rapidly as possible as the basis for improving the quality of life and standard of living. This goal reflects the economic behavior of *Homo sapiens* from a wide variety of political and cultural backgrounds around the world. While this concept is fundamentally materialistic, the collective aspirations of people, expressed through the political process, universally encompass a concern for adequate nutrition, housing, clothing, health care, education, arts and other basic human needs. Concomitantly, there is a universal tendency to value expanded opportunities for the individual and freedom of choice in consumption and production activities. The standard measure used to compare economic progress among nations is the rate of growth in the value of goods and services produced in the economy, expressed in constant prices (real gross domestic product or GDP). The rate of growth in real GDP is compared with the rate of growth of the population to determine if people are, on average, better off.

The second major objective of growth and development in today's world is to distribute production more equitably. Concentration of income and wealth among a small share of the population usually is not sustainable politically. Consequently, more egalitarian sharing of the fruits of economic progress is another important goal of development among countries of all ideological persuasions. This concern often is expressed by strong emphasis on increasing employment opportunities for the growing labor force, which usually is concentrated among lower-income masses, especially in developing countries. It also is expressed in progressive tax systems which redistribute income in favor of the poor and in social welfare programs which transfer resources to meet the basic human needs of poor people. While progressive tax systems and welfare programs tend to be the domain of the developed world, the developing nations are increasingly adopting these mechanisms. Thus, measures of the distribution of income and wealth are other important indices, along with per capita GDP, of achievement of the objectives of economic growth and development.

The role of agriculture in overall economic growth and development has not been well understood, until recently, either by economists, or by economic planners and policymakers in developing countries. Agriculture was consigned to a secondary, policymakers in developing countries. Agriculture was consigned to a secondary, poorly defined role in most of the formal models of economic development that have been in favor during the last few decades. Policymakers compounded the errors inherent in these flawed models as they attempted to make inadequate economic premises fit with political expediency.

A substantial body of new theoretical and empirical knowledge about the role of agriculture in economic development has been produced by agricultural and developmental economists, especially during the last two decades. Policymakers in many developing countries have utilized this new knowledge, albeit with a lag of perhaps a decade or more, as a basis for modifying and improving economic development policies. These countries are in various stages of transition away from the development models of the past and toward more enlightened policy matrices for economic growth which recognize and exploit the potential contributions of agriculture. However, several Latin American countries, including Ecuador, still are following outmoded development models which discriminate against agriculture. As a consequence their economic growth is constrained well below the possible and their distribution of income may be more unequal.

This chapter provides a conceptual foundation for the study of agriculture and its role in Ecuador's economic development presented in the following chapters. The following sections review and analyze: several general economic development models that were the basis for Ecuador's post World War II development strategy and their failure to explain how agriculture is to produce a surplus to fuel the development process; the concept of the agricultural surplus; and the body of more recent, theoretical and empirical findings about the role of agriculture in economic development, the necessary conditions for producing the surplus and the implications of the emerging world economy for developed and developing nations.

Development Models of the Past[1]

Industrialization was proposed as the principal basis for economic development by development economists in the early 1950s. Such a position was rooted intellectually in the dual-sector models and growth-stage models of economic development. It also was based on the dependency theories of economic development advanced about the same time.

Dual-Sector and Growth-Stage Models

Dual-sector models emphasize the dichotomy between the traditional and modern sectors of the economy and suggest that economic growth must be based on development of a modern industrial sector. Dual-sector models can be classified as static or dynamic. The static model was first elaborated by Boeke. Dynamic models are based on the classic article by Lewis and include those developed by Ranis and Fei, and Jorgenson (1961, 1966).

Stage theories of economic growth suggest that the economy moves by steps from a traditional agrarian structure characterized by low productivity to an industrialized state with commercialized agriculture and high productivity. Growth-stage theories can be divided into two schools of thought, structural transformation and leading sectors. The structural transformation school stressed the shift from primary to secondary and tertiary activities as development occurred (Clark). The "leading sectors" school developed later and is credited mainly to Rostow.[2]

The Rostow, Ranis and Fei and Jorgenson models emphasize development of a modern industrial sector in a closed economy. All identify the generation of a surplus as an explicit and initial role for agriculture in promoting general economic development. Both Ranis and Fei and Jorgenson clearly recognize that increases in agricultural productivity will be necessary in order to produce a sustained surplus to drive modernization of the industrial sector.

None of the models adequately explains how the agricultural surplus is to be generated. Indeed, they devote only limited attention to the agricultural surplus, although it is critical to their central thesis. Both Ranis and Fei and Jorgenson argue that agricultural productivity can be increased sufficiently to produce a sustained agricultural surplus through land improvements and other labor-intensive capital formation. In fact, it is now well known that a sustained process of technical change in agriculture requires substantial investments, especially in human capital, and a relatively long gestation period (Hayami and Ruttan 1985, Chapters 5 and 6). A second shortcoming of the models is the assumption that all the agricultural surplus is available for development of the industrial sector. In fact, demand for a whole series of marketing services such as transportation, storage, wholesaling and retailing increases substantially as resources flow from the agricultural to the emerging industrial sector. This occurs because the income elasticity of demand for such services tends to be relatively high. Thus, a substantial portion of the agricultural surplus is drawn off to support development of the services sector which is ignored in the dual-sector and growth-stage models.

A third weakness, explicit in the modern dual-sector models and implicit in the growth-stage models, is the assumption that the industrial sector will generate sufficient new, higher-paying jobs to accommodate labor released from the rural sector. The capital-intensive nature of industrialization generally has limited creation of jobs. Also, industry generally demands skilled labor and rural labor largely is unskilled. Consequently, many migrants are forced to seek employment in the informal service sector.

Dependency Models

The structuralist model of economic development has been the principal conceptual basis for Ecuador's economic development policy since the late 1950s (see Chapter 2). The model was formulated almost simultaneously but independently by Hans Singer and Raul Prebisch (1950). Prebisch (1959, 1963) and his colleagues at the U.N. Economic Commission for Latin America (CEPAL) developed the theory most completely. Their model focuses on a dependency relationship between developing and developed countries. They argued that there is a tendency for the external terms of trade to turn against developing countries that export primary goods, relative to developed countries that export manufactured goods. This occurs because of low income elasticities of demand in the developed countries for primary goods and high income elasticities for industrial products in the peripheral countries. They also argued that primary products had to compete in competitive markets while industrial products were sold in monopolistic markets. Finally, they suggested that productivity growth is much slower in production of primary goods in the periphery than for industrial goods in the center. They concluded that the potential for rapid and sustained economic growth from exports of agricultural products was nil. Their principal policy prescription was for developing countries to promote domestic production of imported industrial products as a much more viable development model. The Prebisch-CEPAL structuralist model of development attracted considerable attention, especially in Latin America, where it has been followed almost dogmatically. Prebisch (1981) has since modified his views about import substitution.

Other dependency models also are relevant to Ecuador because they tend to be identified with and reinforce the policy implications of the structuralist model. The neo-Marxian dependency model, developed about the same time as the structuralist model, also focuses on the economic relationship between the developed center and the underdeveloped periphery (Baran).[3] It argues that the developed center extracts resources from developing countries of the periphery as they become integrated into the world economy. In this view, exportation of advanced technologies from the center results in the development of a coalition in the periphery of newer industrial-commercial interests with the traditional, landed class. This new power group controls the economic and political system and the majority of rural and urban workers are isolated and oppressed.

DeJanvry (1975, 1981) has proposed a dependency model of generalized rural poverty and agricultural development in Latin America along the general lines of the neo-Marxian dependency model. He conceptualizes three levels of exploitation that result in marginalization of the rural poor: (a) the center exploits the periphery through trade of industrial goods for raw materials, *a la* the structuralist model; (b) the emerging industrial-commercial sector of the periphery exploits the subsistence sector and laborers in agriculture; and (c) landlords exploit subsistence farmers and laborers. He argues that farmers are increasingly marginalized by the process of modernization and incorporation in the market economy. He also argues that a coalition of industrial interests and landlords control the political and economic power and conspire to exploit the rural poor.

The DeJanvry model has been criticized on several grounds (Schuh 1984): there is serious doubt that the terms of trade has deteriorated[4]; the labor theory of value, which DeJanvry implicitly assumes, has been generally and widely discredited; trade has evolved principally between the center countries, not between the center and the periphery, which pattern raises serious questions about the predictive power of the model; the substantial political power of urban wage groups throughout Latin America vis-à-vis DeJanvry's industrial-agricultural elite is ignored; the large masses of rural workers are unskilled and have little value to the industrial sector, which requires highly skilled workers; the foreign exchange constraint was not imposed from abroad but was internally generated by a policy matrix that subsidized import-substitution industrialization and neglected the traditional export sector during a period when world trade was growing rapidly; the lag in technological development of the periphery was largely self-imposed and not the result of collusion among the center countries which have had a high degree of competition in research and development; labor services can be made more inexpensive by increasing labor productivity which would have been in the interest of DeJanvry's supposed industrial-agricultural coalition; and high rates of population growth, which explain much of the lag in per capita income of the periphery, are treated superficially. Perhaps the most serious weakness of the DeJanvry model is its failure to clearly specify policies for modernizing agriculture and integrating marginalized rural people into the economy.

The principal conclusion of the dependency models is that rapid and sustained economic growth is possible only by constraining commerce with the center and focusing on development of a modern industrial sector based on internal markets.

Notwithstanding the serious weaknesses of the various models discussed above they have contributed to a better understanding of the development process. Dependency theories focus on trade as one of the important sources of economic growth and development. They also clarify that social and institutional structures are important determinants of the distribution of the gains from trade and of overall social welfare occasioned by trade. These are important factors which the dual sector and growth stage models ignored. The dual sector models provide substantial insight into the interrelationships between the traditional and modern sectors of the economy and especially intersectoral labor markets. They also correctly identify the critical role of the agricultural surplus in fomenting overall economic development. The dependency models failed to address these important elements of the development process. While the various theoretical constructs discussed above each have enhanced understanding, they failed to identify appropriate policies for more rapid and sustained agricultural and economic growth. This failure is due mainly to their simplistic natures and the lack of empirical foundation for many of their questionable assumptions.

Ensuing Strategies and Results

The synthesis of growth-stage, dual-sector, structuralist and neo-Marxian models provided a foundation for broad-based political support for autonomous, internally-focused growth strategies throughout Latin America and much of the developing world for most of the period since World War II. The principal feature of such strategies has been the development of a highly protected, modern industrial sector to produce previously imported consumer durables for the internal market. A second feature has been the isolation of the economy from international economic forces with reliance on growth from expansion of internal markets. A third generalized feature has been the socialist orientation of ambitious welfare and labor legislation that attempts to assure the well-being of poor and disadvantaged groups. Such strategies generally have ignored and depreciated the role of agriculture and tradeables as a basis for more rapid growth because of the weaknesses and shortcomings of the intellectual abstractions underlying these strategies.

Several Latin American countries which adopted import-substitution industrialization in the 1950s had experienced disappointing results from this development model by the mid-1960s (Hirschman). Stagnation occurred as import-substitution opportunities were exhausted and internal markets saturated. Employment generation also was much lower than expected despite initial rapid growth.[5] Subsequently, these countries modified their development policies and have moved toward externally-oriented growth strategies with much greater reliance on agriculture.

Ecuador has followed this general pattern but has lagged well behind other Latin American countries in introducing necessary policy reforms. Macroeconomic policies improved during the 1980s and significant reforms were proposed in early 1990 for implementation during 1990-1993. However, the country still employs an inward-oriented development strategy based on import-substitution industrialization as its primary development model at the beginning of the 1990s, with significant political opposition to the proposed reforms. As a consequence, Ecuador's agricultural development and economic growth continue to be constrained, as agriculture still is taxed to subsidize the industrialization process and urban people (see Chapter 2).

Ecuador's agricultural sector could have and can yet play a much greater role in more rapid, sustained and equitable economic growth and development. The next section briefly reviews the role of agriculture in the development process and the nature of the agricultural surplus. Then the necessary and sufficient conditions for producing a sustained surplus are set forth in the light of new conceptual and empirical knowledge about agriculture's role in economic development.

The Agricultural Surplus

Development of a modern agricultural sector capable of contributing to overall economic growth is a dynamic process whereby the efficiency with which food and fiber products are produced and marketed is increased. Public investment is essential to increase the productive capacity of the sector, to improve efficiency in product and factor markets, and to provide basic social services--especially effective education--if the sector is to be modernized. Provision of these public services induces increased private investments in production and marketing and in the host of service sector activities associated with them. As a consequence of such investments, the productivity of the agricultural sector increases and the intersectoral flows of products and factors is facilitated.

Sustained increases in productivity in the agricultural sector result in what economists have referred to as a "surplus" to facilitate development of the modern sector (Ranis and Fei; Jorgenson 1961, 1966; Nicholls). Increases in productivity cause the supply of agricultural commodities to increase faster than demand. Prices of food and fiber fall and the internal terms of trade (the price of agricultural products relative to nonfarm products) shifts against the agricultural sector.[6] The falling prices of agricultural products put pressure on owners of resources to shift them out of the sector and cause the real incomes of consumers to increase.

The agricultural surplus consists of two main components: (a) redundant resources in agriculture; and (b) increased real incomes. Both components are fundamental to the development process because they provide a source for shifting resources to the nonagricultural sector in support of general economic development, without reducing agricultural output.[7] However, if transfers of resources are to have maximum impact in the nonfarm sector, careful attention must be paid to rural people.[8] Labor is the most important factor of production in agriculture in developing countries but many rural people are illiterate and unskilled. If such people are to find more remunerative employment outside agriculture and the informal sector in urban areas they must be provided with marketable skills. Also, careful attention must be given to improving the efficiency of intersectoral labor markets.

Redundant resources result from decreasing prices of agricultural goods and tend to become relatively more valuable in the nonfarm sector than in agriculture. Owners of such resources must seek alternative employment outside agriculture if they are to earn the same return as before the sustained technical changes began. Subsequent resource transfers facilitated by public investments (such as education) lead to increased levels of production in the economy. The surplus derived from redundant resources may be viewed as the increase in product value that can be obtained if labor and other resources are utilized in their best alternative uses outside agriculture.

Increases in real income, the second component of the agricultural surplus, tend to be realized in both urban and rural areas. In urban areas, increases in real income result only from decreases in the price of agricultural products. Since the demand for these products tends to be price inelastic, expenditures decrease as prices fall. The savings occasioned by reduced agricultural prices also may be viewed as an increase in the real income of urban consumers. Since agricultural products are the most important wage good for the majority of urban consumers in a developing country, the increase in the real income of the average consumer can be substantial.[9] This increased income is available for purchase of wage and investment goods produced in the nonfarm sector and more desireable agricultural products. The result is an increase in demand and investment in those sectors, with increased markets and more rapid development.

In rural areas, decreases in the price of food and increases in productivity both affect real incomes. Just as in urban areas, decreases in the price of food tend to reduce the expenditures for food in rural areas and increase the real income of the rural consumer. Since rural consumers are almost always producers, however, their incomes are simultaneously being reduced by decreasing prices (induced by technical change). Thus, increases in income from decreased food costs tend to be offset by decreases in farm revenues. Technical changes, however, will cause costs of production to fall faster than farm revenues, especially for early innovators. The combined effect will result in increased real incomes for producers who adopt the cost-saving technologies. Others will be under pressure to seek alternative employment for their resources as falling revenues are likely to swamp the effects of lower food costs.

Increased incomes in the rural sector also can be invested or used to purchase consumption goods. The impact of such increases in real incomes can be significant in view of the large proportion of the population concentrated in the agricultural sectors of most developing countries. When combined with the increases in urban incomes, the increase in demand from falling food prices due to technical innovations in agriculture can be substantial. Rising real incomes in both rural and urban areas leads to broader and deeper national markets and contributes to the development of the services and industrial sectors.

The production of an agricultural surplus has three other implications for economic development. First, price decreases tend to shift the distribution of income in favor of the low-income masses, who normally constitute a majority of the population. This happens because low-income people spend a larger proportion of their income on food than the more well-to-do. Second, the nutrition of the population tends to improve as consumers gain access to foods with needed nutrients that were previously too expensive. The improved health of the population can lead to further increases in productivity and production. Third, products of the agricultural sector become more competitive in the world market with subsequent increases in exports, domestic production of previously imported products and increased foreign exchange earnings.

Most developing countries are characterized by a relatively large agricultural sector with low levels of productivity. The conclusion drawn here is that modernization of agriculture and production of a surplus in such countries can contribute substantially to an improved rate of economic growth and a more equitable distribution of income. As noted above, past development models and associated strategies generally have recognized the importance of agriculture and the agricultural surplus. They have failed, however to explain how such surpluses are generated.

What are the conditions for producing sustained increases in agricultural productivity and an agricultural surplus? The next section considers a body of new theoretical and empirical knowledge about agricultural development that addresses this question.

Generating a Sustained Surplus

A substantial body of new theoretical and empirical knowledge about agricultural growth and overall economic development has been developed during the last two decades.[10] This body of knowledge provides much better understanding of the nature of agricultural development and of the policy variables which affect modernization of the sector. It also contains a much clearer explanation of the importance of agriculture in fostering economic development. Increases in agricultural productivity and market incentives are identified as critical elements for generating an optimum rate of economic growth. Concurrent development of the various sectors of the economy, rather than dependence on a leading sector, also is recognized as necessary for rapid and sustained economic growth by most development scholars.

This section briefly reviews three major, interrelated elements of this new set of knowledge, including: (a) a theory of induced agricultural development proposed and refined by Hayami and Ruttan (1971, 1985) which focuses on technical and institutional change; (b) the effects of macroeconomic and sectoral policies on agriculture based on a substantial number of theoretical and empirical studies principally by South American economists (Valdés) and the World Bank (Krueger, Schiff and Valdés 1988); and (c) the implications of the emergence of an international economy for developed and developing countries (Schuh 1974, 1976, 1986 and 1987). These new theoretical constructs and empirical findings provide the principal conceptual bases for the analyses which follow in the rest of this study.

Induced Innovation in Agriculture

Yujiro Hayami and Vernon W. Ruttan (1971, 1985) have proposed a general theory of induced agricultural development, which builds on and extends the seminal work of Schultz. Their model of agricultural development is widely accepted and their book is considered a classic by agricultural economists (Johnson). Schultz, in what has come to be known as the "high-payoff input model" (Hayami and Ruttan 1985, pp. 59-62) hypothesized that poor farmers in developing countries allocate their meager resources efficiently and are constrained by traditional technologies and poverty. Consequently, little or no gains are to be had from reorganizing traditional factors of production. He further argued that agricultural technologies generally are highly location specific and cannot be readily transferred among countries. Schultz suggested that rapid increases in agricultural output can be obtained primarily from technical changes and utilization of more modern factors of production, which form part of the package of inputs necessary to adopt the improved technology.

The policy implications for agricultural development of the high-payoff input model are threefold: (a) development of a publicly supported science base for agriculture which can produce and extend flows of new technology; (b) production of modern inputs which incorporate and complement the new technical knowledge; and (c) education of farmers so that the new technical knowledge can be adopted and utilized. The various hypotheses of the high-payoff input model have been exhaustively tested and generally supported by a large number of empirical studies. Returns to investments in agricultural research, extension and education have been shown to be uniformly high in both developed and developing countries for a variety of individual crops and in aggregate (Evenson, Waggoner and Ruttan; Lockhead, Jamison and Lau; Huffman). Farmers of all economic classes around the world generally have been found to be efficient allocators of factors of production.[11] A significant literature about principles of organization and management of agricultural research, both nationally and internationally, has evolved (Arndt, Dalrymple and Ruttan; Pinstrup-Andersen; Ruttan). This latter body of knowledge strongly supports Schultze's intuitive premise that agricultural technologies are location specific and not easily transferred.

The high-payoff input model clearly has had a substantial impact on agricultural development strategies in many developing and developed countries around the world. The principal contribution of the model is the identification of specific investment targets for increasing agricultural productivity. The model, however, treats technical changes as exogenous and fails to explain how technical changes are induced, especially in the public sector.

The Hayami-Ruttan model of induced innovation in agriculture incorporates all the elements of the high-payoff input model but treats technical changes as endogenous to the sector. In their conceptualization, innovations occur in the public as well as the private sector in response to price signals from the product and factor markets. Furthermore, interactions occur between technical changes and institutions, with induced institutional innovations allowing individuals or groups to internalize returns from technical progress. Finally, in dynamic sequences of technical change and economic growth, technical progress that resolves one critical constraint often leads to another kind of bottleneck with a resultant induced innovation to resolve that bottleneck.[12]

The principal challenge of successful agricultural growth in the Hayami-Ruttan model is to attain an efficient path of technological change which saves the relatively scarce factor of production. In their model, technical changes permit substitution of abundant resources for those in scarce supply. If labor is the limiting resource in the development process then an efficient path of technical change must be labor-saving. Innovations are generally mechanical in this case and permit machines and capital to substitute for labor, thus increasing the use of land and raising the productivity of labor. In essence mechanical innovations permit abundant land to be substituted for scarce labor. If land is relatively limited and labor is in abundant supply, then innovations must save the scarce land. Chemical-biological innovations will permit various technical inputs (such as improved seeds and fertilizers) to substitute for the scarce land, thus increasing its productivity and the use of relatively abundant labor. Thus, chemical-biological innovations permit abundant labor to be substituted for scarce land.

In the induced innovation model of agricultural development, an efficient path of technical change reflects the original endowment of resources and changing relative prices of products and factors. Farmers seek technologies which save the scarce (expensive) factor and reduce their costs. They turn to both public research agencies for improved technologies and to the commercial-industrial sector for modern inputs which can substitute for the limiting factor. Public sector researchers are induced to work on the technological constraints and the private commercial-industrial sector to produce modern technical inputs which incorporate and complement new technical knowledge. This process results in what Hayami and Ruttan (1985 pp. 133-37) conceptualize as a meta-production function which permits the continuous and sustained substitution of new technical knowledge and inputs for the scarce factor of production.

The induced innovation model provides several new insights about agricultural growth and overall economic development. Perhaps most important is that transition from a natural resource-based to a science-based agriculture is the sine qua non of both agricultural and overall economic development. There are several policy implications associated with this finding: (a) substantial resources will be required to develop a viable system capable of producing, extending and adopting continuous flows of new technical knowledge because it is a very capital intensive process; (b) human capital at scientific, technical and general levels must comprise a significant part of the investment in the agricultural science base; (c) the public sector will have to undertake most of the investments in research because the efficient path of technical change for most developing countries is chemical-biological in nature and private investors generally cannot internalize the gains from such research; and (d) organization and management of the public science base for agriculture will be a major challenge and of critical importance to achieving more rapid growth, given the alternative, multiple paths of possible technical innovation.

The induced innovation model also confirms the generally held view among development economists that transfers of the agricultural surplus to the nonfarm sector are essential for higher rates of economic development. An equally important but seldom discussed implication is that how the nonfarm sector is developed with the agricultural surplus has a major, direct effect on the rate of economic growth. In the words of Hayami and Ruttan (1985 pp. 440-41):

> In many developing countries, the income streams generated in the agricultural sector have been used to purchase a nonviable industrial sector or a nonproductive military and administrative bureaucracy....The experience of the last several decades indicates that although it may be easy for poor countries to acquire an industrial sector that produces manufactured products that were formerly imported, it is much more difficult to purchase an industrial sector that is capable of making a sustained contribution to income streams comparable to those generated by the agricultural sector.

> If the intersector income transfers resulting from technical change in agriculture are to result in a cumulative contribution to economic growth, the new sectors purchased by these transfers...must be capable of producing the new industrial materials needed to sustain the process of agricultural development.

The policy implication is clear: economic development policies must recognize the interdependencies of the various productive sectors and exploit the comparative advantages of each, if the rate of economic growth is to be maximized.

A third key finding of the induced innovation model is the important role of market forces in inducing both technical and institutional change. Price distortions in product and factor markets resulting from government policies and interventions have limited the prospects for more rapid and sustained agricultural and general economic growth. These distortions have constrained opportunities in the public and private sector for technical changes and in many countries have constrained the possibility of moving onto an efficient path of technical change. The pricing system must reflect the actual scarcity of products and factors in allocation decisions of public and private sector officials if an efficient path of technical change is to be attained. The policy implications are clear: a more modern system of factor and product markets must be developed with government support for improved information and communication, grades and standards, and transportation and storage within and among principal economic sectors; and distortions and subsidies inherent in misguided public policies must be removed by adopting a more rational macroeconomic and sectoral policy matrix.

While the induced innovation model of agricultural development does recognize the negative effect on agriculture of overvalued exchange rates and price and interest rate controls, the effect of macroeconomic and sectoral policies is not formally incorporated into the model.

Macroeconomic and Sectoral Policies

There is a large and growing body of evidence that the macroeconomic and agricultural sector policy matrix utilized by many developing countries during the last few decades significantly constrained public and private investments in agriculture. These countries almost uniformly adopted policies to promote import-substitution industrialization and self-reliant growth. Principal macroeconomic policies included: overvalued exchange rates; protection of domestic industry through tariff and non-tariff barriers to trade; direct subsides to industry and commerce including tax exonerations and subsidized credit; and highly subsidized importations of capital equipment and intermediate goods.[13] Such countries simultaneously maintained a set of negative sectoral policies for agriculture including: price ceilings for most food and fiber products, which translated into lower producer prices; taxes on exports of primary agricultural products; export prohibitions; state interventions in product and factor markets; and taxes on imports of agricultural inputs in some cases. Finally, such countries also attempted to help agriculture by subsidizing credit and other inputs and through investments in irrigation, storage and transportation infrastructure; land reform and titling; and research, education and extension.

The World Bank has recently completed an exhaustive review of the effect of macroeconomic and sectoral policies on agriculture in 18 countries around the world for the period 1975-1984 (Krueger, Schiff and Valdés 1988). Included are Argentina, Brazil, Chile, Colombia, Ivory Coast, Dominican Republic, Egypt, Ghana, Republic of Korea, Malaysia, Morocco, Pakistan, Philippines, Portugal, Sri Lanka, Thailand, Turkey and Zambia. These countries represent a wide range of development and all the principal low-income regions of the world. Each country was studied independently by different researchers who utilized a common methodology to provide comparability.[14] Each study empirically measured the effect of direct, sector-specific policies (both negative and positive) and of indirect, economy-wide macroeconomic policies on agricultural incentives for principal exportable and importable agricultural products. The impact is measured relative to what prices would have been with a free-trade regime and no direct sectoral interventions (either positive or negative). The reference price is the border price for all tradeables, appropriately adjusted for various marketing costs.

The results indicate clearly that sectoral and macroeconomic policies have discriminated substantially against agriculture in almost all the countries studied. The net effect of direct, positive and negative sectoral policies was equivalent to a tax on exportables (-11 percent on average) and to a subsidy to importables of 20 percent. Thus, direct, sectoral policies favor importable agricultural commodities while depressing incentives for exportables. The indirect effect of macroeconomic policies taxes both exportables and importables at about the same magnitude (-29 and -27 percent, respectively). The indirect effects are relatively large and dominated the direct effects. Moreover, the total effect, on average for the 18 countries, taxed both exportables (-40 percent) and importables (-6 percent). Thus, the average price of exportables is only about 60 percent and of importables is 95 percent of what would have existed under a free-trade macroeconomic policy matrix and no direct sectoral interventions.

These results conclusively demonstrate the pervasive and dominant effect of indirect, macroeconomic policies over sectoral policies for both exportable and importable agricultural commodities throughout a large number and wide variety of developing countries. Producers of agricultural exports have suffered significant reductions in incentives both from direct, sectoral interventions and especially from macroeconomic policies. Producers of importable agricultural commodities have been the recipients of relatively large subsidies from direct policies, only to have these eroded and swamped by indirect policies.

These results illustrate a puzzling anomaly, raised by Krueger, Schiff and Valdés (1988 p. 264): "...agricultural producers often have larger interests in macroeconomic policies than they do in agricultural pricing policies, yet their representatives usually concentrate on the latter." They suggest a partial answer is in the search by consumers of importables and by producers of exportables for internal price stability. However, the magnitude of the disincentives from indirect policies is so great that farmers surely would be greatly concerned if they clearly understood the negative impacts of such policies. The knowledge base about the effect of indirect and direct policies on agriculture is quite new. It is very likely that many farmers do not understand the effects of such policies. Moreover, the urban-commercial-industrial elite, who benefit from directly from the subsidies inherent in such policies, are a strong political coalition which likely would vigorously resist attempts to change the status quo.

There are two other important studies which strongly support the conclusions of the World Bank studies. Valdés provides a summary of the effect of commercial and macroeconomic policies on agricultural growth for South America. He sets forth a valuable methodological contribution by focusing on the real exchange rate, and provides results for Argentina, Brazil, Chile, Colombia, and Peru from several empirical studies.[15] He concludes that agriculture throughout South America has been constrained by inappropriate macroeconomic and commercial policies. He suggests that diversification and expansion of exports may be the most important structural adjustment facing South America. Valdés argues that taking advantage of the opportunities for growth in the international economy, especially for agriculture, will require an alignment of the real exchange rate to stop taxing the sector.

Finally, there is evidence from eight South American countries that agriculture responded positively to post-1982 adjustments in their macroeconomic policy matrices (IICA). These policies were changed in a series of structural adjustments that became necessary after the onset of the international debt crisis in mid-1982, and because of low growth rates and stagnation. These adjustments corrected distortions and reduced or eliminated disincentives associated with import-substitution industrialization and internally oriented growth strategies. While the response of each of the eight countries has been somewhat different, all tended to experience increases in agricultural growth. One principal conclusion of the study is that the macroeconomic policy matrix should continue to be modified in order to eliminate the anti-agricultural policy bias that has existed for decades. The study recognizes the: "...high supply response capacity of the agricultural sector to favorable macroeconomic policies, basically an increase in the real effective exchange rate and free market internal prices." (IICA p. 13, translation by author.)

Sectoral policies will become much more important once macroeconomic policies have been rationalized. Improvements in macroeconomic policies will provide the greatest increase in incentives to agriculture and of about equal magnitude to exportables and importables according to the results of the World Bank studies. Substantial increases in incentives then can be realized through appropriate positive sectoral policies since their effect will not be dampened and swamped by discriminatory macroeconomic policies or negative sectoral policies. The net effect of past positive and negative sectoral policies in the 18 countries studied by the World Bank was to modestly tax exportables and to heavily subsidize importables. These data suggest policymakers will need to be especially careful to introduce more neutral, positive sectoral policies as macroeconomic policies are rationalized and negative sectoral policies are eliminated.

Extracting resources from agriculture through macroeconomic and negative sector policies when no surplus is being produced contributes to an increase in the real internal terms of trade in favor of agriculture (that is, an increase in the shadow price of agricultural commodities relative to non-agricultural products). In this situation there would be pressure for resources to flow into agriculture, if markets were allowed freely to perform their allocation function. Government policies which extract resources from agriculture in such a situation lead to an even more inefficient allocation of resources. The main criticism noted here is that such a policy matrix is not extracting surpluses nor can it stimulate surplus production. While it does extract resources, the real internal terms of trade are turned increasingly in favor of agriculture. The existence of discriminatory macroeconomic and sectoral policies implies that agricultural surpluses do not exist and that agriculture is bearing an unduly heavy tax to support the nonfarm sector. In the long run, such a policy matrix reduces the well-being of all consumers.

An Emerging World Economy

A truly international, global economy began to emerge after World War II, and now is growing vigorously. The world economy is substantially different than it was even in the early 1960s, with increasingly interdependent economic relationships and greater specialization among nations. The reality of the new international economic order, and the high probability that it will continue to grow and develop, has significant implications for both developed and developing countries. Macroeconomic and sectoral policies must be consistent with the realities of the international economy if national economies are to maximize their rate of economic growth and development.

A key factor which appears to underlie the emergence and growth of the international economy is continuing technological innovation in information. Rapid scientific advances in communications and computers have substantially reduced the costs of producing, analyzing and transmitting information. This has resulted in the development of a global communications network in which people in every nation are regularly informed of events around the world.

There have been significant changes in the international economy during the past few decades. These changes have impinged directly on almost every country of the world and especially those with relatively open economies. Schuh (1974, 1976, 1986, 1987) has identified several major changes and analyzed their impact on the U.S. economy.[16] The rest of this section summarizes four of Schuh's main findings and their implications for developing countries in their quest for more rapid and equitable economic growth.

First, there has been a substantial increase in international trade throughout the world, with especially significant increases between the developed countries.

Dependency on imported foreign goods increased in most countries. Concomitantly, exports increased rapidly, especially in countries that exploited economic growth potentials inherent in the emerging international marketplace. Several countries that were underdeveloped in the early 1960s have graduated into the status of newly developed countries by exploiting their comparative advantages in the rapidly growing international economy. Others have experienced much slower development as they have followed internally oriented growth strategies. Almost all countries, however, are much more open than they were twenty-five years ago, and some have experienced quite remarkable changes from basically closed to highly open economies. The expectation is that international trade will continue to grow, and that major opportunities for economic growth for both developing and developed will lie in the international market place.

A second major change is the emergence of a pervasive, well-developed international capital market based, at least in part, on advances in communications technology. The size of the market is phenomenal, at US$42 trillion in 1984 compared to US$2 trillion in international trade (Schuh 1987, p. 2). This market has grown very rapidly and still appears to be expanding. It essentially functions in an international environment, unconstrained by national boundaries. It provides access to the huge pool of international savings for investors in those countries which are willing to recognize and abide by the market forces which allocate capital in the global marketplace. But countries which have erected barriers to the free functioning of this market have found themselves penalized in terms of capital flight, reduced access to international lending and lower credit-worthiness.[17]

Third, there have been major and dramatic changes in comparative advantage of nations and regions. Moreover, changes in comparative advantage are continuing and apparently at a faster pace. Reference has already been made to the emergence of the newly developed countries, primarily of the Far East. Major industries from steel to automobiles to textiles have moved from the older industrialized countries of Europe and especially the U.S. to Japan, and thence to the Republic of Korea, Taiwan, and then on to Brazil and Mexico. One can predict that such industries, which depend on cheap labor and utilize technologies that are not location specific, will continue to be on the move.

Significant resources are being invested in research and development activities oriented to develop comparative advantages vis-à-vis the international marketplace in a large number of forward-looking developing and developed countries. For example, institutional innovations in agricultural research have resulted in the rapid development of thirteen truly international agricultural research centers, focused on assisting developing countries. These centers have developed improved technologies for tropical food crops, which tend to be location specific. Several developing countries simultaneously have strengthened their own capacity for agricultural research. The end result of all of these efforts, in both agriculture, manufactures and services, will be continuing shifts in comparative advantage that will result in significant reallocation of resources among countries and changes in the mix of products and factors within countries. In short, competition in the international economy will become more and more intense and economic integration greater and greater in the years ahead. Those countries which adopt policies to exploit what appears to be a secular change in international specialization will experience substantially greater growth rates and economic progress than those which adopt inward-oriented policies.

A fourth major change documented by Schuh has been the abandonment of the system of fixed exchange rates in 1973. A system of floating exchange rates for the major currencies of the world has been adopted, with other currencies tied to the major currencies. Many people in both the developing and developed world pay little attention to the value of their currency in foreign exchange markets. However, as trade has expanded and the size of the capital market has burgeoned, the exchange rate has become one of the most important prices in the economy. When this price is modified by overt government policy, the distortions introduced will result in misallocation of significant resources relative to opportunities in the international market. The result, again, will be constrained rates of growth and failure to exploit comparative advantages in the growing international market.

The new international world economy developed quite rapidly during the last 25 years and the rate at which it is growing and maturing appears to be accelerating. The future obviously can not be predicted with much precision, especially in the longer term. The recent, rapid changes in the international economic order presage, however, continuing integration of national economies into the emerging international economy. The end result of a continuing integration would be eventually a world-wide economy, with fully integrated markets. The rate a which such integration will take place probably will quicken, although the process likely will be characterized by spurts and lapses rather than a smooth continuum. The technological changes which have driven the substantial integration on the last twenty-five years can be expected to continue. Certainly the extent technical innovation and resultant international economic integration to date would have been difficult to predict in the early 1950s, when most nations existed quite independently.

One of the most important lessons from recent changes in the international economy is that domestic economic policies are increasingly unable to modify the effects of international market forces with impunity. In short, policymakers are becoming subject to economic forces largely beyond their control as world markets emerge. Those nations which attempt to insulate their economies from these pervasive and growing international economic forces will pay a high price in terms of foregone growth and development. Such attempts will consign them to a low-growth path and may cause them to fall permanently behind competitor nations in the race for greater productivity and market shares. Other more enlightened countries which develop policies to exploit significant investment opportunities inherent in the increasingly rapid integration of the world economy will experience much greater rates of growth. Some can be expected to emulate the recent experience of the newly developed countries.

This is not to suggest that policymakers should not be concerned with moderating the impacts of adjustments as a country moves toward an increasingly open economy. It may be economically rational to implement policies which help to stabilize price fluctuations while recognizing that domestic policy can have little effect on secular price levels determined in the world market place. Commodity price policy is a case in point. While recognizing the advantages of trade at international prices Mellor and Ahmed (Chapter 4) recommend a domestic price stabilization policy for developing countries with commodity prices set in reference to the world price.

The Rest of the Study

The new empirical and conceptual knowledge set forth above--the induced innovation model of agricultural development, the effect of macroeconomic and sectoral policies on agricultural growth, and the emergence of a new global economic order--comprise the principal conceptual foundation for the analyses that follow in the rest of this study. The next two chapters provide a perspective on agriculture in overall economic development. Chapter 2 presents a review and analysis of Ecuador's macroeconomic and sectoral policies and provides additional evidence on the negative effects of such policies on agriculture. Chapter 3 reviews economic and agricultural growth; assesses how well agriculture has performed in contributing to economic development in terms of production, foreign exchange earnings and nutrition; and analyzes the extent of rural and urban poverty.

Chapters 4 through 12 treat various aspects of agriculture. Chapter 4 considers the role of natural resources in agriculture, the extent of the agricultural frontier, the general causes of environmental degradation and five critical natural resources issues. Chapter 5 focuses on the demographic characteristics of the population, the labor force and employment and the nature and efficiency of intersectoral labor markets. The production milieu, including production trends, an analysis of the sources of growth in crop production, production of illegal substances and use of modern inputs are treated in Chapter 6. Chapter 7 turns to an analysis of the effectiveness and economic viability of public irrigation and related multipurpose projects and the extent and nature of subsidies to irrigation water. Chapter 8 presents a conceptual framework for analyzing agricultural marketing systems, an assessment of major commodity and input market subsystems and an agenda for market system development. Chapter 9 treats the market for agricultural credit, including subsidized credit policies, principal institutions and the effects of an inflationary macroeconomic policy. Chapter 10 analyzes the role of social institutions in agricultural development based on an original data set gathered for the study, with emphasis on the family and gender issues. The mandates and functions of various public sector institutions serving agriculture, public sector expenditures for agriculture and supporting programs of donor agencies are considered in Chapter 11. Chapter 12 describes and analyzes the human capital and science base serving agriculture, including education, research and extension programs.

The findings and conclusions of the various chapters are integrated and synthesized in Chapter 13 which sets forth the principal obstacles to more rapid agricultural and economic development; lists the accomplishments which serve as a foundation for greater progress; presents recommendations for modernizing agriculture and enhancing overall economic growth; and considers the emerging scenario of Ecuador without petroleum around the year 2000.

NOTES

1. This section considers only those general economic development models that heavily stress industrialization and self-reliant development, the dominant policy thrust of Ecuador during the last three decades. For a more comprehensive review of literature on economic development policy, especially as it relates to agriculture see Hayami and Ruttan (1985 Chapter 1); Eicher and Staatz (Chapter 1); Johnston and Kilby; Johnston; and Mellor. This section draws especially on the insights of Hayami and Ruttan (1985 Chapter 1), and Eicher and Staatz (Chapter 1).

2. Rostow's approach led to the development of several growth-stage models in agriculture. See especially Johnston and Mellor.

3. See Hayami and Ruttan (1985 pp. 33-39) for a more detailed review of dependency models.

4. Spraos concludes that there is no evidence of a clear decline in the terms of trade between primary and industrial goods during 1900-1970. He found a declining trend between 1870 and 1930, however.

5. See Whitaker and Schuh for an analysis of the effects of import-substitution industrialization on labor absorption in Brazil.

6. The dual-sector models of both Ranis and Fei, and Jorgenson (1961, 1966) define the agricultural surplus as a shift in the internal terms of trade against agriculture, which indicates that a process of sustained economic growth is underway.

7. This intersector transfer has been referred to as a production squeeze on agriculture (Owen).

8. Such intersector transfers can be realized either through the market or via public policy instruments. An important question for policy makers concerns the effects of transfers made through alternative public actions on the development process, each relative to the pattern induced by market forces. While this is an important issue, it will not be considered here. Rather, the focus will remain on the nature of the agricultural surplus and its importance in the development of the non-farm sector.

9. The degree to which real income of consumers is increased due to decreasing prices of agricultural products depends on two factors. First, the more inelastic the demand for food and fiber, the greater will be the reduction in expenditures as prices fall. Second, the greater the share of the budget of the average consumer spent on agricultural products, the greater the proportional increase in real income from price decreases.

10. Hayami and Ruttan (1985 Part I) and Eicher and Staatz (Parts I and II) each present a substantial review of literature of the role of agriculture in economic development, and of models and theories of agricultural development, as they have emerged and evolved in the post-World War II period. These two references are highly recommended reading for those who want a better understanding of modern economic thought on agricultural development.

11. See Hopper for a classic example from Asia.

12. For example, original models of grain reapers saved critical harvest labor but led to shortages of labor for raking and binding. This induced invention of self-raking reapers and binders (Hayami and Ruttan 1985, pp. 92-93).

13. The subsidies came both from access to foreign exchange at the overvalued rate and from exonerations from tariffs or prohibitions for importation of capital and intermediate goods.

14. The country study teams met together in Washington, D.C. during February 1988 to compare and evaluate their analyses. A list of the individual country studies and their authors is presented in Krueger, Schiff and Valdés (1988 Footnote 1, p. 257). A summary of the studies is made in Krueger, Schiff and Valdés (Forthcoming).

15. The studies for Argentina, Chile and Colombia cited by Valdés are by the same authors as for the World Bank country studies and are precursors of them.

16. Schuh has provided incisive analyses of the effects of changing international economic conditions on the U.S. economy and particularly agriculture in these four related studies. Most of his findings have equal applicability to any nation facing the challenge of adapting domestic economic policies to the reality of the emerging world economy.

17. Conventional wisdom in South America, and certainly in Ecuador, views the United States and U.S. private banks as the dominant force in this market, *a la* the neo-Marxian dependency thesis. In fact, the center of gravity has shifted from the U.S. and Europe to the Pacific Rim countries. Japan now has the five largest banks in the world and their combined assets are over three times greater than the five largest U.S. banks. Citicorp, the largest U.S. bank, has only about 60 percent of the assets of Japan's fifth largest bank (Economist, The p. 6).

REFERENCES

Arndt, Thomas M., Dana G. Dalrymple and Vernon W. Ruttan. 1977. *Resource Allocation and Productivity in National and International Agricultural Research*. Minneapolis: University of Minnesota Press.

Baran, Paul. 1952. "On the Political Economy of Backwardness." *Manchester School of Economic and Social Studies* 20:January:66-84.

Boeke, J. H. 1953. *Economics and Economic Policy of Dual Societies as Exemplified by Indonesia*. New York: Institute of Pacific Relations.

Clark, Colin. 1957. *The Conditions of Economic Progress*. 3rd ed. London: Macmillan and Co.

DeJanvry, Alain. 1981. *The Agrarian Question and Reformism in Latin America*. Baltimore: The Johns Hopkins University Press.

_____. 1975. "The Political Economy of Rural Development in Latin America: An Interpretation." *American Journal of Agricultural Economics* 57:490-99.

Economist, The. 1989. "International Banking: A Survey." 310(March 25):58 ff.

Eicher, Carl K. and John M. Staatz, eds. 1984. *Agricultural Development in the Third World*. Baltimore: The Johns Hopkins University Press.

Evenson, Robert E., Paul E. Waggoner and Vernon W. Ruttan. 1979. "Economic Benefits from Research: An Example from Agriculture." *Science* 205(September):1101-07.

Hayami, Yujiro and Vernon W. Ruttan. 1985. *Agricultural Development: An International Perspective*. 2nd ed. Baltimore: The Johns Hopkins University Press.

_____. 1971. *Agricultural Development: An International Perspective*. Baltimore: The Johns Hopkins University Press.

Hirschman, Albert O. 1968. "The Political Economy of Import-Substitution Industrialization in Latin America." *The Quarterly Journal of Economics* 82:1-32.

Hopper, David W. 1965. "Allocation Efficiency in a Traditional Indian Agriculture." *Journal of Farm Economics* 47:611-24.

Huffman, Wallace E. 1978. "Assessing Returns to Agricultural Extension." *American Journal of Agricultural Economics* 60:December:973.

IICA (Interamerican Institute for Agricultural Cooperation). 1988. *Ajuste Macroeconómico y Sector Agropecuario in América Latina*. Buenos Aires: IICA.

Johnson, D. Gale. 1989. "Retrospective Review of Hayami, Yujiro and Vernon W. Ruttan, 1971, *Agricultural Development: An International Perspective*, Baltimore: The Johns Hopkins University Press." *American Journal of Agricultural Economics* 71:1062-63.

Johnston, Bruce F. and Peter Kilby. 1975. *Agriculture and Structural Transformation: Economic Strategies in the Late-Developing Countries*. New York: Oxford University Press.

Johnston, Bruce F. 1970. "Agriculture and Structural Transformation." *Journal of Economic Literature* 8:369-404.

Johnston, Bruce F. and John W. Mellor. 1961. "The Role of Agriculture in Economic Development." *American Economic Review* 51:566-93.

Jorgenson, Dale W. 1966. "Testing Alternative Theories of Development of a Dual Economy." *The Theory and Design of Economic Development*. Edited by Irma Adelman and Eric Thorbecke. Baltimore: The Johns Hopkins University Press.

_____. 1961. "The Development of a Dual Economy." *Economic Journal* 93:June:309-34.

Krueger, Anne O., Maurice Schiff and Alberto Valdés. Forthcoming. *The Political Economy of Agricultural Pricing Policies*. 3 Volumes. Oxford University Press.

_____. 1988. "Agricultural Incentives in Developing Countries: Measuring the Effect of Sectoral and Economywide Policies." *The World Bank Economic Review* 2:3:255-71.

Lewis, W. Arthur. 1954. "Economic Development with Unlimited Supplies of Labor." *Manchester School of Economics and Social Studies* 22:May:139-91.

Lockhead, Marlaine E., Dean T. Jamison and Lawrence J. Lau. 1980. "Farmer Education and Farm Efficiency: A Survey." *Economic Development and Cultural Change* 29:October:73-74.

Mellor, John W. and Raisuddin Ahmed. 1988. *Agricultural Price Policy in Developing Countries*. Baltimore: The Johns Hopkins University Press.

Mellor, John W. 1966. *The Economics of Agricultural Development*. Ithaca: Cornell University Press.

Nicholls, William H. 1963. "An 'Agricultural Surplus' as a Factor in Economic Development." *Journal of Political Economy* 71:February:1-29.

Owen, Wyn F. 1966. "The Double Development Squeeze on Agriculture." *The American Economic Review* 56:42-70.

Pinstrup-Anderson, Per. 1982. *The Role of Agricultural Research and Technology in Economic Development*. London: Longman Group, Ltd.

Prebisch, Raul. 1981. "The Latin American Periphery in the Global System of Capitalism." *CEPAL Review* (April):143-50.

_____. 1963. *The Economic Development of Latin America: Toward a Dynamic Development Policy for Latin America*. New York: United Nations.

_____. 1959. "Commercial Policy in the Underdeveloped Countries." *American Economic Review* 64:251-73.

_____. 1950. *The Economic Development of Latin America and its Principal Problems*. Lake Success, NY: United Nations.

Ranis, Gustav and John C. H. Fei. 1961. "A Theory of Economic Development." *American Economic Review* 51:533-65.

Rostow, Walter W. 1959. "The Stages of Economic Growth." *The Economic History Review* 12:August:1-15.

Ruttan, Vernon W. 1982. *Agricultural Research Policy*. Minneapolis: University of Minnesota Press.

Schuh, G. Edward. 1987. "Changes in the International Economy: Implications for the United States." *Assistance to Developing Country Agriculture and U.S. Agricultural Exports: Three Perspectives on the Current Debate*. Edited by CICHE (Consortium for International Cooperation in Higher Education). Washington, D.C.: CICHE.

_____. 1986. *The United States and the Developing Countries: An Economic Perspective*. Washington, D.C.: National Planning Association.

_____. 1984. "The Political Economy of Rural Development in Latin America: Comment." *Agricultural Development in the Third World*. Edited by Carl K. Eicher and John M. Staatz. Baltimore: The Johns Hopkins University Press.

_____. 1976. "The New Macroeconomics of Agriculture." *American Journal of Agricultural Economics* 58:802-11.

_____. 1974. "The Exchange Rate and U.S. Agriculture." *American Journal of Agricultural Economics* 56:1-13.

Schultz, Theodore W. 1964. *Transforming Traditional Agriculture*. New Haven, CN: Yale University Press.

Singer, Hans W. 1950. "The Distribution of Gains between Investing and Borrowing Countries." *The American Economic Review*, 40:473-85.

Spraos, John. 1980. "The Statistical Debate on the Net Barter Terms of Trade between Primary Commodities and Manufactures." *Economic Journal* 90:March:107-28.

Valdés, Alberto. 1986. "Impact of Trade and Macroeconomic Policies on Agricultural Growth: The South American Experience." *Economic and Social Progress in Latin America*. Washington, D.C.: The Inter-American Development Bank.

Whitaker, Morris D. and G. Edward Schuh. 1977. "O Mercado de Trabalho Industrial no Brasil e suas Implicações para Absorção de Mão-de-Obra." *Pesquisa e Planejamento Econômico* 7:August:333-366.

2

DEVELOPMENT POLICY
AND AGRICULTURE

Morris D. Whitaker and Duty Greene

The process of economic development in Ecuador in this century can be divided into two periods each reflecting substantially different economic development models and their associated macroeconomic and agricultural sector policy regimens: (a) the traditional export period from 1900 to the late 1950s; and (b) the import-substitution industrialization period from the late 1950s to the present.[1] Economic growth in the first period was founded on the export of primary commodities, mainly agricultural products from the *Costa* region.[2] The second period saw economic growth based on industrial development through domestic production of import substitutes.

The import-substitution industrialization period has been heavily affected by two other major economic events: (a) the petroleum boom of 1972-1981; and (b) the period of austerity and structural adjustment following the international financial crisis and falling petroleum prices since 1982. The petroleum boom is extremely important in understanding Ecuador's economic and agricultural development. The rapid increase in revenues from petroleum production provided large windfall gains which made it possible to continue subsidies inherent in import-substitution industrialization. The post-1982 period of austerity and adjustment became necessary because of burgeoning public and private expenditures, decreased fiscal revenues and sharply curtailed international credits. More fundamentally, adjustment and austerity became necessary because industrial growth stagnated as internal markets became saturated and import-substitution opportunities were exhausted.

Agricultural growth and economic development have been constrained during the entire 20th Century by macroeconomic and sectoral policies which have, on balance, taxed agriculture. Direct taxes were levied on agricultural exports during most of Ecuador's republican period and were a main source of government revenues until the petroleum boom in 1972. Macroeconomic and sectoral policies have discriminated against agriculture and tradeables and have subsidized industrial and other home goods. Such policies caused significant distortions in relative prices especially during the import-substitution industrialization era. As a result, internal terms of trade moved increasingly against agriculture as resources were extracted by government policy from the sector and transferred into the highly protected industrial sector.

Principal macroeconomic policy distortions which have indirectly taxed the agricultural sector over the last three decades include: an overvalued exchange rate; a

21

agricultural sector over the last three decades include: an overvalued exchange rate; a set of tariff and non-tariff barriers that highly protected domestic industry; and subsidized credit and tax exonerations for industry. Principal sectoral policies which have discriminated directly against agriculture include: taxes on agricultural exports; consumer price ceilings; and state interventions in marketing. Policies which have helped agriculture directly include: subsidized interest rates on agricultural loans; subsidies on fertilizers, rental of farm machinery and irrigation water; construction of roads, irrigation works, storage facilities and other infrastructure; effective price supports for a few crops; and provision of research, extension and education services. The net effect of positive and negative sectoral policies and the macroeconomic policy matrix has been to reduce incentives in agriculture (Scobie and Jardine 1988a).

Reduction of many of these policy distortions, starting in mid-1982, has contributed to a modest rejuvenation of agriculture and the highest sustained agricultural growth rates in Ecuador's history (see Chapter 3). The macroeconomic policy matrix and the setting of price ceilings on many food commodities continue, however, to discriminate against agriculture and to favor urban consumers and industrial development. In fact, import-substitution industrialization and inward-oriented growth still are principal elements of Ecuador's economic development model. This approach continues to have many advocates and was proposed as recently as April 1989 to be the basis for reactivating the economy (Martes Económico p. 3).

This chapter reviews the evolution of the principal economic policies of Ecuador during this century and assesses their impact on agriculture. The following sections review and analyze: the traditional exports period of 1900 to the late 1950s; the import-substitution industrialization period from the late 1950s to the present; the petroleum boom of 1972-1981; the subsequent period of austerity and structural reforms from 1982 to the present including the Roldós-Hurtado, Febres Cordero and Borja administrations; the generally pernicious effects of macroeconomic policies on agriculture during the last three decades based on the findings of several key studies; and illegal drug activities and policies and the impacts of the growing world drug problem on Ecuador. Conclusions and implications for Ecuadorian agriculture are discussed in the last section.

The Traditional Exports Period[3]

Ecuador's development engine from colonial times to the late 1950s was the exportation of minerals and agricultural commodities, with very limited processing. During the 15th century mining and exportation of gold and silver to Spain were the principal economic activities, although they never achieved the degree of importance as in some other Spanish colonies. Exports of textiles also were important in the early colonial period. Such exports were based on wool with some 750,000 head of sheep reported in the fertile intermountain valleys of Northern Ecuador in 1585. The colonial economy underwent a transition from primarily mining in the 15th century to agriculture and livestock during the 16th and 17th centuries. Agriculture dominated the economy by the 18th century. Principal crops included cereals and tubers in the *Sierra* region and tobacco, cacao, coffee, sugarcane and lumber from the tropical Guayas River basin near the port city of Guayaquil. Cacao and tobacco became important exports during the last few decades of the 19th century (Hurtado pp. 6-9).

Cacao, coffee and bananas dominated Ecuador's exports during most of this century. Cacao was the principal export crop from the 1860s through about 1920.

Production was seriously affected by disease during the latter part of this period which restricted exports. Cacao production recovered after World War II with the introduction of improved varieties in response to increasing world prices. Exports of cacao (beans and processed products) increased rapidly during the late 1970s and was the most important agricultural export in 1980.[4] Coffee exports first became important in the late 1920s and represented 17 percent of all exports during the early 1930s, although coffee has been produced since colonial times (Hurtado p. 81). The area planted to coffee expanded rapidly in the late 1960s and the 1970s in response to increased demand and high prices. Coffee emerged as one of the leading earners of foreign exchange during the late 1970s. Banana exports grew rapidly in the early 1950s as weather and disease eroded Central America's near monopoly position in world markets. By the mid-1950s Ecuador was the leading exporter of bananas, a position which it has retained to the present, with the exception of one year of bad weather.

The development model of Ecuador during the 1900s to the late 1950s was production and exportation of primary commodities, principally agricultural. Government programs focused on agriculture, minerals, commerce and industry, with emphasis on technical education, infrastructure and foreign investment. The first 20 years of the century saw continued growth of agricultural exports led by cacao. During this period exports generally exceeded imports and there were large positive balances on the trade account. The advent of serious cacao diseases, declining demand for cacao and trade barriers in the 1910s and 1920s seriously reduced export earnings. Some diversification of exports occurred in the late 1920s and early 1930s, led by coffee but exports did not recover to the levels of the early 1900s until the 1950s. As a result, the economy entered into a period of prolonged recession in the early 1920s which continued until the rapid increase in banana exports in the late 1940s. During the 1920-1950 period the trade balance was rarely positive putting substantial strain on economic development and social programs (Hurtado pp. 70-85).

Macroeconomic and commercial policies tended to discriminate against agricultural and other tradeables throughout the period 1900 to the late 1950s. Fiscal policies, such as taxing agricultural exports, reduced the profitability of investments in agriculture relative to other sectors. Customs duties also were levied on imports; the imports in turn depended on foreign exchange earnings generated by agricultural exports. Such export taxes and customs duties provided the primary source of tax revenues for financing government programs.

These fiscal policies led to government deficits which were inflationary. Government budgets were in deficit from the late 1800s through the 1920s, despite the relatively large income from export taxes and customs duties, as expenditures exceeded tax revenues. The government deficit is estimated to have been S/.25.0 million in 1925 and averaged as much as 80 percent of government expenditures in 1914 (Hurtado p. 323, note 42). Deficits were financed by borrowing from private banks which were largely uncontrolled and could issue their own currency and thus increase the money supply. The result was increasing inflation which became very pronounced after the decline in export earnings in the late 1920s and the early 1930s.

The Sucre was created in 1878 and set at a par with the U.S. dollar and the Ecuadorian peso of 91.67 percent pure gold weighing 1.58 grams (BCE 1986, Part 1, p. 182). The exchange rate remained at par until the mid 1910s when disease decimated cacao exports and foreign exchange reserves were eroded. The Sucre became increasingly overvalued and had to be successively devalued to maintain the competitiveness of the country's exports. The Sucre had fallen to 2.15 per dollar by 1913 when the effects of the cacao disease began to be felt. The exchange rate appreciated to 2.25 in 1920, 5.00 in 1926, 10.80 in 1934, 13.50 in 1949 and 15.00 in 1951 (Hurtado p. 82; BCE 1977, p. 44).

Agricultural exports were taxed and imports were subsidized implicitly with the overvaluation of the Sucre. As the Sucre became increasingly overvalued the prices of Ecuadorian tradeables fell relative to those of home goods. The incentives to produce tradeables were increasingly reduced because of decreased Sucre earnings from exports and relatively lower prices for imported products vis-à-vis locally produced substitutes. The loss of part of Ecuador's share of the world cacao market to other competitors during this period may have been due as much to exchange rate policy as to diseases.

The world prices of coffee, bananas, cacao and other primary goods fell toward the end of the 1950s due to rapidly increasing supplies relative to demand (Rosero de Cevallos pp. 1-3). The result was reduction of both foreign exchange earnings and government revenues which were derived mainly from export taxes and customs duties. Concomitantly, demand for imported industrial goods and scarce foreign exchange was growing in both the public and private sectors. The decrease in foreign exchange earnings coupled with increased demand for imports led to a growing trade deficit which resulted in an increasingly overvalued Sucre at the fixed exchange rate that had prevailed since 1950 (S/.15/US$1). The fiscal situation also worsened which put greater inflationary pressure on the Sucre. In 1960, Ecuador devalued its currency from S/.15 to S/.18/US$1 in an attempt to increase exports and reduce imports.

As the prices of primary goods fell the prices of imported industrial goods, produced mainly in developed countries, were increasing. Thus, the external terms of trade between Ecuador and the developed world deteriorated in the late 1950s, just as it did for many developing countries which were exporters of primary goods.

Import-Substitution Industrialization[5]

The shift in the external terms of trade against Ecuador's primary exports, with the resulting overvaluation of the Sucre and loss of government revenues, precipitated a major and significant change in development policy by the government. A strategy of promoting growth of the industrial sector as the primary basis for rapid and equitable economic progress was adopted in 1957 (Rosero de Cevallos p. 3). This strategy focused on growth of domestic industry and internal markets by protecting selected products and firms from international competition with trade barriers and by cheap food policies.[6] Import-substitution industrialization and internally oriented growth have been the principal elements of Ecuador's economic development model since the late 1950s to the present. Economic growth was especially rapid during the mid-1960s through 1981, a period that corresponded closely to the petroleum boom. Even though growth has been very slow since 1982 the underlying development model has not been fundamentally altered.

In 1957, Ecuador adopted the Law of Industrial Incentives (World Bank 1987, p.13; Rosero de Cevallos p. 3) which formed the initial basis for a heavy thrust into import-substitution industrialization. The incentives introduced in this law were reinforced and extended in the Industrial Development Law of 1962, and further refined in 1971 (Rosero de Cevallos pp. 1-12) and in 1985 (World Bank 1987, p. 13). Tariff and non-tariff barriers were established to protect the domestic production of consumer goods. Relatively low tariffs or exonerations were provided for raw materials, intermediate and capital goods imported for use in protected industries. Relief from income and other taxes also was given to protected industries. Finally, subsidized credits also were made available to import-substituting industries.

A dual exchange rate has been maintained throughout most of the 1950-1990 period. From 1960 through 1970 all foreign trade was pegged at the official rate of S/.18/US$1. A somewhat higher free market rate was in effect for all other transactions. The official exchange rate became increasingly overvalued during the 1960s and was devalued to S/.25/US$1 in 1970. The same pattern occurred in the 1970s and the official rate was again devalued in 1982 to S/.33.15/US$1. The exchange rate policy resulted in underpricing of tradeables (both exports and import substitutes) and clearly discriminated against agricultural producers. It also provided additional subsidies to imports and especially favored imports of industrial inputs which were generally free of tariffs and other non-tariff trade restrictions.

Incentives in agriculture also were reduced by several negative sectoral policies during the late 1950s through 1982. Taxes on exports of agricultural products were maintained throughout most of this period, even after the advent of the petroleum boom in 1973, as agricultural export taxes were seen as an important source of government revenue. Consumer price ceilings were in effect for many agricultural products during much of the period as part of a cheap food policy. And the government intervened in agricultural product and factor markets, especially after the petroleum boom began, in an effort to reduce marketing costs.

The government did provide some limited, direct assistance to the agricultural sector during the import-substitution era, which tended to improve incentives. This took the form of investments in irrigation, transportation and some marketing infrastructure; provision of research, education and extension services; subsidized credit and other inputs such as fertilizers and machinery; price supports for a few crops; and a modest land reform program. In the 1960s, positive government policies and programs focused mainly on diversification into the production of food crops and livestock products instead of traditional export crops as their prices fell in world markets. This strategy was reversed in the 1970s as prices for principal export crops increased rapidly. The government responded by increasing public expenditures to support production of export crops. For example, publicly supported research and extension efforts, with a focus on introduction of higher-yielding varieties and disease and insect control, resulted in increased competitiveness and capacity in coffee, cacao and bananas during the 1970s (Ruff).

Overall, the net effect of the set of macro-economic and sectoral policies in Ecuador was to turn the internal terms of trade against agriculture and other tradeables and in favor of non-traded, protected industrial products and other home goods (Vos p. 1123; Scobie and Jardine 1988a, 1988b). On balance, these policies extracted resources from relatively backward rural areas for development of the rapidly modernizing urban-industrial centers, especially Quito and Guayaquil.

What is often ignored by apologists for import-substitution industrialization in Ecuador is that the small-farm sector, comprising the largest single group of poor people at the time, bore much of the onerous burden of this policy approach. The *campesino* sector, along with other more prosperous farmers, transferred substantial labor and capital to the more well-to-do urban centers. The dominant development model concentrated growth in income and wealth in urban areas, which tended to worsen the distribution of income between rural and urban people and leave rural areas more impoverished (Vos pp. 1130-31).

The Petroleum Boom[7]

The petroleum boom was an exogenous event that made it possible to sustain rapid economic growth via the import-substitution industrialization model during the 1970s and early 1980s.   The effect of the petroleum boom on economic growth and agricultural development, in particular, was significant and pervasive. The period of most rapid industrial growth and greatest agricultural stagnation coincided with the oil boom during the 1972-1981 period even though import-substitution industrialization had been adopted nearly 15 years before as the primary development model. Thus, import-substitution industrialization began to flourish in Ecuador just as it was diminishing in many other Latin American countries. Windfall gains from the oil boom were the primary reason that rapid growth from import-substitution industrialization was sustained in Ecuador well beyond that in other countries.

Petroleum was first discovered in Ecuador in the Santa Elena area of the Guayas Province and was commercialized in the 1920s. In the mid-1960s significant discoveries were made in Ecuador's *Oriente* region (see Chapter 4). Total crude production increased by 54 times between 1970 and 1973 from 1.4 to 76.2 million barrels. At the same time the world price more than quadrupled in 1973 (World Bank 1984, 1987). Thus, Ecuador was the beneficiary of sudden and very large export earnings which were sustained through 1981 and were largely appropriated by the government (Nelson; CORDES; UNDP/World Bank).[8]

The large and unexpected windfall gains from petroleum exports provided the basis for deepening and strengthening import-substitution industrialization. Very ambitious government investments in infrastructure were mounted including upgrading and construction of paved and secondary roads, seaports, national and international airports, power generation and distribution, irrigation, drainage and flood control projects, schools and universities, hospitals, and sports and other community facilities. Significant resources were also devoted to upgrading the armed forces and providing modern equipment. These investments directly complemented the industrialization process and encouraged expansion of manufacturing industry to meet increased demand from oil revenues.

The investment and consumption program of the government, oriented toward production and consumption of home goods, resulted in greatly increased public sector employment.   One estimate indicates that 79 percent of the petroleum revenues between 1972 and 1985 were spent on public sector salaries (CEA 1988). Private sector employment also expanded rapidly during this period as the huge petroleum revenues facilitated industrial development and rapid growth in wholesale and retail trade, transportation, construction, utilities and services.

The ambitious government investment programs and the rapid increase in real per capita incomes, especially in urban areas, resulted in greatly increased demand in both the public and private sectors. The windfall gains from petroleum exports precipitated a buying binge of unprecedented proportions for domestic and imported capital and consumption goods that far exceeded revenue sources. The consequences were deficits on current account, public sector deficits, increasing inflation and an increasingly overvalued official exchange rate. The deficits were financed by external borrowing by both the public and private sector from international banks on the basis of expected increases in petroleum revenues. Domestic savings apparently fell and capital flight increased because of relatively low, fixed domestic interest rates. The limited domestic credit that was available was channeled to selected industries at highly subsidized rates.

The overvalued official exchange rate, used for all trade transactions, served implicitly to subsidize imports and especially imports of industrial inputs, while imports of consumer goods were either highly protected or prohibited.

The rapid increases in income substantially altered the structure of demand for food and fiber with greatly increased demand for animal proteins, fruits, vegetables and seafood especially in urban areas (see Chapter 6). The changing structure of demand induced substantial changes in agriculture toward the production of those foods with higher income elasticities of demand and away from traditional cereals and tubers. This was accompanied by a rapid commercialization of agriculture both in the small-farm subsistence sector and among traditional haciendas. Also, there was a substantial outmigration of rural labor to urban areas where higher-paying jobs were available in construction and services.

The petroleum boom adversely affected agriculture in at least four fundamental ways. First, increasing inflation led to the imposition and enforcement of official retail price ceilings for a large number of basic food commodities in an attempt to mollify the increasingly powerful urban consumers. Second, imported wheat and powdered milk were subsidized directly by the government through importation at the official exchange rate and sale at lower prices than the purchase price. Consumers quickly substituted the consumption of now cheaper bread and noodles from imported wheat for traditional foods. These subsidies (along with the shift in the structure of demand) constrained domestic production of wheat, barley, soft corn, tubers and legumes and increased the public sector deficit. Third, agricultural exports continued to be taxed. While the government started to reduce and eliminate taxes on bananas and sugar in 1973-1974, the inadequacy of petroleum revenues to finance rapidly increasing government expenditures resulted in the taxes on cacao and coffee being retained and raised. Taxes were continued through 1977 for bananas and cacao, and until 1981 for coffee (Keeler, Scobie and Greene p. 53). Fourth, the increasingly overvalued exchange rate meant that the prices of agricultural exports and import substitutes were being depressed.

Negative sectoral policies (fixed prices, imported food subsidies and export taxes) and macroeconomic policies (overvalued exchange rates, protection of the industrial sector and direct subsidies to industry) all greatly reduced incentives to invest in agriculture during the petroleum boom. They extracted resources from agriculture to support the import-substitution industrialization process and urban development. Ironically, the enormous windfall gains from the petroleum boom were not only expended mainly to subsidize the production of industrial and other home goods and benefit urban people; they exacerbated the discrimination against agriculture inherent in the underlying development model. They did this by providing the funding to increase the level and breadth of subsidization to industry and shift the internal terms of trade even further against agriculture.

The government attempted to promote agricultural development directly in several ways during the 1970s. Mention already has been made of investments to rejuvenate production of export crops. The government also promoted food self-sufficiency during the 1970s. An earlier producer price support system that had been largely ineffective was modified in 1972 and applied to crops produced for domestic consumption. The National Agricultural Storage and Marketing Company (ENAC) was established to buy crops at guaranteed minimum prices and to store and sell crops when prices improved. The program has focused almost exclusively on rice, hard corn and soybeans with very limited success in inducing increased production and has been very costly in terms of government subsidies. ENAC generally has been unable to sustain floor prices because of limited funding for purchases, especially in periods of excess supply. In 1971 the government also established the National Company for Basic Products (ENPROVIT) to bypass middlemen and purchase directly from producers for sale to consumers, with the objective of reducing marketing costs and food prices for low-income consumers. Expenditures on ENPROVIT have contributed to the public sector deficit as ENPROVIT also has experienced large operating deficits.[9]

The government invested heavily in development of additional irrigation infrastructure during the 1970s. The primary emphasis was on feasibility studies, arranging loans and developing pilot projects. Projects in Babahoyo and Milagro were completed by 1981 and other major projects were planned for completion in the 1980s. Public irrigation only had limited impact on agriculture during 1972-1981 because the extent of publicly irrigated land was quite small at the beginning of the period and most new projects were not finished until late in the period. Public investments in irrigation generally have been socially unprofitable, highly subsidized and a significant drain on the public sector budget (see Chapter 7).

Substantial amounts of subsidized credit were directed to agriculture through the National Development Bank (BNF). Most credit lines were directed to import-substitute crops especially in the Costa region. The level of subsidization has been very high resulting in decapitalization of the BNF. Moreover, most of the benefits have been captured by relatively large farmers (see Chapter 9).

Finally, the government made modest investments in research, extension, and related programs through the Ministry of Agriculture (MAG) and the National Institute of Agricultural Research (INIAP) in an attempt to improve productivity in the sector. A major share of the expenditures appears to have been in inadequately trained professionals at low salaries with little evidence of increased productivity from these investments (see Chapter 12).

Attempts to enhance agricultural growth in the 1970s through sectoral policies and programs were swamped by the indirect effects of disincentives inherent in the macroeconomic policy matrix and the direct effects of negative sectoral policies (Scobie and Jardine 1988b). The petroleum boom amplified the disincentives to agricultural growth and the subsidies to industry and urban people from macroeconomic and negative sectoral policies. Positive sectoral policies generally had only a limited effect on agricultural production and productivity during the period of the petroleum boom and were a substantial drain on the treasury. In addition, the internal market for domestic industrial products became saturated toward the end of the oil boom. Opportunities for domestic production of additional import-substituting products virtually were exhausted by the early 1980s (World Bank 1987, p. 13; 1988, p. 48). Consequently, industrial production stagnated between 1982 and 1990 which is one of the fundamental causes of the sustained period of economic crisis since 1982.

Austerity and Structural Adjustment[10]

A financial crisis ensued in mid-1982 when foreign banks found that the credit-worthiness of Latin America generally and of Ecuador, specifically, was questionable. Ecuador's foreign debt had increased from US$350 million in 1973 to US$5.8 billion in 1981 largely from pubic sector borrowing, which accounted for 74 percent of the 1981 debt. In 1971 the public sector had a surplus of 3.1 percent of GDP; by 1981 there was a deficit of 5.8 percent of GDP, which increased to 7.5 percent in 1982 at the same time that international interest rates increased. Foreign banks were unwilling to lend further in such an environment (World Bank 1987, pp. 2-5).

The Roldós-Hurtado Government (1979-1984)

The Roldós-Hurtado government continued during 1979-1981 with the inward-oriented macroeconomic and sectoral policies that had been in effect since the late 1950s. The government also continued to make large investments in social programs primarily on the expectation of future oil revenues and external credits.

In early 1982 the government suddenly and somewhat unexpectedly was challenged with the most serious economic crisis in Ecuador's modern history. Foreign credit dried up and the government faced the formidable task of internally financing its burgeoning fiscal deficit. More fundamentally, it had to address the structural problems inherent in nearly three decades of heavily subsidizing industry and urban consumers at the expense of agriculture and rural people. The policy response was the beginning of a continuing period of austerity and structural adjustment throughout the 1980s which reduced somewhat the degree of subsidy to industry and moderately improved investment opportunities in agriculture.

The economic crisis was complicated by the accidental death of President Jaime Roldós on May 24, 1981. The young Vice-President, Oswaldo Hurtado, suddenly was left alone to respond to the formidable problems associated with the emerging economic crisis while he simultaneously had to develop and restructure the political support necessary to govern the country.

The immediate response to the 1982 crisis was to expand credit and the money supply which culminated in the loss of foreign exchange reserves of nearly one-half billion dollars and rapid overvaluation of the Sucre at the official exchange rate. This led to a devaluation of the Sucre in March 1982 from S/.25/US$1 to S/.30/US$1.

The government then appears to have implemented a more integrated and outward-oriented response to the economic crisis. First, the policy of maintaining a fixed and increasingly overvalued exchange rate system was abandoned. The Sucre was devalued to S/.33/US$1 in May 1982 and a system of daily "mini-devaluations" was implemented. The dual exchange markets were maintained which resulted in an overvalued official exchange rate that still subsidized industry and home goods at the expense of agriculture and tradeables. The system of mini-devaluations continued throughout the Hurtado administration; in addition the Sucre suffered two macro-devaluations and was at S/.72/US$1 in mid-1984. Second, strict import controls and restrictions were established in 1982. As a result, the large deficit in the current account balance was reduced substantially in 1983. Third, the Hurtado government entered into an austerity program with restrictions on government spending that sharply curtailed the ambitious social programs of the first two years of the Roldós-Hurtado administration. These measures effectively eliminated the public sector deficit in 1983 and removed some of the inflationary pressure from the economy. The success of these measures permitted an expansion of the credit available for the private sector and the government raised interest rates although they still were less than the rate of inflation. Also, the government rescheduled its debt, assuming that of the private sector with the "Sucretization" program of October 1983 (Nickelsburg). It also negotiated a standby agreement with the International Monetary Fund (IMF).

The austerity measures compounded by bad weather precipitated a recession in 1983 and GDP fell by 2.8 percent. Disastrous weather referred to as the "El Niño" phenomenon was a major factor in the economic downturn. Unprecedented rainfall caused flooding and loss of roads, railroads, communication infrastructure and bridges, and destroyed crops and livestock. Agricultural production fell by 13.9 percent. In 1984 the economy recovered somewhat and the public sector budget had a surplus for the first time in years.

The Febres Cordero Government (1984-1988)

The Febres Cordero government took office in August 1984 and refined and expanded substantially the policy initiatives of the Roldós-Hurtado administration. One major adjustment was to move gradually toward a unified exchange rate and away from the dual system which tended to be overvalued and favored industry and home goods at the expense of agriculture (World Bank 1987, pp. 4-8; 1988, pp. 9-13). Initial steps in late 1984 involved shifting some foreign exchange transactions from the official rate of S/.66.5/US$1 to the intervention rate of S/.96.5/US$1. Then in September 1985 all international trade was unified at the intervention rate which was devalued to S/.108.5/US$1 in January 1986. Finally, in August 1986 the Sucre was floated, with a single market-determined rate for all foreign exchange transactions. The unified rate that was established initially in the free market of S/.145/US$1 represented a devaluation of the Sucre of 25 percent compared to the intervention rate of S/.108.5/US$1.[11] The unified rate remained relatively constant for several months and then began to appreciate. By August 1987 it was S/.200/US$1, a devaluation of 28 percent compared to the free-market rate of a year earlier. The rapid devaluation of the Sucre after August 1986 made agricultural products much more competitive in world markets (World Bank 1987, pp. 10-11).

A second major policy reform was to free interest rates on all savings and loans except those on subsidized loans from the Central Bank to specific sectors. The Febres Cordero government also undertook measures to raise public sector revenues and helped generate the 1984 budget surplus and sustain it in 1985. The government also was able to obtain another stand-by agreement from the IMF and to reschedule its external debt with private banks (World Bank 1987, p.7).

The Febres Cordero government also implemented several new policies which attempted to reverse the excesses of import-substitution industrialization and to improve incentives for agriculture (World Bank 1987, pp. 8, 11). First, the government eliminated almost all consumer price ceilings in 1985. In addition, the number of products subject to minimum price supports through ENAC buying and selling operations were limited to rice, corn, soybeans and cotton. Second, the operations of ENAC were curtailed by selling some of its storage facilities and a system of issuing negotiable certificates for ENAC-stored commodities was implemented. Third, an agricultural commodities exchange market was established in 1986 to facilitate marketing of agricultural products. Fourth, the government eliminated all export taxes on agricultural products except for a very small tax to finance customs services.

The government simultaneously embarked on an ambitious program to reduce and eliminate restrictions and prohibitions on the importation of industrial goods that have been at the heart of Ecuador's economic development model of import-substitution industrialization for nearly three decades. Restrictions were removed for a significant number of imports, primarily final consumer goods, in April 1985 and January 1986. Tariffs were reduced for many items and the average tariff, including surcharges, for all items on the import list fell from 51 to 38 percent (World Bank 1987, pp. 13-15). Finally, the government eliminated its monopoly in fertilizer imports and sales and permitted the free importation of fertilizers and other agricultural inputs.

Exogenous events in 1986 and 1987 severely constrained attempts to diversify the economy and move toward a more efficient path of sustained economic growth. First, the price of petroleum fell precipitously in 1986 to about US$12 per barrel from an average of US$25 in 1985. This sharply reduced government revenues and led to a budget deficit of 5.1 percent of GDP in 1986 (World Bank 1988, p. 11). At the same time, imports had to be sharply curtailed as foreign exchange reserves were reduced by about US$1.0 billion. Second, there was a major earthquake on March 5, 1987 which destroyed a section of the trans-Andean pipeline and essentially eliminated most of Ecuador's petroleum exports for nearly six months. This event caused the postponement of approximately another US$1.0 billion of foreign exchange earnings. The combined effect of these exogenous events was the reduction in public sector revenues from 28 percent of GDP in 1985 to only 22 percent in 1987. The Febres Cordero government was concomitantly engaged in a very expansionary fiscal policy that saw public sector expenditures increase from 26 percent to 31 percent of GDP during the same period. As a result the public sector deficit increased substantially to 10.5 percent of GDP in 1987 and the foreign exchange position worsened. In late 1987 and early 1988, the Sierra experienced a drought during most of the prime growing season and the production of food crops declined in 1988.

These exogenous shocks created a major economic crisis in late 1987 and early 1988. The rate of inflation, the public sector deficit and the Sucre/US$ exchange rate all increased rapidly. The government subsequently reversed some of its innovative policy reforms. In February 1988 price ceilings for primary consumption products, principally agricultural, were reinstated. In early March 1988 a multiple exchange rate system was reestablished. All government transactions were set at S/.250/US$1, and all private imports and exports were required to be transacted at a "controlled free-market" rate of up to S/.275/US$1. The free market rate for all other transactions was at nearly S/.400/US$1, so the fixed rates were highly overvalued, which led to massive imports and disincentives to export through the official market. The free market exchange rate surged to S/.560/US$1 by July 1988.

This reversal of price and exchange rate policy was a major step backward in the effort to free market prices and to promote a more outward-oriented economy. This policy change, instituted only a few months before the Febres Cordero government left office, also provided a mechanism to transfer significant resources to those who received import licenses and subsequent access to foreign exchange at highly subsidized rates. In any case, the free-market policies of the Febres Cordero government were ended primarily because of the exogenous shocks combined with expansionary fiscal policy mentioned above and the desire to control the ensuing rapid devaluation of the Sucre and increasing inflation.

The Borja Government (1988-Present)

The Borja government inherited a rapidly deteriorating economic situation when it assumed power on August 10, 1988. The fiscal deficit was estimated to be at 13.8 percent of GDP, inflation was increasing rapidly and foreign exchange reserves were exhausted (Monetary Board, Ministry of Finance and Central Bank of Ecuador 1990a, p. 6A). As a consequence, an emergency economic plan was announced on August 30, 1988 for the first year of the government. It focused on economic stabilization and control of inflation as highest priorities along with several social welfare programs to repay the "social debt" (U.S. Embassy/Quito; MAG/PAU).

The highly overvalued Sucre at the intervention rate was devalued to about 80 percent of the free market level (S/.390/US$1) and a weekly mini-devaluation of S/.2.50 was implemented with the announcement of the emergency economic plan. As a result, the exchange rate policy became more favorable to the production of agricultural goods and tradeables than it was at the end of the Febres Cordero administration. However, the multiple exchange rate structure established near the end of the Febres Cordero government was maintained as was industrial protection through trade restrictions and tariffs.

The Borja administration also imposed a very tight monetary policy and limited the growth of the money supply to about 60 percent of the inflation rate. Imports were restricted for most capital and some consumer goods unless financed abroad. Prices of domestic petroleum products and electricity were raised significantly, regular monthly price increases were established and a substantial subsidy on imported wheat was eliminated. Petroleum export prices strengthened, averaging over US$16/barrel during 1989. Consequently, international monetary reserves increased by US$533 million between August 1988 and December 1989 with a positive balance of US$203 million at the end of the period while the deficit on the current account balance fell from 7.0 percent to 4.4 percent of GDP. The fiscal deficit, which had reached a projected high of 13.8 percent of GDP in August 1988 was reduced to 5.1 percent of GDP in 1988 and to 2.2 percent in 1989 (Monetary Board, Ministry of Finance and Central Bank of Ecuador 1990a, p. 6A). The intervention exchange rates, which tended to become increasingly overvalued, were adjusted to market levels through the weekly mini-devaluations and several macro-devaluations in the base rate since August 1988.

Inflation was gradually reduced during 1989. The annual rate, which had been increasing since July 1988, approached 100 percent in March 1989. Food prices surged in early 1989, especially rice and sugar and the government was forced to import both these items during 1989. Inflationary pressures abated during late 1989 to an annual rate of about 50 percent and monthly rates during the last quarter that averaged about 40 percent on an annual basis. It has been very difficult to reduce the inflation rate below this level as the perennial fiscal deficit has continued to push aggregate demand.

Several interrelated factors suggest that inflation will increase during 1990. The monthly inflation rates increased modestly during the first quarter of 1990 relative to the last quarter of 1989 suggesting a possible increasing trend (BCE 1990, p. 50). The 1990 winter crop was severely affected by a prolonged drought in both the Sierra and the Costa regions which contributed to increasing food prices during April and May 1990. Petroleum prices fell substantially during the second quarter of 1990 as they dropped below US$13 per barrel and are expected to remain weak for the rest of the year. Coffee prices have been severely depressed since July 1989, shrimp and cacao exports are down, the economy is stagnant and the foreign debt renegotiation is not progressing well as of June 1990. The decrease in foreign exchange earnings and government revenues could be further aggravated by external events such as a continued fall in the price of petroleum, or disruptions in its supply. Inefficiency in the public sector and wasteful public spending on subsidies to various special interest groups are structural aspects of fiscal deficits and inflation which continue to be major constraints to economic stabilization. The Borja administration has not yet articulated an adequate fiscal policy to control and limit expenditures and, although it has improved its taxation policy, revenues and foreign exchange earnings are falling because of declining petroleum prices and other exogenous events beyond the government's control. This pessimistic scenario suggests a strong tendency to growing fiscal deficits and inflation during 1990. A stagnant economy during the Borja administration has led to increasing demands from the private sector to relax monetary policy in order to stimulate investment and economic growth, which could further contribute to inflationary pressure.

The foreign debt is another major problem facing the Borja administration. It was US$12.4 billion in April 1990, including an accumulated arrearage of US$1.2 billion with US$5.6 billion being owed to international private banks (CEA 1990). The proposed Brady plan may serve to reduce some of the debt burden although renegotiation of the debt will not be possible on the highly favorable terms sought by the government. The debt service is very large relative to Ecuador's capacity to pay. Payment of the debt will tend to limit growth and could contribute to inflation.

Reactivation of the economy is the second major priority of the Borja government. There is great concern that focusing on inflation for too long and exclusively may result in a major recession. CONADE made a pessimistic preliminary estimate of economic growth in GDP for 1989 of .5 percent (Cifra p. 9). **Well informed sources in the government indicate, however, that soon-to-be-released official statistics from the Central Bank will show a decline in GDP of about 2 percent for 1989. The Borja administration has set a goal of 3.5 percent growth in 1990. The actual rate is likely to be much lower given the country-wide 1990 drought, low and falling export prices, decreases in shrimp production, strong prospects for increasing inflation and the relatively inhospitable investment climate. If economic growth decreased by 2 percent in 1989, the liklihood of increasing inflation and low growth is even greater. The level of the fiscal deficit of 2.2 percent reported by the government is underestimated since it was based on the assumption of growth of .5 percent in GDP. A higher deficit is consistent with and would explain much of the inflationary pressure in the economy.

CONADE announced its economic development plan in mid-1989 (CONADE 1989a). The primary economic theme and development model of the CONADE plan was continued emphasis on producing for the internal market, which incorporates import-substitution industrialization and self-sufficiency. For example, the proposed CONADE plan for agricultural development was focused on cooperative production for the internal market and simultaneous achievement of social and equity objectives, with little emphasis given to programs to increase productivity (CONADE 1989b, pp. 5-10). This was fully consistent with the governing political party's position on economic development during the campaign (Izquierda Democrática pp. 19,22). A "new" industrial development strategy to activate the economy also was proposed (Martes Económico p. 3). This scheme suggested import-substitution industrialization based on production of food, clothing and housing for the internal market as the primary strategy for economic growth. The CONADE plan and the "new" industrial development strategy are seriously flawed and have been largely ignored by the press and economic policymakers in the government.

The Ministry of Finance, the Central Bank and the Monetary Board have been moving cautiously but consistently toward a more outward-oriented set of macroeconomic policies since the beginning of the Borja administration, in contrast to CONADE's inward-oriented plan. They also have been increasingly involved in setting economic development policies. These three government agencies jointly announced a new economic action plan in early 1990 in letters to the World Bank and to the International Monetary Fund (Monetary Board, Ministry of Finance and Central Bank of Ecuador 1990a, pp. 6-7A; 1990b, pp. A6-7). This action plan is based on opening the economy, reducing and eliminating trade barriers, reducing government deficits and liberalizing prices and interest rates. These official communications signaled a shift in power within the government in the formulation of economic policy from CONADE to the Ministry of Finance, the Central Bank and the Monetary Board. They also implied a shift in policy from import-substitution industrialization toward an outward-oriented economy (Hoy p. 3A).

The emerging development plan of the Borja administration appears likely to substantially alter past, inward-oriented policies and establish an outward-oriented growth strategy for the 1990s. The government implemented an ambitious reduction in tariffs in June 1990, just a few months after they were announced as part of the economic plan. If all of the elements of the plan were to be fully implemented, Ecuador's economic development model would be substantially altered and lead to a more dynamic, competitive economy.

The plan, however, has its limitations. There is no integrated policy for agricultural development and improvement in the production of tradeable commodities. For example, the plan fails to free agricultural trade with substantial barriers on both exports and imports based on the outmoded and inefficient notion of self-sufficiency in food production. It fails completely to address the fundamental need for greater productivity as the primary basis for competitiveness in the international marketplace both for agriculture and the rest of the economy. It is seriously deficient in addressing the fiscal deficit and especially the oversized, inefficient public sector and the large, recurring subsidies in the economy. Finally, the time-frame for implementation appears to be too long with a piecemeal approach, which may lead to economic crisis before more rapid growth is realized. Nevertheless, the economic action plan of the Borja administration and its implementation to date are improvements over past inward-oriented policies.

Effects of Macroeconomic Policies

There is a growing body of literature which analyzes the effect of macroeconomic and commercial trade policies on agriculture in Ecuador and other developing countries. These studies generally conclude that agricultural production and exports have been constrained by such policies relative to a more neutral set of policies.

Keeler, Scobie and Greene examined the effects of macroeconomic and commercial policies on the structure and performance of Ecuador's agricultural sector during 1960-1985. They calculated effective exchange rates to take into account the variations in exchange rates and inflation rates of Ecuador's major trading partners. They also calculated equivalent exchange rates to account for the effects of taxation and subsidization policies on exports and imports. The effective and equivalent exchange rates were aggregated into the effective equivalent exchange rate to determine how competitive Ecuadorian importers and exporters were in the international market.

Their study found that a steady appreciation of the effective exchange rate between 1961 and 1982 made conditions steadily worse for Ecuadorian exporters, and made importable goods less expensive, ceteris paribus. The effects of subsidies and taxes on imports and exports, as accounted for in the equivalent exchange rate, further discriminated against agricultural exports, and especially against the traditional exports of bananas, cacao and coffee which comprise the majority of agricultural exports. These trade policies generally had the effect of encouraging import-competing activities and of discriminating against export production. While the equivalent exchange rate for the aggregate of all imports was generally higher than that for exports, the study notes that imports of raw materials and capital goods for industry faced a much lower equivalent exchange rate than for imports of highly protected final goods.[12]

The Keeler, Scobie and Greene study, unfortunately, did not disaggregate the equivalent exchange rate for industrial raw materials and capital goods relative to final goods. The study documents, however, a series of tariff reductions and exonerations and exemptions from other non-tariff barriers to import raw materials and capital goods, especially for industry. It is likely that the equivalent exchange rate for the importation of such goods was lower than any of the equivalent rates for exports, suggesting a significant subsidy to such imports. The study's general conclusion is that commercial policies made the production and export of agricultural commodities steadily less attractive, especially during the period 1970-1982. The study also concluded that: (a) protection to industry was maintained at relatively high levels in the first half of the 1980s, even though policy changes after 1982 increased incentives to agriculture; and (b) commercial and macroeconomic policies favored production of home goods (generally industrial) at the expense of tradeable goods (generally agricultural).

Scobie and Jardine (1988a) reviewed the performance of the agricultural economy of Ecuador in the context of macroeconomic policies applied to the general economy during the 1970-1987 period. They argue that the secular performance of agriculture was relatively poor and that sustained stagnation was a function of both sectoral and macroeconomic policies. They demonstrate that most of the products of agriculture are tradeable and that, therefore, prices of most agricultural products are subject to international market forces. They argue that because the agricultural economy is so open, that incentives in the sector are influenced by macroeconomic policies which change the competitiveness of Ecuadorian agriculture relative to the rest of the world.

A key variable in their analysis is the real exchange rate, defined as the price ratio of tradeables to non-tradeables (or home goods). They demonstrate that this rate turned increasingly against tradeables (mainly comprised of agricultural products) during 1960-1981, and especially during the years of the oil boom (1973-1981), and in favor of home goods (an important share of which was comprised of industrial products and public services). The study suggests that this occurred in spite of increased, direct public sector investments and policies supporting agricultural development (such as infrastructure, research and extension and price supports). In essence, macroeconomic policies (especially the overvalued exchange rate and industrial protection), and negative sectoral policies (such as taxes on traditional agricultural exports) overwhelmed the effects of positive sectoral policies.

The Scobie and Jardine study (1988a) concluded that changes in the macroeconomic policy matrix implemented in 1981 as part of the readjustment program of the Roldós and Hurtado administrations and enhanced during the Febres Cordero administration from 1984 through 1987, improved the internal terms of trade in favor of tradeables, with a generally more favorable set of incentives for agriculture. They argued that the recovery of the agricultural sector during 1984-1986 was a direct response to the more favorable incentives induced by the policy changes. The study also concluded that any implementation of the macroeconomic and trade policies of the 1970s which taxed agriculture so heavily will constrain growth and reduce welfare.

Scobie and Jardine (1988b) also tested the effect of different macroeconomic policies on the performance of the agricultural sector with an empirically estimated econometric model. Because Ecuadorian agriculture is so open to international economic forces, the price of tradeables is hypothesized to be very sensitive to changes in macroeconomic policies which modify the relative profitability of tradeables and home goods. The real exchange rate (the ratio of the prices of tradeable to home goods) is hypothesized to be a function of macroeconomic policies and to be affected directly by changes in them. The real exchange rate first was estimated as a function of fiscal, monetary, exchange rate and commercial policies. The second equation of this recursive model then estimated the relationship between the real exchange rate and the relative output of tradeables (agricultural goods) and home goods (non-agricultural). The estimated coefficients of this model indicate that much of the decline in the relative output of agriculture that occurred in the 1970s can be explained by appreciation of the real exchange rate, caused by macroeconomic policies.

The Scobie and Jardine (1988b) study found, utilizing the econometric results and simulation models, that agriculture could have grown at over 5 percent in real terms between 1970 and 1986 with a more appropriate set of macroeconomic policies. Real agricultural output (GDP) in 1986 would have been more than three times what was actually produced. Trade policies, with high protection to industry for domestic production of import substitutes, an overvalued exchange rate and taxes on tradeables were found to be major constraints to increased agricultural production.

The Scobie and Jardine (1988b) study simulated the level of protection to importables that would have been necessary in order to maintain the relative output of agriculture at average levels of the 1960s. They found that importables would have to have been taxed (through subsidies to imports) rather than protected just for agriculture to have remained even. This suggests that protectionist policies for industry severely taxed agriculture and reduced potential economic growth. Results of the study also suggest, very strongly, that agriculture had resources extracted from it to subsidize the industrialization process. This study also suggests that macroeconomic policies offset attempts to stimulate agriculture through direct investments.

The inescapable conclusion of the recent studies of the effects of macroeconomic policies on agriculture in Ecuador is that the agricultural sector was heavily taxed to support an inefficient import-substitution industrialization process and the production of home goods.

This conclusion is consistent with similar findings for many other developing countries around the world. There is a growing body of evidence that the macroeconomic policy matrix associated with import-substitution industrialization reduced public and private investments in agriculture in many Latin American countries (Valdés). There also is evidence from 18 countries in Asia, Africa, Europe, and Latin America that the negative effects on agriculture of discriminatory macroeconomic policies and negative sectoral policies were much greater than the positive effects of policies intended to help the sector (Krueger, Schiff and Valdés). Finally, there is evidence from eight South American countries that agriculture responded positively to post-1982 adjustments in their macroeconomic policy matrices which corrected distortions and reduced or eliminated disincentives associated with import-substitution industrialization (IICA).

The lesson for Ecuador, from the specific studies from Ecuador and from studies of other developing countries, is consistent and clear. Ecuador must continue to move toward a more outward-oriented set of macroeconomic and trade policies, and then sustain this policy set if it is to achieve a more rapid rate of economic growth. This modified policy matrix clearly should incorporate movement away from protection of industry with its production primarily for the internal market, toward production for competitive external markets. The World Bank (1988) presents projections of economic growth in Ecuador which indicate that movement to an outward-oriented strategy will result in much more rapid rates of growth, albeit with the poor bearing a disproportionate share of the adjustment costs in the short run.

The World Bank (1988) report also recommends removal of protection and an export-oriented strategy to revitalize industry. The stagnation of the industrial sector is largely a result of inward-oriented macroeconomic and trade policies. The internal market for most of the products of industry is relatively small and is growing very slowly. The market is generally saturated and opportunities for additional import-substitution are nil. Moreover, subsidies to imports of capital equipment for industry have tended to constrain utilization of labor and reduce employment over what it might have been under a more appropriate set of macroeconomic and trade policies (Lal and Rajapatirana; World Bank 1986; 1987, p. 13). There is evidence however, that some parts of industry (e.g., milling and bakery products, fish, cigarettes, weaving, sawmill products, furniture, soaps, perfumes and cosmetics, tires, cement and electric home appliances) are relatively efficient (World Bank 1988, Annex C). Movement toward a more outward-oriented macroeconomic and commercial policy matrix will improve incentives for both agriculture and industry, although inefficient firms in both sectors will be subject to competition and possible reallocation of resources. In the longer term, the net effect will be more rapid economic growth and development than is possible under protectionist policies of the past.

Illegal Drug Activities and Policies

As an Andean nation Ecuador has been affected significantly by the very large growth in the World's drug economy during the decade of the 1980's. The two drugs that are of most concern for their actual or potential impacts on agriculture are marijuana and cocaine with nearly all the attention on the latter. This section discusses the situation and policies with respect to drug production, use and trafficking in Ecuador. Information on production is reported in Chapter 6.

Narcotics production, processing, dealing and use are illegal in Ecuador and the government has attempted strongly to control such activities within existing resource constraints. However, the country is wedged between Peru and Colombia which together with Bolivia produce and process some 80 percent of the world's cocaine (Casalduero; Gonzales Carrero and del Giudice). Ecuador, Brazil and Venezuela have been affected by drug trafficking largely as result of pressures from drug dealers within the three main producing countries to find alternative supply and marketing routes, as well as production and processing sites. Illegal drugs are economically attractive because huge sums of money can be made and drug activities present, therefore, potentially serious problems.

The primary drug concerns and policies in Ecuador relate to the use of the country as a bridge for trans-shipment of cocaine, as a source of chemical inputs for cocaine processing, as an intermediary for laundering drug money, as a location for producing and processing coca leaves and for the problems caused by the internal consumption of drugs. Most of the information on drugs is derived from activities of the government to control the drug problem and have been compiled by the International Organization of Criminal Police (INTERPOL); these are summarized for 1985-1989 in Table 2.1. Other information has been obtained from a compilation of abstracts of 1984-1988 Ecuadorian newspaper articles about drugs (DINACONTES).

The trans-shipment of drugs is of especial concern to the agricultural sector due to the use and attempted use of agricultural exports as covers for drug shipments, activities that could prejudice continuation of such exports. Shipments of drugs have been discovered in wood, chocolate products, bananas, oranges, plantains, flowers and

Table 2.1 Repression and Control of Illegal Drug Activities, 1985-1989

Activity	1985	1986	1987	1988	1989
Persons Arrested					
For Drug Dealing	115	197	210	269	227
For Possession	5	26	26	11	72
For Use	139	168	216	132	153
For Chemicals				31	11
Drugs Confiscated					
Cocaine (grams)	673,805	332,233	49,093	33,330	321,539
Marijuana (grams)	8,384	4,391	38,911	32,490	98,116
Liquid Cocaine (liters)	800	8			
Plants (number)	872,162	1	68,448	42,852	74,591
Money Confiscated					
Sucres	1,355,390	5,995,000	184,305	3,314,870	23,856,985
Pesos	25,420	5,962,000	7,100	17,606	253,621
Dollars	749	11		106,251	17,652
Laboratories Destroyed	14		4		1
Chemicals Confiscated					
Ether (liters)		3,900	25,300	220	920
Caustic Soda (sacks)			33		525
Permanganate (grams)			208		390
Acetone (liters)			220	23,280	46,910
Sulfuric Acid (liters)				320	640
Thiner (liters)				220	1,980
Mehtyl exano (liters)				12,760	960
Others (liters)				19,480	7,510
Vehicles Confiscated					
Automobiles		1	11	19	
Airplanes, small				2	
Motorcycles				1	1

Source: INTERPOL unpublished data.

palm hearts.

Ecuador has been considered a leader among South American countries in fighting drug trafficking (DINACONTES p. 73). It's drug control activities are encompassed in the 1988 National Integrated Plan for the Prevention of Production, Traffic and Consumption of Drugs (Borja). A major weakness, in addition to inadequate resources, is that current laws do not prohibit the sale of chemicals and other inputs to drug processors. However, the Borja government has submitted a proposal for a new law that would strengthen its drug enforcement capabilities (El Comercio).

Conclusions

Economic growth in Ecuador for the first sixty years of this century relied primarily on the exports of three primary agricultural commodities: cacao, bananas, and coffee. Taxes on exports of these commodities provided the major source of government revenues during this period. Export taxes and an overvalued real exchange rate discriminated against the production of agricultural and tradeable goods. Growth in demand for industrial goods and increased supply of primary commodities after World War II resulted in falling relative prices of primary products on the world market and a deterioration in the external terms of trade for most developing countries. As a result there were increasing incentives and pressures to move toward a model of import-substitution industrialization in Ecuador, as in most of the developing world.

Ecuador adopted import-substitution industrialization as its model of economic development in the late 1950s and has continued with it to the present although the country edged toward a more outward-oriented economy during the 1980s. The industrial sector was seen as the basis for rapid economic growth while the role of agriculture was depreciated. Industry was protected from foreign competition through a variety of tariff and non-tariff barriers to trade that resulted in a rapid expansion of the sector. The Sucre was overvalued during most of the last three decades which reduced the price of exports and imports on average. Imports of final goods that competed with domestic industry were heavily taxed, while imports of raw materials and capital equipment for industry were either exempt from import taxes and restrictions or taxed at very low rates. In essence, the industrial sector has had access to foreign exchange at subsidized rates for imports of raw materials and capital goods during the last three decades. Industry also has enjoyed subsidized lines of credit and exemption from, or reduction or deferment of various taxes. In contrast, agriculture generally has been taxed, directly and indirectly, through a variety of policy instruments to provide government revenues and to subsidize import-substitution industrialization.

The policy reforms of the 1980s induced by the economic crisis of 1981 were more of degree than of fundamental change in development strategy. The dominant policy thrust throughout the 1980s has been import-substitution industrialization, with a brief flirtation and some experimentation with a more outward-oriented, free-market approach especially during the Febres Cordero administration. Even though there was relative improvement in macroeconomic policies in favor of agriculture during the 1980s, post-1982 macroeconomic and sectoral policies continued to subsidize industry and urban areas while taxing agriculture and rural people. While the Borja administration has announced its plan to move toward an outward-oriented economy, the industrial sector and urban dwellers still remain highly protected and subsidized at the beginning of the 1990s.

NOTES

1. The present refers to June 1990 when this Chapter was finalized.

2. Continental Ecuador comprises three principal geographic regions: the *Costa*, the *Sierra* and the *Oriente*. These three regions are referred to throughout the book by their Spanish names since they are the formal names of Ecuador's main geographic regions. The Costa is a strip of tropical lowlands along the Pacific coast from the Colombian border on the north to Peru on the south and inland about 200 km at its widest point to the western foothills of the Andes Mountains. The Sierra is a zone of mountains and intermontane valleys of the Andes east of the Costa region and includes a wide range of elevations and climates from cold to temperate to subtropical. The Oriente region is a vast area of tropical lowlands east of the Sierra region covered mainly with native rain forests. The Sierra and the Oriente regions also border Colombia and Peru. Ecuador's fourth principal region, the Galápagos Islands in the

Pacific Ocean west of continental Ecuador, is not included in this study since it has almost no agricultural activity. See Chapter 4 for a description of Ecuador's three principal geographic regions and eight major agro-ecological zones.

3. This section draws on Hurtado. While Hurtado's work focuses on the rise of Ecuador's political parties it contains a brief but excellent analysis of Ecuador's economic history from the colonial period until 1950. It is highly recommended reading for students of Ecuador's economic development.

4. See Chapter 3 for a detailed analysis of agricultural trade during 1965-1987.

5. All exchange rates reported in the rest of this chapter are taken from BCE (1977, 1978, 1988, 1990) unless otherwise noted.

6.The policy stance Ecuador adopted was heavily influenced by dependency, dual-sector and growth stage theories of economic development discussed in Chapter 1.

7. This section draws on data and analyses by the World Bank (1987, 1988); Pachano (1986, 1987); and Scobie and Jardine (1988a, 1988b).

8. See also Brogan and Gibson for more information on the role of petroleum in Ecuador's economy.

9. See Chapter 8 for more information about the agricultural marketing system.

10. The discussion of adjustments by the Roldós-Hurtado and Febres Cordero governments in this Section is based partially on studies by the World Bank (1987, 1988).

11. The free-floating, unified rate initially depreciated to S/.145/US$1 compared to the free market rate of S/.164.5/US$1 that existed in July 1986, immediately prior to the float. The free market rate of July 1986 pertained to only a small segment of the total foreign exchange market, while the lower intervention rate (S/.108.5/US$1) covered the largest share of the market. When these two segmented markets were unified after August 1986 the free-floating rate averaged somewhat less than the July free market rate for several months but was substantially more than the intervention rate.

12. The overvalued nominal exchange rate also had the general effect of subsidizing imports and therefore discouraging domestic production of import-competing goods, especially some agricultural products such as wheat and barley, whose importation was allowed and even directly subsidized by the government. In addition, imports of capital equipment and raw materials for producing import-competing products had access to foreign exchange at the overvalued rates and low average import tariffs, compared to final goods whose importation was either prohibited, or imported at a very high average tariff.

REFERENCES

BCE (Central Bank of Ecuador). 1990. *Información Estadistica Mensual*. Quito: March.
_____. 1988, 1978. *Boletin Anuario*. Quito: Nos. 11 and 1.
_____. 1986. *Pensamiento Monetario y Financiero*. 2 Parts. Quito: Corporación Editora Nacional.
_____. 1977. *Series Estadisticas Básicas*. Quito.
Borja, Rodrigo. 1988. "Plan Nacional de Prevención Integral a la Producción, Trafico y Consumo de Drogas." Quito: *Registro Oficial* Numero 141, pp.2-10, March 3.
Brogan, Christopher. 1984. *The Retreat from Oil Nationalism in Ecuador: 1976-83*. London: University of London.
Casalduero, Vincente. 1990. "Las Rutas de la Cocaína." *Hoy*. Quito.
CEA (Center for Studies and Analysis). 1990. *Renegociación y Conversión de la Deuda Externa*. Quito: April 20, No. 60.
_____. 1988. *Rentas Petroleras y Gastos en Remuneraciones*. Quito: Feb. 26, No. 4.
Cifra. 1990. "La Producción en 1989" *Hoy*. Quito: Dinediciones, January 11, p. 9.
CONADE (National Development Council). 1989a. "Plan Nacional de Desarrollo Económico y Social: Resumen Ejecutivo." Quito: Secretaria General de Planificación.
_____. 1989b. "Plan Nacional de Desarrollo, Programa I: El Sector Agrícola." Quito: Preliminary Document.
CORDES (Corporation for Development Studies). 1985. *Sector Petrolero: Resultados de 1984, Pronóstico de 1985*. Quito: Apunte Técnico No. 2.
DINACONTES (National Directorate for the Control of Narcotics). 1988. *Recortes de Prensa*. Quito: Centro de Información, May.
El Comercio. 1990. "En Dicusión Ley Antidrogas." Quito: June 1, p. A8.
Gibson, Charles R. 1971. *Foreign Trade in the Economic Development of Small Nations: The Case of Ecuador*. New York: Praeger Publishers.
Gonzales Carrero, Alfredo and Alfredo del Giudice. 1984. "La Geodroga." Caracas: CONACUID (National Commission Against the Illegal Use of Drugs).
Hoy. 1990. "Adiós a la Sustitución de Importaciones." Quito: February 16, p. 3A.
Hurtado, Osvaldo. 1985. *Political Power in Ecuador*. Translated by Nick D. Mills, Jr. Boulder: Westview Press.
IICA (Interamerican Institute for Agricultural Cooperation). 1988. *Ajuste Macroeconómico y Sector Agropecuario en América Latina*. Buenos Aires: IICA.
Izquierda Democrática. 1988. "Plan de Gobierno de la Izquierda Democratica." Quito: Documento No. 1.
Keeler, Andrew G., Grant M. Scobie and Duty D. Greene. 1988. *Exchange Rates and Foreign Trade Policies in Ecuador: 1960-85*. Raleigh, NC: Sigma One Corporation, May, Working Paper No. EMT.WP.06.
Krueger, Anne O., Maurice Schiff and Alberto Valdés. 1988. "Agricultural Incentives in Developing Countries: Measuring the Effect of Sectoral and Economywide Policies." *The World Bank Economic Review* 2:3:255-71.
Lal, Deepak and Sarath Rajapatirana. 1987. "Foreign Trade Regimes and Economic Growth in Developing Countries." *The World Bank Research Observer* 2:2:189-216
MAG (Ministry of Agriculture)/PAU (Policy Analysis Unit). 1988. "Review of the Economic Program of the Borja Government (Emergency Plan of August 30, 1978)." Quito: PAU, September.

Martes Económico. 1989. "Proponen Nuevo Modelo de Desarrollo." *El Comercio.* Quito: April 11, p. 3.

Monetary Board, Ministry of Finance and Central Bank of Ecuador. 1990a. "Plan de Acción Económica (Letter of January 30, 1990 to the World Bank)." *Hoy.* Quito: February 17, pp. 6-7A.

_____. 1990b. "Carta de Intención con el FMI (Letter of February 2, 1990 to the International Monetary Fund)." *El Comercio.* Quito: February 18, pp. A6-7.

Nelson, David D. 1987. "Petroleum Production and Economic Growth in Ecuador." Unpublished Masters Thesis, University of Maryland.

Nickelsburg, Gerald. 1985. "Sucretización y Estabilización de Precios." *Cuestiones Económicos* 11:January:39-49, Banco Central del Ecuador.

Pachano B., Abelardo. 1987. *Políticas Económicas Comparadas: Ecuador 1981-1987.* Prepared for CORDES Seminar: "Neoliberalismo y Políticas Económicas Alternativas." Quito: CORDES, July 6-8.

_____. 1986. *Endeudamiento Global y Requisitos de la Intervención Estatal: Experiencias y Perspectivas.* Quito: CORDES, Apunte Técnico No. 8.

Rosero de Cevallos, Janett. 1984. "La Protección Arancelaria del Estado Ecuatoriano a las Actividades Productivas, en el Período 1965-1980." Unpublished Masters Thesis, Facultad Latinoamericana de Ciencias Sociales (FLACSO) at Quito.

Ruff, Samuel. 1984. *Agricultural Progress in Ecuador, 1970-82.* Washington, D.C.: United States Department of Agriculture, Economic Research Service, Foreign Agricultural Economic Report No. 208.

Scobie, Grant M. and Verónica Jardine. 1988a. "Efectos de las Políticas Macroeconómicas de Ajuste Sobre el Sector Agrícola y Alimentario del Ecuador." *Ajuste Macroeconómico y Sector Agropecuario en América Latina.* Edited by IICA (Interamerican Institute for Agricultural Cooperation). Buenos Aires: IICA.

_____. 1988b. "Macroeconomic Policy, The Real Exchange Rate and Agricultural Growth in Ecuador." Quito: Ministry of Agriculture and Sigma One Corporation, Working Paper No. 04, May.

UNDP (United Nations Development Program)/World Bank. 1985. *Ecuador: Issues and Options in the Energy Sector.* Washington, D.C.: UNDP/World Bank, Report No. 5865-EC.

U.S. Embassy/Quito. 1989. *Economic Trends Report for Ecuador.* Quito: February 28.

Valdés, Alberto. 1986. "Impact of Trade and Macroeconomic Policies on Agricultural Growth: The South American Experience." *Economic and Social Progress in Latin America.* Washington, D.C.: The Inter-American Development Bank.

Vos, Rob. 1985. "El Modelo de Desarrollo y El Sector Agrícola en Ecuador, 1965-1982." *El Trimestre Económico* 52:4:1097-1140.

World Bank. 1988. *Ecuador: Country Economic Memorandum.* Washington, D.C.

_____. 1987. *Ecuador: Country Economic Memorandum.* Washington, D.C.

_____. 1986. "Trade and Pricing Policies in World Agriculture." *World Development Report 1986, Part II.* New York: Oxford University Press, pp. 61-84.

_____. 1984. *Ecuador: An Agenda for Recovery and Sustained Growth.* Washington, D.C.: World Bank, Report No. 5094-EC.22

3

THE PERFORMANCE

OF AGRICULTURE

Morris D. Whitaker and Jaime Alzamora

A more efficient and productive agriculture generally is necessary in order to achieve faster, sustained economic growth in developing countries. The agricultural sector of most such countries is relatively large and, in many cases, is the primary economic basis from which overall growth and development must proceed. Agriculture produces much of the principal wage and subsistence goods in these economies--food and fiber. With appropriate policies and public sector investments it can: release labor and generate savings and capital for investment in the production of nonagricultural goods and services; generate increased foreign exchange earnings to pay for imports of capital and consumer goods, including food; and provide a nutritious diet at decreasing real prices.

Chapter 2 argued that achievement of more rapid and sustained economic growth in Ecuador in the post-World War II period was seriously constrained by macroeconomic policies which discriminated against agriculture while subsidizing industry. It concluded that the policy environment and incentives facing agriculture improved somewhat in the post-1982 austerity period, but that subsidization of industry at the expense of agriculture continued. How well has agriculture done in this restrictive environment?

This chapter analyzes the performance of agriculture and its contribution to general economic development. The following sections review and analyze: growth rates and the changing importance of the principal sectors of the economy with comparisons of the main period of import-substitution industrialization (1965-1981) with the post-1981 austerity period; growth in agriculture's subsectors and their changing relative importance, compared for the same periods; agricultural trade and agriculture's important contribution to foreign exchange earnings; the effective role of agriculture in meeting the nutritional needs of the population; and the interrelated issue of the cost of the diet, economic access to food by the poor and poverty. The last section contains conclusions. Employment generation in agriculture is treated in Chapter 5.

Development of the Principal Sectors

National account data from the Central Bank of Ecuador (BCE) provide the basis for analyzing the relative performance of the principal sectors of the economy during

Table 3.1   Rates of Growth in Gross Domestic Product by Sector for Selected Periods[a] (Percent, Calculated from GDP in Constant 1975 Prices)

Sector	Import Substitution (1965-81)	Austerity Period		Total Period (1965-88)
		(1982-88)	(1984-88)	
Agriculture	3.4	6.2	8.1	3.2
Petroleum and Mining[b]	6.1	2.1	-3.5	4.6
Industry	9.3	0.2	1.3	7.0
Utilities	9.5	15.6	14.2	10.0
Construction	5.8	-1.1	-0.4	3.6
Wholesale/Retail Trade	7.6	1.2	2.5	5.6
Transportation/Communications	10.7	4.3	5.0	8.5
Total Services	7.7	0.9	1.2	6.3
Financial Services	7.9	-0.2	0.9	6.1
Household Services	6.0	2.7	2.6	6.0
Government Services	8.7	0.9	0.6	6.6
Total GDP (at market prices)	8.2	2.3	2.5	6.2

Source: Whitaker, Colyer and Alzamora Appendix Table 3.1.

[a]The annual average growth rate calculated by fitting a curvelinear (exponential) trend line to the data. The formula utilized is $y = ae^{bx}$ where a>0, and y>0.
[b]Data for petroleum between 1965 and 1971 are negative, due to an accounting procedure in the national accounts. Growth rates calculated with 1972 and later data.

for analyzing the relative performance of the principal sectors of the economy during 1965-1988 (BCE 1982a, 1982b, 1988a, 1989). This section compares sectoral growth and structure within and between the main part of the import-substitution industrialization period (1965-1981) and the following austerity period (1982-1988).[1]

Growth during the Import-Substitution Period

Economic development proceeded at a historically high rate during the heart of the import-substitution industrialization period. Gross Domestic Product (GDP, or value added) grew in real terms at an average rate of 8.2 percent from 1965-1981 which is high by any standard (Table 3.1). Growth in this period was led by the petroleum sector which expanded by 54 times between 1970 and 1973 (World Bank 1987, p. 1).[2] Not only did production and exports increase rapidly but world prices rose by more than four times in 1973, swelling foreign exchange reserves and providing the economic basis for rapid growth in industry and related sectors for the rest of the decade (World Bank 1984, p. i). The transportation and communications sector grew at an annual average rate of 10.7 percent, followed closely by utilities and industry at 9.5 and 9.3 percent, respectively. Services grew at 7.7 percent led by a very rapid increase in government services. Construction, the slowest growing sector except for agriculture, still grew at nearly six percent per year.

In contrast, agriculture grew relatively slowly at only 3.4 percent during 1965-1981, barely faster than the rapid population growth experienced in this period. This general pattern reflects the petroleum boom and the subsidization of industry, transportation and communications, utilities and urban areas at the expense of agriculture and rural people via macroeconomic and sectoral policies (see Chapter 2). It also resulted from strong linkages between industry and the other sectors of the nonagricultural and predominantly urban-based economy.

The Austerity Period (1982-1988)

There was a major reversal of the sectoral growth pattern of 1965-1981 during the austerity period of 1982-1988 and economic growth stagnated. Growth in GDP was only 2.3 percent reflecting the effects of the financial crisis and subsequent recession of 1982, the devastating El Niño rains and floods of 1983, destruction of part of the trans-Andean petroleum pipeline in a 1987 earthquake and modest changes in macroeconomic policies in favor of agriculture throughout the period.

Agriculture responded to the improved incentives and was one of the leading sectors of the economy during the austerity period. It experienced an average annual growth rate of 6.2 percent between 1982-1988, almost three times as fast as the overall economy and about twice the rate of the 1965-1981 period.[3]

In contrast, most of the rest of the economy grew very slowly. GDP in the important industrial sector was stagnant, growing at only .2 percent per year during the austerity period. The industrial sector, which was heavily protected since 1957, was relatively inefficient. Even though only gradually and partially exposed to market forces since 1982 by changes macroeconomic and sectoral policies it was unable to compete. Moreover, the import-substitution industrialization process had about run its course, with a relatively saturated and constrained domestic market, which also dampened growth.

The recession of 1982 and stagnation in industry had a chilling effect throughout the rest of the nonagricultural economy. GDP in construction fell by an average of 1.1 percent per year during 1982-1988. Services grew by only .9 percent and wholesale and retail trade grew only slightly faster at 1.2 percent. GDP in transportation and communications grew at 4.3 percent, about two times slower than in the earlier period, while the small utilities sector grew at 15.6 percent. The relatively rapid growth of transportation and communications and utilities during the austerity period reflects continued large government subsidies. These sectors continued to receive waivers of import controls and tariffs and heavily subsidized prices for petroleum derivatives (gasoline, diesel fuel, etc.). The petroleum sector grew at only 2.1 percent on average during 1982-1988 primarily because of the ruptured pipeline in 1987. When 1987 data is removed from the calculation petroleum and mining output grew at 10.3 percent. Depressed petroleum prices have nullified the potential benefits of increased production however.

The dichotomy in the pattern of sectoral growth between the import-substitution industrialization era and the austerity period is even more pronounced when data for 1984-1988 are compared with the 1965-1981 period. During 1984-1988 GDP in agriculture grew at an annual average rate of 8.1 percent while the overall economy grew at 2.5 percent. The large annual increases in agricultural production in 1984, 1985, 1986, 1987 and 1988 reflect primarily responses to the set of improved incentives inherent in the modified policy environment relative to disincentives and slow growth during 1965-1981. Part of the relatively large increase in agricultural production in 1984 and in 1985 also reflected recovery from the El Niño floods and rains of 1983.

Table 3.2   Sectoral Structure of Gross Domestic Product for Selected Periods,
            1965-1988 (Percentages)

Sector	Import Substitution		Austerity Period		
	1965-67	1979-81	1982-84	1986-88	1988
Agriculture	25.6	14.5	14.0	16.6	16.8
Petroleum and Mining[a]	-1.6	10.8	12.4	12.3	14.8
Industry	15.6	18.5	18.9	17.2	16.8
Utilities	0.6	0.7	1.0	1.5	1.7
Construction	6.3	4.8	4.4	4.0	3.5
Wholesale/Retail Trade	17.1	16.5	15.4	15.0	14.5
Transportation/Communications	4.7	6.8	6.9	7.6	7.3
Total Services	26.7	26.4	27.6	26.1	24.8
Financial Services	11.6	11.6	11.9	10.8	11.4
Household Services	6.9	5.6	6.3	6.4	6.8
Government Services	8.2	9.1	9.4	8.8	8.4
Others[b]	5.0	1.2	-0.7	-0.2	-0.2
Total GDP (at market prices)	100.0	100.0	100.0	100.0	100.0

Source: Whitaker, Colyer and Alzamora Appendix Table 3.1.

[a]Data for petroleum between 1965 and 1971 are negative due to an accounting procedure in the national accounts; consequently the share for 1965-1967 is negative.
[b]Includes net customs taxes and imputed bank services.

Sectoral Shares of GDP

The structure of the economy changed substantially during the main period of import-substitution industrialization (Table 3.2). Agriculture, which accounted for 25.6 percent of GDP during 1965-1967 (at the beginning of the period) produced only 14.5 percent of GDP by 1979-1981 (the end of the period) as the sector grew much more slowly than total GDP. The petroleum sector increased its share from nearly zero to 10.8 percent of total GDP during 1965-1981, while industry, and transportation and communications modestly increased their share of GDP.[4] These latter two sectors benefitted heavily from the subsidies provided in the import-substitution industrialization strategy and grew somewhat faster than overall GDP. The contribution to GDP declined slightly for wholesale and retail trades, construction, and services.

The policies implemented during the austerity period reversed the changes in the structure of the economy that had taken place during the import-substitution industrialization period. The share of agriculture, which had fallen further to 14.0 percent during 1982-1984 primarily because of the effect of the El Niño weather phenomenon, increased to 16.6 percent of GDP on average during 1986-1988 and stood at 16.8 percent in 1988. In contrast, the share of industry fell from 18.9 to 17.2 percent during the austerity period and was down to 16.8 percent in 1988. The shares of transportation and communications, and utilities increased slightly, maintaining the trend of the past, in response to continued subsidies during the austerity period. All other sectors of the economy declined in relative importance, although the decline in petroleum's share is due mainly to the destruction of the trans-Andean pipeline in the March 1987 earthquake. Petroleum accounted for 12.3 percent of GDP on average

Table 3.3 Structure and Growth Rates of Gross Domestic Product in Agriculture and its Subsectors for Various Periods, 1965-1988[a]

Time Period	Bananas Cacao & Coffee	Other Crops	Livestock Production	Forestry	Hunting & Fishing	Total
Growth Rates[b] (%)						
1965-81	1.2	2.0	4.6	9.6	11.7	3.4
1982-88	2.4	8.1	3.8	1.8	16.7	6.2
1984-88	4.4	10.4	4.5	3.1	20.3	8.1
1965-88	0.2	1.7	4.3	7.6	12.5	3.2
Structure[c] (%)						
1965-67	26.4	38.8	29.2	3.3	2.3	100.0
1970-74	22.2	39.4	30.3	4.4	3.7	100.0
1979-81	19.4	32.3	34.0	7.1	7.1	100.0
1982-84	15.4	29.7	37.6	7.9	9.5	100.0
1986-88	13.7	32.2	33.5	6.7	14.0	100.0

Source: Whitaker, Colyer and Alzamora Appendix Table 3.2.

[a]Calculated from GDP in constant 1975 prices.
[b]The annual average growth rate as calculated by fitting a curvelinear trend line to the data. The formula utilized is $y = ae^{bx}$ where a>0, and y>0.
[c]The share of the subsector in total agricultural GDP.

for 1986-1988 and 14.8 percent in 1988, shares somewhat higher than at the end of the import-substitution period.

Agriculture's Subsectors

The national accounts divide agriculture into five subsectors: (a) bananas, coffee and cacao (export crops); (b) other crops; (c) livestock; (d) forestry; and (e) hunting and fishing (which includes shrimp farming). Performance among the subsectors of agriculture has been highly variable over the last two decades and the structure of the sector has changed considerably (Table 3.3).

Growth Rates

Growth in the both the export and other crops subsectors was relatively low on average during the import-substitution industrialization era. Export crops grew by only 1.2 percent during 1965-1981 and other crops fared only slightly better at 2 percent. In contrast, forestry, and hunting and fishing grew at relatively rapid rates of 9.6 and 11.7 percent, respectively, while livestock performed reasonably well at 4.6 percent. Rapid growth in hunting and fishing is partially explained by growth in demand for shrimp and fish in the export market. The high rates of growth in livestock production, and forestry are at least partially explained by the strong backward linkages from protected domestic industries to these two sectors which produced raw materials for the rapidly expanding internal market.

The pattern of growth changed substantially during the austerity period 1982-1988.

The rates of growth in livestock production and forestry both fell as domestic industry stagnated following the recession of 1982. The growth rates in the other subsectors increased substantially as the new policy matrix provided increased incentives to tradeables. These policies induced greater production of export crops which grew at 2.4 percent during 1982-1988 and other crops which grew at 8.1 percent. It also further stimulated shrimp farming, so that hunting and fishing grew at 16.7 percent during the austerity period. This pattern is even more pronounced during 1984-1988 after recovery from the 1982 recession and the 1983 El Niño floods.

Changes in Structure

These variable rates of growth caused the structure of the agricultural sector to change considerably. Export crops fell continually from an average of 26.4 percent of agricultural GDP during 1965-1967 to 13.7 percent in 1986-1988, while other crops fell from 38.8 to 29.7 percent between 1965-1967 and 1982-1984. Other crops recovered somewhat due to its very high recent growth rate and accounted for 32.2 percent of agriculture's GDP during 1986-1988. Hunting and fishing registered the largest increase from 2.3 to 14.0 percent of GDP between 1965-1967 and 1986-1988. Forestry more than doubled its share to 6.7 percent, and livestock production increased from 29.2 to 37.6 percent between 1965-1967 and 1982-1984 before falling back to 33.5 percent at the end of the austerity period (1986-1988). The large decline in the share of traditional exports was offset by a similar increase in the share of fish and shrimp exports under the rubric of hunting and fishing. The decrease in the share of other crops was offset by modest increases in the share of GDP in livestock production and in forestry. It is important to note, however, that other crops and livestock still accounted for 65.7 percent of agricultural GDP (average in 1986-1988) down only slightly from 68.0 percent early in the import-substitution industrialization period (1965-1969). When bananas, coffee and cacao are added to this, traditional agriculture continues to constitute the major share of sectoral GDP at 79.4 percent.

Agriculture and Trade[5]

Agricultural exports long have been an important element of the Ecuadorian economy. The relative importance of such exports, however, decreased dramatically and substantially with the advent of the petroleum boom in 1973. The petroleum sector has since received much of the attention from economic analysts and government planners, even though agricultural exports continued to be a major component of foreign trade and their relative importance has increased substantially in recent years. This section analyzes the extent and nature of the contribution that agriculture has made to the foreign exchange earnings of Ecuador between 1965 and 1987. This is done by comparing agricultural exports and imports and calculating the agricultural trade balance from trade data published by the BCE (1978, 1988b).

Exports

Agricultural exports are defined to include products from the five principal sectors of agriculture in the National Accounts: (a) export crops (bananas, coffee, and cacao); (b) other crops; (c) livestock; (d) forestry; and (e) fishing and hunting. They also are defined to include processed or manufactured products from these same five groups

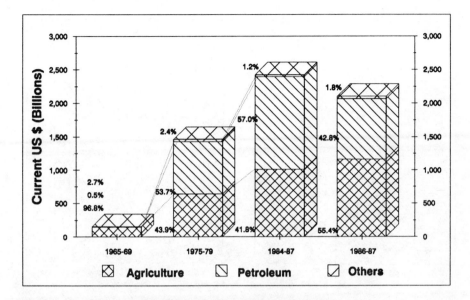

Figure 3.1 Principal Exports (Annual Average Value, FOB)
Source: Whitaker, Colyer and Alzamora Appendix Table 3.3.

that are included in the manufacturing sector of the national accounts. For example, agricultural exports include cacao as beans and processed cacao products such as cocoa. This definition is utilized to account for exports of all products of agricultural origin, whether they are exported directly from agriculture as primary products or as processed industrial products.

Agricultural exports are a very important component of total exports (Figure 3.1). Before the advent of the petroleum boom in 1973 agricultural exports accounted for almost all exports (e.g., 96.8 percent during 1965-1969). With the very large increase in petroleum production and prices in 1973 the value of petroleum exports exceeded those of agriculture for the first time and the share of agriculture fell to 43.9 percent during 1975-1979 and to 41.8 percent during 1984-1987.

The relative importance of agricultural exports recovered substantially in 1986 and 1987 primarily because of exogenous shocks to the petroleum sector. In 1986 the world price of petroleum fell precipitately and the value of Ecuador's petroleum exports fell by nearly one billion dollars. This was followed by the destruction of the trans-Andean pipeline in March 1987 as a direct result of a severe earthquake which cut petroleum exports for about six months, causing postponement of another approximately one billion dollars in export earnings in 1987. As a result of these two exogenous shocks agricultural exports exceeded petroleum exports in both 1986 and 1987 and averaged 55.4 percent of total exports during 1986-1987. Agricultural exports likely will be more important than petroleum exports during the 1990s because of lower petroleum prices compared to the boom years of the 1970s and declining petroleum production.

Ecuador long has been dependent on the export of traditional, primary agricultural products as principal earners of foreign exchange, with cacao, coffee and bananas being

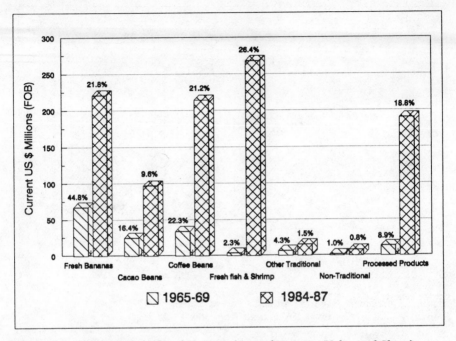

Figure 3.2 Principal Agricultural Exports (Annual Average Value and Share)
Source: Whitaker, Colyer and Alzamora Appendix Table 3.4.

the most important during the last two decades (Figure 3.2; Whitaker, Colyer and Alzamora Appendix Table 3.4). Exports of coffee and cacao beans and fresh bananas together accounted for 52.5 percent of total agricultural exports on average during 1984-1987, down from 83.5 percent during 1965-1969.

Exports of fresh (chilled and frozen) shrimp, lobster and fish increased rapidly during the last decade. This class averaged 26.4 percent of total agricultural exports during 1984-1987 with shrimp exports being dominant. This was up from only 2.3 percent in 1965-1969. Fresh shrimp, which primarily are raised in ponds, became the single most important agricultural export in 1987, accounting for 33.1 percent of the total, well ahead of bananas or coffee.

Non-traditional agricultural exports have received considerable attention in the popular press, with recurring articles about exports of cut flowers, strawberries, asparagus, and other fresh fruits and vegetables. During 1984-1987, however, all these products combined accounted for only 0.8 percent of agricultural exports and the share of this class declined slightly between 1965-1969 and 1984-1987. The products in this class appear to offer limited potential for substantial improvements in agriculture's commercial balance compared to other major crops (see below).

Four primary product groups now dominate agricultural exports instead of three, with fresh bananas, cacao beans, coffee beans, and fresh seafood (mainly shrimp) accounting for 79.0 percent of all agricultural exports during 1984-1987 (Table 3.4). This share, however, is down somewhat from 1965-1969, when these four products were 85.8 percent of total agricultural exports.

Table 3.4 Exports of Primary and Processed Agricultural Products, Annual Averages, 1965-1969 and 1984-1987

Years	Bananas	Cacao	Coffee	Fish & Shrimp	Subtotal	Others	Total
Value (US$ 1,000)							
1965-69							
Total	67,391	26,202	33,606	4,747	131,947	18,531	150,478
Primary	67,388	24,614	33,605	3,481	129,088	8,050	137,138
Processed	3	1,588	2	1,266	2,859	10,481	13,340
1984-87							
Total	224,800	162,926	236,107	340,916	964,749	48,105	1,012,853
Primary	220,777	97,058	214,184	267,805	799,824	22,917	822,740
Processed	4,024	65,868	21,923	73,111	164,925	25,188	190,113
Shares (%)							
1965-69							
Total	44.8	17.4	22.3	3.2	87.7	12.3	100.0
Primary	44.8	16.4	22.3	2.3	85.8	5.3	91.1
Processed	0.0	1.1	0.0	0.8	1.9	7.0	8.9
1984-87							
Total	22.2	16.1	23.3	33.7	95.3	4.7	100.0
Primary	21.8	9.6	21.1	26.4	79.0	2.3	81.2
Processed	0.4	6.5	2.2	7.2	16.3	2.5	18.8

Source: Whitaker, Colyer and Alzamora Appendix Table 3.5.

The decline in the share of exports of primary agricultural products reflects increased exports of processed agricultural products, especially cacao, coffee and fish and shrimp. Exports of processed agricultural products increased as a direct result of government incentives and taxes on the export of primary (unprocessed) agricultural products. Processed agricultural products were 18.8 percent of total agricultural exports during 1984-1987 up from only 8.9 percent during 1965-1969. The elimination or reduction of export taxes on primary products in the early 1980s reduced incentives to invest in processing, but exports of processed coffee, cacao and seafood continued at relatively high levels compared to the late 1960s.

When exports of processed bananas, cacao, coffee, and seafood are added to primary exports of these four products, their combined importance as foreign exchange earners increases from 79.0 to 95.3 percent of all agricultural exports during 1984-1987. Exports of all other minor primary and processed agricultural products are relatively small amounting to 4.7 percent of total agricultural exports during 1984-1987, down from 12.3 percent during 1965-1969.

Imports

Agricultural imports are defined to include: (a) agricultural consumer goods for direct consumption (foodstuffs, tobacco and alcoholic and other beverages); (b) inputs for agriculture (animal feeds, fertilizers, chemicals and other factors of production); (c) capital goods for agriculture (machinery and implements, tractors and transportation

Table 3.5 Principal Imports, Annual Averages, 1965-1969, 1975-1979 and 1984-1987

Years	Agri- culture[a]	Industrial Consumer Goods[b]	Raw Materials & Capital for Industry[c]	Construc- tion[d]	Transport, Fuel & Misc.[e]	Total Imports
Value (US$ 1,000,000)						
1965-69	56.3	27.7	74.5	14.1	37.6	210.2
1975-79	218.0	125.4	601.5	72.3	231.0	1,248.1
1984-87	334.3	150.0	916.6	57.7	356.3	1,814.8
Share (%)						
1965-69	26.8	13.2	35.5	6.7	17.9	100.0
1975-79	17.5	10.0	48.2	5.8	18.5	100.0
1984-87	18.4	8.3	50.5	3.2	19.6	100.0

Source: Whitaker, Colyer and Alzamora Appendix Table 3.6.

[a] Foods, beverages, tobacco, agricultural inputs and capital goods, and raw food products and fibers for industrial processing.
[b] Pharmaceuticals, clothing, other nondurables and consumer durables.
[c] Minerals, chemicals, other nonagricultural raw materials and capital goods for industry.
[d] Construction materials.
[e] Transportation equipment, fuels and lubricants and miscellaneous.

equipment and other agricultural equipment); and (d) raw materials of agricultural origin for industrial processing (unprocessed or semiprocessed foods, fibers and hides).[6] The category "raw materials of agricultural origin for industrial processing" is included to permit the calculation of a commercial balance of agricultural trade and highlight its relative importance.

Agricultural imports are a relatively small proportion of total imports accounting only for 18.4 percent in 1984-1987, down from 26.8 percent during 1965-1969 (Table 3.5). In contrast, imports of nonagricultural raw materials and capital goods for industry have increased in relative importance throughout the last two decades from 35.5 percent of total imports in 1965-1968 to 50.5 percent of total imports during 1984-1987. When imports of raw materials of agricultural origin for industrial processing are counted as part of industrial imports, industry's share of total imports increases from 50.5 to 62.4 percent for 1984-1987 and agriculture's share falls from 18.4 to only 6.6 percent.[7] Thus, the industrial sector is by far the largest demander of foreign exchange for imports. The transportation sector (which is defined to include transportation equipment, fuels and lubricants and miscellaneous imports) is the second most important demander of foreign exchange with 19.6 percent of all imports on average during 1984-1987. Thus, the industrial and transportation sectors dominate imports. Industrial consumer goods accounted for 8.3 percent of total imports and construction materials were 3.2 percent.[8]

The most important class of agricultural imports is raw materials of agricultural origin for industrial processing at 64.4 percent of the total during 1984-1987, down from 71.0 percent in 1965-1969 (Table 3.6; Whitaker, Colyer and Alzamora Appendix Table 3.7). The most important imports in this class are wheat, barley, unrefined vegetable oils, powdered milk, cotton, wool, hides and other food products for processing.

Table 3.6 Principal Agricultural Imports, Annual Averages, 1965-1969,
1975-1979 and 1984-1987

Year	Agricultural Consumer Goods[a]	Fertilizer & Other Inputs[b]	Capital Goods[c]	Agricultural Raw Material for Industry[d]	Total
Value (US$ 1,000 CIF)					
1965-69	6,387	4,649	5,297	39,925	56,258
1975-79	34,464	32,378	35,693	115,416	217,951
1984-87	27,705	63,074	28,098	215,395	334,271
Share (%)					
1965-69	11.4	8.3	9.4	71.0	100.0
1975-79	15.8	14.9	16.4	53.0	100.0
1984-87	8.3	18.9	8.4	64.4	100.0

Source: Whitaker, Colyer and Alzamora Appendix Table 3.7.

[a] Foods, beverages and tobacco.
[b] Fertilizer, animal feeds, pesticides and other inputs.
[c] Machines and implements, tractors and transportation equipment, and other agricultural equipment.
[d] Cereal grains, unrefined vegetable oils, powered milk and other unprocessed foods, natural fibers, and hides.

Agricultural consumer goods for direct consumption (food, beverages, and tobacco) were 8.3 percent of agricultural imports during 1984-1987, down from 11.4 percent in 1965-1969.[9] Operating and capital inputs for agriculture accounted for 27.3 percent of agricultural imports on average during the 1984-1987 period, up from 17.7 percent two decades ago (see Chapter 6 for more information on agricultural inputs).

An Agricultural Trade Surplus

Agricultural exports have exceeded agricultural imports by a substantial margin during the last two decades (Figure 3.3; Whitaker, Colyer and Alzamora Appendix Table 3.8). The trade surplus ranged from US$80 million in 1965 to US$866 million in 1986, a ten fold increase (measured in current dollars). The surplus averaged US$94 million per year during 1965-1969, US$425 million during 1975-1979 and US$679 million during 1984-1987. The surplus approached the US$1 billion level during 1986 and 1987.

Agricultural exports have been sufficient to pay for all imports of: (a) food, beverages and tobacco for direct human consumption; (b) inputs and capital goods for agriculture; (c) raw materials of agricultural origin for industrial processing (primarily food products, wool, cotton and hides); and (d) all costs associated with these imports, including customs charges, insurance and freight, with relatively large surpluses left over. These surpluses have contributed significantly to the foreign exchange earnings of Ecuador, and have been utilized to subsidize and sustain the import-substitution industrialization approach to economic development during the last three decades..

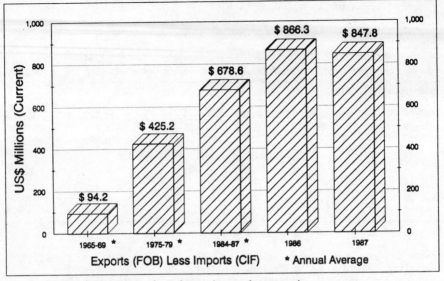

Figure 3.3 Agricultural Trade Balance (Annual Average)
Source: Whitaker, Colyer and Alzamora Appendix Table 3.8.

The agricultural trade surplus has been sufficiently large to pay for all or most of industry's imports of other raw materials (besides those of agricultural origin) and capital goods depending on the period under consideration (Table 3.7). During 1965-1969 agricultural trade surpluses were 126.4 percent of industrial imports and 74.0 percent of the much larger industrial imports during 1984-1987. Thus, agriculture has made and continues to make a major contribution to economic growth and development through the generation of very large surpluses of foreign exchange. This is a remarkable accomplishment when the disincentives to invest in agriculture inherent in the macroeconomic policy matrix and the general neglect of the sector are considered (see Chapter 2).

Improving the Agricultural Trade Balance

Agricultural exports are very important earners of foreign exchange but Ecuador's continued reliance primarily upon five principal exports should be a cause for concern. Producers in Ecuador face elastic world prices for their exports and are unlikely to be able to influence prices which are determined by constantly changing market conditions outside Ecuador. One reality of world markets is the volatility of prices in response to changes in international supply and demand, so that Ecuador's foreign exchange earnings always are subject to substantial variation which are beyond the influence of domestic policies. The devastating consequences of the precipitate fall in petroleum prices in 1986 and coffee prices in 1989 are grim reminders of the painful adjustments such price swings can impose on a small, open economy such as Ecuador.

Changes in world market conditions also can result in erosion or loss of Ecuador's market shares to international competitors as has happened with cacao (Ghana and

Table 3.7 Agricultural Trade Balance, 1965-1987 (US$ 1,000,000)

Years	Agricultural Exports (FOB)	Agricultural Imports (CIF)	Trade Balance	Raw Materials & Capital for Industry	Trade Balance as Share of Industrial (%)
1986	1,174.5	308.2	866.3	944.4	91.7
1987	1,157.9	310.1	847.8	1,097.8	77.2
Average					
1965-69	150.5	56.3	94.2	74.5	126.4
1975-79	643.5	218.0	425.2	601.5	70.7
1984-87	1,012.9	334.3	678.6	916.6	74.0

Source: Whitaker, Colyer and Alzamora Appendix Table 3.8.

Brazil), bananas (Colombia) and is happening with shrimp. There are many countries in Asia and Central America that will strongly challenge Ecuador's share of the fresh shrimp market in the next few years, as their productive capacity develops. The recent incursion into the market by China is a case in point. Technological improvements in both production and marketing processes will determine which countries are able to consolidate their shrimp industries and remain as significant suppliers in the highly competitive North American and European markets.

A potential exists for increasing the agricultural production for export and for domestic consumption of several of the food and fiber items now imported for direct consumption or industrial processing. The value of potential exports or of savings from production of import substitutes in agriculture is an estimated US$100 million (Whitaker and Alzamora 1988b, pp. 23-27). Ecuador probably could supply close to one-third of its wheat and all of its vegetable oils, milk, hides, and wool and possibly have surpluses for export. There also is potential for exports of rice and vegetable oils to Andean neighbors which import large amounts of these items. Ecuador has perhaps the best agricultural base of any of the Andean countries for producing rice and vegetable oils with evidence of comparative advantage in their production (IDEA; Stewart and Cuesta). Domestic production of fertilizers based on natural deposits of phosphates and abundant natural gas also is a possibility although the economies of scale required for production of nitrogen fertilizer are large (Hammond and Hill). Again, however, there may well be opportunities for export of any surplus fertilizer production to Andean neighbors.

Nutritional Status and Agriculture

Agriculture in Ecuador contributes to the availability of food in two fundamental ways. First, it produces a wide variety of crops and livestock products primarily for domestic consumption. Second, it generates a substantial foreign exchange surplus after paying for all imports of food and fiber and inputs and capital for agriculture. Thus, it can be argued that the agricultural sector has made Ecuador self-reliant in meeting its food needs in that it has provided all of the available food, both domestic and imported, and has generated significant additional foreign exchange for development of the rest of the economy.

The adequacy of the available food supply in meeting the needs of Ecuador has two principal dimensions. The first is the nutritional requirements of the population which is treated in this section. This dimension is concerned with whether there is enough food and of sufficient quality to provide, on average, the minimum level of nutrition necessary for a healthy and productive life for each member of society. The second is the cost of food which is considered in the following section.

Conventional Wisdom and Data

It is commonly believed in Ecuador that there is not enough food available, on average, to meet the minimum nutritional needs of the population. This viewpoint has been a continuing theme of the popular press and of some institutions and observers over the last two decades (see, e.g. Freire and Polanco). This school of thought has criticized the large imports of food and the shift of lands out of Sierra cereals, tubers and legumes and into pastures and production of animal proteins (see Chapter 6). It has called for increased production of traditional Sierra crops and argues for the anachronistic notion of self-sufficiency in meeting the nutritional needs of the population. It has not recognized the critical role of agricultural exports in paying for food imports nor of past government policies which subsidized imports of food to the detriment of domestic production.

Data for measuring the nutritional status of the Ecuadorian population are limited and confined almost exclusively to small case studies or to estimates of apparent consumption from secondary data. There have been only two national nutrition surveys and neither was representative of the total population. The first was carried out in 1959 by the Ecuadorian military, the Ecuadorian National Institute of Nutrition (INNE) and the Interdepartmental Committee on Nutrition for National Defense (ICNND) of the U.S. Departments of State and Defense (see ICNND). The second was a national survey of children through five years of age carried out by the National Development Council (CONADE) in 1986 which relied on anthropometric measurements (Freire et al.).

Past Analyses of Apparent Consumption

Several analyses of food balances for various years between 1961 and 1980 comprise the principal sources for inferring that there has not been enough food to meet minimum nutritional requirements of the population. Estimates of apparent consumption were made by Freire and Polanco, the United Nations Food and Agriculture Organization (FAO 1977, 1980), the United Nations Economic Commission for Latin America (CEPAL) and FAO, and Ribadeneira Baca. The general approach of each of these studies was to calculate the apparent consumption of food by adjusting production for imports, exports, stocks, losses in marketing, animal feeds, seeds, industrial processing losses and food preparation losses. The edible balance was converted to nutrient content (energy, protein, vitamins, etc.) by use of standard factors to determine the amount of nutrients available per capita per day. Minimum daily requirements, as recommended by various national and international agencies, were adapted to the body-weight regime and the age and sex distributions of the population to determine weighted average per capita requirements. The comparison of average daily per capita availability with weighted average per capita daily requirements (or standards) indicated whether the particular nutrient was surplus or deficit.[10]

Table 3.8 Daily Availability of Energy and Protein per Capita in Ecuador, Based
on Calculation of Apparent Consumption from Various Studies, 1961-1980

Year	Study	Apparent Consumption		Standard Utilized[a]		Apparent as a Share of Standard	
		Energy (k calories)	Protein (grams)	Energy (k calories)	Protein (grams)	Energy (%)	Protei (%)
1961	CEPAL-FAO	1,885	46	2,300	45	0.82	1.02
1961-63	FAO (1977)	1,845	46	2,290	--	0.81	--
1968	CEPAL-FAO	2,023	48	2,300	45	0.88	1.07
1968	Freire-Polanco	1,748	41	2,300	62	0.76	0.66
1968	Ribadeneira-Baca	1,618	42	2,100	57	0.77	0.74
1969-71	FAO (1977)	2,062	--	2,290	--	0.90	--
1972-74	FAO (1977)	2,087	47	2,290	--	0.91	--
1974	CEPAL-FAO	2,109	48	2,300	45	0.92	1.07
1974	Freire-Polanco	1,985	37	2,300	62	0.86	0.60
1975-77	FAO (1980)	2,109	50	--	--	--	--
1980	Freire-Polanco	1,755	44	2,300	62	0.76	0.71

Source: See references to this chapter for the detailed citation of each study.

[a]The standards utilized vary according to the study. They generally are weighted-average per capita requirements, but for a weight regime of a typical developed country taken from FAO-WHO. An exception is the 62 grams of protein from Freire which is the FAO-WHO "safe level" at a score of 60 percent for moderately active adult males weighing 65 kilos. Freire incorrectly compares this to per capita consumption, rather than to consumption per adult male equivalent. See text.

The results of these analyses vary considerably for both energy and protein availability (Table 3.8). The studies found deficiencies in energy, as measured by kilocalories, for various years between 1961 and 1980 ranging from 77 to 92 percent of the standard utilized. The CEPAL-FAO and FAO studies each revealed a trend of increasing levels of energy consumption from about 80 percent of the standard in 1961 to over 90 percent by 1974. The Freire and Polanco, and Ribadeneira Baca studies found much lower levels of energy consumption in 1968 than did the CEPAL-FAO and FAO studies for 1968 and 1969-1971, respectively. The Freire and Polanco study showed the same increasing trend as CEPAL-FAO and FAO between 1968 and 1974, then a decrease by 1980 to 1968 levels.

The CEPAL-FAO study found per capita protein consumption, measured by grams, exceeded the standard in 1961, 1968 and 1974, with a slight increase between 1961 and 1968 and then maintenance of this level in 1974. Freire and Polanco and Ribadeneira Baca found substantially lower levels of protein consumption in 1968 than CEPAL-FAO at only 66 and 74 percent of the standard, respectively. Moreover, Freire and Polanco's results indicated a strong decrease in per capita protein consumption by 1974 to only 60 percent of the standard and then an increase by 1980 to 71 percent, back to near the 1968 level.

Great care must be exercised in interpreting the results of these studies because they all appear to contain errors.[11] They tend to overestimate protein and energy standards and hence conclude that deficits are greater and surpluses are less than they actually are.

First, all the studies apparently use standards based on average body-weights more representative of a developed than a developing country. These standards are based on recommendations of FAO and the United Nations World Health Organization (WHO) but appear to have been erroneously adapted from those for FAO-WHO's typical developed country rather than its typical developing country. For example, Freire and Polanco (p. 30) describe their reference or standard man as that for "...developing countries, being a man of 29-39 years of age, with a weight of 65 kilograms (kg), healthy and able to work 8 hours per day in moderate activities." (Translation by author.) However, 65 kg is the weight of the reference man for FAO-WHO's typical developed country; that for a typical developing country is only 53 kg (FAO-WHO p. 82). They also are based on recommendations of the National Institute of Nutritional and Social-Medical Research (ININMS) which uses a body-weight regime that is nearly identical to FAO-WHO's typical developed country and was adapted from data for Central America (Oleas p. 5; INCAP). Thus, the body-weight regime utilized in these studies is not even based on studies of body-weight in Ecuador which has people of relatively small stature. To the extent the body-weight regime utilized is heavier than that of the Ecuadorian population, the protein and energy standards are too high and protein and energy deficits are overestimated (or surpluses are underestimated).

Second, the Freire and Polanco study also substantially overestimated the magnitude of the protein deficit because it compared the protein requirement for a standard or reference man with the per capita availability for the population. The study should have compared the weighted average requirement for protein for the population (adjusted for body-weight and weighted by the age and sex distribution of the population) with the per capita availability.

Third, the protein standard in Freire and Polanco is further overestimated because of an unduly pessimistic assumption about the quality of protein in the Ecuadorian diet. The ININMS's standards assume that only 60 percent of the protein is high quality, equivalent to milk or eggs, with all the essential amino acids (Oleas). FAO-WHO (p. 73) indicates that countries like Ecuador have a protein quality that averages 70 percent and that a quality of 60 percent is typical of only the very poorest developing countries where "...70-80 percent of the diet comes from such foods as cassava and maize and virtually none from animal foods..." The CEPAL-FAO study corrected its protein standard to 65 percent in recognition of this reality (Szretter p. 207), but the other studies apparently implicitly utilized the 60 percent ININMS'S score.

Apparent Consumption: 1985

Apparent consumption was calculated for 1985 utilizing the same general methodology employed in the studies cited above. Domestic production was adjusted for imports and exports, stocks (when available), animal feed, seeds, and processing, marketing and food preparation losses. The remaining edible portion was converted to energy and protein equivalents utilizing factors published by INNE (1955), the predecessor agency of ININMS. This analysis indicated daily, per capita consumption in 1985 of 2,354 calories of energy and 46.6 grams of protein (Table 3.9). Not included in this total are an estimated 207 calories consumed in the form of sugarcane-based alcohol and home made brown sugar (*panela*).

The per capita requirements for energy and protein consumption were calculated for the Ecuadorian population in 1985, based on the published recommendations and average body-weights of ININMS (Oleas) and projections of the population for 1985

Table 3.9 Food Balance Sheet for Ecuador, 1985

Food Source	Production	Imports	Exports	Seeds	Animal Feed	Losses & Wastage	Apparent Consump.	Availab. per/cap.	-Daily per capita- Energy[a]	Protein
	------------------------------------ (metric tons) ------------------------------------							(kgs/yr)	(k calories)	(grams)
Total	9,594,128	573,820	2,045,658	116,603	257,841	3,444,304	4,303,544	458.90	2,354.27	46.55
Grains	660,104	265,531	16,984	55,096	204,708	36,276	612,571	65.32	576.54	14.73
Legumes & Nuts	122,253	1,456	0	10,347	0	40,740	72,622	7.74	60.49	3.52
Tubers	669,759	0	10	48,999	0	30,840	589,910	62.90	188.91	3.05
Oils and Fats	546,962	267,649	5,458	2,161	53,133	584,974	168,885	18.01	436.26	0.00
Vegetables	215,659	0	0	0	0	23,528	192,131	20.49	20.07	0.67
Fruits	3,563,071	1,627	1,649,173	0	0	412,461	1,503,064	160.28	451.37	4.46
Animal	871,117	37,557	62,944	0	0	27,700	818,030	87.23	225.35	17.81
Other	2,945,203	0	311,089	0	0	2,287,784	346,330	36.93	395.27	2.31

Source: Whitaker, Colyer and Alzamora Appendix Table 3.9.

[a]An additional 207 calories per capita of energy are consumed in the form of alcohol and home-made brown sugar, produced from sugar cane. This amount is not included in the total because most of these calories are believed to be consumed mainly as alcohol (definitive data are lacking).

Table 3.10 Daily per Capita Apparent Consumption of Energy and Protein Compared to
ININMS Standards and to Corrected Standards for Ecuador, 1985

Class	Energy (k calories)	Protein (grams)
1. Apparent Consumption[a]	2,354	46.6
2. ININMS's Consumption Standards[b]	2,285	49.2
3. Corrected Consumption Standards[c]	2,020	37.3
4. Available as Share of Standards		
(a) ININMS (%)	103.0	94.7
(b) Corrected (%)	116.5	124.9

Source: Whitaker, Colyer and Alzamora Appendix Tables 3.9, 3.10, and 3.11.

[a] Not including 207 grams from sugarcane-based alcohol and panela (home-made brown sugar).
[b] Weighted by Ecuador's age and sex distribution in 1985.
[c] Protein score of 70 percent instead of 60 percent, and body-weight regime similar to that of a developing, instead of a developed country.

by the National Institute of Statistics and Census (INEC), CONADE and the Latin American Demographic Center (CELADE). The average requirements for energy and protein for each age and sex class of given body-weight, and for lactating and pregnant females were weighted by the share of the population in each age and sex group.[12] The resulting per capita requirement was 2,285 calories of energy and 49.2 grams of protein.

Comparison of per capita availability with the ININMS based standards indicates that there was enough energy to meet the requirements of the population, on average at 103.0 percent of the standard not including that from alcohol from sugarcane (Table 3.10). Protein availability was only 94.7 percent of the minimum standard.

The ININMS per capita energy and protein requirements for 1985 were corrected to account for too low a protein score and for body-weights that appear to be too heavy for Ecuador. The protein score was assumed to be 70 instead of 60 percent per FAO-WHO findings (p. 73) which reduced the weighted average protein requirement from 49.2 to 42.2 grams. The modified protein requirement and the energy requirement also were adjusted downward to reflect the body-weight regime of FAO-WHO's typical developing country (p. 82).[13] When this correction is made the protein requirement falls further to 37.3 grams and the energy requirement falls from 2,285 to 2,020 calories.

Utilizing these corrected and more realistic standards indicates apparent consumption of energy and protein in 1985 were 116.5 percent and 124.9 percent, respectively, of the average requirements for Ecuador in 1985. Moreover, the protein availability per capita as calculated in all the apparent consumption studies cited above is greater than the corrected standard excepting in the Freire and Polanco results for 1974. The level of apparent consumption of energy per capita is very close to the corrected energy requirement in six of the eleven previous studies and estimated deficits are much smaller than with the higher standards utilized in the studies.

Table 3.11 Quality of the Diet in Terms of Energy Sources

| Food Class | Source of Energy (k calories) | | | Total |
	Protein	Fat	Carbohydrates	
Grains	61.8	30.0	494.2	586.0
Legumes & Nuts	14.8	15.4	33.3	63.5
Tubers	12.4	1.2	172.1	185.6
Oils and Fats	0.0	458.4	0.2	458.6
Vegetables	2.8	1.8	23.1	27.7
Fruits	19.2	19.7	474.5	513.4
Animal Foods	73.0	116.2	40.9	230.1
Other	9.5	46.1	377.6	433.2
Total	193.5	688.8	1,615.8	2,498.2
Percent of total	7.75	27.57	64.68	100.00
Percent of Recommended Diet (ININMS)	9-11	30-35	54-61	

Source: Whitaker and Alzamora 1988a, Appendix Table 4.

Quality of the Diet

The quality of the average diet also was analyzed in relation to a suggested ININMS standard for sources of energy and found to be reasonably good (Table 3.11). The apparent consumption of various foods was converted to calories derived from protein, fat and carbohydrate sources by utilizing average conversion factors (White, Handler and Smith). The calculated percentage distribution of calories from each of the three energy sources was compared to the ININMS standard to measure the quality of the diet. The comparison indicated that too little of the average diet came from proteins and from fats and that too much came from carbohydrates. The deviations from the ideal were not large, however, suggesting that the quality of the average diet is reasonably good. No attempt was made to adjust these results for the corrected energy and protein standards but the implication is that the quality of the diet is somewhat better than indicated.

Average versus Minimum Requirements

The surplus of energy and protein on average found in the 1985 analysis of apparent consumption does not imply either: (a) that all people are consuming the minimum nutritional requirement; or (b) that excess food supplies exist which can be allocated to those consuming below the minimum requirement. In fact, the term "surplus" is a misnomer because all the available food supply is consumed with higher-income groups consuming more than the minimum requirements and the lowest-income groups consuming less than the minimum. The supply of food would have to be increased to raise consumption up to the minimum standard for all those consuming below it. Thus, even with a "surplus" compared to average requirements a food deficit may exist when compared to meeting total nutritional requirements at the margin.

Ecuador has a highly unequal distribution of income. This suggests a significant number of people have limited economic access to food relative to the situation that would exist with a more equitable distribution of income. The more optimistic findings of the 1985 analysis of apparent consumption relative to the earlier studies are ones only of degree; as will be shown below there is a significant proportion of the population who do not have economic access to a minimally nutritious diet suggesting a food deficit relative to total nutritional needs.

Nutritional Deficiencies

Thomason found that energy consumption in 1953 and 1954 among lower income groups in the rural and urban Sierra was deficient. The national level ICNND survey of civilian and military populations found inadequate consumption of riboflavin, thiamin, niacin and calcium among both groups. Civilians had a high incidence of goiter (iodine deficiency) in the Sierra and anemia (iron deficiency) in the Costa, with inadequate energy intake, especially in the rural Sierra (ICNND). The endemic level of goiter appeared to be declining in later years in response to use of iodized salt and is no longer considered a serious nutrition problem. Several studies of specific population groups and geographic regions, however, have found very high levels of nutritional anemia (Freire and Polanco p. 41).

A study by INNE (1973) found that malnutrition was greater in rural than in urban areas and more prevalent in the Sierra than the Costa. The same study found infants, preschool children and pregnant and lactating females to be most at risk. A number of studies over the last two decades based on samples of local population groups have found evidence of growth faltering which has been attributed by some analysts to protein-energy deficiencies among children (Meneses and Proaño).

The national-level survey by CONADE in 1986 provides the first comprehensive analysis of malnutrition among children (Freire et al.).[14] The study utilized anthropometric measurements to determine the incidence of acute, chronic and global malnutrition among children ages 0-59 months.

Acute malnutrition (underweight for height) appears in the second semester of life among 2 percent of children, rises to 16 percent in the second year, falls to 7 percent in the third year and then to zero. This is an alarming statistic because it indicates that a relatively large number of children are malnourished during one of the most critical phases of physical growth and development--the weaning period. The resultant loss of body weight, if it is sustained, leads to permanent stunting. Acute malnutrition disappears after age three, suggesting that nourishment becomes adequate for children after weaning.

Permanent stunting because of acute malnutrition during the weaning period is evidenced by the increasing proportion of children suffering chronic malnutrition (too short for age). The Freire et al. study showed that 16 percent of infants 0-5 months were too short for their age, increasing to 56 percent of five-year-olds. The short height for age of 16 percent of newborns and infants is inconsistent with the almost complete absence of acute malnutrition in this age group. The explanation appears to be that a significant proportion of mothers are of relatively small stature and give birth to short babies. If infants are classified as chronically malnourished when, in fact, they were born short, the Freire et al. study may overestimate the incidence of chronic and global malnourishment (Nelson). Global malnutrition (underweight for age) is negligible among infants but jumps to 47 percent of children ages 12-23 months, reflecting the combined effects of acute and chronic malnutrition. Global malnourishment then declines to 38 percent for ages 24-59 months, suggesting that some children who were previously underweight for their age gained enough weight to drop out of the classification. This finding is consistent with the disappearance of acute malnutrition in older children and suggests that some children receive sufficient food after age two to reverse some of the earlier effects of acute malnutrition.

A key question is the reason for the high incidence of acute malnutrition (underweight for height) during ages 6-35 months and especially during ages 11-23 months. One possible explanation is that has gained wide acceptance in Ecuador is that there is not enough food available to meet minimum nutritional requirements of children and especially weanlings. This is the rationale for the plethora of feeding programs that have been implemented with the assistance of various international donors.

Another explanation focuses on diseases and feeding practices during the weaning period (Nelson; Jonnson). There is evidence that traditional but improper feeding practices, in association with unfounded home remedies for treatment of diseases, severely limit energy consumption among infants of weaning age (Nelson p. 4; Grijalva, et al.). One study clearly demonstrates that mothers routinely fed inadequate food during weaning and in the presence of disease, because of poor feeding practices and remedies based on folklore (Novotny). The weaning period coincides almost perfectly with the very high incidence of acute malnutrition observed by Freire et al. when most permanent stunting occurs.

Almost nothing is known about the nutritional status of older children, youth and adults in Ecuador due to lack of representative studies of these groups. The next section, however, will demonstrate that access to food by many families is severely constrained by economic realities and that the cost of food again is increasing relative to other consumption goods. The implication is that some in these population subgroups are malnourished because of insufficient quantity or quality of food and that the magnitude of the problem may be worsening. Thus, it appears that malnutrition among children is a function of poor feeding practices, diseases and of absolute lack of food for some families, and the interaction of these variables.

The Cost of the Diet

The level of income necessary to meet minimum nutritional needs and other basic requirements, the number of people who fall below this level and the degree of their poverty are of critical importance to government agencies concerned with health and welfare and more generally with development planning. The trend in food prices also is of concern in understanding the dynamics of access to food by the poor. Finally, poverty and relative food prices affect prospects and options for agricultural and economic development. Each of these factors is considered in turn.

The Degree of Poverty

Critical poverty is defined as having insufficient income to afford even a minimally nutritious diet. The threshold of critical poverty is the level of income needed to just purchase adequate food to meet minimum nutritional needs and is referred to as basic-food income. Relative poverty is defined as having enough income to meet minimal nutritional needs but not enough for all other basic necessities. The threshold of relative poverty is the level of income needed just to meet all basic needs and is referred to as basic-needs income. The terms "basic-food income" and "threshold of critical poverty" are used synonymously, as are the terms "basic-needs income" and "threshold of relative poverty". The usual approach for determining the degree of critical and relative poverty is as follows. The basic-food income is estimated by calculating the cost of the minimally nutritious diet from nutritional recommendations and food prices. This threshold of critical poverty then is divided by the Engel coefficient (the share of income spent on food out of total expenditures) in order to estimate basic-needs income or the threshold of relative poverty. These two thresholds then are compared with the distribution of income to determine the share of the population which falls below them and thus measure the magnitude of critical and relative poverty.

This approach identifies three groups: those which have incomes above the threshold of relative poverty and can afford a nutritious diet and other basic necessities, with surpluses for other wants; those whose incomes fall between the thresholds of relative poverty and critical poverty who can afford an adequate diet, but not all of the other basic necessities; and those whose incomes are below the threshold of critical poverty, who can not afford even basic food.

Several studies have examined the issue of critical and relative poverty and the distribution of income in Ecuador or provide sufficient data to make gross estimates of the poverty thresholds and degree of poverty: Barreiros and Teekens, Vos, World Bank 1979, Ministry of Agriculture (MAG) and France's Office of Overseas Science and Technology Research (ORSTOM), and the National Planning Commission (JUNAPLA--a predecessor agency of CONADE) and BCE. Unfortunately, data on income distribution and household consumption patterns are for the mid-1970s so estimates of the magnitude of critical and relative poverty are based on data which now are 15 years old.

The results of these studies and estimates by the authors based on data presented in them suggests substantial levels critical and relative poverty in both rural and urban areas (Table 3.12).[15] The three estimates of poverty in urban areas are quite similar and suggest 21-25 percent of urban people are below the critical poverty level and another 29-35 percent are in relative poverty. These results indicate that 50-60 percent of all urban people are in critical or relative poverty. The two estimates of rural poverty are quite different from each other ranging from 13-28 percent in critical poverty and another 19-62 percent in relative poverty. The higher estimates are based on a field survey by MAG-ORSTOM that enjoys a reputation for quality and the higher-level estimates are deemed more accurate. If they are, rural poverty is more pronounced than in urban areas, with 85-90 percent of rural people in critical or relative poverty. The data upon which these results are based are quite old however and these conclusions are subject to validation for the present.

Prices of Food

The relative changes in the price of food, compared to the price of all other non-food items in the consumer price index have been calculated for Quito, Guayaquil and Cuenca for 1965-1988 (Figure 3.4). These data, reported in BCE (1987, 1988b) illustrate that food and non-food items experienced a modest secular trend of increasing prices. The price of food has tended to increase at about the same rate as for non-food items, for most of the period. There are, however, two important exceptions and what appears to be the beginning of a third.

Table 3.12 Magnitude of Critical and Relative Poverty in Ecuador, 1975

Class:	---------- Urban ----------			-------- Rural -----	
	Barreiros- Teekens	World Bank	JUNAPLA	Synthesis[d]	MAG-ORSTOM
	(1984)	(1979)	(1977)		(1978)
Type of Poverty	(per capita)	(per family)	(per family)	(per family)	(per family)
Critical Poverty Threshold (Sucres, 1975 prices)	5,000	23,170	23,170	18,900	18,900
Share of Population Below Threshold[a] (%)	21	25	25	13-16	26-28
Relative Poverty Threshold (Sucres, 1975 prices)	12,800	59,410	59,410	48,461	48,461
Share of population in class[b] (%)	29	35	30	19-25	59-62
Share of population Below Threshold[c] (%)	50	60	55	32-41	85-90

Source: See References for full citation of each of the studies.

[a] Those in a state of critical poverty.
[b] People with incomes above critical poverty, but below the threshold of relative poverty, or in a state of relative poverty.
[c] All those below the threshold of relative poverty including those below the threshold of critical poverty.
[d] Estimates by authors based on World Bank, Vos, and MAG-ORSTOM sources.

The first is the period 1973-1975 where the price of food increased much more rapidly than the cost of other basic consumption goods. One explanation is the El Niño phenomenon of 1973 which reduced supply, causing a relatively larger increase in price because of inelastic demand. Another explanation is based on increased demand for food from the large windfall gains from the petroleum boom. A large percentage of these gains went to civil servants and urban workers in the form of higher wages and were translated into increased demand because of relatively high income elasticities of demand for many food items.

The second period when food prices increased much more rapidly than non-food items was during 1982-1984. The large increase in relative food prices is explained by the El Niño phenomenon where food production was reduced drastically in 1983 and had not fully recovered by 1984. Once recovery had occurred, food prices increased at the same rate as non-food items during 1985-1987. The relative increase in food prices appears to have started again between 1987 and 1988.[16] This is at least in part due to the drought in the Sierra during the winter crop season of 1987 (September 1987-February 1988) and also may reflect the clandestine export of foodstuffs to Colombia and Peru.

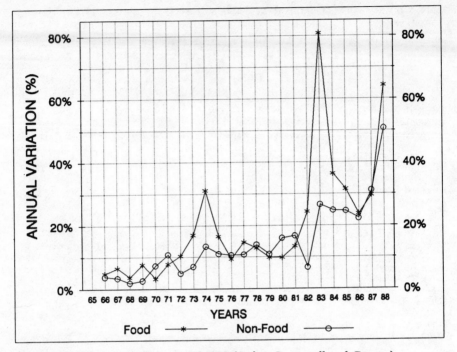

Figure 3.4 CPI Growth Rates: 1965-1988 (Quito, Guayaquil and Cuenca)
Source: Whitaker, Colyer and Alzamora Appendix Table 3.12.

Conclusions

The agricultural sector responded to improved macroeconomic policies during the austerity period of 1982-1988 and grew at an annual average rate of over six percent in contrast to its relatively poor performance during 1965-1981 as production for export and domestic consumption burgeoned. Exhaustion of import- substitution possibilities resulted in complete stagnation of industry. This pattern affected most of the other urban-based economic sectors which also had negative or very low growth rates.

The agricultural sector has made a major contribution to economic growth and development by generating trade surpluses in every year of both the import-substitution and austerity periods. Agricultural exports have been great enough to pay for all imports of capital equipment and inputs for agriculture and all imports of final foods and unprocessed food and fiber, with a relatively large surplus of foreign exchange earnings for purchasing capital equipment, raw materials and consumer goods for the rest of the economy.

While incentives for agricultural production increased due to the more outward-oriented macroeconomic policies, such policies still discriminate against agriculture and tradeables generally. Significant potential remains for increasing and diversifying agricultural production both for export and domestic consumption.

Two major changes are required in order to exploit this potential. First, the macroeconomic and sectoral policies need to be modified in order to provide equal incentives throughout the economy (see Chapter 2). Such policies have resulted in greater imports of raw materials and capital goods for industry and of foodstuffs while dampening incentives for increasing and diversifying agricultural production and exports. They continue to subsidize industry, home goods and urban people while penalizing agriculture, tradeables and rural people.

Second, the science and technology base for agriculture will have to be substantially improved and productivity raised, if farmers are to reduce costs, increase profits and improve their competitive position in the world markets. Ecuadorian farmers still utilize, on average, relatively high cost, low-productivity technologies which keep the country from exploiting its potential comparative advantage (see Chapter 12). Both these changes will require the government to recognize the importance of agriculture in economic growth and development, provide the requisite additional funding for the science base, and give leadership and support for modifying the policy environment.

Agriculture also has made a much more significant contribution to the provision of an adequate food supply than conventional wisdom would suggest. The agricultural sector provides all food for the population, either from domestic production, or through the generation of sufficient foreign exchange to pay for food imports four times over. The 1985 analysis of apparent consumption indicates that there was enough food to exceed the average, minimal nutritional requirements of the population by 25 percent for protein and 17 percent for energy. It also showed a continuation of the increasing trend of past studies. This trend suggests that the improved policy environment and greater incentives for agriculture in the 1980s had a salubrious effect on availability of food.

There are a significant number of people at the margin who do not have economic access to a minimally nutritious diet, notwithstanding the surplus of food on average. The magnitude of poverty should be a cause for serious concern. According to data from the late 1970s, an estimated 20-25 percent of Ecuadorians were in critical poverty with not enough income to purchase even a minimally nutritious diet. Another 25-35 percent were in relative poverty with income for basic food but not enough to meet other basic necessities. Moreover, the situation was more aggravated in rural than urban areas. Thus, roughly half the population were in a state of poverty relative to a very modest standard of well-being. While more recent global data are not available the situation probably has not improved.

The high incidence of poverty reflects one of the more fundamental socioeconomic problems facing Ecuador--its highly unequal distribution of income. It reveals the absence of a large middle income class and a major discontinuity between a large, poverty-stricken segment of the population and a relatively small, urban elite. Lack of effective demand for food and other basic necessities among as much as 60 percent of the population constrains and limits prospects for agricultural development and growth in other economic sectors producing basic consumption goods.

The hungry people of Ecuador, whose incomes fall below the threshold of critical poverty, tend generally to be the indigenous populations, especially in rural areas (*campesinos*) and those working in the informal sector, primarily in self-employment and outside the minimum wage structure in urban areas (Moncayo). They are most likely to be recent migrants, illiterate, have large families and tend to perpetuate the conditions in which poverty breeds. They have extremely limited upward economic mobility which precipitates social and political unrest and contributes to destabilizing the very system which can begin to address the fundamental causes of inequities. According to Barreiros and Teekens, education and family planning are most likely to be effective in breaking the vicious cycle of poverty among these people (pp. 31-42).

A national nutrition strategy for Ecuador would need to be closely coordinated with agricultural and economic development programs. One element of the strategy would be to exploit Ecuador's comparative advantage in agriculture by increasing productivity, production and exports. This leads to the same two policy recommendations as for improving the agricultural trade balance: an improved macroeconomic and sectoral policy environment; and research, extension and education programs for increasing agricultural productivity.

A second important element of any nutrition strategy is a welfare program focused on the poorest and most malnourished groups in the population. This element would identify such population subgroups and provide transfers to address the most urgent and pressing cases of malnutrition and poverty. This element also would comprise education programs to address problems of feeding and associated health care practices, which should be directed more broadly to include lower-middle income groups, as well as the poor.

The burden of increasing food production and export earnings must be focused on commercial agriculture, if the urban poor are to be helped through greater supply responses and downward pressure on food prices. Agricultural development programs focused mainly on resource-poor, part-time farmers (see Chapter 10) will fail to generate the requisite increases in production and productivity. Focusing such programs on commercial agriculture can be justified on welfare as well as efficiency grounds, given the large number of rural and urban people in critical and relative poverty and the urgent need to increase food supply and lower prices. Also commercial agriculture comprises most Ecuadorian farmers, large and small, and programs to improve their productivity will simultaneously and directly improve the welfare of large numbers of farm families. They also will generate off-farm employment and higher incomes for part-time and subsistence farmers. Such productivity-increasing programs in commercial agriculture clearly can be justified as part of a broader social agenda.

NOTES

1. The import-substitution industrialization period spans from the late 1950s to the present. The principal period of rapid industrialization occurred during the late 1960s through 1981 and corresponds closely to the petroleum boom. The period since 1982 has been characterized by austerity measures and economic stabilization with some movement toward a more outward-oriented economy. Nevertheless, the internally oriented development model based on import-substitution still dominated the economy at the beginning of the 1990s (see Chapter 2).

2. The growth rate for petroleum of 6.1 percent during 1965-1981 in Table 3.1 is substantially underestimated because of an accounting procedure in the national accounts which resulted in negative levels of production in the petroleum and mining sector between 1965 and 1971. The growth rates for the import-substitution industrialization period of 1965-1981 and for 1965-1988 were estimated with post-1971 data.

3. This growth rate has taken into account the poor harvest of 1983 due to the El Niño floods. When 1983 is removed from the calculation the growth rate increases slightly to 6.3 percent.

4. The negative share of petroleum in total GDP during 1965-1967 is an anomaly of national accounting methodology (see Note 2). In fact, petroleum production was positive but very small during 1965-1967.

5. This section is summarized from Whitaker and Alzamora (1988b) which contains a more detailed analysis of Ecuador's foreign agricultural trade.

6. Capital goods for agriculture do not include vehicles which are reported only as a class and not allocated to each of the productive sectors.

7. Calculated from data in Whitaker, Colyer and Alzamora Appendix Tables 3.6 and 3.7.

8. "Industrial consumer goods" is defined to include consumer durables and the non-durables (pharmaceutical, clothing and others) not included in agricultural imports. See the footnotes to Whitaker, Colyer and Alzamora Appendix Table 3.6.

9. It is important to recognize that this share is distorted by inclusion of "raw materials of agricultural origin for industrial processing" as part of agricultural imports. If they were not included, the share of "agricultural consumer goods" in the smaller total would be much higher.

10. The terms "requirements," "standards" and "recommendations" are used synonymously throughout this study to describe the requisite minimum nutritional intake for both energy and protein.

11. See Whitaker and Alzamora (1988a) for a detailed analysis of the methodological errors in each of these studies.

12. The individual requirement for energy is the average for a particular age and sex class of given body size. The requirements for an individual vary from the average depending on body-weight, ambient temperature, level of physical activity, altitude and the particular metabolic characteristics of the individual. The individual requirement for protein is the minimum safe level of intake for a particular age and sex class of given body-weight defined as two standard deviations above the average requirement for the class. Thus, protein requirements are estimates of the upper range of individual requirements with only 2.5 percent of individuals with physiological requirements above these levels. In contrast, energy requirements are averages.

13. See Whitaker and Alzamora (1988a pp. 7-9) for more detail on how ININMS's standards were corrected for the body-weight regime of FAO-WHO's typical developing country.

14. The following discussion is based in part on the critique by Nelson (1986) of the 1986 CONADE study (Freire).

15. See Whitaker and Alzamora (1988a pp. 14-18) for a detailed description of the assumptions underlying the estimation of poverty thresholds and the share of the population in each poverty class.

16. See Spurrier (1988) for a review of increases in the consumer price index during 1987 and early 1988.

REFERENCES

Barreiros, Lidia and Rudolph Teekens. 1984. "Poverty and Consumption Patterns in Urban Ecuador, 1975." The Hague: ISS-PREALC, July.

BCE (Central Bank of Ecuador). 1989, 1988a, 1982a, 1982b. *Cuentas Nacionales del Ecuador*. Quito: Nos. 12--Preliminary Summary, 11, 3 and 2.

_____. 1988b, 1978. *Boletín Anuario*. Quito: BCE, Nos. 11 and 1.

_____. 1987. "Indice de Precios al Consumidor: Area Urbana." Quito: División Técnica. CEPAL and FAO (U.N. Economic Commission for Latin America and U.N. Food and Agriculture Organization). 1975. "Food Supply Analysis." Quito: September.

FAO (U.N. Food and Agriculture Organization). 1980 *Anuario de Producción: 1979*. Vol. 33. Rome.

_____. 1977. *La Cuarta Encuesta Alimentaria Mundial de la FAO*. Rome.

FAO and WHO (U.N. World Health Organization) Joint, ad hoc Expert Committee. 1973. *Energy and Protein Requirements*. Geneva: Technical Report No. 522.

Freire, Wilma B., et al. 1988. *Diagnóstico de la Situación Alimentaria, Nutricional y de Salud de la Población Ecuatoriana Menor de Cinco Años*. Quito: CONADE, January.

Freire, Wilma and Nancy Polanco. 1984. *La Situación Alimentaria y Nutricional de la Población Ecuatoriana*. Quito: CONADE, August.

Grijalva, Y. et al. 1986. *Proyecto de Evaluación y Mejoramiento del Programa de Asistencia Alimentaria Materno-Infantil, Informe Final*. Quito: ININMS.

Hammond, L. L., and J. M. Hill. 1984. "Fertilizer Status Profile of Ecuador." Muscle Shoals, AL: International Fertilizer Development Center, August.

ICNND (Interdepartmental Committee on Nutrition for National Defense of U.S. Departments of State and Defense). 1960. *Ecuador Nutrition Survey*. Washington, D.C.: U.S. Government Printing Office.

IDEA (Agricultural Policy Institute). 1988. *Alternativas para la Estrategia de Comercialización de Maíz y Arroz in El Ecuador*. Quito: May.

INCAP (Nutrition Institute of Central America and Panama). 1973. *Recomendaciones Dietéticas Diarias para Centro América y Panamá*. Publication E-109, December.

INEC, CONADE and CELADE (National Institute of Statistics and Census, National Development Council and Latin American Demographic Center). 1984. *Ecuador: Estimaciones y Proyecciones de Población*. 1950-2000. Quito: CONADE, December.

INNE (Ecuadorian National Institute of Nutrition). 1973. *Planificación de Programas Nutricionales*. Quito.

_____. 1955. *Table de Composisición de Alimentos Ecuatorianos*. Quito: Casa de la Cultura Ecuatoriana.

Jonnson, Urban. 1988. *Final Report of the JNSP-Mission to Ecuador, 17 October-15 December 1988*. Quito: WHO/UNICEF Joint Nutrition Support Programme.

JUNAPLA and BCE (National Planning Commission and Central Bank of Ecuador). 1977. *Análisis de la Coyuntura Económica*. Quito: JUNAPLA, No. 8, August.

MAG (Ministry of Agriculture). 1985. "Estimaciones de la Superficie Cosechada y Producción." Quito: Dirección General de Informática.

MAG and ORSTOM (Ministry of Agriculture and France's Office of Overseas Science and Technology Research). 1978. *Diagnóstico Socio-Económico del Medio Rural Ecuatoriano*. Quito: MAG, Documents Nos. 3 and 7.

Meneses, S. and M. Proaño. 1982. "Experiencias de Trabajo de Plan Padrinos." *Las Jornadas de la Lucha Contra el Hambre*. Ambato, Ecuador.

Ministry of Finance. 1985. "Anuarios de Comercio Exterior." Quito: Departamento de Comercio Exterior de Tributación Aduanera.

Moncayo, Jaime. 1988. "Una Visión Actualizada de la Pobreza en El Ecuador." Quito: USAID, May.

Nelson, David. 1988. "Draft Position Paper on Feeding Programs." Quito: USAID.

Novotny, Rachel. 1986 "Preschool Child Feeding, Health and Nutritional Status in Highland Ecuador." Unpublished Ph.D. Thesis, Cornell University.

Oleas, Mariana. 1983. *Recomendaciones Nutricionales para la Población Ecuatoriana*. Quito: Ministerio de Salud Pública, ININMS.

Ribadeneira Baca, Mario. 1971. "Hoja de Balance de Alimentos del Ecuador en 1968." Unpublished Tesis de Grado, Central University of Ecuador.

Stewart, Rigoberto and Mauricio Cuesta. 1988. "La Política de Precios del Arroz y sus Efectos en el Ecuador: 1970-1987." Quito: MAG/Policy Analysis Unit, March.

Spurrier, Walter. 1988. *Analysis Semanal* 18:16.

Szretter, Héctor I. 1982. "La Nutrición y la Oferta de Alimentos Básicos." Santiago, Chile: PREALC, May.

Thomason, M.J. 1957. "Dietary Studies in Ecuador," *American Journal of Clinical Nutrition* 5:3:295-304.

Vos, Rob. 1981. "Ecuador, Rural Households: Savings and Investment, 1974-75." Quito: ISS-PREALC, Research Paper No. 2, December.

Whitaker, Morris D. and Jaime Alzamora. 1988a. "Feeding the Population." Quito: USAID, September 7, Assessment of Ecuador's Agricultural Sector, Working Paper No. 8-88.

_____. 1988b. "Agriculture and Trade." Quito: USAID, October 14, Assessment of Ecuador's Agricultural Sector, Working Paper No. 9-88.

Whitaker, Morris D., Dale Colyer and Jaime Alzamora. 1990. *The Role of Agriculture in Ecuador's Economic Development*. Quito: IDEA (Agricultural Policy Institute).

White, Abraham, Philip Handler and Emil L. Smith. 1960. *Principles of Biochemistry*, 3rd Ed. New York: McGraw-Hill Book Company.

World Bank. 1987. *Ecuador: Country Economic Memorandum*. Washington, D.C.

_____. 1984. *Ecuador: An Agenda for Recovery and Sustained Growth*. Washington, D.C.: Report No. 5094-EC.

_____. 1979. *Development Problems and Prospects of Ecuador: Special Report. Vol. I: The Main Report, and Vol. III: Technical Annexes and Statistical Appendix*, 3 vols. Washington, D.C.: Report No. 2373-EC, June 18.

4

DEVELOPMENT OF ECUADOR'S

RENEWABLE NATURAL RESOURCES

Douglas Southgate

Development of renewable natural resources is central to Ecuador's economy. Many of the country's farmers enjoy the benefits of fertile agricultural land and adequate rainfall. Exploiting the biological productivity of the Costa ecosystems, Ecuador has developed a large shrimp industry. Timber and fuel wood are extracted from the country's forests. In addition, Ecuador has linked its economic growth to hydroelectricity production, the expansion of irrigated agriculture and other forms of water resource development.

Given the importance of soil, water and natural ecosystems to the national economy, the costs of resource degradation in Ecuador are great. Soil erosion hinders agricultural production and jeopardizes a large share of the anticipated benefits of water resource development. Disturbance of Costa ecosystems harms mariculture and offshore fishing. Likewise, mismanagement of forests bodes ill for future growth of the timber industry.

This chapter addresses human interaction with the country's natural environment and identifies reforms needed to encourage resource conservation. The following sections describe and analyze: the country's varied geography and its eight major agro-ecological zones; agricultural land use and the potential for agriculture to continue its geographic expansion; the general causes of environmental degradation in Ecuador; five critical natural resource issues (destruction of Costa ecosystems, degradation of tropical forests, erosion of prime agricultural land, waste and misallocation of water, and pesticide contamination); and support that donor agencies could give to conservation initiatives in Ecuador.

All natural resource development issues currently facing Ecuador cannot be covered in a single chapter. Management of offshore fisheries, extraction of petroleum and other mineral resources and development of the Galápagos Islands (which is a matter of global concern) are not addressed here. Even the coverage of environmental problems in rural areas of continental Ecuador is not entirely complete. For example, preservation of the country's biological diversity, which is the subject of a recently completed report (Cabarle et al.) is not discussed. In spite of such omissions, the reader will find that major issues associated with the development of Ecuador's soil, water and natural ecosystems are addressed.

73

Ecuador's Environmental Diversity

With 26,266,000 hectares of territory on the South American mainland and 801,000 hectares in the Galápagos Islands, Ecuador is a little larger than West Germany or the state of Colorado. Nevertheless, its geography is astonishingly varied (Figure 4.1). From the deserts of the Santa Elena peninsula, west of the Costa metropolis of Guayaquil, one need travel no more than 150 kilometers (km) to reach the humid tropics. Nowhere is Ecuador's coastal plain, known as the Costa region, wider than 200 km. It is bounded on the east by the precipitous western range of the Andes, which is dominated by Mount Chimborazo (6,310 meters above sea level). Next come temperate intermontane valleys of the highlands, or Sierra region, where elevations generally exceed 2,500 meters. After the eastern range of the Andes has been crested a rapid descent into the Amazonian rain forest of the eastern lowlands, or Oriente region, begins. An Amazonian frontier town, Nueva Loja (formerly called Lago Agrio) is only 400 km from the Pacific Ocean and 300 meters higher than the surface of the Atlantic Ocean, which is more than 3,000 km due east.

In Ecuador, dramatic topography is matched by marked variations in climate and by biological diversity. Twenty-five of the 30 life zones identified by Holdridge are found in the country (Cabarle et al. p. 5). In addition, the number of plant and animal species living in or endemic to Ecuador compares to similar numbers for larger countries in the Western Hemisphere (Cabarle et al.).

Clearly, all of Ecuador's heterogenous environments cannot be captured in a map that is visually tractable. The eight agro-ecological zones described in this section, however, represent a reasonable breakdown of the country, given criteria generally used to describe Ecuador's renewable natural resource base.

Criteria for Geographical Classification

Five criteria are typically used to distinguish one part of Ecuador from another. The first is temperature, and because Ecuador straddles the equator, a location's temperature is generally a direct function of its altitude. The country's temperature gradient averages a decline of 0.55° centigrade (C) for every 100 meters increase in elevation. Water, the second criterion, varies considerably throughout the country. The amount available for crop and livestock production in different parts of the country depends both on precipitation and stream flow. Data on temperature and rainfall, both their yearly averages and monthly variability, are collected at the meteorological stations of the National Institute of Meteorology and Hydrology (INAMHI). Hydrological data are collected by IHAMHI, the Ecuadorian Institute of Water Resources (INERHI) which is a part of the Ministry of Agriculture (MAG) and by regional authorities. The third criterion is soil quality which is important for deciding whether land should be used for intensive agricultural production, in permanent pasture, or forested. MAG's National Program for Agrarian Regionalization (PRONAREG) considers the following soil characteristics: depth, erodibility, rock content, fertility, salinity, drainage and susceptibility to flooding. Maps prepared by PRONAREG are used to assess soils' agricultural productivity. The fourth criterion is land use. Regions with extensive natural vegetation (e.g., primary forests) are distinguished from those where most land is used for crop or livestock production.

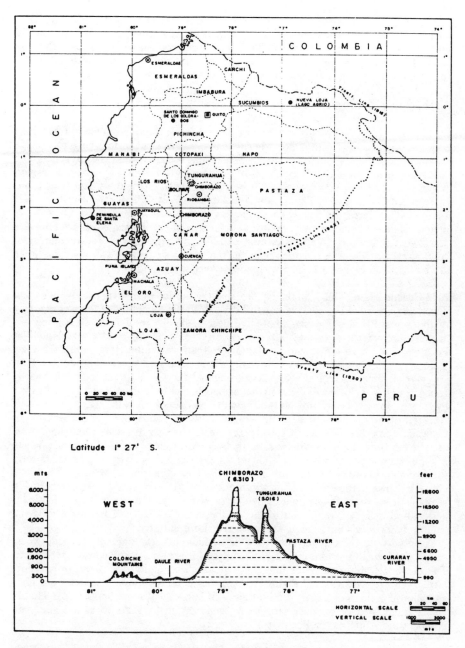

Figure 4.1 Provinces and Geographical Profile of Ecuador
Source: IGM (Military Geographic Institute).

The Center for the Survey of Natural Resources by Remote Sensing (CLIRSEN) as well as MAG's National Forestry Directorate (DINAF) are sources of data on land cover. The final criterion is accessibility which is determined by use of maps showing roads, railways and navigable rivers to rate how well a region is linked with the rest of the country. Mapping is the responsibility of the Military Geographic Institute (IGM).

Eight Agro-Ecological Zones

The dichotomy between the Sierra region where Ecuador's population was long concentrated and the Costa region where the majority of Ecuadorians currently reside antedates the country's independence. When one keeps in mind the preceding five criteria used to describe different parts of the country, however, neither major region comes close to being homogeneous. It is appropriate to divide the Costa region into three zones: Arid Coastal Plains, Southern Humid Coastal Plains and Northern Wet Littoral. The Sierra, defined by convention as all land in central Ecuador above 1,200 meters, is divided among four regions: Outer Faces of the Andes, Northern Hillsides and *Páramos*, Northern Valley Bottoms, and the Southern Sierra. The remainder of continental Ecuador, the Oriente region, is treated as a single zone. Zonal boundaries are indicated in Figure 4.2. A description of each zone follows.

Arid Coastal Plains Between the equator and the border with Peru, land within a few dozen kilometers of the coast is hot and dry. With the exception of the western part of the Santa Elena peninsula, where the heat is slightly moderated by marine air, average temperatures throughout the region are well above 24°C. Rainfall at Portoviejo, some 20 km inland, averages less than 450 millimeters (mm) per year. Salinas, a resort city at the tip of the Santa Elena peninsula, receives little more than 100 mm of rain in a typical year. As throughout the Costa, precipitation is heavily concentrated in a single rainy season that usually begins in January and is typically over by May or June. Stream flow in the region's few rivers is likewise seasonal.

Vertisols are common along the coast between the equator and the Gulf of Guayaquil. South of Portoviejo, calcium carbonate concentrations are often high. Soils around the Gulf of Guayaquil are saturated with salt water. Except for small pockets of pasture interspersed with cropland (principally along rivers) dry forests and deserts predominate between the equator and the Gulf of Guayaquil. Most of Ecuador's coffee is grown in the hills east and south of Portoviejo. Irrigation water being readily available from rivers flowing out of the Sierra, banana production is the predominant agricultural activity around and to the northeast of Machala. That city also is the center of Ecuador's burgeoning shrimp mariculture industry.

Limited water is a major constraint on agricultural development along the coast between the equator and the Gulf of Guayaquil. It is also a costly constraint to relax. The planned transfer of water into the region will be quite expensive. In addition, farmers in the Arid Coastal Plains face significant competition for water from non-agricultural users. For example, withdrawals of irrigation water from the Poza Honda reservoir, in Manabí province, are greatly reduced in dry years to assure adequate potable water supplies for Portoviejo.

Southern Humid Coastal Plains Lying immediately east of the Arid Coastal Plains is a considerably more humid part of the Costa region. The northern and northwestern

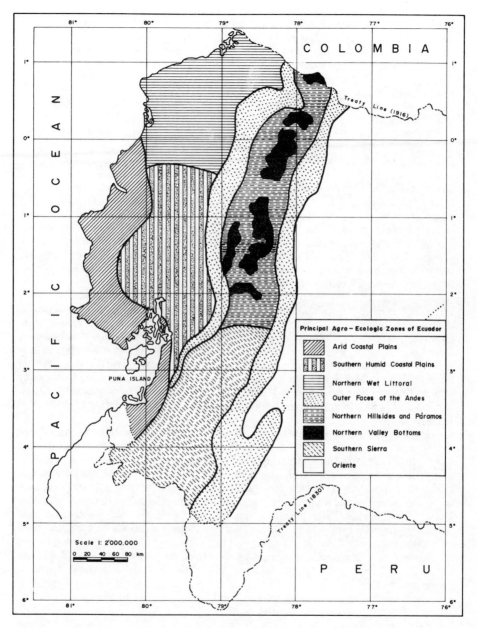

Figure 4.2 Principal Agro-ecological Zones of Ecuador
Source: Prepared by author.

borders of the Southern Humid Coastal Plains coincide with the northern and western limits of the Guayas River Basin, which occupies over half of the Costa region. From a point 50 km due west of Guayaquil, the boundary runs southeastward to within 20 km of the port city, traverses the Guayas River and then runs almost directly south. Consistent with conventional practice for determining where the Costa ends, the eastern boundary of the Southern Humid Coastal Plains is defined to be wherever the altitude of the western range of the Andes rises above 1,200 meters. The southern tip of this wedge-shaped region nearly touches the Peruvian border.

Temperatures in the region are as high as in the arid lands immediately to the west. Soils in the Southern Humid Coastal Plains are generally deep and fertile. Except in the low Andean foothills the land is flat or gently sloped. Consequently, soil erosion is not a major hindrance to agricultural development. The agricultural frontier in the Southern Humid Coastal Plains was all but closed by the early 1970s, with only a few forests left standing in the region's Andean foothills. The Southern Humid Coastal Plains are now the agricultural heartland of Ecuador (Bromley). For several decades, rice production has been the dominant agricultural activity in the Guayas river delta. Farther inland, bananas are grown around Babahoyo. Moving northward, up the Guayas river basin, one sees a mixture of cattle pastures, cropland planted to corn, soybeans, sorghum and other annual crops, and tree crops (e.g., oilpalm and citrus). At slightly higher elevations, coffee and cacao production predominate.

The major problem facing farmers in the Southern Humid Coastal Plains is extremely variable precipitation and stream flow. Nearly all the 1,000 mm of rain in Guayaquil, 1,800 mm in Babahoyo (60 km inland from Guayaquil) and 2,100 mm in Quevedo (an additional 80 km inland) falls during a single wet season that begins in December or January and concludes in June. Stream flow in the region is similarly variable. For example, the Daule River crests with a flow exceeding 800 cubic meters (m^3) a second in March and April, two months after the beginning of the Costa rainy season. By July flow has fallen to 100 m^3 a second. Late in the dry season the Daule River is little more than a stream, with a flow of 20 m^3 a second during the month of November.

Flooding during the rainy season could be alleviated by constructing more large catchments (like the Daule-Peripa reservoir) by adding more culverts, by protecting forests that remain in the upper watershed or by combining these three approaches. Reservoir construction also would ease agricultural water shortages always experienced during the dry season. If reducing seasonal fluctuations in water availability proves not to be too expensive then opportunities to take additional advantage of the Southern Humid Coastal Plains' rich soils should arise. For example, the two crops of rice currently harvested each year in the lower Guayas River Basin could be complemented by a third.

However, dams, culverts, and other public works are very costly. The first phase of the Daule-Peripa project, undertaken to control flooding and to provide irrigation water and hydroelectricity, is costing US$403 million in 1988 dollars (Chapter 7). Clearly, sound economic analysis of the benefits and costs of improved engineering control of water resources is essential.

Northern Wet Littoral Extending from the upper reaches of the Guayas River Basin, a little south of the equator, to the Colombian border is the Northern Wet Littoral. As in the rest of the Western Ecuador, temperatures in the region vary little from month to month and average readings are generally above 24°C. Rainfall is likewise very high with annual precipitation in over half of the Northern Wet Littoral exceeding

3,000 mm. Water availability during the dry season is less of a problem there than it is farther south both because rain falls throughout the year and because rivers flowing through the region originate in the Andes, where monthly fluctuation in precipitation is relatively modest.

Until the 1960s the Northern Wet Littoral was a backwater. Agricultural colonization accelerated rapidly at that time when a new highway linking Quito and Guayaquil passed through Santo Domingo de los Colorados (Bromley). With improvement of the road connecting Santo Domingo to the northwestern port city of Esmeraldas still more farmers flocked into the region. MAG's Ecuadorian Institute for Agrarian Reform and Colonization (IERAC) has adjudicated more land flanking the highway to Esmeraldas than in any other part of the country (Barsky et al.).

After 25 years of agricultural development much of the Northern Wet Littoral has been deforested. Cattle pastures and african oilpalm plantations now dominate the landscape around Santo Domingo. Farther to the northwest, towns like Quinindé are surrounded by small farms where various crops and livestock are raised.

Development of additional infrastructure threatens the Northern Wet Littoral's remaining forests. Long in construction, a new highway connecting Ibarra with Ecuador's northernmost port of San Lorenzo is now three-quarters complete. Similarly, a road running northwest from Quito to La Independencia, west of Santo Domingo is in the final stage of construction. This road will reduce travel time from Quito to Esmeraldas from five to three and one-half hours. Finishing these projects will stimulate additional colonization.

Many, both inside and outside of Ecuador, are concerned over continued deforestation in the Costa. The domestic timber industry, which is centered in the Northern Wet Littoral, argues that domestic supplies of wood products could be reduced if forests continue to be converted into pastures and cropland. In addition, fragile soils now covered with forests are not, in general, highly productive for agriculture. Finally, environmental groups in Ecuador and around the world, hoping to maintain national and global biological diversity, propose that measures be taken to protect sites like the Awa Reserve from encroachment.

Outer Faces of the Andes Because the Andes are a relatively young mountain chain, the transition from the Costa to the Sierra is abrupt as is the descent into the Oriente, farther to the east. The thin strips of land lying between 1,200 and 3,000 meters on the two outer faces of the Andes are wet, generally receiving at least 2,000 mm of precipitation a year. More than 6,000 mm of rain falls each year in Lita, in Northwestern Ecuador. At 1,200 meters above sea level, median average temperature is around 20°C. At 3,000 meters, it is a little above 10°C.

Building and maintaining roads in wet, steeply sloped areas is a considerable challenge. Consequently, the Outer Faces of the Andes have remained largely inaccessible and covered with forests. However, human pressure, especially on the western face, has grown considerably during the past twenty-five years. Logging is widespread and, although soil erosion from steeply sloped, deforested parcels is often severe, agricultural colonists are penetrating from the Costa. Much of the eastern face of the Andes remains undisturbed. Even there, however, penetration from the Sierra is steadily increasing.

Northern Hillsides and Páramos Distinct from the land lying below 3,000 meters in elevation on the eastern and western faces of the Andes are the Northern Hillsides and Páramos. This zone extends from the Colombian border on the north almost to

Cuenca and includes the steeply sloped lands bordering the Northern Valley Bottoms (which are a separate agro-ecological zone) as well as the gently sloped alpine grasslands (páramos) of the high mountains.

Rainfall varies dramatically throughout the region. Average yearly precipitation south of Quito and along the Colombian border exceeds 1,500 mm. In general, rainfall as well as temperature are functions of elevation. Páramos generally receive at least 1,000 mm of rain a year. At 3,000 meters above sea level, average temperatures are a little over 10°C. A thousand meters higher up, average readings are below 6°C and the risk of frost is appreciable.

Soils in the Northern Hillsides and Páramos are generally of recent volcanic origin. *Cangagua*, which is hard-packed and sterile, covers at least 35 percent of the region (Caujolle-Gazet and Luzuriaga p. 60).

Although land use statistics in Ecuador are highly aggregative it is clear that the agricultural frontier has been advancing steadily into the Northern Hillsides and Páramos for several decades. *Hacienda* owners had long planted wheat, barley, and other crops on the hillier portions of their estates. Agricultural pressure on the hillsides increased after the 1964 land reform. Holding onto more productive agricultural land in valley bottoms, hacienda owners only allowed marginal hill lands to be redistributed, as *minifundios*, to their former tenants (Commander and Peek).

Soil erosion is a constant problem in the Sierra. Many small farmers gave up trying to farm steeply sloped lands rising from valley bottoms and moved to the higher-elevation páramos. This pattern of migration, which seems to be especially strong around Latacunga and Ambato, might have been promoted in recent years by global warming, which reduces the risk of frost at higher elevations. PRONAREG personnel claim, for example, that crops are being produced in protected "eco-niches" located some 4,000 meters above sea level.

Northern Valley Bottoms The mild climate of the Andean valleys has long attracted settlement. Average annual temperatures in Northern Valley Bottoms are, in general, above 12°C. In some locations (e.g., Ibarra) average readings approach 18°C. The transition from warm afternoons to cool nights is far more pronounced than monthly variation in temperature.

With the exception of the area south of Quito, the Northern Valley Bottoms tend to be the driest places in the Sierra. Around Ibarra and west of Latacunga, Ambato and Riobamba, less than 500 mm of rain falls in a typical year. However, precipitation in surrounding hills insures that streams flowing through the valley bottoms are a dependable source of irrigation water. The region's soils are similar to those of the surrounding Northern Hillsides and Páramos (see above).

Because the prices of dairy products and meat have generally increased relative to those of wheat, barley and other traditional Andean crops, extensive agricultural holdings in the Northern Valley Bottoms have been shifted to livestock production. Because that activity is less labor intensive than crop production, the conversion of cropland into pasture was also strongly reenforced during the 1970s and early 1980s by strong growth in urban demand for labor, which pulled up wages in the countryside (Commander and Peek). In spite of the shift to livestock production, production of beans, potatoes and other crops remains significant in the Northern Valley Bottoms.

Southern Sierra The Southern Sierra, which runs from the Peruvian border to slightly north of Cuenca, is similar in many ways to the rest of Ecuador's Andean highlands. Average yearly rainfall varies from 600 mm to over 1,000 mm. Median temperatures are likewise very mild. Depending on elevation, average readings range from 10 to 15°C.

The most important distinguishing characteristic of the Southern Sierra is its soils which are not of recent volcanic origin. Vertisols with a high calcium carbonate content are common in the hills around Cuenca. Kaolinite clays, which are easily compacted, are found in abundance around Azogues and Loja.

Another difference between the Northern and Southern Sierra is that the latter region's river valleys, where good agricultural land is concentrated, tend to be narrow. Since the region's major cities are also located in river valleys, there is intense urban competition for land well suited for crop production.

Crop production outside of the river valleys is difficult. Poverty-stricken minifundios surround Cuenca and Azogues and cattle ranching is a predominant activity throughout the region. Much of the Southern Sierra, however, is covered with dry forests and other natural vegetation.

Oriente The Oriente is similar in many ways to the Northern Wet Littoral. Average temperatures in the region vary from 20 to well over 24°C. Rainfall is torrential, totalling more than 3,200 mm a year at Limoncocha, a little southeast of Nueva Loja. Precipitation is higher closer to the Andes with over 4,400 mm of rain falling each year at Puyo. Different from precipitation in the Costa, rainfall in Eastern Ecuador follows no strong seasonal pattern and there is no regularly "dry" month. For this reason, stream flow in the Oriente is less variable than it is on the western side of the Andes.

Regardless of President Plaza Lasso's warning that "the Oriente is a myth," many Ecuadorians and their political leaders continue to think that the region has great agricultural potential. Ongoing surveys of the Oriente, however, indicate that limited soil fertility and poor drainage render sustainable crop production uneconomical in most of the region. MAG has found that no more than 16 percent of Northeastern Ecuador should be in cropland or pasture.

Agricultural colonization of the Oriente was confined largely to a few lower Andean valleys until the late 1960s. Extensive road construction in the region, mostly undertaken to service oil production around Nueva Loja, began during the 1970s. Improved infrastructure, in turn, has stimulated rapid settlement. For example, although forests continue to cover well over half of Northeastern Ecuador, 36 percent of the region has been claimed by agricultural colonists, each of whom is gradually deforesting his respective parcel (MAG).

Agricultural Land Use in Ecuador

As indicated in the preceding section, the agricultural frontier has expanded in several parts of the country during the last few decades. Farmers have penetrated the forests of the Northern Wet Littoral and the Oriente. At the same time, agricultural land use has been increasing in the Northern Hillsides and Páramos.

Existing data do not allow for documentation of changes over time in agricultural land use in each of the eight zones discussed in the preceding section. In this section, those changes are only summarized for the Costa, Sierra and Oriente as a whole and the current extent of cropland and pasture is compared to PRONAREG assessments of appropriate land use in continental Ecuador. Also, the implications for Ecuadorian forestry of additional land clearing can only be assessed by referring to forest inventories conducted during the 1980s.

Table 4.1 Agricultural Land Use Trends (Hectares)

Land Class	1965-69	1980-85[a]	Change
Land Planted to Sierra Crops[b]	571,606	234,414	-337,192
Land in the Costa and Oriente Planted to Tropical Crops[c]	1,166,106	1,311,174	+145,068
Total Cropland	1,737,712	1,545,588	-192,124
Pasture	1,718,946	4,292,830	+2,573,884
Sierra	955,456	1,838,194	+882,738
Costa	516,500	2,033,630	+1,517,130
Oriente	247,000	421,006	+174,006

Source: Chapter 6 Tables 6.5 and 6.6.

[a]Data for 1983 are excluded from the average because of extremely bad weather which caused abnormally low production.
[b]Include barley, fruits, legumes, potatoes, soft corn, vegetables and wheat.
[c]Include bananas, cacao, cassava, castor oil, coffee, cotton, fruits, hard corn, manila hemp, oil palm, peanuts, plantains, rice, soybeans and sugar cane.

Changes in Agricultural Land Use

Through 1985, MAG collected data on agricultural land use and crop and livestock production in each of Ecuador's provinces. No single year's estimate of cropland or pasture is very reliable since it is based on information provided by an under-funded and under-manned network of extension agents. However, some trends in agricultural land use are indicated by the MAG data set.

The area planted to tropical crops (almost entirely in the Costa) increased by 145,068 hectares between the middle 1960s and the middle 1980s (Table 4.1). This increase was exceeded, however, by a simultaneous 337,192 hectare decline in Sierra cropland. Meanwhile, pastures in the five Costa provinces (El Oro, Guayas, Los Ríos, Manabí and Esmeraldas) were quadrupling, from 516,500 to 2,033,630 hectares. The area in pastures also more than doubled in the Sierra to 1,838,194 hectares.

MAG data yield a misleading impression of changes in agricultural land use in Sierra provinces for two reasons. First, the Costa region's agricultural frontier has traversed the western portions of several of Sierra provinces (e.g., Cañar, Cotopaxi and Pichincha) in recent years. Second, far from being intensively managed grasslands, much of the area classified as pasture in the Sierra is unproductive, abandoned cropland on which livestock occasionally graze. Consequently, MAG's report that highland pastures doubled between the middle 1960s and middle 1980s actually masks a significant decline in the quality of a large area in the Ecuadorian Andes that used to be planted to crops.

Twenty-five years ago the area planted to crops in the Oriente was negligible. As MAG surveys indicate that area had risen to 63,100 hectares by 1985. Cattle graze on most of the agricultural land in the Oriente, however. Pastures increased from 247,000 to 421,006 hectares between the middle 1960s and the middle 1980s (Table 4.1).

Table 4.2 Potential Land Use, Sierra and Costa Combined[a]

Category	PRONAREG Classifications	Area (hectares)	Share (%)
Prime farmland	C1a through C3b	3,081,700	21.7
Marginal Cropland	C3c through C4d	1,307,000	9.2
Pastures Only	Pa through Pd	2,451,900	17.3
Forests Only	Ba through Bd	5,905,300	41.7
No Use	S	1,451,900	10.2
Totals		14,197,700	100.0

Source: PRONAREG.

[a]Evaluation of potential use of the areas around Jipijapa and Salinas had not been completed at the time this chapter was being written. The area includes most of the lower slopes of the Andes of the Oriente region in Eastern Ecuador.

Current versus Potential Land Use

The application of improved technology contributed significantly to increased agricultural production in Ecuador during the past quarter century (Chapter 6). However, extension of the agricultural frontier has been a more important cause of increased production in the country. The latter approach to agricultural development cannot continue for long because the quality of land not now being used for crop or livestock production is, by and large, fairly poor.

The primary source of information on land use capabilities in Ecuador is PRONAREG. That agency is completing a detailed study of potential land use in the Sierra and Costa with only the marginal land around Jipijapa and Salinas remaining to be classified. Also the area surveyed includes most of the lower slopes of the Andes in the Oriente region (Table 4.2).

Although PRONAREG reports data on precipitation and average temperature, it ranks land primarily according to soil characteristics. It has determined that approximately 3,100,000 hectares of land in the western two-thirds of Ecuador (corresponding closely to the Sierra and the Costa regions) are relatively fertile, well drained, not highly erodible and free of other serious natural limitations. Consequently, those 3,100,000 hectares are an excellent site for intensive crop production, provided that water is available and temperatures do not drop too low. Agricultural land use depends on the relative prices of different commodities and not just on the suitability of soils for crop production. Consequently, it is best to regard the 3,100,000 hectares as "prime farmland," rather than as prime cropland.

Sustained crop production on an additional 1,300,000 hectares in the Sierra and Costa is possible once measures to deal with serious erosion or drainage problems, for example, have been put in place. Livestock grazing is the only suitable agricultural use of an additional 2,500,000 hectares of land with fragile soils. Finally, in addition to the 5,900,000 hectares of fragile lands that PRONAREG has determined can be used for production forestry, there are 1,500,000 hectares that should remain undisturbed.

Although data on the exact use of the 3,100,000 hectares classified by PRONAREG as prime farmland are not available, virtually all that land appears to be planted to crops or in intensive pasture. Observing that forages are produced on many of those 3,100,000 hectares, some critics argue that under-utilization of prime farmland is a major problem. Sometimes, such a claim reflects a misreading of PRONAREG's sound recommendation that pastures be established where crop production would cause excessive soil degradation. Quite often, however, the charge of under-utilization of prime farmland reflects economic ignorance. Improved pastures are among Ecuador's most intensively used agricultural lands, particularly in the Sierra, and the decision to establish pastures rather than to raise crops should be regarded as a rational response to market forces. Forage crop production is often an efficient use of prime farmland.

To assess agricultural use of other land in the Costa and Sierra, it is appropriate to assume that all of the two regions' 3,100,000 hectares of prime farmland is in intensively managed pasture or planted to crops and that half (i.e., 919,097 hectares) of the Sierra area classified as pasture by MAG is actually degraded and abandoned cropland (see above). These two assumptions imply that current agricultural land use in the Costa and Sierra is 4,498,315 hectares (cropland, Costa pastures and one-half of Sierra pastures) and exceeds prime farmland in the same two regions by 45 percent. Current agricultural land use even exceeds the sum of prime farmland and marginal cropland (i.e., 3,100,000 plus 1,300,000 hectares) by a slight amount. In some parts of the country, then, the agricultural frontier has already extended onto lands characterized by PRONAREG as very fragile.

Increased settlement of the Oriente does not constitute a satisfactory solution to the problem of scarce prime farmland in Ecuador. MAG (p. 60) has determined that slightly more than 850,000 hectares in Northeastern Ecuador (approximately 16 percent of its land area) can be used for agriculture and that the remaining 4,490,000 hectares (or 84 percent) of the region should remain covered with forests. However, 1,120,000 hectares has already been colonized or is in the process of being settled by farmers and ranchers (MAG p. 14).

Even if good agricultural land remains covered with trees in the Oriente, the investment in infrastructure needed to link that land with agricultural markets in the rest of the country will be sizable. Indigenous inhabitants of the region will reject outsiders' attempts to take over land for intensive agricultural production. Also, continuing to deforest the Oriente will do additional harm to the region's biological diversity. Finally, clearing land in the Oriente with limited agricultural potential carries a sizable opportunity cost in the form of foregone development of the region's timber resources.

Almost certainly, the net social benefits of continued agricultural colonization in Eastern Ecuador are negative.

Standing Timber in Primary Forests

Ecuador's forest resources are considerable by any measure. Alone, standing commercial timber in the Costa's major forests approaches 61 million metric tons (Table 4.3). Since commercial demand for timber in Ecuador is less than 2.5 million metric tons (Montenegro and Durini p. 12) those forests, which yield most of the country's supply of wood, could supply the timber and wood products industry with raw materials for several decades to come. When the additional, enormous commercial

Table 4.3 Standing Timber by Region

Region	Inventoried Area (hectares)	Total Wood[a] ----(1,000,000 metric	Commercial Timber[a] tons)----
Costa:			
Esmeraldas Province	800,000	71.0	50.1
W. Rio Guayas Basin	176,000	11.2	4.8
E. Rio Guayas Basin	110,000	11.5	5.9
Oriente:			
Napo Province	2,492,300	220.0	--
Pastaza Province	3,229,600	371.2	207.8
Southeast	1,897,600	219.6	83.2

Source: AIMA 1985 for the Costa; DINAF and CLIRSEN surveys for the Oriente.

[a]Assumes .7 metric tons per m^3 of wood.

timber reserves of the Oriente are taken into account, the danger that excessive logging will significantly restrict timber supplies in the foreseeable future is very remote.

The future adequacy of timber supplies is threatened, instead, by the planting of crops and the establishment of pasture where forests used to stand. DINAF officials indicate that the current deforestation rate is approximately 200,000 hectares a year. Land use conversion is particularly rapid in the northeastern part of the Oriente where agricultural colonists settle alongside roads leading to centers of oil exploration and extraction and in the Northern Wet Littoral, which is the heart of the country's timber industry. As indicated in the preceding subsection, a little over 20 percent of Northeastern Ecuador has been or is now being colonized. More than half of the land in Esmeraldas province, which was covered with forests 25 years ago, is now or soon will be used for crop or livestock production (MAG p. 14).

Relative to the pace of deforestation, cumulative reforestation has been negligible. From 1962 through the middle 1980s around 100,000 hectares had been planted to trees (AIMA 1985, p. 43). A significant portion of reforested area was in the Sierra, where few natural forests had survived into the current century. Virtually nothing has been done to reverse deforestation in Ecuador's humid lowlands.

Causes of Environmental Degradation

Reviewing the ample evidence of resource degradation in developing countries and bearing in mind that human populations in Africa, Asia, and Latin America are expanding rapidly, one is tempted to explain depletive human interaction with third world natural environments in simple Malthusian terms. Certainly, blaming resource degradation in Ecuador on solely on population growth is appealing since the country is the most densely populated in South America.

Accepting a Malthusian perspective hardly causes one to be optimistic about the prospects for resource conservation in a place like Ecuador. Fertility rates have been declining in the country since the middle 1970s (INEC). However, median age, 17.6 years in 1982, is low (United Nations). Given that the number of women of child-bearing age will increase for several more years, Ecuador's population is projected to grow by 2.6 percent a year through the turn of the century (INEC, CONADE and CELADE).

Ultimately, conservation of renewable natural resources probably requires that population growth be checked because of direct increases in the demand for food and the reality that agriculture in Ecuador is largely based on exploiting natural resources. But the Malthusian perspective alone fails to suffice as a comprehensive explanation of resource degradation. As is the case throughout Latin America, inappropriate tenurial arrangements, discriminatory macroeconomic policies, governmental interference with market forces, and inadequate investment in research and extension both for agriculture and natural resources are major reasons for overuse and degradation of Ecuador's renewable natural resources. Conservation policy must address these deficiencies, as well as high population growth rates if renewable natural resources are to be conserved.

Inappropriate Tenurial Arrangements

That severe institutional crises often underlies environmental degradation in Ecuador is most obvious where government properties are being managed poorly. Those properties are extensive. Subsurface resources have always been under government control. With passage of the 1972 Water Law all water resources were nationalized. Costa wetlands are national patrimonies. Similarly, most of the country's tree-covered land is designated as forest patrimony (*patrimonio forestal*) or is part of a publicly owned park or reserve.

These claims far outstrip the government's capacity to manage resources or even to ensure that its claims are honored by the public at large. Consequently, encroachment on public sector properties is widespread. "Trespassers" tend to treat the resources as a free good, neglecting the costs society as a whole associates with environmental degradation. This is the crux of what Hardin calls the "tragedy of the commons," which describes well the state of many public properties in Latin America.

In many cases, the Ecuadorian government tacitly recognizes that environmental damage results from an imbalance between its extensive formal claims on natural resources and its limited capacity to manage them and to control access. It chooses, then, to vest property interests in users of "idle" lands (*tierras baldias*) which are nominally under governmental control. However, those property rights are rarely structured so as to encourage resource conservation. Destruction of natural vegetation is usually a prerequisite for formal tenure in a colonized parcel.

The Ecuadorian government also influences the use and management of privately held natural resources by rendering private tenure in those resources insecure. To approve a private claim for formal land tenure, IERAC executes ten separate procedures (Seligson). Because its record-keeping system is extremely cumbersome (IERAC did not acquire its first computer until the late 1980s) adjudication can take years. In the meantime, the property rights of the individual making a claim are insecure. Tenure insecurity discourages the adoption of soil conservation measures and other land improvements partly because the National Development Bank (BNF) is reluctant to issue loans to farmers lacking title (Ramos p. 34). In addition, farmers with insecure tenure do not make land improvements because they cannot be sure that they will capture the long-term benefits of their investment.

However, redistributing property rights to or within the private sector is usually a politically charged undertaking. Ideologues of the right argue that all natural resources should be divided among private holdings, since the owners can be expected to develop their properties efficiently. Ideologues of the left doubt that market exchange of private property rights can ever result in the wise use of natural resources. Both extremes tend to ignore the value of "intermediate" tenurial arrangements: the rules and procedures governing resource use that local communities tend to develop to avoid environmental degradation (Hayami).

Achieving tenurial solutions to Ecuador's environmental problems requires hard-headed economic objectivity. That is, all costs and benefits of different tenurial approaches to any particular environmental issue must be carefully assessed. For example, before deciding to draw on the undeniable strengths of private property rights, the costs of establishing and administering such a regime, which can be considerable, need to be investigated (Runge). Similarly, heavy reliance on community-level arrangements is best when trade-offs associated with natural resource development are confined to a small area. Finally, even when the impacts of resource degradation are broadly distributed, governmental action is called for only if expected improvements in environmental quality compare favorably with the costs of that action.

Governmental Intervention in Markets

Public sector interference with market forces has long been a prominent feature of third-world economies. Among major features of development strategies pursued by the Latin American region's governments are overvalued exchange rates, tariff and non-tariff barriers to protect domestic industry from foreign competition, controlled prices of agricultural and natural resource commodities and extensive subsidization (Valdés). Import-substitution industrialization has clearly been the aim of the Ecuadorian government since the late 1950s (Chapter 2).

By arresting the growth of agriculture and other sectors of the rural economy, this approach to development diminishes the derived value of land, water, forests, and other renewable resource inputs. Consequently, incentives to manage and to conserve those resources are reduced.

Governments also interfere with factor markets in agriculture in an attempt to compensate for development strategies biased toward urban areas and industry. Compensation in the form of subsidized prices for agricultural inputs, however, can result in inefficiency and pollution in the countryside. Subsidizing pesticides, for example, often causes environmental concentrations of toxic chemicals to rise (Repetto). The waste of irrigation water in Ecuador as well as strong political pressure to pursue inefficient irrigation projects are explained largely by the low prices public agencies charge for water (Chapter 7).

On a larger scale, Ecuador's long-standing policy of subsidizing the use of gasoline, electricity and other forms of energy has led to widespread waste and inefficiency. One consequence of that policy has been to encourage excessive expansion of the agricultural frontier.

Failure to Invest in the National Scientific Base

While the Ecuadorian government has often extended subsidies and otherwise interfered with market forces, it has been slow to develop the national scientific base on which growth in agriculture, forestry and fishing depends (Chapter 12). Research and extension networks tend to be fractured. Separate entities created for agriculture, forestry and fishing do not usually cooperate on basic scientific research. In addition, coordination among narrowly focused and disparate public and private entities providing extension services is often poor. Funding of research and extension institutions is also meager, as is investment in human capital and especially sine qua non scientists and technicians.

Inadequate investment in the national science base has, in turn, led to the mining of land and other renewable natural resources to meet increased demand from high population growth. Weak agricultural research and extension, for example, has translated into low crop and livestock yields. If agricultural productivity exhibits no strong, increasing secular trend, then growing demand for agricultural commodities must be met primarily by bringing additional land, which is usually of marginal quality, into production and exploiting other natural resources. In Ecuador, roughly two-thirds of the increases in crop production occurring between the mid 1960s and the mid 1980s were accounted for by an expanding agricultural frontier. Improved productivity explained only the remaining third (Chapter 6).

Research and extension for crop and livestock production should always reflect an agricultural economy's factor endowments. Like many other Latin American countries, however, Ecuador continues to under-invest in agriculture's scientific base even though most suitable land has long been used for crop or livestock production. Under these circumstances, the pressure to bring environmentally fragile lands with limited agricultural potential into production will be strong for years to come.

Critical Natural Resource Issues

The causes of environmental degradation have been discussed in broad terms, as have general approaches to natural resource policy. Let us consider now some of the specific natural resource issues facing Ecuador. As indicated in this section, applying a combined program of tenurial reform, deregulation of markets for natural resource commodities and technological innovation would contribute greatly to the solution of problems like the destruction of Costa ecosystems, tropical deforestation, soil erosion and water misallocation. The problem of pesticide contamination is somewhat different in that increased, rather than reduced, regulation is appropriate. However, reforming policies and programs that discourage efficient development of soil, water and other natural resources should free up public sector resources needed to promote the safe and effective use of agricultural chemicals.

Disturbance of Costa Ecosystems

During the past fifteen years, Ecuador's shrimp industry expanded rapidly. This growth has come about exclusively through mariculture development. About 8,000 metric tons of shrimp have been captured off the Ecuadorian coast each year since the late 1970s. Meanwhile, the amount of shrimp collected from maturation ponds has increased from less than 5,000 metric tons in 1979 to around 50,000 in 1987.

Problems Mariculture development has been achieved largely at the expense of Costa ecosystems that support the shrimp industry. Of the 117,729 hectares of shrimp maturation ponds established between 1969 and 1987, 28,524 hectares displaced mangrove swamps, where all shrimp must spend a portion of their lives (CLIRSEN). Thus, 14 percent of the mangrove swamps existing in Ecuador in 1969 had been

Table 4.4 Area in Shrimp Maturation Ponds and Mangrove Swamps, Selected Years

| Year | Shrimp Ponds | | Mangrove Swamps (hectares) |
	Total (hectares)	From Mangroves (hectares)	
1969	0	---	203,700
1984	89,368	21,587	182,108
1987	117,729	28,524	175,126

Source: CLIRSEN.

displaced by the middle 1980s, almost exclusively from construction of shrimp ponds (Table 4.4). In some localities, the impacts of mariculture development have been far more extreme. In El Oro province (south of Guayaquil), which is the center of the Ecuadorian shrimp industry, extensive tracts of mangrove swamps have been lost. Between 1969 and 1987, 10,231 hectares (equal to 30 percent of the original 33,634 hectares) were displaced there (CLIRSEN). The situation is even more extreme in Manabí province where almost half of the original mangrove area of 12,371 hectares has been converted to shrimp ponds.

Mangrove swamp displacement is accelerating. Recent surveys conducted by CLIRSEN indicate that 6,937 hectares of Costa swamps were converted to shrimp ponds between 1984 and 1987, as compared to 21,587 in the preceding fifteen years. Moreover, the area of shrimp ponds authorized by government permits as of the mid-1980s exceeded pond area existing at that time (Zapata and Fierro p. 70). Consequently, more wetlands have been lost during the late 1980s.

The expansion of shrimp farms has caused increasing environmental damage according to a 1989 study by the Agricultural Policy Institute--IDEA (Espinoza). Even when mangrove swamps are not directly displaced, Costa ecosystems are affected by the discharge of waste water from ponds. That effluent tends to be highly saline and to feature high concentrations of algae (Snedaker et al. p. 32). In addition, Costa ecosystem disturbance takes the form of over-fishing. Excessive collection of larvae and egg-laden female shrimp, which is undertaken to help stock maturation ponds, is a cause of declining shrimp populations along the coastline. Larvae used to stock shrimp maturation ponds are captured with hand-held nets in shallow Costa waters. This method results in damage to all organisms in that environment because larvae fishermen dispose of all undesired species (Espinoza). Over-fishing for crab in mangrove swamps and for shrimp and other species in the ocean likewise takes a toll.

Determining the environmental impacts of mariculture development is difficult. The effects of water quality changes have not been determined. Neither do reliable estimates of marine populations of commercial species exist. However, it is apparent that reduced shrimp populations are affecting the Ecuadorian economy. By the middle of 1988, the price of an egg-laden female shrimp had risen US$10.00. Another indicator of declining populations is the 23 percent reduction in the volume of shrimp exports occurring between the first half of 1988 and the first half of 1989, which has been attributed to the cumulative impacts of excessive larvae collection (EIU p. 10).

Causes Other than periodic over-valuation of the Ecuadorian Sucre and a modest export tax, Ecuador's shrimp producers are relatively free of public sector intervention in markets for their output. However, tenurial incentives to conserve the industry's natural resource base are weak. At the same time, the chances that Costa ecosystems will be mined rather than managed are enhanced by inadequate investment in the scientific base for mariculture and fishing.

Depletive management of Ecuador's Costa ecosystems has much to do with property rights. By law, wetlands are a national patrimony. But because the government has virtually no capacity to control access to those areas, they are, in effect, the property of no one. For example, a community of crab fishermen has established itself without any sort of governmental approval or interference in the Churute Ecological Reserve, a mangrove swamp 40 km south of Guayaquil.

Unrestricted access, in turn, guarantees resource depletion. Excessive collection of female shrimp and shrimp larvae, like other forms of over-fishing, are classic tragedies of the commons. Any fisherman knows that he can capture the benefits of extra fishing effort (in the form of payments for his catch). By contrast, the costs associated with decreased breeding populations and other forms of fishery depletion are shared by all who make their living, directly or indirectly, from the sea.

But Costa ecosystem disturbance is worse than a standard tragedy of the commons since Ecuadorian property law obliges the shrimp industry to encroach on swamps. A maricultural enterprise can secure a formal legal interest (i.e., a use permit) in a parcel of Costa wetlands only by promising to destroy that parcel (i.e., by constructing a maturation pond).

The future of Ecuador's Costa wetlands and marine shrimp populations depend on the state of the country's scientific base. If that base does not improve significantly Ecuador will lose its comparative advantage in shrimp production to the United States, Mexico and several Asian nations, which have technologically superior mariculture. Losing comparative advantage will, in turn, enhance the temptation to "mine" mangrove ecosystems and other Costa and marine resources in an attempt to maintain production and exports. Knowing that the long-term prospects for mariculture are unfavorable, no individual producer will ever hesitate from damaging mangrove habitats or collecting excessive numbers of larvae to enhance short-term profits.

Solutions Costa wetlands could continue to be treated as a national patrimony. However, the government would have to devote far more effort to controlling access. The additional budgetary and manpower costs needed for such an effort to be effective would be considerable. As an alternative, the government should consider divesting itself of more Costa wetlands. Destruction of natural ecosystems should not continue to be a prerequisite for the acquisition of private tenure. Instead, where a well-defined community is making use of a tract of wetlands, the government could deed that tract to the community. The onus would then be on the community, itself, to develop a system of rules governing management of the tract's fishery resources. Where no such well-defined community exists, wetland leaseholds could be auctioned off to private enterprises. Winning bids would reflect some of the economic value of mangrove swamps and the funds generated by these auctions could be allocated to public sector management of wetlands.

Firms and communities cannot be given complete control of Costa wetlands since complete internalization of the costs associated with the degradation of that resource is impossible. In particular, any enterprise or community would regard the decline in offshore fishing or Costa larvae collection associated with the destruction of or excessive fishing in wetlands as an external cost. Recognizing this, the government would have to include strict conservation guidelines in wetland leaseholds. A company's or community's failure to abide by guidelines governing land use and fishing in its tract would result in that company or community losing current property rights as well as the prerogative to acquire other wetland tracts in the future. Bonds could be posted to assure compliance with conservation guidelines and would be subject to forfeiture.

Just as leasing Costa wetlands should be possible, the government can issue rights to collect larvae along given stretches of the Ecuadorian coastline to specific groups or people. They would then undertake to manage their resources as efficiently as they know how, subject to conservation guidelines stipulated in larvae collection leases.

The legal interests of private firms and communities in mangrove swamps and other Costa and marine resources need to be transferable. If a prospective owner thinks he can use a resource more profitably than the current owner, then the former should be able to buy out the latter. As long as conservation guidelines stated in the original leasehold agreement continue to be observed, then government should facilitate the transaction.

Finally, investment in the scientific base underpinning the shrimp industry should reduce the temptation to mine mangrove swamps and other Costa and marine resources for two reasons. First, excessive larvae collection should abate. Second, maricultural enterprises using larvae bred in laboratories will have a much weaker incentive to construct ponds in or close to the ecosystems that are the natural source of larvae.

Forest Depletion and Deforestation

As Cabarle et al. point out, tropical deforestation is the major threat to biological diversity in Ecuador. Those same authors also indicate specific measures for protecting threatened species. Those measures are not reiterated here. Instead, this analysis of forest depletion and deforestation focuses on opportunities for timber industry development that are lost as tree-covered land is cleared by agricultural colonists. Policy reforms needed to encourage forest conservation are also identified.

Problems Compared to maricultural enterprises and shrimp fishermen, the timber industry's contribution to the national economy is modest. Because domestic demand for pulp and paper is satisfied almost entirely through imports, Ecuador generally runs a negative balance of trade in forest products. Central Bank data indicate that logging accounts for 0.9 percent of Ecuador's gross national product. The processing of wood products, broadly defined to include furniture manufacturing, accounts for an additional 0.8 percent. Montenegro and Durini (p. 13) estimate that extracting, transporting and processing timber and manufacturing wood products employs around 45,000 Ecuadorians. These figures probably understate the economic importance of the forest products industry since the volume of fuel wood extracted from Ecuador's forests far exceeds the volume of wood used in other ways (AIMA 1987, p. 4; Montenegro and Durini p. 12) and since fuel wood is exchanged largely outside of the formal economy.

The capacity of the forest products industry to contribute more to gross national product and net exports while generating additional employment is seriously threatened by deforestation. As indicated earlier, at least 200,000 hectares of tree-covered land is being converted into cropland and pasture each year. This current annual rate exceeds the 100,000 hectares reforested between the early 1960s and the middle 1980s

(AIMA 1985, p.43). Land clearing is particularly rapid in the Oriente where agricultural colonists settle alongside roads leading to centers of oil exploration and extraction, and in the Northern Wet Littoral, which is the heart of the country's timber industry (MAG p. 14).

The immediate waste of timber associated with deforestation is enormous. Addressing the efficiency with which agricultural colonists harvest commercial timber, DINAF officials indicate that at least 25 percent (and perhaps as much as two-thirds) of standing commercial timber is destroyed when colonists clear their parcels and that poor transport and handling techniques severely damages a good portion of the timber delivered to sawmills and other assembly points. Over the long term, of course, raising crops and livestock on sites with major forestry potential (e.g., in the Northern Wet Littoral) carries a very high opportunity cost.

Causes Deforestation in Ecuador is a clear illustration of how inappropriate tenurial arrangements, governmental intervention in markets and inadequate investment in research and extension combine to cause resource degradation.

As indicated earlier in this chapter, most of the country's tree-covered land is designated as forest patrimony or is in a park or reserve. However, the government's capacity to control access to its forests is modest. For example, no rangers have been assigned to the 2,000,000 hectares of forest patrimony delimited in Northwestern and Northeastern Ecuador (MAG). Funds and personnel allocated to parks and reserves, covering about 2,100,000 hectares in continental Ecuador, are negligible. In 1987, a mere two administrators, 25 technicians, and 119 permanent and seasonal rangers were assigned to parks and reserves (DINAF).

Implicitly acknowledging that a discrepancy between extensive public sector claims and limited public sector capacity to control access can provoke a tragedy of the commons, the Ecuadorian government allows for the transfer of its forest lands to private parties. However, the terms of that transfer assure ecosystem destruction. By law, IERAC must insist that at least half of a 50 hectare claim be cleared before it adjudicates that claim. The only direct fiscal check on the conversion of forests into agricultural land is the adjudication fee, which was raised in 1989 from a nominal US$2 to a minor US$20 per hectare. Furthermore, tenure insecurity associated with the many years IERAC requires to adjudicate a colonist's claim on frontier lands accelerates deforestation, as Southgate, Sierra and Brown have demonstrated in a statistical analysis of the causes of settlement and land clearing in eastern Ecuador.

The tenurial regime inducing colonists to clear the forest patrimony causes indigenous inhabitants of Ecuador's tropical forests to follow suit. Macdonald reports that the periodic fallowing scheme long practiced by the Amerindian community of Pasu Urcu, in the eastern part of the country, was abandoned during the 1970s after members of that community had been informed by IERAC agents that fallow lands could be claimed by agricultural colonists, who were 50 km away at the time.

To the list of tenurial factors discouraging efficient development of Ecuador's tropical forests, one must add the ban on logging concessions imposed in 1982. That ban makes the forest products industry in lowland Ecuador almost entirely dependent on agricultural colonists, who inefficiently harvest and sell timber to sawyers. The degree to which prohibiting logging concessions enhanced the importance of timber sales to colonists is indicated by the increase in chainsaw imports during the early 1980s. In 1981, imports amounted to US$1.8 million (CIF, 1988 dollars). In 1985, three years after the ban went into effect, US$5.2 million worth of chainsaws were brought into the country (Montenegro and Durini) as colonists switched to clearing techniques allowing for the marketing of commercial species.

Along with inappropriate tenurial arrangements, the Ecuadorian government's interference with market forces discourages forest conservation. Gasoline prices rarely rose above US$0.10/gallon during the 1970s or US$0.30/gallon during the 1980s. As a result, migration to far flung areas in the Oriente and elsewhere was heavily subsidized. In addition, prohibiting log exports has depressed domestic prices for unprocessed timber and, hence, reduced private incentives to manage existing forests or to establish new stands of trees. The severity of price distortions associated with the log export ban, which in effect has converted the domestic market for timber into a local monopsony, are illustrated by the price offered in early 1989 by a Spanish firm for 10 meter eucalyptus logs: US$30 each. The prevailing domestic price ranges from US$2 to US$4 a log. Among the impacts of such price distortions is negligible reforestation.

Finally, inadequate investment in the scientific base for agriculture and forest management complements tenurial and pricing policies as a cause of deforestation in Ecuador. As has already been discussed, there is strong pressure to use increasing amounts of land for agricultural production when crop and livestock yields are low and exhibit no strong temporal trend. In addition, weak forestry research and extension diminish the returns to forest management. Aside from one or two companies undertaking species trials, private sector research in Ecuador is nil. Governmental forestry research is correspondingly negligible and, for all intents and purposes, there is no forestry extension service. Under these circumstances, no individual colonist is likely to perceive that the conversion of forests into cropland or pasture involves a substantial opportunity cost.

Solutions Central to any strategy for encouraging the efficient development of Ecuador's forests is the removal of tenurial conditions and timber market regulations that currently encourage people to degrade the country's tree-covered land. In addition, the future management of forests depends greatly on improved forestry research and extension.

A ban on logging would be exactly the wrong kind of tenurial reform. Countries imposing such bans (e.g., the Dominican Republic) have found them very difficult to enforce because forest guards, who tend to be poorly paid and few in number, are easy to bribe. More importantly, prohibiting timber harvesting removes all private incentive to reforest land, or to manage forests.

Instead, the Ecuadorian government needs to strengthen private incentives to conserve the country's forests. More important than anything else, neither agricultural colonists not indigenous groups should have to clear land to acquire property rights. By the same token, the government should allow for leaseholds in logging sites. Payments for leaseholds should not take the form of a severance tax (i.e., a charge on timber removed from a parcel) since such a tax tends to encourage "high-grading" of timber resources. Neither should a tax on standing timber be assessed since such a tax interferes with an efficient schedule of resource extraction. Government revenues should be collected as "front-end lump sums" paid by firms offering the highest bids in auctions for forested parcels. In addition to encouraging efficient extraction of timber, an auction system would raise funds that could be used to underwrite management of the forest patrimony.

Reservations about transferring natural resources from government to the private sector arise from the suspicion that prices offered for public sector resources will fall short of the true value of those resources. Perhaps the best way to address this problem is to expand the number of bidders participating in resource auctions. Where auctions have only been open to domestic firms, for example, foreign companies could be invited to participate. Another strategy for raising bids is to use an auction method proposed by William Vickery, a North American economist, during the 1950s. The distinguishing characteristic of a "Vickery auction" is that the firm submitting the winning bid does not have to pay the amount it offered. Instead, it pays the second-highest amount offered. Firms participating in a Vickery auction of some natural resource are reluctant to understate the value they associate with that resource, because doing so might allow some competitor to obtain the resource at a low price.

Investing in forestry research and extension also would contribute to the conservation of tree-covered lands. For example, if information on improved forest management and timber extraction techniques can be extended to colonists who have tenure in tree-covered land, then that group will be less inclined to convert their properties to cropland or pasture. Similarly, the net returns that the timber and forest products industry associates with the management of tree-covered land depends on the scientific base underpinning Ecuadorian forestry, which is currently rudimentary for the most part.

Finally, the log export ban should be abolished. Free trade will drive up timber prices in Ecuador. As a result, land owners will have a stronger incentive to reforest cleared land and to take better care of existing forest lands.

Soil Erosion

Many consider erosion to be rural Ecuador's most serious environmental problem. The potential for soil loss is great in 47.9 percent of continental Ecuador, principally along the precipitous outer faces of the Andes and the sides of intermontane valleys.

Problems Erosion is "active" or in the process of becoming active in 12.1 percent (3,150,000 hectares) of the country (Figure 4.3; de Noni and Trujillo p. 6). Major soil loss occurs in the Costa hills of Manabí province and along agricultural frontiers in the Northern Wet Littoral and in the Oriente. In addition, soil erosion is particularly severe in the Sierra. As in other parts of the world, soil erosion in Ecuador induces a temporal decline in land productivity. For a few years, farmers can apply fertilizer to compensate partially for erosion's impact on yields. But after cumulative land degradation crosses a threshold, crop production often becomes economically infeasible. In the Sierra, that threshold has been reached quickly on the steep hillsides surrounding intermontane valley bottoms. Stopping crop production allows for natural land regeneration, which is a very slow process. However, soil continues to be lost from many Sierra fields formerly planted to crops because livestock are routinely allowed to graze on abandoned land.

Soil erosion is not simply a problem for agriculturalists who use Ecuador's fragile lands. It also impedes water resource development. Serious reservoir sedimentation problems have arisen at the Paute complex, which produces a major share of the country's hydroelectricity (Southgate and Macke). Similarly, plant nutrients in eroded soils contribute to water quality problems that have arisen in Poza Honda and other reservoirs in the Costa.

Causes Where land is steeply sloped and soils are easily displaced, which is the case in much of Ecuador, natural erosion can be appreciable. However, soil loss is

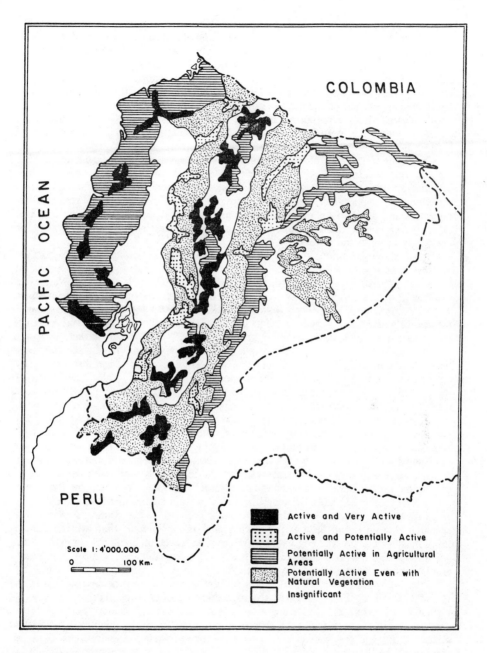

COLOMBIA

PACIFIC OCEAN

PERU

Scale 1: 4'000.000

0   100 Km.

Active and Very Active

Active and Potentially Active

Potentially Active in Agricultural Areas

Potentially Active Even with Natural Vegetation

Insignificant

Figure 4.3 Soil Erosion in Ecuador
Source: de Noni and Trujillo.

considerably accelerated by human activity. Policies can influence expansion of the agricultural frontier onto fragile lands, the adoption of soil conservation practices inside agriculture's extensive margin, as well as the state of abandoned cropland.

Tenurial incentives that foster excessive land clearing in the humid tropics (described above) are in force along other agricultural frontiers in Ecuador. Article 48 of Ecuador's Land Reform Law, for example, stipulates that "idle" Andean páramos, like tropical forests, are subject to agricultural colonization. Inevitably, colonization accelerates soil loss. Another parallel with tropical deforestation is that agriculture's expansion into the páramos and other Sierra hinterlands is a consequence of inadequate investment in the scientific base for crop and livestock production.

Government policies also contribute to rapid erosion from farms within the agricultural frontier. Tenure insecurity, associated with IERAC's cumbersome adjudication procedures, is widespread among the owners of Ecuador's small farms (*minifundios*). As a result, those owners are not inclined to invest in soil conservation measures and other forms of land improvement. That disinclination is reinforced as *minifundistas* suffer the consequences of policy-induced distortions in markets for agricultural inputs and outputs.

Consider, for example, who bears the costs of credit rationing brought about by interest rate controls. Among others, Gonzalez Vega documents that lenders restricted from charging more than a certain rate allocate credit to larger borrowers with substantial collateral. This practice allows them to minimize loan processing costs as well as the riskiness of loan portfolios. Denied access to formal credit lines, small farmers rely on informal credit markets in which interest rates are considerably higher than those that would be observed in an unregulated formal credit market.

Sporadic attempts to maintain producer prices above market clearing have not helped Ecuador's small farmers either. The financial resources and warehouse capacity committed to the government's price support schemes have typically fallen short of what is needed for those schemes to succeed. With relatively good access to market information, larger farmers tend to be the "first in line" to sell their output to government warehouses at the support price. Small farmers, by contrast, are more apt to sell their grain after efforts to maintain minimum prices have collapsed. Receiving relatively low prices for their output and paying high interest rates for informal credit, minifundistas are less willing than they would be in an unregulated market economy to invest in soil conservation measures. In addition, soil conservation on Ecuador's minifundios is discouraged by inadequate research and extension since small farmers are unlikely to benefit from whatever limited improvements are made in the country's scientific base. Because of resource constraints, scientists at the country's agricultural research centers spend little time working on farming systems that would enhance minifundistas' income and conserve soil. Even if improved technologies for controlling soil erosion were available, Ecuador's fractured, uncoordinated extension programs would not be able to reach enough small farmers to make a difference.

Tenurial, research and extension policies also contribute to excessive erosion from abandoned lands. IERAC regards abandoned cropland as tierras baldias and, hence, subject to colonization. This attenuation of former land users' property rights reduces private incentives to invest in restorative measures (e.g., the planting of pasture grasses). Even if tenurial disincentives to restore degraded abandoned lands were overcome, land restoration would still be seriously impeded by limited investment in the national scientific base. Other than a few trials with *setaria* (a genus with species that are indigenous to the Sierra) during the 1970s, no research has been done on grass and legume species that promote soil formation or simply hold remaining soil in place.

Solutions Since soil erosion is severe along expanding agricultural frontiers, removing tenurial incentives that promote excessive land clearing (e.g., article 48 of the Land Reform Law) will contribute to soil conservation in tropical forests, páramos, and other areas in Ecuador. Similarly, poor management of privately owned agricultural land is largely a consequence of macroeconomic, pricing, and trade policies that penalize the agricultural sector. As those policies are reformed, farmers will be more inclined to adopt erosion control measures and to invest in the management of their soil resources.

Special attention should be given to correcting the policies that discourage small farmers, whose soil resources tend to be especially fragile, from adopting conservation measures. In particular, IERAC's land adjudication procedures need to be streamlined so that small farmers' tenure will be more secure. This will, in turn, improve their access to formal sources of credit, which can then be used to finance investments in erosion control. Also, information on improved erosion control and agricultural production techniques needs to be extended to small farmers working on erodible lands. The likely influence of policy reform should not be exaggerated, however. As off-farm employment opportunities improve, as they did in Ecuador throughout the 1970s, then wages are pulled up. In turn, this discourages the adoption of some soil conservation measures. For example, terracing and other labor-intensive measures are difficult for a land owner to justify when wages are high. In contrast, other soil conservation measures may be enhanced, such as reduced tillage and other labor-saving techniques.

Finally, reducing soil erosion from open access, abandoned lands requires tenurial reform as well as technical innovation. Communities and individuals could bid for government contracts to recuperate unused, degraded parcels. Contractors would receive not only a government payment for successful establishment of tree plantations or pastures but also title to recuperated lands. To enhance the effectiveness of such a scheme, however, considerably more research on trees and pasture grasses that can survive on degraded lands is needed. As indicated above, the absence of research on pasture grasses that can be planted on degraded abandoned cropland is particularly deficient at present.

Water Misallocation

Between 80 and 140 billion m^3 of surface water flow from continental Ecuador into the Pacific Ocean each year. Alone, this annual runoff could cover the country's 1,600,000 hectares of cropland with 5 meters of water, when the average required on INERHI's irrigation projects is 1.9 meters. In addition, 210 to 370 billion m^3 a year flow toward the Amazon River. There are also several aquifers in the country that have consistently provided significant quantities of water. It is no exaggeration to say that Ecuador is abundantly endowed with water resources (Delavaud pp. 12-13).

Problems As pointed out in this chapter, however, those resources are unevenly distributed, both geographically and seasonally. In general, precipitation is meager along the Costa, in Southwestern Ecuador and in many intermontane basins. In addition, a unimodal rainfall pattern typical of the tropics is pronounced throughout the Arid Coastal Plains as well as the Southern Humid Coastal Plains. River hydrology in those two regions is correspondingly unimodal.

Given geographic and temporal variations in precipitation and hydrology, farmers in several parts of the country vigorously demand access to irrigation water. Over the years, INERHI and other public agencies have responded to this demand by committing over S/.100 billion (1988 Sucres) to irrigation investment. Water utilization at many projects is extremely inefficient. For example, currently operating INERHI projects were designed to deliver water to 79,300 hectares. However, irrigation water was used on only 65.6 percent of that area in 1987 (see Chapter 7 for a detailed analysis of irrigation).

Whereas substantial sums have been expended addressing Ecuadorian farmers' water *quantity* problems, relatively little has been said about agriculture's emerging water *quality* problems. The latter are serious. Citing studies conducted by INERHI in 1983 and 1984, Landázuri and Jijón (pp. 55-60) report that *E. coli* and other pollutants are very high in the waterways carrying untreated sewage from Quito and neighboring towns. Irrigating crops with water drawn from those rivers and streams can be hazardous to human health. By the same token, agriculture is a significant contributor to water quality problems in Ecuador's cities (see below).

Causes Optimistic assumptions about the efficiency with which irrigation water is or will be used account for part of the marked discrepancy between areas originally projected to benefit from irrigation projects and areas that actually receive water (Chapter 7). However, low water prices are the major cause of inefficient use of irrigation water throughout the country. INERHI water tariffs cover only 4.2 percent of irrigation systems' capital and operating expenses.

When the prices of irrigation water are low, farmers with reliable supplies of cheap water do not monitor water use carefully. They also substitute water for other inputs. As a result, their water use will be far more than had been anticipated by the planners of irrigation projects. This behavior reduces the reliability of water supplies for other farmers. To avoid risks, the latter group tends not to plant crops requiring large amounts of water. This explains the "under-utilization" of land at the margins of irrigation projects.

Pricing irrigation water far below its cost also intensifies political pressure to undertake additional irrigation projects. Potential beneficiaries of new projects count on society as a whole to bear most of the financial burden. One wonders, for example, how many of the farmers who will benefit from the Santa Elena project would be keen to see it go forward if they had to internalize its capital costs, which will exceed US$9,000 for each hectare of irrigated land.

There is another opportunity cost of heavily subsidizing irrigation water. The 1972 Water Law gave INERHI broad authority to regulate and to develop the country's water resources. However, because water tariffs cover a small portion of the costs of on-line projects and because INERHI is under strong political pressure to undertake new, heavily subsidized irrigation projects, over 95 percent of that agency's budget is absorbed by operating expenses and by the planning and construction of new projects. This leaves INERHI in a poor position to deal with urban and agricultural water pollution problems.

Solutions Irrigation water will never be used efficiently as long as the price farmers pay for that commodity is significantly less than its cost (Chapter 7). In addition, the political demand to undertake expensive new projects will remain strong as long potential beneficiaries know that subsidies will remain high.

To dampen the latter demand, the government should make clear that water tariffs paid by the beneficiaries of future projects will fully cover operating and maintenance as well as capital costs of the water they receive. Subsidization of projects that are already on line can only be reduced over a period of time. If subsidies were curtailed immediately, many of those projects' beneficiaries would go bankrupt (because the value of their land, which reflects low water prices, would plummet).

The public sector might find collecting payments for non-subsidized irrigation water from individual farmers difficult since "metering" can be expensive in the countryside. As an alternative, it can sell its water to communities of water users (at prices approaching efficient levels). Each community would then develop a scheme for allocating water among and collecting payments from its members.

Pesticide Contamination

Concern over careless use of agricultural chemicals in Ecuador was initially aroused by a Fundación Natura report on pesticides. Particularly alarming was a list of twenty-three chemicals, including DBCP and 245T, that had been banned or that could only be used subject to restriction in several countries around the world. Because of these bans and restrictions, the international prices of those chemicals were relatively low and Ecuador's imports of them were rising steadily (Sevilla Larrea and Pérez de Sevilla).

Problems By now, pesticides have worked their way to the "top" of the food chain. Agricultural chemicals are washed into streams from which downstream cities withdraw drinking water. Those chemicals are also found in food. In a study carried out in Esmeraldas, Guayaquil and Quito, MAG/CONACYT found human breast milk contained BHC, Aldrin, DDT and other hazardous agricultural substances.

Causes The other environmental problems discussed in this section are exacerbated by governmental interference with the market mechanism. For example, the log export ban discourages forest conservation. Similarly, excessive soil erosion is partly a consequence of failed commodity price support programs and interest rate controls. By contrast, pesticide contamination is excessive in Ecuador precisely because the government's regulation of the sale and use of agricultural chemicals is weak.

One should bear in mind, however, that laissez faire treatment of the market for agricultural chemicals is, in a sense, a consequence of misdirecting government resources. For example, heavy subsidization of irrigation water leaves INERHI with virtually no financial, technical and human resources to fulfill its statutory obligations to manage water resources. As a result, anyone wishing to use Ecuador's rivers and streams as a dumping ground for hazardous substances faces no serious regulatory impediments.

Solutions An economic perspective on the allocation of scarce public sector resources goes a long way to explain the importation of sizable volumes of "dirty dozen" substances, like Aldrin and Dieldrin, into the country (Sevilla Larrea and Pérez de Sevilla) in recent years. So too does such a perspective explain why relatively little has been done to inform farmers about the safe and effective use of agricultural chemicals.

As Ecuador discards regulations and subsidies that hinder efficient development of soil, water, and natural ecosystems, the personnel and budgets needed to control the importation and internal sale of potentially hazardous agricultural chemicals should become available. So too should it be possible to expand extension programs for informing farmers about the safe and effective use of those substances.

Donor Agencies and Resource Conservation

Recommendations for donor agency action to promote resource conservation in Ecuador follow from this chapter's analysis of the causes of environmental degradation in the country. That is, donor agencies should assist Ecuador as it addresses tenurial, regulatory, and technological factors contributing to the mismanagement of soil, water, and natural ecosystems.

The preceding description of property arrangements that discourage resource conservation is preliminary. Future study of those arrangements, which should be a top priority for donor agencies, should focus on the transition to alternative regimes. Among specific topics to be addressed would be how to structure efficient auctions for transferring government-owned resources to the private sector and what restrictions to be written into leasehold interests in Costa wetlands, the forest patrimony, and other properties. Technical assistance should also be provided to governmental initiatives to address tenurial crises underlying visible environmental problems.

Donor agency support is also needed to phase out subsidies and regulations in markets for natural resource commodities. For example, donor agencies can facilitate studies and provide technical assistance needed to develop a schedule for eliminating subsidies on irrigation water. Similar action might be needed to eliminate the log export ban.

Finally, it is important to support improvements in the scientific base directly serving renewable natural resources. Support of forestry research and extension by the United States Agency for International Development (USAID) for example, should be continued and expanded.

Two other major policy reforms suggested elsewhere in this study for strengthening and improving agriculture and general economic growth also are of critical importance in conserving renewable natural resources. The first is improvement in the science base serving agriculture (Chapter 12) while the second is improvement in macroeconomic policies (Chapter 2). These two reforms will induce the production of new technical knowledge and modern, industrial inputs for agriculture. These inputs can be substituted directly for the renewable natural resources upon which agriculture now is largely dependent and thus save these increasingly scarce endowments. These two policy reforms are clearly of major importance to better conservation of natural resources. The recommendations presented in this chapter are complementary to them and will have only limited impact on improving the conservation of natural resources if these two more pervasive reforms are not implemented.

REFERENCES

AIMA (Wood Industry Association). 1987. "Análisis de la Situación del Sector Forestal y Maderero del Ecuador." Quito.
_____. 1985. *Diagnóstico Actualizado del Sector de la Madera en el Ecuador*. Quito.
Barsky, Osvaldo, Eugenio Dias Bonilla, Carlos Furche and Robert Mizrahi. 1982. *Políticas Agrarias, Colonización, y Desarrollo Rural en Ecuador*. Quito: CEPLAES.
Bromley, Raymond. 1981. "The Colonization of Humid Tropical Areas in Ecuador." *Singapore Journal of Tropical Geography* 2:15-26.

Cabarle, Bruce J., et al. 1989. "An Assessment of Biological Diversity and Tropical Forests for Ecuador." Washington: Center for International Development and the Environment of the World Resources Institute, Draft Report to USAID.

Caujolle-Gazet, Alain and Carlos Luzuriaga. 1986. "Estudio de un Tipo de Cangagua en el Ecuador: Posibilidades de Mejoramiento Mediante el Cultivo." *La Erosión en el Ecuador.* Quito: CEDIG (Documento de Investigación No. 6).

CLIRSEN (Center for the Survey of Natural Resources by Remote Sensing). 1988. *Actualización del Estudio Multitemporal de Manglares, Camaroneras y Salinas.* Quito: MICEI/Subsecretary of Fisheries and Directorate of the Merchant Marine.

Commander, Simon and Peter Peek. 1986. "Oil Exports, Agrarian Change, and the Rural Labor Process: The Ecuadorian Sierra in the 1970s." *World Development* 14:79-96.

Delavaud, Anne Collin (ed.). 1982. *Atlas del Ecuador.* Paris: Les Editions J.A.

de Noni, Georges and German Trujillo. 1986. "La Erosión Actual y Potencial en Ecuador: Localización, Manifestaciones, y Causas." *La Erosión en el Ecuador.* Quito: CEDIG (Documento de Investigación No. 6).

DINAF (National Forestry Directorate). 1988. *Plan de Acción Forestal para el Ecuador: Diagnóstico del Sector Forestal.* Quito: Ministerio de Agricultura y Ganadería.

EIU (Economist Intelligence Unit). 1989. *Ecuador: Country Report No. 3.* London.

Gonzalez Vega, Claudio. 1984. "Credit Rationing Behavior of Agricultural Lenders." *Undermining Rural Development with Cheap Credit.* Edited by Dale W Adams, Douglas H. Graham and J.D. von Pischke. Boulder: Westview Press.

Hardin, Garrett. 1968. "The Tragedy of the Commons." *Science* 168:1243-1248.

Hayami, Yujiro. 1988. "Community, Market, and State." Elmhirst Memorial Lecture presented at XX International Conference of Agricultural Economists, Buenos Aires.

Holdridge, Leslie. 1967. *Life Zone Ecology.* San Jose, Costa Rica: Tropical Science Center.

Espinoza, Fernando. 1989. *Situación Actual de la Maricultura del Camarón en el Ecuador y Estrategias para su Desarrollo Sostenido.* Quito: IDEA (Agricultural Policy Institute), Documento Técnico No. 21.

INEC (National Institute of Statistics and Census). 1982. *Encuesta Nacional de Fecundidad, 1979.* Quito.

INEC, CONADE and CELADE (National Institute of Statistics and Census, National Development Council and Latin American Demographic Center). 1984. *Ecuador: Estimaciones y Proyecciones de Población, 1950-2000.* Quito.

Landázuri, Helena and Carolina Jijón. 1988. *El Medio Ambiente en el Ecuador.* Quito: Instituto Latinoamericano de Investigaciones Sociales.

Macdonald, Theodore. 1981. "Indigenous Responses to an Expanding Frontier: Jungle Quichua Economic Conversion to Cattle Ranching." *Cultural Transformations and Ethnicity in Modern Ecuador.* Edited by Norman Whitten, Jr. Urbana: University of Illinois Press.

MAG (Ministry of Agriculture). 1987. *Informe Final de la Limitación del Patrimonio Forestal del Estado.* Quito.

MAG/CONACYT (Ministry of Agriculture and National Council on Science and Technology). 1986. "Proyecto de Determinación de Residuos de Pesticidas Clorados en Leche Materna." Quito.

Montenegro S., Fernando and Manuel Francisco Durini T. 1989. "Ecuador: Una Potencia Forestal?" Quito: Corporación Forestal J.M. Durini.

PRONAREG (National Program for Agrarian Regionalization). 1984. "Mapa de Aptitudes Agrícolas." Quito: Instituto Geográfico Militar.

Ramos, Hugo. 1984. "Agricultural Credit Situation." Quito: USAID.

Repetto, Robert. 1985. "Paying the Price: Pesticide Subsidies in Developing Countries." Washington: World Resources Institute Research Report No. 2.

Runge, C. Ford. 1986. "Common Property and Collective Action in Economic Development." *World Development* 14:623-635.

Seligson, M. 1984. "Land Tenure Security, Minifundization, and Agrarian Development in Ecuador." Quito: USAID.

Sevilla Larrea, Roque and Pilar Pérez de Sevilla. 1985. "Los Plaguicidas en el Ecuador: Mas Allá de una Simple Advertencia." Quito: Fundación Natura.

Snedaker, Samuel C., Joshua C. Dickinson, III, Melvin S. Brown and Enrique J. Lahmann. 1986. "Shrimp Pond Siting and Management Alternatives in Mangrove Ecosystems in Ecuador" Quito: USAID, Final Report, Grant No. DPE-5542-G-SS-4022-00.

Southgate, Douglas and Robert Macke. 1989. "The Downstream Benefits of Soil Conservation in Third World Hydroelectric Watersheds." *Land Economics* 65:38-48.

Southgate, Douglas, Rodrigo Sierra and Lawrence Brown. Forthcoming. "A Statistical Analysis of the Causes of Deforestation in Eastern Ecuador." *World Development*.

United Nations. 1982. *National Demographic Indicators: Estimates and Projections*. New York.

Valdés, Alberto. 1986. "Impact of Trade and Macroeconomic Policies on Agricultural Growth: The South American Experience." *Economic and Social Progress in Latin America*. Washington, D.C.: Inter-American Development Bank.

Zapata, Bernardo and Miguel Fierro. 1988. "Diagnóstico del Sector Pesquero y Camaronero." Guayaquil: Fundación Pedro Vicente Maldonado.

5

THE HUMAN FACTOR

AND AGRICULTURE

Morris D. Whitaker

The rates of agricultural growth, economic development and the distribution of production are highly dependent on the nature of population growth and the size and quality of the labor force. Economic growth and improvements in equity also are highly dependent on how efficiently labor markets mobilize human resources and allocate them among economic sectors, regions and rural and urban areas. Ecuador's population and labor force continue to grow very rapidly. Agricultural and overall economic growth must occur at even higher rates in order for per capita consumption to improve and levels of employment to increase, on average. Thus, high rates of population growth tend to limit improvements in individual wellbeing. Such improvements are further constrained to the extent that labor markets function inefficiently.

This chapter examines the human factor in agricultural growth in the context of its relationship with the development of the rest of the economy. The following sections review and analyze: several characteristics of Ecuador's population including size, geographic and rural-urban distribution, growth of cities, density and migration patterns; growth and composition of the labor force and the extent and nature of unemployment; the level of sectoral employment, absorptive capacity by sector and underemployment; labor markets, including rigidities and market segmentation in the public sector; and how efficiently labor markets have allocated labor between the productive sectors and between rural and urban areas. Conclusions are presented in the last section.

Population Characteristics[1]

Censuses of the population were carried out on November 29, 1950 (Ministry of Economy); November 25, 1962 (INEC 1964); June 8, 1974 (INEC 1977); and November 28, 1982 (INEC 1985b); all tended to underestimate the population.[2] In 1984 the National Institute of Statistics and Census (INEC) the National Development Council (CONADE) and the Latin American Demographic Center (CELADE) published adjusted, global census data, estimates of the population from 1950 to 1980 and projections from 1980 to 2000 (see INEC, CONADE and CELADE). The estimates of population are only modestly greater than the censuses of population and the growth rates are very similar. Projections were made under assumptions of low,

Table 5.1   Population and Growth Rates According to Adjusted Censuses:
            Estimates and Projections

| Year | Population | Growth Rates | |
		Period (years)	Annual Average (%)
Adjusted Censuses:			
November 29, 1950	3,310,080	---	---
November 25, 1962	4,695,805	12.00	2.96
June 8, 1974	6,829,467	11.53	3.30
November 28, 1982	8,606,116	8.47	2.77
Estimates/Projections:			
1990	10,781,613	8.00	2.86
1995	12,314,210	5.00	2.69
2000	13,939,400	5.00	2.51

Source: INEC, CONADE and CELADE.

the growth rates are very similar. Projections were made under assumptions of low, medium and high global rates of fecundity with the medium rate being generally accepted as most likely. INEC (1985a) completed a more refined and detailed set of projections of rural and urban population by age and sex and by province and canton for 1982-1995, with global projections consistent with the 1984 projections.

Size and Growth

Total population in 1990 is estimated to be 10,781,613 and is expected to grow to nearly 14,000,000 by the year 2000 (Table 5.1). The population has more than tripled since 1950, growing at a relatively high annual average rate of 3.0 percent for the 40 year period.

Population growth between 1950-1962 was 2.96 percent due to a very high birth rate of about 47 per thousand and a relatively high death rate of about 17 per thousand (CONADE and UNFPA Chapters 2 and 3). The growth rate increased to 3.3 percent between 1962-1974 because of a combination of large fall in the death rate to about 11 per thousand accompanied by a modest decrease in the birth rate to around 43 per thousand. During 1974-1982 the birth rate fell to less than 37 per thousand, while the death rate fell a little more than one point causing a decrease in the population growth rate to 2.77 percent.

The population growth rate is projected to increase slightly to 2.86 percent during the 1982-1990 period because the death rate is expected to decline slightly faster than the birth rate. Then population growth is projected to fall to 2.69 percent between 1990-1995 and to 2.51 percent between 1995-2000 as the birth rate is expected to fall more rapidly than the death rate. At this still relatively high rate the projected population of 13,939,400 in 2000 would double to nearly 28,000,000 by 2028.

Geographic Distribution[3]

The distribution of population among the principal regions has shifted substantially since 1950, with major political, economic and social implications. The Costa has

Table 5.2   Population, Share and Growth Rates by Regions, Census Years and
            Projections

	Unadjusted Censuses				Projections		
	1950	1962	1974	1982	1982	1990	1995
Population							
Ecuador	3,202,757	4,476,007	6,521,710	8,060,712	8,606,116	10,781,613	12,314,210
Sierra	1,856,445	2,271,345	3,146,565	3,801,839	4,047,182	4,926,776	5,527,360
Costa	1,298,495	2,127,358	3,179,446	3,946,801	4,214,289	5,359,743	6,171,622
Oriente	46,471	74,913	173,469	263,797	275,690	407,330	513,873
Galápagos	1,346	2,391	22,230	48,275	68,955	87,764	101,355
Shares (%)							
Ecuador	100.0	100.0	100.0	100.0	100.0	100.0	100.0
Sierra	58.0	50.7	48.2	47.2	47.0	45.7	44.9
Costa	40.5	47.5	48.8	49.0	49.0	49.7	50.1
Oriente	1.5	1.7	2.7	3.3	3.2	3.8	4.2
Galápagos	0.0	0.1	0.3	0.6	0.8	0.8	0.8
Growth Rates[a] (%)							
Ecuador	---	2.83	3.32	2.53	---	2.86	2.69
Sierra	---	1.70	2.87	2.26	---	2.49	2.33
Costa	---	4.20	3.55	2.59	---	3.05	2.86
Oriente	---	4.06	7.55	5.07	---	5.00	4.76
Galápagos	---	4.90	21.34	9.59	---	3.06	2.92

Source: Whitaker, Colyer and Alzamora Appendix Tables 5.1 and 5.2.

[a]Rates are for each inter-census or inter-projection period and are the compound
(geometric) growth rate. For example the rates in the column labeled "1962" are
for the inter-census period 1950-1982 (12 years).

replaced the Sierra as Ecuador's most populous region and the Oriente has nearly
tripled its population, although it is still relatively small (Table 5.2).[4] The share of the
population located in the Costa increased between 1950 and 1990 from about 40.5 to
nearly 49.7 percent while the Sierra's share fell from 58.0 percent to 45.7 percent. The
Costa has become more influential in politics and has emerged as the dominant
economic region of Ecuador. The changing concentration of population among
principal regions of the country reflects differential rates of population growth. The
Costa experienced more rapid rates of population growth than the Sierra during all
three inter-census periods, although population growth rates declined in both regions
during 1974-1982. The Oriente experienced higher rates of population growth and
more than doubled its share of the population between 1950 and 1990. The Galápagos
grew faster than any other region but on a very small base and accounted for .8 percent
of the population in 1990. Nevertheless, the rapid population growth of the Oriente
and Galápagos is a cause for major concern, given the fragile ecologies of these two
regions and especially the Galápagos with its unique and internationally acclaimed flora
and fauna.

The trend of increasing concentration of population in the Costa is expected to
continue according to INEC projections (1985a). The Costa will grow at nearly 3.0
percent during 1982-1995 while the Sierra is projected to grow at about 2.4 percent for
the same period. The Oriente is projected to have the most rapid rates of population
growth of any of the regions at about 5.0 percent through 1995. Growth in the

Table 5.3 Distribution of the Rural and Urban Population by Geographic Area for Census Years, and Projections

	Unadjusted Censuses				Projections		
	1950	1962	1974	1982	1982	1990	1995
Population (1,000)							
Ecuador	3,203	4,476	6,522	8,061	8,606	10,782	12,314
Urban	914	1,612	2,699	3,968	4,226	5,977	7,237
Rural	2,289	2,864	3,823	4,093	4,380	4,805	5,077
Sierra	1,856	2,271	3,147	3,802	4,047	4,927	5,527
Urban	485	744	1,203	1,707	1,817	2,513	3,008
Rural	1,371	1,527	1,944	2,095	2,230	2,414	2,519
Costa	1,298	2,128	3,179	3,947	4,214	5,360	6,172
Urban	423	858	1,470	2,199	2,343	3,354	4,085
Rural	875	1,270	1,709	1,748	1,871	2,006	2,087
Oriente	46	75	173	264	276	407	514
Urban	5	10	23	58	61	102	134
Rural	41	65	150	206	215	305	380
Galápagos & oth.	1	2	22	48	69	88	101
Urban	0	0	2	4	5	8	11
Rural	1	2	20	44	64	80	90
Share (%)							
Ecuador	100.0	100.0	100.0	100.0	100.0	100.0	100.0
Urban	28.5	36.0	41.4	49.2	49.1	55.4	58.8
Rural	71.5	64.0	58.6	50.8	50.9	44.6	41.2
Sierra	58.0	50.7	48.2	47.2	47.0	45.7	44.9
Urban	15.2	16.6	18.4	21.2	21.1	23.3	24.4
Rural	42.8	34.1	29.8	26.0	25.9	22.4	20.5
Costa	40.5	47.5	48.8	49.0	49.0	49.7	50.1
Urban	13.2	19.2	22.5	27.3	27.2	31.1	33.2
Rural	27.3	28.4	26.2	21.7	21.7	18.6	16.9
Oriente	1.5	1.7	2.7	3.3	3.2	3.8	4.2
Urban	0.2	0.2	0.4	0.7	0.7	0.9	1.1
Rural	1.3	1.4	2.3	2.6	2.5	2.8	3.1
Galápagos & oth.	0.0	0.1	0.3	0.6	0.8	0.8	0.8
Urban	0.0	0.0	0.0	0.1	0.1	0.1	0.1
Rural	0.0	0.1	0.3	0.5	0.7	0.7	0.7

Source: Whitaker, Colyer and Alzamora Appendix Tables 5.1 and 5.2.

Galápagos is expected to slow substantially to about 3.0 percent but still will be faster than the national average. As a result of these differential growth rates, the Costa will have more than half of Ecuador's population in 1995, the Oriente will have over 4 percent, the Galápagos' share will increase to nearly 1 percent while the Sierra's share will decline further to less than 45 percent.

Rural-Urban Distribution

There also have been large relative increases in the urban population between 1950 and 1990 (Table 5.3).[5] In 1950 Ecuador was a predominantly agrarian society with 71.5 percent of its 3.2 million people living in rural areas. By 1990 this scenario was reversed with 55.4 percent of the population of 10.8 million living in urban areas. The urban population increased by over six times between 1950-1990--an absolute increase

Table 5.4   Global, Rural and Urban Population Growth Rates by Region, Census Years
            1950, 1962, 1974, 1982; Projected for 1982, 1990 and 1995

Growth Rates (%)	Inter-censuses			Inter-projections	
	1950-62	1962-74	1974-82	1982-90	1990-95
A. Ecuador	2.83	3.32	2.53	2.86	2.69
Urban	4.84	4.57	4.66	4.43	3.90
Rural	1.88	2.54	0.81	1.16	1.11
B. Sierra	1.70	2.87	2.26	2.49	2.33
Urban	3.63	4.25	4.22	4.13	3.66
Rural	0.90	2.12	0.89	1.00	0.86
C. Costa	4.20	3.55	2.59	3.05	2.86
Urban	6.07	4.79	4.87	4.59	4.02
Rural	3.15	2.61	0.26	0.87	0.80
D. Oriente	4.06	7.55	5.07	5.00	4.76
Urban	5.37	7.09	11.45	6.72	5.69
Rural	3.87	7.63	3.79	4.48	4.44
E. Galápagos & other	4.90	21.34	9.59	3.06	2.92
Urban	---	---	7.92	6.85	6.14
Rural	4.90	20.16	9.77	2.74	2.57

Source: Whitaker, Colyer and Alzamora Appendix Table 5.2.

of 5.1 million inhabitants--which severely tested municipal governments' capacity to
provide requisite services.

The trend of increases in urban population have been especially strong in the Costa.
In 1950 the Sierra had the largest share of urban dwellers in the total population of any
region at 15.2 percent while the urban population of the Costa accounted for 13.2
percent of Ecuador's population. By 1990 Costa urban dwellers had increased to 31.1
percent of the total population, while the Sierra's urban population increased at a more
modest rate to 23.3 percent of the total. The Costa region now has the largest urban
population, with nearly one out of three Ecuadorians living in urban areas of the Costa.

Even though Ecuador has been transformed into a society with a majority of urban
people there has been a significant increase in the absolute number of rural people
who still account for 44.6 percent of the population. There are 4.8 million rural people
in 1990, an increase of 2.5 million since 1950, which also strained government's capacity
to meet their needs. The largest rural population is located in the Sierra with 2.4
million in 1990 (50.2 percent of the total) compared to 2.0 million (41.7 percent) in the
Costa and .4 million (8.1 percent) in the Oriente and Galápagos.

The rural population grew at much lower rates than the urban population reflecting
fairly rapid rural to urban migration in all the inter-census periods (Table 5.4). The
rural population growth rate plummeted to .81 percent during 1974-1982 because of
significant decreases in the birth and death rates combined with greatly increased rural
to urban migration. The quickened pace of outmigration was in response to relatively
greater employment and income opportunities in urban areas associated with the oil
boom and the urban-biased macroeconomic policies focused on import-substitution
industrialization (see Chapter 2). The rural population of the Sierra grew at only .89
percent during this period, a decrease of 58 percent from 1962-1974, while that of the

Table 5.5   Seventeen Principal Cities in Ecuador by Census Years, Ranked by Size

City	Province	Capital	1982	Rank	1950	Rank
Guayaquil	Guayas	yes	1,199,344	1	258,966	1
Quito	Pichincha	yes	866,472	2	209,932	2
Cuenca	Azuay	yes	152,406	3	39,983	3
Machala	El Oro	yes	105,521	4	7,549	15
Portoviejo	Manabí	yes	102,628	5	16,330	7
Ambato	Tungurahua	yes	100,454	6	31,312	4
Manta	Manabí	no	100,338	7	19,028	6
Esmeraldas	Esmeraldas	yes	90,360	8	13,169	11
Milagro	Guayas	no	77,010	9	13,736	10
Riobamba	Chimborazo	yes	75,455	10	29,830	5
Loja	Loja	yes	71,652	11	15,399	8
Santo Domingo	Pichincha	no	69,235	12	NA	17
Quevedo	Los Rios	no	67,023	13	4,168	16
Ibarra	Imbabura	yes	53,428	14	14,031	9
Babahoyo	Los Rios	yes	42,266	15	9,181	13
Chone	Manabí	no	33,839	16	8,046	14
Tulcán	Carchi	yes	30,985	17	10,623	12

Source: INEC 1985b; Ministry of Economy.

Costa fell by 90 percent to grow at only .26 percent.

Rural population is expected to grow at about 1.1 percent per year during 1982-1995, slightly faster than the last inter-census period. A total of 696,505 people will be added to the rural population with 24 percent of these in the Oriente. However, the share of the rural population will fall to 41 percent by 1995. The Oriente will experience growth rates of rural population nearly twice the national average and will about double its rural population. The rural population of the Sierra is expected to grow at about .9 percent during 1982-1995 and the Costa at about .8 percent, both much slower than the global growth rate.

Urban population growth is expected to slow to 4.4 percent during 1982-1990 and to 3.9 percent during 1990-1995 but still will be substantially faster than the global population growth rate. There will be an additional 3,011,589 urban residents during 1982-1995, over four times the increase in rural population. Urban growth is expected to be fastest in the Oriente and Galápagos, followed by the Costa, with Sierra experiencing the slowest urban population growth of any region, but still much faster than the national average.

Provincial Capitals and County Seats

Ecuador's cities grew very rapidly during the last three decades which severely strained their capacity to provide for the needs of their burgeoning populations (Table 5.5). For example, Santo Domingo, Quevedo and Machala have emerged from relative obscurity to become major secondary cities.

Increases in urban population tend to be concentrated in the provincial capitals,

Table 5.6   Changes in Rural and Urban Population Between 1950 and 1990

	1950	1990	Differences	Share of Differences (%)		
				National	Urban	Capitals
Ecuador	3,202,757	10,781,613	7,578,856	100.00	- -	- -
Urban	913,932	5,976,833	5,062,901	66.80	100.00	- -
Capitals	683,458	4,386,820	3,703,362	48.86	73.15	100.00
Quito	209,932	1,281,849	1,071,917	14.14	21.17	28.94
Guayaquil	258,966	1,764,170	1,505,204	19.86	29.73	40.64
Others	214,560	1,340,801	1,126,241	14.86	22.24	30.41
County seats	230,474	1,590,013	1,359,539	17.94	26.85	- -
Rural	2,288,825	4,804,780	2,515,955	33.20	- -	- -
Sierra	1,856,445	4,926,776	3,070,331	100.00	- -	- -
Urban	485,475	2,512,670	2,027,195	66.03	100.00	- -
Capitals	375,386	2,047,522	1,672,136	54.46	82.49	100.00
Quito	209,932	1,281,849	1,071,917	34.91	52.88	64.10
Others	165,454	765,673	600,219	19.55	29.61	35.90
County seats	110,089	465,148	355,059	11.56	17.51	- -
Rural	1,370,970	2,414,106	1,043,136	33.97	- -	- -
Costa	1,298,495	5,359,743	4,061,248	100.00	- -	- -
Urban	422,893	3,354,241	2,931,348	72.18	100.00	-
Capitals	305,195	2,293,682	1,988,487	48.96	67.84	100.00
Guayaquil	258,966	1,764,170	1,505,204	37.06	51.35	75.70
Others	46,229	529,512	483,283	11.90	16.49	24.30
County seats	117,698	1,060,559	942,861	23.22	32.16	- -
Rural	875,602	2,005,502	1,129,900	27.82	- -	- -
Oriente	46,471	407,330	360,859	100.00	- -	- -
Urban	5,564	101,789	96,225	26.67	100.00	- -
Capitals	2,877	43,223	40,346	11.18	41.93	100.00
County seats	2,687	58,566	55,879	15.48	58.07	- -
Rural	40,907	305,541	264,634	73.33	- -	- -
Galápagos & Other	1,346	87,764	86,418	100.00	- -	- -
Urban	0	8,133	8,133	9.41	100.00	- -
Capitals	0	2,393	2,393	2.77	29.42	100.00
County seats	0	5,740	5,740	6.64	70.58	- -
Rural	1,346	79,631	78,285	90.59	- -	- -

Source: Whitaker, Colyer and Alzamora Appendix Table 5.1.

especially in Quito in the Sierra and in Guayaquil in the Costa. The population of these two cities increased by a combined total 2,577,121 people between 1950-1990, and accounted for 50.9 percent of the increase of 5,062,091 in urban population (Table 5.6). An additional 22.2 percent is explained by increases in the population of other provincial capitals, while the balance of 26.9 percent is accounted for by growth in the population of county seats. Urbanization in the Sierra is heavily concentrated in the capital cities. Quito alone accounted for 52.9 percent of the increase in the urban population of Sierra, with the other provincial capitals accounting for 29.6 percent and only 17.5 percent of the increase was in Sierra county seats.

The increase of urban population is more disperse in the Costa. The principal city, Guayaquil, accounted for 51.4 percent of the increase in the urban population of the Costa, about the same share as for Quito in the Sierra. However, a relatively large

Table 5.7   Population Density by Regions and Provinces, Ecuador, 1950, 1982 & 1990

Regions and Provinces	Area (km^2)	Total Population (1,000)			Persons/km^2		
		1950	1990	1995	1950	1990	1995
Ecuador[a]	269,055	3,203	10,782	12,314	11.9	40.1	45.8
Sierra	63,608	1,856	4,927	5,527	29.2	77.5	86.9
Carchi	3,750	77	151	159	20.4	40.2	42.4
Imbabura	4,466	147	300	323	32.9	67.2	72.3
Pichincha	12,870	386	1,984	2,369	30.0	154.2	184.0
Cotopaxi	6,248	166	333	355	26.5	53.3	56.9
Tungurahua	3,128	188	403	439	60.1	129.0	140.2
Chimborazo	6,523	218	384	398	33.4	58.8	61.0
Bolivar	4,106	109	168	172	26.6	40.9	41.9
Cañar	3,185	98	213	231	30.7	67.0	72.5
Azuay	8,118	251	563	627	30.9	69.3	77.2
Loja	11,214	217	427	455	19.3	38.1	40.6
Costa	66,778	1,298	5,360	6,172	19.4	80.3	92.4
Esmeraldas	15,152	75	335	387	5.0	22.1	25.5
Manabí	18,744	401	1,126	1,241	21.4	60.1	66.2
Guayas	20,247	582	2,842	3,331	28.8	140.4	164.5
Los Rios	6,825	150	592	668	22.0	86.7	97.8
El Oro	5,811	89	465	546	15.4	80.0	93.9
Oriente	130,659	46	407	514	0.4	3.1	3.9
Napo	53,764	18	192	254	0.3	3.6	4.7
Pastaza	29,135	8	44	52	0.3	1.5	1.8
Morona	25,785	16	99	118	0.6	3.9	4.6
Zamora	21,975	5	71	89	0.2	3.3	4.1
Galápagos	8,010	1	88	101	0.2	11.0	12.7

Source: INEC 1985a; Ministry of Economy; INEC, División de Cartografía, unpublished data on area.

[a]Undefined areas not included (1,611.7 km^2).

32.2 percent of the increase in the urban population of the Costa was in its county seats while only 16.5 percent was due to increases in the urban population of other provincial capitals. The Costa accounted for almost 70 percent of the increase in the population of county seats nationally between 1950-1990. Given the initially larger populations of the Costa county seats and their more rapid growth, the divergences between the urban populations of the county seats of the two regions has become more pronounced. In contrast, the increase in population of the provincial capitals is more evenly divided between the two regions, with the Costa accounting for 54 percent.

Population Density

Population density increased from 11.9 to 40.1 people per square kilometer (p/km^2) between 1950 and 1990 and is expected to be at 45.8 p/km^2 by 1995 (Table 5.7).[6] The Costa and Sierra each have about one-fourth the total land area and their population densities are very similar at 80.3 and 77.5 p/km^2 in 1990, respectively. The Costa surpassed the Sierra as the most densely populated region of the country in the mid-1970s as its population density more than quadrupled between 1950-1990. The Sierra's population grew more slowly than the Costa but its population density still increased by 2.7 times between 1950-1990. The Oriente, with about half of the total land area, is very sparsely populated with only 3.1 p/km^2 in 1990. However, its population density increased by nearly eight times between 1950-1990 due to a rapid influx of settlers during the 1970s and 1980s. The permanent population density of the Galápagos increased the most dramatically, by over 55 times and now is 11.0 p/km^2. This permanent increase, along with rapid influxes of tourists has imposed significant stress on the fragile ecology of the Galápagos and threatens the survival of this important nature reserve.

These averages mask important differences among provinces. Pichincha and Guayas provinces which contain the principal cities of Quito and Guayaquil have population densities of 154.2 and 140.4, respectively and are the most densely populated provinces of Ecuador. The next greatest population density is in Tungurahua province, Ecuador's smallest, at 129.0 p/km^2. The most sparsely populated province (outside the Oriente) is Esmeraldas in the Costa, followed by Loja in the Sierra.

Rural to Urban Migration

Differences in the global, rural and urban population growth rates for Ecuador and its regions reflect differences in underlying determinants of population growth including the death rate, the birth rate, net migration and reclassification of parishes (*parroquias*) from rural to urban between censuses. Limited data make it difficult to disaggregate the relative importance of each of these determinants of net population growth rates. There is evidence, however, that migration from rural to urban areas is very important in explaining the rapid rates of urban population growth and the relatively low rates of rural population growth. Data on death and birth rates for rural and urban areas indicate that the natural rate of population growth is somewhat higher in rural than urban areas, primarily because of a much higher levels of fecundity (CONADE and UNFPA Chapter 2). Since the observed population growth rates are much higher in urban areas, rural to urban migration and reclassification of rural areas as urban must explain a significant share of urban population growth.

Rural to urban migration can be estimated by assuming that the rate of population growth in rural and urban areas is the same as the national average, projecting rural and urban populations at this rate and calculating the difference between actual and projected rural and urban populations (Table 5.8). Since the natural rate of population growth likely is higher in rural than in urban areas, this assumption will result in a lower-limit estimate of net rural to urban migration. These estimates will include actual rural to urban migration and reclassification of rural parishes as urban.

Rural to urban migration is estimated to have been about 632,500 between 1974-1982 using this procedure.[7] The same analysis for 1962-1974 suggests rural to urban migration of approximately 350,000. These results indicate that a little less than one-third of the increase in Ecuador's urban population between 1962-1974 was due to rural to urban migration. Migrants were a much more important share of the increase in urban population of 1,269,640 between 1974-1982, accounting for almost half.

A recent study by Padilla came to a similar conclusion. It found that between 1962-1974 a little more than 35 percent of urban population growth was explained by net migration from rural to urban areas, including rural to urban migration per se and

Table 5.8 Estimates of Rural to Urban Migration, 1962-1974 and 1974-1982

Year	Unadjusted Census	Projected[a]	Estimated Migration (difference)
1982			
Rural	4,092,350	4,724,007	(631,657)
Urban	3,968,362	3,334,769	633,593
1974			
Rural	3,822,988	4,173,190	(350,202)
Urban	2,698,722	2,349,652	349,070

Source: Whitaker, Colyer and Alzamora Appendix Table 5.1; projections by author.

[a]Projected from previous census year at Ecuador's average growth rate of 2.53 percent between 1974-1982 (8.47 years) and at 3.32 percent between 1962-1974 (11.53 years).

reclassification of jurisdictions from rural to urban. Between 1974-1982 more than 50 percent of urban growth was explained by such transfers. The study estimated that the natural growth of population in rural areas was reduced by 29 percent between 1962-1974 and by 75 percent between 1974-1982 by rural to urban migration and reclassification of parishes from rural to urban.

CONADE and UNFPA (pp. 244-46) estimated the effects of reclassification of rural areas as urban as relatively minor. They found that the population of areas reclassified as urban represented 6.6 percent of urban population growth during 1962-1974 and 5.8 percent during 1974-1982. This suggests that the major part of net rural to urban migration as estimated here and by Padilla is due to rural to urban migration. Moreover the increase in the share of urban population growth due to rural immigrants, from about 35 percent to over 50 percent between the two inter-census periods indicates that the rate of rural to urban migration increased substantially during 1974-1982.

One striking aspect of the rural and urban migration patterns is their complexity. It is tempting to conclude that rural to urban migration is a dominant pattern but this is not so. Data from the 1982 population census for "last migratory movement" tabulated by rural and urban areas illustrate the nature of rural and urban migration patterns (Table 5.9). The largest outmigration was from urban areas and at 1,071,355, was substantially greater than outmigration of 644,810 from rural areas. While most urban outmigration was to other urban areas, a substantial portion was to rural areas. Moreover, this flow of people from urban to rural areas offset more than half of rural to urban migration as captured in the 1982 census by people reporting a "last migratory movement."[8]

The Labor Force

A country's labor force, or economically active population (EAP) usually is defined to include all those who are employed and those who are unemployed and actively seeking employment, including new entrants into the job market. The size of the labor force at any point in time is dependent upon two principal variables: the share of the

Table 5.9 Rural and Urban Migration Patterns, According to "Last Migratory Movement," 1982

	Emigrants From:					
	Ecuador	Rural	Urban	Sierra	Costa	Oriente
Immigrants to:						
Ecuador	1,716,165	644,810	1,071,355	863,756	811,752	40,657
Rural	418,078	63,081	354,997	202,458	199,684	15,936
Urban	1,298,087	581,729	716,358	661,298	612,068	24,721
Sierra	731,746	263,341	468,405	565,180	148,769	17,797
Costa	881,585	339,799	541,786	230,087	647,862	3,636
Oriente	102,834	41,670	61,164	68,489	15,121	19,224

Source: INEC 1985b.

population of working age, which in turn depends on past demographic trends; and the rate of participation in the labor force of various segments of the population of working age. Growth in the labor force depends on how these two variables change over time.

Recent Growth

The 1962, 1974 and 1982 censuses of population present data on the labor force, defined to include those age 12 and over, but female participation rates were substantially underestimated. The censuses under-counted women, because many indicated they were housewives (defined in the censuses as not economically active) when in fact they were employed, especially in agricultural activities. The 1962 and 1982 census data on EAP were corrected by the Institute of Social Studies of Holland (ISS) and the United Nations Regional Employment Program for Latin America and the Caribbean (PREALC) (1984a, 1984b) and by INEC (1979) for 1974. Corrected data were reported in Gutiérrez (1984a Table 11) and are summarized here.

There were an estimated 2.9 million people in Ecuador's labor force in 1982, up from 2.3 million in 1974 and 1.7 million in 1962. The rate of growth in the labor force also increased from 2.2 percent between 1962-1974 to 2.9 percent between 1974-1982. These data suggest the annual increases the labor force more than doubled in 20 years, from 39,000 in 1963 to 83,000 in 1983.

The increase in rate of growth of the labor force between the two inter-census periods reflects the net effect of changes in two key variables. The first is the share of the population of working age in the labor force (commonly referred to as the participation rate). The second is the growth rate of the population of working age.

Gutiérrez (1984a pp. 15-19) documented a continual decline in the first key variable--the participation rate--from 60.7 percent in 1962 to 54.0 percent in 1974 to 51.8 percent in 1982. This decline reflected primarily: (a) greatly increased enrollment in school among 12-24 year old men and women in both rural and urban areas, but especially for rural males; (b) much broader social security coverage among older workers and especially for urban males over age 55; and (c) the process of urbanization which provided greater access to school and social security for urban people.[9] The continual decline in the participation rate between 1962-1974 and between 1974-1982 tended to reduce the rate of growth of the labor force.

The rate of growth of the population of working age--the second determinant of labor force growth--increased from 3.29 percent during 1965-1975 to 3.44 percent between 1975-1985 (INEC, CONADE and CELADE Tables 2 and 9).[10] This increase placed significant upward pressure on the rate of growth of the labor force.

The net effect of changes in the two prime determinants of labor force growth between the inter-census periods was to increase the rate of growth. The positive effect of the increased rate of growth of the population of working age was greater than the negative effect of declining participation rates and the pace of growth in the labor force increased by almost 32 percent during 1974-1982 relative to 1962-1974.

Future Labor Force Growth

CONADE and UNFPA (pp. 289 ff.) made projections of growth in the labor force for five-year intervals from 1985 to 2000 using the uncorrected census data as a basis. Consequently, these projections started from too low a base because the 1982 census had significantly under-counted rural women in the EAP. As a result, the projected levels of the EAP also are too low, especially for women. For example, the 1985 projections were for a total EAP of 2,854,100, while the corrected census data reported an EAP of 2,864,800 in 1982, three years earlier. Also, the number of women in the labor force in 1982 according to corrected census data was 893,818, while the CONADE and UNFPA projections were for 592,600 in 1985.

The rates of growth in the CONADE-UNFPA projections appear to be more reliable and consistent with the rapid growth of the population of working age discussed above. They indicate a rapid increase in the labor force of 3.2 percent annually between 1985-2000, with especially high rates of growth during 1985-1990 of 3.4 percent.

Estimates of the labor force were made utilizing the corrected 1982 census data as the base, the 2.9 percent inter-census growth rate in the labor force between 1974-1982 (from corrected census data) for projecting the EAP in 1985, and the growth rates for the five-year intervals implicit in the CONADE and UNFPA projections for projecting the EAP in 1990, 1995 and 2000 (Table 5.10). These estimates indicate an annual increase in the labor force of 104,579 in 1986, 117,789 in 1991, 131,848 in 1996 and 153,293 in the year 2001, about 10 percent greater each year than in the CONADE-UNFPA projections.

Characteristics of the EAP

There were significant changes in the nature of the labor force between 1962 and 1982 with respect to rural and urban location, gender and age.

The labor force became increasingly concentrated in urban areas, especially since 1974 (Gutiérrez 1984a, Table 9). In 1962, only 29.8 percent of the labor force was in urban areas; this increased to 36.7 percent by 1974 and 44.6 percent by 1982. This phenomena reflects the subsidization of industry and other mainly urban-based economic sectors at the expense of agriculture and rural people (see Chapter 2). As a result, employment opportunities became much more lucrative in nonagricultural activities, the pace of rural to urban migration quickened, the urban labor force grew rapidly and agricultural employment actually declined (see below). The labor force is projected to become even more concentrated in urban areas, reaching 64 percent of the total by 2000, up from 54.0 percent in 1985 (CONADE and UNFPA p. 301).

Another important change in the labor force is the increasing share of women.

Table 5.10 Corrected Censuses and Projections of the Labor Force

	EAP (1,000)	Annual Average Growth Rate[a] (%)	Annual Average Increase[b]
Corrected Censuses			
1962	1,745.6	---	39,175
1974	2,278.3	2.24	66,179
1982	2,864.8	2.90	83,215
Projections			
1985	3,121.8	2.90	104,579
1990	3,680.9	3.35	117,789
1995	4,308.8	3.20	131,848
2000	5,009.6	3.06	153,293

Source: Growth rates, 1985-2000, derived from estimates of EAP by CONADE & UNFPA (p.300); 1962-1982, Gutiérrez (1984a Table 11); projections of EAP by author.

[a]The annual average rate between the census or projection years. For example, the rate of 2.24 percent is for the period 1962-1974.
[b]Calculated from the EAP in the base year and the growth rate for the period. For example, 39,175 is the annual increase in 1963 given the 1962 base and the annual average growth rate of 2.24 percent between 1962-1974. The increase for 2001 is calculated at the same rate as for 1995.

Corrected census data indicated that 28.9 percent of the labor force were women in 1962 and this increased slightly to 31.2 percent in 1982 (Gutiérrez 1984a, Table 10). The participation rate for women has remained relatively constant although a decline in fecundity likely will result in increased participation rates, especially among women of childbearing age. Also, increased levels of education may increase the participation rate, particularly for urban women over school age.

Finally, the composition of the labor force tended to become more concentrated among people ages 25-64. This is because the younger ages increasingly are in school instead of the labor force and because older people are covered by social security and are not working. In 1962, 58.7 percent of the EAP was concentrated in ages 25-64; this had risen to 64.0 percent in 1982 (Gutiérrez 1984a Table 9).

Unemployment

Unemployment is an emotional issue in Ecuador. Discussion of its extent and how to resolve it composes a significant part of the national public debate about economic issues (see, e.g. El Comercio p. B-1). This debate is rendered more subjective by inadequate data and differing concepts about what is meant by unemployment. Periodic surveys by the National Employment Institute (INEM) to measure unemployment started in 1987. Past occasional studies and surveys of unemployment tended to use different methodologies and concepts so the results are not strictly comparable. The unemployed in Ecuador traditionally are defined to include all those who are seeking employment for the first time and those who are looking for work after quitting or being dismissed from their jobs.

The magnitude of unemployment is relatively low, although it appears to have increased since the mid-1970s. Urban unemployment, as measured by data from the uncorrected censuses and three different household surveys, ranged from 4.4 to 5.8

percent of the EAP through the 1970s and early 1980s, with a modest trend of increasing unemployment in both the census and survey data (Gutiérrez 1984a, p. 59). In one survey of poorer neighborhoods in Quito and Guayaquil the rate was 9.7 percent in 1983, a year of severe economic recession, compounded by the El Niño floods. Rural unemployment measured in the 1974 and 1982 censuses was much less than urban unemployment but shows the same increasing trend. There are no data for rural unemployment more recent than the 1982 census but rural unemployment probably continues to be much lower than in urban areas. Also the trend of increasing rural unemployment between 1974-1982 probably reversed in the 1980s. Agricultural growth recovered substantially after 1982, after being relatively stagnant in the 1970s (see Chapter 3). Indeed, agriculture has led economic development since 1982 and likely has generated new jobs, although data are lacking on this point.

The most recent primary data on unemployment are from household surveys in Quito, Guayaquil and Cuenca during November 1987 (INEM). This survey revealed an urban unemployment rate of 7.24 percent for the three principal cities. This rate suggests that the trend of rising unemployment during the 1970s and early 1980s continued through the mid-1980s. This interpretation is consistent with the general stagnation of the economy after 1982 and especially in urban-based economic sectors.

The INEM survey data also reveal an unemployment rate for females twice that for males and a rate for female heads of households three times that for male heads. The data also indicate that unemployment is much higher among young workers, those with less education and new entrants into the labor force.

The level of unemployment indicated in the INEM survey is relatively low and close to the norm for frictional unemployment. Matching displaced workers and new entrants into the labor market with jobs consumes time and resources. Because of this, levels of unemployment of less than 6 percent are considered to be compatible with full employment in developed economies. Viewed in this light, the unemployment rate of 7.2 percent in the three principal cities of Ecuador is relatively low, considering the likely greater inefficiencies in the information system and corresponding greater delays in matching skills and jobs.[11]

Employment and Labor Absorption

There have been significant changes in the capacity of the economy to generate new jobs and to absorb the burgeoning labor force. The sectoral composition of employment experienced a significant transformation and absorptive capacity changed greatly over the last three decades.

Changing Sectoral Composition

Agriculture was the largest employer of any economic sector in 1982 with 1,172,700 workers but its share had declined to 44.7 percent of the total from over 59.0 percent in 1970 (Table 5.11). Agriculture's capacity to generate employment and to absorb increases in the labor force actually declined absolutely during 1974-1982, after reasonable performance during 1970-1974. Agriculture accounted for 36,600 new jobs in the earlier period, or 22.8 percent of the total increase. However, agricultural employment declined by 19,800 during 1974-1982 as rural people sought more lucrative jobs in other sectors of the economy.

The sharp decline in agriculture's capacity to generate new jobs is explained by

Table 5.11 Employment by Sector, 1970, 1974, and 1982 (Thousands)

Sector	1970	1974	1982	Growth 1970-74	Growth 1974-82
Total	1,959.2	2,119.7	2,626.3	160.5	506.6
Agriculture	1,155.9	1,192.5	1,172.7	36.6	-19.8
Mining/Petroleum	5.1	6.2	7.1	1.1	0.9
Industry	203.5	228.0	270.6	24.5	42.6
Construction	70.9	86.4	153.6	15.5	67.2
Utilities	6.9	8.7	12.4	1.8	3.7
Commerce	155.5	190.6	253.1	35.1	62.5
Transportation	50.1	54.8	104.9	4.7	50.1
Finances	16.3	20.0	37.6	3.7	17.6
Services	295.0	332.5	614.3	37.5	281.8
Other[a]	43.2	72.3	57.6	29.1	-14.7
Shares (%)					
Total	100.0	100.0	100.0	100.0	100.0
Agriculture	59.0	56.3	44.7	22.8	-3.9
Mining/Petroleum	0.3	0.3	0.3	0.7	0.2
Industry	10.4	10.8	10.3	15.3	8.4
Construction	3.6	4.1	5.8	9.7	13.3
Utilities	0.4	0.4	0.5	1.1	0.7
Commerce	7.9	9.0	9.6	21.9	12.3
Transportation	2.6	2.6	4.0	2.9	9.9
Finances	0.8	0.9	1.4	2.3	3.5
Services	15.1	15.7	23.4	23.4	55.6

Source: Gutiérrez 1984a, Table 19.

[a]Not included in total since it cannot be allocated among sectors.

three interrelated factors. First, agricultural growth stagnated relative to the rest of the economy as the macroeconomic policy matrix subsidized industry and urban development at the expense of agriculture. Second, agricultural wage rates increased as labor was pulled out of the sector by the lure of higher wages and other nonpecuniary benefits of urban-based employment. Agriculture responded to reduced incentives and more expensive labor by adopting production processes which substituted capital for labor. Third, the macroeconomic policy matrix also resulted in the subsidization of capital which further enhanced agriculture's adoption of capital intensive techniques.

Services, which includes both government and households, was the second most important sector in terms of employment in 1982 at 614,300.[12] It accounted for 37,500 new jobs between 1970-1974, slightly more than agriculture and on a much smaller base. Then, between 1974 and 1982 it nearly doubled its employment absorbing a very large 281,800 new entrants into the labor force, or 55.6 percent of the increase in the total economy for the period. As a result, its share increased from 15.1 percent of employment in 1970 to 23.4 percent in 1982.

Industry and commerce were the third and fourth most important sectors in terms of employment in 1982 at 270,600 and 253,100 employees, respectively. Both however, reduced their rates of labor absorption during 1974-1982 relative to the earlier period, with commerce accounting for 12.3 percent of increases in employment for the period and industry only 8.4 percent. Construction, the fifth the most important sectoral employer in 1982, accounted for more of the increase in employment between 1974 and

1982 (67,200) than any other sector excepting services. Transportation and finances also increased their employment of the growing labor force, with each nearly doubling the number employed between 1974 and 1982.

Absorptive Capacity

The capacity of each of the sectors to generate employment is quantified in employment elasticities (Table 5.12). These elasticities measure the percentage change in employment relative to the percentage change in Gross Domestic Product (GDP) over a given period. The absorptive capacity of the economy increased substantially between 1970-1974 and 1974-1982 from .13 to .43. This global increase masked some important changes in the structure of employment generation, however. The threefold increase in the capacity of the economy to employ new workers was due to very large increases in the employment elasticity in construction, transportation, finances and services which collectively accounted for 39 percent of GDP in 1982. These increases were sufficiently large to offset the large decline in the employment elasticities in agriculture and industry and modest decreases in commerce and utilities.

Underemployment

The concept of underemployment is less precise than unemployment. The underemployed are, by definition, a subset of that part of the labor force which is employed in some way. The literature on employment problems in developing countries generally identifies two kinds of underemployment: (a) open underemployment where a worker is employed for fewer hours per day or week than some standard; and (b) disguised or hidden underemployment where the worker is employed full time but earns less than some standard, usually related to a minimum wage or similar index of well-being (Fletcher, Marquez and Sarfaty pp. 37-40). Obviously, the magnitude of open and hidden underemployment depends on the absolute level of the standards utilized. The higher the standard the greater will be the observed levels of underemployment. Thus, subjectivity in defining the standard impinges directly on the magnitude of underemployment.

Open underemployment in Ecuador is measured in the INEM survey in relation to the legal workweek of 40 hours. The rate of open underemployment in November 1987 was relatively low at 4.8 percent of the labor force. This low rate reflects labor law in Ecuador which limits less than full-time employment in almost all circumstances by setting a 40-hour work week and making hourly hiring generally illegal. The low rate also reflects the reality that unemployed workers quickly become self-employed in the services sector where they can earn enough to support their families by working long hours. Finally, most employed workers in a recessionary economy are unwilling to participate in arrangements for sharing work even where labor law so permits.

Hidden underemployment in Ecuador is a much more serious problem, with a rate of 21.9 percent for Quito, Guayaquil and Cuenca in 1987 according to the INEM survey. This rate was established by comparing earnings of full-time workers with the minimum wage, including all compensation established by law.

The rate of hidden underemployment in Ecuador does not distinguish between the causes of hidden underemployment. The concept of hidden underemployment basically is concerned with measuring the extent to which workers with the same skills earn different wages, because of segmentation in the labor market. However, lack of

Table 5.12 Employment Elasticities, 1970-1974 and 1974-1982

Sector	1970-74	1974-82	Percentage Change
Total[a]	0.13	0.43	238.4
Agriculture	0.16	(0.07)	-147.7
Industry	0.31	0.19	-39.5
Construction	0.52	2.56	388.0
Utilities	0.58	0.54	-6.6
Commerce	0.57	0.46	-19.2
Transportation	0.23	0.91	301.4
Finances	0.56	1.17	110.3
Services	0.41	1.08	163.3

Source: Table 5.11; Whitaker, Colyer and Alzamora Appendix Table 3.1.

[a]"Others" not included in total since it cannot be allocated among sectors. "Mining and Petroleum" not included in total because of its relative unimportance in employment and negative GDP in 1970.

requisite wage data usually precludes measurement of hidden underemployment caused by market segmentation.[13] Such is the case with the INEM estimates which used the minimum wage as the standard. Consequently, the hidden underemployment rate can not be interpreted solely as a measure of labor market segmentation. The high level of hidden underemployment more likely reflects limited investments in human capital, especially in rural areas, rather than market segmentation. The majority of rural emigrants appear to be trapped in low-paying jobs in urban areas because of their limited skills.

Workers are trapped in low-paying jobs, not only because of their extremely limited education and skill levels, but because very few higher-paying jobs are being created by the internally oriented model of economic development employed in Ecuador during the last three decades. There is little incentive for poor people to invest in literacy, or improved skills if prospects for recouping such investments are constrained by a stagnant economy and very slow growth in better jobs.

The Labor Market

There is a continuing debate about the extent to which labor markets function efficiently in developing countries. One body of evidence suggests that markets are efficient and that employment problems originate in the distortions introduced by macroeconomic and sectoral policies (Kannappan; Berry and Sobot; Kahnert; Gregory). There are a few studies which suggest that competition can not produce a common wage for workers with similar skills (Uthoff; Krueger and Summers). Increased investment in human capital, especially in primary and secondary education and improved skills are the best way to increase incomes and wellbeing of poor people when labor markets are relatively efficient. But if institutionally induced wage differentials exist, the basic policy approach would be to foster growth in employment in the high-wage industries, or to reduce or eliminate institutional barriers, including labor laws, to inter- and intra-sectoral labor mobility.

There are no empirical studies on the degree of segmentation in labor markets in Ecuador. One study argues intuitively that some segmentation must exist in high-wage industries, because it does in a few other countries (Fletcher, Marquez and Sarfaty). A second study (Hachette and Franklin) found some limited segmentation in the industrial sector but argues that markets have been relatively efficient. It also argued that one important sector of the economy--public services--appears to be segmented from the rest of the economy.

Principal Characteristics

Ecuador's labor markets are characterized by regionalization, fragmentation, informality and high opportunity costs associated with finding employment consistent with skills and abilities. Public support for the labor market is practically nonexistent. Employment services, which match unemployed workers with jobs in many countries do not exist. There is no unemployment insurance so that the costs of being unemployed are borne completely by the individual. This, in turn, tends to force the mismatching of skills with jobs as the individual can not afford to wait for the "right" job. The inadequate and increasingly costly communication system also tends to limit the efficient functioning of the labor market. However, a relatively good system of roads and highly subsidized fuel prices have facilitated the movement of people and have enhanced the efficient functioning of the labor market.

Labor markets tend to operate informally. The principal cities are centers for matching people to jobs, with interrelated markets in smaller, secondary cities. Most information about jobs, especially those requiring unskilled labor, is spread via informal communication networks. Newspaper advertisements are utilized to solicit applications for skilled labor, professional services and some lower skill jobs (such as maids) in the urban areas. But no formal, publicly supported system for matching workers with jobs exists.

The combination of limited public support, regionalization and fragmentation and the informal nature of labor markets results in high opportunity costs associated with employment. Individuals must spend substantial time and effort to explore the job opportunities that may be available to them even in the context of a local labor market.

Rigidities and Market Segmentation

One major rigidity affecting the labor market generally, is the Ecuadorian labor code, or *Código del Trabajo*. This law, a very ambitious pieces of social legislation, was promulgated during the liberal era of the late 1930s and was intended to improve income distribution by increasing payments to labor. It was substantially revised and broadened during the euphoria of the petroleum boom and rapid economic expansion of the late 1970s. It provides for minimum wages for firms with less than 15 workers, domestic servants, agricultural workers and employees of large firms; a 40 hour work week; long-term contracts; three extra monthly salaries; and a variety of other compensations associated with tenure of employment, transportation and dismissal. In addition, workers also are covered by social security legislation, which requires significant additional payments. The transactions costs associated with compliance with these laws are substantial and are an additional element of labor costs. The principal effect of labor and social security legislation is to make labor relatively more expensive as it receives compensation unrelated to its productivity. Labor concomitantly tends to become a relatively fixed factor of production with a quasi-permanent commitment by employers, which is an important element of its increased cost. These effects, in conjunction with heavy subsidies to capital inherent in the macroeconomic policy matrix, have encouraged substitution of capital for labor throughout the economy but especially in industry.

The share of the labor force which is employed under the aegis of the labor code is not known. It is known, however, that particular elements of the labor force work outside purview of the law. A large share of agricultural labor in the Costa is employed by the day. It is common to employ unskilled labor in Quito and Guayaquil for temporary jobs by the day, by going to certain locations and selecting laborers from groups that congregate there. Entrepreneurs have circumvented the labor code in a variety of inventive ways. One approach is to contract with a number of individuals, or small firms to produce something from delivered components, such as sewing clothing by the piece. Since no employer-employee relationship is established, minimum wages and other provisions of the labor code are not in effect.

Fletcher, Marquez and Sarfaty (p. vi) argue for Ecuador from one study in the U.S. and three unpublished studies for other Latin American countries, that "...some labor market segmentation and nonpure competition most likely exists...in high-wage industries while too many poorly paid workers are trapped in the low-productivity informal sector..." They suggest that the reduction of labor regulations and institutional arrangements will help to alleviate such segmentation but do not identify specific regulations, institutional arrangements or cases of segmented markets. A recent review of literature on the subject from various developing countries suggests, however, that urban labor markets are quite efficient, with little evidence of segmentation (Kannappan).

There may be segmentation of the labor market in the public sector. Public sector employees fall under two different laws: the labor code, which encompasses lower-skill workers; and the civil service code, which covers professionals and administrators. All public sector employees are subject to one of the two laws, each of which is fully complied with across the gamut of public sector entities, including autonomous agencies.

Public sector jobs are highly sought after. The work load usually is perceived of as light and the compensation as relatively good. Job tenure is practically guaranteed for life, especially among the lower skill workers who are organized into unions (*sindicatos*). The low productivity of public sector employees is notorious. If low-skill, public employees were to have to work in another sector of the economy, most undoubtedly would be required to work longer hours or more intensively, at higher levels of productivity to earn the same wages. If so, wages of low-skill workers in the public sector are higher than people with similar skills in the rest of the economy, and the labor market is segmented by enforcement of the labor code in the public sector.[14] The implication is that the labor code needs to be revised to permit a reduction in the wages for public servants, or to increase their productivity.

Evidence of Efficiency

Labor markets in Ecuador are quite competitive and have transferred significant numbers of people to higher-paying jobs. Data indicate that labor productivity is converging between economic sectors and between rural and urban areas. This indicates that intersectoral and interregional labor markets are relatively efficient in an economic sense. It also implies that employment problems are mainly a function of distortions in the macroeconomic policy matrix, the stagnant economy and extremely limited investments in human capital.

Intersectoral Labor Markets

Labor markets have allocated human resources efficiently among the principal economic sectors according to relative changes in GDP per worker (Table 5.13). These data indicate a convergence of the productivity gaps between the agricultural sector, and the construction, services, transportation and finance sectors, and maintenance of the differentials between agriculture and the commerce and utilities sectors. Industry was the only sector whose labor productivity diverged (grew faster) significantly from agriculture.

These data must be used with care in attempting to draw inferences about the efficiency of national labor markets. Ideally, such analysis requires comparison of the real wages of labor at the margin for the same skill classes among economic sectors, regions or areas. Such data are not available and average GDP per worker is used instead. GDP per worker, however, measures income from all productive factors, not just labor. Payments to low-skill labor probably constitute the largest share of GDP, especially in the agricultural, construction and services sectors and is an important element in most of the other economic sectors. If so, average GDP per worker would tend to converge between the sectors as labor transfers occur, if labor markets are functioning efficiently.

GDP per capita in agriculture rose between 1974-1982 by 24.3 percent to S/.19,699 as massive rural-urban migration was occurring and sectoral employment declined. The most likely sectors of employment for those leaving agriculture, who generally had low skills, was in construction and services. These two sectors had much higher levels of GDP per capita in 1974 than agriculture and together accounted for 68.9 percent of the increase in employment between 1974-1982. The GDP per capita in construction declined substantially between 1974 and 1982 and slightly for the services sector. In both cases the absolute level of GDP per capita in 1982 still was about two times greater in services and 2.4 times greater in construction, than in agriculture. This differential probably still was wide enough to provide continued attraction of rural workers after 1982 to seek employment in the low-skill economic sectors, especially in urban areas.

The relatively small decrease in GDP per worker in the aggregate services sector is explained by the importance of higher-salary government services, relative to household services.[15] In 1982, professional government workers constituted over 30 percent of employment in the services sector, another 27 percent were lower-skill government employees covered by the labor code, while only 43 percent were in household services (INEC 1985b, Tables 34A and 36A).[16] Household services clearly was the principal market for many unskilled, rural emigrants and constituted an important component of the informal sector. Consequently, there probably was a much sharper decline in GDP per capita for household services between 1974-1982, than the small decrease for the aggregate services sector. GDP per worker in the total services sector tended to be sustained by the rapid increase in the number of higher-salaried government employees during the 1970s. Unfortunately, disaggregated data for 1974 are not reported in the census and the magnitude of changes in the government and household components of the services sector could not be determined.

These data suggest that labor markets moved large numbers of people from lower-paying jobs in agriculture to higher-paying jobs in construction and household services

Table 5.13   GDP Per Worker by Sector, 1970, 1974 and 1982

Sector	1970	1974	1982 Amount	Agriculture Relative	Growth 1974-82
Total[a]	31,002.4	47,094.9	59,097.2	3.00	25.5
Agriculture	13,591.1	15,844.0	19,699.0	1.00	24.3
Industry	53,086.0	65,508.8	109,327.4	5.55	66.9
Construction	55,571.2	64,641.2	47,428.4	2.41	-26.6
Utilities	69,130.4	79,655.2	100,080.6	5.08	25.6
Commerce	69,009.6	78,483.7	100,995.7	5.13	28.7
Transportation	75,149.7	97,189.8	101,878.0	5.17	4.8
Finances	462,331.3	530,500.0	494,414.9	25.10	-6.8
Services	34,210.2	39,780.5	38,466.5	1.95	-3.3

Source: Table 5.11; Whitaker, Colyer and Alzamora Appendix Table 3.1.

[a]"Others" not included in total since it cannot be allocated among sectors. "Mining and Petroleum" not included in total because of its relative unimportance in employment, and negative GDP in 1970.

and probably into low-skill government services. GDP per capita converged between agriculture and these sectors which is fully consistent with an efficiently functioning labor market.

Only industry's GDP per worker grew significantly faster than that for agriculture during the 1974-1982 period. As noted above, macroeconomic policies subsidized capital-intensive industrialization during the petroleum boom of the 1970s. Thus, the divergence in GDP per employee between agriculture and industry could well be consistent with convergence of agricultural and industrial wages, since an increasingly important share of industrial GDP was earned by capital throughout the period. Evidence from several developing countries indicate that wage differentials between manufacturing jobs and the self-employed in the informal sector overlapped substantially for the same skill levels (Kannappan p. 47).

Rural and Urban Linkages and Efficiency

A similar analysis for rural and urban areas indicates a convergence of GDP per capita between 1974-1982. This suggests that labor markets also are efficiently moving people from rural to urban employment.

The rapid rates of rural to urban migration between 1974-1982, and the concomitant decline of agricultural employment are consistent with the notion that nonagricultural productive sectors are located in urban areas, while rural areas contain predominantly agricultural activities. The corollary of this idea is that rural people are employed primarily, if not exclusively, in agriculture. Data on the distribution of the EAP between rural and urban areas by productive sector expose these intuitive conclusions as fallacious and misleading (Table 5.14)[17]. More than one-third of the EAP in rural areas was engaged in nonagricultural activities in 1982, an increase from just over one-fourth in 1974. In fact, 60.6 percent of the EAP in petroleum and mining, 36.2 percent in construction, 33.4 percent in manufacturing, 26.2 percent in utilities, 25.9 percent in transportation, 23.0 percent in services and 18.4 percent in commerce reported that they lived in rural areas in 1982.[18] Only finance can be considered a mainly urban

Table 5.14 Distribution of the Economically Active Population (EAP) by Rural and Urban Areas and by Productive Sector, Unadjusted Censuses 1974 & 1982

Productive Sector	1974			1982		
	Total	Rural	Urban	Total	Rural	Urban
Total	1,816,946	1,083,596	733,350	2,224,366	1,091,623	1,132,743
Agriculture	896,894	835,847	61,047	786,972	724,471	62,501
Non Agriculture	920,052	247,749	672,303	1,437,394	367,152	1,070,242
Petroleum/Mining	6,155	3,758	2,397	7,406	4,485	2,921
Manufacturing	226,266	95,147	131,119	286,530	95,635	190,895
Utilities	8,470	2,468	6,002	13,183	3,450	9,733
Construction	86,192	30,178	56,014	158,009	57,182	100,827
Commerce	189,072	40,036	149,036	271,914	49,921	221,993
Transportation	54,650	13,594	41,056	101,321	26,286	75,035
Finance	19,694	933	18,761	44,116	2,405	41,711
Services	329,553	61,635	267,918	554,915	127,788	427,127
Shares (%) Total[a]	100.0	100.0	100.0	100.0	100.0	100.0
Agriculture	49.4	77.1	8.3	35.4	66.4	5.5
Non Agriculture	50.6	22.9	91.7	64.6	33.6	94.5
Petroleum/Mining	0.3	0.3	0.3	0.3	0.4	0.3
Manufacturing	12.5	8.8	17.9	12.9	8.8	16.9
Utilities	0.5	0.2	0.8	0.6	0.3	0.9
Construction	4.7	2.8	7.6	7.1	5.2	8.9
Commerce	10.4	3.7	20.3	12.2	4.6	19.6
Transportation	3.0	1.3	5.6	4.6	2.4	6.6
Finance	1.1	0.1	2.6	2.0	0.2	3.7
Services	18.1	5.7	36.5	24.9	11.7	37.7

Source: INEC 1977, 1985b.

[a]Not included are new entrants to the labor force, and "others" that could not be classified by sector.

sector, with only 5.5 percent of the EAP living in rural areas. In contrast, over 5 percent of agricultural workers lived in urban areas.

Thus, a significant number of people who lived in rural areas (367,152 or 33.6 percent of the rural EAP) were employed in nonagricultural activities in 1982. Moreover, employment in the nonagricultural sectors in rural areas increased by 119,403 between 1974-1982, primarily from increases in services, construction, transportation and commerce, while employment in rural agriculture declined. Given the relatively large and increasing share of rural people in nonagricultural employment and the weight of their incomes in rural income, it is possible that rural people were better off than conventional wisdom would suggest and that their lot was improving relative to urban people.

Data on the EAP, GDP and population for 1974 and 1982 were utilized to estimate the GDP per capita in rural and urban areas, to test the hypotheses that: (a) the average income of rural people is closer to that of urban people than commonly assumed; and (b) rural people have become relatively better off compared to urban people during the inter-census period 1974-1982. Rural and urban GDP by productive sector were estimated from total GDP per sector in proportion to the EAP in rural and urban areas by productive sector (Table 5.15).

Rural areas had about one-half the GDP per capita of urban people in 1974 and improved their relative position to over 60 percent by 1982 (Table 5.16). These results

Table 5.15   GDP in Rural and Urban Areas by Productive Sector, 1974 and 1982
(Millions of 1975 Sucres)

Productive Sector	1974			1982		
	Total	Rural	Urban	Total	Rural	Urban
Total	102,046	43,783.42	58,262.58	155,265	57,438.78	97,826.22
Agriculture	18,894	17,607.98	1,286.02	23,101	21,266.33	1,834.67
Non Agriculture	83,152	26,175	56,977	132,164	36,172	95,992
Petroleum/Mining	15,597	9,522.91	6,074.09	15,527	9,403.00	6,124.00
Manufacturing	14,936	6,280.73	8,655.27	29,584	9,874.24	19,709.76
Utilities	693	201.93	491.07	1,241	324.77	916.23
Construction	5,585	1,955.45	3,629.55	7,285	2,636.37	4,648.63
Commerce	14,959	3,167.57	11,791.43	25,562	4,692.96	20,869.04
Transportation	5,326	1,324.82	4,001.18	10,687	2,772.56	7,914.44
Finance	10,610	502.65	10,107.35	18,590	1,013.44	17,576.56
Services	13,227	2,473.79	10,753.21	23,630	5,441.61	18,188.39
Other	2,219	745.59	1,473.41	58	13.50	44.50

Source: BCE 1982, 1986; Table 5.14.

Table 5.16   Gross Domestic Product per Capita in Rural and Urban Areas, 1974 & 1982

	Population		Gross Domestic Product (million 1975 sucres)		Gross Domestic Product Per Capita	
	1974	1982	1974	1982	1974	1982
Total	6,521,710	8,060,712	102,046	155,265	15,647.12	19,261.95
Rural	3,822,988	3,968,362	43,783	57,439	11,452.67	14,474.18
Urban	2,698,722	4,092,350	58,263	97,826	21,588.95	23,904.66
Rural/Urban (%)	141.7	97.0	75.1	58.7	53.05	60.55

Source: Population from INEC (1985b, 1977); GDP from Table 5.15.

suggest that intersectoral labor flows have narrowed the productivity gap between rural and urban areas and that labor markets have been relatively efficient in moving labor to new employment opportunities in rural and urban areas. They also indicate that rural people are, on average, relatively better off than commonly thought.

Changing Rural Labor Markets

Significant changes took place in the rural labor markets during the 1970s, in concert with rapid growth of the economy and the increased pace of urbanization. Commander and Peek found two interrelated factors had impacted directly on rural labor. First, the import-substitution model of development led to rapid urban growth and rapidly expanding demand for wage goods, especially food. The land reform of 1964 was implemented as part of the overall development model, in an attempt to increase agricultural productivity and production of food and fiber for the burgeoning population. Second, the petroleum boom of the 1970s provided windfall gains to fuel the import-substitution industrialization process and resulted in average growth of 8.2 percent annually between 1965-1981 and accelerated urban growth.

These factors had two principal effects on agriculture. First, they resulted in greatly increased demand for food and fiber in the growing and newly prosperous urban centers. Agriculture generally became more commercial among all farm sizes, both because of the prod of expropriation and because of rapidly expanding demand. A large share of subsistence farmers shifted to commercial production, with even the smallest farms marketing most of their production (MAG and ORSTOM). Second, demand for unskilled labor increased rapidly in urban centers, especially in the construction and services sectors. This resulted in greatly increased rural to urban migration and rising rural wages.

The commercialization of agriculture and the rapid emigration substantially altered the use of labor in agricultural production. In essence, the rural areas of Ecuador were faced with a growing labor shortage during the petroleum boom of the 1970s and responded by economizing the use of labor. Large farms substituted temporary labor for permanent labor as they moved from traditional *hacienda* agriculture toward commercial farming. This was done to reduce labor costs and reflected the increasing demand for seasonal labor. The rising cost of labor, along with subsidies to capital resulted in labor-saving technical changes and shifts to less labor intensive enterprises, such as pastures and dairying.

Labor use on smaller farms also was substantially modified. Farmers simultaneously faced rapidly growing urban markets for their produce and lucrative off-farm employment opportunities for excess family labor. They responded by shifting from subsistence to commercial farming and by hiring temporary labor, instead of utilizing traditional labor exchanges, so that family members could seek higher-paying off-farm employment. One result has been the increasing involvement of women, the aged and children in small-farm agriculture, as men and younger women worked for other farmers or emigrated to urban areas. Also, the phenomena of circulation of rural people between urban employment and rural homes has increased substantially, in part from heavy subsidies to transportation (Chapter 10).

The net effect of greatly increased demand for food and labor was to create a new class of part-time farmers, as farmers with small holdings commercialized their agriculture and sought off-farm employment to maximize family incomes. Smaller farmers derived the majority of their family income from off-farm sources in the mid-1970s (Vos Table 20). And the smallest farmers earned higher family incomes than farmers with small to medium-sized holdings (Vos Table 9).

The recession of the 1980s probably has substantially worsened the situation for the small-farm sector. Demand for wage goods has not expanded nearly as rapidly as in the 1970s and growth in the urban economy has been nearly stagnant, with much more limited employment growth. While no data are at hand, it is likely that much of the gains of smaller farmers have been eroded. While agriculture has grown rapidly since 1984, it had moved to a more capital intensive structure and likely had a low employment elasticity during the last decade.

Conclusions

Ecuador's population is growing rapidly and will increase by 3.2 million during the

1990s to reach nearly 14.0 million in the year 2000. The urban population has exploded due to high levels of rural to urban migration with concentration in Quito and Guayaquil. Rapid growth of the urban population imposed a major burden on local governments to provide necessary services (health care, education, sewer and potable water, electricity, and transportation). These demographic patterns have been heavily affected by macroeconomic and sectoral development policies which subsidized industry and urban development at the expense of agriculture and rural areas.

The labor force of Ecuador is growing even faster than the population and will add an average of 135,000 new job-seekers to the labor market each year during the 1990s. The stagnant economy and few new jobs in the face of the burgeoning labor force poses a major challenge to policymakers and portends social and political crisis.

Labor markets functioned quite efficiently between 1974 and 1982, both between sectors and between rural and urban areas. They transferred substantial numbers of workers from lower-paying agricultural employment to higher-paying jobs in other sectors and from rural to urban areas. As a result, agricultural labor productivity converged with most of the other economic sectors, as did rural and urban labor productivity. Employment actually declined absolutely in the agricultural sector between 1974 and 1982. Employment in the industrial sector increased but was highly constrained by the capital intensive nature of the import-substitution industrialization process. Most new jobs were generated in the rest of the economy, especially in the services sector in urban areas. These jobs were usually low-paying and required minimal skills.

These data cast doubt on intuitive arguments that segmentation of the labor market is a major employment problem. They suggest the best way to improve the wellbeing of poor people is to substantially increase investments in human capital through primary and secondary education and special skills so that upward mobility is enhanced. There is indication that labor markets are segmented in the public sector for low-skill workers. At the same time, the labor code probably contributed to capital-intensive investments throughout the economy and may have introduced some degree of market segmentation in the productive economic sectors where labor unions are strong. To the extent market segmentation exists, revision of the labor code to allow for greater competition will result in increased employment and more efficient production.

The principal employment problem is based on unnecessarily low growth rates inherent in Ecuador's internally oriented development model. The stagnant economy has cast a pall over the labor market and employment growth since 1981. The primary problem is to get the economy and employment growing again through implementation of a more outward-oriented macroeconomic policy matrix (see Chapter 2), and greater investments in human capital and a science base for agriculture (see Chapter 12).

The labor market, per se, appears to be making reasonably strong contribution to development by mobilizing labor and moving it to its highest-paying alternatives, given the low skill level of the labor force. The labor market could benefit from investments to facilitate the matching of people with jobs, such as employment services. Also, modification of the ponderous labor code would undoubtedly result in increased employment and more rapid economic growth. These latter reforms are likely to be very difficult, politically, and will not result in significant gains if more rapid and sustained economic growth is not realized.

NOTES

1. This section is based primarily on Whitaker and Alzamora which contains a more detailed analysis of various census data and projections and detailed data tables. Also see CONADE and UNFPA for an excellent, detailed analysis of the demographic and socioeconomic implications of the four censuses of population.

2. CONADE and UNFPA (pp. 1-2) estimate the omissions at 4.3 percent in 1950; 5.9 percent in 1962; 4.3 percent in 1974 and 7.6 percent in 1982.

3. All official data, including the censuses and projections of population, are presented for four major geo-political regions with the same names as the major geographic regions but defined in terms of groupings of provinces rather than by strictly geographic criteria (see Chapter 2 Note 2). The four geo-political regions are defined in Table 5.7. Each of the four geo-political regions corresponds roughly to the four main geographic regions, consistent with common usage in Ecuador.

4. The data for 1950, 1962, 1974 and 1982 for the analyses of changes in various aspects of population in the rest of this section are from the unadjusted census data because adjustments and projections were not made for the population subsets being analyzed. Thus, growth rates for the global population calculated from the unadjusted data are slightly different from those based on the adjusted data but reveal the same general trends.

5. Urban population is defined in the Censuses and in the INEC projections as the population of capital cities of provinces, plus the population of county seats (*cabeceras de cantones*). Each county (*cantón*) is divided into one urban parish (*parroquia*) and several rural parishes. Each provincial capital and county seat is located in an urban parish which may contain a rural area outside the city, but inside the boundary of the urban parish, referred to in the census as the periphery (*periferia*). The rural population is defined as the population of all rural parishes, plus the population of the periphery of urban parishes. These geo-political criteria result in some small county seats of less than 1,000 people being counted as urban, while some fairly large cities of more than 20,000 people are counted as rural because they are in a rural parish. The net effect appears not to bias estimates of rural and urban population although estimates for counties may be distorted (CONADE and UNFPA pp. 217, 223-24).

6. While overall population density has increased, population relative to agricultural land has declined due to increases in the area in pastures, with large decreases in the Costa and Oriente and a slight decrease in the Sierra (Whitaker and Alzamora Appendix Table 8).

7. This estimate assumes rural and urban population both grew at 2.53 percent between 1974 and 1982 (the average rate for Ecuador based on the original census data). If so, the rural population in 1982 would have been 631,567 larger than it was (or alternatively, the urban population would have been 633,593 smaller than it was) with rural to urban migration and reclassification accounting for the difference. The estimate of 632,625 is the average of these two data.

8. The net effects of rural and urban migration calculated from 1982 census data on "last migratory movement" are not as great as those made above. The data on "last migratory movement" indicate a net rural to urban migration of about 227,000 people. However, these data are only for the last migratory movement of those enumerated in the 1982 census and not for all rural to urban migration between 1974 and 1982.

9. See Gutiérrez (1984b) for a more detailed analysis of the labor force participation rates.

10. Data are for the population 15 years of age and older, as corrected data were not available for the census definition of the EAP--people age 12 and older.

11. Fletcher, Marquez and Sarfaty report a calculation from secondary data of a national unemployment rate of 12 percent by the National Development Council (CONADE). They argue convincingly that this rate is too high because of flawed methodology and because rural unemployment tends to be lower than the urban rate. The INEM estimate of 7.2 percent for the three principal cities suggests strongly that the national rate is not any greater.

12. Data are not available to separate employment in government services from household services.

13. See Fletcher, Marquez and Sarfaty for a more detailed analysis of problems in defining and measuring hidden underemployment in Ecuador.

14. The case of segmentation for higher skill workers is not as clear. Salaries appear to be higher in the private sector, but jobs are limited relative to public sector employment. Many public sector professionals have other employment or businesses in order to augment their low salaries.

15. Many analysts assume services, or the even more aggregate tertiary sector to be the sector of employment of last resort and typify it as employing the lowest-skill laborers and comprising the informal sector (see e.g., Fletcher, Marquez and Sarfaty pp. 17-18).

16. GDP per capita in 1982 for government services was S/.44,959 and was only S/.31,572 for household services.

17. Unadjusted census data were utilized since corrected data do not provide the breakdown by rural and urban areas for 1974 and these data are required for the analysis of changes in GDP per capita in rural and urban areas which follows. Consequently, these data are not strictly comparable with those for EAP from the corrected censuses cited above.

18. This does not necessarily mean that the place of employment was located in rural areas, although there is probably a strong correlation. What is significant is that an important share of the EAP who live in rural areas are productively employed in nonagricultural pursuits.

REFERENCES

BCE (Central Bank of Ecuador). 1986, 1982. *Cuentas Nacionales del Ecuador*. Quito: BCE, Nos. 6 and 3.

Berry, A. and R. Sobot. 1981. "Labor Market Performance in Developing Countries." in *Recent Issues in World Development*. Edited by P. Streeten. New York: Pergamon Press, 1981.

Commander, Simon and Peter Peek. 1986. "Oil Exports, Agrarian Change, and the Rural Labor Process: The Ecuadorian Sierra in the 1970s." *World Development* 14:79-96.

CONADE and UNFPA (National Development Council and U.N. Fund for Population Activities). 1987. *Población y Cambios Sociales*. Quito: Editorial Nuestra América.

El Comercio. 1989. "Ganarás el Pan con el Sudor de tu Frente." Quito: August 31, p. B-1.

Fletcher, Lehman B., Gustavo A. Marquez and David E. Sarfaty. 1988. *Formulating a Strategy for Employment Generation in Ecuador: Issues and Priorities*. Washington, D.C.: Development Alternatives, Inc., Report Prepared for USAID.

Gregory, Peter. 1986. *The Myth of Market Failure: Employment and the Labor Market in Mexico*. Baltimore: The Johns Hopkins University Press.

Gutiérrez, Alejandro. 1984a. *Empleo y Crecimiento en Ecuador 1970-82: Tendencias Recientes y Lineamientos de Política*. Santiago, Chile: ISS/PREALC, December.

_____. 1984b. *La Tasa de Participación en Ecuador*. Quito: ISS/PREALC, Working Paper Q/8405.

Hachette, Dominique and David Franklin. 1990. "Employment and Incomes in Ecuador: A Macroeconomic Context." Quito: Sigma One Corporation.

INEC (National Institute of Statistics and Census). 1985a. *Proyecciones de la Población Ecuatoriana (1982-1995)*. Quito: November.

_____. 1985b. *IV Censo de Población, 1982, Resultados Definitivos, Resumen Nacional*. Quito: May.

_____. 1979. *Proyecciones de la Población Económicamente Activa Por Areas, Grupos de Edad, Sexo y Ramas de Actividad*. Quito.

_____. 1977. *III Censo de Población, 1974, Resultados Definitivos, Resumen Nacional*. Quito: April.

_____. 1964. *II Censo de Población, 1962, Resultados Definitivos, Resumen Nacional*. Quito.

INEC, CONADE and CELADE (National Institute of Statistics and Census, National Development Council and Latin American Demographic Center). 1984. *Ecuador: Estimaciones y Proyecciones de Población, 1950-2000*. Quito: CONADE, December.

INEM (National Employment Institute). 1987. *Household Employment Survey*. Quito, November.

ISS and PREALC (Institute of Social Studies of Holland and the U.N. Regional Employment Program for Latin America and the Caribbean). 1984a. "Población Económicamente Activa Corregida 1962-1974." Quito: ISS/PREALC, Working Document Q/8410.

_____. 1984b. "Población Económicamente Activa Corregida 1982." Quito: ISS/PREALC, Working Document Q/8411.

Kahnert, Friedrich. 1987. *Improving Urban Employment and Labor Productivity*. Washington, D.C.: World Bank, Discussion Paper No. 10, May.

Kannappan, Subbiah. 1989. "Urban Labor Markets in Developing Countries." *Finance and Development* June:46-48.

Krueger, Alan and Lawrence H. Summers. 1988. "Efficiency Wages and the Inter-Industry Wage Structure." *Econometrica* 56:259-93.

MAG and ORSTOM (Ministry of Agriculture and France's Office of Overseas Science and Technology Research). 1978. *Diagnóstico Socio-Económico del Medio Rural Ecuatoriano*. Quito: MAG, Documents Nos. 3 and 7.

Ministry of Economy. 1960. *I Censo de Población del Ecuador, 1950*. Quito.

Padilla, Cecilia Moreno de. 1984. *Características y Tendencias del Proceso de Concentración en Ecuador*. Quito: UNFPA/CONADE, Proyecto ECU-80-PO4.

Uthoff, A. 1984. "Changes in Earnings Inequality and Labor Market Segmentation: Metropolitan Santiago, 1969-1978." *Journal of Development Studies* 22:2:300-26.

Vos, Rob. 1981. *Ecuador: Rural Household Savings Capacity and Investments: 1974-1975*. Quito: Netherlands Institute of Social Studies and PREALC, December.

Whitaker, Morris D. and Jaime Alzamora. 1988. "Characteristics and Indicators of Ecuador's Population." Quito: USAID, August 29, Assessment of Ecuador's Agricultural Sector, Working Paper No. 4-88.

6

PRODUCTION AGRICULTURE:

NATURE AND CHARACTERISTICS

Morris D. Whitaker and Jaime Alzamora

Agricultural production in Ecuador is highly varied both with respect to the technologies utilized and the crops and livestock produced. The country has a large number of distinct agro-ecological zones and numerous microclimatic areas and is capable of producing a wide range of tropical, subtropical and temperate-zone agricultural products (see Chapter 4). There are a variety of enterprise combinations and technologies utilized in the production of each of the major crops and livestock. Techniques of production range from centuries-old farming systems based on animal power and internal generation of inputs to modern agriculture utilizing mainly industrial inputs such as machinery and fertilizers in combination with high-yielding varieties to exploitative slash and burn agriculture in new-lands areas.

Sierra crops and livestock, comprised of tubers, legumes, soft corn, small grains, vegetables, fruits and dairy cattle have traditionally been utilized almost exclusively for internal consumption. These products are produced in a temperate climate largely on smaller farms ranging up to 10 hectares which account for most of the farmland, with larger farms usually involved in dairy production. Crops and livestock produced in the Costa provide an important component of the diet especially rice, sugar, plantains, vegetable oils and beef, while hard corn and soybean meal are utilized by the broiler industry. The Costa also produces major export crops of bananas, coffee, cacao and pond-raised shrimp, which collectively accounted for over half of all foreign exchange earnings in recent years (see Chapter 3). In contrast to the Sierra, Costa crops are produced in a tropical or subtropical climate on relatively large farms of 50 to 100 hectares or more, especially the cereals. The Oriente also produces coffee, oilpalm, livestock and other subtropical and tropical crops. Except for oilpalm, the Oriente crops and livestock are relatively unimportant in total agricultural production, although coffee and livestock are becoming more important. The term "Costa crops," as it is used throughout the rest of this chapter, refers to crops produced in the Costa and in the Oriente.

The analysis of production agriculture is constrained by two data deficiencies. First, 1986-1988 data for cropland and yields are not comparable with the pre-1986 data series because of a change in the methodology for collecting crop production data. Second, there is not a series of reliable data for livestock numbers and census data for 1954 and 1974 are not strictly comparable to the data that do exist.

1954 and 1974 are not strictly comparable to the data that do exist.

This chapter describes and analyzes the production milieu in Ecuadorian agriculture and its evolution since 1965. The following sections review and analyze: the current structure of production agriculture based on the farmgate value of production; trends in the production of the principal crops; the relative importance of technical changes and changes in harvested area in explaining changes in crop production; the growing importance of livestock, poultry and shrimp production; production of illegal substances; the use of modern factors of production; and the causes of major changes in agricultural production and associated factor use during the last two decades. The implications of the findings are discussed in the last section.

Structure of Production Agriculture

The structure of production agriculture, as measured by the current farmgate value of various products, changed substantially between 1971 and 1988 (Table 6.1).[1] Farmgate value for each crop and livestock product was determined from the price received by the farmer and level of production. Current prices were used instead of constant prices to account for the importance of changing relative prices as well as changes in production in determining changes in the relative importance of each product in the agricultural economy.

Milk was the most important product in 1988, maintaining its number one position since 1971. Shrimp was in second place, jumping from 15th place in 1971. Moreover, almost all the 1971 production was wild shrimp, while most of 1988 shrimp production was pond-raised. Rice occupied 3rd place in 1988, increasing rapidly in relative importance from 11th place in 1971. The three export crops, bananas, cacao and coffee maintained their importance in the top ten crops, although their ranking shifted as world prices varied and other domestic crops increased in value. Beef was the 6th most important product in 1988, falling from 3rd place in 1971. Chicken and oilpalm both became much more important, with chicken moving up quickly from 16th to 8th place and oilpalm coming from relative obscurity in 36th place in 1971 to 9th place in 1988. Potatoes rounded out the top ten products in 1988, but slipped substantially from 5th place in 1971.

Other major changes in rank include eggs, soybeans, watermelons, tomatoes and manila hemp which all jumped substantially. In contrast, pork, soft corn, sugarcane, domestic bananas, cassava, wheat, barley, oranges, peas and castor oil declined rapidly in relative importance between 1971 and 1988.

These data expose some important myths about the relative importance of various crops and livestock products. Few would pick milk, a predominately Sierra product, to be more valuable at the farmgate than Costa export crops such as shrimp. Wheat and barley, which receive prominent attention in the popular press were relatively unimportant in 1971 and are even less so in 1988. Eggs, plantains, watermelons, tomatoes, domestic bananas, dry beans, cassava and onions--usually considered of minor importance--all have greater farmgate value than wheat and barley, some by several times.

There was a substantial decline in the farmgate value of Sierra crops relative to those of the Costa between 1971 and 1988 (Table 6.2).[2] Sierra crops accounted for 31.5 percent of the total farmgate value of production in 1971; this had declined to only 17.2 percent in 1988. The rapid decrease in the relative importance of Sierra crops resulted from major crop diversification programs and subsidies focused mainly on

Table 6.1 Farmgate Value and Rank for Principal Crops and Livestock, 1988, 1982,
1978 and 1971 (Million of Current Sucres)

	1988		1982		1978		1971	
Product	Value	Rank	Value	Rank	Value	Rank	Value	Rank
Milk [a]	70,703.96	1	8,002.90	1	4,067.57	1	1,112.64	1
Shrimp [a]	58,019.06	2	2,670.30	10	295.60	21	253.15	15
Paddy Rice	50,866.90	3	2,690.45	9	1,171.04	9	396.94	11
Bananas(Exp)	50,593.87	4	3,602.55	5	2,305.89	4	1,106.01	2
Cacao	33,496.74	5	3,971.07	4	4,006.93	2	570.63	8
Beef	32,443.98	6	4,386.08	3	1,300.88	8	989.07	3
Coffee	28,088.19	7	2,826.80	7	2,571.98	3	621.74	7
Chicken	27,283.78	8	5,446.04	2	1,589.90	5	243.25	16
Oilpalm	21,842.46	9	1,206.15	15	356.87	18	24.56	36
Potatoes	19,396.34	10	2,769.19	8	1,427.55	6	722.49	5
Hard Corn	18,151.35	11	1,739.55	11	616.89	14	278.72	13
Eggs	17,833.49	12	2,833.97	6	1,301.25	7	242.05	17
Plantains	11,767.91	13	1,341.27	14	820.41	11	257.06	14
Soybeans	9,970.02	14	385.41	25	248.92	24	4.26	44
Pork	9,132.79	15	1,445.59	13	530.80	15	655.27	6
Soft Corn	8,583.14	16	589.56	22	257.66	23	567.50	9
Watermelon	7,184.35	17	145.33	37	114.05	34	21.08	40
Sugarcane	6,699.63	18	962.27	16	737.80	13	449.29	10
Tomatoes	6,630.46	19	397.59	24	174.55	26	71.92	30
Bananas(Dom)	6,101.86	20	878.37	17	765.50	12	739.79	4
Beans	6,034.01	21	766.85	19	274.94	22	154.86	22
Manila Hemp	5,788.60	22	172.10	34	152.22	30	22.68	39
Cotton	4,287.29	23	333.01	27	301.61	20	42.44	31
Cassava	3,406.05	24	706.29	20	386.35	17	289.54	12
Onions	3,268.42	25	612.13	21	146.64	32	159.24	20
Barley	2,967.89	26	231.00	30	112.28	35	155.97	21
Wheat	2,038.66	27	282.42	28	131.51	33	172.93	18
Oranges	1,805.09	28	1,466.44	12	931.80	10	122.52	23
Peanuts	1,488.52	29	149.82	36	176.68	25	79.95	26
Apples	1,410.49	30	431.14	23	305.20	19	40.57	32
Naranjillas	1,166.52	31	230.32	31	157.51	29	78.01	27
Pineapples	1,030.27	32	841.01	18	434.96	16	87.09	24
Tangerines	853.38	33	265.24	29	149.71	31	24.04	37
Avocados	806.06	34	357.73	26	163.54	27	36.11	34
Peaches	638.88	35	55.91	41	26.31	42	9.75	41
Lemons	637.94	36	162.84	35	51.85	38	22.74	38
Peas	561.63	37	180.77	32	59.67	37	86.76	25
Garlic	537.42	38	104.93	38	32.05	40	40.23	33
Broad Beans	533.13	39	82.32	40	27.13	41	34.41	35
Sheep	486.10	40	172.92	33	63.96	36	160.41	19
Lentils	230.35	41	23.38	43	7.63	43	9.08	42
Cabbage	211.24	42	87.71	39	160.67	28	75.35	29
Sweet Potatoes	113.05	43	24.50	42	6.28	44	8.35	43
Castor Oil	59.49	44	22.23	44	44.35	39	76.52	28

Source: Whitaker, Colyer and Alzamora: Appendix Table 6.1, prices; and Appendix
Table 6.2, crop production. Tables 6.12 and 6.14 for livestock, poultry and shrimp
production.

[a] Whole Shrimp production for 1988 and 1982 was converted to shrimp tails using the
factor 1.73, since only prices of shrimp tails were available after 1979.

Table 6.2 Comparison of Farmgate Value of Sierra and Costa Crops, 1988, 1982,
1978 and 1971 (Million of Current Sucres)

	1988		1982		1978		1971	
	Value	Share	Value	Share	Value	Share	Value	Share
Total	319,248	100.0	31,096	100.0	19,784	100.0	7,661	100.0
Sierra[a]	55,015	17.2	7,203	23.2	3,439	17.4	2,415	31.5
Costa	264,233	82.8	23,893	76.8	16,345	82.6	5,246	68.5

Source: Table 6.1.

[a]Sierra crops include: Potatoes, Soft corn, Tomatoes, Beans, Onions, Barley, Wheat,
Apples, Naranjilla, Avocados, Peaches, Peas, Garlic, Broad beans, Lentils, Cabbage
from Table 6.1. The balance of 21 crops from Table 6.1 are classified as Costa.

Costa crops which grew at rapid rates while Sierra crop production declined in most
cases.

Trends in Crop Production

Analyses of trends in crop production, yields and area are complicated by a change
in statistical methodology after 1985. Gathering and publication of official production
statistics were the responsibility of the Ministry of Agriculture (MAG) through 1985
(MAG 1965-1985). MAG agents, located in the various counties (*cantones*) made
estimates of area, yields and production based on surveys and interviews. These
estimates then were aggregated and published. The National Institute of Statistics and
Census (INEC) established the National System of Agricultural Statistics (SEAN) and
changed the methodology to area sample frames of yields and area for 1986 and later
(INEC/SEAN). Thus data for 1986-1988 are not strictly comparable with earlier
years.[3] The analyses of crop production trends utilize data through 1985 in order not
to confound the results with a different data series for the three most recent years.[4]

There is a markedly different pattern of changes in production of Costa as
compared to Sierra crops between the annual averages of 1965-1969 and 1980-1985
(Table 6.3).[5] Production increased rapidly for almost all the Costa crops, while it fell
at relatively high rates for all the Sierra crops except for a few minor fruits and
vegetables.[6]

Growth in production of Costa crops between 1965 and 1985 was led by soybeans
and oilpalm at very high annual average rates of 39.9 and 28.6 percent, respectively.[7]
Hard corn, plantains and rice production increased at relatively high rates of 4.9, 4.4
and 3.3 percent, well ahead of the rate of population growth. Production of cacao and
coffee increased at 2.5 and 2.0 percent, respectively, while cotton production increased
by 1.3 percent. Production of manila hemp, tangerines, watermelons, oranges, and
pineapples also increased at rapid rates. Banana production fell by 2.4 percent
annually as excess capacity was reduced, while large decreases in castor bean
production of 13.0 percent per year resulted from development of synthetic substitutes

Table 6.3 Crop Production, Annual Averages, 1965-1969 and 1980-1985; and Growth Rates, 1965-1985

	Production (metric tons)			Annual Growth Rates[b] (%)
Crop	1965-69	1980-85[a]	Change	
Costa Crops				
1. Soybeans	218	42,908	42,690	39.9
2. Oilpalm	6,998	336,890	329,892	28.6
3. Manila Hemp	242	11,154	10,912	25.0
4. Tangerines	11,310	32,922	21,612	8.3
5. Watermelon	10,170	28,370	18,200	7.5
6. Oranges	162,372	412,378	250,006	6.2
7. Hard Corn	114,098	250,064	135,966	4.9
8. Plantains	417,708	791,078	373,370	4.4
9. Pineapples	56,986	109,414	52,428	4.0
10. Paddy Rice	227,702	406,772	179,070	3.3
11. Cacao	51,164	89,612	38,448	2.5
12. Coffee	261,440	383,508	122,068	2.0
13. Cotton	16,544	26,722	10,178	1.3
14. Peanuts	8,672	9,080	408	-0.7
15. Lemons	21,364	17,748	-3,616	-0.7
16. Sugarcane	7,921,094	5,993,118	-1,927,976	-1.3
17. Cassava	263,362	223,612	-39,750	-2.2
18. Bananas	2,619,204	1,984,980	-634,224	-2.4
19. Sweet Potatoes	8,418	5,346	-3,072	-3.0
20. Castor Beans	21,826	3,222	-18,604	-13.0
Sierra Crops				
1. Apples	3,056	31,752	28,696	17.4
2. Tomatoes	23,618	49,186	25,568	4.6
3. Avocados	25,778	30,336	4,558	1.8
4. Peaches	2,710	3,108	398	0.9
5. Potatoes	420,808	388,796	-32,012	-1.3
6. Beans	35,870	27,098	-8,772	-2.3
7. Garlic	3,664	2,440	-1,224	-3.9
8. Soft Corn	74,380	48,162	-26,218	-3.9
9. Onions	97,996	44,020	-53,976	-5.3
10. Wheat	76,504	30,940	-45,564	-6.2
11. Cabbage	77,856	26,098	-51,758	-6.8
12. Peas	17,480	6,388	-11,092	-7.2
13. Lentils	1,096	404	-692	-7.3
14. Naranjillas	47,462	12,446	-35,016	-7.3
15. Barley	81,074	27,708	-53,366	-7.5
16. Broad Beans	18,892	4,550	-14,342	-9.1

Source: Whitaker, Colyer and Alzamora Appendix Table 6.2.

[a] Data for 1983 are excluded from the average because of extremely bad weather which caused abnormally low production.
[b] See Note 6.

in the international market. Modest decreases in sugarcane production reflect the cost-price squeeze suffered by this industry and the relative profitability of other Costa crops. Cassava production, principally a subsistence crop, also fell, as did several minor crops.

Production of all the major Sierra crops fell at fairly rapid rates, with wheat, barley

Table 6.4   Harvested Cropland and Pastures, Annual Averages for 1965-1969 and
            1980-1985 and Growth Rates for 1965-1985

Class of Land	Area (hectares)			Annual Growth Rates[b] (%)
	1965-69	1980-85[a]	Change	
Cropland	1,788,138	1,600,854	-187,284	-0.8
Principal Crops	1,737,712	1,545,588	-192,124	-0.9
Other Crops	50,426	55,266	4,840	0.4
Pastures (Total)	1,718,946	4,292,830	2,573,884	6.2
Total Agricultural Land	3,507,084	5,893,684	2,386,600	3.6

Source: Whitaker, Colyer and Alzamora Appendix Table 6.3.

[a]Data for 1983 are excluded from the average because of extremely bad weather which
caused abnormally low production.
[b]See Note 6.

and most legumes falling at rates ranging from 6.2 to 9.1 percent per year, on average, between 1965 and 1985. Production of potatoes and dry beans both fell, but at substantially lower rates. Only a few minor fruits and tomatoes experienced increases in production. The Sierra did experience rapid growth in livestock production, especially in dairy cattle, as cropland was shifted into improved pastures (see the section in this chapter on livestock production and trends).

Sources of Growth in Crop Production

Ecuador has been blessed with abundant land resources and it is commonly accepted that most increases in agricultural production during the last few decades have been due to expansion of the land base. As a corollary, it also is widely believed that expansion of the agricultural frontier can serve as the primary means of meeting Ecuador's food and fiber needs well into the 21st Century. In fact, only limited potential exists for expanding land area under cultivation as all of the good, arable land now is in use (see Chapter 4). Production is expanding onto more marginal lands in terms of location and quality and increasingly higher social and private costs must be incurred to bring them into production. Expansion of agriculture onto the fragile soils of the Oriente and Northwestern Ecuador is a case in point.

Land under Cultivation

Total land in agricultural production, including harvested cropland and pastures, nearly doubled in the last two decades. Such lands grew from an annual average of 3.5 million hectares during 1965-1969 to 5.9 million hectares during 1980-1985, an average annual rate of 3.6 percent (Table 6.4). Harvested cropland decreased by 187,284 hectares for the same period to 1.6 million hectares, while land in principal crops fell by 192,124 hectares. Thus, all the increase in land in agricultural production was due to increases in pastureland, which grew at an annual average rate of 6.2 percent.

The aggregate decrease in harvested cropland masks important shifts in land

Table 6.5   Harvested Area of Principal Crops Classified by Region and Direction of Change, Annual Averages, 1965-1969 and 1980-1985 (Hectares)

Area/Crop	1965-69	1980-85[a]	Change
A. Total	1,737,712	1,545,588	-192,124
B. Costa Decrease	394,774	215,650	-179,124
1. Bananas	197,000	65,062	-131,938
2. Castor Beans	21,582	3,576	-18,006
3. Sugarcane	108,856	96,084	-12,772
4. Cotton	23,524	17,470	-6,054
5. Cassava	28,942	23,458	-5,484
6. Peanuts	12,142	9,068	-3,074
7. Sweet Potatoes	2,728	932	-1,796
C. Costa Increase	771,332	1,095,524	324,192
1. Coffee	199,538	340,546	141,008
2. Rice	106,096	135,718	29,622
3. Plantains	37,720	67,176	29,456
4. Oilpalm	1,642	28,380	26,738
5. Soybeans[b]	252	26,076	25,824
6. Fruits	15,288	36,414	21,126
7. Hard Corn	153,800	172,786	18,986
8. Cacao	256,672	273,742	17,070
9. Manila Hemp	324	14,686	14,362
D. Net Costa	1,166,106	1,311,174	145,068
E. Sierra Decrease	566,234	225,166	-341,068
1. Barley	140,996	29,658	-111,338
2. Soft Corn	143,406	57,156	-86,250
3. Legumes	143,316	65,810	-77,506
4. Wheat	78,618	28,992	-49,626
5. Potatoes	45,522	33,430	-12,092
6. Vegetables[c]	10,458	6,930	-3,528
7. Fruits[d]	3,918	3,190	-728
F. Sierra Increase	5,372	9,248	3,876
1. Fruits[e]	3,490	6,124	2,634
2. Tomatoes	1,882	3,124	1,242
G. Net Sierra	571,606	234,414	-337,192

Source: Whitaker, Colyer and Alzamora Appendix Table 6.3.

[a] Data for 1983 are excluded from averages because of extremely bad weather which caused abnormally low production.
[b] Includes citrus, pineapple and watermelon.
[c] Includes garlic, onions and cabbage.
[d] Includes peaches and naranjillas.
[e] Includes avocados and apples.

devoted to individual crops (Table 6.5).[8]   Costa crops, defined to include those produced in the Costa and Oriente, experienced a net increase of 145,068 hectares between the annual average of 1965-1969 and 1980-1985. There was a decline of 179,124 hectares in seven Costa crops, led by a fall in bananas of 131,938 hectares and a major reduction of area in castor beans. Concomitantly, there was an increase of 324,192 hectares in nine other Costa crops, with coffee accounting for 43 percent of the increase and rice, plantains, oilpalm and soybeans accounting for another 34 percent.

Table 6.6   Pasture Lands in Ecuador by Region, Annual Averages, 1965-1969 and
            1980-1985 (Hectares)

Region/Year	1965-69	1980-85[a]	Change
Ecuador (Total)	1,718,946	4,292,830	2,573,884
Sierra Provinces	955,456	1,838,194	882,738
Costa Provinces	516,500	2,033,630	1,517,130
Oriente Provinces	247,000	421,006	174,006

Source: Whitaker, Colyer and Alzamora Appendix Table 6.3.

[a]Data for 1983 are excluded from averages because of extremely bad weather which
caused abnormally low production.

Most of the increased area in coffee, cacao and rice was new lands, while increases
in area in soybeans, hard corn, plantains, oilpalm and manila hemp were primarily on
land previously in bananas and cotton. The balance of the land taken out of bananas,
cotton and sugarcane was converted to improved pastures, roughly estimated at about
30,000 hectares.

The harvested area in Sierra crops decreased on net by 337,192 hectares between
1965-1969 and 1980-1985, a decrease of 59 percent in two decades. Seven major crops
or crop groups experienced decreases in land area totaling 341,068 hectares. Over one-
third of the total was due to decreases in barley, one-fourth each was due to decreases
in soft corn and legumes, and most of the balance was due to decreases in wheat and
potatoes. A small amount (3,876 hectares) of the lands taken out of the seven crop
groups was shifted to the production of tomatoes and fruits. The balance of 337,192
hectares was converted to improved pastures primarily for dairy production, was
abandoned or used for seasonal grazing.

Area in pastures more than doubled during the last two decades, increasing from
an annual average of 1.7 million hectares in 1965-1969 to 4.3 million hectares in 1980-
1985 (Table 6.6). Data for pastures are less reliable than those for crops and the
indicated changes should be interpreted more as general trends and magnitudes than
as precise measures. Pastures in Sierra Provinces increased by about 900,000 hectares,
with almost 40 percent of this from land taken from Sierra crop production.[9] The
balance is new pastureland in the Western foothills and lowland areas of the Sierra
Provinces.[10]

Pastureland in the Costa Provinces increase by 1.5 million hectares, with an
estimated 30,000 of this from lands taken out of crop production and the balance from
new lands brought into use as pastures. The Sierra Provinces had more than half of
Ecuador's pastures during 1965-1969 and almost twice as much land in pastures as the
Costa. By 1980-1985, however, Costa pastures had nearly quadrupled and the Costa
surpassed the Sierra as the leading pasture region. Oriente pastures increased by
about 175,000 hectares and nearly doubled, with all of the increases on virgin lands.

Crop Yields

Decreases in cropland have had a downward effect on agricultural production but
this has been offset to some extent by increases in yields (Table 6.7). There is a clear
secular trend of increasing yields for all the major Costa crops, except coffee and

Table 6.7   Crop Yields: Annual Averages, 1965-1969 and 1980-1985; and Growth Rates, 1965-1985

| Area/Crop | Yields (kilograms/hectare) | | | Annual Growth Rates[b] (%) |
	1965-69	1980-85[a]	Change	
Costa Crops:				
1. Oilpalm	4,012	11,750	7,738	7.5
2. Watermelon	6,504	13,664	7,160	6.7
3. Bananas	13,359	30,445	17,087	5.3
4. Sweet Potatoes	3,135	5,745	2,610	4.2
5. Soybeans	870	1,632	763	3.8
6. Hard Corn	774	1,453	679	3.5
7. Cotton	719	1,434	714	2.8
8. Cacao	200	325	125	1.8
9. Paddy Rice	2,179	3,005	826	1.7
10. Peanuts	736	968	232	1.3
11. Plantains	11,116	11,773	657	0.1
12. Cassava	9,049	9,545	496	-0.1
13. Sugarcane	72,670	62,502	-10,168	-0.4
14. Castor Beans	987	911	-75	-0.6
15. Lemons	12,758	10,818	-1,940	-0.7
16. Tangerines	12,311	10,036	-2,275	-0.8
17. Oranges	20,274	17,506	-2,768	-0.9
18. Pineapples	19,179	16,882	-2,296	-1.0
19. Coffee	1,325	1,146	-179	-1.5
20. Manila Hemp	746	742	-4	-1.5
Sierra Crops:				
1. Apples	3,879	10,373	6,494	7.9
2. Soft Corn	497	840	344	3.0
3. Barley	576	932	356	2.7
4. Lentils	382	579	197	2.7
5. Peaches	4,236	6,120	1,884	2.6
6. Garlic	3,619	5,106	1,486	2.0
7. Beans	471	575	104	1.2
8. Potatoes	9,260	11,619	2,359	1.2
9. Avocados	9,517	9,959	441	0.9
10. Tomatoes	14,043	15,661	1,618	0.7
11. Broad Beans	584	688	104	0.6
12. Wheat	974	1,059	85	0.5
13. Peas	564	586	22	-0.2
14. Onions	14,008	8,840	-5,168	-2.7
15. Cabbage	35,483	17,914	-17,569	-4.1
16. Naranjillas	14,389	4,571	-9,817	-6.0

Source: Whitaker, Colyer and Alzamora Appendix Table 6.4.

[a]Data for 1983 are excluded from averages because of extremely bad weather which caused abnormally low production.
[b]See Note 5.

sugarcane. Oilpalm, bananas, soybeans and hard corn had annual average increases in yields between 1965 and 1985 of 7.5, 5.3, 3.8, 3.5 percent, respectively, which are very high rates by any standard for a two decade period. Cotton, cacao and rice also had respectable rates of growth in yields, ranging from 2.8 to 1.7 percent per year. Yields of plantains and cassava were stagnant, while yields of sugarcane and castor beans fell modestly. Coffee and hemp were the only Costa crops to experience significant declines in yields. Yields of watermelons increased rapidly, while citrus and pineapple yields fell modestly.

All of the major Sierra crops also experienced increases in yields but the magnitude was less than for Costa crops. Soft corn, barley and lentils had the greatest rates of increase in yields at 3.0, 2.7 and 2.7 percent, respectively. Yields grew for both potatoes and dry beans at the rate of 1.2 percent per year, while yields of wheat and broad beans increased at about .5 percent per year. Only four Sierra crops (peas, onions, cabbage and naranjillas) experienced decreases in yields.

Crop yields are relatively low in comparison to those in neighboring countries and to experiment station yields in Ecuador (see Chapter 12 Table 12.1). The modest successes to date and Ecuador's still relatively low yields and labor productivity, suggest significant opportunities to modernize technologies and thereby increase land and labor productivity, farmers' incomes and agricultural production.

Explaining Changes in Production

Changes in crop production can be conceptualized as resulting from: (a) changes in land area under cultivation; and (b) changes in technology which encompass increased use of modern factors of production, improvements to the land such as irrigation and leveling and use of better quality land.   The following analysis demonstrates that technical changes explained an important part of changes in production for many of Ecuador's crops over the last two decades and were more important than changes in land area for several principal crops.

The sources of change in production of various crops can be measured with a more formal accounting model.[11] This model utilizes data for yields and harvested area for each crop to explain how changes in factor use have contributed to changes in production. It disaggregates the separate effects of changes in technology and in land area on changes in production.

The model permits the calculation of the relative importance of changes in: land area; yields; and the interaction between changes in land area and yields. A more detailed, and formal algebraic specification of the model is presented in Whitaker, Colyer and Alzamora Chapter 6, Appendix I. The three elements of the model can be easily explained in graphic form (Figure 6.1). The rectangle $0A_oX_oY_o$ is production in the initial period (P_o), and $0A_tX_tY_t$ is production in the end period (P_t). The rectangle $A_oA_tZX_o$ is the increase in production from an increase in land area with yields held constant at Y_o. The rectangle $Y_oX_oBY_t$ is the increase in production due to an increase in yields, with land area held constant at A_o. The rectangle X_oZX_tB is the increase in production due to the interaction of increases in area and yields. Note that the graph illustrates increases in yields and area; any combination of increases and decreases in yields and area can be graphed in a similar manner.

Average production, harvested area and yields for 1965-1969 and 1980-1985 were utilized to measure the relative importance of changes in each of the three components of the accounting model in explaining changes in production.

Results of the Analysis

The results provide strong evidence that technical changes in agriculture have been relatively important for almost all crops. Technical improvements usually either contributed substantially to increases in production or cushioned decreases in production from reductions in land area (Table 6.8). Results for three crops, which

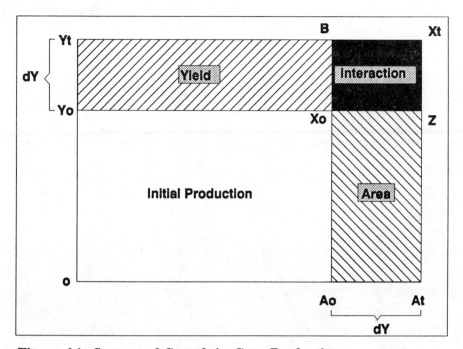

Figure 6.1 Sources of Growth in Crop Production

illustrate three different combinations of changes in yields and area, are explained in detail to facilitate interpretation. Included are: paddy rice, which experienced increases in area and yields; soft corn, with decreases in area and increases in yields; and coffee with increases in area and decreases in yields.

Paddy rice production increased by 176,662 metric tons between the average of 1965-1969 and 1980-1985.[12] Increases in land explained 64,558 metric tons of the total increase in production, with yields held constant in 1965-1969. Increases in yields (technical advances) explained 87,637 metric tons, with land held constant. The interaction of increases in yields and increases in land area explained another 24,468 metric tons.

Production of soft corn decreased by 23,180 metric tons. It would have fallen by 42,823 metric tons from decreased land area with yields held constant but increases in yields helped to cushion the effects of reductions in area. Production would have increased by 49,285 metric tons from increases in yields, with land area held constant in 1965-1969. But land area fell and the interaction of this decrease with increases in yields reduced the potential increase in production from increased yields by 29,642 metric tons. This is the foregone production that would have been realized at the higher yields if land area had not been reduced.

Coffee production increased by 125,884 metric tons due completely to increases in land area as yields declined. Production would have increased by 186,831 metric tons from increases in land area with yields held constant at 1965-1969 levels. Decreases in yields resulted in a decrease in production of 35,711 metric tons with land area held constant. But land area increased so that the interaction of decreases in yields and

Table 6.8   Source of Changes in Crop Production Between the Annual Average of
1965-1969 and 1980-1985[a] (Metric Tons)

Area/Crops	Change in Production	Source of Change		
		Land Area	Yield	Interaction
Costa Crops:				
1. Hard Corn	132,033	14,696	104,444	12,893
2. Paddy Rice	176,662	64,558	87,637	24,468
3. Cacao	37,659	3,414	32,109	2,135
4. Plantains	371,550	327,432	24,773	19,345
5. Oilpalm	326,876	107,272	12,706	206,898
6. Watermelon	17,937	3,031	11,570	3,336
7. Soybeans	42,345	22,462	192	19,691
8. Manila Hemp	10,653	10,718	-1	-64
9. Tangerines	21,583	29,054	-2,102	-5,369
10. Pineapples	50,531	65,246	-6,903	-7,812
11. Oranges	238,524	302,128	-22,347	-41,256
12. Coffee	125,884	186,831	-35,711	-25,236
13. Cotton	8,123	-4,355	16,803	-4,324
14. Bananas	-650,843	-1,762,526	3,366,041	-2,254,359
15. Cassava	-37,994	-49,626	14,351	-2,719
16. Sweet Potatoes	-3,198	-5,630	7,119	-4,687
17. Peanuts	-159	-2,262	2,817	-713
18. Castor Beans	-18,040	-17,770	-1,628	1,358
19. Lemons	-3,283	-51	-3,240	8
20. Sugarcane	-1,905,123	-928,141	-1,106,848	129,866
Sierra Crops:				
1. Tomatoes	22,496	17,441	3,045	2,010
2. Apples	28,759	8,874	5,026	14,858
3. Avocados	4,644	3,293	1,199	153
4. Peaches	407	-551	1,202	-245
5. Potatoes	-33,101	-111,971	107,399	-28,528
6. Barley	-53,524	-64,087	50,220	-39,657
7. Soft Corn	-23,180	-42,823	49,285	-29,642
8. Beans	-9,254	-14,163	8,024	-3,115
9. Wheat	-45,839	-48,316	6,718	-4,241
10. Broad Beans	-14,169	-14,858	3,338	-2,649
11. Garlic	-1,717	-2,425	1,704	-996
12. Peas	-10,884	-11,130	680	-434
13. Lentils	-734	-869	585	-450
14. Naranjillas	-34,934	-8,604	-32,200	5,871
15. Onions	-55,646	-29,837	-36,817	11,008
16. Cabbage	-51,482	-25,832	-38,440	12,790

Source: Whitaker, Colyer and Alzamora Appendix Table 6.5; and accounting model in
Appendix I.

[a]Data for 1983 are excluded from averages because of extremely bad weather which
caused abnormally low production.

increases in land area reduced the potential increase in production from increases in
land area by another 25,236 metric tons. This is the foregone production from the
increased land area that could have been realized if yields had not declined.

Increases in yields explained the majority of increases in production of the
important Costa crops of rice, hard corn and cacao and all the increase in production
of cotton. Yields also were of major importance in cushioning and limiting decreases
in the production of bananas as area declined substantially. Yield increases also

limited the impact of reduced area on production of cassava, sweet potatoes and peanuts. Increases in land area were more important than increases in yields in explaining increases in production of plantains but yield increases still explained part of the increase. Increases in the production of coffee are explained by relatively large increases in land area, as yields declined. Coffee production would have increased much more rapidly if yields could have been sustained. Decreases in yields also contributed to decreased production of castor beans and sugarcane.

Technical improvements also have been important in explaining changes in production in the Sierra. All the principal Sierra crops experienced decreases in production between the annual average of 1965-1969 and 1980-1985 and most decreases were relatively large. The decreases in production of potatoes, barley, soft corn, beans and lentils would have been significantly greater if not tempered by relatively large increases in yields. Yields of wheat, broad beans and peas increased slightly and modified somewhat the effects of decreases in land area.

The effects of technical change on production also are captured in the interaction term, which generally reflects a significant role for technical change. For example, oilpalm and soybean production increased from large increases in area and yields (see Tables 6.5, 6.7) with an important share of the effect of such changes on production measured by the interaction term. Examination of the effects of yields alone (in Table 6.8) would lead to the conclusion that increases in yields were not very important in explaining increases in either oilpalm or soybean production when, in fact, their output would be much lower in the absence of technical change. The interaction term also is relatively large for crops (mainly Sierra) that experienced decreases in land area and increases in yields. In these cases, the negative interaction term is measuring foregone production that could have been realized at the higher yields, if land area had not declined. In both cases, the magnitude of the interaction term generally reflects the effects of important levels of technical progress.

The general conclusion that technical changes have been relatively important in explaining changes in crop production must be tempered by a possible measurement problem. It may be that increases in yields, especially in the Sierra, measured concentration of traditional Sierra crops on better quality land, as croplands were shifted to pastures, abandoned or left fallow, as well as improvements in technology. Rapid expansion of crop production onto new, more marginal lands in the Costa would tend to lower yields. The negative effect of decreasing coffee yields on production could be measuring decreases in the quality of land, as well as any retrogression in technical practices. Thus, the yield variable measures changes in the quality of land, as well as technical improvements, with no way to distinguish their separate effects.

Livestock, Poultry and Shrimp

The livestock subsector became an increasingly important component of the agricultural economy and now is nearly as important as the combined export crops (bananas, coffee and cacao) and traditional crops subsectors (as defined in the national accounts). These latter two subsectors comprised 65.2 percent of agricultural GDP during 1965-1967 compared to only 29.2 percent for livestock (see Chapter 3). During 1986-1988 the share of the two crops subsectors had fallen to 45.9 percent of GDP, while the share of the livestock sector had increased to 33.5 percent. The increase in the relative importance of the livestock subsector reflects more rapid growth rates in livestock than in crops. The hunting and fishing subsector also grew rapidly from 2.3

to 14.0 percent for the same period mainly because of the rapid increase in the production of pond-raised shrimp. Shrimp are discussed along with livestock and poultry in this section because they are raised in captivity in a maricultural process completely analogous to agricultural production.

Livestock and poultry production increased rapidly during the past three decades. It is more difficult to measure the magnitude of change because of inadequate data. As Sarhan (p. 6) has noted, official data lack consistency. For this reason the data on livestock numbers utilized in this analysis are from the 1954 and 1974 censuses and from INEC/SEAN for 1988 as reported in a recent statistical bulletin by MAG's Livestock Development Project (PROFOGAN). The PROFOGAN bulletin, prepared with technical assistance from the Federal Republic of Germany, is the most recent and consistent set of data on livestock numbers, production and technical information. Data on shrimp production are from unpublished sources from the Ministry of Industry and Commerce (MICIP) and its predecessor, Ministry of Industry, Commerce and Integration (MICEI).

Location and Numbers

Principal livestock in Ecuador include dairy cattle, beef cattle, dual-purpose cattle, chickens, swine and sheep, with shrimp being the only major aquatic species raised in captivity. Minor livestock include goats, rabbits, guinea pigs (*cuyes*), turkeys, ducks and geese, donkeys, horses, mules and llamas. The minor animals generally are kept as barnyard animals for subsistence consumption or as beasts of burden and as a store of wealth for unanticipated expenditures. In contrast, the principal livestock and shrimp are produced mainly for market, usually on larger production units. These two sets are not mutually exclusive with some minor animals, such as turkeys, produced mainly for commercial purposes, while an important share of some of the principal livestock, such as sheep and hogs, are raised for subsistence consumption.

The principal livestock are located throughout the country but with important regional concentrations. Dairy cattle, mainly Holstein and some Brown Swiss, are concentrated in the Northern and Central Sierra, with a small but increasing number in the Baeza area of the Oriente. Beef and dual purpose cattle, usually a mix of criollo and imported Zebu, are produced mainly in the dryer areas of the Costa. Production of beef cattle has become increasingly important in the Oriente during the last two decades but transportation is a major constraint to increased production. Commercial production of chickens is located mainly in Manabí to serve the Guayaquil market and in the area around Santo Domingo de los Colorados in Pichincha province to serve the Quito market. Chickens are kept by almost all rural families throughout Ecuador and by a surprisingly large number of urban families as well. Sheep production is concentrated in Cotopaxi, Chimborazo and Azuay provinces but is spread throughout the Sierra. Limited numbers of tropical breeds of sheep are found in the Costa and Oriente. Commercial swine production is spread throughout the country with Manabí in the Costa being the most important province, followed by the Sierra provinces of Pichincha, Loja, Azuay and Chimborazo. Pigs also are kept by most rural and some urban families for subsistence consumption. Shrimp are raised in maturation ponds in the Costa with wild shrimp fisheries accounting for only a small share of total production. Guayas is by far the most important province in shrimp production, followed by El Oro and Manabí.

Livestock numbers increased at relatively rapid rates between the 1954 and 1974

Table 6.9 Cattle, Swine, Sheep and Goat Populations by Region, 1954, 1974 and 1987

Livestock	1954	1974	1987	Annual Growth Rate[a](%) 1954-74	1974-87
	--------(thousand head)--------				
Cattle	1,215.9	2,494.0	3,884.1	3.5	3.2
Sierra	786.3	1,170.6	1,847.6	1.9	3.3
Costa	429.6	1,136.4	1,669.6	4.7	2.8
Oriente	---	187.0	366.9	---	4.9
Swine	683.1	1,038.3	1,620.1	2.0	3.2
Sierra	429.8	536.2	925.5	1.1	4.0
Costa	253.3	474.9	596.8	3.0	1.7
Oriente	---	27.2	97.8	---	9.6
Sheep	1,350.6	1,033.3	1,293.0	-1.3	1.6
Sierra	1,338.0	1,022.4	1,274.6	-1.3	1.6
Costa	12.6	7.0	15.5	-2.8	5.8
Oriente	---	3.9	2.9	---	-2.1
Goats	136.7	218.2	261.9	2.3	1.3
Sierra	107.3	166.4	188.2	2.1	0.9
Costa	29.4	51.4	73.0	2.7	2.5
Oriente	---	0.4	0.7	---	4.1

Source: PROFOGAN pp. 48-53.

[a]Compound, average annual growth rates between each of the years.

agricultural censuses and especially between the 1974 census and the INEC/SEAN survey data for 1987 (Table 6.9). There were a reported 3.9 million dairy, dual-purpose and beef cattle in 1987. Cattle numbers increased at an annual rate of 3.2 percent between 1974 and 1987, somewhat slower than the 3.5 percent growth rate between 1954 and 1974. The slower growth rate in the latter period reflects much higher rates of slaughter in the late 1970s because of greatly increased demand for meat, prolonged drought and controlled milk prices which favored urban consumers and reduced producer incentives. Subsidized credit for importation of breeding stock, higher prices for milk and meat and technical assistance have since led to increased cattle numbers.

The INEC/SEAN data summarized by PROFOGAN do not distinguish clearly between dairy cattle, dual-purpose cattle and beef cattle and estimates of milk cow numbers appear to be too small. PROFOGAN (p. 65) reported 522,000 milk cows in production in 1987 but this number is inconsistent with reported production of 1,130 million liters of milk (p. 62) and it does not distinguish between dairy and dual-purpose breeds. Given national production of 1,130 million liters, average production per cow of 3.8 liters per day and assuming an average lactation of 310 days would imply nearly 1,000,000 milk cows in lactation during 1987. The total dairy and dual-purpose herd would be about 1.5 million or more head when accounting for dry cows and those nursing calves. Earlier MAG data reported 1,000,000 dairy cattle in 1986, but did not indicate if dual-purpose cattle were included (Sarhan p. 2).

The Sierra is the most important dairy area, producing an estimated 75 percent of milk from 60 percent of the milk cows, which are largely dairy breeds (PROFOGAN pp. 64-65). The balance of the dairy and dual-purpose herd is located in lowland areas, primarily in the Costa, and is comprised mainly of dual-purpose, tropical breeds,

Table 6.10 Chicken Population, Selected Years and Growth Rates, 1970-1988 (1,000)

Year	Layers	Broilers	Roosters	Total
1970	1,615	2,744	1,780	6,139
1980	5,577	21,647	5,400	32,624
1988	5,496	39,853	4,548	49,897
Annual Growth[a] (%)	7.4	15.1	5.8	12.0

Source: PROFOGAN p.55 for 1970-1987; unpublished data from the National Directorate of Livestock, MAG for 1988.

[a]Continuous growth rates for 1970-1988 calculated by fitting an exponential curve: $Y = ae^{bx}$, where a>0 and Y>0.

although some Holstein herds are located near Guayaquil. Most of the dual-purpose breeds are located in the lowlands areas of Pichincha province near Santo Domingo de los Colorados and are probably no more than 20-25 percent of the total of dairy and dual-purpose cattle. An important share of meat in the Sierra is from culled dairy cattle.

The balance of the 3.9 million cattle in 1987 are beef cattle, estimated to be about 2.4 million head not including the dual-purpose cattle. According to the above estimates, there are probably 300,000 to 400,000 dual-purpose cattle, for a total beef and dual purpose herd of about 2.9 million head.

Swine numbers grew at 3.2 percent between 1974 and 1987, a faster rate than during the earlier inter-census period and stood at 1.6 million head in 1987. There were 1.3 million head of sheep in 1987 and the sheep population grew at 1.6 percent during 1974-1987, after declining during 1954-1974. The decrease in numbers during the earlier period reflects the effects of the land reform and the expropriation of the large farms of the National Association of Sheep Growers (ANCO). The return of these lands and the reestablishment of ANCO in 1985 have resulted in a resurgence of interest in commercial sheep production.

Chicken numbers have increased more dramatically than any other class of livestock, growing at an average of 12.0 percent per year between 1970 and 1988 (Table 6.10). There were a total of 49.9 million chickens in 1988 up from only 6.1 million in 1970. This dramatic increase resulted from surging demand during the 1970s fueled by increased income from the oil boom and from rapid growth of the population.

The area in shrimp ponds also has expanded rapidly, with nearly 118,000 hectares in 1987, according to a study by the Center for the Survey of Natural Resources by Remote Sensing (CLIRSEN), up from zero in 1969. Approximately 25 percent of the shrimp ponds were constructed from mangrove swamps and 33 percent from *salinas* (flat, salty areas flooded by tides) with the balance (42 percent) of the area from other higher-altitude agricultural land inward from the seacoast. The expansion of shrimp farms into mangrove swamps has caused increasing environmental damage according to a 1989 study done for the Agricultural Policy Institute--IDEA (Espinoza).

Livestock Products

Production of livestock products has grown at about the same rate as livestock

Table 6.11   Livestock Slaughter and Production of Red Meat, Selected Years and Growth Rates, 1974-1988 (1,000 Head and 1,000 Metric Tons)

Year	Cattle		Swine		Sheep/Goats		Total Meat
	Slaughter	Meat	Slaughter	Meat	Slaughter	Meat	
1971	---	56.0	---	34.0	---	11.0	101.0
1974	346.7	54.5	466.0	18.3	206.1	4.0	76.8
1980	440.4	72.3	484.9	22.9	256.4	4.2	99.4
1988	620.3	102.3	611.6	27.5	129.0	1.7	131.5
Annual Growth[a] (%)	4.0	4.4	0.9	2.7	-1.7	-2.2	3.8

Source: PROFOGAN pp. 71-72 for 1974-1987; unpublished data from the Department of Agricultural Statistics, MAG, for 1971; unpublished data from the National Directorate of Livestock, MAG for 1988.

[a]Continuous growth rates for 1974-1988 calculated by fitting an exponential curve: $Y = ae^{bx}$, where a>0 and Y>0.

numbers. Red meat production grew at an average of 3.8 percent between 1974 and 1988 led by growth in beef production of 4.4 percent per year (Table 6.11). Pork production grew at 2.7 percent while sheep and goat meat production declined. The annual slaughter in 1988 included 620,300 head of cattle, 611,600 head of swine and 129,000 head of sheep and goats. Milk production increased by 3.6 percent per year and was 1,388 million liters in 1988 (Table 6.12). About 33 percent of the milk is used on the farm for human consumption and rearing calves, 14 percent is pasteurized, 22 percent is consumed raw, 24 percent is processed in cottage industries (mainly into cheese) and 7 percent is used for industrial processing.

Production of chicken meat grew at the very rapid annual rate of 11.6 percent between 1970 and 1988 led by growth in broiler production of 15.2 percent and egg production of 7.6 percent per year (Table 6.13). Production of shrimp has grown at very high annual rates since the mid-1970s and was 82,580 metric tons (whole shrimp) in 1988, with 52,500 metric tons (shrimp tails) being exported, almost exclusively to the United States. The majority of the production in early years was from wild shrimp while an estimated 80 percent of production in 1988 was from cultivated shrimp.

Degradation of the mangroves and associated reduced availability of wild larvae is beginning to negatively affect shrimp production according to the IDEA study. Only 51 percent of installed capacity was in production in 1988, the share has been declining for nearly a decade and is expected to decline further during the early 1990s (Espinoza p. 135).

Consumption patterns of livestock products changed substantially during the 1970s and 1980s as production of animal proteins increased in response to growing demand. Meat consumption per capita increased from 12.2 kilograms (kg) in 1970 to 17.2 kg in 1987, a 41 percent increase (PROFOGAN p. 75). The increase of 5.0 kg per capita was comprised of increases in consumption of about 1.9 kg of beef and 4.0 kg of chicken, with decrease of about .4 kg of pork and .5 kg of sheep and goat. In 1970, 61 percent of meat consumption was from beef, 29 percent from pork, sheep and goats and 10 percent from poultry. By 1987 poultry had increased to 31 percent of meat consumption, while pork, sheep and goat meat had fallen to only 15 percent and beef declined slightly to 54 percent. Egg consumption increased by 113 percent from 39 to 83 eggs per capita. No official consumption data for shrimp are available, but there

Table 6.12 Milk Production and Utilization, Selected Years and Growth Rates,
           1973-1988 (1,000,000 Liters)

| | | --------- Off-Farm Utilization ----------- | | | | |
Year	Production	Pasteurized	Raw	Home Processed	Industry Processed	Farm Use
1973	717	178	142	136	32	229
1980	897	110	232	223	44	287
1987	1,130	160	252	266	90	362
1988	1,388	---	---	---	---	---
Annual Growth[a] (%)	3.6	-1.9	4.2	5.0	7.7	3.1

Source: PROFOGAN p. 62 for 1973-1987; unpublished data from Department of Livestock Marketing, MAG, for 1971; unpublished data from the National Directorate of
Livestock, MAG for 1988.

[a]Continuous growth rates for 1973-1987 (1973-1988 for Production) calculated by
fitting an exponential curve: $Y = ae^{bx}$, where a>0 and Y>0.

Table 6.13 Chicken and Shrimp Production, Selected Years and Growth Rates,
           1970-1988 (Metric Tons)

Year	Eggs	Broilers	Layers	Roosters	Total Chicken	Shrimp[a]
1970	12,986	2,881	2,018	2,226	7,125	---
1975	20,906	8,054	3,250	3,412	14,716	5,548
1980	44,844	22,729	6,972	6,750	36,451	17,500
1988	44,197	41,846	6,870	5,684	54,400	82,580
Annual Growth[b] (%)	7.6	15.2	7.2	5.5	11.6	22.8[c]

Source: PROFOGAN p. 74 for chicken for 1970-1987; unpublished data from the
Subsecretary of Fisheries, MICIP and MICEI for shrimp; unpublished data from the
National Directorate of Livestock, MAG for chicken in 1988.

[a]Whole Shrimp.
[b]Continuous growth rate calculated by fitting an exponential curve:
$Y = ae^{bx}$, where a>0 and Y>0.
[c]Based on 1975-1988 data.

was apparent consumption of .75 kilograms of shrimp tails per capita in 1988.

Production of Illegal Substances

There is very little information about the areas and levels of production of crops
used for illegal drug production. The information that is available is based on
plantations that have been discovered and destroyed by the police and army, which
are likely to be only a fraction of the amounts produced. The two main drugs that
affect Ecuadorian agriculture are marijuana from the hemp plant and cocaine from the

coca plant. The poppy from which heroin is made grows wild throughout the Sierra, but is not known to used for drug production.

Some marijuana is produced in Ecuador, nearly all for the illegal domestic market. Ecuador is too far from major world markets for marijuana to be a viable competitor to Colombia which is a major supplier of that relatively bulky product. Thus, the effect of marijuana production on food production probably is extremely small, although its contribution to the incomes of a few rural people may be substantial.

The climate and soils of Ecuador are amenable to the production of the coca plant but, unlike in Peru and Bolivia, that has never been a customary or legal activity. Ecuador was part of the Incan Empire where the chewing of coca leaves to relieve hunger and fatigue was practiced, and still legally is in parts of Bolivia and Peru. This practice did not spread to Ecuador, which was incorporated into the Empire very late in its existence. The legal production of coca leaves in Peru and Bolivia for hundreds of years has led to a large production base comprising many small farmers scattered throughout various parts of each country. That reality greatly complicates policing illegal production, since it is difficult to distinguish between the legal and illegal product. The fact that coca has never been a legal crop in Ecuador has helped to prevent the initiation of extensive plantings among small farmers.

While it is not known how large a total area is planted to the coca plant, it cannot be large. Representatives of the International Organization of Criminal Police (INTERPOL) indicate that there are no extensive plantations in Ecuador. The small size of the country and the relative accessibility of most of the area where coca can be produced make it very difficult for large plantations to be initiated or maintained. The police and army have discovered and destroyed a number of small fields during the last several years (DINACONTES; El Comercio). The coca plantations that have been discovered and destroyed were along border areas with Colombia, in Esmeraldas and Napo (now Sucumbíos) provinces. Although the area was not reported, the Ecuadorian police destroyed 100,258 coca plants in 1989 which would translate into a very small area (El Comercio). Thus, even if the area in production is several times that discovered it would still be relatively small and would have little impact on the county's overall agricultural situation.

Modern Inputs

Use of modern technologies and associated industrial inputs generally is limited. Most of the major crops are produced with traditional or semi-modern technologies. Only a small proportion of most crops is produced with a fully modern technological package including improved seeds and fertilizer, although there is significant variation among crops. The lack of a comprehensive data base makes measurement of the nature and extent of technical practices by crop and region difficult. There are several studies of individual inputs and crops which permit general inferences to be made.

Levels of Technology

The levels of technology vary substantially within and among crops, with a wide range of technical practices employed (Table 6.14). Potatoes and bananas, for example, are mainly produced with modern technologies, while coffee and cassava are produced largely with traditional, low-productivity techniques. Most crops are produced with semi-modern technologies which incorporate some modern inputs, such

Table 6.14 Technology Classes Used for Producing Principal Crops

	------ Percent Produced Using Technology Class: ----		
Crop	Modern	Semi-Modern	Traditional
Potatoes	62	26	12
Tomatoes	59	40	1
Bananas (Export)	48	52	0
Onions	40	57	3
Soybeans	29	71	0
Sugarcane	21	76	3
Wheat	14	68	18
Rice	14	67	19
Barley	12	66	22
Dry Beans	11	69	20
Soft Corn	2	78	20
Hard Corn	2	66	32
Cacao	2	59	39
Coffee	2	26	72
Cassava	0	24	76
Citrus	0	17	83

Source: Adapted from Economic Perspectives, Inc. 1987a, Appendix Table 1.

as improved seeds, fertilizers, pesticides and herbicides but stop short of a complete package of modern technical practices. A majority of producers have shifted from traditional to semi-modern technologies and a smaller proportion have moved all the way to modern technologies. This is consistent with the trends of increasing yields for most crops and with the relative importance of technical changes in explaining increases in production.

The three classes of technical change set forth in Table 6.14 are gross abstractions of the range of technical practices which exist for each of the crops. For example, IDEA and Grupo Consultores Asociados (pp. 14-16) identified five major technologies utilized in rice production. The range of practices varies widely within each technology. Similar variations in technical practices are found among all the crops of Ecuador, although technical advances have occurred more rapidly in some crops than others.

Fertilizer Use[13]

Fertilizer use is much below the recommended levels for the principal crops, on average. Hammond and Hill estimated that fertilizer use for 16 crops averaged 44.7 kilograms per hectare in 1982, which was only 24.1 percent of requirements for all nutrients, based on soil analyses for the 16 crops (p. 45). Use relative to requirements for the three principal nutrients was 24.7 percent for nitrogen, 30.1 percent for phosphorous, and 17.6 percent for potassium. A similar analysis for 14 major crops in 1986 by Economic Perspectives, Inc. (1987a) found nitrogen use at 32 percent of recommended levels, phosphorous at 24 percent and potassium at 21 percent, at an average of 61.2 kilograms per hectare.

The relative price of fertilizer has fallen, especially in the post-1981 austerity period. The prices of fertilizer and other inputs were implicitly subsidized by the overvalued exchange rate during the import-substitution era and especially during the oil boom in the 1970s. The price of agricultural products was simultaneously constrained to artificially low levels by the overvalued exchange rate and other macroeconomic policies. Adjustments and structural reforms during the 1980s removed most of the exchange rate subsidies to agricultural inputs and simultaneously allowed the price of agricultural products to increase. The net effect was a fall in the price of fertilizers relative to product prices between 1980 and 1986 (Economic Perspectives, Inc. 1987a, p. 11). For example, it required eight kilos of bananas to purchase one kilo of urea in 1980; this had fallen to 1.6 kilos of bananas by 1986.

These favorable price relationships resulted in increased levels of fertilizer use with an annual growth rate of 14.9 percent between 1976 and 1986.[14] It is estimated that fertilizer use will double by the year 2000 (Economic Perspectives, Inc. 1987a, p. i).

The gap between average fertilizer use and recommended levels still is relatively large, even after discounting the recommended technical levels to an economic optimum.[15] The large gap is indicative of the relatively low levels of technology being utilized. Major constraints to increased rates of fertilizer use include: limited support for reliable soil testing, lack of studies on economically optimum rates of fertilization, an extremely weak applied research and technology transfer system, uncertainty about government price policy for products and inputs, unreliable supplies of fertilizer with spot shortages of various nutrients, structural deficiencies in the fertilizer industry, and a general lack of farm management research (Hammond and Hill pp. 1-5; Economic Perspectives, Inc. 1987a, pp. i-iii).

The fertilizer industry is dominated by the Ecuadorian Fertilizer Company (FERTISA) a quasi-private enterprise owned mainly by the public sector. All nutrients are imported and then mixed and bagged. FERTISA had about 50 percent of the market prior to 1986 when prices and imports were tightly controlled. In 1986 the government allowed unrestricted importation of fertilizers and FERTISA suddenly was faced with intense competition. Prices fell substantially which contributed to the increased use of fertilizers and resulted in an operating loss for FERTISA given its high cost structure. The Borja government reimposed import controls in 1988, but is considering relaxing trade restrictions for fertilizers. Given relatively large world supplies of urea and attractive prices, the government can facilitate increased fertilizer use and greater productivity if it eliminates trade barriers for this important input.

Improved Seeds[16]

Use of improved seeds is relatively limited, although comprehensive data are not available for a detailed analysis. Production of certified seed is confined to wheat, barley, rice, hard corn, soybeans, cacao, oilpalm and a few minor crops (Flores p. 43). There is a National Seed Program, with the National Institute of Agricultural Research (INIAP) and the National Seed Company (EMSEMILLAS) as principal participants. INIAP is responsible for developing promising new lines and for quality control in the production of basic, registered and certified seeds. It tests improved genetic material, then produces foundation seed, basic seed and registered seed (first, second and third generations). It then contracts with private growers to produce certified seed (fourth generation) which is processed and sold by EMSEMILLAS. Several private firms also are engaged in the production of improved rice, corn and barley seeds and have processing facilities, as does the National Cotton Program which produces certified cotton seed.

Data for the principal crops that utilize seed from Ecuador's certified seed program suggest relatively high levels of use for Costa crops and low levels for Sierra crops

Table 6.15 Shares of Main Sierra and Costa Crops Planted With Certified Seed

| ------------ Costa ------------------ | | ------------- Sierra --------------- | |
Crop	Share (%)	Crop	Share (%)
Hard Corn	58	Wheat	9
Rice	65	Barley	7
Soybeans	95	Soft Corn	3
Cotton	100	Potatoes	3

Source: Economic Perspectives, Inc. 1987c, Table 1.

(Table 6.15). Improved seeds for the other major crops must be imported and data are not available for estimating the share of cropland sown with improved varieties. Use of improved legume seeds is nil and almost all pasture, grass and vegetable seeds are imported. Use of improved varieties must be relatively high for some of the vegetable crops, which require fresh seed for germination. This is reflected in the relatively high share of tomatoes and onions that are produced with modern or semi-modern technologies (Table 6.14 above).

There are several problems which have constrained expanded use of improved seeds (Flores; Economic Perspectives, Inc. 1987c). Principal among these has been the government policy of setting low prices for improved seeds and overvalued exchange rates, which have simultaneously subsidized seed imports. These two factors have combined to substantially reduce incentives to develop and strengthen domestic production of improved seeds, although the subsidized price has tended to encourage increased use of improved seeds. A second major problem is limited accessibility to improved seed. The distribution system is highly centralized and there is almost no retail distribution in production areas, thus significantly increasing the transactions costs associated with use of improved seeds. A third problem has been the policy of the National Seed Council to deny import permits until proposed parent varieties can be tested by INIAP. INIAP has limited capacity to respond quickly to such requests, thus delaying import of improved seeds.

Perhaps the most serious constraint to increased use of improved seeds is the extremely limited science base serving agriculture, the limited amount of proven technical information and the low level of education and experience in the use of improved seeds and other modern technical practices. Closely related to this is the tendency to promote and sell modern inputs independently (e.g. fertilizer via FERTISA and seeds via EMSEMILLAS). What is needed are increased efforts to validate and extend packages of improved technologies, rather than selling just seeds, or fertilizer.

Other Modern Inputs

Use of other modern inputs also is relatively limited, although definitive data are not available. One study of the agricultural chemicals in Ecuador found their use quite limited (Economic Perspectives, Inc. 1987d). They tend to be used in the production of Costa cereals where they are a larger cost item than fertilizers. Application rates per hectare have been relatively stable. All pesticides are imported with three firms controlling 82 percent of the total sales. There is little reliable applied research on optimal application rates by crop and region and farmers are generally ignorant about proper handling and use of pesticides. There is evidence of serious environmental contamination from use of farm chemicals (see Chapter 4).

Machinery use increased fairly rapidly between 1975 and 1984, with tractors increasing at 4.6 percent per year and harvesting equipment at 2.9 percent (Economic Perspectives, Inc. 1987b, p.6). There was an estimated inventory of 7,600 tractors and 650 combines in 1984. The fairly rapid increase in machinery during this period is related to the rapid rural to urban migration and the absolute decline in agricultural employment during the same period.

The degree of mechanization is relatively limited. Assuming the average tractor was able to cover 75 hectares, the 7,600 tractors would cover 570,000 hectares or 36 percent of harvested cropland in 1984. This provides a rough index of the degree of mechanization in Ecuadorian agriculture.

The government provides mechanization services through the National Program for Agricultural Mechanization (PRONAMEC) of MAG. This agency rents machinery services to farmers who can not afford their own equipment. Other agencies such as the Ecuadorian Institute of Water Resources (INERHI) also have machinery pools which tend to duplicate MAG services. Such programs are notoriously inefficient and provide services at highly subsidized prices. While ostensibly focused on resource-poor farmers, there is evidence that much of the subsidy may be going to larger farmers who use their influence to obtain the subsidized services.

Technological Improvements in the Longer Term

The above discussion of modern inputs for agriculture has focused on the need to shift from a traditional technology to a modern, high-input technology. The traditional technology utilizes mainly inputs produced within agriculture while the modern technology is based on high-yielding varieties, which require high levels of industrial inputs and human capital (fertilizers, chemicals, irrigation equipment, tractors, harvesters, other equipment, scientists, technicians and better-educated farmers).

The degree to which the modern technology is sustainable has been the subject of concern by ecologists for more than a decade (Cox and Atkins). The high social costs associated with use of chemicals and intensive irrigation are well documented and widely understood. The principal question concerns the sustainability of these high-input systems relative to other systems which are less productive, but are more profitable because of substantially lower private and social costs. For the immediate future in Ecuador, it appears that the modern, high-input system offers higher social returns given the relative prices of products and factors. Moreover, it will generate substantially higher growth rates necessary to fuel more rapid economic development consistent with Ecuador's high rate of population growth. Research should be designed to address the question of sustainable agriculture and public and private sector entities should clearly consider the alternatives to high-input technologies as they formulate investment plans and public policy.

Understanding Changes in Production

Several interrelated factors help explain the changes in the crop production, land use and yields described above. Included are the macroeconomic policy matrix, the petroleum boom and sectoral policies intended to accelerate agricultural development. These three factors collectively generated substantial shifts in relative prices and incomes which, in turn, induced changes in land use and yields among crops and regions and caused the structure of agricultural production to be altered substantially.

Macroeconomic Policies and the Petroleum Boom

The government's economic development policy since the mid-1950s has been import-substitution industrialization and internally oriented growth (see Chapter 2 for a detailed analysis). The net result was to shift the internal terms of trade strongly in favor of industry and urban development and against agriculture. In essence, the macroeconomic policy matrix subsidized urban-based economic growth at the expense of agriculture and rural people.

The petroleum boom resulted in greatly increased demand for better-quality food because of rapid, sustained economic growth during the 1970s. One immediate result was a rapid increase in real per capita incomes during the 1970s, especially in urban areas. As incomes increased, demand for higher-quality foods and especially for animal proteins grew. Since the income elasticity of demand for such products is relatively high, especially among lower income groups, the demand for such foods increased rapidly. A second major result of the oil boom was greatly reduced demand for traditional subsistence crops. The boom precipitated rapid rural to urban migration which caused the rural population growth rate to plummet to .8 percent. The relatively large decreases in rural population growth caused sharp decreases in the demand for traditional subsistence crops in rural areas.

One policy of the government was to provide cheap food to the burgeoning urban population. In the 1970s the government provided subsidies and controlled prices to hold down food costs for the rapidly growing urban population. Wheat imports were heavily and directly subsidized and both wheat and barley imports were authorized at the highly overvalued, official exchange rate. Consumer acceptance of the imported hard wheat, which had superior milling and baking qualities compared to domestic soft wheat, was quick and pervasive. These subsidies and the consumer acceptance substantially reduced the profitability of producing wheat and barley. In addition, maximum prices were set at the consumer level for most basic foods to protect urban consumers and the government embarked on programs to stimulate the production of other basic food crops and feed grains.

Sectoral Policies

Four major government initiatives for agriculture directly affected and conditioned changes in production of crops and livestock between the mid-1960s and the present. First, the government embarked on an ambitious program of Costa crop diversification in the mid-1960s toward food crops, feed grains and pastures for livestock production as Ecuador faced a secular decline in the prices of export crops. Second, the rehabilitation and rejuvenation of export crops were emphasized in the 1970s when export prices recuperated. Third, the government implemented an agrarian reform program in 1964 as a complement to its import substitution program in an attempt to produce cheaper wage goods for the growing urban population. Finally, the government devoted significant resources to improving livestock production in the Sierra.

Costa Crop Diversification The government initiated a major effort in the 1960s and early 1970s to diversify Costa crop production, primarily by shifting land out of bananas and, to a lesser extent, coffee and cacao. Banana production had increased rapidly during the 1950s in response to favorable world prices growing markets and production problems in Central America. By the early 1960s output substantially exceeded demand, while a new, disease-resistant variety resulted in substantially increased yields per hectare. This allowed production to remain relatively high while freeing land for other uses.

Principal government policy instruments to induce diversification were: (a) subsidized credit (Chapter 9); (b) guaranteed minimum prices (Chapter 8); (c) focused technical assistance (Chapter 12); and (d) highly subsidized irrigation projects (Chapter 7). The main recipients of subsidized credit, guaranteed minimum prices, technical assistance and subsidized irrigation water were the politically influential farmers with larger holdings.

Export Crop Rehabilitation World prices of coffee and cacao rose to unprecedented levels in the mid-1970s, after a period of sharp price declines in the 1960s. The government responded by implementing renovation programs for coffee and cacao, while continuing with policies which encouraged production of food and feed crops and livestock. The export crop programs provided subsidized credit from the National Development Bank (BNF) for rehabilitation of plantations, through replacement of older trees with higher yielding varieties supplied mainly from INIAP's Pichilingue experiment station. The program also focused on improved technical practices including control of insects and diseases.

Agrarian Reform Agrarian reform constituted one element of the broader strategy of internally oriented growth in an attempt to increase productivity and the production of food for the growing urban population. The land reform affected crop production and factor use in several fundamental ways. It resulted in the fairly rapid incorporation of idle or underutilized land into production because of the threat of expropriation and farms of all sizes generally became more commercial (Colyer). This permitted small farmers to shift quickly from production of subsistence to commercial crops as demand rose in urban areas during the oil boom. Agrarian reform also resulted in the fragmentation of crop areas, especially for wheat and barley, as large farms were broken up. As a result, the economies of scale necessary for efficient small-grains production were rapidly eroded. Many Sierra farmers were denied access to the limited BNF production credit because they lacked titles to their land and were unable to provide the necessary collateral. Many also sought off-farm employment, thus reducing the labor available to agriculture.

Sierra Livestock Government policies for the Sierra during the 1970s and 1980s were directed mainly at increasing livestock production, especially dairy cattle. These programs provided subsidized credit, guaranteed minimum prices and technical assistance. There also was some limited technical assistance for some crops, especially wheat, barley and potatoes, and some investment in irrigation infrastructure, which was relatively small compared to the large Costa irrigation projects. The agricultural potential of the Sierra was inherently more limited than the Costa at the beginning of the petroleum era as nearly all agricultural land was in production. Hence, any increases in production had to come from improved yields, or from reducing the area in other crops.

Most Sierra crops were subject to market prices in both the factor and product markets and were not shielded from the negative effects of the macroeconomic policy matrix (see Chapter 2). In contrast, subsidized credit and minimum prices at least partially counteracted the restrictive effects of macroeconomic policies for the dairy sector, wheat, barley and most Costa crops.

Effects on Crop Production and Factor Use

The combination of macroeconomic and sectoral policies resulted in a decline in the producer prices of Sierra crops relative to livestock and Costa crops. As a consequence, several shifts in land use and crop production occurred during the 1970s and 1980s.

In the Sierra provinces, larger farmers converted cropland to pastures from traditional crops, while the small farm sector shifted from production of subsistence crops to higher-value crops in response to burgeoning urban markets (see Chapter 5).[17] New lands were brought into pasture production in the Costa and the lowlands areas of the Sierra provinces for dairy and beef production, and for rice, oilseeds, oilpalm, cacao and coffee. Moreover, land was shifted out of bananas and into feed grains and oilseeds production in the Costa to support the broiler industry and to augment vegetable oil production.

There also were major changes in factor use. The total area devoted to principal crops decreased by 192,124 hectares, or by 11 percent. There was a massive emigration from rural areas and employment in agriculture declined absolutely between 1974 and 1982 (Chapter 5). Modern factors of production were substituted for land and labor. Agriculture became more capital-intensive as tractors and other machinery increased. Improved varieties of plants which required complementary fertilization and controlled water were adopted. As a consequence, use of chemical fertilizers and other chemical inputs intensified, although use still is limited. The livestock sector imported pure-blooded livestock and semen. Finally, irrigation of cropland grew rapidly with an estimated 25 percent being irrigated in 1990, mostly from private systems. Machinery, improved seeds and livestock, chemical inputs and irrigation have substituted for limited land and labor which sustained production through increased yields as land area and labor inputs decreased.

Implications for the Future

All of Ecuador's good and marginal agricultural land is in production and the remaining poorer-quality land entails increasingly higher costs of production. Improvements in yields are likely the most cost-efficient way to increase agricultural production. The gap between average yields in Ecuador and the rest of South America, or those obtained by Ecuador's most progressive farmers, still is relatively large for most crops and livestock. Thus, it is fully within the realm of possibility to significantly increase yields at relatively low costs using proven technologies.

The science base for agriculture will have to be substantially improved, however, if Ecuador is to realize this potential (Chapter 12). Extant capacity for applied and adaptive research, technology transfer and agricultural education is practically very limited. Greatly increased investments in research, education and extension institutions; scientists and technicians; and in improved linkages to the international network of agricultural science will be needed. Finally, incentives to invest in more modern technologies and industrial inputs which incorporate and complement the improved technologies will have to be provided through an appropriate macroeconomic and sectoral policy matrix.

It is significant that average yields have increased at relatively rapid rates during the two-decade period in which macro-economic and many sectoral policies discriminated against agriculture. Despite these pervasive constraints, substantial technical changes also were taking place, which augurs well for future investments in research, education and extension, even in a less-than-optimal policy environment.

NOTES

1. Agriculture is divided into five subsectors in the national accounts: export crops (bananas, coffee and cacao); other crops; livestock; forestry; and fishing and hunting (Chapter 3). Production agriculture in this chapter is defined to include the principal commodities from the first three subsectors, plus shrimp from the hunting and fishing subsector. Products from the rest of the hunting and fishing, and forestry subsectors are harvested from naturally occurring populations and consistent data series for them are unavailable. Consequently they are not considered in this chapter.

2. Livestock products could not be apportioned between the Sierra and Costa and are not included in Table 6.2.

3. There is a significant disparity between the two data sets for yields and area while the production data appear more consistent. Yields fell substantially while harvested area increased for most crops between 1985 (the last year of MAG data) and 1986 (the first year of INEC/SEAN data). For example, the MAG data show harvested cropland of 1,730,540 hectares for 1985 while INEC/SEAN data indicated 2,238,920 hectares for 1986, or 29 percent greater. While some of this gap may be due to expansion cropland between 1985 and 1986, it also suggests that MAG data probably underestimated 1985 harvested area while overestimating yields. The net result of greater land area and lower yields in the 1986 SEAN data was a change in production for most crops between 1985 and 1986 that appears to be more in line with trends in the earlier MAG data series.

4. This is not to suggest that the SEAN data for 1986-1988 are not accurate, only that they are based on a different methodology, and therefore are not comparable with the earlier data series. In fact, the SEAN data likely are more accurate since they are based on a more objective methodology. A complete and accurate census is needed to help determine the accuracy of the SEAN data.

5. Data for 1983 are excluded from the average for 1980-1985 in all the analyses in this chapter because of the extremely bad weather caused by the *El Niño* phenomenon and the resulting very low levels of production.

6. Some crops are grown in the Costa and Sierra but there were no data to make this distinction. Such crops were classified in the region where production is more concentrated.

7. All growth rates in this chapter were calculated with an exponential curve fit of the form $Y = ae^{bx}$, where a>0 and Y>0, and thus are continuous growth rates. Consequently, the direction of growth along the trend line may be different than that indicated by comparing the data for a beginning year (1965-1969 average) with an end year (1980-1985 average).

8. The following analysis considers changes in the area harvested of the principal crops. "Other Crops" are excluded because this category changes over time as crops are added to or dropped from the list of official production statistics.

9. MAG classifies abandoned land used only for seasonal grazing, as pasture.

10. The reader should keep in mind that the descriptive terms of Sierra, Costa and Oriente refer both to major geographical regions and to aggregations of Provinces for presentation of official statistics (see Chapter 4 and Chapter 5 Note 3). While the geographical and geo-political regions are roughly homogeneous, this is not always the case. Inferring that all Sierra pastures are highland pastures, or that there are no virgin lowland areas in the Sierra provinces is a case in point.

11. The model used here is adapted from Pray, with assistance from Hugo Ramos, senior author of Chapter 9.

12. The changes in production presented in Table 6.8 are slightly different than those presented in Table 6.3. This is because the average production data in Table 6.3 are calculated directly from annual production data while average production data in Table 6.8 are calculated from the averages of harvested area and annual yields. These two methods of calculating the average are not mathematically equivalent. See Whitaker, Colyer and Alzamora Appendix Tables 6.2, 6.3, 6.4 and 6.5.

13. See Economic Perspectives, Inc. (1987a); and Hammond and Hill for excellent reviews of the fertilizer industry in Ecuador.

14. Continuous growth rate calculated from data presented in Economic Perspectives, Inc. (1987a p. 11) by fitting an exponential curve.

15. Recommended fertilization rates in Ecuador generally are based on technical optimums that maximize production and are greater than the economic optimum where profits are maximized. The economic optimum is less than the technical optimum because of the law of diminishing returns to increased applications of fertilizer. The rate of fertilizer application should be increased as long as the additional revenue from increased production exceeds the additional cost of the fertilizer. The economic optimum is attained when the added revenue from one additional unit of fertilizer is equal to the cost of the fertilizer.

16. See Economic Perspectives, Inc. (1987c); and Flores for excellent reviews of the improved seed situation in Ecuador.

17. There was a significant reduction of land area in the Sierra in leguminous crops, potatoes, barley, wheat and soft corn as farmers shifted to pastures or abandoned depleted, eroded cropland. The legumes were consumed along with the cereals as part of a principally vegetarian, subsistence diet of rural people prior to the petroleum boom and provided a complete protein. The Ecuadorian diet changed substantially in the aftermath of the petroleum boom as animal products were substituted for the legumes. At the same time imported wheat, Costa cereals and plantains were substituted for the Sierra cereals and tubers.

REFERENCES

CLIRSEN (Center for the Survey of Natural Resources by Remote Sensing). 1988. *Actualización del Estudio Multitemporal de Manglares, Camaroneros y Salinas*. Quito: CLIRSEN, MICEI/Subsecretary of Fisheries and the Directorate of the Merchant Marine.

Colyer, Dale. 1989. "Land Tenure and Agrarian Reform." Quito: USAID, January 23, Assessment of Ecuador's Agricultural Sector, Working Paper No. 11-89.

Cox, George W. and Michael D. Atkins. 1979. *Agricultural Ecology: An Analysis of World Food Production Systems*. San Francisco: W. H. Freeman and Company.

DINACONTES (National Directorate for the Control of Narcotics). 1988. *Recortes de Prensa*. Quito: Centro de Información, May.

Economic Perspectives, Inc. 1987a. *An Economic Review of the Fertilizer Industry in Ecuador*. McLean, VA: July.

_____. 1987b. *La Industria de la Maquinaria y Equipo Agrícolas en El Ecuador*. McLean, VA: July.

_____. 1987c. *An Economic Review of the Certified Seed Industry in Ecuador*. McLean, VA: August.

_____. 1987d. *The Agricultural Chemical Industry in Ecuador*. McLean, VA: September.

El Comercio. 1990. "En Dicusión Ley Antidrogas." Quito: June 1, p. A8.

Flores, Jaime. 1984. *Information on Seeds in Ecuador*. Quito: Consulprode Cia. Ldt., August.

Hammond, L.L. and J.M. Hill. 1984. *Fertilizer Status Profile of Ecuador*. Muscle Shoals, AL: International Fertilizer Development Center.

Espinoza, Fernando. 1989. *Situación Actual de la Maricultura del Camarón en el Ecuador y Estrategias para su Desarrollo Sostenido*. Quito: IDEA, Documento Técnico No. 21.

IDEA (Agricultural Policy Institute) and Grupo Consultores Asociados. 1987. *Estudio del Sistema de Mercadeo de Granos en la Región Costera del Ecuador: Vol. III, Mercadeo de Arroz*. Quito: Technical Bulletin No. 2, July.

INEC/SEAN (National Institute of Statistics and Census, National System of Agricultural Statistics). 1986-1988. *Encuesta de Superficie y Producción por Muestreo de Areas*. Quito: INEC.

MAG (Ministry of Agriculture). 1965-1985. *Estimación de la Superficie Cosechada y de la Producción Agrícola del Ecuador*. Quito: Dirección General de Informática.

Pray, Carl E. 1979. "The Economics of Agricultural Research in Bangladesh." *The Bangladesh Journal of Agricultural Economics* 2(December):1-34.

PROFOGAN (The Livestock Development Project). 1988. *Estadísticas Pecuarias del Ecuador, 1950-1987*. Quito: MAG.

Sarhan, M. E. 1988. *The Livestock and Meat Subsector in Ecuador*. Research Triangle Park, NC: Sigma One Corporation.

Whitaker, Morris D., Dale Colyer and Jaime Alzamora. 1990. *The Role of Agriculture in Ecuador's Economic Development*. Quito: IDEA (Agricultural Policy Institute).

7

IRRIGATION AND

AGRICULTURAL DEVELOPMENT

Morris D. Whitaker and Jaime Alzamora

The status of irrigation and its role in the development of Ecuadorian agriculture is reviewed and analyzed in this chapter. The primary focus is on the economic viability of relatively large investments in public irrigation works. Such investments include the study, design, construction, operation and maintenance of irrigation systems. They also encompass complementary services such as technical assistance, machinery pools, demonstration farms and subsidized inputs. A secondary focus is on the distribution of benefits from irrigation projects. Such projects are intended to increase the productivity and incomes of resource-poor farmers and project benefits are supposed to be widely distributed.

The following sections review and analyze: Ecuador's water resources and the need for irrigation; the principal public irrigation agencies and their irrigation activities; the extent and effectiveness of public and private irrigation systems now in operation; future irrigation projects including those under construction and design and study; the process for financing irrigation projects; the costs of irrigation projects and their impact on the foreign debt; the subsidies to public irrigation via the water tariff; the economic viability of public projects; and the size and distribution of economic benefits of irrigation projects. The last section presents conclusions and recommendations for enhancing the contribution of public irrigation to agricultural development.

Water Resources and Irrigation

Ecuador has been endowed with abundant water resources that are reasonably well distributed throughout the country. There are eighty-four river basins, the majority of which flow into the Pacific Ocean (Keller, et al. p. 91). The total annual discharge of these rivers ranges between 210 and 370 billion cubic meters (m^3) toward the Atlantic Ocean and between 80 and 140 billion m^3 toward the Pacific Ocean (Delavaud, et al. pp. 12-13). The smaller of these amounts of water would provide Ecuador's 1.6 million hectares of cropland with 183,500 m^3 of water per hectare, or a depth of 18.4 meters. In comparison, the 52,004 hectares of land irrigated from the Ecuadorian Institute of Water Resources (INERHI) systems in 1987 required an average of 19,129 m^3 per hectare, or a depth of 1.9 meters. Thus, there is enough surface water to irrigate about

161

hectare, or a depth of 1.9 meters. Thus, there is enough surface water to irrigate about ten times Ecuador's current total cropland. Less is known about the amount of subterranean water but there are several aquifers that have consistently provided significant quantities of water. Several irrigation systems in the Sierra and Costa have been developed utilizing subterranean water.

The demand for irrigation water is determined generally by the distribution and level of rainfall relative to the location of agricultural land. Other variables besides rainfall, which affect the need for irrigation, are temperature, gradient, elevation, the kind of plants and soil characteristics. There is great variability among each of these factors across Ecuador and consequently a large number of agro-ecologic zones.[1] This suggests that the need for irrigation varies considerably from zone to zone.

Eight major climatic zones have been identified based on distribution of rainfall, temperatures and level of rainfall (Delavaud, et al. pp. 17-20). These zones suggest the need for irrigation is greatest in the Sierra and the Central and Southern Costa.

Rainfall in the Sierra generally is equatorial with a bimodal distribution, peaking in April and again in November. The rainy season starts in October and continues through May with reduced precipitation during July through September. The principal agricultural season (winter) corresponds with the beginning of the rains in October. The secondary season (summer) follows the heavy April rains. The amount of rainfall varies considerably from less than 500 millimeters (mm) to 2000 mm throughout the Sierra. The primary demand for irrigation water during the winter season is for supplementary irrigation. The demand for irrigation water rises significantly during the summer season, especially in areas of low average precipitation and in dry years. Almost all irrigation infrastructure in the Sierra is designed for supplementary irrigation, with no storage for irrigation during the dry season. This reflects the bimodal distribution of rainfall and the generally lower temperatures which limit summer crops.

In contrast, the Central and Southern Costa have a tropical pattern of rainfall characterized by a single peak, usually in March. Rainfall begins in December, increases through March and falls off sharply in May. There is a pronounced dry season from June through mid-December, with little rainfall. River flows drop substantially during the dry season. Demand for irrigation during the winter season is small unless December and early January rains are late. If so, some supplementary irrigation may be required especially in rice. Demand for irrigation in the Costa is primarily for producing a second or third crop in the dry season. As a consequence, irrigation projects in the Costa, especially the newer ones, have storage facilities. Those that do not are severely limited in the area they can irrigate.

Public Agencies[2]

There are six principal public agencies involved in irrigation: INERHI, the Study Commission for the Development of the Guayas River Basin (CEDEGE); the Center for the Rehabilitation of Manabí (CRM); the Center for the Economic Recovery of Azuay, Cañar and Morona Santiago (CREA); the Regional Program for the Development of Southern Ecuador (PREDESUR); and the National Institute of Meteorology and Hydrology (INAMHI). In addition several other entities, including provinces, municipalities and national government agencies are engaged in irrigation programs. Each of these institutions is briefly described.

INERHI

INERHI was created on November 10, 1966 from the National Bureau of Irrigation and the Directorate of Water Resources of the Ministry of Agriculture (MAG). It is a semi-autonomous, public institution with its own budget and administrative unit. It is attached to MAG and the Minister appoints the director, serves as chair of the Board of Directors and has some influence through the budgetary process. It has the greatest area under irrigation of any of the public institutions.

INERHI assumed the responsibilities of its two predecessors as it was created in 1966. A new Water Law, issued in 1972, substantially expanded INERHI's responsibilities. The new law nationalized all water resources clearly stating that all water that had been considered private property was now a public resource. However, previous owners could continue to use the water under terms of the new law. These terms included efficient use of the water and the concession of a water-use permit issued by INERHI which was not transferable by the user. Under the previous Water Law of 1936 water rights were held privately and could be freely bought and sold or rented separately from the land. Modifications in this law between 1936 and 1972 moved toward the radical reform inherent in the 1972 law. In the euphoria of the oil boom, the new law also provided substantial subsidies to users of irrigation water.

INERHI has three primary functions which were defined in the law creating it and in the Water Law of 1972. First, it is to plan, administer and regulate, as ultimate authority for the Government, the use of all the water resources of the country for all purposes, public and private, rural and urban. Specifically it is to: (a) issue, regulate and control water-use permits; (b) locate water and evaluate water quality and quantity; (c) protect water resources; (d) inventory and evaluate use of water; and (e) plan for the use and protection of water.

Second, INERHI is to plan and administer, as maximum authority, all irrigation, drainage and flood control activities for the country. Its specific functions in this area are to: (a) prepare and execute a national plan for irrigation, drainage and flood control; (b) inventory and evaluate irrigation works and water use for irrigation; (c) regulate, control and approve all irrigation, drainage and flood control programs and projects; and (d) promote and support the development of irrigation and drainage by the private sector and other public sector entities.

Third, INERHI is to study, construct and operate irrigation systems. Specifically it is to: (a) carry out requisite pre-feasibility and feasibility studies including technical, economic and social aspects; (b) construct irrigation works and take all actions necessary to achieve complete implementation of the projects; (c) operate and maintain infrastructure; and (d) promote economic and social development in areas of irrigation.

INERHI's efforts, as measured by its budget allocations since 1985, have been concentrated mainly on its third function, the development of irrigation, drainage and flood control systems (Table 7.1). Nearly 87 percent of its budget was devoted to construction and operation of irrigation systems on average during 1985-1988. Only 3.3 percent of its budget was spent on its first function of planning, administering and regulating the use of water resources. Almost nothing has been done to carry out the second function of irrigation management, with only .1 percent of its budget devoted to this task.

IHERHI's organizational structure may be impeding its ability to play a more vigorous role in carrying out its first two mandates. The Directorate of Administration of Water which is responsible for planning, administering and regulating Ecuador's

Table 7.1   INERHI Expenses by Programs and Activities, Annual Average 1985-1988
(Million of 1988 Sucres)

| | INERHI Functions | | | | | |
	Central Management	Water Management	Irrigation Management	Construction & Operation	Inst. Planning	Total by Activity
Studies	0.71	6.09	0.30	186.21	1.45	194.76
Construction	19.55			4,331.32		4,350.87
Operation				75.89		75.89
Maintenance	8.20			108.33		116.53
Ag. Development				52.30		52.30
Administration	415.77	60.09	9.06	1,040.67	32.17	1,557.77
Fixed Assets	75.02	4.03	0.06	332.85	0.86	412.82
Public Debt	50.77					150.77
Water Agencies		160.60				160.60
Total by Function	670.02	230.81	9.42	6,127.58	34.47	7,072.30
Share (%)	9.47	3.26	0.13	86.64	0.49	100.00

Source: Whitaker, Colyer and Alzamora Appendix Tables 7.1 and 7.2.

water resources, is attached administratively to the Technical Directorate. The Technical Directorate studies, designs, builds and operates INERHI's irrigation systems.[3] At the field level, the Water Agencies, which process water concessions, are subordinate to the Chief of the Irrigation District. Thus, the administrative unit of INERHI with responsibility to allocate water among all its competing uses is administratively subordinate to a unit of INERHI which develops water for irrigation. The Department for the National Irrigation Plan is part of the Directorate of Planning which serves as a staff office to the Executive Directorate. There is no line office responsible for carrying out the second function of planning and administering all irrigation and drainage at the national level. This reflects the low priority of this function and the minuscule budget allocations to it.

INERHI also has labor problems which may be constraining its performance. Salaries for its 811 professional staff (civil servants) have declined in real terms in every year since 1985 and are low compared to private sector alternatives (Whitaker, Colyer and Alzamora Appendix Table 7.3). Consequently, it is difficult to develop and maintain a critical mass of experienced staff. Its 1,357 laborers work under a collective labor contract. This union paralyzed INERHI during the peak of the dry season in 1988 by declaring a national strike and closing the Pisque irrigation project for nearly 90 days. The unionization of INERHI's laborers clearly limited its ability to provide basic irrigation services. Finally, INERHI has suffered from a high turnover of senior staff with four Executive Directors during 1985-1990. The politicization of INERHI has resulted in instability and discontinuity of leadership in an agency that is largely technical in nature.[4]

CEDEGE

CEDEGE was created in 1965 and is a semi-autonomous public agency attached to MAG and to the Office of the President (Orquera p. 22). It is located in Guayaquil, has its own endowment and is governed by a Board of Directors. It was created to carry out studies of ways to develop the Guayas River Basin. In 1970, its jurisdiction was expanded to include the Santa Elena Peninsula and in 1972 it was given authority to design and implement projects as well as carry out analyses and studies. In 1979 CEDEGE was given responsibilities of implementing the multipurpose Jaime Roldós Aguilera project (known popularly as the Daule-Peripa project) which strengthened its function of regional planning and interinstitutional coordination.

CEDEGE will have over 100,000 irrigable hectares when the Daule-Peripa and related Santa Elena projects are fully implemented. These projects are being completed in stages, however, with only 17,000 hectares planned in the first phase starting in 1990. The balance of the 100,000 hectares will be irrigated under three later phases.

CRM

CRM was created in 1962 in response to a severe drought that resulted in emergency conditions in the Province of Manabí. It a semi-autonomous public agency attached to the MAG. It has its own budget, is located in Portoviejo and has jurisdiction only in the Province of Manabí.

CRM has focused primarily on potable water systems with some limited involvement in irrigation. It plans to greatly expand its involvement in irrigation with construction of the multiple-purpose Carrizal-Chone project in the near future and rehabilitation of the Poza Honda project. These and several smaller projects will add about 31,000 additional hectares under irrigation. CRM also plans to bring water from the Daule-Peripa reservoir to the La Esperanza reservoir (as part of the Carrizal-Chone project) and thence to the Poza Honda reservoir. This additional water will meet increasing urban demands for potable water in the Portoviejo area and resolve a growing conflict between agricultural and urban water users.

CREA

CREA was created in 1958 and also is a semi-autonomous public agency attached to the MAG. It is a legal entity with its own budget and is located in Cuenca. CREA has some very small irrigation projects which it has developed but no data are available. It is working with INERHI to improve the management of watersheds and better utilize water resources. It has no plans to implement new irrigation projects.

PREDESUR

PREDESUR does not exist as a separate legal entity; it is an element of the Executive Directorate of the Ecuadorian Subcommission for the Development of the Puyango-Túmbez and Catamayo-Chira River Basins. The Executive Directorate was created in 1972 with its own budget in accord with a 1971 bilateral agreement with Peru. The bilateral agreement called for the establishment of subcommissions by Peru and Ecuador to exploit the binational water resources of the two river basins. The Executive Directorate of the Subcommission established PREDESUR in 1975 and is legally responsible for it.

PREDESUR's principal involvement in irrigation has been the Puyango-Túmbez project which includes the Tahuín dam. The Tahuín dam project was transferred to INERHI after the dam was about 60 percent complete. When the Puyango-Túmbez project is completed (including two more dams) it will irrigate about 70,000 hectares in Ecuador. Another smaller project of 6,000 hectares (Zapotillo Alto) is under study.

INAMHI

INAMHI is a semi-autonomous public agency created in 1979 and attached to the Ministry of Natural Resources and Energy. Its primary function is to gather, analyze and provide, in coordination with other agencies, meteorologic, climatic and hydrologic data and information. INAHMI has very limited resources for carrying out its important assignment. The number and level of training of its staff are inadequate to the task at hand. Its meteorologic stations are antiquated and many probably give inaccurate measurements. Several other institutions also have substantial networks of meteorologic stations, including the Ecuadorian Electrification Institute (INECEL), the National Institute of Agricultural Research (INIAP), CEDEGE, CRM and CREA. While the Board of Directors of INAMHI is comprised of representatives from some of these agencies, the data from their stations are not ratified by INAMHI nor incorporated into a national data system. The data generated by INAMHI are fundamental to rational allocation of water concessions by INERHI but the two agencies tend to work very independently.

Other Public Agencies

There are several other public national and regional entities that are engaged in the operation of irrigation systems. Included are provincial and municipal governments, MAG, INIAP and the Military (CAME). The most important of these in terms of irrigated area is the Provincial Council of El Oro with approximately 12,000 hectares in four irrigation systems. The provincial councils of Loja and Cotopaxi also have irrigation systems. Fifteen municipal governments, mainly in the Sierra, collectively irrigate 6,600 hectares mainly from small and simple irrigation systems. MAG irrigates 1,000 hectares and INIAP and CAME each about 250 hectares on their farms.

Irrigation Extent and Effectiveness

There were approximately 418,000 hectares of land irrigated in 1987 (Table 7.2). This includes land irrigated from both public and private projects throughout the year and does not account for irrigation of multiple crops. Irrigated agriculture is relatively important, accounting for about 27 percent of the cropland of the country.[5]

The extent of private irrigation has been estimated but there are no reliable data and the estimates have to be considered approximations. Keller, et al. (p. 103) estimated the area under private irrigation to be 323,000 hectares in 1981. A more recent estimate by Carrera de la Torre of 330,000 hectares is consistent with the first. It also is cited by Orquera (p. 31) as an accepted estimate. Cox, Cox and Tolosa (p. 20) argued that the 1981 estimate was too high and made a more conservative, but undocumented estimate for 1988 of 231,00 hectares. The estimate of 330,000 hectares is judged to be the most reliable on the basis of consistency with the 1981 estimate. INERHI, with assistance from the Office of Overseas Science and Technology Research of France (ORSTOM) is carrying out a study of irrigation by river basin that will provide more accurate data about the extent and location of private irrigation. The study will not be completed until the early 1990s.

Table 7.2 Irrigation Projects in Operation, 1989

Entity	Command Area[a] "Superficie Dominada" (hectares)	Irrigable Area "Superficie Regable" (hectares)	Area Irrigated in 1987 (hectares)	Irrigable as Share of Command (%)	Irrigated as Share of Irrigable (%)
GRAND TOTAL	510,735	445,244	417,959	87.2	93.9
Private	330,000	330,000	330,000	100.0	100.0
Public	180,735	115,244	87,959	63.8	76.3
INERHI	139,630	79,289	52,004	56.8	65.6
CEDEGE	9,000	4,700	4,700	52.2	100.0
CRM	3,500	2,650	2,650	75.7	100.0
CREA	4,200	4,200	4,200	100.0	100.0
Provinces	16,315	16,315	16,315	100.0	100.0
Municipalities	6,600	6,600	6,600	100.0	100.0
MAG, INIAP, CAME	1,490	1,490	1,490	100.0	100.0

Source: Whitaker, Colyer and Alzamora Appendix Tables 7.4 and 7.5.

[a]See Note 8.

The private sector accounts for nearly 80 percent of all irrigation, accepting the estimate of 330,000 hectares in private irrigation. About 33,000 hectares of private irrigation is in 14 farms, ranging from 1,000 to 5,000 hectares per farm (Orquera p. 32). The balance is in smaller, simpler systems thought to be located primarily in the Sierra.[6] INERHI has been involved since 1985 in a modest program to improve the privately owned *acequias* (distribution systems--primarily primitive ditches) and shallow wells of small farmers. In 1987 this effort improved irrigation on 23,000 hectares and benefitted 15,300 families (INERHI 1987a).

There were a reported 87,959 hectares irrigated in public projects in 1987 located throughout the country (Figure 7.1). INERHI accounted for 52,004 hectares (59 percent) while seven other regional, provincial and local government agencies collectively irrigated nearly 36,000 hectares (Table 7.2). The single most important of these is the Provincial Council of El Oro, which irrigated 12,000 hectares.

INERHI irrigation systems have not realized their planned potential.[7] The area planned at the design stage to be irrigated (command area) was 139,630 hectares. There is only sufficient infrastructure, however, for an irrigable area of 79,289 hectares or 57 percent of the planned command area. More critically, the irrigable area is greatly underutilized with only 52,004 hectares actually under irrigation in 1987 (66 percent of irrigable area).[8]

Inefficient utilization of irrigation water, especially on farms, likely is the main reason that one-third of the irrigable area is not irrigated. Keller, et al. (p. 45-48) found on-farm efficiencies were especially low at only 2-15 percent for earth systems and 20-45 percent for lined systems. The same study noted that almost all Ecuador's irrigation systems are stream diversions and that irrigation must occur 24 hours per day to take full advantage of available water. Night irrigation was found to be very inefficient, especially on steeper slopes in the Sierra. As a result there may be as little as one-half the water effectively available as supplied. These stark realities expose the overly optimistic nature of feasibility studies which assumed much higher rates of

168

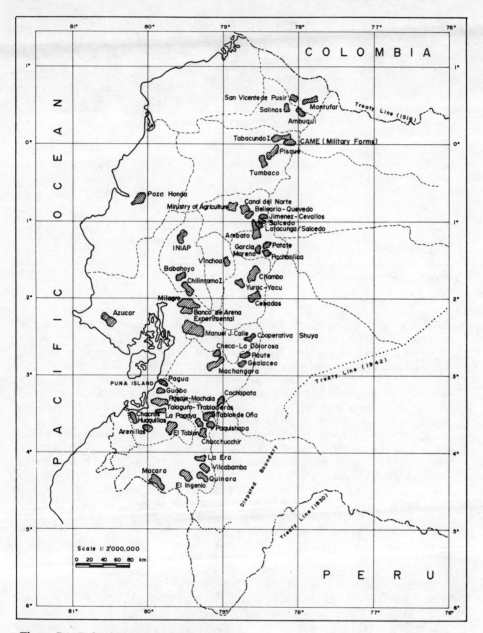

Figure 7.1 Irrigation Projects in Operation
Source: Prepared by authors from data provided by the various irrigation agencies. See
Whitaker, Colyer and Alzamora Appendix Tables 7.4 and 7.5.

efficiency in the main system and in on-farm applications than are being realized.

Efficiencies appear to be relatively lower in on-farm applications than in the main systems in all public projects (Keller, et al. 1982, p. 47). This suggests that on-farm water management should be the initial focus of technical assistance and training. There clearly is opportunity for substantial improvement in efficiency of on-farm water applications in Ecuador with already proven technologies. If efficiencies were improved by only one-third, there would be sufficient water to irrigate all the land that is currently irrigable in INERHI projects (79,289 hectares). Water resources sometimes prove insufficient to fully develop a project, despite initial hydrologic studies which document adequate supplies. The problem appears primarily to be incorrect measurements of available water supply at the feasibility stage of the project. This is due, at least in part, to several institutions being involved in water measurement. There currently is no system for linking these diverse networks into an integral information system. As a result, data on water supplies are less accurate than they might be and overestimations of flows occur. Projects which suffer from overestimations of water flows and also have inefficiencies in on-farm water applications obviously are constrained to much less irrigable area than planned.

Lack of funding also has constrained development of irrigation infrastructure and restricted expansion of the irrigable area toward the contemplated command area. INERHI has expended, on average, for all of its operating irrigation systems, only 79 percent of planned total project costs (Whitaker, Colyer and Alzamora Appendix Table 7.4). Only 16 of INERHI's 35 operational systems are 90 percent or more completed, as measured by accumulated expenditures as a share of total project costs. Construction tends to be delayed primarily because of funding shortfalls. Given inefficient on-farm water management and inadequate water supplies, the postponement of further investments in infrastructure has been efficient.

Future Irrigation Projects

There are a relatively large number of public irrigation projects either under construction or under serious study or design programmed for completion during the 1990s. If completed as planned these projects will substantially increase irrigated cropland in Ecuador but at very high costs and increased public foreign debt.

Projects under Construction

Projects currently under construction will expand the irrigated area by 108,109 hectares when and if fully implemented (Table 7.3, Figure 7.2). INERHI is the most important agency in terms of numbers and magnitude of new projects. It has 25 projects under construction with a planned command area of 62,318 hectares. The most important of these is Phase I of the Jubones Project of 15,600 hectares located in El Oro province. Other important projects include the Ambato-Huachi-Pelileo and Píllaro projects in Tungurahua province and the Tahuín project in El Oro province. The latter was part of PREDESUR's Puyango-Túmbez project but has been transferred to INERHI. The other 21 INERHI projects are much smaller, ranging from 170 to 3,100 hectares and are located throughout the country.

CEDEGE is the next most important irrigation agency in terms of new projects. It will add 32,691 hectares when three projects currently under construction are completed and fully implemented. The most important of these is the first phase of

Table 7.3 Irrigation Projects under Construction, January 1989

Entity/project	Province	Planned Command Area (hectares)	Expected Termination Date (year)
GRAND TOTAL		108,109	---
INERHI		62,318	---
Ambato-Huachi-Pelileo	Tungurahua	9,885	1990
Píllaro	Tungurahua	8,870	1995
Tahuín	El Oro	7,400	1994
Jubones Phase I	El Oro	15,600	1995
Others (21 Projects)	Various	20,583	---
CEDEGE		32,691	
Daule-Peripa Phase I	Guayas	17,000	1990
Santa Elena Phase I	Guayas	15,691	1990
Samborondón (Drainage)	Guayas	—	1991
CRM		13,100	
Poza Honda Rehabilitation	Manabí	6,500	1990
Jama	Manabí	2,000	1990
Briceño	Manabí	1,000	1990
Small Dams (9 Projects)	Manabí	3,600	---

Source: Whitaker, Colyer and Alzamora Appendix Tables 7.6 and 7.7.

the Daule-Peripa multipurpose project.[9] It includes the dam on the Daule River which was completed and placed in operation in 1988. Infrastructure for irrigation of 17,000 hectares on the right bank of the Daule has been completed but will not be operational until 1991. The second phase will add generation of electricity and the third will provide infrastructure to irrigate 33,000 hectares on the left bank of the Daule River.[10]

CEDEGE's second most important construction project is the first phase of its Santa Elena project.[11] The Santa Elena project utilizes water stored in the Daule-Peripa Reservoir for both irrigation and potable water throughout the Santa Elena Peninsula. The first phase of the project will pump water from the lower Daule River, near La Toma in Guayas Province, up 75 meters to an aqueduct which will carry it to the Chongón dam and distribution system for irrigation of 15,691 hectares in the Chongón-Playas area and potable water for Playas. The second phase of the project, which is under study and design, will irrigate another 27,192 hectares and provide potable water for Salinas and La Libertad. Water will be pumped uphill another 73 meters from the Chongón Reservoir and distributed via aqueducts and canals to various sites in the Western Santa Elena Peninsula.

CRM has three principal projects under construction, rehabilitation of the Poza Honda and Briceño projects and construction of the Jama project, which will irrigate 9,500 hectares in total. CRM has nearly completed rehabilitation of the Poza Honda project, which was damaged by flooding, and plans to add a net of 6,500 hectares to the 2,650 hectares that are now irrigable. The Jama project will add 2,000 hectares. The Briceño project is being rehabilitated and a net of 1,000 hectares will be added. CRM also is constructing nine small dams which will irrigate 3,600 hectares.

The actual increase in the area under irrigation from projects currently under construction probably will be smaller and slower than implied by their planned

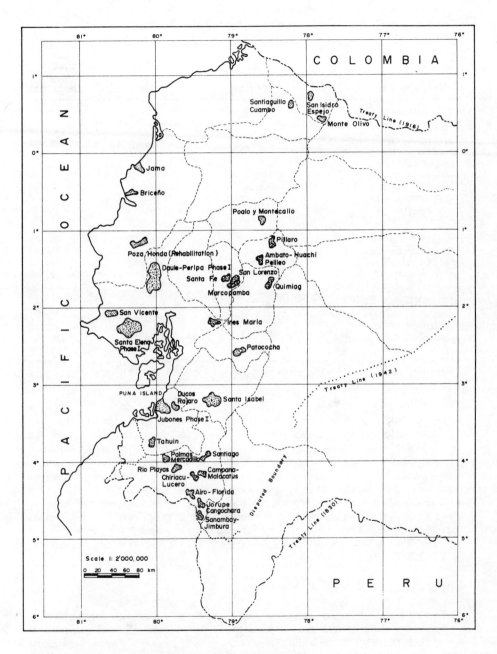

Figure 7.2 Irrigation Projects under Construction
Source : Prepared by authors from data provided by the various irrigation agencies
and Whitaker, Colyer and Alzamora Appendix Tables 7.6 and 7.7.

Table 7.4   Irrigation Projects under Design or Serious Study, January 1989

Entity/Project	Province	Stage of Study or Design	Planned Command Area (hectares)
GRAND TOTAL			294,308
INERHI			132,116
Artezon-Mira-El Angel	Carchi	Feas.	9,000
Tabacundo II (Tunnel)	Pichincha	Design	8,889
Chaupi Paloma	Cotopaxi	Feas.	10,700
Chalupas	Cotopaxi	Feas.	18,600
Banco de Arena	Guayas	Feas.	12,800
Catarama	Los Rios	Feas.	5,800
Jubones Phase II	El Oro	Design	38,400
Others (13 Projects)	Various	Des.-Feas	27,927
CEDEGE			68,192
Daule-Peripa Phase III	Guayas	Design	33,000
Santa Elena Phase II	Guayas	Design	27,192
Pedro Carbo	Guayas	Pre-Feas.	8,000
CRM			18,000
Carrizal-Chone	Manabí	Design	18,000
PREDESUR			76,000
Puyango-Túmbez	Loja	Feas.	70,000
Zapotillo Alto	Loja	Design	6,000

Source: Whitaker, Colyer and Alzamora Appendix Tables 7.8 and 7.9.

command area of 108,109 hectares. Financial and other constraints likely will slow down the completion of infrastructure. The result will be smaller irrigable areas than the planned command areas, even several years after planned completion dates in the early 1990s. Moreover, inefficient use of water at both the system and farm levels probably will limit the area actually irrigated to less than the irrigable area. Lack of complementary resources such as improved technological packages and associated modern factors of production (improved seeds, pesticides and fertilizers) will limit the profitability of irrigation and further constrain full utilization of the irrigable areas. These realities already have been demonstrated in the experience of INERHI's many operating irrigation systems. There is no reason to expect a greatly improved pattern in INERHI's new projects, or that CEDEGE or CRM, with less institutional capacity than INERHI, will fare any better.

Projects under Design or Study

There are a number of irrigation projects under design or serious study which have a planned command area of 294,308 hectares (Table 7.4, Figure 7.3). These projects include only those which are in the design phase or under feasibility study. In addition to these, there are a large number of other projects that are at the preliminary stages of identification and study which are not treated in this chapter. For example, INERHI alone has 36 other projects (besides those listed in Table 7.4) which are under

173

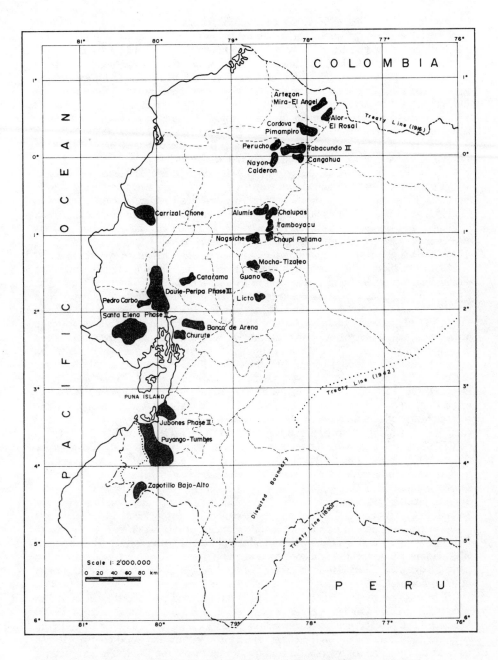

Figure 7.3 Irrigation Projects under Design or Serious Study
Source: Prepared by authors from data provided by the various irrigation agencies
and Whitaker, Colyer and Alzamora Appendix Tables 7.8 and 7.9.

preliminary study that would irrigate another 152,058 hectares.[12]

INERHI is the most important public irrigation agency in terms of projects now under design or in serious study, with 132,116 hectares, followed by CEDEGE with 68,192, PREDESUR with 76,000 and CRM with 18,000. Several are second and third stages of projects currently under construction and likely will advance to the construction stage by the early to mid-1990s. They will be subject to the same funding and operational constraints discussed above for projects now under construction. It is unlikely that projects now under design or study will be completed before the late 1990s or increase the area irrigated in any significant way until after 2000.

INERHI's most important project is Phase II of the Jubones project with an additional 38,400 hectares of planned command area, which is at the design stage and is expected to move to construction in the early 1990s. The Tabacundo II project (8,889 hectares) also is designed and construction will begin when financing can be arranged. Other important projects include Artezon-Mira-El Angel in Carchi province, Chalupas and Chaupi Palama in Cotopaxi province and Catarama and Banco de Arena in Guayas and Los Rios provinces, respectively. INERHI also has 13 other projects at design or feasibility stage totaling 27,927 hectares.

INERHI is planning the rehabilitation of five of its older irrigation systems at a cost of US$17.3 million. The most important of these is the Chambo system which was designed with too small a diversion dam to irrigate the planned command area. The cost of this modification is projected to be US$12.0 million, which seems very high for the benefits expected. Other systems planned for renovation include Salinas, Pisque, Tumbaco and Manuel J. Calle. The latter is afflicted with serious drainage problems which, if not resolved, may obviate the utility of recent improvements in the distribution system. INERHI also is continuing its program to repair and improve the acequias and shallow wells of small farmers. While INERHI had planned to continue its flood control program in the Lower Guayas River Basin, this activity was transferred to CEDEGE early in 1989, along with responsibility for the Catarama irrigation project. Moreover, it is possible that INERHI's three large irrigation projects in the region (Milagro, Chilintomo and Manuel J. Calle), which are an integral part of flood control infrastructure, also could be transferred to CEDEGE.

CEDEGE has two major projects in the design stage and is seeking financing for them. One is the Phase III of the Daule-Peripa project which will construct infrastructure to irrigate 33,000 hectares on the right bank of the Daule river. The second is Phase II of the Santa Elena project which will provide irrigation water for an additional 27,192 hectares in the Santa Elena Peninsula and potable water for Salinas and La Libertad. Each of these sub-projects is closely related to investments made in the first phases and the economic viability of the Daule-Peripa and Santa Elena projects depends on completion of all the phases of both projects. It is expected that funding will be secured and construction on these two sub-projects will start in the early 1990s. CEDEGE also is in process of final design of the Pedro Carbo project of 8,000 hectares.

CRM has one major project which has been designed and shortly will be under construction. The Carrizal-Chone project has a planned command area of 18,000 hectares. The project includes construction of the La Esperanza dam on the Carrizal river and the Grande dam on the Chone river for irrigation and flood control. It also includes an aqueduct for inter-basin transfer of water from the Daule-Peripa reservoir to the La Esperanza reservoir and from there to the Poza Honda reservoir to augment the supply of potable water for Portoviejo. Construction of the La Esperanza dam is expected to begin in late 1990.

PREDESUR is just letting contracts for the feasibility studies of the Puyango-Túmbez project which will irrigate an estimated 70,000 hectares in Loja when it is completed (PREDESUR). The initiation of construction is likely several years away,since financing still has to be secured.

Nothing is known about the status of any current construction or plans for private irrigation. Even after completion of public projects currently under construction, private irrigation at the current level of 330,000 hectares will substantially exceed public irrigation of 196,068 hectares. The actual gap will probably be even greater as the planned command areas of public projects will not be realized.

The total area under public and private irrigation if all public projects in construction and under design and study were fully implemented would be 820,376 hectares, nearly doubling the area currently under irrigation.[13] INERHI will continue to be the dominant irrigation agency even if all the projects under construction and study by other agencies are fully implemented. Because of the constraints discussed above, the irrigable area from new public projects is expected to be much smaller than the planned command areas and the irrigated areas smaller than the irrigable areas. Also, it will require much longer to bring these reduced areas under irrigation than planned in overly ambitious schedules.

Financing Irrigation Projects

The process for approving and financing public irrigation projects in Ecuador is largely decentralized and highly subjective. There is only a limited attempt by the National Development Council (CONADE) to enforce the application of objective criteria and procedures in setting national priorities for allocation of investment capital (Cox, Cox and Tolosa 64 ff.). The result is intense interinstitutional competition for financing development projects.

Funding for irrigation projects for every public entity comes from two principal sources, domestic (government) and external (primarily bilateral and multilateral development agencies). Domestic resources for the public irrigation agencies include funds from taxes earmarked for specific activities, revenues from tariffs and other services, funds from the general budget, internal credits and donations from domestic agencies.

The sources of funds limit flexibility in applying objective criteria to allocation of funds. For example, INERHI receives earmarked tax proceeds from the *Plan Loja* which must be used for irrigation projects in the Loja province. It also receives funds from a tax on Central Bank credits that goes into a National Fund for Irrigation and Drainage (FONARYD) half of which must be used for the Jubones irrigation project. International and domestic credits and donations almost always reflect perspectives and interests of the funding sources. The flexibility represented by income from water tariffs and direct budget support is relatively small. Tariffs have averaged about 3-4 percent of INERHI's income in recent years and much smaller shares for CEDEGE and CRM (Cox, Cox and Tolosa p. 64). Direct budget support has averaged about 25-30 percent.

The decentralized and politicized system for financing irrigation projects has several undesirable effects. An unhealthy competition has ensued between the principal irrigation agencies. Another undesirable effect of decentralized project development and financing is the failure to complete projects while undertaking new projects. Another manifestation of problems with the decentralized approval and financing

Table 7.5   INERHI Investments in Infrastructure in its Operational Irrigation
            Systems, through 1988

| Irrigation System (name) | Share Completed (%) | Costs to Date (1988 sucres) | | Inferred Total Costs (million) |
		Total (million)	Per Irrigable Hectare	
INERHI Total	79.4	75,313.1	949,855	94,839.8
Montufar	96.8	6,845.0	2,444,632	7,073.8
San Vicente de P.	100.0	337.9	844,625	337.9
Ambuquí	81.5	1,307.0	986,415	1,603.1
Salinas	96.8	3,243.0	1,544,281	3,351.4
Tabacundo I(Wells)	100.0	425.5	236,635	425.5
Pisque	93.8	13,145.3	2,094,873	14,012.0
Tumbaco	72.5	2,574.2	1,336,563	3,552.1
Lat./Sal./Ambato	98.0	6,017.7	716,389	6,138.7
Jiménez-Cevallos	100.0	89.1	127,300	89.1
Canal del Norte	67.0	158.0	158,020	235.9
Pujilí		147.4	733,483	
Pachanlica	89.0	354.2	590,250	397.9
Garcia Moreno	90.2	325.5	325,530	360.9
Patate	66.7	116.7	166,743	175.1
Chambo	56.7	13,809.1	2,191,913	24,354.2
Cebadas	100.0	384.9	641,533	384.9
Yurac-Yacu	96.2	57.3	190,967	59.5
Vinchoa	79.8	54.1	135,325	67.9
Machángara	73.8	2,225.3	2,674,663	3,016.4
Tablón de Oña	86.4	266.9	266,870	308.9
Macará	86.1	3,327.2	1,848,428	3,866.0
La Papaya	83.0	333.5	476,400	401.7
La Era	100.0	169.8	424,575	169.8
El Ingenio	90.7	241.6	604,050	266.4
Paquishapa	88.6	225.0	562,475	253.9
Chucchucchir	100.0	77.7	310,960	77.7
Quinara	100.0	504.9	1,262,200	504.9
Vilcabamba	100.0	168.3	561,133	168.3
Milagro	89.8	11,992.5	1,050,135	13,354.3
Chilintomo I	51.9	184.1	167,355	0.0
Manuel J. Calle	58.1	5,785.9	262,993	9,959.6
Azúcar	80.5	185.8	764,403	230.6
Banco de Arena	28.6	35.5	132,045	124.3
Chacras-Huaqui.	61.9	92.5	370,000	149.5
El Tablón	100.0	104.7	149,600	104.7

Source: Whitaker, Colyer and Alzamora Appendix Tables 7.4 and 7.10.

system is the tendency to construct interrelated elements of projects out of sequence,
such as occurred in the Santa Elena project.

Costs and Public Debt

Expenditures on public sector irrigation and water resources have averaged nearly
40 percent of the public sector budget for agriculture for nearly two decades (see
Chapter 11 Table 11.3).   In contrast, the area actually irrigated by public sector
projects in 1987 of 87,959 hectares is about 6 percent of average cropland during 1980-

Table 7.6 Cost of New, Public Irrigation and Multipurpose Projects
           (Million, 1988 Prices)

Entity	Under Construction		Under Design and Study		Total Under Design or Construction	
	(sucres)	(dollars)	(sucres)	(dollars)	(sucres)	(dollars)
TOTAL	480,867.0	1,102.4	489,370.6	1,121.9	970,237.6	2,224.3
INERHI	72,446.8	166.1	201,563.5	462.1	274,010.3	628.2
CEDEGE	384,375.0	881.2	205,323.6	470.7	589,698.6	1,351.9
CRM	24,045.2	55.1	28,788.5	66.0	52,833.7	121.1
PREDESUR	0.0	0.0	53,695.0	123.1	53,695.0	123.1

Source: Whitaker, Colyer and Alzamora Appendix Tables 7.7 and 7.9.

1985 (see Chapter 6). The share of agriculture's GDP derived from publicly irrigated agriculture is not known but probably is not much different than 6 percent. Thus, public expenditures to operate irrigation systems seem disproportionately large relative to the importance of irrigated cropland.

The cost of infrastructure for INERHI's 35 operating irrigation systems through 1988 is estimated to be S/.75,313.1 million in 1988 constant prices, or US$172.7 million, at the free market exchange rate of S/.436.19/US$1 in 1988 (Table 7.5).[14] The value in 1988 prices of other public irrigation infrastructure is estimated at S/.34,152.0 million or US$78.3 million.[15] Thus, the total value of all public irrigation systems now in operation is S/.109,465.1 million or US$251.0 million, on the basis of these estimates. These estimates do not include the costs of operations and maintenance, services, institutional development, central administration, national level water and irrigation and drainage management, nor water measurement by INAMHI.

The costs of INERHI's infrastructure per irrigable hectare averaged S/.949,855 (US$2,177.62) in 1988 but varied considerably among operational irrigation systems. Such costs range from a low of S/.127,300 per irrigable hectare in Jiménez-Cevallos to S/.2,674,663 in Machangara. The great variability in costs suggests some projects may be viable with much lower benefits relative to higher-cost projects.

As noted above, more than half of INERHI's 35 operational irrigation systems are less than 90 percent complete and average only 79 percent complete based on accumulated costs as a share of total costs. The total cost in 1988 prices of these projects is estimated at S/.94,839.8 million or US$217.4 million.[16] Thus, INERHI needs another US$44.7 million just to finish the partially completed projects that are in operation.

The proposed cost of new irrigation and multipurpose projects under construction is US$1.1 billion and those under design and study another US$1.1 billion, or a total of US$2.2 billion (Table 7.6). This estimate includes only those projects currently under construction and those under design or study that are under serious consideration for implementation. It does not include a large number of projects that are under preliminary review and that currently are low priority.[17]

Financing of these projects has contributed significantly to Ecuador's foreign debt (Table 7.7). The debt from irrigation and multipurpose projects in operation and under construction is estimated to be US$1.1 billion or 11.6 percent of the foreign debt.[18] When only the irrigation component is considered the amount is US$312.3 million and 3.3 percent of the foreign debt, still significant levels. If multipurpose and

Table 7.7   Importance of Irrigation and Multipurpose Projects in the Foreign Debt
(Million of 1988 Dollars)

Item	Operating Systems (a)	Under Construction (b)	Subtotal (a+b)	Under Design and Study (d)	Total (a+b+d)
Total Cost	251.0	1,102.4	1,353.4	1,121.9	2,475.3
Irrigation Cost[a]	251.0	235.4	486.4	640.9	127.3
Irrigation/Total (%)	100.0	21.0	36.0	57.0	46.0
Financed Abroad[a] (All Components)	100.4	992.2	1,092.6	1,009.7	2,102.3
Financed Abroad[b] (Irrigation Component)	100.4	211.9	312.3	576.8	889.1
Foreign Debt[c]	9,395.0	9,395.0	9,395.0	10,516.9	10,516.9
Financed Abroad/Debt (All Components)	1.1%	10.6%	11.6%	9.6%	20.0%
Financed Abroad/Debt (Irrigation Component)	1.1%	2.3%	3.3%	5.5%	8.5%

Source: Tables 7.5 and 7.6; BCE 1989, pp. 85-86 for data on the foreign debt.

[a]The cost of the irrigation component was estimated from the cost of infrastructure per hectare for INERHI projects (US$2,177.62 at the 1988 free market exchange rate of S/.436.19/US$1) multiplied by the command area of projects under construction, or under design and study from Table 7.5.
[b]See Note 18 for assumptions.
[c]The cost of projects under design and study is added to the 1988 debt for calculation of the debt share for such projects.

irrigation projects currently under design and study are implemented, the magnitude of the debt burden will increase by US$1.0 billion, to US$2.1 billion or to 20.0 percent of the foreign debt. Moreover, projects under design and study are much more irrigation intensive than projects under construction, with irrigation components accounting for 57 percent of total costs for the former and only 21 percent for the latter. As a result, the share of the public debt from irrigation components of projects will rise sharply to 8.5 percent of foreign debt when projects under design and study are implemented.

Subsidies and the Water Tariff

Public irrigation projects in Ecuador are heavily subsidized. Ecuadorian law stipulates that such subsidies be given through the water tariff. Thus, irrigation water is priced much lower than the cost of providing it. The irrigation subsidy is one of the largest provided by the government and has contributed substantially to recent budget deficits.

INERHI is responsible legally for establishing water tariffs for all public irrigation projects. The water tariff has two components, the basic tariff which recovers some capital costs and the volumetric tariff which is supposed to recover all the costs of operation and maintenance.

The basic tariff is for "...amortizing the capital invested by INERHI in constructing infrastructure in its irrigation systems..." (INERHI n.d., p. 2, translation by authors.) The total cost of the infrastructure is updated annually to account for new investments but is not adjusted for inflation. The law stipulates that 25 percent of the cost of infrastructure and all of the interest on capital be given as subsidies to water users. The period of time over which the reduced capital costs are to be recovered is 75 years for surface irrigation and 12 years for wells. The cost per year then is divided by the number of irrigable hectares to determine the basic tariff per hectare. A single, average tariff is calculated each year for all surface systems and individual tariffs for each subterranean system.[19] The basic tariff in equation form for surface systems is:

$$\text{Basic Tariff} = \frac{(\text{Total Investment})(.75)}{(\text{Irrigable Area})(75)}$$

The second component is the volumetric tariff. The Water Tariff Regulation specifies that it is to be calculated by dividing the operation and maintenance costs for all projects by the volume (cubic meters) of water used to calculate a uniform tariff (INERHI n.d., p. 4). INERHI converts the volumetric tariff to a per hectare basis because measurement of water supplied to individual farmers is not widespread. This is done by using standard water requirements for each crop, by soil and climate and then applying these requirements to the crop mix for each irrigation project to determine the water requirement per hectare. The cost per hectare is obtained by multiplying the cost per cubic meter of water by the requirement per hectare. The volumetric tariff charged to each farmer then is determined by multiplying the per hectare water requirement by the number of hectares irrigated.

The magnitude of the subsidy inherent in the basic tariff can be estimated by comparing it with the annual cost of amortizing the irrigation infrastructure. The basic tariff for 1989 for INERHI's 35 operating irrigation systems is calculated to be S/.686 per irrigable hectare. This estimate is based on the sum, in current prices of each year (S/.5,436.5 million) of all past capital investments using the above formula (Table 7.8; Whitaker, Colyer and Alzamora Appendix Tables 7.4 and 7.10).[20] INERHI investments in the same systems through December 1988 in 1988 prices were S/.75,313.1 million.[21] The cost to amortize this amount over 40 years (a typical term for a loan for irrigation infrastructure) using an interest rate of 6 percent is S/.63,129 per hectare per year. The difference (S/.62,443) between this and the basic tariff is the per hectare subsidy paid by the government to construct irrigation infrastructure. Thus, the government is subsidizing 99 percent of the costs of irrigation infrastructure in the 35 INERHI systems currently in operation. This subsidy will have to be paid every year for 40 years, under the assumptions of this example, to pay all the interest and capital costs.

The volumetric tariff also is subsidized. It is estimated that S/.1,861.1 million (constant 1988 prices) on average per year during 1985-1988 related closely to the operation and maintenance of irrigation systems but were not accounted for in the volumetric tariff.[22] These costs were one-fourth of INERHI's average annual budget during 1985-1988 and nearly fifteen times the 1987 operations and maintenance costs of S/.98.0 million, which were included by INERHI in the calculation of its 1988 volumetric tariff. This is an additional subsidy of S/.23,472 per irrigable hectare (79,289 hectares). The INERHI volumetric tariff for potatoes, which demand

Table 7.8   INERHI: Capital, and Operation and Maintenance Costs; the Water Tariff;
            and the State Subsidy in 1988, per Irrigable Hectare (1988 Sucres)

Item	Capital Costs	Operations & Maintenance	Total Costs	Share (%)
Actual Cost	63,129	26,534	89,663	100.0
Water Tariff	686	3,062	3,748	4.2
Subsidy	62,443	23,472	85,915	95.8

Source: Calculated by authors (see text).

substantial water, was S/.3,062 per hectare in 1988. This upper-limit tariff is assumed to represent the average volumetric tariff for all INERHI water users in 1988 in this analysis of subsidies (INERHI 1987b, p. 11). Thus, the volumetric tariff charged by INERHI is much lower than it would be if all relevant costs were included.

The total subsidy is estimated to be S/.85,915 per irrigable hectare for INERHI projects comprised of the subsidy to capital of S/.62,443 and to operations and maintenance of S/.23,472 (Table 7.8). This amounts to 96 percent of the total costs of providing the water and is a major drain on government resources.

Other regional irrigation agencies are supposed to charge a water tariff based on the same criteria as INERHI and under INERHI's supervision. In fact, CEDEGE, CRM, CREA and PREDESUR have established their own criteria for water tariffs with generally greater subsidies than INERHI (Cox, Cox and Tolosa p. 102).

The magnitude of the annual government subsidy to all operational public irrigation systems as of December 1988 is estimated to be S/.9,901.2 million, or US$22.7 million based on the INERHI subsidy per hectare of S/.85,915, the irrigable area of 115,244 hectares in all operational projects and the 1988 free market exchange rate of S/.436.19/US$1.0 (see Whitaker, Colyer and Alzamora Appendix Table 7.11). Government subsidies to irrigation will increase by another US$21.3 million in the next few years to a total of US$44.0 million as large new projects now under construction are completed, assuming the same subsidy per hectare and an irrigable area of 108,109 hectares. A similar calculation reveals that the subsidy will increase by another US$58.0 million to US$102.0 million when high-priority projects under design or study with a command area of 294,308 hectares become operational.

The very large current subsidies and the likelihood that they will double in size when projects now under construction are completed is cause for serious concern. Such subsidies increase the debt burden, contribute to fiscal stress and greater budget deficits, reduce foreign exchange reserves and make it more difficult to contain inflationary pressures. The large subsidies also result in waste of water resources. When water is so substantially underpriced, farmers use more than is needed. Greatly underpriced water explains, in large part, the very low levels of efficiency in on-farm applications of water and why public irrigation projects generally yield low economic returns to relatively large public investments.

Economic Viability of Irrigation

There is evidence that irrigation systems in Ecuador generate much smaller economic returns than estimated in the economic analyses of feasibility studies, which tend to be unduly optimistic. *Ex ante* economic evaluations of proposed irrigation projects likely have overestimated the internal rate of return or benefit-cost ratio. A review of 34 feasibility studies by INERHI revealed that 31 of the 34 had estimated ex ante internal rates of return ranging from 12 to 40 percent and all were positive.[23] These studies generally assumed that: (a) all infrastructure for the planned command area would be constructed and in an unrealistically short time; (b) all the planned command area would be irrigated also in an unrealistically short time; (c) water would be used at relatively high levels of efficiency both at the system levels and in on-farm applications; (d) the water flow was sufficient for the planned command area; (e) farmers would be able to significantly increase productivity and yields; (f) water tariffs and fees would be collected fully; and (g) costs of project construction and operation would not increase.

There are only two ex post facto economic evaluations of the actual performance of irrigation projects in Ecuador in contrast to the large numbers of ex ante feasibility studies. These are evaluations of the Montufar and Milagro projects by Inter-American Development Bank (IDB) and the World Bank, respectively. Thus, there has been almost no attempt by INERHI or other regional or planning agencies in Ecuador to measure the actual performance of irrigation systems, relative to what was predicted.

The results of these two studies and other evidence indicate that actual economic returns to public investments in irrigation are much lower than estimated in feasibility studies. The IDB evaluation of Montufar found that the harvested area was only 29 percent of project design and the increase in profits per hectare was only 43 percent of project design. The net result was that profits had increased by only 17 percent of what was planned in project design, five years after completion of infrastructure and with lined tertiary canals. The project had 3,500 hectares of irrigable land but was irrigating only 1,800 hectares. It experienced a cost overrun of 64 percent with a total cost of US$6.9 million, or US$3,833 per irrigated hectare. The internal rate of return was only 5 percent compared to an estimated rate of return of 26 percent in the feasibility study. Even today the Montufar project shows signs of low returns, with a reduced irrigable area of only 2,800 hectares and an irrigated area of 2,238 hectares.

Similar results were obtained by the World Bank in a 1982 review and evaluation of the Milagro project. Milagro is clearly one of INERHI's most inefficient projects. There had been only a modest increase in the irrigated area of the project since 1973. Even today, only 3,150 hectares are irrigated out of an irrigable area of 11,420 hectares. There are large investments in a machinery pool and other complementary inputs which are relatively unproductive. The mix of crops has changed very little and increases in profits per hectare are very small.

The ex post facto evaluations of specific projects and the general evidence lead to the conclusion that expected benefits do not begin as soon nor in nearly as large a magnitude as projected in feasibility studies. The major portion of costs, however, tend to occur before the irrigation system is operational and well before any substantial flow of benefits. Costs also tend to be greater than those planned at the design stage. It is well known that the internal rate of return, or benefit-cost ratio is very sensitive to the timing of the flow of project benefits relative to costs. If benefits are not realized for several years later than projected, the internal rate of return will be substantially smaller. And if the benefits not only are postponed but are smaller than expected, the internal rate of return will be even smaller. Finally, if costs are greater than planned, the rate will be smaller still.

There are three main reasons why net benefits to public irrigation projects are lower than expected. First, projects usually begin operation only partially completed because of cost overruns and slowdowns in construction. Second, technical efficiency of water use is much lower than assumed, or less water is available at the source than estimated, which limit the area that can be irrigated. Third, complementary inputs and improved technical practices are not adopted on the irrigated land as quickly or as widely as was planned. Thus, yields and net increases in income (profits) from irrigation remain relatively low.

The Size and Distribution of Benefits

Irrigation projects permit farmers who begin to irrigate their land to realize increased profits (project benefits), with the better farmers producing relatively greater benefits. These benefits are produced because irrigation and complementary inputs allow farmers to increase productivity, production and profits. Project benefits are defined as the increase in profits per unit of irrigation water utilized, after paying for all the additional inputs required to adopt irrigation and associated technological packages.

Project benefits from irrigation generally continue year after year. They tend to be capitalized into the value of the land when the right to use the water is tied to the land because they are perceived as permanent increases in profits due to adoption of irrigation. Thus, the original owners of the land receive all the economic rents as a lump sum (present value of future net project benefits) from irrigation projects when they sell the land. Private benefits from irrigation are in direct proportion to original land ownership. Consequently, land values will tend to fall for all owners if the government raises the water tariff in an attempt to pass on more of the cost to farmers. Second owners will be decapitalized when user fees are raised because they paid the original owners a higher price of land reflecting the lower water tariff.[24]

Private investments to utilize irrigation water from public projects in Ecuador will realize higher rates of return than the public investments in the project, because of the large government subsidy to irrigation water. Utilization of irrigation water from public projects (instead of relying of rainfall) entails additional private costs for the water tariff and other complementary inputs (such as infrastructure for on-farm irrigation, improved seeds, fertilizers, etc.). Once these costs have been covered by the value of increased production, the farmer realizes an increase in profits and private investments to utilize irrigation water from the public system are profitable.

However, the water tariff covers only about 5 percent of the total costs of delivering water to the farm, with a government subsidy in 1988 of S/.85,915/irrigable hectare/year. The increase in private profits must be sufficient to pay for all of the subsidy in order for public investments in irrigation projects to become socially profitable. When the increase in profits exceeds the subsidy the social benefit-cost ratio is greater than one and the internal rate of return is positive.[25] The size of project benefits is of critical concern, both in terms of measuring the degree to which farmers capture government subsidies and of determining if public investments are socially profitable.

Table 7.9 Weighted Average of the Differences in the Value of Irrigated and Unirrigated Land of Similar Quality for Operational Irrigation Projects, January-May, 1989

System	Number of Observations	Mean Difference in Value of Land (1,000 sucres)	Irrigable Area (hectares)	Total Value (1,000 sucres)
INERHI				
Montufar	6	450	2,800	1,260,000
San Vicente de P.	1	1,350	400	540,000
Ambuqui	1	1,350	1,325	1,788,750
Salinas	1	650	2,100	1,365,000
Tabacundo I(Wells)	1	250	1,789	447,250
Pisque	1	200	6,275	1,255,000
Lat./Sal./Ambato	3	700	8,400	5,880,000
Chambo	2	1,125	6,300	7,087,500
Cebadas	1	650	600	390,000
Milagro	3	370	11,420	4,225,400
Manuel J. Calle	2	325	22,000	7,150,000
CRM (Poza Honda)	2	410	2,650	1,086,500
CEDEGE (Babahoyo)	1	250	4,700	1,175,000
TOTAL	25	476[a]	70,759	33,650,400

Source: Informal survey conducted during January-May of 1989 (see Whitaker, Colyer and Alzamora Appendix Table 7.12).

[a] Weighted Average.

One method for estimating the magnitude of project benefits is to determine the increase in the value of land due to irrigation. As noted above, the annual net benefits from irrigation projects which accrue to farmers, tend to be capitalized into the value of farmers' land. Informal surveys of knowledgeable people (farmers, real estate agents and officials of the Chambers of Agriculture) during January-May 1989 revealed substantial differences between the value of irrigated land and the value of unirrigated land of similar quality near the irrigation project in question (Table 7.9). The survey included 25 observations in all the major irrigated areas of the country and covered projects that account for 61 percent of the irrigable area of all public projects currently in operation. Differences in the value of irrigated and unirrigated land are highly variable, ranging from S/.160,000 to S/.1,700,000 per hectare and reflect the present value of the stream of expected benefits produced by the irrigation project.

The difference between the value of unirrigated and irrigated land necessary to reflect a benefit stream sufficiently large to pay the irrigation subsidy is S/.1,292,703/hectare. This "break-even" value is easily calculated as the present value of a benefit stream equal to the irrigation subsidy of S/.85,915 per hectare, given some time period over which the annual benefits flow and a discount rate. Utilizing the same parameters as in the estimate of the subsidy to public projects (40 years and 6 percent interest) permits comparison of the estimated average subsidy with the benefit stream implicit in the difference in land values.[26] The observed differences in land values indicate that most irrigation projects produce net benefit streams that are substantially less than the average subsidy, although a few projects are socially profitable. Farmers reap some or all of the public irrigation subsidy in the form of

Table 7.10 Allocation of Subsidies and Benefits of Public Irrigation Projects in
           Ecuador, 1989 (Million of Sucres and Million of Dollars, 1988 Prices[a])

Item		Subsidy	Benefit	Difference (Loss)
Per Hectare(sucres)	S/.	85,915.0	31,636.0[b]	54,279.0
Present INERHI	S/.	6,812.1	2,508.4	4,303.7
(79,289 hectares)	US$	15.6	5.8	9.9
Present Public	S/.	9,901.2	3,645.9	6,255.3
(115,244 hectares)	US$	22.7	8.4	14.3
Under Construction	S/.	9,288.2	3,420.1	5,868.0
(108,109 hectares)	US$	21.3	7.8	13.5
Total (Current &	S/.	19,189.4	7,066.0	12,123.4
Under Construction)	US$	44.0	16.2	27.8
(223,353 hectares)				

Source: Tables 7.2, 7.3 and 7.8.

[a] Sucres converted to dollars at the average free market rate for 1988 of S/.436.19
per dollar.
[b] Calculated by authors from difference in land values (see text).

increased profits that are reflected in higher land values. In those projects where
benefits are not sufficient to pay for all the costs of water, part of the subsidy is wasted.
All projects which have a difference in land values less than the break-even of
S/.1,292,703 are socially unprofitable and part of the subsidy is lost.

The amount of the subsidy that is wasted can be roughly approximated from the
survey data on land values. The weighted average of the differences in the value of
irrigated and unirrigated land of S/.476,000 is an estimate of the average increase in
the value of land due to irrigation. The average annual benefit stream from public
irrigation projects reflected in this average of increased land values due to irrigation
is S/.31,636, assuming the same parameters of 40 years and a discount rate of 6
percent. Farmers actually receive, on average, only 37 percent of the subsidy of
S/.85,915 and the balance is completely wasted. Project benefits are substantially less
than predicted and planned and are not sufficient to cover the costs of providing the
water. This analysis suggests that public irrigation projects are socially unprofitable on
average, with a benefit-cost ratio of less than one.

The allocation of subsidies and benefits is summarized for operating irrigation
systems and for those under construction (Table 7.10). The estimated annual subsidy
to public irrigation systems in operation was US$22.7 million. Farmers capture US$8.4
million of this subsidy each year in the form of increased profits, which tends to be
capitalized into the value of their land. The value of land is increased by an estimated
S/.54,857.3 million or US$125.8 million, which is received as a windfall gain when the
land is sold.[27]

The balance of the annual subsidy, amounting to US$14.3 million is lost and wasted
in the form of unproductive irrigation infrastructure. Given the limited demand for
used dams and lined canals, there is little likelihood that such losses ever will be
recovered without significant complementary investments to make existing projects
more efficient and productive. When projects under construction are completed the
amount of the annual subsidy will nearly double to US$44.0 million, with US$16.2

million being captured by farmers and the balance of US$27.8 million being lost.

The distribution of benefits from irrigation is directly proportional to the distribution of land ownership. Unfortunately, data on land ownership in public irrigation projects is extremely limited. The only data available were for the Pisque project for 1981 (S.A. AGRER N.V. and INERHI Annexes, p. 286). These data, based on a sample of about one-third of 2,569 water users, indicate that land ownership is highly concentrated. Since project benefits are directly proportional to land ownership, this means that benefits from the Pisque project are distributed very unequally with a relatively small number of landowners receiving the bulk of the benefits as a government subsidy. The 53 largest land owners constituted only 5.5 percent of all farmers but owned 45.2 percent of the land. In contrast, the 1,521 farmers with the smallest holdings were 52.9 percent of all farmers but had only 13.7 percent of the land (720 hectares).

Thus, a small number of farmers with large land holdings are the principal beneficiaries of public irrigation projects. The conventional wisdom that such projects benefit primarily small farmers is a myth. Moreover, relatively few farmers utilize public irrigation with only an estimated 64,200 doing so in 1988. Justification of irrigation projects on social grounds (i.e., improving the wellbeing of poor farmers with small holdings) is as poorly founded as the ex ante attempts to rationalize such projects on the basis of economic (efficiency) criteria.

Conclusions and Recommendations

There are several results from this study which indicate that public resources dedicated to irrigation are used very inefficiently. These findings suggest the need for substantial reallocation of these scarce development resources if more rapid agricultural development is to be realized. The major conclusions of the study are summarized and recommendations for more productive public investments are made.

Conclusions

Irrigation is an important aspect of agriculture, with nearly one in four hectares of cropland under irrigation in 1987 and nearly 80 percent of this in private irrigation. The area irrigated by private systems is widely accepted estimate but needs to be confirmed. Case studies indicate private systems are less capital intensive and more carefully managed than public systems, with greater efficiency in on-farm applications of water and higher yields than in public projects.

Projects under construction, and design or serious study would nearly double the irrigated area from 417,959 to 820,376 hectares if fully implemented. Expansion of the area under irrigation is not likely to materialize nearly as quickly, nor in the magnitudes planned in project designs and studies. On the basis of past INERHI experience, additional area under irrigation from projects now under construction will be about 40,670 hectares, not the 108,109 hectares planned and this would not be in production until the mid-to-late 1990s. Another 110,718 hectares would be brought into irrigation from projects now under design or study by 2000-2010 not the 294,308 hectares planned. This would add 151,388 hectares to that now irrigated (89,959 public and 330,000 private) for a total of 569,347 hectares, compared to a planned total of 820,376 hectares. If this is the actual experience of these projects, then project benefits will be lower than predicted and economic returns will be much smaller.

Public irrigation projects are, on average, not economically viable, with costs that exceed benefits. While ex ante economic studies exude optimism, ex post facto studies present a more sobering picture of cost overruns and of much smaller and later benefits than predicted. Annual benefits are estimated to average about 35 percent of the annual subsidy to irrigation water in INERHI systems and are likely no higher in other public projects.

Public irrigation projects are highly subsidized, with farmers paying only about 4 percent of the total costs of irrigation water, on average. The balance of the costs are a government subsidy that is estimated at US$23.3 million per year in 1988. Farmers receive about US$8.6 million of the subsidy annually in the form of increased profits (project benefits) from irrigation. The balance of US$14.7 million is wasted in sunk costs of unproductive and unsalable irrigation infrastructure. Project benefits would have to increase by the amount of the lost subsidy (US$14.7 million) before projects become, on average, socially profitable. And if the increased profits were substantially later than the investments in infrastructure, the projects still could be uneconomic.

Financing of public, multipurpose irrigation projects comprises a significant part of the foreign public debt. The value of foreign financing of projects now in operation and under construction is estimated to be US$1.1 billion. This is 11.6 percent of the public foreign debt and imposes a substantial burden on the economy, especially in terms of balance of payments and inflationary pressures. When projects currently under design and study are financed the debt share will increase to 20.0 percent. The negative impact of these debts is magnified because the investments are so unproductive. They represent a continued drain on the economy rather than contributing significantly to economic growth and development. The government will have to pay the relatively large irrigation subsidy for many years to come with little hope of project benefits ever covering all the cost of providing the water.

Benefits from irrigation projects are very unequally distributed, with large landowners receiving disproportionately large shares. Annual project benefits tend to be capitalized into the value of the land and accrue to the original owner of the land when it is sold. Thus, project benefits are proportional to the size of land holdings of the original owners.

Project benefits are very small and later than expected because of low levels of efficiency in on-farm applications of water. Efficiency is so low that the area irrigated is nearly one-third less that installed capacity. Benefits also are less than predicted because the installed capacity is less than planned. This is a secondary concern since the existing infrastructure is being utilized at much less than capacity.

Yields and profits are much lower than expected because of inadequate public investments in technology development and diffusion--one of the major deficiencies in Ecuadorian agriculture. Lack of adequate support in science and technology related to soil, water and plant relationships and in on-farm use of water has seriously constrained the viability of investments in irrigation infrastructure. Public irrigation agencies have attempted to address the problem of low productivity through machinery pools, subsidized fertilizer, demonstration farms and technical assistance. These efforts have been very small and disparate, and duplicate other programs. Investments in irrigation have been further constrained by the unfavorable macroeconomic policy environment which has depressed the price of agricultural products and subsidized industry.

The national-level functions of planning, administering and regulating: (a) water use; and (b) irrigation, drainage and flood control have been given very limited budget support and leadership. INERHI, which is assigned these functions by law, has concentrated the major share of its resources on its third function, the construction and operation of irrigation systems. INERHI's organization structure subordinates the first two functions to the third. This likely both partially explains and is a result of the allocation of most resources to building and operating irrigation systems.

The process and criteria for setting national priorities for investments in irrigation, drainage and flood control systems is highly and increasingly politicized. There is no procedure which requires public irrigation and water projects be approved, in the context of national priorities, before foreign financing can be obtained, although CONADE does review and attempt to coordinate the financing of such projects. Strong regional interests actively promote their pet projects and vie with each other for external funding support. Objective social and economic criteria often are given only limited weight in the process of deciding whether to proceed with a project and feasibility studies generally are deficient.

There is an increase in the degree of inter-regional competition among the principal irrigation agencies. This is manifest in competition for external funding for various projects. It also is apparent in attempts to extend control over more projects. The most recent winner is CEDEGE, which has obtained external credits for its Daule-Peripa and Santa Elena projects and which recently was assigned responsibility for two important projects previously under INERHI jurisdiction. CRM and PREDESUR also have been successful in obtaining relatively large levels of external funding. Tensions in INERHI are heightened and employee morale is low as some view these events as precursors of greater "losses."

Recommendations

A moratorium should be declared on all new irrigation projects, pending a careful review and analysis. Public investments in irrigation are much less socially and economically viable than has been predicted. The review and analysis should set priorities for all future investments in irrigation. It also should establish a uniform process, to which all irrigation agencies would be subject, for deciding which projects would be advanced to design stage and financed after the moratorium was lifted. Projects under construction also should be reviewed to determine how they could be more sharply focused. Only those components with demonstrated high pay-offs should be continued.

Resources should be focused on improving the efficiency of existing irrigation systems. Public irrigation agencies should focus and concentrate their limited budgets on increasing the efficiency of water use both on the farm and at the system level. They should work closely with research and extension agencies to enhance the utilization of higher-yielding varieties and complementary inputs.

Significant resources should be allocated to technology generation and transfer for irrigated agriculture. INIAP, the Foundation for Agricultural Development (FUNDAGRO), the Program for the Development of Agricultural Technology (PROTECA) and the national production programs of MAG should work closely with the public irrigation agencies to develop, adapt and disseminate improved technologies focused on soil-plant-water relationships. Productivity must be raised in irrigated agriculture, which affects one in four hectares of cropland. Investments in public irrigation projects will become more profitable as yields increase.

A clear division of labor should be implemented between public irrigation agencies and technology transfer institutions and duplication of effort eliminated. Public irrigation agencies should focus on the technical aspects of irrigation systems and on-farm water management. Research and extension agencies should focus on soil-water-plant relationships and on increasing agricultural productivity. The agricultural development component of public irrigation agencies (demonstration farms, machinery pools, subsidized fertilizer and propagation and sale of plants and animals) should be transferred to the appropriate agencies such as INIAP and MAG.

The water tariff should be increased as productivity and project benefits increase. It seems abundantly clear that Ecuador can not afford to continue to subsidize irrigation water. The 1972 Water Law, which was passed in the euphoria of the oil boom, needs to be changed and the costs of irrigation water shifted substantially to the private users of the resource. The government should carefully reconsider the advisability of maintaining property rights for water as a public good. Increases in the water tariff must be implemented carefully, however, since large, wholesale increases will tend to decapitalize second and later owners of irrigated land. Increases in the tariff must be closely correlated with increases in productivity. Unfortunately, the current benefits of irrigation appear to be much lower than the costs, on average, so that some part of the investments in infrastructure are being lost. Unless productivity is increased substantially, it will be impossible to pass on all the costs to private users through increased tariffs, who will stop irrigating before they suffer losses.

Management of public irrigation projects needs to be turned over to water users' associations, with the State involved primarily in maintaining complex structures. When users have the responsibility to manage the system, they will tend to minimize the costs of operation and routine maintenance. There appears to be a substantial waste of resources by public agencies which are too heavily involved too far down the irrigation system.

INERHI should provide increased support to improvement of private irrigation systems, especially maintenance of the primary and secondary canals and water diversion structures. INERHI has the expertise and experience to provide such services, which should be done on a cost basis. The private sector should make investments in necessary infrastructure with technical assistance from INERHI.

INERHI's national-level functions of planning, administration and regulation of: (a) water resources; and (b) irrigation, drainage and flood control should be made autonomous from its dominant function of construction and operation of irrigation systems. These extremely important functions are subordinate administratively to the function of construction and operation of irrigations systems and both have received a disproportionately small budget. These two functions are very important and should be carried out independently from the operation and construction of irrigation systems, with substantially increased budget support. One approach would be to create a new independent water and irrigation board. INERHI would continue with construction and operation of irrigation, drainage and flood control systems and would have the same status as other public irrigation agencies. All entities which construct and operate irrigation, drainage and flood control systems would be subject to the norms and standards set by the proposed national-level water and irrigation board.

A uniform and streamlined process for review and approval of all new irrigation projects should be developed by the proposed national-level water use and irrigation board. This process should specify the various steps for approval (project identification, feasibility studies, design, financing and construction). It should specify the criteria for project identification and the review and approval procedures at each step of the process. The national water use and irrigation board should have authority to approve all projects and access to national and foreign financing and credits.

Investments to raise the productivity of rainfed agriculture also should be increased substantially (see Chapter 12). Rainfed crop and pasture lands comprise more than three times the irrigated area. Productivity on rainfed lands also is very low and more modern technologies can have a major impact on increasing agricultural production and incomes of farm families. Public investments to raise productivity of rainfed and irrigated agriculture are far more likely to meet the future food needs of Ecuador's rapidly growing population, than continued investments in irrigation infrastructure. Ecuador has substantially overinvested in irrigation infrastructure while substantially underinvesting in technology generation and transfer for rainfed agriculture.

NOTES

1. See Chapter 4 for a detailed description of land use and eight principal agro-ecologic zones.

2. There are several studies which provide more detail on the legal and institutional aspects of Ecuador's irrigation sector and are a partial basis for information provided in this Section. See Cruz, Orquera and Salazar; Orquera; Cox, Cox and Tolosa; and Keller, et al.

3. This anomaly has been noted in other studies. See Orquera; Cox, Cox and Tolosa; and Louis Berger International and PROTECVIA Ltd.

4. The same problem affects many of the public agencies serving agriculture. See Chapter 12 for the case of INIAP, Ecuador's public research agency.

5. Average cropland was 1,545,588 hectares during 1980-1985 (Chapter 6 Table 6.5). Part of irrigated land is in improved pastures which are not included in cropland. Data on irrigated pastureland are not available but such lands are a small proportion of total pastures. If irrigated pastures were 25 percent of all irrigated land, then the share of irrigated land in the total of cropland and irrigated pastures would fall from 27 to 25 percent.

6. According to Anderson (p. 80) there were 250 water user's associations in the Sierra and one in the Costa in 1973.

7. It is highly probable that the discussion which follows about INERHI also applies to the other principal irrigation agencies. Unfortunately data are not available for a similar analysis.

8. Data on command area, irrigable area and area irrigated in 1987 were available only for INERHI, CEDEGE and CRM. Data for the other entities were taken from secondary sources and were purported to measure irrigated area. To the extent that these data measure command or irrigable areas and the area actually irrigated was less, the area irrigated in 1987 is overestimated.

9. See Marshall & Associates for a description of the Daule-Peripa project.

10. Design work has been completed as of 1990 for the 33,000 hectares but financing has not yet been secured.

11. The Santa Elena project is closely related to the Daule-Peripa project and is sometimes referred to as if it were part of the Daule-Peripa project. It is, however, a separate project. See CEDEGE/CEDEX.

12. Unpublished data provided by INERHI, Directorate of Planning.

13. This assumes all the planned command areas of projects under construction and in design or study are irrigated and that the area under irrigation in existing public and private systems continues to be irrigated.

14. These estimates are based on INERHI data on the annual value of investments in infrastructure in current prices. INERHI maintains annual data for all its projects since 1966 and the total amount for each project since its inception. The difference between the sum of the annual amounts since 1966 and the total since inception is the sum in current prices of all investments for projects that began prior to 1966. The annual values were converted to constant 1988 Sucres using the Consumer Price Index. The sum of investments prior to 1966 was assumed to have been incurred in 1965. To the extent investments occurred before 1965, the constant value in 1988 prices is underestimated. The dollar value is calculated at the average free market exchange rate for 1988 of S/.436.19/US$ (BCE 1990, p. 46).

15. The average cost of INERHI infrastructure per irrigable hectare (S/.949,855) is multiplied by the number of irrigable hectares in other public irrigation systems of 35,955 hectares (Table 7.2). The result is S/.34,152.0 million or US$78.3 million.

16. The degree of completion in Table 7.5 (share of accumulated cost in total cost both in current prices) is used to estimate the total cost in 1988 prices of completing the project.

17. For example, INERHI has an additional 36 such projects on its "wish list." These projects would cost another S/.38,357.2 million or US$87.9 million (at the 1988 average free market exchange rate of S/.436.19/US$1.0) according to unpublished INERHI data. All are at the prefeasibility stages of study.

18. This assumes: 50 percent of the costs of operating projects have been repaid and 80 percent of the balance is financed abroad, 90 percent of projects under construction are financed abroad, and 90 percent of the projects under design and study will be financed abroad.

19. Charging the average tariff to all water users in surface systems means that more efficient irrigation systems and water users subsidize the less efficient.

20. The 1989 tariff estimated here is based on the sum of all past investments through December 1988, including those incurred prior to 1966, in the 35 operational irrigation systems considered in this analysis, all in current prices in accordance with current INERHI practice. INERHI does not adjust the value of total investments for inflation when calculating the basic tariff, although doing so has been analyzed by the staff and considered by the Board of Directors during the last two years.

21. Total costs are presented in constant 1988 prices to account for the opportunity costs of investment in irrigation infrastructure. Amortizing the value of past investments in 1988 prices accounts explicitly for the costs society must bear for having invested in irrigation infrastructure. The Consumer Price Index on a 1988 base was used to deflate the current investment in each year. The value of irrigation infrastructure in 1988 likely is underestimated because all investments prior to 1966 are assumed to have been made in 1965 (see Note 14).

22. The estimate of an annual average subsidy of S/.1,861.1 million is calculated as follows. First, the costs of studies and construction (S/.4,517.5) and operations and maintenance (S/.184.2 million) are subtracted from total costs since these are accounted for in the basic and volumetric tariffs. Then the costs of water management (S/.230.8 million) and irrigation management (S/.9.4 million) which are nationwide functions not related to INERHI's irrigation systems, are subtracted from the undistributed balance of S/.2,370.5 million. Finally, the costs of central management and institutional planning associated with the functions of water management, irrigation management and construction are subtracted from the balance of S/.2,316.5 million. These costs were estimated at S/.455.4 million, in proportion to the importance of

water management, irrigation management, and construction (65 percent) in total costs. The balance of S/.1,861.1 million is the part of INERHI's budget that is allocable to operations and maintenance of irrigation systems but not accounted for in the volumetric tariff (see Table 7.1; Whitaker, Colyer and Alzamora Appendix Tables 7.1 and 7.2).

23. From an unpublished table, "Estudios de Proyectos de Riego," prepared by the Sección Agro-Socio-Economía of INERHI.

24. Original owners are also decapitalized from an increase in the water tariff because the value of their land also falls. Thus, they will suffer a loss in terms of foregone income when the land is sold. But original owners paid a much lower price for the land before the value of irrigation benefits were capitalized into it so they suffer a "paper" loss. Second owners suffer an direct loss since they paid more for the land than it is worth after the increase in the tariff.

25. This conclusion needs to be qualified to accommodate the timing of costs and benefits. A positive net benefit stream at some point in the life of the project is a necessary but not a sufficient condition for an economically viable project. Annual benefits may eventually exceed the annual costs of amortizing the capital investments and paying for operations and maintenance. However, if capital costs are realized primarily in the initial years of the project and project benefits do not begin in a substantial way until several years later, the internal rate of return still may be negative.

26. Note that if a higher interest rate is utilized, the size of the subsidy increases, as does the annual flow of project benefits. The relationship between them remains basically the same, however.

27. The increased value of land is estimated as the present value of the annual benefit streams, amortized over 40 years at 6 percent interest (to be consistent with parameters used throughout this analysis) multiplied by the amount of irrigable land in operational projects.

REFERENCES

Anderson, D. Craig. 1973. "The Management of Irrigation Water in Ecuador." Unpublished Master's Thesis, Utah State University, 1973.

BCE (Central Bank of Ecuador). 1990. *Información Estadística Mensual*. Quito: March 15, No. 1633.

_____. 1989. *Memoria Anual: 1988*. Quito: November 22.

Carrera de la Torre, Luis. 1987. *Los Recursos Hidráulicos y el Riego en el Ecuador*. Quito: Fundación Natura. Presented at the First Ecuadorian Congress on the Environment.

CEDEGE/CEDEX (Study Commission for the Development of the Guayas River Basin/Center for Water Studies of Spain). 1984. *Plan Hidraúlico Acueducto Santa Elena: Evaluación Económico*. Guayaquil: CEDEGE, July.

Cox, Maximiliano, Tomás Cox and Juan Tolosa. 1988. "Diagnóstico Preliminar de Riego en Ecuador." Quito: Inter-American Development Bank, December (preliminary draft).

Cruz, Roberto V., Arturo Orquera and Alex Salazar. 1988. *El Riego en El Ecuador*. Quito: INERHI.

Delavaud, Anne Collin, et al. 1982. *Atlas del Ecuador*. Paris: Les Editions J.A. and Banco Central del Ecuador.

IDB (Inter-American Development Bank). 1981. *Expert Evaluation of the Montufar Irrigation Project*. Washington, D.C.

INERHI (Ecuadorian Institute of Water Resources). 1987a. *Informe de Labores, Año 1987*. Quito: Annex Table 2.

_____. 1987b. *Tarifa de Riego, 1988*. Quito: Dirección Operación y Desarrollo de Sistemas de Riego, December.

_____. No Date. *Reglamento de Tarifas por Servicio de Riego*. Quito: Ministerio de Agricultura y Ganaderia.

Keller, Jack, et. al. 1982. *Ecuador: Irrigation Sector Review*. Logan, UT: Utah State University, USAID/WMS Report 12.

Louis Berger International/PROTECVIA Ltd. 1985. *Diagnóstico de la Estructura, Organización y Operación del INERHI*. Quito: Louis Berger International.

Marshall & Associates. 1984. Reorganización Administrativa de CEDEGE: Diagnóstico . Institucional. Guayaquil: CONSUPLAN, December.

Orquera Cárdenas, Arturo. 1986-1987. *El Riego en el Ecuador*. Quito: Instituto de Altos Estudios Nacionales.

PREDESUR (Regional Program for the Development of Southern Ecuador). 1988. *Desarrollo Regional del Sur del Ecuador*. Cuenca, Ecuador: Oficina de Coordinación de la Subcomisión Ecuatoriana.

S. A. AGRER N. V. and INERHI. 1982. *Proyecto El Pisque: Plan Maestro Quinquenal*. Quito: INERHI, July.

Whitaker, Morris D., Dale Colyer and Jaime Alzamora. 1990. *The Role of Agriculture in Ecuador's Economic Development*. Quito: IDEA (Agricultural Policy Institute).

World Bank. 1982. *Informe de Evaluación Ex Post, Ecuador: Proyecto de Riego Milagro (Crédito 425EC)*. Washington, D.C.: Department of Evaluation of Operations, October 7 (draft).

8

THE AGRICULTURAL MARKETING
SYSTEM

David Tschirley and Harold Riley

The Ecuadorian agricultural marketing system presents a complex set of problems reflecting several basic conditions including the geographic and related agricultural diversity of the country, the export orientation of a major portion of the agricultural sector and the relatively weak infrastructure and institutional support for marketing. Assessment of the Ecuadorian agricultural marketing system should recognize that private enterprises are and will likely continue to be the primary providers of marketing services. Thus, a major policy issue is the appropriate role of the public sector in regulating and promoting development within a fundamentally entrepreneurial system.

During the past two decades this system has been under substantial pressures associated with rapid urbanization, continued high rates of population growth and a surge in per capita income during the oil boom of the 1970s, followed by a persistent economic recession in the 1980s as oil revenues dropped sharply. The development of national highway and communication networks has supported the growth of a more geographically coordinated marketing system allowing greater regional and farm-level specialization in agricultural production. However, the forces of technological and socioeconomic change continue to create opportunities for more efficient, innovative methods of arranging transactions, transporting, storing, processing and distributing agricultural products and delivering low-cost farm inputs. Such progress will be critical as the importance of marketing activities continues to increase in relation to farm-level production.

The government regulates prices and intervenes directly in the purchase, storage and sale of selected basic commodities. Parastatals have been formed to provide a more extensive agricultural input distribution system. These interventions have been costly to the government and in some instances have served as disincentives to producers and private sector marketing firms. A lack of public sector support for private marketing enterprises stems in large measure from a deeply ingrained bias, resulting in continued efforts to replace them or to strictly control their activities.

This chapter examines agricultural marketing issues and problems. The following sections present and analyze: the food marketing system with a conceptual framework for the analysis of marketing systems and the changing environment within which agricultural marketing takes place; a descriptive and diagnostic assessment of the organization and performance of the major commodity and input marketing subsystems; and an agenda for market system development focused on subsidies, price policy, strategic public and private sector investments, market regulations and public sector marketing support services.

The Food Marketing System

The current problems within the Ecuadorian food system are similar to those in many other countries, especially in Latin America. The rapid growth of large urban centers and the general trend to urbanization has been a dominant force in the transformation of Latin American food systems; Ecuador is no exception. Large public and private sector investments are required to expand transport, storage, processing, wholesaling and retailing facilities as urban populations overtake and exceed those in rural areas. Insufficient investment in these facilities can seriously impede the transition from a traditional to a dynamic, market-oriented agricultural economy.

A Conceptual Perspective

The conceptual basis for this analysis is developed from the extensive research and technical assistance experience of Michigan State University (Harrison, Henley, Riley and Shaffer; Riley; Riley et al.; Weber et al.). This approach places emphasis on the role of dynamic market processes, within the context of *scientific industrialization* of the food and agricultural system (Shaffer). Scientific industrialization involves the creation and adoption of new technologies and institutional arrangements that lead to greater specialization of labor, increased productivity and shifting labor from farm to non-farm activities, often in small-scale agricultural processing and service functions. Over time, there is substantial migration to towns and cities and shifting patterns of food consumption, both of which contribute to a rapid increase in the demand for marketing services. The principal changes in food consumption patterns include a relatively rapid increase in the demand for livestock products, fruits, vegetables and processed foods and decreasing demand for basic grains and starchy tubers. The pattern of change proceeds more rapidly when there are significant and sustained increases in per capita income.

The concept of a *food system* provides a framework for describing the changing organization of the marketing system, diagnosing problems and formulating strategies to improve the system. The food system includes all of the steps of productive activity required to move food from the initial producer to the final consumer (Figure 8.1). This process includes international as well as domestic markets and marketing agents. Also included are policy and program elements and the supporting institutions providing credit, education, research and information. The coordination of these functional activities is achieved largely through market forces, though government intervention can and does have significant impacts on the coordination process. The advantage of viewing marketing activities as they relate to one another in a food system context is that one is better able to identify constraints and possible opportunities for improving overall system performance.

For diagnostic and prescriptive purposes it is useful to divide the food system into commodity subsystems since each commodity group has unique characteristics that must be accommodated in the marketing process. The desired attributes of such a subsystem are: (a) the matching of supply and demand over space, form and time at each stage in the production-distribution system; (b) efficiency in the physical transformation, handling and delivery of commodities, as well as in arranging and

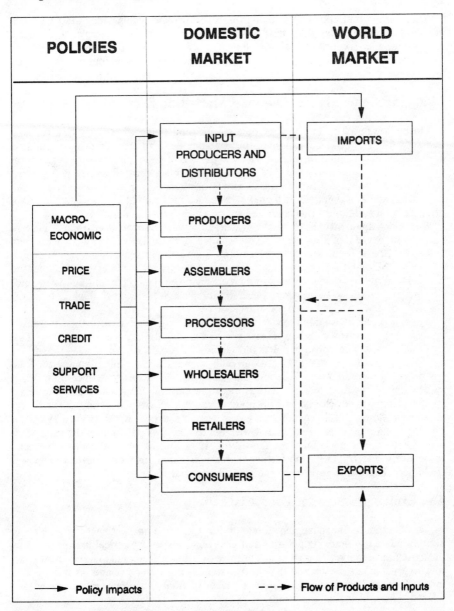

Figure 8.1 Principal Components of a Food System

carrying out transactions; (c) progressiveness in developing new products and in adopting more productive technologies, management methods and institutional arrangements; and (d) equity in returns to subsector participants in relation to value added to the final product, costs and risks incurred.

There are potential conflicts among these performance goals which must be taken into consideration in designing new policies and programs. For example, equity goals may sometimes conflict with those of progressiveness and efficiency. One of the challenges for marketing analysts is to clarify the trade-offs among goals, so that policymakers can make more informed choices.

Changing Demands for Food and Marketing Services

During the development process, demand for food changes both quantitatively and qualitatively. The principal causes of this changing demand are increasing population and increasing consumer income. As a consequence of population growth in Ecuador, the demand for food at the national level has probably increased by nearly 3 percent per year during the past two decades. However, demand for marketing services will have increased at a significantly higher rate reflecting the additional logistical costs of bringing food to families that migrated to the cities (see Chapter 5).

Real per capita income grew at an average annual rate of more than 5 percent during the decade of the 1970s. This income growth likely increased per capita demand for basic foodstuffs by approximately 3 percent per year, assuming an income elasticity of demand for food of 0.4 to 0.6. However, rising incomes probably caused per capita retail food expenditures to increase by more than 3 percent annually, since the income elasticity of demand for marketing services is much higher than the elasticity of demand for basic foodstuffs.

Thus, it seems reasonable to conclude that total retail demand for food increased by an average of seven or more percent per year during the decade of the 1970s. This very rapid growth in consumer demand changed dramatically with the onset of the economic crisis during the 1980s. As a result, aggregate per capita demand for food has probably increased very little and may have decreased for lower-income groups.

Though survey data indicate that average protein and caloric intake of the lower income group has not changed significantly since 1986, food and beverage expenditures as a proportion of total expenditures has increased sharply. From 1986 to 1989, this proportion rose in urban areas from 49 percent to nearly 64 percent. In the rural areas near Quito and Guayaquil, the figures for 1989 are 70 percent and 76 percent, respectively (CEDATOS). Any further decrease in these households' purchasing power could soon begin to compromise their nutritional status.

The Evolving System of Food Marketing

To respond to the changing demands for food and marketing services and to accommodate the changing patterns and increasing volume of agricultural production, the agricultural marketing system must evolve over time. Regional markets must move toward greater integration and the entire system of infrastructure and institutions that moves food and food products from the farm to final consumers must expand and adapt to these changing conditions.

Geographic Perspective Mainland Ecuador consists of three distinct geographic regions, the Costa, Sierra and Oriente, that are being drawn into a more integrated, national, agricultural marketing system. The wide range of soil, water and temperature conditions in Ecuador provides opportunities for the production and consumption of a large variety of products. This creates the possibility of organizing the production and delivery of perishable products over a broad spectrum of the year, reducing seasonal supply fluctuations and the need for processing and storage activities. But to achieve this potential requires increasingly better-informed and technically progressive enterprise managers in the private sector.

The two largest cities, Quito in the Sierra and Guayaquil in the Costa, are the dominant trading centers that link these two regions into a growing national agricultural marketing network. The Oriente has no trading center comparable to Quito and Guayaquil, but is increasingly integrated into the Sierra and Costa marketing system. Secondary marketing cities in the Sierra are Cuenca, Ambato, Latacunga, Riobamba, Loja and Ibarra. In the Costa, the major secondary market cities include Machala, Manta, Esmeraldas, Portoviejo, Milagro, Daule and Quevedo. Santo Domingo is an important market city located between the two regional networks. Also, numerous rural assembly centers exist throughout the country. Farm production generally moves first to these rural assembly points. Assemblers then either sell directly to consumers, or to wholesalers who move the product to the primary and secondary cities for consumption there or to the secondary cities for transhipment to Quito and Guayaquil.

All-weather highways connect the primary and secondary cities, but flooding in the Costa and landslides in the Sierra often create traffic interruptions. The lack of good secondary and farm-to-market roads in rural areas, especially in the Costa, is widely cited as a major transportation problem which contributes to high marketing costs and the inability of many farmers to move products to market during the rainy season. Hence, the development and maintenance of an improved road and highway network should be a high priority in any comprehensive market development program.

Urban Food Distribution Most food reaches urban consumers through many very small retailers. Within each urban center there are one or more municipal market facilities in which the municipality makes tiny stalls available to retailers at subsidized rental rates. As urban populations have grown, food wholesale and retail activities have spread into buildings and streets surrounding the municipal markets, creating traffic congestion and product handling difficulties. Concurrently, retailers have established small food stores in various locations within the expanding residential areas. The heavy influx of rural migrants, the lack of employment opportunities and the ease of entry into some form of food retailing contributes to the small-scale, extremely fragmented system of retail food distribution.

Modern, self-service supermarkets have successfully entered the Quito and Guayaquil markets, but as yet handle only a modest percentage of retail food sales. According to management of the largest chain, Supermaxi, their national market share of retail rice sales is only 2.0 to 2.5 percent. Shares in Quito, their major center of operations, would be significantly higher. Supermaxi has its own wholesale warehouse in Quito, from which it supplies its branch stores with nearly all their product line. It also has a special facility for receiving, cleaning and packaging fresh fruits and vegetables, and is vertically integrated in the production of milk, beef and chicken. Supermarkets will make a long-term contribution to the development of a larger-scale, more technically efficient system of urban food distribution and a related food processing industry. This process should eventually reduce the cost and improve the variety and quality of food products reaching all urban consumers. Prices of basic foodstuffs in modern supermarkets are consistently below those in the large "popular markets" and neighborhood stores frequented by low income consumers (Table 8.1).

A modern, wholesale market was built on the outskirts of Quito in 1980. The

Table 8.1   Average Prices of Basic Foodstuffs in Supermarkets, "Popular Markets"
and Neighborhood Stores, Quito, 1989

	Type of Store		
Food	Super-market	"Popular Market"	Neighborhood Store
Rice (Sucres per Pound)	125	133	142
Sugar (Sucres per Pound)	78	78	89
Oil (Sucres per Liter)	500	500	511
Soft Corn (Sucres per Pound)	250	255	268

Source: MAG 1988.

project was initiated by the municipality with financial assistance from the Inter-American Development Bank. The land and buildings are the property of the municipality but the market is operated by a mixed enterprise composed of 30 shareholders, including the provincial chamber of agriculture, the local association of wholesale grocers, two producer cooperatives and a supermarket firm. This market has become established as a wholesale center for rice, food legumes, dry groceries, potatoes and eggs, but has not yet attracted a high volume of fresh fruits and vegetables.

The need for more modern and logistically efficient food wholesaling facilities in the larger cities continues to be assessed by municipal and national planning units. Feasibility studies have been made for marketing facilities in Guayaquil and Cuenca. Additional studies are needed for a comprehensive market development program.

Rural Markets   Rural periodic markets continue to be important institutional arrangements for organizing the purchase and sale of agricultural products and the distribution of farm inputs and consumer goods (Bromley). Municipalities provide space, rudimentary facilities and the supervision of market activities. The market day has great social, religious and political as well as commercial significance in the life of the community. With the improvement of transportation and communication services, these markets are increasingly drawn into the regional and national market network. This broadens the variety of products available in local markets and creates additional potential competition among buyers of surplus agricultural commodities that can be transhipped to other markets.

As rural trading centers grow, there is often increased interest in improved market facilities and services. This provides an opportunity for public sector assistance in planning investments and institutional arrangements, which could increase the efficiency and effectiveness of rural markets (Weber).

ENPROVIT   The National Company for Basic Products (ENPROVIT) is a government-owned enterprise created in 1971 and attached to the Ministry of Agriculture (MAG). Its function is to regulate prices of basic commodities for low-income consumers. During the period 1980-85, ENPROVIT operated 250-275 retail outlets, including 30 supermarkets. These outlets were located throughout the country but the bulk of the sales took place in the major cities. The main products handled have been rice, pastas, powdered milk, oatmeal, sugar, salt and a few household items and processed foods. However, the supermarkets carried a wider range of food and non-food products. The basic foodstuffs have been sold at official prices and at margins considerably below operating costs.

Over the past decade most outside marketing experts have viewed ENPROVIT as a relatively high cost and ineffective mechanism for the distribution of food and basic consumer goods. Efforts to improve its operations have not significantly changed this situation. Recommendations have ranged from closing it down to converting it into a strictly wholesaling operation. Given the Ecuadorian political-economic environment, it is likely to continue operations in some form as a means to demonstrate government concern over food prices and food availability to the poorer segment of the population. However, the highest priority for food subsidization should be carefully targeted to the poorest segments of the population and the most vulnerable from a nutritional perspective, eg., pregnant mothers and small children (see Chapter 3). Such a policy would require active participation by public agencies responsible for health, education and social services.

Commodity Marketing Subsystems

The principle agricultural marketing subsystems are Costa grains, Sierra food crops, poultry, beef, milk, oil crops, fruits and vegetables and export crops.

Costa Food and Feed Grains

The principal food and feed grains cultivated in the Costa are rice, hard corn and soybeans. Rice is used for direct human consumption while rice milling by-products are used predominantly in the manufacturing of poultry and shrimp feed. Soybeans yield oil for human consumption and meal for use in poultry and shrimp feed. Hard corn is used almost entirely in poultry feed. Production trends have been highly positive for each crop (Chapter 6).

Production and Marketing All three Costa grains share two distinct growing seasons. The rainy season, December to June, accounts, on average, for 80 percent of hard corn production and 60 percent of rice production.[1] Dry season plantings take place primarily during June, with subsequent harvests most concentrated in October. This harvest accounts for the vast majority of soybean production. The three grains, however, show great variety in their structure of production. Hard corn is the most geographically dispersed, the smallest scale and is served by the poorest transportation infrastructure. Soybean production is the most geographically concentrated and the largest scale and is served by an excellent road system. Rice production lies between those two crops in all three characteristics (Tschirley 1988; Ramos 1989a, 1989b).

Despite the numerical dominance of small and medium-sized hard corn farmers, marketings are clearly dominated by the largest producers. According to Tschirley (1988) 5 percent of farmers accounted for 78 percent of all 1987 rainy season sales, while nearly 40 percent of all farmers made no sales. Rice production is also quite concentrated. Twenty percent of farmers made over three-quarters of all sales during 1988. Twenty-four percent of the soybean farmers accounted for 70 percent of total sales during the 1987 dry season harvest.

Hard corn goes through an average of 2.2 transactions to reach poultry feed manufacturers. During the 1987 rainy season harvest, nearly 90 percent of the marketed surplus was sold by farmers to rural traders. These traders then sold over

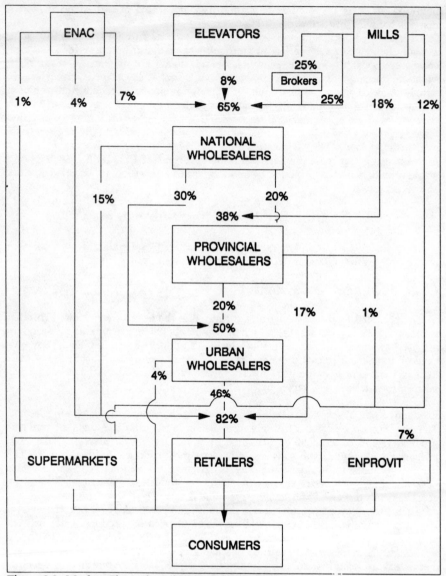

Figure 8.2 Market Channels and Flows of Milled Rice
Source: Ramos 1989a

one-half of their purchases to feed manufacturers and more than 40 percent to wholesalers (Tschirley 1988). Hard corn marketing at the rural assembly level appears to be very competitive. Nearly three-quarters of all hard corn sold in rural markets was sold in towns with more than five traders. Only 2 percent was sold in towns with one trader. Small quantities of hard corn generally receive the same price as larger quantities if the two are of comparable quality (Tschirley 1988).

Competition at the wholesale and feed manufacturer level for hard corn also appears to be adequate. Feed manufacturing during 1986 and 1987 had a low concentration level, as measured by the commonly used CR4 ratio.[2] In addition, feed manufacturers in the Costa must compete with Sierra wholesalers for purchases from rural traders. It is highly unlikely, then, that these manufacturers could unilaterally depress the price received by producers or rural traders.

Since rice is consumed directly by humans, its marketing requires more transactions than does that of hard corn and soybeans. Most rice passes through five marketing agents before reaching its final consumers, an initial sale to rice millers, followed by sales to three levels of wholesalers (national, provincial and urban), and finally a sale to retailers (Figure 8.2). Nearly 1,000 commercial rice mills compete for farmers' grain in the relatively small rice producing area. Too, the fifteen largest millers process only 15 percent of total production (Ramos 1989a, 1989b).

It is possible that rice wholesalers are able to exercise some market power. A large percentage of milled rice eventually passes through the hands of between twelve and twenty large, national wholesalers. These wholesalers have excellent access to commercial bank credit and are the major lenders to rice millers. Most rice stored in rice millers' warehouses is owned by wholesalers, who retrieve it when necessary. The level of excess profits that these traders may extract requires a closer examination. Currently, despite their large scale and access to capital, it remains doubtful that they form a cartel with the ability to unilaterally influence prices.

Soybean marketing is the most direct of the three grains, going through an average of 1.3 transactions to reach soybean crushers. During the 1987 dry season harvest, nearly two-thirds of all producer sales were to crushers, with nearly one-quarter to traders and the remainder to the marketing parastatal, the National Agricultural Storage and Marketing Company--ENAC (Tschirley 1988). The greatest possibility of insufficient assembly level competition occurs in the marketing of soybeans, due to extreme concentration among crushers. Nevertheless, the presence of ENAC is sufficient to practically force crushers to pay the official price. Also, soybean farmers have the option of selling to competitive local traders instead of crushers.

Rural traders and rice millers provide two important services to producers. One is a competitive local market alternative to more distant soybean crushers, feed manufacturers and rice wholesalers. The other is an immediate cash payment, which helps farmers improve their liquidity in preparation for the following crop cycle. The fact that so many farmers choose to sell to these traders, even in the presence of alternatives, attests to the service they provide.

Finally, routine observation and formal analyses indicate that spatially separated Costa grain markets are well integrated. This integration extends to neighboring Colombia and Peru (Tschirley 1988) and provides additional evidence supporting the view that marketing of basic grains in the Costa of Ecuador is generally quite competitive.

Public Sector Participation Although the private sector plays a dominant role in the marketing of Costa grains, the government has significantly influenced these processes through regulation and direct participation. The State has controlled imports, bought and sold in all three markets and controlled prices.[3]

The Government of Ecuador (GOE) controls all imports. These are implemented by prohibition of some private imports or by strictly enforced quotas when the private sector is permitted to import. The Ministries of Agriculture and Industry also must

Table 8.2   Percent ENAC Participation in Rice, Hard Corn and Soybean Markets in
            Ecuador, 1974-1988

	ENAC Participation (%)		
Year	Rice	Hard Corn	Soybeans
1974	3.5	0.0	0.0
1975	9.5	0.0	0.0
1976	1.9	2.0	0.0
1977	7.1	4.0	0.0
1978	5.6	18.0	0.0
1979	2.8	15.0	0.0
1980	15.3	18.0	0.0
1981	9.6	36.0	0.0
1982	11.5	11.0	0.0
1983	0.0	0.0	0.0
1984	0.0	10.0	50.0
1985	5.1	42.0	0.0
1986	22.1	20.0	0.0
1987	32.4	1.0	15.0
1988	0.0	0.0	0.0
Average:[a]	8.4	11.8	10.8
Coefficient of Variation:	1.04	1.09	1.69

Source: Rice: Stewart and Cuesta; corn and soybeans: Tschirley 1988; Consultores
Asociados 1988.

[a]Average and coefficient of variation for soybeans are calculated beginning in
1983, the first year that an official producer price was set for this crop.

approve each individual import. Prohibitions have been most common for rice, while
quotas have been more commonly applied to hard corn, soybeans and soybean meal
and oil. In addition, import levies or subsidies are used to equalize import and official
domestic prices of rice and hard corn. To encourage domestic processing of soybeans
a value-added import tax of between 70 percent and 80 percent is imposed on
processed oil and 10 percent on meal. Soybeans and crude soybean oil enter the
country tax free (Stewart, Cuesta and Acosta).

Direct government participation consists of buying and selling grains through
ENAC, which purchases the grains from farmers at official support prices (Table 8.2).
ENAC sells a very small proportion of its rice to ENPROVIT for retail distribution,
but channels the largest volume to wholesalers. ENAC sells hard corn to feed
manufacturers or wholesalers and soybeans to oilseed processors. ENAC's
participation in the rice, hard corn and soybean markets reached historical highs during
the period 1985-1987.

ENAC purchases of over 20,000 metric tons in 1989 were insufficient to enforce
official hard corn prices (Figure 8.3). This can be attributed to the inability of ENAC
to purchase all that it is offered at the official price. In contrast, the concentration of
soybean production and consumption has allowed ENAC intervention to practically
impose official prices during years in which they exceeded domestic equilibrium market
prices (Tschirley 1988). ENAC's influence in the rice market lies between these two

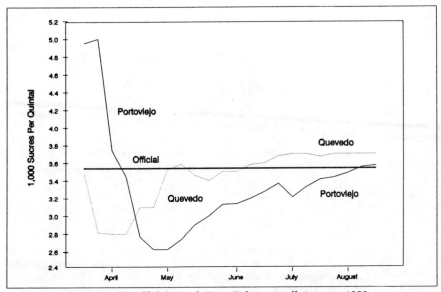

Figure 8.3   Market and Official Hard Corn Prices, April-August, 1989

extremes. Although farmers may be willing to sell to millers and traders at a discount from the support price, ENAC's presence often causes market prices to closely track official prices.

Price controls have been in place since 1973 and in 1977 the Economic Front began to fix maximum consumer and minimum producer prices. In practice, the only grain for which consumer prices have been enforced is rice. This has been attempted through ENAC sales, as well as legal sanctions against traders selling above the official price. Legal measures include the seizing (with payment at official prices) of relatively small amounts of rice from warehouses.[4] The pattern price control activities indicates that enforcement becomes most severe during periods of shortage and consequent high prices. The market disruptions that often result are severe.

Principal Marketing Problems The principal problems affecting the marketing of rice and hard corn in Ecuador are supply and resulting price instability. Severe shortages and price increases have affected markets in 1983-1984, 1987-1988 and 1988-1989. To differing degrees, domestic production shortfalls and large unofficial sales to Colombia were the causes of the initial shortages. However, the extreme price shocks were largely a result of great uncertainty regarding the timing and volume of imports to cover the shortages, as well as delays in import arrival. The causes of these delays are unreliable data regarding production and stocks, the highly political nature of imports and inconsistent relative price policies.

The official estimates of hard corn production provided by the National Corn and Soybean Program of MAG are at best "ballpark" figures. Unofficial estimates come from the Association of Feed Manufacturers (AFABA) and from the National Agricultural Commodities Exchange (*Bolsa de Productos*). AFABA estimates are based primarily on aerial surveys and are consistently the lowest of the three. National

Exchange estimates are also somewhat ad hoc and tend to fall between the other two. The uncertainty created by unreliable production data is compounded by a very active unofficial border trade and by the complete absence of reliable stock data. Rice production estimates from MAG's National Rice Program are more accurate than those for hard corn. The Program also collects relatively reliable stock data from rice millers. However, both data series could be significantly improved.

Rice and hard corn prices are available daily at the Guayaquil and Quito wholesale markets and hard corn prices also are available at feed manufacturing plants. Border prices with Colombia and Peru are available at least once a week. Border and domestic price differentials, used in combination with domestic price movements and the available production estimates, might be sufficient to allow adequate import/export decisions, were it not for the highly political nature of these decisions. An overriding policy objective in Ecuador is self-sufficiency in basic food and feed grains. Shortfalls are considered a policy failure and tend to be politically costly for the government. Shortages are therefore often denied until they reach crisis proportions.

Finally, relative official prices of hard corn and soybeans have contributed to hard corn supply instability during at least two years. Between 1986 and 1987, the official soybean price nearly doubled relative to the official hard corn price. As a result, volume of hard corn marketed may have fallen by more than two months of consumption. In 1989, the relative soybean price ratio remained very high. Farmers planted almost exclusively soybeans during the dry season, resulting in the smallest dry season hard corn harvest in many years.

A secondary problem affecting both hard corn and rice marketing is the absence of systematic price incentives for improved quality. Prices at each level in the marketing system are only loosely related to quality. As a result, at least 20 percent of hard corn sold at the rural assembly level exceeds the maximum mold content accepted by the more progressive feed manufacturers (Tschirley 1988).

ENAC presence in the soybean market appears to have been sufficient to prevent monopoly pricing of the grain by soybean crushers. Nevertheless, soybean meal prices have consistently exceeded soybean prices, reversing the price relationship found in international markets and imposing higher production costs on the poultry industry. This pattern is due to oligopoly market power exercised by the crushers in the absence of competition from imported soybean meal.

Sierra Food Crops

By order of farmgate value in 1988, the principal food crops produced in the Sierra are potatoes, soft corn, tomatoes, dry beans, onions, barley and wheat (Chapter 6). Tomatoes and onions will be treated along with other vegetables in a later section. Wheat, barley and potato production have declined, with barley and wheat showing the most drastic decreases (Table 8.3). Soft corn and dry bean production have been highly variable, with no clear positive or negative trends.

Sierra food crop production is characterized by very small land holdings. The average farm size in many areas of the Sierra is less than two hectares. All five Sierra food crops are generally sold in small lots to local assemblers by individual farmers. Marketed surplus (the proportion of total production which is marketed) ranges from 43 percent for soft corn to 72 percent for barley and dry beans (Consultores Asociados 1989a, 1989b, 1989d).

Functional distinctions can be made between the marketing of wheat and barley on

Table 8.3   Indexes of Sierra Crop Production, 1975-1987

Year	Wheat	Barley	Soft Corn	Dry Beans	Potatoes
1975	100	100	100	100	100
1976	72	98	117	127	110
1977	62	65	60	100	84
1978	45	35	43	72	69
1979	48	33	202	89	51
1980	48	39	50	101	65
1981	64	43	54	114	78
1982	60	56	61	109	83
1983	42	47	49	78	63
1984	39	40	63	100	78
1985	29	43	68	141	85
1986	51	70	118	104	78
1987	48	48	111	97	71

Source: Consultores Asociados 1989a, 1989b, 1989c, 1989d, 1989e.

the one hand, and potatoes, dry beans and soft corn on the other. Wheat and barley are industrialized, wheat being used primarily for bread and pasta and barley for beer. Marketing channels for domestically produced grain are short, commonly with two transactions for the grain to arrive to millers and brewers. Post-harvest losses are relatively low. Seasonal price movements are modest, due in part to year-round imports of each grain. Wheat imports increased 120 percent between 1973 and 1987, and represented over 95 percent of total supply in 1988. Barley imports tripled between 1976 and 1985 and comprised 31 percent of total supply in 1988. Both millers and brewers prefer imported grain due to its higher quality and more streamlined marketing process. As a result, brewers purchased only 17 percent of national barley production between 1978 and 1988. Millers buy a larger proportion of national wheat production, although probably not over 50-60 percent.

Potatoes, beans and soft corn are with few exceptions not industrialized. Marketing channels are long and the retail distribution system is extremely fragmented. Sales volumes tend to be small, losses large, margins high and quality poor. Total physical losses of potatoes between the farm and retail levels are estimated to be as high as 22 percent (Consultores Asociados 1989e). Soft corn losses are lower but still high. Seasonal price movements can be extreme, especially in outlying markets. This problem is especially severe in potatoes, where the ratio of the seasonal high price to the seasonal low price at the retail level often exceeds 2.5 in Guayaquil and Quito and reaches as high as 5.0 in outlying markets.

Direct state participation in Sierra food-crop markets is almost non-existent. ENAC purchased dry beans only in 1981 and has never purchased any other Sierra crop. Indirect state participation includes the setting of minimum producer and maximum consumer prices for each crop, periodic shutting of borders to stop dry bean-sales to Colombia and Peru and direct and indirect subsidies on imported wheat and locally produced wheat flour. No effective system of grades and standards exists. Minimum producer and maximum consumer prices are seldom enforced. Wheat and wheat flour subsidies were by far the most important government policy affecting Sierra agriculture, prior to their elimination in late 1988. They had major impacts on domestic wheat and dairy production and on consumption patterns. Periodic border closings to impede the flow of dry beans to Colombia also have drastically depressed prices received by Ecuadorian producers in certain years. Given the very small internal market for the type of bean sold to Colombia, allowing unimpeded foreign sales would significantly benefit producers, while imposing little or no cost on Ecuadorian consumers.

The principal problems affecting the marketing of Sierra food grains include poor quality, relatively high marketing margins and price instability. Poor quality affects all crops and physical losses are relatively high in potatoes and soft corn. High margins and a fragmented retail distribution process principally affect potatoes, soft corn and beans. Elevated margins are due largely to related high marketing costs. Price instability is most severe in potatoes due largely to weather, frosts and droughts. Soft corn also shows relatively large seasonal and interyear variations.

Poultry and Eggs

The poultry industry in Ecuador has been among the most dynamic in the country. Growth rates were rapid and real prices fell steadily throughout the 1970s and into the 1980s. These trends, combined with rapidly growing urban populations and per capita income, place eggs and chicken within the financial reach of a large share of the population.

Nevertheless, the industry has experienced serious difficulties in recent years. According to MAG Poultry Division data, per capita consumption of chicken has fallen slightly since 1982, while per capita consumption of eggs had a pronounced decline. Currently, chicken is moderately more expensive than beef and is considered a luxury good by many consumers. Slow productivity growth will likely preclude falling real prices of hard corn and soybean meal in the absence of a more liberalized trade policy. Thus, the fundamental challenge facing this industry over the next five to ten years is to maintain or increase per capita consumption of poultry products in the face of rising or stagnant input prices and falling or stagnant real per capita incomes.

An econometric supply and demand analysis (Tschirley 1988) indicates that population growth, and to a lesser extent changes in consumer preferences, will cause total chicken and egg demand to continue to increase significantly, even with stagnant real prices and per capita incomes. Expected increases in chicken demand between 1987 and 1996, are 23 percent under a "low" scenario of falling real incomes and increasing real prices, 81 percent under an "intermediate" scenario of constant real prices and incomes and 169 percent under a "high" scenario of falling real prices and rising real incomes. Expected increases in derived demand for hard corn and sorghum, and soybean meal are relatively large (Table 8.4).[5]

It appears realistic to expect an increase in hard corn, sorghum and soybean meal demand at least equal to that in the intermediate scenario. The challenge faced by the country is illustrated by the fact that hard corn and sorghum production since 1985 (a year of self-sufficient domestic production) would have had to increase at a compound annual rate of 4.1 percent just to assure sufficient domestically produced supplies under the "medium" scenario. In fact, production has fallen since that time and it appears quite unlikely that Ecuador can attain the necessary productivity growth to satisfy its feed grains needs solely through domestic production.[6]

Feed grain price and import policies thus become critical issues for this subsector. It will be necessary for Ecuador to design a comprehensive policy that encourages efficient domestic production, while guaranteeing stable and sufficient domestic and

Table 8.4 Projected Increases in Derived Demand by the Poultry Industry for Hard
Corn, Sorghum and Soybean Meal in Ecuador, 1987-1996

	Increase Over 10 Years (%)	
Scenario	Hard Corn and Sorghum	Soybean Meal
Low	106	112
Intermediate	49	53
High	8	11

Source: Tschirley 1988.

imported supplies to the feed manufacturing industry. This policy must be complemented by aggressive agricultural research to increase productivity and reduce the prices of feed grains.

Beef

Beef is the main meat consumed in Ecuador. In 1986, per capita consumption was 11.5 kilograms (kg) compared to 2.3 kg of pork and 5.6 kg of poultry (Sarhan). Beef produced in the Sierra comes largely from dairy herds. In the Costa and Oriente most cattle herds are composed of beef animals, usually a combination of native breeds and Cebu. Live cattle are trucked from surplus provinces to the larger cities for slaughter and immediate distribution, most frequently without refrigeration. In 1986, there were 113 slaughterhouses scattered throughout the country, nearly three-fourths of which were municipal enterprises that provide custom services to wholesalers who assemble live cattle and sell dressed beef. The fees charged by the municipal slaughterhouses are low and usually subsidized by local governments. Although there is a strict law establishing sanitary standards, it is not enforced.

The specialized group of intermediaries called *introductores* are the main coordinators of the beef marketing system. They buy live cattle from producers, assemble truck load lots and arrange for slaughter and delivery of carcass beef to retailers. This is a closely knit system that provides a reasonably stable meat supply and short-term operating credit to retailers. Most beef is sold to consumers by small retailers in public markets. Meat handling generally is unsanitary, cutting methods are crude and gross margins are relatively large. A high percentage of the beef carcass and viscera are sold for human consumption.

The beef marketing system has received a great deal of criticism. Producers are believed to be at a disadvantage in selling live animals to the introductores. Buyers are alleged to have an information advantage and to be more skilled than producers at estimating live cattle weights. Assembly market facilities are non-existent or deficient and relatively unregulated. Slaughterhouses are unsanitary and a threat to human health. Competition among wholesalers also has been questioned.

Improvements are being made by both the public and private sectors. One supermarket chain (Supermaxi) and a few hotels have direct supply arrangements with producers. The animals are slaughtered in private abattoirs. Several municipalities are planning new slaughtering facilities. Much remains to be done to facilitate the development of an efficient and sanitary system of beef marketing. Proposals for the

Table 8.5 Destination of Marketed Milk in Ecuador, 1987

Destination	Percent
Fluid consumption	54
Pasteurized milk	16
Raw Milk	36
Reconstituted imported powder	02
Milk Products (cheese, powder, butter, ice cream, yogurt)	46
Industrial plant production	10
Small plant production	36
Total	100

Source: Echeverria.

consolidation of slaughtering into a few large, regional facilities with refrigerated transport and distribution systems should be approached with caution. This alternative may prove to be desirable for the long run, but in the short run much could be done to improve the functioning of assembly markets and the organization of more competitive and technically adequate slaughtering and retailing channels.

Milk

More than three-fourths of all milk is produced in the Sierra, where agro-ecological conditions favor dairying. Substantial volumes of fresh milk are transported by refrigerated trucks from the Sierra to Guayaquil and other Costa urban markets. Total milk production has increased at about three percent per year over the past decade. Annual consumption has held steady near 80 liters per person, including fluid milk and the fluid equivalent of milk products. Approximately one-third of the total milk output is used on farms to feed calves.

The government sets minimum prices for milk at the farm level and maximum prices at the consumer level. The law provides for the control of milk quality. The Economic Front reviews and adjusts prices periodically, taking into consideration cost-of-production studies by a milk producer association and the MAG.

However, it is alleged by producers that the controlled prices do not cover production costs, especially during inflationary surges. As a result, herds are being reduced or liquidated (Echeverria). In practice, price controls are easier to monitor on pasteurized, packaged fluid milk than on raw milk. The latter has a reputation of being unsanitary, diluted with water and dispensed with non-standardized ladles from milk cans. Furthermore, there are no price controls on processed milk products. This creates opportunities for greater profit by diverting milk from pasteurized to unpasteurized fluid use, or to cheese, butter and other processed products. Clandestine sales to Colombia and Peru also have been means of realizing higher prices for dairy products.

The GOE has very limited capacity to enforce the law on sanitary handling of milk. More than two-thirds of the milk used in fluid form is unpasteurized (Table 8.5) and there is little if any control of handling practices from farm to consumer. Likewise, more than three-fourths of manufactured milk products are produced in small, relatively unsupervised plants.

Table 8.6 Edible Oil Production, Imports and Total Availability in Ecuador, 1977-1987 (Metric Tons)

Year	Cotton, Sesame, and Peanuts		Soybeans		African Palm		Total Avail.	%Dom. Prod.
	Domestic Prod.	Imports	Domestic Prod.	Imports	Domestic Prod.	Imports		
1977	4,526	0.8	3,854	10,014	26,110	10,993	55,498	62
1978	4,054	114.5	5,060	20,733	31,715	500	62,176	66
1979	6,574	0.5	5,981	21,062	29,648	498	63,764	66
1980	7,021	20.7	6,719	21,168	44,087	4,428	83,444	69
1981	6,781	0.1	6,637	16,134	54,000	0	83,552	81
1982	3,498	6.8	7,484	53,398	55,672	0	120,059	56
1983	1,752	1.4	2,815	54,905	63,761	0	123,235	55
1984	2,250	1.7	9,422	54,222	67,040	0	132,936	59
1985	3,576	0.6	12,577	33,650	82,421	0	132,224	75
1986	4,312	0.6	14,080	10,082	88,201	0	116,675	91
1987	3,892	0.0	23,772	0	92,061	0	119,725	100

Source: Centeno, Plúa and Veliz.

Oil Crops

Production and consumption of vegetable oils have grown very rapidly since the early 1970s. Between 1977 and 1987, total availability (domestic production and imports) of these oils increased by nearly 115 percent, while imports fell from 38 percent to 0 percent of total availability (Table 8.6). Some estimates indicate that as much as 30 percent of this total supply is traded illegally to Colombia and Peru. Rapid growth in per capita income into the early 1980s clearly boosted per capita consumption. African oilpalm and soybeans are the primary sources of oil supply, accounting for nearly 97 percent of the total in 1987. Palm oil use has increased and in 1987 represented over 75 percent of the total.

African oilpalm fruit is produced primarily on large plantations located in Los Ríos and Pichincha provinces in the Costa and Napo province in the northeastern part of the Oriente. There is a great deal of forward and backward integration in this industry. Six of the top 11 and three of the top four crushers have invested in plantations in the Oriente, while at least three of the largest plantations have crushing and refining plants. The crushing of palm fruit is not highly concentrated, with at least 27 crushers active in the country. Nevertheless, the two largest crushers have over one-third of all crushing capacity and could begin to increase their market share. Refining of crude palm oil is far more concentrated; four firms dominate the industry with nearly 70 percent of production.

The concentration in this industry raises difficult policy questions regarding the best manner to encourage efficiency and avoid oligopoly and oligopsony pricing. These issues will be addressed below.

Fruits and Vegetables

The production and marketing systems for fruits and vegetables present many problems. Production tends to be small-scale and geographically scattered. The transport costs tend to be high, especially for the more perishable products.

A network of new urban wholesale markets has been considered as a major element in improving the marketing of fruits and vegetables. These markets could be the focal points for introducing new classification, packaging and handling methods, and could serve also as centers for price formation. Market information systems could then provide traders and producers with useful data on prices and volumes traded. These activities have been initiated at the Quito wholesale market and are being extended to other major trading centers. Ambato has been an important concentration market for cool-climate fruits and vegetables to be transhipped to Guayaquil and other cities in the Costa as well as to Quito. A new wholesale transhipment facility was under construction in 1989. The wholesale markets also can serve as assembly centers for nearby producers who can deliver products directly to them, but rural assembly markets will be needed to serve more distant producing areas.

Agricultural Export Commodities

Cacao, coffee and bananas have been produced primarily for export for many decades. Shrimp and other seafood exports have expanded rapidly in the past two decades. The relative importance and the historical trends in agricultural exports are described and analyzed in Chapter 3.

Bananas The banana industry is dominated by a few large exporting firms, the three largest being Noboa, Standard Fruit and Reybanpac. Several thousand growers have production contracts with the main exporters. There are thousands of other growers who produce outside the contract system and sell through export agents located in the production areas. When the export market is weak, or when there is surplus production, substantial quantities are left unharvested or fed to livestock.

The major markets for Ecuadorian bananas are the United States, West Germany, Belgium, Luxembourg and Italy. There is little reason to expect significant increases in export sales above the slow upward trend of the past two decades, although some increase may develop as the Eastern European market opens up. The major problem facing the banana industry is the intense competition in international markets but Ecuador has been able to maintain its leading position.

Cacao For many decades Ecuadorian cacao had an excellent reputation for its distinctive flavor. It therefore commanded a significant price premium. However, this reputation has been severely eroded over the past 20 years and a substantial proportion of Ecuadorian cacao now sells at a discount. Disease problems have further reduced export revenues from this crop.

A recent study of the international market for Ecuadorian cacao (Harrison, Schulte and Baker) documents of the quality problems with the Ecuadorian product. The authors identified the post-harvest handling and marketing practices that contribute to the quality problem. They recommended vigorous industry-wide efforts to regain a solid reputation for a high quality product. An aggressive educational program and public sector research and extension were strongly recommended. It was also suggested that the industry consider a self-imposed export tax to generate funds to support research, education and market development activities. Implementation will be a major challenge since cacao is produced by a large number of small farmers who sell their beans to many small assemblers. At present there is very little price incentive of Ecuadorian cacao now sells at a discount. Disease problems have further reduced export revenues from this crop.

A recent study of the international market for Ecuadorian cacao (Harrison, Schulte and Baker) documents of the quality problems with the Ecuadorian product. The authors identified the post-harvest handling and marketing practices that contribute to the quality problem. They recommended vigorous industry-wide efforts to regain a solid reputation for a high quality product. An aggressive educational program and public sector research and extension were strongly recommended. It was also suggested that the industry consider a self-imposed export tax to generate funds to support research, education and market development activities. Implementation will be a major challenge since cacao is produced by a large number of small farmers who sell their beans to many small assemblers. At present there is very little price incentive for improved quality reflected through the market channels to producers.

Coffee The coffee production and marketing system probably involves over a million people in various aspects of growing, processing and marketing. There are approximately 120,000 farms producing coffee, some as their principal commercial enterprise and others as a supplemental cash crop. The main domestic marketing problems stem from the relatively low level of technology used in the production, harvesting, drying and sorting of coffee beans. In addition, wide international price fluctuations, such as occurred in 1988-1989, have created significant market risks, especially for coffee producers. The termination of the International Coffee Agreement has increased price instability. The Ecuadorian coffee industry will find it necessary to improve quality and reduce production and marketing costs if is to compete effectively with other exporting countries.

Shrimp The rapid growth of the Ecuadorian shrimp industry is often cited as one of the success stories in the promotion of nontraditional exports. The initiative came from the private sector with some support from public financial institutions. The United States and Japan have been the principal markets for Ecuadorian shrimp. During the late 1980s, international competition has increased, especially from China, Taiwan and Indonesia. Meanwhile, the Ecuadorian shrimp industry has experienced serious production problems due to the inadequate supply of shrimp larvae needed to stock the growing ponds. The apparent solution is to expand the artificial production of larvae but this has met with limited success. The industry also is confronted with growing public concerns regarding the ecological impacts of the ponds (Espinoza; and Chapter 4).

Continued growth in the demand for shrimp in international markets will stimulate efforts to maintain and expand Ecuadorian production for export. Although there are about 180 exporting firms the Association of Shrimp Producers considers that only 25 to 30 are capable of offering an export-quality product. Access to investment and operating credit, export tax reduction or elimination and increased scientific research are priority concerns if Ecuador is to maintain a position as a leading shrimp exporter.

Non-Traditional Agricultural Exports Since the early 1980s the GOE has expressed a strong interest in expanding non-traditional exports to diversify and expand foreign exchange earnings. Agricultural production, processing and exporting enterprises are being promoted but growth has been slow and export levels remain very low. A flower-export industry is becoming established and a few, small initiatives are emerging in fruits and vegetables. For these to expand significantly requires a combination of macroeconomic policies that provide incentives for exporting; less time-consuming, costly legal requirements for arranging export transactions; and public sector research, extension and market information programs. The expansion of non-traditional exports should be approached as a long-term effort that takes place in conjunction with the further development of efficient and progressive domestic production and marketing systems.

Marketing Margins

Marketing margins are important indicators of a marketing system's performance. A margin is the difference between the price of a product at one level in the system and the price of a similar product at a higher level. This margin represents the price paid for necessary marketing services. Marketing services involve costs which must be covered if they are to be provided by the private sector.

A typical farm-consumer gross margin for potatoes in 1987 was 41 percent of the consumer price (Consultores Asociados 1989e). Gross wholesale-retail margins as a percentage of wholesale prices ranged from a low of 20 percent in Quito to a high of 37 percent in Portoviejo. However, relatively stable absolute margins and highly variable prices resulted in margins that often exceeded 50 percent during harvest. Spatial margins are tremendously variable. Between Quito and outlying markets, the general pattern is one of slightly negative margins during February through April, followed by pronounced increases through September or October. Both wholesale-retail and spatial wholesale potato margins indicate probable marketing inefficiencies which merit further attention.

A typical farm-consumer gross margin for rice during the 1988 winter harvest was 49 percent of the consumer price (Ramos 1989a). Of this, nearly 17 percent was earned by the rice miller and covered assembly, farm to mill transportation, drying, cleaning and milling.[7] Twenty-three percent was earned by between one and three wholesalers and covered transportation and distribution costs. Finally, 9 percent was earned by retailers for the purchase, transport and sale of the rice in one pound bags. A 23 percent margin for wholesalers appears to be above the level which could be justified by simple cost considerations and therefore raises the possibility of market power. A definitive answer on this issue must await further investigation.

With some exceptions, marketing margins for agricultural commodities in Ecuador appear to be reasonable, given the existing marketing and institutional infrastructure. For the most part, returns to labor are low and returns to capital are highly variable. Little evidence exists to support frequent allegations that middlemen as a group are earning consistently high and unwarranted profits. On the contrary, the earnings of thousands of small retailers, assemblers and transporters are less than or equal to the minimum wage. For many intermediaries, this low income represents their best employment opportunity.

Input Marketing Subsystems

This section focuses on the marketing systems for pesticides, fertilizers, seeds, machinery and equipment. Pesticides, fertilizers, seeds and machinery, in conjunction with the scientific knowledge base, are major determinants of the productivity of the agricultural sector. It is, therefore, critical that these products be readily available, of consistently high quality and priced consistent with competitive conditions. The GOE has taken a direct role in the marketing of all except pesticides. It created parastatals to market certified seeds and fertilizer and a mechanization program to sell machinery services to farmers.

Seeds

The National Seed Company (EMSEMILLAS) was created to produce and market certified rice, hard and soft corn, soybean, cotton, wheat, barley and potato seeds developed by INIAP. It dominates the certified seed market, selling 71 percent of all rice, hard corn and soybean seed, and 63 percent of certified seeds of all types in 1987 (Economic Perspectives, Inc. 1987c). Six other firms along with INIAP share the remaining 37 percent of the market. EMSEMILLAS has the processing capacity to supply the entire Ecuadorian certified seed market and is the only firm capable of cold storage, giving it a further strategic market advantage.

Certified seed quality generally is good and use in the Costa has increased tremendously over time, despite prices which rose relative to product prices. Between 1981 and 1986 seed:product price ratios rose nearly 7 percent for soybeans, 15 percent for rice and 114 percent for hard corn. Average ratios in 1986 for the top four Sierra food crops (potatoes, soft corn, wheat and barley) were 1.44, compared with 2.57 for the top three grains in the Costa (rice, hard corn and soybeans). Table 6.16 in Chapter 6 shows the approximate percentage of land in each crop which is planted with certified seeds. These data indicate that use of certified seed in the Sierra is much lower than that in the Costa. One reason for this differential may be the inadequate marketing system relative to farm size. Sales outlets are located in and around larger towns and cities in both regions. Since farm size and its resource base are much smaller in the Sierra, the costs of obtaining improved seed is relatively greater for most Sierra farmers. Also, urban centers of the Costa are more widely dispersed than in the Sierra (Chapter 5). As a result, small and medium farmers of the Sierra use unimproved seed almost exclusively.

Pesticides

Although precise data is not available, pesticide use per hectare appears to have remained relatively stable during the past 10 years. Most pesticides are used by technified and semitechnified farmers in the Costa, for whom these chemicals comprise a larger proportion of production costs than do fertilizers (Economic Perspectives, Inc. 1987d). In the Sierra, potatoes are the most intensive users of pesticides. All pesticides are imported without quantitative restrictions, but the industry is nevertheless tremendously concentrated. Between 1984 and 1986, the top three firms controlled 52 percent of all imports.

Fertilizers

The fertilizer industry also is dependent entirely on imports (Economic Perspectives, Inc. 1987a). Overall, it suffers from problems nearly identical to those affecting the chemical inputs industry. Local market power can be very strong and service to small and medium farmers is relatively poor. The Ecuadorian Fertilizer Company (FERTISA) is the government parastatal charged with rectifying this situation. In the past, it has imported simple fertilizers and mixed them to produce compound fertilizers. Its production and mixing capacity would allow it, if functioning efficiently, to dominate the fertilizer market. However, as of December 31, 1988, its accumulated losses were equal to 92 percent of its total capital and it made no sales in 1989. Its major shareholders, the National Development Bank (BNF) with 65 percent of all shares, the National Finance Corporation (CFN) with nearly 21 percent and MAG with nearly 6 percent, have been unable to reach agreement on a solution to FERTISA's financial problems (see Chapters 6 and 11).

Farm Equipment

All motorized farm equipment and 80 percent of non-motorized farm equipment is imported. Although the import process is cumbersome, any individual can import machinery. Nevertheless, the industry is quite concentrated. In terms of total value, the top five firms imported 50 percent of all machinery in 1986 and the top 10 imported 66 percent. Concentration is significantly higher within sub-groups. For example, the top three firms in 1986 imported nearly 90 percent of all harvesters and milking equipment and 75 percent of all replacement parts.

The National Mechanization Program (PRONAMEC) within the MAG is the government's response to this highly concentrated industry structure (Economic Perspectives, Inc. 1987b). Operating out of 17 centers, 11 in the Sierra and six in the Costa, it sells machinery services to farmers in direct competition with private sellers of the same services. It was created in 1974 and by 1985 had acquired 435 tractors and 36 harvesters, as well as 784 other pieces of equipment. The program suffers from a number of serious problems, fundamentally related to a lack of funds and ineffective management. By 1987, only 313 tractors and 28 harvesters were in working order. Other problems include a personnel management system in which staff and workers are assigned by a government agency with little knowledge of the program and its needs. There also is a lack of systematic attempts to forecast demand for services and thereby plan its activities. Unless these problems are addressed, PRONAMEC will inevitably play a diminishing role in the provision of machinery services to the agricultural sector.

An Agenda for Market System Development

The development of an improved market system must focus on five interrelated issues: (a) the general issue of subsidies; (b) price policy; (c) strategic investments in market system development; (d) market regulations; and (e) public sector support services to facilitate development of an efficient market system.

Subsidies

Subsidies have become ubiquitous in Ecuadorian agriculture. For every winner from these subsidies, there also are losers. Overall, they have exacted a high price in terms of both total output and its distribution. As a general recommendation, most if not all untargeted subsidies should be eliminated. It is critical that the exchange rate be allowed to closely track its real level. Positive real interest rates should be established. ENAC support prices should not automatically cover all fixed and variable costs of production, plus profits. Finally, ENAC purchases and sales should be at prices that allow it to at least recover interest costs and depreciation on its facilities. The objectives of efficiency and market stabilization should be separated from that of providing welfare assistance to low-income producers and consumers.

As generalized subsidies are eliminated, the savings they generate should be used to fund a small number of carefully designed, targeted subsidies. In this regard, ENPROVIT's role needs to be reoriented to provide a small number of basic foods to a carefully delineated target population of nutritionally vulnerable consumers.

Price Policy

Grains Basic grains in Ecuador have for many years received special attention with regard to price policy. The GOE will in all likelihood continue to intervene in some way in its grain markets. The objective, then, is to design a system that in the words of Ahmed and Bernard (p. 9) "...would minimize economic waste but preserve the elements that address food security and price support concerns arising from severe price instability."[8] Such a system must acknowledge the inescapable role of markets in allocating resources and attempt to modify only the more extreme results of market forces. It is therefore recommended that a "rule-based" price band policy be applied to rice, hard corn and perhaps to wheat, barley and soybeans.[9] The band consists of floor and ceiling prices. No legal sanctions of any kind are used to enforce these price limits. Market participants can freely buy and sell at whatever market-clearing price results. However, "rules of the game" are set so that the equilibrium price will generally lie between the floor and ceiling. In principle, two alternative mechanisms can be utilized to achieve this result. It can be accomplished solely through direct government purchases at the floor price and sales at the ceiling price. Alternatively, the band can be implemented exclusively through variable duties and/or subsidies on imports and/or exports. The variable duties and subsidies are set so that importers always pay the ceiling price and exporters always receive the floor price. Imports are subsidized if the world price exceeds the ceiling and taxed if they are below it. Similarly, exports are taxed if the world price exceeds the floor price and subsidized if they are below it. In practice, some combination of the trade and government intervention approaches will likely be necessary to effectively defend the price floor and ceiling.

The system would be rule-based in the following sense. The announcement of floor and ceiling prices prior to planting establishes the price levels facing importers and exporters and which trigger government purchases and sales. Once these prices are announced, the system becomes largely self-regulating. The government acts predictably according to the buy/sell and variable levy/subsidy rules implied by the band and private sector participants choose freely to buy and sell domestically or internationally at whatever market price they face. Such a rule-based system saves very scarce administrative and analytical capacity and thereby improves the probability of the policy's success.

Two cases relevant to Ecuador can be identified in which the recommended mix of policy instruments (direct government intervention versus trade) differs: the import case and the self-sufficiency case. The import case refers to a situation in which a country imports significant quantities of grain every year and faces no realistic probability of being a self-sufficient or surplus producer. This case currently applies very well to wheat and barley. In the self-sufficiency case a country is on the edge of adequacy, sometimes facing deficits and sometimes surpluses. Rice and hard corn are currently such crops in Ecuador. Briefly, direct government participation is relatively less important in the import case and more important in the self-sufficiency case. In the self-sufficiency case, imports or government sales at the price ceiling and exports or government purchases at the price floor are both necessary.[10]

Requirements to ensure the success of the policy include administrative and operational flexibility, sufficient annual budgets and credit lines to finance the required interventions, a balanced and stable relationship between the level of the band and the level of border prices, timely and accurate situation and outlook information on world and domestic markets and the ability to analyze this information and recommend timely appropriate. Finally, in determining the floor and ceiling prices--the *level* and *width* of the band--the floor price should not be located "too" far above the minimum producer price and the ceiling price should not be fixed "too" far below the maximum consumer price which would result without State intervention. The width of the band should be sufficient to allow "normal" seasonal price movements without government intervention. This movement will be closely related to normal trading margins and direct financial costs of storage. If seasonal price movements are unduly restricted, public storage will begin to replace private storage and the cost of the policy may reach unacceptable levels. In general, the band should closely track world price trends.

In summary, attempting to impose a very high, low, narrow or complicated band, or one divorced from world market prices, will result in an expensive and unsustainable policy. By limiting its actions to the elimination of extreme fluctuations in prices, the government will avoid the large expenses and chronic financial losses that so often lead to the failure of well-intentioned price policies.

Other Products The relatively perishable nature of potatoes and soft corn, rules out the type of active price policy suggested for the basic grains. In these cases, the government should encourage strategic investments in their marketing systems in order to increase efficiency and adaptability and contribute to lower costs, more stable prices and fewer post-harvest losses. Milk and beef price controls probably should be eliminated, given the near impossibility of enforcing them. The GOE should focus its efforts on enforcing sanitary regulations, useful grades and standards and market information.

Significant market concentration at the processing level in the sugar and oilseed markets requires that these processors be exposed to world market competition. Quantitative restrictions on foreign trade should be eliminated for raw, intermediate and final products. The access to alternative markets that this policy gives to retailers and farmers might be expected to negate the market power that processors currently enjoy.

Inputs The agricultural input marketing system has a highly concentrated structure, a relatively rudimentary state of development and government intervention has failed to solve existing problems. The first characteristic presents the danger of prices significantly above competitive levels, while the second results in much better service to larger farmers than to their smaller neighbors. The failure of efforts to improve input marketing systems indicates that existing policies are seriously flawed.

The capacity of EMSEMILLAS and FERTISA to supply the entire Ecuadorian market with certified seed and fertilizer has important policy implications. It implies that three alternatives to the current ineffective approach could be used to capitalize on the economies of scale this situation offers, while avoiding monopoly pricing: (a) a government monopoly could be imposed; (b) the sector could be privatized but subject to government price setting; or (c) the sector could be privatized and subjected to vigorous price competition from imported materials, without government price setting.

The current financial and administrative problems of FERTISA and EMSEMILLAS argue against government monopoly as a recommendable policy. The third alternative, private ownership subject only to import competition, may be well suited to fertilizers. This approach would probably not be successful in the seed industry, since imported seed generally needs to be adapted to local conditions prior to use. Thus if EMSEMILLAS is to be privatized, there seems little choice but to subject it to government regulation.

The chemical industry, though clearly not a natural monopoly, shows signs of market concentration. In this case and that of fertilizers, a free import policy will not create effective competition unless local farmer organizations and other cooperative institutions have unhindered access to imported products. This will require not just new laws or executive decrees, but streamlining of the bureaucratic import process, increased managerial capability within the organizations, training in the intricacies of the import process and innovative institutional arrangements to channel credit to these organizations. If these problems can be successfully addressed, the third option could effectively correct the distorted prices which result from the structural failures in input markets. If the weaknesses of farmer and cooperative organizations remain pricing problems probably will continue to exist in these industries.

Strategic Public Sector Investments

During the 1970s and early 1980s the Ecuadorian government was able to make substantial investments in a highway network that facilitated the development of a more integrated national market for food and agricultural commodities. However, the depressed economic conditions since 1982 have greatly reduced the ability of the government to maintain the existing highway system or to extend and improve roads serving rural communities. Further exploitation of the agricultural potential can be accelerated by strategic investments in the road system. Additionally, export enterprises will need improved seaport and airport facilities if they are to compete internationally, especially in perishable commodities. Some combination of user fees, domestic taxes and long-term international loans will be needed to finance these infrastructure investments. Investments in electric energy generation and distribution and water systems also are necessary for the development of new and expanded agricultural processing industries.

The rapid growth of the larger cities requires planning and construction of new wholesale market facilities to lower marketing costs through improved logistics and greater transparency of the price formation process. Improved market facilities in smaller towns also are important to improve the efficiency of the entire system.

The deplorable sanitary conditions in existing slaughter plants should be corrected and clandestine, unsupervised slaughter eliminated. New investments are being made in livestock slaughter plants operated by municipalities. However, over the longer run there should be greater support for the entry of privately owned slaughter plants along with more effective government supervision of sanitary conditions.

Existing government-owned grain storage facilities are operated by insufficiently trained technicians and lack the maintenance necessary to function efficiently. Alternative courses of action are to upgrade government facilities and staff, to transfer the ownership and operation of the facilities to the private sector or to lease the facilities to the private sector on a long-term basis. In the latter two cases ENAC could intervene in grain markets simply by purchasing and selling warehouse receipts and maintaining reserve stocks in privately operated storage facilities. This would increase the efficiency of government intervention, in terms of the cost required to obtain a given level of price stability.

Market Regulations

There are always laws, regulations or informal rules that structure the incentives confronting market participants and place limitations on their behavior. Regulations can facilitate trading and contribute to the development of efficient market systems, but can also serve as barriers to the exploitation of new economic opportunities. This is likely to be the case when regulations become obsolete due to changing technologies and business practices, or when unrealistic rules and standards have been established at the outset.

Ecuador has made considerable progress in establishing standard weights and measures but enforcement capabilities are limited. Quality standards on agricultural inputs are not well developed and the standards that exist are not adequately enforced. The Ecuadorian Institute for Normalization (INEN) has issued quality standards for more than 1,500 processed food products but much remains to be done to extend this effort and to focus attention on problems with processed foods where consumer health may be compromised.

Specific areas of concern being addressed by INEN include the following: (a) a lack of sanitation in food processing that results in the transmission of toxic pathogens to consumers; (b) fraudulent labeling regarding ingredients, nutritional content and net weights; and (c) chemical residues in food from pesticide application at the farm level and chemical additives used in food processing (see Chapter 4).

Descriptive quality grades for raw agricultural commodities are beginning to emerge along with an expanding market information system. The widespread use of grading criteria in the pricing of commodities is badly needed to provide economic incentives for improving product quality. However, care must be taken to develop and promote the acceptance of realistic grades and standards without requiring mandatory use throughout the private trading system.

The government has important regulatory functions in the development of efficient and equitable food systems. In Ecuador, there is a strong disposition to control private trading. This has resulted in increased risks and costs to private sector entrepreneurs and has not contributed significantly to the achievement of stated development goals. Hence, a general recommendation is that government policymakers and administrators be sensitive to the societal cost of regulations that have negative effects on the food industry.

Public Sector Support Services

For markets to function effectively, the GOE must provide direct market support services to actively improve market performance. These include providing information and analyses, financial assistance, research and education.

Agricultural Information and Market Analyses Over the past several years the agricultural statistics and market information service within the MAG has had very limited ability to produce and disseminate reliable and timely estimates of crop and livestock production, storage stocks and current market price information. Several other government agencies have made independent estimates of agricultural production and marketing statistics. The result has been incomplete, inconsistent and often conflicting data sets which fail to provide the information needed to support sound administrative decisions by government and well-informed production and marketing decisions in the private sector.

The crucial importance of improving agricultural statistics and market information system was recognized in the design of the Agricultural Sector Reorientation Project. A major objective of the project has been to strengthen the technical capabilities of two agencies, the National Institute of Statistics and Census (INEC) and the MAG, to develop a more coordinated national agricultural information system. The activities that have been supported include: (a) an expanded market news service; (b) a crop and livestock reporting service; (c) agroclimatic data collection and analysis for use in crop production forecasts; and (d) a computerized data management system.

The market news service has regular reporting from 26 market centers covering some 60 commodities (MAG 1988; Abt Associates). Prices and related market information are disseminated daily. Weekly printed reports were given limited distribution until the end of 1989, when insufficient funding forced their suspension. Personnel have been partially trained and a market information office has been organized. Much additional work is needed to improve the quality of the information through the use of generally accepted grades and standards. Quantity data also would be extremely useful to enable a better understanding of how the different markets function. Finally, the usefulness of market information could be substantially increased with carefully prepared commodity market analyses.

Much also remains to be done to improve crop and livestock production estimates. An area frame sample is being used to estimate crop production. Yield forecasting is being attempted and will be assisted by the on-going agroclimatic data collection and analysis.

An important constraint facing all these efforts has been the difficulty of coordinating activities between INEC and MAG and in obtaining adequate long-term funding support from the GOE to maintain a trained staff and the necessary facilities (Abt Associates). An additional constraint is the negative public sector attitude toward the private sector and especially toward processors and traders. Distrust of government also exists within the private sector and reduces their willingness to share data with publicly sponsored, market-information services. It will take considerable time and demonstrated objectivity in the gathering and use of market data before this distrust can be overcome.

Marketing Credit and Financial Institutions There has been relatively little credit for medium and long-term, private sector investments in marketing facilities and equipment. Commercial banks have been the primary source of short-term credit to finance inventories held by agricultural commodity processors and wholesalers. Small traders and many processors depend to a great extent on their own funds and various schemes for deferring payments for products purchased from farmers or other traders. Rice millers depend to a large extent on cash advances from large wholesalers. The concentration of capital in relatively few wholesalers' hands may inhibit effective competition at this level. Thus, limited access to credit has continued to constrain the development of a more modern, cost effective marketing system (see Chapter 9).

Research, Extension and Education The agricultural research and extension programs carried out by INIAP and the Foundation for Agricultural Development (FUNDAGRO) are directed almost entirely toward production technology. Marketing problems are not being seriously addressed by these institutions. This is an issue that deserves priority attention as a means to facilitate better economic adjustment between agricultural production and market opportunities. Applied research and extension should provide decision support to farmers, private sector intermediaries and public sector administrators. Poorly informed decisions contribute to market failures, missed opportunities and inefficient allocation of resources.

It is particularly important that an institutional capability be established to improve post-harvest handling and processing of agricultural commodities. This capability would reduce product losses and expand the potential for the delivery of higher quality products. Success in promoting the export marketing of non-traditional, perishable commodities can only be achieved through a demonstrated capability to supply a dependable volume of high-quality merchandise. The development of post-harvest technologies and effective institutional arrangements will require close cooperation between the public and private sectors. All of this will take time and can only occur with a major investment in human resources.

The lack of trained personnel is a serious constraint to the development of a more efficient and progressive system of agricultural marketing. At the operational level, there is a need to train people to operate more modern systems of product handling, storage, processing and distribution. Specialized training also is needed in food processing, wholesaling and retailing. More comprehensive academic training is needed to prepare managers, administrators, analysts and planners for leadership positions in both the public and private sectors of the agricultural marketing system. The project paper for the U.S. Agency for International Development (USAID) Agricultural Sector Reorientation Project called attention to the almost complete lack of professionals trained in the field of agricultural economics.

The experience of the MAG and the Agricultural Policy Institute (IDEA) in arranging contract studies has verified the extreme shortage of qualified professionals to carry out high-quality, applied marketing and policy analyses. IDEA has begun organizing agricultural economics courses at a local university and is committed to work with the university toward the development of a comprehensive agricultural economics curriculum. However, the effort is not apt to succeed without the support of a long-term, donor-assisted program. This program should include further graduate training of qualified students and existing faculty and be supplemented with in-service training of public sector personnel. In addition, extension education should be undertaken to address the marketing problems facing private sector groups.

A Concluding Statement

The Ecuadorian agricultural marketing system has played a key role in the country's overall economic development by adding value to farm production and by providing employment to a broad cross-section of society. As population grows, rapid urbanization proceeds and per capita incomes rise, this system must play an increasingly important role in the development process. The efficiency and progressiveness of the system will determine whether it impedes or facilitates this process.

The agricultural marketing system been subject to a great deal of stress over the past twenty years. In general, it has responded positively to the growing demands placed upon it and has, in the process, contributed to the formation of a nationally integrated agricultural market. It, nevertheless, continues to be affected by a number of problems. Foremost among these might be public attitudes towards private sector marketing agents (middlemen) and their activities. A persistent and deeply embedded bias against private marketing agents has resulted in widespread government attempts either to replace these agents with public ones, or to rigidly control their activities. One result of this bias has been insufficient public and private investment in the creation of a more efficient and progressive marketing system.

An alternative approach which can best be summarized as *helping markets work* stands in contrast to both the government's deep mistrust of markets and to the idea that markets must be simply allowed to work. It is based on an appreciation for the tremendous efficiency of markets in allocating resources to their most productive uses, but it also recognizes that market system performance is directly determined by the legal framework within which it operates, the availability of information, the level and distribution of human and physical capital, the ease of entry and the performance of each of the individual markets within the system.[11] The government can and must play a role in helping create an environment within which markets can function efficiently and equitably. This requires the design of more neutral and market-oriented macroeconomic policies, sectoral price policies which simplify and reduce government intervention and clarify the conditions under which it will occur and improved market regulations which contribute to rather than impede efficient market performance. These reforms must be accompanied by strategic investments in marketing infrastructure, support services and training to increase the private sector's ability to respond positively to the improved policy environment.

Finally, even efficient markets will not meet the needs of all members of society. Cost-efficient, targeted interventions must be designed to protect the nutritional status of the most vulnerable population groups. In the long-run, emphasis must be continually placed on providing viable economic opportunities to these groups, so that they may more fully participate in the development process.

NOTES

1. The relative proportions are especially variable in hard maize, due to the substitutability in production between this crop and soybeans during the dry season. Relative price policy between the crops has very significant effects on production of each. Erratic policies in the past have seriously disrupted the corn market.

2. The Four Firm Concentration Ratio (CR4), which indicates the percentage of a market's total production under the control of the four largest firms, is a widely used measure of industry concentration. According to Marion, the CR4 can be divided as follows: highly concentrated oligopoly, 65 percent or more; oligopoly of high-medium concentration, 50 to less than 65 percent; oligopoly of low concentration, 35 to less than 50 percent and unconcentrated market, less than 35 percent.

3. Macroeconomic policies have had very significant indirect effects. See Chapter 2 for a general overview and Scobie and Jardine (1988a, 1988b, 1989) for detailed discussions of these policies.

4. Payment at the official price implied very steep losses during February through April, since the market price exceeded the official price by more than 100 percent at that time. Although the volume of seized grain was minor in both instances, these

actions cause uncertainty in the market. Based on discussions with traders and govern-ment price reporters, there is reason to believe that, in times of shortage, such actions induce withholding of grain from the market rather than its release. The conventional wisdom is the opposite, i.e., that seizures will cause existing grain to flow more quickly to the market.

5. Hard corn and sorghum are direct substitutes in the production of poultry feed.

6. See Tschirley (1989) for more information on this issue.

7. All calculations are done in milled rice equivalents. Thus, the calculated margin covers only the cost of drying, cleaning, and milling. It does not cover the weight loss which occurs during these processes.

8. Ahmed and Bernard have a helpful and concise discussion of the economic justifications for grain stabilization policies. See also Timmer or Streeten for excellent discussions of, as Timmer's subtitle phrases it, "the scope and limits of price policy."

9. Variations on the basic price band approach to price stabilization have been utilized in Indonesia Kenya, and Chile, among other countries. Research on the approach has been carried out in Costa Rica, Honduras, Belize, Peru and Southern Africa. See Ahmed and Bernard; Pinckney; Edwards and Ducci; Paz-Caferatta and Escobal; and Rebolar.

10. For a detailed discussion of the recommended mix of policy instruments in each of these cases see Tschirley, Ramos and Hugo.

11. For example, an inefficient domestic capital market can greatly reduce competition in domestic commodity markets.

REFERENCES

Abt Associates, Inc. 1989. *Evaluation of the Agricultural Sector Reorientation Project*. Quito: USAID.

Ahmed, Raisuddin and Andrew Bernard. 1989. *Rice Price Fluctuation and an Approach to Price Stabilization in Bangladesh*. Washington, D.C.: IFPRI Res. Rpt. No. 72.

Bromley, Ray. 1981. "Market Center and Market Place in Highland Ecuador: A Study of Organization, Regulation, and Ethnic Discrimination." *Cultural Transformations and Ethnicity in Modern Ecuador*. Edited by Norman C. Whitten, Jr. Urbana: University of Illinois Press.

CEDATOS (Center for Studies and Data). 1989. "Estudio de Consumo Familiar, Estrato de Bajos Ingresos." Quito: IDEA.

Centeno, Elena, Juan Plúa and Mauricio Veliz. 1988. "La Industria de Aceites Comestibles en el Ecuador." Quito: MAG, Unidad de Análisis de Políticas.

Consultores Asociados. 1989a. *Producción y Comercialización de Productos de la Sierra: Maíz Suave*, Vol. II. Quito: IDEA, Documento Técnico No. 20.

_____. 1989b. *Producción y Comercialización de Productos de la Sierra: Cebada*, Vol. III. Quito: IDEA, Documento Técnico No. 20.

_____. 1989c. *Producción y Comercialización de Productos de la Sierra: Trigo*, Vol. IV. Quito: IDEA, Documento Técnico No. 20.

_____. 1989d. *Producción y Comercialización de Productos de la Sierra: Frejol*, Vol. V. Quito: IDEA, Documento Técnico No. 20.

_____. 1989e. *Producción y Comercialización de Productos de la Sierra: la Papa*, Vol. VI. Quito: IDEA, Documento Técnico No. 20.

_____. 1988. *El Impacto de las Políticas de Importaciones y Sustentación de Precios de la ENAC en los Mercados de Maíz Duro y Soya*. Quito: IDEA, Documento Técnico No. 12.

Echeverria, Jorge. 1989. "Un Diagnóstico Sobre Mercadeo de la Leche Cruda y Procesada en el Ecuador." Quito: Subsecretaría de Comercialización, MAG.

Economic Perspectives, Inc. 1987a. *An Economic Review of the Fertilizer Industry in Ecuador*. McLean, VA: July.

_____. 1987b. *La Industria de la Maquinaria y Equipo Agrícolas en El Ecuador*. McLean, VA: July.

_____. 1987c. *An Economic Review of the Certified Seed Industry in Ecuador*. McLean, VA: August.

_____. 1987d. *The Agricultural Chemical Industry in Ecuador*. McLean, VA: September.

Edwards, Gonzalo and A. Ducci. 1986. *Alternativas de Estabilización de Precios Agropecuarios*. Santiago, Chile: Departamento de Economía Agraria, Pontificia Universidad Católica de Chile, Serie de Investigación No. 54.

Espinoza, Fernando. 1989. *Situación Actual de la Maricultura del Camarón en el Ecuador y Estrategias para su Desarrollo Sostenido*. Quito: IDEA, Documento Técnico No. 21.

Harrison, Kelly, Don Henley, Harold Riley and James Shaffer. 1974. *Improving Food Systems in Developing Countries: Experiences from Latin America*. E. Lansing, MI: Latin America Studies Center Research Report No. 6.

Harrison, Kelly, R. Bruce Schulte and John D. Baker. 1988. *Market Potential for Ecuadorian Arriba Cocoa*. Quito: IDEA, Documento Técnico No. 17.

MAG (Ministry of Agriculture). 1988. *Boletín de Información de Precios y Noticias de Mercado*. Quito: Subsecretaría de Comercialización.

Marion, Bruce. 1985. *The Organization and Performance of the U.S. Food System*. Lexington, MA; Lexington Books.

Paz-Caferatta, J. and J. Escobal. 1989. "Opciones de Políticas de Precios Agrícolas: El Caso de las Bandas de Precios." Lima.

Pinckney, Thomas. 1988. *Storage, Trade, and Price Policy Under Production Instability: Maize in Kenya*. Washington, D.C.: IFPRI, Research Report No. 71.

Ramos, Hugo. 1989a. *El Crédito para la Comercialización del Arroz: Memorias del Seminario*. Quito: Documento Técnico de IDEA No. 19.

_____. 1989b. "The Financial System Supporting Rice Marketing in Ecuador." Ph.D. Thesis, Michigan State University.

Rebolar, Jaime. 1989. "La Oferta y Demanda de Trigo en Chile y el Impacto de la Banda de Precios." Tesis de Grado, Título de Ingeniero Agrónomo, Pontificia Universidad Católica de Chile.

Riley, Harold. 1989. "Developing Agroindustrial Capabilities to Exploit Domestic and International Market Opportunities." Paper presented at a policy seminar on agroindustrial development in Latin American and the Caribbean, sponsored by IICA, CIDA and Banco do Brasil, Brasilia.

Riley, Harold, et al. 1970. *Market Coordination in the Development of the Cauca Valley Region--Colombia*. E. Lansing, MI: Latin American Studies Center Research Report No. 5.

Sarhan, M. E. 1988. *The Livestock and Meat Subsector in Ecuador*. Research Triangle Park, NC: Sigma One Corporation.

Scobie, G. and Verónica Jardine. 1989. *Trade Policies in Ecuador: Who Gains and Who Loses?*. Quito: Ministry of Agriculture and Sigma One Corporation.

_____. 1988a. "Efectos de las Políticas Macroeconómicas de Ajuste Sobre el Sector Agrícola y Alimentario del Ecuador." *Ajuste Macroeconómico y Sector Agropecuario en América Latina*. Buenos Aires: IICA.

_____. 1988b. *Macroeconomic Policy, the Real Exchange Rate, and Agricultural Growth in Ecuador*. Quito: Ministry of Agriculture and Sigma One Corporation, Working Paper No. 4.

Shaffer, James. 1968. "Changing Orientation of Marketing Research." *American Journal of Agricultural Economics* 50:1437-1453.

Stewart, Rigoberto and Mauricio Cuesta. 1988. *La Política de Precios del Arroz y sus Efectos en el Ecuador, 1970-1987*. Quito: MAG, Unidad de Análisis de Políticas Documento No. 1.

Stewart, Rigoberto, Mauricio Cuesta and Mónica Acosta. 1988. *La Política de Incentivos y la Ventaja Comparativa del Ecuador en la Producción de Soya*. Quito: MAG, Unidad de Análisis de Políticas Documento No. 3.

Streeten, Paul. 1987. *What Price Food? Agricultural Price Policies in Developing Countries*. Ithaca: Cornell University Press.

Timmer, C. P. 1986. *Getting Prices Right: The Scope and Limits of Agricultural Price Policy*. Ithaca: Cornell University Press.

Tschirley, David. 1989. "La Futura Demanda de Productos Avícolas y de Maíz Duro y Sorgo en el Ecuador." Quito: *Avicultura Ecuatoriana* No. 21. Fourth Quarter, pp. 5-10.

_____. 1988. "Market Coordination and Supply Management in the Feed Grains/Poultry Subsector of Ecuador." Ph.D. Thesis, Michigan State University.

Tschirley, David, Hugo Ramos and Cornelius Hugo. 1989. *La Utilización de Bandas de Precios para Estabilizar los Precios de Granos Básicos en el Ecuador: Una Agenda de Cambio*. Quito: Documento Técnico de IDEA No. 23, PMA No. 2.

Weber, Michael. 1976. "An Analysis of Rural Food Distribution in Costa Rica." Ph.D. Thesis, Michigan State University.

Weber, Michael, et al. 1988. "Informing Food Security Decisions in Africa: Empirical Analysis and Policy Dialogue." *American Journal of Agricultural Economics* 70:5:1044-1052.

9

CREDIT AND

CREDIT POLICIES

Hugo Ramos and Lindon Robison

This chapter analyzes agricultural credit and credit policies. The goal is to explain how these have influenced the development of Ecuador's agricultural sector. Since agricultural credit and credit policy are the major themes, they are first defined. Credit is the ability to borrow. Thus credit is a reserve or a resource that can be exchanged for loans or maintained as a reserve to be used when needed. The amount of credit available to an individual borrower depends on lenders having funds to lend and borrowers having demonstrated they are trustworthy. Loans then are not credit but what is exchanged for credit.

Credit is important in agricultural development because all investments in agriculture require an initial commitment of funds in return for expected future profits. As a result, there will be a lapse between the time funds are committed to the investment and when the investment generates the income necessary to repay the costs of the investment. Few firms have the liquid funds (cash and legal instruments easily converted to cash) necessary to pay for investments initially and therefore will need credit to invest. Unless there is a well-functioning credit system that provides loan funds on a timely basis and at a reasonable cost, investments and resulting increased productivity will be reduced and economic development retarded.

Ecuador's agricultural credit policy consists of the private and public terms and conditions under which savers save and borrowers borrow and how these terms are enforced in the agricultural sector. These policies are important in agricultural development because they influence the access to and cost of loan funds. This, in turn, helps determine which firms will make the investments required to produce, process and distribute agricultural products. Those firms with adequate access to credit will have significant advantages over firms without such access. Thus, the organization of the agricultural sector will be influenced by agricultural credit policies. Agricultural credit policies also affect consumers because the organization of production helps to determine the price and availability of food products.

Evidence presented in this chapter supports the conclusion that the policy of administered and subsidized interest rates has created a condition of excess demand for agricultural loans. This, in turn, has resulted in non-market allocations of loan funds through processes that are dominated by the interests of large and well-to-do farmers who often divert loans from their more productive uses in agriculture.

farmers who often divert loans from their more productive uses in agriculture. Subsidized interest rates for loans lead to below-market rates of interest on savings, which discourages savers from depositing funds with banks. A further consequence of the subsidized interest rates is the decapitalization of the National Development Bank (BNF), agriculture's major source of loan funds. The evidence also indicates that macroeconomic policies have caused inflation, which has discouraged long-term investments in agriculture (Barry and Robison).

The following sections describe and analyze: Ecuador's agricultural credit supply policies and the role of the Central Bank; private financial intermediaries and public financial organizations serving agriculture; the policies of administered and subsidized credit and the effects of these on large and small farmers; and the influence of inflationary macroeconomic policies on agricultural credit and liquidity. The last section presents conclusions and recommendations for improving Ecuador's agricultural credit policies.

Ecuador's Credit Supply Policy

Sources of loan funds for Ecuador's agricultural sector include private savings, government agencies, and foreign loans. The government, through the Central Bank of Ecuador (BCE), is the supplier of credit for the sector.

The Role of the Central Bank

The main source of loanable funds for banks and other financial institutions serving the agricultural sector is the Central Bank. The BCE obtains funds from the Government of Ecuador's (GOE) budget allocations, foreign loans, contributions of Ecuadorian private banks and other financial organizations, and sales of bonds in the national capital markets. The GOE's budget allocations increased rapidly during the petroleum boom but diminished during the 1980s. Foreign lenders and donors to Ecuador's agricultural sector include the International Bank for Reconstruction and Development (World Bank), the Inter-American Development Bank (IDB), regional organizations such as the Andean Finance Corporation (CAF) and private, foreign banks. Funds from foreign lenders and donors increased during the 1970s but began to shrink after the 1982 financial crisis. BCE funds obtained from private financial organizations in Ecuador are basically BCE stock purchases and private bank deposits.

The BCE influences the supply of money through the purchase and sale of bonds. Both the GOE and private financial institutions issue bonds which the public is supposed to purchase. In practice, these bonds have been purchased by the BCE and have never been sold in the national capital market. The BCE could sell bonds in the stock market to withdraw money from the economy, or it could buy bonds whenever the economy needs cash. Currently (1990) the bonds are not being sold privately because the yield on them is well below the inflation rate and the BCE is unwilling to discount them enough to make them attractive to private investors.

The BCE provides credit through its rediscount operations, by offering direct loans and advances, issuing bankers acceptances and providing emergency loans. Financial intermediaries participating in the BCE's rediscount operations act in some ways like a loan officer making loans on behalf of the BCE. They first grant a loan to a borrower. Then the note associated with this loan is submitted to the BCE which lends to the financial intermediary a percentage (usually 80) of the original loan. The interest rate the BCE charges the bank is called the rediscount rate. Banks are allowed to add a margin (spread) to this rate which is supposed to cover the banks' costs of administering such loans. The rediscount rate plus the margin is the interest rate paid by borrowers who obtain loans from the financial intermediaries serviced by the BCE. By adjusting this spread, the BCE influences the amount of money lenders are willing to lend.

The BCE offers direct loans to banks, finance companies and private firms to finance specific programs or projects. Examples of this type of operation are BNF advances used to finance the National Agricultural Storage and Marketing Company's (ENAC) intervention in the grains market. Bankers' acceptances are BCE operations by which financial institutions are able to rediscount their loans to private traders, especially to exporters of agricultural products. Finally, emergency loans are made by the BCE to financial institutions unable to meet the legal reserve requirement.

Another way the BCE provides credit is through established credit lines which are accessed mainly through rediscount operations. The Financial Funds Mechanism (FFM) and the Marketing Line of credit (*Regulación* 696) are the BCE's most important agricultural lines of credit. The FFM was created at BCE to channel the large flow of oil revenues and funds from domestic and foreign resources to the various sectors of the economy. The FFM organizes the loan funds into five basic categories: the agricultural and livestock fund, the industry and artisan fund, the integrated development projects fund, the export promotion fund, and the external resources fund. Another special fund known as the Regulación 696 is available to finance marketing activities.

Administered Credit Policies

Ecuador's credit policies are administered rather than market determined. That is, interest rates on loans, reserve requirements and distribution of loans are the result of government policies and associated administrative decisions rather than a response to market forces.

Credit policies of the BCE are established by the Monetary Board. The Monetary Board includes representatives from the Presidency, Ministries, agriculture, industry, artisans and small industry, and chambers of commerce. The board prepares its annual budget and loan policies in coordination with and in support of the National Development Council's (CONADE) development plan.

Once the Monetary Board has decided on the allocation of loan funds the BCE implements its plan, basically by making credit lines available to the financial institutions. Most credit lines are defined by the Monetary Board as preferential and are offered at subsidized interest rates.

The Monetary Board discriminates among their preferential credit lines. For example, in 1984 the BCE advance and rediscount rates were set at 11 percent for the Fund for Marginal Rural Development (FODERUMA), 13 percent for the BNF and 18 percent for private banks. By mid-1989 the rates had risen to 18 percent for FODERUMA, 27 percent for BNF and 31 percent for private banks.

The Monetary Board also sets the margin between what it charges participating financial institutions and what they can charge their borrowers. By the middle of 1989, BNF was allowed to charge a margin of five points, placing an upper limit of 32 percent on the loan rate for borrowers. The margin for private banks, however, was seven points, allowing them to set a maximum rate of 39 percent.[1]

Private banks, and to a' lesser extent the BNF, currently can provide loans to the agricultural sector from privately supplied funds at market determined rates. However, these so-called "market" rates are not completely free since the Monetary Board limits the rate to 17 percentage points over a "reference rate" estimated and published by the BCE. The reference rate is calculated as the average rate paid by banks on savings and 90-day certificates of deposit. Financial companies are allowed to charge 19 percentage points over the reference rate but they are not allowed to receive monetary deposits. The rates paid on savings and 90-day certificates of deposit are determined competitively. In mid-1989, the average deposit rate was about 36 percent, setting the private bank loan rates at about 53 percent.

Another way BCE discriminates among lenders is by requiring different levels of reserves. Since the late 1970s, the legal reserve rate for the BNF has been set at 10 percent. Meanwhile this rate has varied for the private banks. In 1984 it was 22 percent; by mid-1989 it had increased to 31 percent. In February of 1988 the reserve requirement reached a peak of 37 as the BCE tried to restrict the money supply and to reduce inflation. Despite efforts to restrict the money supply with increased reserve requirements on private banks, Ecuador's money supply tripled from 1984 to 1988 and increased by 16 percent from December 1988 to September 1989 (BCE).

BCE's allocation of loanable funds discriminates against the private financial sector in favor of the BNF. In 1980 BNF use of BCE credit lines represented 15 percent of the total credit available at BCE and private banks utilization represented 28 percent; by mid-1989 the shares were 22 percent for the BNF and 16 percent for private banks. Private banks claim that the margin between the loan rate they are allowed to charge their borrowers and the rediscount rate paid to BCE does not cover their costs. Thus, they cannot justify fully utilizing BCE credit lines. On the other hand, BNF is becoming more and more dependent on BCE funds, as well as on foreign loans, because of its continuing decapitalization and its inability to attract private savings and monetary deposits.

Financial Intermediaries

Financial intermediaries are firms whose main activity is obtaining funds and providing loans. Examples of financial intermediaries include private banks, private finance companies, credit unions and savings cooperatives. In addition, informal lenders provide important financial services to the agricultural sector. This section describes and discusses the most important public and private financial intermediaries and other organizations that supply loans to agriculture (Figure 9.1). For each organization this section presents a brief history, purpose, source of loanable funds, the unique credit policies under which it operates, the clients it serves and the interest rate it charges.

Public Financial Institutions

BNF The BNF was created as the Mortgage Bank (*Banco Hipotecario*) during the 1926-1933 progressive banking years. In 1947 the Mortgage Bank was reorganized and transformed into the BNF banking system. According to its charter (*Ley Orgánica*), the bank's main purpose is to help medium and small farmers and producers to increase production and improve productivity. Since its creation, the BNF has constantly expanded its operations, especially during the 1970s when oil revenues significantly increased the amount of loanable funds in Ecuador's financial

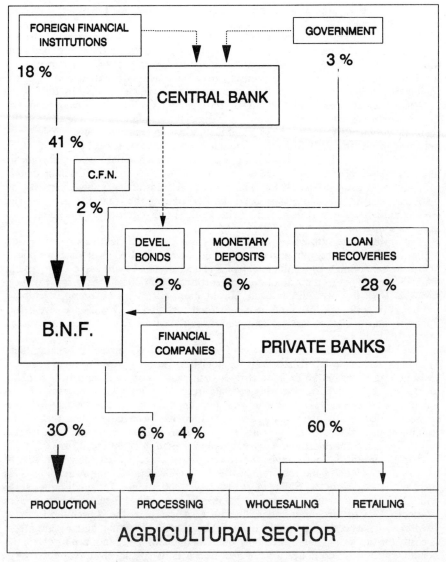

Figure 9.1 Sources of Funds for the BNF and Flow of Funds to the Agricultural Sector (Percentages are Averages for the Period 1980-1988).

system.

The BNF is the single most important institutional source of credit for the agricultural sector. During the 1980s it provided, on average, 36 percent of the funds used in agriculture. The loans provided by the BNF have been funded mainly by the BCE through the FFM, the development bonds and the marketing fund programs. The use of the FFM by the BNF has been facilitated by its extensive infrastructure (72 bank offices) and the location of its branch offices in many cities and towns not served by commercial banks.

Another important source of funds for the BNF are foreign loans contracted directly with multinational financial institutions. The IDB and the World Bank have been the most important such suppliers of financial resources. This source of funds is becoming more and more important as other sources, mainly monetary deposits and savings, are rapidly diminishing due to the low savings and term deposit rates paid by BNF.

The monetary deposits of public institutions were a significant source of funds for the BNF until 1980, when the government changed the regulations. The changes in the regulations obligated public agencies and institutions to transfer all disposable funds held as deposits in the BNF to the National Treasury Account opened at the BCE. Since the public funds deposited in its branches by municipalities, provincial councils and other public institutions were used to provide loans, they could not be immediately recalled for deposit at the BCE. The process of transferring public funds to the National Treasury Account destabilized the BNF during the transition period. The BNF could not repay part of its rediscounts to the BCE requiring it to negotiate two debt consolidations.

The savings rate offered by the BNF has not been sufficient to attract private depositors. The interest rate paid on savings deposits at the BNF is at least two points below the rate offered by commercial banks and savings and loans associations and at least 25 percent below the rate offered on certificates of deposit. As a consequence, saving at BNF has been discouraged. In addition, borrowers obtaining BNF loans frequently deposit their loan funds in commercial banks, where they also receive better financial intermediation services and where their deposits can be used to leverage private bank loans.

The BNF offers basically two types of loans, a training loan and a banking loan. Training loans are designed exclusively for small borrowers by providing them technical assistance and funds at lower interest rates than charged on banking loans. Banking loans are directed to borrowers who graduate from the training loan program, who no longer need technical assistance or who are supposed to be able to pay for such services. Historically, the banking loan portfolio has been larger than that of the training loans. BNF's bank loans are treated much like a commercial loan from a private bank, except that the interest rate is lower than in commercial banks.

To obtain BNF loan funds, borrowers must meet a cumbersome set of requirements. One of the requirements is the certification of land ownership. This turns out to be one of the BNF's most restrictive requirements for small farmers. In addition, there are other requirements that may be especially difficult for small farmers to meet. One of these is the identification card issued by the Agricultural Center (*Centro Agrícola*) certifying that the borrower is a farmer. Meeting these requirements is costly for the farmers and when only small amounts of loan funds are involved, the benefits of the loan do not justify the high transactions cost involved (Ramos 1984).

CFN The National Finance Corporation (CFN) was created in 1953 as the Commisión de Valores and received its current name in 1977. Its primary purpose was to serve the small industry and artisan sectors of the economy. Later, the purpose was expanded to include the financing of non-traditional agricultural export products. As with other financial companies, the CFN is not allowed to receive deposits. Therefore, its sources of funds are limited to loans from multinational lending organizations and the central government, through financial allocations of funds managed by the BCE.

Within the CFN there is a special credit program called the Small Industry and

Artisan Fund. This program is important to the agricultural sector because it supports agro-industrial investments such as processing equipment and storage.

The Export Promotion Fund Program is another special program of CFN. It is funded by rediscounts from the BCE and by direct loans from foreign governments and agencies. This program finances the export of non-traditional agricultural products such as flowers, shrimp, exotic fruits and vegetables.

The interest rates charged by the CFN, like those charged by the BNF, are set by the Monetary Board. Investment loans carry a lower interest rate than short-term loans such as those for shipping expenses. The average term for short-term loans is 180 days and the maximum term is two years. The term for long-term loans ranges from five to twelve years, including a grace period varying from two to four years.

CFN loans, like those of the BNF, are supervised. The loans require a pre-investment inspection. The loans are granted in increments that depend on completion of intermediate steps and favorable reports from credit supervisors. Supervisory visits increase the transaction costs of the loan, causing the CFN to favor large investment projects.

Private Financial Intermediaries

Private Banks Private banks were created primarily to provide financial intermediation services to the private sector. The private banks of the Costa region served the financial needs of producers of traditional export crops such as cacao, coffee and bananas. The private banks of the Sierra mainly financed large farms (*latifundios*) and the country's interregional trade.

Ecuador's private banking system is highly concentrated. It consists of 32 banking institutions, including four foreign banks (Citibank, the largest foreign bank, *Holandés Unido*, Lloyds Bank and Bank of America). Ecuador's five largest private banks, based on a three year average (1986-1988), hold about 45 percent of the assets of the private banking system. They also hold 44 percent of the loan portfolio, more than 50 percent of the monetary deposits (including certificates of deposit) and about 42 percent of the total capital and reserves of all private banks. The remaining 27 private banks are medium and small banks created mainly by industrial investors who are eager to gain access to the subsidized credit available at the BCE through the FFM.

The main sources of funds for private banks have been the monetary deposits (demand and time deposits and savings) and foreign loans. Since 1985, private banks have aggressively competed for domestic savings through the issuance of certificates of deposit and by offering market determined interest rates.[2] The BCE became an important source of funds for private banks as the gap between the inflation and the interest rates widened. Private banks are required to make 10 percent of their loans to the agricultural sector. They meet this obligation by allocating large amounts of resources to a few large borrowers to reduce transaction costs.

The majority of funds lent to the agricultural sector by private banks have been to finance short-term investments, basically annual crops and trade (Ramos 1984). The rest of the funds have been targeted to a few large, long-term investments secured by land, processing plants and the goods financed by the loan, such as cattle, machinery and equipment. During the last few years, private banks have reduced their financing of long-term investments, recognizing that the acceleration of the inflation rate vis-à-vis fixed interest rates was resulting in large financial losses. Private banks have been financing long-term investments by permitting short-term loans to roll over.

The interest rate charged by private banks on their agricultural loans is higher than that charged by public financial institutions such as the BNF and the CFN. However, many borrowers express the viewpoint that after adding the transactions costs of BNF loans, the total cost of a loan from a private bank is less than the cost of obtaining a loan from the BNF or CFN.

Private Financial Companies (PFCs) Private financial companies are basically new institutions, created during the 1970s. The largest and most closely linked to the agricultural sector is the Ecuadorian Finance Corporation. The main purpose of PFCs is to provide specialized financial intermediation services to such groups as home and office builders, consumer groups and selected agricultural enterprises.

The existing monetary laws do not permit private financial companies to receive deposits although they can borrow private resources to be channeled to private borrowers. Private financial companies have access to the BCE's FFM rediscount window. During 1988, BCE provided about 22 percent of the loanable funds of PFCs.

The role of PFCs in the agricultural sector has been limited. Most of their loans have financed capital investments and operating expenses in the dairy and beef industries, oilpalm plantations and shrimp farms. The share of agricultural loans in the portfolio of these financial companies during 1988 was about 22 percent. The rest of their loans financed industrial and manufacturing investments (about 38 percent) and construction (approximately 20 percent).

The interest rate PFCs charge agricultural borrowers is determined by the Monetary Board. In addition to the interest rate, however, financial companies charge additional fees for commissions, inspections, insurance and other administrative expenses, making their loans even more expensive than private bank loans.

Credit Unions Credit Unions were created to provide deposit and short-term loan services to their members. It is estimated there are about 1,000 credit unions throughout Ecuador, of which 150 are approved and supervised by the Credit Union Federation of Ecuador compared to only 39 Savings and Loans Co-ops that were registered by the Superintendency of Banks in 1988. The majority of credit unions are located in the urban areas and serve specific groups of people such as employees, artisans and small industrial firms. Credit unions in rural areas, however, are community-oriented and their members include farmers as well as others.

Credit unions are not allowed to receive demand deposits but they can accept savings deposits in the form of shares. Nor do the credit unions have access to the BCE's rediscount window. Thus, the funds they have for lending are self-generated. Their widespread distribution has made them the principal means for mobilizing savings in many communities where neither banks nor financial companies have offices. Yet, restrictions on receiving demand deposits and using the BCE rediscount mechanism limit the range of financial services they can provide.

The loans provided by credit unions are mostly for commercial activities, urban construction and small industrial production. Credit unions direct their agricultural loans to mainly small producers and to finance marketing operations.

Informal Credit Suppliers Informal credit suppliers include moneylenders, processors of agricultural goods, wholesalers advancing money for the purchase of agricultural products under a future delivery type of contract and agricultural input suppliers.

Moneylenders generally finance their operations with their own savings, while processors and wholesalers finance their loans with both their own resources and with bank loans. Agricultural processors usually have access to subsidized credit from the BNF. Those vertically integrated with production add these funds to loans obtained from banks to finance their production activities. Part of the processors' resources are used to develop agricultural production, lending them again then to small producers who are unable to borrow directly from the BNF or private banks because of their size or bad credit history.

Agricultural input suppliers, especially those located in the rural areas and close to their farmer customers, often provide credit in kind; that is, they advance agricultural inputs with payment expected at harvest. The credit they provide is based on their own resources, loans from banks, or credit from larger suppliers who allow them to make purchases using post-dated checks (checks redeemable after 15 or more days).

The cash resources obtained through informal channels are used mainly to finance the harvest and the trade (including some processing activities) of agricultural produce. In some cases, these funds are used to finance production activities as well, especially when the planted area is estimated to be low and processors want to guarantee their supply of raw products.

Credit arrangements in the informal financial markets are secured mostly with personal confidence and trust developed through many years of doing business or relationships established in other contexts. First-time participants in the informal credit market are required to secure their loans, handing in valuable assets to lenders, such as jewelry, consumer durables or small equipment not necessary for agricultural activities (sewing machines, for example).

Although the transactions costs of closing loans in the informal credit market are lower, the interest rates charged are higher than rates charged in the formal credit market. During May-June 1989 a field survey of rice marketing revealed that this rate was, on average, 10 percent per month, not compounded. The survey revealed also that the terms of these loans was usually less than two months (Ramos 1989).

External Financial Institutions and Donors

The World Bank The World Bank has been a major supplier of funds to Ecuador. In January of 1986, the World Bank granted an agricultural sector loan of US$100 million to be monitored by the BCE through its FFM mechanism. In January of 1987 it granted another loan to Ecuador for US$48 million (Loan 2752-EC) to help finance the development of agricultural exports.

IDB The IDB has been an important source of external funds for the agricultural sector and especially for the BNF. Past IDB funds have been provided directly to the BNF. During the 1980s the IDB provided a total of US$374 million to finance three global agricultural credit programs executed by the BNF. In December of 1983, loans identified as 463/OC, 464/OC and 743/SF, totaling US$54 million, were negotiated to help finance the First Global Agricultural Credit Program intended to help boost productivity of agricultural products directed to local markets. In 1985 a new loan, 510/OC, equal to US$120 million was approved to help finance the Second Global Agricultural Credit Program. A Third Global Agricultural Program, EC-245, for US$200 million was approved to increase agricultural production and to improve agricultural productivity.

Table 9.1 Comparison Between the Inflation Rates and the Average Interest Rates
          Charged on Loans by the National Development Bank

Year	Price Index	Inflation Rate (%)	Interest Rate[a] (%)	Real Interest Rate[b] (%)
1980	1.00	12	11	-1
1981	1.15	15	13	-2
1982	1.34	16	13	-3
1983	1.98	48	15	-33
1984	2.60	31	17	-14
1985	3.33	28	19	-9
1986	4.10	23	21	-2
1987	5.31	30	23	-7
1988	8.31	57	27	-30

Source: BCE.

[a] Average interest rate charged on loans.
[b] Defined as nominal interest rate minus the inflation rate.

Other Foreign Lenders Among other foreign lenders who provide credit to Ecuador's agricultural sector is the Andean Development Corporation (CAF). The CAF has provided loans directly to the BNF and the CFN to finance specific investments. Three recent loans to BNF have been used to finance oilpalm plantations in Pichincha and Esmeraldas provinces. The U.S. Agency for International Development (USAID) also has provided a credit line to help support the export of non-traditional agricultural products. It also has provided limited credit lines as part of rural development projects.

The government of Ecuador has also received grants and loans from other governments, both in cash and in machinery and equipment, to help the country to develop its agricultural sector. The governments of West Germany, Denmark, Czechoslovakia and, lately, Italy, have provided credit to Ecuador (see Chapter 11).

Consequences of Subsidized Credit

Since the BNF is the most important credit source for Ecuador's agricultural sector, this section focuses on how the credit policy of administered interest rates affects the BNF and the agricultural borrowers it is directed to serve.

Ecuador's credit policy is one of administered interest rates on loans. It consists of charging below-market rates of interest to privileged borrowers. Then, because the rates paid savers cannot exceed the rate charged on loans, the interest rate paid on deposits also is below the market rate required to induce individuals to save.

The interest rates charged on new BNF loans were always less than the rate of inflation during the 1980s (Table 9.1). Moreover, during 1983 and 1988, the inflation rate was at least 30 percent higher than BNF's interest rate. This means that BNF borrowers were being paid by the bank to borrow money since the real rate of interest on their loans was negative. Clearly, BNF borrowers have been offered a good deal.

Concentration of Loan Benefits

BNF's loans at below-market rates of interest have largely benefitted their large

Table 9.2   The Distribution of the National Development Bank's Loans by Loan Size
            (Million of 1980 Sucres)

Year	Size of Loans							Total Annual Loans
	< 0.1	0.1-0.5	0.5-1	> 1[a]	1-5	5-20	> 20	
				million sucres				
1980	1764	2258	832	1242	0	0	0	6095
1981	1532	2411	915	1513	0	0	0	6371
1982	1236	2270	875	1413	0	0	0	5794
1983	1025	2403	1078	2508	0	0	0	7014
1984	748	2545	1302	3878	0	0	0	8474
1985	539	2645	1663	0	3726	1546	0	10119
1986	389	2334	1708	0	3647	2433	0	10512
1987	257	1968	1708	0	3161	1620	0	8715
1988	114	1214	1420	0	2412	1464	310	6934
				%				
1980	29	37	14	20	0	0	0	100
1981	24	38	14	24	0	0	0	100
1982	21	39	15	24	0	0	0	100
1983	15	34	15	36	0	0	0	100
1984	9	30	15	46	0	0	0	100
1985	5	26	16	0	37	15	0	100
1986	4	22	16	0	35	23	0	100
1987	3	23	20	0	36	19	0	100
1988	2	18	20	0	35	21	4	100

Source: BNF.

[a]Until 1984 all the loans greater than 1 million Sucres were included into one
category because there were few loans greater than 5 million Sucres and none
greater than 20 million Sucres.

borrowers, although according to its charter the bank's main purpose is to help
medium and small farmers and producers. The BNF was to accomplish this purpose
by providing the medium and small borrowers the credit necessary to make needed and
timely investments. The evidence is that the BNF has not accomplished its purpose
(Table 9.2).

The percentage of small loans (less than 100,000 1980 Sucres) fell from 29 percent
in 1980 to 2 percent in 1988, while loans larger than one million Sucres increased from
20 percent in 1980 to 60 percent in 1988. Thus, assuming that large loans are granted
to borrowers with greater equity and influence, the benefits of the BNF subsidized loan
program are increasingly being concentrated in the hands of more well-to-do
borrowers.[3]

The concentration of BNF loans in the hands of fewer and larger borrowers may
be explained partly as BNF's effort to reduce their transactions costs or to reduce the
effective demand for BNF loans. Consider how such pressures might concentrate the
benefits of BNF's loan program.

Credit markets are in equilibrium when the demand for loans equals the supply of
loans. When financial institutions such as the BNF offer credit at below-market rates
of interest, the demand for loans exceeds the supply of loans. Nevertheless, the supply
of credit must be distributed among borrowers; because interest rates no longer serve
as an allocation device non-market mechanisms are used.

Excess demand for credit, the result of BNF's below-market interest rates, invites political patronage, bribes and similar mechanisms for allocating loan funds. Moreover, those with the most influence are more apt to be granted loans. These are not necessarily those who can use the loan funds most productively.

BNF helps equate the supply of loans to the demand for loans at below-market interest rates by increasing the transactions costs of obtaining loans. Transactions costs that reduce the profitability of BNF loans and hence reduce the demand for loans include increases in the collateral required for loans, increases in the number of times a borrower must come to the bank before receiving his or her loan funds, increases in the number of forms documenting the loan, reductions in the amount available for specific loans, delays in receiving the loans funds and a shorter term of loan. The BNF has imposed all of these non-interest costs on its borrowers. These, however, represent a fixed cost which decreases per Sucre borrowed as the size of the loan increases. Smaller borrowers pay a higher cost per Sucre borrowed than do large borrowers. Thus the demand for BNF loans by small borrowers has been reduced, because of transaction costs induced by the policy of subsidized interest rates.[4]

Subsidized credit policies result in higher costs for smaller than larger borrowers. This helps explain the concentration of loans from the demand side. It is also important to examine whether or not a subsidized interest rate encourages the BNF to lend to large borrowers. The conclusion reached here is that it does. Since the BNF does not have the authority to charge borrowers the market rate of interest on loans, they attempt to remain viable by reducing the cost of granting loans. Experience has demonstrated that loan-servicing costs are directly related to the number, not the size of loans (Araujo and Meyer). Recognizing this fact has encouraged the BNF to make fewer and larger loans.

Transactions costs for the BNF also can be reduced by lending to repeat borrowers since these loans may not require reinspection and collateral for the loan often is already secured. Finally, the bank's transactions cost of lending may be reduced by offering loans only to financially secure firms whose default risk is low. But offering large amounts of credit to repeat borrowers who are financially secure serves to concentrate the benefits of the subsidized loans in the hands of larger, more well-to-do borrowers.

Constrained Savings Mobilization

Agricultural finance researchers have repeatedly concluded that subsidized loans and negative real interest rates result in a failure to mobilize savings in the rural sector (Adams; Gonzalez Vega). This result is especially likely when the only depository services are those available from public financial intermediaries. Ecuador's experience offers particular support for this conclusion. In the private economy, impressive increases occurred in savings in the form of certificates of deposit when private banks were allowed to offer market determined rates of interest during the 1985-1987 period.

In partial response to Ecuador's financial crisis, the Febres Cordero government freed interest rates on all savings and loans except those subsidized by the BCE for specific sectors.[5] This policy, however, had minimal effects on the agricultural sector because the Monetary Board refused to remove interest rate restrictions on the BNF. Nevertheless, allowing interest rates to be market-determined for the private sector demonstrated how important savings mobilization could be when stimulated with positive real interest rates.

In 1985, private banks were allowed to issue certificates of deposit at market determined rates of interest. In the first year, the total amount issued reached 33.2 billion Sucres. By the end of 1986 the total amounted to 58.5 billion and by the end of 1987 reached 88.5 billion--equivalent to 21 percent of the total liabilities of the commercial banks to the private sector.[6]

The impressive saving mobilization role provided by the certificates of deposit testify to the availability of financial savings. Moreover, by lending these funds in the sector in which they are saved, a multiplier effect is generated on other savings and loans. Unfortunately, there are no data that distinguishes the quantities of certificates of deposits provided by rural savers. Nevertheless, the BNF has the rural branches available to receive deposits that would be mobilized if they could offer incentives to savers. Then deposits would increase and so would the loanable funds of the BNF.

Savers suffer an additional cost of not being able to save at positive real interest rates. It means they must hold physical goods or make investments for which they may be ill-prepared to manage. Thus the failure to provide profitable alternative depository opportunities precludes the separation of the savings and investment functions and the advantages which this separation offers. Moreover it forces many potential savers into investments less profitable and less liquid than could be earned if the credit market were allowed to function properly. Finally, it results in capital flight to secure capital markets operating in foreign countries.

The negative real domestic interest rate paid on Sucre-denominated financial assets, relative to the rate paid on financial assets held in dollars offers a substantial interest rate arbitrage gain. Additionally, holding dollar-denominated assets has been perceived as a secure way to save and hedge against economic instability and inflation. The amount of money that has been expatriated under these conditions has not been documented. However, Connolly notes that Ecuadorian private sector monetary deposits in U.S. banks is over five billion dollars, equivalent to about 50 percent of the Ecuadorian foreign debt.

Decapitalization of BNF

Offering loans at negative real rates of interest, unless there are individual savers or donors willing to save at negative rates of interest, will eventually decapitalize financial intermediaries. The explanation is simple. With inflation, Sucres are devalued. If the interest rate on loans is less than inflation, loan principal and interest repaid the bank will be worth less than the original loans received by borrowers. If the bank is lending its own capital funds, which is the case of the BNF, then offering negative real interest rates on savings guarantees its decapitalization.

The BNF has been obligated by the Monetary Board to offer interest rates that are less than the rate of inflation. Moreover, the negative real interest rates offered savers has not attracted deposits from the private sector in any significant amount. Thus, its continued operation is made possible only by continued infusions of capital by BCE, CFN, the GOE and foreign donors (Table 9.3).

In 1980, 1981 and 1982, when BNF's interest rate was on average only 2 percent less than the rate of inflation, the percentages of funds from loan repayments were 34, 54 and 60 percent, respectively. In 1986, 1987 and 1988 the rate of inflation exceeded BNF's loan rate by over 20 percent. As a consequence, the percentages of funds obtained from loan recovery fell to 21, 22 and 27, respectively. Meanwhile, the percentage of loan funds provided by foreign loans increased from about 2 percent to

Table 9.3 The National Development Bank's Sources of Loan Funds

Year	Monetary Deposits	BCE & CFN	Foreign Loans	Development Bonds	GOE Capital	Loan Recovery	Annual Loans
				(million sucres)			
1980	878	2,624	284	40	221	2,048	6,095
1981	411	2,044	147	444	314	3,959	7,319
1982		2,300	194	418	186	4,646	7,744
1983		6,884	277	1,535	844	4,369	13,909
1984	2,360	7,089	514	1,668	2,197	8,219	22,047
1985	339	17,043	7,708	400	1,146	7,066	33,702
1986	1,229	21,098	11,293	220		9,228	43,068
1987	5,317	21,698	8,940	479	944	10,277	47,655
1988	3,346	22,797	14,050	257	1,595	15,604	57,649
				%			
1980	14	43	5	1	4	34	100
1981	6	28	2	6	4	54	100
1982	0	30	3	5	2	60	100
1983	0	49	2	11	6	31	100
1984	11	32	2	8	10	37	100
1985	1	51	23	1	3	21	100
1986	3	49	26	1	0	21	100
1987	11	46	19	1	2	22	100
1988	6	40	24	0	3	27	100

Source: BNF.

well above 20 percent. Foreign lenders, however, are not likely to continue to subsidize large BNF borrowers that eventually decapitalize their loans. Evidence of this is the IDB's late 1989 suspension of disbursements of a credit to the BNF until its subsidized credit policy was modified.

Subsidized interest rates encourage borrowers to repeatedly renew their loans and to default. This is because of the inherent subsidy in loan payments which are increasingly smaller in real terms due to the effects of a nominal interest rate below the rate of inflation, and rapid inflation. The longer period that a borrower can maintain control over a loan, the larger is the subsidy that can be claimed. Control is maintained by renewing the loan under the same terms, or by defaulting. These practices, however, tend to reduce the real value of BNF's funds for lending, and contributes to the concentration of BNF funds among the same clientele.

BNF has penalized defaulted loans, but the penalty was not sufficient to discourage loan delinquency. Normal banking standards would expect less than 2 percent of a lending institution's funds be overdue. At BNF, however, the rate averaged over 10 percent during the 1980s (Table 9.4). Some farmers believe that the transactions costs to obtain a new loan or to renew the outstanding one are higher than the extra 2-4 percentage points charged as a default rate. These borrowers have decided to default on the loan and continue to use the funds at the slightly higher interest rate, rather than obtaining a new loan. This study concludes that, unless there are strong limitations against renewing a loan indefinitely and significant penalties for defaulting, that subsidized interest rates encourage a high default rate and concentration of loans in the same clientele.

The evidence to support the conclusion regarding the effect of subsidized interest

Table 9.4 Total and Overdue Loans of the National Development Bank

Year	Overdue Loans	Total Loans	Overdue Loan Rate
1980	1,781	13,879	13
1981	2,065	16,129	13
1982	2,479	17,927	14
1983	2,525	23,386	11
1984	3,068	33,901	9
1985	4,760	51,551	9
1986	7,203	70,674	10
1987	9,388	88,857	11
1988	9,877	105,774	9

Source: BNF.

rates on loan repayments comes from the BNF's own experience. During 1988, the BNF adopted a policy that stipulated that overdue loans be treated as normal commercial loans bearing the market interest rate after the due date. According to BNF's officials, this mechanism seems to be effective in reducing loan defaults, although it has raised strong opposition from some groups of producers.[7]

Other Issues

Investment Practices Another conclusion regarding the use of BNF's subsidized credit is that much of it is not used for the purposes for which it was loaned. This, of course, depends on the amount of loan supervision provided by BNF and may not be all bad considering that many times loans are made for unproductive investments.

The demand for a loan is derived from the expected return from its use in a productive activity. But when subsidized credit is available, and particularly when it is targeted to a specific investment, the specific investment may be undertaken even though it is not the most profitable one and would not be undertaken if the loan funds were acquired at competitive interest rates.[8]

On the other hand, if loan supervision is weak, the loan recipient may benefit by not using the loan funds for the purpose intended. This will be the case when the credit line is directed towards investments that do not represent the highest and best use of the resources. For example, consumer credit is often the most costly and is rarely subsidized in Ecuador's economy. Consequently, cheap loan funds made available for agricultural investments often are used to purchase consumer goods such as cars, boats and vacations abroad.

Evidence to support this assertion is difficult to obtain, nor are there reliable estimates of the significance of the diversion. But among agricultural producers and even BNF's credit officials, the diversion of the loans is well known.

In addition, the fungible nature of the loans, even with tight loan supervision, is unlikely to increase the total amount of loan funds invested in agriculture as a result of subsidized and targeted loan programs. Loan funds for worthwhile projects simply substitute for investment funds that would have been made without the loan program. One undesirable diversion of funds is their conversion into dollar-denominated financial assets that effectively make the funds not available for either the agricultural sector or for domestic use and reduces the foreign reserves of the BCE.

Table 9.5   National Development Bank's Loans for Irrigation, Land Improvements,
and Agricultural Machinery, as Compared to Total Annual Loans

Year	Irrigation Loans	Land Improvement Loans	Machinery Loans	Total Annual Loans
	------------------------- (million sucres) -----------------------			
1980	73	202	271	6,095
1981	89	213	456	7,319
1982	91	217	257	7,744
1983	104	347	601	13,909
1984	398	1,027	1,607	22,047
1985	1,054	863	1,907	33,702
1986	1,062	1,537	3,226	43,068
1987	527	1,224	2,386	47,655
1988	725	2,072	2,438	57,649
	----------------------------- % -----------------------------			
1980	1.20	3.32	4.44	100
1981	1.22	2.91	6.24	100
1982	1.18	2.80	3.31	100
1983	0.75	2.49	4.32	100
1984	1.81	4.66	7.29	100
1985	3.13	2.56	5.66	100
1986	2.47	3.57	7.49	100
1987	1.11	2.57	5.01	100
1988	1.26	3.59	4.23	100

Source: BNF.

Capitalized Gains from Targeted Credit   Earlier, the Monetary Board's policy of administratively allocating loan funds to specific purposes rather than letting the market do it was discussed. Within the line of credit allocated to production agriculture, a significant proportion of funds has been directed to irrigation and land improvement (Table 9.5).

Thus far these investments have been unproductive and their benefits have largely been capitalized into land values, benefitting the current owners of the now-improved land who are primarily large farmers. Meanwhile, Ecuador's agricultural productivity remains among the lowest in South America (Chapter 6).

Targeting agricultural loans allocates credit based on criteria other than profitability of the investment. Thus, many unproductive investments are made because of the availability of low cost loans. In addition, many productive investments are not made because the loan funds have already been committed to another purpose.

A peculiarity of Ecuador's agricultural credit policy is to exclude wholesalers and processors from any significant amount of credit. By failing to recognize the credit needs of these and other agricultural sector participants, those most dependent on capital investments have been denied public sector loan funds. As a consequence, the entire agricultural chain from producers to consumers has been constrained (Chapter 8).

Subsidized Interest Rates and Welfare Programs   In most large organizations, and especially in government organizations, programs multiply and the leadership of the programs are decentralized and coordination is weak, two likely outcomes occur. First, certain programs may duplicate each other. Or worse, programs may exist with conflicting goals. Both of these consequences have occurred in the agricultural credit policy of Ecuador.

The policies intended to transfer income to small and medium farmers, via subsidized credit, have had just the opposite effect. They, in fact, concentrate cheap loans in the hands of borrowers who have the greatest collateral for securing their loans and who often have friends in the banks who help them obtain their loans. Thus, neither the goals of increasing production nor improving the well-being of the poor are being achieved by the policy of administered interest rates or administratively determined credit allocations.

Subsidized Credit and Financial Intermediation Services Subsidized interest rate policies have another undesirable effect that has not been discussed. It reduces the supply of financial intermediary services available in rural areas. Private banks and other financial intermediaries are more dependent on savings mobilization than are the parastatal lenders such as the BNF. Consequently, it is unlikely they will develop and profitably operate in areas where they do not have significant deposit and loan activity.

In the rural areas, however, private lenders are not likely to be able to compete for loans with the BNF which offers subsidized credit. Although there likely exists opportunities for savings mobilization by offering market rates of interest, inability to compete for loans will discourage private lenders from establishing themselves in rural areas.

In addition, if private lenders cannot compete for loans, they are unlikely to successfully compete for deposits either, since one of the significant incentives for depositors establishing a relationship with the financial intermediary is that it creates credit. For the reasons above, private banks and financial intermediaries tend to locate in areas where lending activity is at the market rate of interest and where the savers often become the borrowers from the bank as well. Thus, subsidized credit discourages financial services from developing in rural areas (Araujo and Meyer).

Macroeconomic Policies and Liquidity

Macroeconomic policies leading to inflation increase interest rates and lower the credit available to firms. In addition, they create a liquidity problem that is not usually recognized nor well understood. An inflationary economy is the consequence of an irresponsible fiscal and monetary policy at the national level (Chapter 2).

During an inflationary period, unless influenced by relative changes in demand or supply, the prices of physical goods, such as agricultural land and machinery, will increase at the rate of inflation. Also in a free capital market, the price of borrowing increases with inflation. This increase is required to maintain the ability of savers to purchase higher-priced physical goods in future periods.

Now consider what gives rise to the liquidity problem. The price of money, the interest rate, rises with the rate of inflation. But profits on investments do not rise sufficiently to pay for the higher interest costs on loans because total earnings on assets are reflected mostly in capital gains. Thus, an investment may be profitable once capital gains are included with the cash return but still may not be earning sufficient liquid returns to meet the required interest and principal payments on a loan, especially during the initial years (Robison and Brake).[9]

The consequences of the liquidity problem are severe, especially during the early periods of an investment, when repayment of the loan may require subsidies from the firm's equity. This again, however, limits investments to those already well-off and equity-strong. Thus, inflation will be much more of a restraint for small borrowers than for large ones.

Another consequence of the inflation-induced liquidity problem is that it discourages long-term investments. Obviously, the shorter the life of an investment, the less effect inflation has on liquidity. To illustrate, suppose a farmer has a one year investment. Then that investment, if profitable, will pay for itself and interest costs in one year and there is no liquidity problem. In general, the shorter the economic life of a durable, the less severe will be the liquidity problems created by inflation.

The relationship between the inflation and liquidity problem has important implications for Ecuador's agricultural sector. This is because most agricultural investments (new technology and human capital improvements) are long-term (Chapter 12). Of all sectors in the economy, agriculture is likely to be the one most adversely affected by the inflation-induced liquidity problem because its investment base has the longest economic life.

An inflationary economy creates one more problem, perhaps the most severe of all. It often leads policymakers to take inappropriate actions that do not solve the liquidity problem, that create new problems, or make the liquidity problem worse. The appropriate action is to attack the inflation problem directly through fiscal and monetary responses. The incorrect responses taken by the government have been to blame the inflation problem on certain participants in the economy, especially the merchant class, and to adopt a subsidized credit policy.

This section has pointed out that offering subsidized credit is not likely to solve the liquidity problem created by inflation except in the case of extremely large subsidies. Since the initial liquidity problem is directly related to the magnitude of the inflation problem, subsidized interest rates could be negative in real terms and still not solve the liquidity problem.

Conclusions and Recommendations

The principal conclusion of this chapter is that the dominant agricultural credit policy of administered and subsidized interest rates has impeded rather than facilitated development in the agricultural sector. It has supplied evidence that the following undesirable consequences can at least in part be attributable to this policy.

First, the agricultural credit policy of administered and subsidized interest rates has created a condition of excess demand for agricultural loans. This condition, in turn, has required non-market allocations of loan funds that are dominated by the interests of larger, more well-to-do farmers who may divert loans from their most productive use in agriculture. Thus, subsidized interest loan programs have largely benefitted the large farmers.

Second, in response to the excess demand for loan funds, the BNF has increased the transactions costs of securing its loans. These increased transactions costs have fallen more on the resource-poor and small borrowers. Consequently their effective demand for BNF loans has decreased.

Third, although the BNF was created with the explicit purpose of aiding small farmers, in practice it has failed in this mission. This is because it has been necessary for the BNF to reduce total transactions costs by lending to fewer and larger, more secure borrowers to both survive and to offer subsidized interest rates.

Fourth, offering subsidized interest rates on loans generally results in a below-market rate of interest offered savers. Thus, in the agricultural sector where deposits are needed, they are not forthcoming because of the negative real interest rates being offered potential savers. Consequently, there is a lack of savings mobilization forcing the BNF to reduce its lending activities and to depend on funding sources other than deposits of savers.

Fifth, the subsidized interest rate policy of the BNF is a major cause of its decapitalization. It is increasingly dependent on outside sources of funds to maintain its viability. Evidence is that foreign lenders are not willing to continue to see their loans used in such clearly unproductive and resource-concentrating loan programs.

Sixth, strong evidence supports the conclusion that subsidized interest rates cause more borrowers to default or to postpone their loan repayments. Consequently, BNF has sustained an unacceptably high default rate by most banking standards.

Other possible consequences of subsidized interest rates include inflation, discouragement of the development of private financial intermediaries and diversion of the loan proceeds to purposes for which they were not intended.

Finally, inflation creates liquidity problems. It often is argued that the apparent liquidity problem is a profitability problem that requires a subsidized interest rate to solve. Nothing could be further from the actual facts. What is needed is to establish reduced loans repayments in the early years of the investment project.

To overcome many of the problems discussed in connection with the policy of subsidized interest rates, the following changes in Ecuador's agricultural credit policies are recommended.

First, it is recommended that the policies of administratively determined credit allocation and interest rates be eliminated for all sectors. The elimination of subsidized credit for all sectors will allow credit to be supplied on nearly equal terms to potential borrowers who will employ it in more productive uses. Market interest rates also will lead to much greater savings mobilization. Such a policy change will also permit the government to separate agricultural production policies from welfare policies, maintain the BNF as a reliable source of agricultural loan funds and reduce its dependence on foreign donors and discourage political patronage and high transactions costs for borrowers.

Second, innovations in the disbursal and collecting of loan funds must be adopted for the agricultural sector to compete for loan funds with other sectors demanding credit. One such solution has been proposed to the BNF and has been adopted on a trial basis (Ramos 1989). The program builds on an existing business network between millers and producers of rice. The miller in essence becomes a financial intermediary for the BNF and receives a line of credit, secured by the mill, to support producers who use the services of the mill. Having millers provide credit to producers reduces the supervision costs of producer loans to the BNF and facilitates, at a reduced cost, a function already being performed informally by the millers. The result of improving the efficiency of credit allocation to the agricultural sector is its increased ability to compete for loan funds.

Third, it is recommended that the discriminatory credit allocation system that now exists be eliminated. There is no justification for the selective credit bias against certain agricultural sector participants who provide important marketing services. Adequate access to credit by all agricultural sector participants is needed to develop more competitive trading structure (Chapter 8).

Fourth, as long as there are significant levels of inflation there will be liquidity problems associated with long-term investments. These liquidity problems will not be solved through loan subsidy programs as experience has demonstrated. To overcome the liquidity problem the following approach is recommended. Establish loan terms based on the real balance of the loan. During periods of high inflation this may require that nominal loan balances be increased in each period. It also implies a system of graduated loan payments. One reason lenders are reluctant to extend loan terms or adopt graduated payment plans is because inflation and the possibility of changing inflation rates increase their risk. To overcome this reluctance and to maintain their viability as financial institutions it is recommended that a system of variable interest rates be adopted. This variable interest rate scheme has been employed successfully by many banking systems and could be effectively employed in Ecuador.

NOTES

1. Both the BNF and the private banks are allowed to add another 2 to 3 points to these rates as charges for social services institutions such as the Fire Department and Health Research Centers, and bank commissions and insurance fees, raising the cost of the loans even further but having no effect on the banks' earnings.

2. The interest rate charged by private banks is not completely market-determined because the government limits the spread between the rate banks pay savers and the rate they can charge on their loans. As inflation increases, the real value of this spread decreases.

3. The inference that large loans are made to well-to-do borrowers with large amounts of equity is defensible because they are the only borrowers with the collateral required to secure large loans.

4. Most BNF borrowers recognize the real cost associated with subsidized loans and would prefer credit to be available on a timely basis and at market rates of interest rather than pay the high transactions cost of obtaining a BNF loan. Evidence of this feeling among farmers comes from a seminar sponsored by the Agricultural Policy Institute (IDEA) in Guayaquil. Farm sector participants at this conference concluded by proposing the following (IDEA): "...that BNF charge market interest rates but deliver the loans on time and in adequate amounts."

5. See Chapter 2.

6. Other benefits of positive interest rates for savings include the integration of markets, the encouragement to hold larger proportions of wealth in domestic financial assets rather than unproductive inflation hedges or foreign assets, reduced transactions costs and the establishment of bank-customer relationships that may extend to loan arrangements.

7. Once a loan payment is not fulfilled, the BNF transfers the loan from the subsidized line of credit (where borrowers pay 38 percent in 1990) to the commercial loan portfolio, where the interest rate is near the market determined rate (about 50 percent).

8. Investments in irrigation projects discussed in Chapter 7 exemplify this point.

9. Another way to describe how inflation creates liquidity problems for borrowers, and hence discourages long-term investment, is to examine the reduction in the average

real balance on loans, holding the term of the loan constant but increasing the inflation rate. Consider the following.

Suppose a borrower takes out a loan of 100 million Sucres which is to be repaid in equal annual installments of 20 million Sucres for five years. If there is no inflation, then the real average outstanding balance over the five years is: $(100+80+60+40+20)/5 = 60$ million Sucres. Now suppose that the economy is suffering a 100 percent annual rate of inflation. Moreover, assume the term of the loan is not changed. Then the average real balance of the loan must be calculated anew. The first year's real balance with 100 percent rate of inflation is 50 million Sucres (S/100/2.00); 20 million (S/80/4.00) in the second year; 7.5 million in the third year; 2.5 million in the fourth year; and .6 million in the fifth year. On average then, the real balance has fallen to $(50+20+7.5+2.5+.6)/5=16.1$ million Sucres instead of 60 million Sucres. This represents a decrease of over 70 percent is the average real balance of the loan over its term because of inflation.

REFERENCES

Adams, Dale. 1984. *Undermining Rural Development with Cheap Credit*. Boulder: Westview Press.

Araujo, Paulo F. C. and Richard L. Meyer. 1977. "Agricultural Credit Policy in Brazil: Objectives and Results." *American Journal of Agricultural Economics* 59:957-961.

BCE (Central Bank of Ecuador). Various Years. *Información Estadística Mensual*. Quito.

BNF (National Development Bank). 1989. *Boletín Estadístico 1970-1988*. Quito: Gerencia Técnica.

Barry, Peter J. and Lindon J. Robison. 1986. "Economic versus Accounting Rates of Return for Farm Land." *Land Economics* 62:388-401.

Connolly, Michael. 1990. "Interest Rate Arbitrage and Capital Flows Between Ecuador and the United States: 1985-1989." Quito: Sigma One Corporation, Preliminary Report, April 15.

Gonzalez Vega, Claudio. 1986. "The Ohio State University Approach to Rural Financial Markets: A Concepts Paper." Columbus, OH: Occasional Paper No. 1248, Department of Sociology, Ohio State University, February.

IDEA (Agricultural Policy Institute). 1989. *El Crédito para la Comercialización del Arroz*. Quito: Documento Técnico No. 19, January.

Ramos, Hugo. 1989. "The Financial System Supporting Rice Marketing in Ecuador." Ph.D. Thesis, Michigan State University.

_____. 1984. "Agricultural Credit Situation." Quito: USAID.

Robison, Lindon J. and John R. Brake. 1980. "Inflation, Liquidity and Growth: Some Implications for the Farm Firm." *Southern Journal of Agricultural Economics* 12:131-137.

10

SOCIAL INSTITUTIONS, GENDER

AND RURAL LIVING CONDITIONS

Rae Lesser Blumberg and Dale Colyer

Social, economic and other factors influencing rural living conditions in Ecuador vary tremendously. Life is affected by the region, farm size and type and social class and ethnic group of the farm family. Other important sources of variation include climate, soil, topography, education and public services. These factors interact and effects of one may be modified by those of another. In addition, there are significant differences within regions, farm sizes and types and ethnic groups so that making generalizations based on specific situations can be misleading.

However, there are commonalities within the overall social, cultural and economic environments of rural Ecuador. One is the hegemonic Latin culture with its tradition of male domination, close family relationships and kinship ties that operate at the expense of societal cohesiveness and effective functioning of the public sector. Another shared experience is the economic crisis that has affected the country for the last decade. For a very large proportion of Ecuador's rural residents this means continuing to endure lives of poverty, due to low levels of resources, technology and productivity, coupled with large families.

Analyses of these factors are hampered by a lack of current data. The 1982 censuses of population and housing provide some relatively recent information but there has been no agricultural census since 1974 and most of the other reliable general information and data about rural living conditions also date from the mid-1970s. The Sierra has been the subject of a relatively large number of studies which provide information on living conditions for specific situations and localities but there are few similar studies for the Costa and Oriente. Thus, for the purposes of this study, existing information was supplemented by fieldwork using rapid rural appraisal (RRA) methods.

The following sections describe and analyze: gender roles in Ecuadorian agriculture based on previous analyses; the results of the RRA survey to supplement previous studies; rural community life, including governmental, educational, economic, organizational, religious and social characteristics; and part-time farming by low-resource farmers.

Gender Roles in Agriculture

The Ecuadorian constitution recognizes equal rights for women. Paragraph 5, Article 19 states: "Women, whatever their civil status, have equal rights and opportunities to men in all aspects of public, private and family life..." (Translation by the authors.) But Spanish American culture, like many others, continues to be characterized by *machismo* and women often must defer to men, at least in appearance. This generalization applies in the agricultural sector as much if not more than in other areas. Women, however, contribute very importantly and directly in the production and distribution of farm products. In addition, the extent of their actual subordination varies by region, ethnicity and social class. Indeed, as in other aspects of Ecuadorian life there are notable differences in sex roles between regions (women are more active in farming in the Sierra than in the Costa) and ethnic groups (women are more active in farming among Indians versus whites and mestizos). Furthermore, both a recent empirical study (Alberti) and the RRA found a noteworthy interaction among gender, ethnicity and social class.

Production Activities

Census data from 1982, the last population census, indicated that only a relatively small percentage (7.5) of farm women were economically active, i.e., participants in the measured labor force (Chapter 5). Women's activities were reported as being concentrated on "household activities," which that greatly understated their agricultural contributions (Luzuriaga and Fiallo). Haney summarized information from a number of surveys and other studies which documented that women contributed substantially more to the agricultural labor force than reported by the census. A national study of the agricultural labor force was conducted for 1974-1975 (Torres, Cañadas and Ribadeneira). These data, summarized in Tables 10.1, 10.2 and 10.3, show that women participated more in the agriculture of the Sierra than they did in the Costa but even there about one-fifth of the family farm labor was supplied by women (Table 10.1). This is related to both the ethnic composition of producer groups and the types of agriculture practiced in the two regions (see also Phillips 1985a, 1985b, 1987).

A high proportion of the agricultural population in the Sierra consists of indigenous population groups in which women play a more important role in farming than in nonindigenous populations (Alberti). The Costa population is composed of a much smaller proportion of indigenous groups than is true for the Sierra. Agricultural production in the Costa tends to be on larger farms, to be more strongly oriented to commercial production, uses larger amounts of hired workers and concentrates on export crops, situations where the participation rates of women are lower than is typical of smaller family farms and subsistence units found in the Sierra. An exception in the Costa is that women frequently pick coffee for pay. Women also participate less in the larger commercial operations in the Sierra, except for some dairy operations where they are hired for milking, a role that has declined with mechanization (Stolen).

While, among the indigenous groups in the Sierra, women participate extensively in nearly all farming activities, there tends to be a division of labor by sex, with men's activities being concentrated on crop production and women devoting relatively more

Table 10.1   Division of Man-Days of Labor by Gender for All Farming Activities
Ecuador, 1975

Activity	Sierra	Costa	Oriente	Ecuador
Family Labor				
Male	48,666,529	37,995,759	6,791,453	93,453,741
Female	36,038,849	10,937,697	1,808,579	48,785,125
Permanent Hired				
Male	3,943,540	2,427,680	133,139	6,504,359
Female	559,955	99,748	0	659,703
Temporary Hired				
Male	21,911,431	18,755,980	1,302,901	41,970,312
Female	982,190	46,391	1,483	1,030,064
Help/Exchange				
Male	1,948,829	1,203,850	89,565	3,242,244
Female	619,368	375,586	21,616	1,016,570
All Labor				
Male	76,470,329	60,383,269	8,317,058	145,170,656
Female	38,200,362	11,459,422	1,831,678	51,491,462
Grand Total	114,670,691	71,842,691	10,148,736	196,662,118

Source: Torres, Cañades and Ribadeneira.

Table 10.2   Division of Man-Days of Labor by Gender for Crop and Livestock
Production, Ecuador 1975 (Thousands)

Activity	--- Sierra ---		--- Costa ---		-- Oriente --		-- Ecuador --	
	Crop	Livestock	Crop	Livestock	Crop	Livestock	Crop	Livestock
Family Labor								
Male	19,046	7,529	17,624	4,263	2,331	1,531	39,001	13,323
Female	8,310	11,129	2,679	2,339	581	537	11,570	14,005
Permanent Hired								
Male	2,059	1,045	754	1,024	9	79	2,822	2,148
Female	142	350	13	81	0	0	156	432
Temporary Hired								
Male	19,325	488	16,809	177	660	57	36,794	723
Female	717	166	44	1	1	0	763	167
Help/Exchange								
Male	1,898	4	1,110	0	79	0	3,087	4
Female	567	0	375	0	22	0	963	0
All Labor								
Male	42,328	9,068	36,298	5,464	3,079	1,667	81,705	16,198
Female	9,738	11,646	3,112	2,422	604	537	13,453	14,604
Grand Total	52,066	20,713	39,409	7,886	3,682	2,203	95,156	30,802

Source: Torres, Cañades and Ribadeneira.

Table 10.3   Man-Workdays Used for Crop Production by Gender and Size of Farm
             Ecuador 1975 (Thousands)

| Size Range | -- Sierra -- | | -- Coast -- | | -- Oriente -- | | -- Total -- | |
(hectares)	Male	Female	Male	Female	Male	Female	Male	Female
0-0.99	2,074	1,591	2,260	470	18	7	4,352	2,068
1-1.99	2,889	1,798	2,195	363	32	9	5,116	2,170
2-4.99	4,762	2,390	5,377	873	90	54	10,229	3,316
5-9.99	3,752	1,463	4,130	601	154	44	8,036	2,107
10-19.99	2,012	489	3,833	428	395	67	6,240	984
20-49.99	2,731	482	4,130	554	916	222	7,776	1,258
50-99.99	820	66	871	60	577	174	2,268	300
100 & Over	294	36	751	110	149	4	1,194	149
Totals	19,334	8,314	23,546	3,457	2,331	581	45,211	12,351

Source: Torres, Cañades and Ribadeneira.

time to livestock raising activities (Table 10.2). Women's participation is especially large on the small farms which are very important in terms of numbers and in the use of labor since the level of mechanization is very low (Table 10.3). Most small farms raise some livestock in addition to producing crops for the market as well as home use (Cornick; Ibarra; Pomeroy). The livestock include cattle, hogs, sheep, chickens, rabbits and guinea pigs. Since the amount of land and forage per farm is very limited, to assure effective utilization, the livestock generally are not pastured in the open but rather are carefully herded or tethered to control their grazing or the forage is cut and taken to them. All these techniques are labor-intensive with women and children performing a large share of the work. Men generally do the heavier field work, such as land clearing and plowing, with women being more involved in planting, weeding and harvesting crops. In addition, women care for the children and do the housework. Men are more apt than women to participate in farm labor markets, working as day or permanent laborers on larger farms.

Marketing Activities

Farm women in the Sierra participate somewhat equally with men in the marketing of the products produced on their farms (Haney; Torres, Cañadas and Ribadeneira). Women also play very important roles in the agricultural marketing system, i.e., as intermediaries. This is especially important in the traditional marketing system which consists of *ferias*, the market days held one or more times per week in most rural towns. Bromley estimated that 75 percent of the intermediaries are women, although the larger merchants and wholesalers tend to be men. Women also operate a large share of the retail market outlets in the market centers and the small community stores in cities such as Quito and Guayaquil. While supermarkets have been growing in importance, the majority of food products are still handled by smaller merchants (see Chapter 8).

Impacts of Changes

Women's roles in agriculture are continuing to evolve in response to changing conditions in the sector as well as in the country's economy and society generally. As a result of the agrarian reform movement in the 1960s and 1970s, Ecuador's farm sector was further dichotomized into a group of a relatively few medium and larger commercial farms and a much larger group of small farms. The smaller farms had a substantial subsistence base prior to the petroleum boom, although most have since entered primarily into commercial activities. Women have much larger roles on the smaller than on the larger farms (Haney).[1] Participation by both indigenous and nonindigenous women is greater on the small farms, since conditions make their participation essential for economic survival.

A second factor has been the growing need for the small farm families to obtain off-farm income for economic survival, since many of the farm units are too small to support the family. The development of home-produced crafts and off-farm employment are used for attaining additional income (Brea-Porteiro; Meier; Muratorio 1980, 1981; Poeschel; Balarezo, et al.; Schroder). Women are frequently the producers of crafts, while men are more likely to do off-farm work. Off-farm work may consist of labor on neighboring larger farms, seasonal migration or commuting to other farm areas or to the cities.[2] As a result, adult males tend to be absent from the farm during the day, week or season. Maintenance and control of the family plot fall increasingly on the women (Salamea and Likes). This phenomenon also has contributed to the decline in production of typical food crops which tend to require more and heavier labor.

Attitudinal Impacts

Social custom dictates that women, especially of the dominant white-mestizo culture, defer to men in public matters. This is reflected in the title of Wendy Weiss's 1985 doctoral thesis, *Es El Que Manda* (It Is He Who Commands). Despite this custom, the role of women is important and the changing social and economic circumstances are altering the perceptions as well as reality. Women inherit equally with men and thus own and control property. Their increasingly important roles as income earners further add to their power and influence (Weiss). Illiteracy remains higher among women but educational levels have improved and the numbers of female students in university agricultural curriculums have been growing more rapidly than those of males (Izurieta and Pinto). Cornick, et al. found that objectives of farming systems research were often frustrated because scientists failed to account for the influence and control of resources by women. Agreements reached with the men would not be carried out because the women who controlled part of the resources would not cooperate. This was not apparent during negotiations because the village women did not participate when the farming systems research team was composed of males. The team recommended that all research teams contain females to assure that women's views were adequately taken into consideration. This seems relevant for most economic development activities involving small farms.

Findings of the Rapid Rural Appraisal

The objectives of the rapid rural appraisal were to examine the social and economic situations of rural families in the Sierra, Costa and Oriente, with special attention to the division of labor and resources by gender, age, ethnicity and social class. For this, RRA fieldwork was conducted in Chimborazo (Sierra), Manabí (Costa) and Napo and

Sucumbíos (Oriente). The methodology of RRA is based on "triangulation," i.e., obtaining more than one source of data about a limited and focused number of issues. The process began with the selection of sites that had both recent agro-socioeconomic diagnostic research by Ecuadorian or U.S. social scientists and a project sponsored by the U.S. Agency for International Development (USAID). These provided base-line data. Additional data were generated via a variety of methods.[3] The RRA fieldwork did not involve random samples, so that the results from the cases studied cannot be generalized.

Family, Gender and Agricultural Development

The results of the RRA help to confirm the drastic underestimation of the female contribution to Ecuadorian farming by the *1982 Census of Population (INEC)*. The official census statistics indicated that only 7 percent of rural women were economically active. This under-counting is due mainly to the use of a question that tends to exclude women from being classified as economically active. When asked about their occupation, women, or their husbands, generally answer that it is *quehaceres domésticos* (housework) or *ama de casa* (housewife). A totally different picture emerges when the question is about the extent of participation in farming activities by family members. A 1974-1975 sample survey shows much higher rates of female participation in family agricultural labor than does the census (Torres, Cañadas and Ribadeniera). The RRA and a 1989 study by Balarezo indicate that the levels of female involvement in farming are higher than those reported by the 1974-1975 study.

The RRA results for the Sierra are in line with the high rates of women's involvement in all phases of farming found in recent studies of Sierra populations (Alberti; CIM; Poeschel). The RRA and Balarezo results for the Costa, however, indicate a dramatically higher female participation than the few other published studies, which indicated that women do almost no agricultural work (Leonard; Luzuriaga; Phillips 1985a, 1987). The Torres, Cañadas and Ribadeniera study also indicated substantial Costa female participation in 1974-1975. In the Oriente, the RRA was one of the first efforts to ascertain the gender division of labor among colonists. It found a level of female involvement intermediate between that of the Sierra and Costa.

Sex and Age Division of Labor and Resources

Among the Sierra Indians, few farmers are very well off but, *regardless of level of wealth*, women generally participate as *equal partners* in the *division of agricultural labor*. These findings have been well-documented by the RRA and other recent studies of Chimborazo villages based on random samples (Alberti; CIM). Women work with the men--as often do children--in every main crop task except plowing and chemical applications. When a man is not available for those tasks, the women do the work, hire labor, organize a *minga* or obtain help from a male with obligations due to kinship or other ties. Women also care for small and medium animals, with the help of their children. Caring for chickens, guinea pigs and rabbits are almost 100 percent female activities while sheep and pigs are predominantly female obligations. Cattle and horses tend to be male-dominated enterprises.

Seasonal migration by men tends to be subordinated to involvement in the main crop months, except among those Indians who have too little land to provide even for subsistence needs. This proved the case in the community of Magipamba, where the typical landholding is less than one-fourth hectare and where most men migrate and come back only once or twice a year. In contrast, in the communities of Chimborazo and Yacupamba, with larger farms, prime-age men migrate only when they are not crucially needed for farming. In both Chimborazo and Pisicaz, however, many of the men live at home but work off-farm on neighboring haciendas or in a nearby cement factory.[4]

With respect to the *division of resources* by age and sex it was found that from very early ages, children may be given a chicken or a guinea pig to care for. It is their animal and they will benefit from its proceeds. As they get older, they gain access to larger animals. Similarly, inheritance customs mean that land is divided equally among sons and daughters. In Alberti's Indian sample, over 80 percent of the women had some land. For married couples, a joint decision-making pattern is dominant (the RRA; Alberti; CIM; Poeschel). The husband and wife will reach a consensus on both sales and use of the proceeds. Women frequently sell small animals or artisan items in the market for funding household subsistence but men generally have more access to cash income. Studies of Sierra Indian populations emphasize women's stronger adherence to ethnic identity, language and customs and attribute this, in part, to women's reluctance to trade their greater relative gender equality as Indians for the subordinate position of mestiza women (Alberti; Poeschel).

Among the mestizos, the ideal is that a woman is economically dependent and should not have to work in the fields (Alberti; Stolen; Weiss). The higher the social class and/or economic level, the more likely the ideal is to be realized. The RRA found this among mestizos in the Oriente and the Costa; Alberti provides empirical documentation for her sample villages in Chimborazo Province in the Sierra. Among other things, this pattern means that the women of the better-off mestizo families have less household leverage vis-à-vis their husbands than do the women from poorer mestizo families. This is because the poorer the family, the more active the woman is likely to be in agricultural production and/or other income-generating activities (Alberti; Blumberg 1989). But the situation is complicated by high levels of seasonal migration among mestizos youths, household heads, and some young, single women. The head of the Ecuadorian Center for Agricultural Services (CESA) in Riobamba and a USAID/Ecuador official (citing a 1979 USAID study) indicated that for much of the year in many mestizo villages in Chimborazo Province, the population consists overwhelmingly of women, old men and young children. Under such circumstances, women do most of the agricultural work, although most of the income may come from off-farm activities.

Comparing the relative economic and social status of Indian and mestiza women, the Indian women not only play more important and equal roles in production, their status is further enhanced by strong cultural norms of "full partnership" that give them more household leverage than one might expect from their low cash incomes in comparison with their seasonally migrating husbands. Mestiza women may do as much work in poorer families and in areas of high male migration but strong cultural norms of economic dependence reduce the household leverage of these women.

The RRA area for the Costa was carried out around Portoviejo, Manabí Province, which is an overwhelmingly mestizo area. Women have been described as doing virtually no field work in the Costa region, except for working in the coffee harvest. However, according to both men and women in the five communities surveyed for the RRA, women also are involved in family farming activities, performing substantial amounts of field work, much of the animal care and sometimes raising a garden. With respect to field crops, women were acknowledged as having important roles in planting, harvesting and post-harvest processing. In addition, women pointed out that they also helped in land preparation, weeding and seed selection. A common daily work pattern for roughly six months of a typical agricultural cycle is for the woman to spend the morning doing domestic and farm-related chores near the house. They then prepare lunch, take it out to their husbands and spend the afternoon working in the fields. In the coffee-growing areas, where harvesting was in progress during the RRA visit, the women did not hesitate to tell how much they were paid for a day's labor harvesting coffee. This was their principal source of independent income during the year and they said that they used almost all of it for their children's food and other needs.[5]

As of the 1982 population census, some 30 percent of the 115,000 inhabitants of Napo Province were lowland *Quichua* Indians. They farm by horticultural methods, specifically by "slash and mulch" cultivation and claim, like the Sierra Indians, an equal partnership pattern in field operations for most principal crops. But the equal partnership may involve more sexual differentiation among crops than in the Sierra. For example, cassava is largely a woman's crop. It also is their principal subsistence crop, consumed in both solid and liquid (*chicha*) forms. Women take primary care of the children and fill in when men leave for temporary migration.[6] They, however, tend to have less direct access to cash income than their female counterparts in the Sierra, since local markets are not as developed and ubiquitous. Thus, the women are less likely to be market sellers in the few local ferias than in the Sierra.

Among the mestizo colonists, the usual norm about women's ideal role as housewife prevails, but the norm is observed even less than in the Costa. Pioneering on a remote farm is labor-intensive and both women and children, especially male children, work in agricultural tasks. Women colonists described the same pattern for farm work as found in Manabí. After a morning doing chores, women prepare lunch, deliver it to their husbands in the fields and remain to spend the afternoon working. However, getting to and from the cultivated areas of their two-kilometer-deep, still-largely forested parcels is a more formidable task than in the Costa region. In many areas colonists have settled as far back as the eighth or ninth tier of properties from the main road (see below).[7]

In the northern area of the Oriente, there is no real dry season, so male migration is not confined to any particular season. When there is an urgent need for money or when oil companies or a neighbor are hiring, the man may undertake outside work, leaving the wife and children to carry on as best they can. However, a report by Darío, Seré and Luzuriaga indicates that only about a fifth of the colonists work off the farm and that most of those are the newer immigrants who have not fully established their farms.

Wives of the colonists have fewer opportunities to earn and spend cash income than in the other regions. Coffee is the main cash crop and some women work for pay in its harvest, but it is difficult for those who live away from the main roads to leave for a stint picking coffee or shopping. However, most of the farming in the study area is a family business so that day labor opportunities are very limited, for men as well as women. Thus, while women do a significant portion of the work, they have less access to cash income than their female counterparts in the other regions, and less opportunity to spend it.

Temporary Migration/Circulation/Commuting[8]

The RRA results indicate that, except for three situations (two are in Chimborazo

Province, in the Quichua village of Yacupamba and the ten mestizo villages of Chingazo-Pungales, and the third involves the Associations of Cassava Producers and Processors (APPYs) of Manabí) men increasingly work away from the farm.[9] The primary reason given was that the economic crisis had caused an increase in the cost of living. For the Oriente, the recent declines in coffee prices have reduced farm incomes, further aggravating the situation. The increased off-farm work includes all three activities: temporary or seasonal migration, circulation and daily commuting to nearby jobs. The latter range from day labor for local landowners to work in a cement factory (in the indigenous villages of Chimborazo and Pisicaz). The net result is that women and others not in prime labor force years (the young and old) do more of the farmwork. It also was evident that more of their production was being used for consumption than sale, unless a development project had enhanced their agricultural productivity.

Markets in the Sierra and Oriente

"Mini-censuses" of several markets in both the Sierra and the Oriente were undertaken as a follow-up to earlier, more extensive studies of Sierra markets. Bromley had found that women accounted for some 65 percent of the market sellers, including 85-90 percent of those retailing fresh foodstuffs. Counts taken in four Sierra markets indicate that quite similar patterns still exist. In Otavalo's textile/artisan market, 63 percent of the sellers were women. In the small/medium animal market of Guamote women were found to be the exclusive sellers of chickens and guinea pigs and to be in the majority (some 55-60 percent) of the sellers of hogs and sheep; whereas cattle, horses and donkeys were sold almost exclusively by men. All of the wholesalers observed buying the sheep and hogs were women. In the main, fruit, vegetable and miscellaneous market of Saquisilí, 85 percent of the vendors were women. In the Riobamba textile market about half the sellers were women, due to a preponderance of male tailors and male Otavaleños selling textiles from that area. In the Oriente, women were 65 percent of the sellers in the weekly market in Coca and 57 percent in Sacha's weekly market. A less precise count of the large Lago Agrio market found at least two-thirds of the sellers were women.

Community Life

Although rural life in Ecuador tends to be centered around family and kinship interrelationships, community activities also are important. These include governmental, educational, economic, organizational, religious and social functions, activities that typically are interrelated.

Local Government

Ecuadorian local government units are *cantones* (counties), *parroquias* (parishes), *municipios* (municipalities) and *comunas* (communities). The latter is the smallest administrative unit and the one with which a *campesino* is apt to have greatest contact (Colyer). The comuna is a form of economic and community organization recognized by the 1979 Constitution. To be legally recognized the comuna must be registered with the Ministry of Agriculture, as is the case for most other agricultural organizations. In 1983 there were 1,844 registered comunas with a total population of

682,663 (FIDA p. 83).

Most comunas are indigenous groupings, located primarily in the Sierra but with some in the Oriente and Costa. Historically, they possessed both communal land and individual family parcels, with the communal land often located in the high pastureland areas (*páramos*). With increasing population pressures, the comunas have tended to subdivide the common land so that new families could have their own land. Comunas operate through general assemblies consisting of all members 18 years of age and older, which develop policies and elect a council (*cabildo*) to carry out the policies. In addition, there are the *comuneros* consisting of the household heads, primarily men, who have the obligation to participate in community activities. A principal function is the administration of communal property but they also conduct other community business and promote development, education, health and other services.

Public Services

Public services in rural areas were upgraded substantially during the oil boom years, a process that has continued but at a much slower pace due to the economic crises of the 1980s. Rural electrification was expanded, roads were constructed, schools built, water was piped into many communities and health centers were installed. The "rural year" required for completion of medical degrees has made health services more available, as has the campesino health insurance program. School construction was expanded so that most communities are served by at least a primary school (six grades).

Medium-sized to larger farms tend to have adequate services. With access to electricity, such farms can install water and waste disposal systems. They can afford bottled natural gas or other fuels. These farms tend to be on or to have access to all-weather roads and most of the owners have trucks for transporting their products. They either live in communities with both primary and secondary schools or can send their children to private schools. Many of the owners of larger land units live in cities such as Quito, Guayaquil or the larger provincial cities and towns.

However, the same situation does not prevail for the majority of owners of small farms, who cannot afford to privately install such services. Large numbers of rural people do not have many of the basic services. According to the *1982 Census of Housing*, 31.6 percent of the rural houses had electricity, 23.7 percent had running water (either within or outside the house), 28.6 percent had indoor or outdoor toilets and 15.5 percent had waste water disposal facilities such as septic tanks (Jordán p. 237; Páez, Ordoñez and Torres). Only about one fourth of the rural households (24.1 percent) obtained their water from public systems, with the remainder about equally divided between wells and springs (38.6 percent) and other sources such as rivers and streams (37.3 percent). Less than 30 percent of the rural houses were classified by census personnel as acceptable or better.

Important differences in the availability of water and electric services exist both within and between regions (Table 10.4). A higher proportion of rural households in the Sierra (28.7 percent) obtain their water from public sources than in either the Costa (16.3 percent) or Oriente (15.8 percent). In the Sierra the percentages vary from 22.0 in Bolívar to 45.6 in Imbabura while the variation in the Costa is from 4.1 in Esmeraldas to 44.8 in El Oro and for the Oriente the range is 8.2 in Napo to 31.4 in Zamora Chinchipe. About two thirds of the rural households in both the Sierra and Costa regions are without electricity, while over 85 percent of those in the Oriente lack

Table 10.4   Rural Housing Characteristics, Ecuador 1982

Province	Number of Houses	-- Water Source -- Public	Wells	Other	Percentage Without: Elec.	Toilet	Sewage
Sierra	436,297	28.7	35.4	36.8	64.9	81.7	88.0
Azuay	60,660	25.8	44.1	30.1	67.2	87.4	90.0
Bolívar	24,940	22.0	53.0	25.0	79.6	78.7	86.4
Cañar	31,395	22.7	52.7	24.6	66.9	83.5	84.9
Carchi	14,620	25.2	29.8	71.8	55.1	83.3	88.5
Cotapaxi	50,140	22.1	35.2	42.7	71.8	84.6	88.9
Chimborazo	54,340	32.4	49.2	18.4	78.0	84.1	88.1
Imbabura	31,542	45.6	23.2	31.2	64.6	82.4	85.2
Loja	47,560	29.5	51.3	19.2	83.2	95.2	96.8
Pichincha	77,360	39.0	23.3	37.7	50.4	63.3	72.4
Tungurahua	43,740	29.9	14.3	55.8	45.7	71.0	84.8
Costa	299,053	16.3	40.6	43.1	67.0	55.6	79.1
El Oro	21,760	44.8	30.2	25.0	62.1	64.8	73.2
Esmeraldas	22,220	4.1	21.1	74.8	77.6	73.4	92.1
Guayas	109,760	14.9	31.2	53.9	51.8	54.1	73.3
Los Ríos	54,739	12.3	53.5	34.2	79.8	73.2	77.6
Manabí	90,574	16.5	51.5	32.0	76.2	40.2	85.1
Oriente	36,711	15.8	38.3	45.9	85.8	83.3	90.4
Morona-Santiago	9,974	15.1	44.9	40.0	86.2	85.8	92.3
Napo	16,170	8.2	39.8	52.0	88.9	81.8	90.8
Pastaza	3,709	22.2	19.9	57.9	71.8	74.4	80.3
Zamora-Chinchipe	6,858	31.4	35.1	33.5	85.3	88.1	91.9
Galápagos	346	24.9	7.5	67.6	60.1	50.6	76.6
Unassigned Areas	7,545	12.5	56.2	31.3	66.2	41.4	75.3
Combined Areas	779,942	24.1	38.6	37.3	67.2	70.6	83.3

Source: Páez, Ordoñez and Torres.

such services. Less than half the rural houses in Tungurahua lack electricity, compared to nearly 89 percent in Napo.

While most of the primary roads are paved, the vast majority of the secondary roads are gravel or dirt and tend to be poorly maintained. Thus, transportation for both people and products is a serious problem for many small farms, especially those located at a distance from main roads or population centers, since they generally must depend on public transportation. Those who live away from main roads often have to walk, or use horses or donkeys, to transport themselves and their products to markets or to a point on a main road where they can access public transportation systems.

In the Sierra and Costa regions most farms are located on or close to roads, although the road quality may be poor. The colonization process in the Oriente, however, has resulted in a large number of farms that do not front a main road. Colonization has followed the construction of roads for oil exploration and production. Each colonist receives 50 hectares from the Ecuadorian Institute for Agrarian Reform and Colonization (IERAC) in a parcel that is 250 meters wide and 2 kilometers deep. These are organized in tiers, with the 250 meters being road frontage for the first tier of farms along each side of the road. The second tier begins at the end of the first, the third is at the end of the second, etcetera. Typically, colonization occurs in 4 or 5 tiers but there may be 10 or more. Thus, most colonists must walk or ride horses or donkeys on narrow paths along property boundaries for several kilometers for access to the main road and public transportation, schools and other public services and markets.

Many communities have piped water systems but most small farms depend on wells, rivers, rainwater or water hauled in by tank trucks. Many families must devote considerable amounts of time to obtaining water, a task generally performed by the women and children of the household. Water quality also is a problem with much of the water contaminated. This contributes very significantly to rural health problems, especially for children where gastro-intestinal infections and diarrhea are common.

Health services also remain a problem in many rural areas. While health centers have been established in some communities, others do not have such services or have them on a part-time basis. Health problems are more serious for more isolated farms, in all areas but particularly in the Oriente, where they are exacerbated by the lack of transportation that permits quick access to medical services in emergency situations. Although access to family planning services was not studied in detail, many women in all three regions indicated the need for more and improved services.

Access to a primary school is relatively easy in nearly all rural areas, although distances can be substantial for the more isolated farms. Secondary school access is more problematic for many smaller communities or for the children from more isolated farms, since such schools tend to be located in larger communities and to serve several communities. Thus, relatively few farm children go to secondary schools because of the difficulty and costs of accessing the schools. Many farm families indicated they would like to send more of their children to secondary schools but cannot because of the cost.

In addition, some of the more isolated areas, primarily in the Oriente, have problems with obtaining or retaining teachers who are assigned by the Ministry of Education. In such places there may be only one teacher for all six grades and if she (or he) becomes ill or leaves in mid-term, another teacher may not be assigned, causing the loss of an entire year of education.

Historically, fewer girls than boys attended or completed primary school so that more women than men were illiterate. This was especially true in many indigenous areas where the women often spoke only Quichua. Most of the disparity has been eliminated in the 1980s (Chapter 12). Currently, a literacy campaign aimed at completely eliminating illiteracy is being waged. Part of the campaign requires high school students to teach reading and writing for four months to receive their diplomas (*bachilleratos*).

Organizations

A large number of organizations of various types exist in or to serve rural areas of Ecuador (FIDA; Jordán). The country's constitution requires that campesinos receive state support in organizing and promoting their interests. Under the Agricultural Development Law, Agrarian Reform Laws and Law of Comunas, the Ministry of Agriculture (MAG) is charged with assisting and developing such organizations. All have to be officially registered by MAG to have legal standing, a status that is essential for receiving services such as training and credit.

Organizations which have membership of individuals are classified as first degree units, while unions or federations of first degree organizations are classed as second degree units. The FIDA study indicated that in 1987 there were 27 second degree organizations with a membership of 291 first degree associations. These second degree organizations can be of associations, cooperatives, comunas or combinations of these. National or third degree organizations generally consist of aggregations of second degree units. They attempt to represent their groups at the national level and to obtain political benefits for their members. Such groups represent, especially, campesino and indigenous interests. Examples are the National Federation of Campesino Organizations, which represents some 15 small farmer organizations and the Union of Natives of the Ecuadorian Amazon which is composed of indigenous groups.

Official organizations, mandated by law, include the agricultural centers (*Centros Agrícolas*), organized at the cantonal level and to which farmers must belong to obtain farmer identification cards. These are federated into four regional chambers of agriculture (*Cámaras de Agricultura*) which in turn are part of a national federation, although this latter unit is weak and lacks the influence of the regional chambers. The centers vary in activities but many provide services such as input stores, marketing and technical assistance.

Associations are groups of farmers organized for specific purposes, often to promote production of a particular product or improvement of farmer interests in a given geographical area. There are associations of large- as well as small-farm owners. Associations tend to be relatively easy to form but to be legally recognized they must be registered with the Ministry of Agriculture. Members of producer associations must have land titles or certificates of possession but the same rule does not apply to marketing associations. An example of first degree associations are the APPYs in Manabí Province. Through a second degree organization, the Union of Cassava Producers and Processors (UAPPY) and with the assistance of the International Center for Tropical Agriculture (CIAT), USAID, MAG and the National Institute of Agricultural Research (INIAP), some 350 cassava producers have developed cooperative activities to process cassava into a dried product for use in mixed feeds for livestock and shrimp (Huffstutler; Romanoff and Toro).

Through May 1987, there were 2,245 MAG-registered, agriculturally related cooperatives with 77,589 members (FIDA p. 84). Many of these are traditional organizations that provide goods and services for their members. There also are production cooperatives that were formed as a result of agrarian reform requirements, especially for receiving land that had been state-owned.[10] Decree 1001, issued in 1970 during the last Velasco Ibarra dictatorship was specifically for rice sharecroppers in the Costa region (Phillips 1985a, 1987). To be eligible for land expropriated under the decree, an individual had to be a member of a production cooperative, which received the land and other services. Colonists also must form or join a cooperative or pre-cooperative to obtain land under the colonization programs in the Oriente. Many are cooperatives in name only since individuals join only to receive land. The units are then operated as independent farms; many of the cooperatives are not active organizations. In other cases, cooperatives have been formed because the government provides benefits that accrue only to cooperatives. Coffee marketing cooperatives, for example, were organized because of a law that granted them a proportion of the country's coffee quotas under the International Coffee Agreement.

Labor unions are a form of organization to which some rural agricultural workers belong but these are relatively few due to legal requirements and other factors. Unions are permitted where there are more than 15 workers with permanent employment. Employers often avoid union activities and other labor law requirements by contracting workers for short periods of time. Thus, unions are apt to exist only for relatively large agro-industrial firms.

Women's and youth organizations exist in some rural areas but the total numbers and membership are very small compared to the potential. Women can be members of associations and cooperatives although by law membership is limited to one member per household, who almost universally will be the head of the household, the husband. Associations and cooperatives for women's activities include, for example, two in cassava production and processing in Manabí Province. They produce cassava starch, a process that is more labor-intensive than cassava flour production. But they are having difficulties becoming registered with the government as a producer association, since the land titles or certificates of possession required are not in their names. Lack of registration, in turn, limits their access to credit. Despite the equality of men and women proclaimed in the Constitution and that the government began a new push in the summer of 1989 to abolish laws in conflict with the Constitutional guarantee of equality, there are no current plans to modify the laws permitting only one member of a household to belong to a producer association or cooperative and awarding land titles or certificates of possession to the head of the household (González).

The primary rural youth organizations are the 4-F clubs, an organization run by a foundation with support from the Ministry of Agriculture.[11] These clubs are for farm youth, both sexes, between the ages of 14 and 25. The 4-F clubs have produced very positive results for their members, but benefit relatively few. There are only about 110 clubs with some 3,500 members out of around a million eligible for membership.

Finally, there are school-related organizations. The most important are the Parents Associations, which conduct efforts to maintain and improve local school systems. There also are student associations or clubs within some schools, generally the secondary schools. The majority of these, however, are involved with sports activities.

Religion

Ecuador remains a largely Catholic country although some Protestant denominations have made inroads in some rural areas (see, for example, Muratorio 1980, 1981). Church activities revolve around services, marriages, baptisms and religiously related festivals. Many rural areas do not have permanent priests but are serviced by circuit riders who come to the community to hold services, hear confessions and perform marriages and baptisms. The Church has been active in promoting agricultural, educational and community improvements. These include, especially, activities by the Center for Social Action (CEAS) in the Riobamba area.[12] The Church also has been active in missionary, educational and development activities among the Indians groups in the Oriente with resources provided through the Catholic Relief Services.

While the total numbers are still relatively small, Protestant denominations-- especially fundamentalist and evangelical groups--have become important community forces in many rural areas. They have changed community standards with respect to activities such as drinking. Some contribute substantially to community, health, education and other economic development activities. World Vision, for example, has carried out important development activities in the community of Chimborazo west of Riobamba, including development of a cheese factory, a water system, outdoor latrines and a trout production facility. These development projects were mentioned prominently by villagers when discussing their recent conversion. Conversely, however, villagers in Magipamba, which has had Protestant missionaries for over 25 years, only mentioned receiving traditional charity activities (clothing and food for the neediest, rides to a hospital for the sick, etc.) from the missionaries.

Community Activities

Although family and kinship ties (*compadrazgo*) dominate in the social and economic lives of most rural Ecuadorians, some activities occur as community functions. One of the more important of these is the minga, the joining together of a group to accomplish some objective by use of voluntary and unpaid labor. These are used commonly and extensively by the indigenous communities but also are practiced by many other groups. They may involve the entire community or some smaller group. Mingas are used for activities such as constructing facilities, maintaining infrastructure or carrying out some specific project. In some Indian communities, mingas are used for preparing ground, planting, cultivating and harvesting crops. This can be especially important in areas where many of the males migrate or work away from the farm during periods of critical farming operations, since it permits carrying out those critical functions even for families with limited labor supplies.

In nonindigenous communities, mingas may be used for specific community-related tasks such as building a community center, school or other activity with common benefits. These also may be activities of an entire community or of some specific group within the community. Both the male and female APPYs, for example, have used mingas to carry out some of their association activities. These have included constructing and maintaining the facilities and preparing for the new production season.

Another common community-based activity is the festival. Festivals tend to be based on religious or related activities and are held at a time when nearly everyone in the community can participate. Community resources are pooled to finance the festival and individuals with more resources are expected to contribute more. During the *huasipungo* era, the large landowners (*hacendados*) helped finance festivals, although often complaining of the time lost from work. Those festivals were used to distribute bonuses, food, clothing and other items, to the farm workers. Crain documents the economic losses that accompanied the abandonment of one such festival after the 1964 agrarian reform. However, even today larger farms and employers in an area generally contribute to particular community festivals as a way to help relieve the tedium of arduous farm labor and to maintain good relationships with their workers.

Market days also can be considered community functions since the markets squares (*plazas*) are public facilities. Larger towns in an area will generally devote one day per week to the feria, a time when rural and other residents come to the town to sell and buy farm products, livestock, clothing, artisan goods and other products. The market days vary considerably in the Sierra but tend to be on weekends in the other regions.

Part-Time Farming

A large percentage of the Ecuadorian farm families earn substantial proportions of their incomes from off-farm or nonfarm sources, including work on other farms, according to data reported by a Ministry of Agriculture-Office of Overseas Science and Technology Research (ORSTOM) study (Table 10.5). These data were developed during an early year of the petroleum era and do not fully reflect the impacts of the oil boom on nonfarm employment opportunities. They do, however, indicate that very small farms, those with two hectares or smaller holdings, earned half or more of their incomes from nonfarm sources. Although recent data are not available, studies of

Table 10.5 Percentage of Farm and Nonfarm Income by Farm Size, Ecuador 1974

Source	Farm Size Range (hectares) 0>1	1>2	2>5	5>10	10>20	20>50	50>100	100+	All Sizes
Farm[a]	28.2	50.7	67.3	78.6	84.2	88.8	86.9	89.3	68.7
Product Sales	21.4	38.0	53.9	65.3	70.4	78.8	81.6	87.1	59.5
Home Use	6.8	12.7	13.4	13.3	13.8	10.0	5.3	2.2	9.2
Nonfarm[a]	71.9	49.3	32.7	21.4	15.8	11.3	13.0	11.6	31.4
Trade	7.9	3.9	4.5	4.9	4.6	2.7	4.4	4.2	4.9
Artisan Products	4.4	1.4	0.6	0.8	0.1	0.8	0.6	1.0	1.4
Agr. Wages	31.6	26.2	17.1	8.1	5.1	2.3	1.1	0.3	12.8
Nonagr. Wages	27.3	17.0	9.8	7.3	5.2	4.6	6.3	3.9	11.4
In Kind Income	0.7	0.8	0.7	0.3	0.8	0.9	0.6	2.2	0.9

Source: Torres, Cañades and Ribadeneira.

[a]Totals may not sum to 100 due to rounding.

economic activities in several areas of the country indicate that local day labor, seasonal migration, circulation, artisan production, trade and other nonfarm activities continue to be important economically and that farm families with limited resources continue to depend on such sources for substantial portions of their incomes.

Recent trends probably have increased the dependence on off-farm work for many of the smallholders. This proved generally true in the RRA, although, as described above, campesinos in three areas indicated that they are now working away less than in previous years. Factors that tend to increase off-farm work are a greater pressure on land, due to subdivision as new generations reach maturity and form new households, and a deterioration in economic well-being that the economic crises have produced. During the 1970s, there were economic inducements to migrate from farms mainly to urban areas as employment opportunities expanded, due to the construction boom and increases in other economic activities. Some of this resulted in permanent migration as farmers and farm workers moved to urban areas, a factor that helped relieve some of the pressure on land. The economic crisis of recent years has reduced off-farm employment opportunities and may be limiting off-farm employment.

The net result has been a further "feminization of farming" in areas where men are away for much of the crop cycle.[13] While many farm households reduce their production and rely increasingly on the men's off-farm earnings, the records of two development projects that introduced productivity-enhancing interventions in areas of high male seasonal migration offer food for thought. In the APPYs, which receive assistance from USAID, cassava production activities are contra-cyclical, beginning when the men normally would migrate. A market is being created for cassava and evidence indicates that male migration is down. Recent studies do show that on-farm income is up sharply for APPY members (Chávez). In the Chingazo-Pungales area of Chimborazo, an irrigation project has dramatically increased incomes and reduced male migration. Previously, according to the CESA head for Riobamba, about 90 percent of income came from men's off-farm earnings. Since irrigation water began flowing, farm income has risen from 10 to about 60 percent of family earnings, while male migration is down 6-7 percent (Martínez).

Further research is needed before it can be concluded that productivity-enhancing efforts for part-time, "feminized", smallholdings merit a substantial slice of the agricultural development budgetary pie. Rather, what is needed is greater realism; present projects aimed at smallholders tend to ignore male migration and women farmers, often to the detriment of project viability.[14] Future aid should seek for a better balance by farm size and gender. In this way donors would be able to target those actually contributing to Ecuadorian agricultural productivity and food security.

NOTES

1. Indigenous Sierra women worked on the household plot (*huasipungo*) assigned to the family in exchange for work during the *hacienda* era.

2. The petroleum and construction boom resulted in more off-farm employment opportunities and made both permanent and temporary migration feasible.

3. Techniques used included: (a) interviews with key informants; (b) group meetings with village, farmer and indigenous groups; (c) semi-structured interviews with men and women farmers; (d) a limited amount of participant observation; (e) "mini-censuses" of four markets in the Sierra and three in the Oriente; (f) secondary analyses of census and other large-scale data sets on Ecuadorian agriculture; and (g) a literature review of gender and agriculture in Ecuador. In total, data were obtained from 115 men and 115 women in the three regions and, in the Quito area, from an additional 30 key informants and workers in an agroindustrial firm growing flowers for export.

4. Since the neighboring haciendas tend to be on the same agricultural calendar, men who spend considerable time as day laborers may find that the *hacienda* work conflicts with functions on their own farms and women do more of the farm work.

5. The women who belonged to the only women's Association of Cassava Producers and Processors (APPY) that had operated through an entire farming season (in San Vicente) also stated that they spent their income on food and their children's health, education and clothing. This pattern of women more single-mindedly spending income under their control on basic needs and, especially, children's nutrition, health and welfare, is found worldwide (Blumberg 1988, 1989). The women stressed that the income brought them greater self-confidence, respect from their husbands and families and more voice in household decisions.

6. There appears to relatively little migration of the older men although many of the young men work for the oil companies. The main purpose of this work is to enable the youths to save funds to pay for marriage ceremonies.

7. It was impractical to interview on the back tiers of farms, but in the group meetings, colonists living on the third and fourth tier--and one man living on the eighth--were interviewed. The man from the eighth tier (16 kilometers from the main road) would take his wife and children "outside" their farm only once a month, for a one- or two-day trip for marketing, meetings, etc. The key woman informant who had worked as an interviewer on a recent study by the Foundation for Agricultural Development (FUNDAGRO) had interviewed as far back as the fourth tier. Her subjective impression was that health and children's education are negatively related to living farther away from the road.

8. Temporary or seasonal migration refers to leaving the farm for a distant area for several weeks or months where returns to the home base are infrequent. Circulation refers to leaving to work in an area away from the home base but where returns are frequent, generally every week or two. Commuting is where the individual travels daily to either temporary or permanent work.

9. The men of Yacupamba have been devoting more effort to agriculture lately in the hopes of wresting some sort of harvest from their increasingly deteriorated agricultural base. In the ten *mestizo* villages an irrigation project (constructed largely by women) has enabled the villages to raise impressive quantities of alfalfa, corn, peas, fruits and vegetables, thus reducing male migration and increasing farm income. Finally, men of three APPYs migrate less since work at the processing plants provides them with increased incomes.

10. These State-owned lands were confiscated from the Catholic Church as a result of the Liberal Revolution of 1905 and rented to individuals.

11. The 4-F clubs are similar in concept to the 4-H clubs of the United States. The Fs are from four words in the Spanish club pledge, "fe" (faith), "fecunda" (fertile or productive), "fortaleza" (support) and "felicidad" (happiness).

12. CEAS activities were the result of efforts by Monsignor Leonides Proaño, a leader in the Latin American liberation church movement, to make the Church a more effective force for improving living conditions in indigenous communities.

13. In some *mestizo* areas of high male migration, it appears that female-headed families, *de facto* or *de jure*, are increasing. Balarezo, for example, found almost 30 percent female-headed units in the Jipijapa area of Manabí.

14. The RRA found a clear example in the Guamote Integrated Rural Development Project. The three top technical officials mentioned that their biggest problem was the lack of continuous male participation, due to migration. They admitted that women were heavily involved in the crops and animals (especially sheep) they were targeting for assistance. But they did not work with women farmers. In contrast, the agent for Chimborazo Province of the USAID-assisted National Association of Sheep Growers (ANCO) sheep project is beginning to work with women as well as men, with positive results. Blumberg (1989) reviewed worldwide evidence on gender and agricultural development and found that bypassing of women, even given male absence, is the prevalent practice.

REFERENCES

Alberti, Amalia M. 1986. "Gender, Ethnicity, and Resource Control in the Andean Highlands of Ecuador." Ph.D. Thesis, Stanford University.

Balarezo, Susana, et al. 1984. *Mujer y Transformaciones Agrarias*. Quito: Corporación Editora Nacional.

Balarezo, Susana. 1989. Personal communication.

Blumberg, Rae Lesser. 1989. *Making the Case for the Gender Variable: Women and the Wealth and Well-Being of Nations*. Washington, D.C.: Agency for International Development, Office of Women in Development.

_____. 1988. "Income Under Female vs. Male Control: Hypotheses from a Theory of Gender Stratification and Data from the Third World." *Journal of Family Issues* Vol. 9, No. 1, March.

Brea-Porteiro, Jorge A. 1986. "Effects of Structural Characteristics and Personal Attributes Upon Labor Mobility in Ecuador." Ph.D. Thesis, Ohio State University.

Bromley, Ray. 1981. "Market Centers and Market Places in Highland Ecuador." *Cultural Transformation and Ethnicity in Modern Ecuador*. Edited by Norman E. Whitten, Jr. Urbana: University of Illinois Press.

Chávez, Napoleon. 1989. Personal communication.

CIM (Interamerican Commission on Women). 1987. *Investigación Socio-Económica*. Quito: Comisión Interamericana de Mujeres/Ministerio de Agricultura y Ganadería, Proyecto de Tecnología Apropiada para la Mujer Campesina.

Colyer, Dale. 1988. "Agriculture and the Public Sector." Quito: Working Paper no. 6-88, U.S. Agency for International Development.

Cornick, Tully R., et al. 1985. *Institutionalizing Farming Systems Research and Extension: Cornell University's Experience in Ecuador and the Philippines*. Ithaca: Cornell International Agriculture Mimeograph 115.

Crain, Mary M. 1989. *Ritual Memoria Popular y Proceso Político en la Sierra Ecuatoriana*. Quito: Corporación Editora Nacional y Ediciones Abya-Yala.

Darío Estrada, Rubén, Hugo Seré and Carlos Luzuriaga. 1988. *Sistemas de Producción Agrosilvopastoriles en la Selva Baja de la Provincia del Napo, Ecuador*. Cali, Colombia: Centro Internacional de Agricultura Tropical.

FIDA (International Fund for Agricultural Development). 1988. *Informe de la Misión Especial de Programación a la Republica Ecuador*. Quito: Informe No. 0098-EC.

González, Gladys. 1989. Personal communication.

Haney, Wava G. 1985. "Women of Highland Ecuador: Work and Reality." Paper presented at the Midwest Sociological Society Annual Meeting, St. Louis.

Ibarra, Alicia. 1985. *Los Indígenas y el Estado en el Ecuador*. Quito: Ediciones Abya-Yala.

INEC (National Institute of Statistics and Census). 1985. *IV Censo de Población, 1982, Resultados Definitivos, Resumen Nacional*. Quito: May.

Huffstutler, Steven. 1989. *UAPPY, Unión de Asociaciones de Productores y Procesadores de Yuca de Manabí, Ecuador: Evaluation and Recommendations*. San Jose, Costa Rica: Agricultural Cooperative Development International.

Izurieta, Leonardo and Ernesto Pinto. 1985. *Análisis de la Población Estudiantil, 1973 a 1983*. Guayaquil: Las Facultades de Ciencias Agropecuarias de Ecuador.

Jordán Bucheli, Fausto. 1988. *El Minifundio: Su Evolución en el Ecuador*. Quito: Corporación Editora Nacional.

Leonard, Olin. 1947. "Pichilingue, A Study of Rural Life in Coastal Ecuador." U.S. Office of Foreign Agricultural Relations, Report No. 17, 1947.

Luzuriaga C., Carlos. 1980. *Situación de la Mujer en el Ecuador*. Quito: USAID Documento Interno No. 5. Also published in 1982 by Gráficos San Pablo.

Luzuriaga, Carlos and Monserrath Fiallo. 1988. "El Empleo en la Agricultura Ecuatoriana." Quito: MAG, Unidad de Análisis de Políticas.

Martínez, Nelson. 1989. Personal communication.

Meier, Peter C. 1980. "Peasant Crafts in Otavalo: A Study in Economic Development and Social Change in Rural Ecuador." Ph.D. Thesis, University of Toronto.

Muratorio, Blanca. 1981. "Protestantism, Ethnicity and Class in Chimborazo." *Cultural Transformation and Ethnicity in Modern Ecuador*. Edited by Norman E. Whitten, Jr. Urbana: University of Illinois Press.

_____. 1980. "Protestantism and Capitalism Revisited, in the Rural Highlands of Ecuador." *Journal of Peasant Studies* 8:1:37-60.

Páez Molestina, Francisco, José Ordóñez S. and Magdalena Torres Q. 1985. *Población y Desarrollo Socioeconómico en el Ecuador*. Quito: Centro de Estudios de Población y Paternidad Responsible and Centro para el Desarrollo Social.

Phillips, Lynne E. 1987. "Women, Development, and the State in Rural Ecuador." *Rural Women and State Policy: Feminist Perspectives on Latin American Agricultural Development*. Edited by Carmen Deere and Magdalena Leon. Boulder: Westview Press.

_____. 1985a. "Gender, Class and Cultural Politics: A Case Study of Rural Vinces, Ecuador." Ph.D. Thesis, University of Toronto.

_____. 1985b. "Gender, Class and Development in Rural Coastal Ecuador." Toronto: Working Paper No. 50, Centre for Research on Latin America and the Carribbean.

Poeschel R., Ursula. 1988. *La Mujer Salasaca*, 2nd ed. Quito: Ediciones Abya-Yala.

Pomeroy, Cheryl S. 1986. "Environment, Economics, and Family Farm Systems: Farm Expansion on the Western Slopes of Andean Ecuador." Ph.D. Thesis, University of Illinois.

Romanoff, Steven and Guillermo Toro. 1986. *La Yuca en la Costa Ecuatoriana y Sus Perspectivas Agroindustriales*. Quito: Instituto Nacional de Investigaciones Agropecuarias (INIAP).

Salamea, Lucia and Mary Frances Likes. n.d. "The Changing Role of Rural Women in Ecuador." Quito. Manuscript.

Schroder, Barbara C. 1984. "Haciendas, Indians and Economic Change in Ecuador." Ph.D. Thesis, Rutgers University.

Stolen, Kristi Anne. 1987. *A Media Voz: Relaciones de Género en la Sierra Ecuatoriana*. Quito: Ediciones Abya-Yala.

Torres G., Jaime, Luis Cañadas C. and Mario Ribadeneira B. 1982. *Diagnóstico Socio-Económico del Medio Rural Ecuatoriano: Descomposición de la Mano de Obra*. Quito: Ministerio de Agricultura y Ganadería.

Weiss, Wendy A. 1985. "Es El Que Manda: Sexual Inequality and Its Relationship to Economic Development in the Ecuadorian Sierra." Ph.D. Thesis, Bryn Mawr College.

11

AGRICULTURE
AND THE PUBLIC SECTOR

Dale Colyer

Agriculture has played an important role in Ecuador's turbulent political history. Conflicts between agricultural interests and disagreements with government policies have contributed to the country's political instability. In over a century and a half since achieving independence the country has had numerous changes in government with only a few democratically elected administrations that completed their terms in office. Although completed terms have become more common in the last forty years, there were interruptions in constitutional rule in both the 1960s and 1970s.

The Ecuadorian political situation developed within a conservative/liberal dichotomy, where the conservative forces tended to be concentrated in Sierra agricultural interests and the liberal views in Costa agricultural and associated commercial interests (Hurtado; Kasza). However, politics came to be dominated more by individuals with followings based as much on personality as on ideology; this is reflected in the long political life of J. M. Velasco Ibarra, who was popularly elected or appointed President five times from 1932 to 1968. Cultural and historical factors, economic forces, regional and personal conflicts led to internal disputes within the liberal and conservative parties and to the formation of many political movements and parties with no party being able to command support of a majority of the voters. Thus, election to power does not necessarily carry with it the popular mandate needed for effective governance.

The current political situation has been affected significantly by the discovery and development of oil in the Oriente. The era began with a period of military rule in 1972 when Velasco Ibarra was overthrown close to the end of his fifth term as President. The military government developed the policies and programs for exploiting and using the revenue from the oil. The approach included the nationalization of a large share of the oil industry and an import-substitution industrial policy. Other nationalistic policies were the development of additional state or mixed state-private sector enterprises, stronger economic regulation including price controls and a substantial expansion of the bureaucracy with increased activities in agriculture, education, health and public works as well as expanded military forces and hardware.

The following sections review and analyze: the organizational structure of the Government of Ecuador (GOE); the Ministry of Agriculture (MAG), its organization, functions and activities; other GOE agencies with activities that affect the agricultural sector; linkages between the government and the private agricultural sector; the sector; linkages between the government and the private agricultural sector; the government's budget and programs for agriculture; and the activities of agriculturally related foreign assistance programs in Ecuador.

Governmental Organization

The current Ecuadorian constitution, its 17th, was adopted in 1978 and revised extensively in 1983 (Constitución de la República del Ecuador). The governmental structure is highly centralized, but there are provincial, county (*cantón*) and municipal (local) government units with varying degrees of power and autonomy. Under the new constitution all literate citizens 18 years of age or older have the right and obligation to vote, except that members of the armed forces and national police cannot vote. The new constitution extended suffrage to include the illiterate, although they are not required to vote. It recognized four economic sectors (public, private, mixed and communal) and provided encouragement for organization and mobilization of the populace. A reform also requires a runoff for president between the two top candidates if no one receives over 50 percent in the first round of elections. The new charter continues the U.S. type of structure with separate executive, legislative and judicial branches.

Executive

The executive branch is headed by a President and Vice President who run on the same ticket and serve a four year term. The President is limited to a single term, i.e., can never be reelected.[1] The system is basically one of strong executive power where the President and executive agencies have fairly wide authority to carry out their functions. The executive branch consists of 12 ministries and several other agencies. The President can create ministries "as needed" and appoints the Ministers and other agency heads, a process that does not require legislative confirmation, although such individuals can be impeached and then removed from office by a simple majority vote of the Congress. There are numerous other agencies to carry out administrative functions.

Economic policy is essentially an executive function. Major actors in developing and implementing economic policy, in addition to the President, are the Ministry of Finance, Central Bank, Monetary Board (*Junta Monetaria*) and Economic Front (*Frente Económico*) plus, at least in the planning stage, the National Development Council (CONADE). Within this group, the Monetary Board and Economic Front tend to be the more important policy-making bodies. The Monetary Board comprises a presidentially appointed head; a General Secretary; the Ministers of Agriculture, Finance, Energy, and Industries; the Secretary General of CONADE; the General Manager of the Ecuadorian Development Bank; two representatives from Chambers of Agriculture, Commerce, Industries, and Construction--one from the Costa-Galápagos Islands and one from the Sierra-Oriente; a representative of the Private Banks; the Superintendent of Banks; and the General Manager of the Central Bank. The Economic Front is comprised of the Ministers of Agriculture, Finance, Industry, and Public Works. The Monetary Board is concerned with monetary policy and develops programs implemented by the Central Bank. The Economic Front develops general economic policies, especially on macroeconomic issues although it also sets prices for controlled products.

Legislative

The legislative branch was completely overhauled under the new constitution. It was converted to a unicameral system instead of the traditional Senate and House of Representatives, which had been used in Ecuador under most previous constitutions. The legislature consists of 72 deputies, with 12 elected nationally and the remainder popularly elected in each province, with the number per province determined by population. There is one provincial representative for each 100,000 population up to 2, with an additional representative for each additional 300,000 people or fraction thereof.[2] National deputies are elected for four-year terms and provincial deputies are elected for two-year terms with elections held during the first presidential round (January every fourth year) and at the midterm. A deputy cannot be immediately reelected but is eligible for reelection after one term out of office. The legislature meets in regular session only 60 days beginning on the 10th of August (9th in Presidential election years) each year. Additional special sessions can be called for by either the leadership of the legislature, the President, or by petition of the membership. Other interim legislative matters are handled by four commissions (committees) or a plenary of the four. The commissions are for agriculture, budget, labor and social matters. They must approve major new activities of the executive such as the budget or new regulations.

The main function of the congress is to legislate, although it also has certain appointive powers and the power to evaluate, criticize and judge the actions of the executive branch. This includes the power to impeach and remove the President, Vice President, Ministers of State and heads of major government agencies. The President and Vice President can only be impeached for treason or other grave offenses against the State. Ministers and others can be removed for offenses committed in the prosecution of their duties. The Congress also has the right to vote amnesty for political offenses and pardons for common offenses. With each new administration Congress appoints the judges for the Supreme Court and associated tribunals. From lists submitted by the President, it also appoints the heads of three control agencies, the Solicitor General and members of the Electoral and Constitutional Guarantees tribunals. For the latter the Supreme Court and other agencies also submit lists from which some members are selected.

Judicial

The judiciary consists of a Supreme Court of Justice with lower provincial and cantonal courts, the Fiscal Tribunal and the Tribunal for Administrative Disputes. Separate courts exist for the national police and military. The Supreme Court and Tribunal Justices are appointed each four years by the Congress. Provincial judges are appointed by the Supreme Court and cantonal judges are appointed by the provincial courts. Their primary functions are to try civil and criminal cases, although the Supreme Court has some power to settle contradictions in laws.

In addition there are two parajudicial organizations, the Tribunal of Constitutional Guarantees (TGC) and the Supreme Electoral Tribunal (TSE). The TGC oversees compliance with the constitution and can suspend laws (not retroactively) which are contrary to the Constitution although Congress is the final arbiter of constitutionality (Torres). The TSE is charged with directing, overseeing and guaranteeing the electoral process. For example, the TSE certifies the winners for the President and Vice

President who Congress is then obligated to install.

Provincial and Local Government

There are parallel national and local government organizations at the provincial, cantonal (county) and parochial (parish or township) levels. Appointed central government officials carry out national programs with local applications which are implemented through an hierarchial system. This includes Governors (appointed by the President) at the provincial level, Political Chiefs (*Jefes Políticos*) in the cantones and Political Lieutenants (*Tenientes Políticos*) in the parishes. While once very powerful officials they now have more limited powers and functions, although as agents for the central government with its resources and powers they can have significant impacts on local activities. These central government appointees differ from the relatively autonomous, elected provincial and local government officials who have strictly local functions.

The provincial and lower-level government units are both considered to be local for public sector financial accounting. At the provincial level a council and prefect (*prefecto*) are elected to four year terms. The prefect is the executive and presides at the provincial council meetings. Provincial units are not strong governments when compared to, say, state governments in the United States. Local governments correspond to cantones, each of which is a municipality for government purposes. There are two types: (a) provincial capitals and other cantones with over 50,000 population; and (b) all other cantones. Both elect a municipal council which is the governing body for the municipality (cantón). The main difference is that the first type elects a mayor (*alcalce*) while the second elects a council president but both perform executive functions. These local government units have considerable functional, economic and administrative autonomy. They have legislative authority by the passage of municipal ordinances and are relatively strong as local government units. *Comunas*, discussed below, also have governance functions but are not formal government units.

Public Administration

Public administration in Ecuador is carried out by an extensive civil service bureaucracy that was expanded greatly during the years of the petroleum boom. The administrative structure is based on a set of institutions created and laws passed in the late 1920s and 1930s (Torres). The institutions include the Monetary Board, Central Bank, Superintendency of Banks and Office of the Controller General. Laws were developed for managing the budget, monetary system, international trade, banking and tariffs and labor. A set of major administrative reforms were made in the 1960s when the Civil Service, Administrative Career and Municipal Government laws were passed and when modern techniques for personnel administration, administrative analysis, simplified procedures and program budgeting were introduced. Administration of the agricultural sector follows the general pattern described above, with the MAG being the principal focus of public sector agricultural activities.

Ministry of Agriculture

The Ministry of Agriculture was re-established in 1973, when it was separated from the Ministry of Production. Previously it had existed as a separate ministry and the

1973 realignment was only the last of several that the ministry has undergone. The MAG, along with most Ecuadorian institutions, expanded very rapidly during the 1970s as the public sector took on more extensive and intrusive roles in the economy. New agencies were created and the sizes and functions of the existing units expanded. Thus, it consists of an extensive bureaucracy with many functions and numerous agencies to carry them out. Its main offices are in a large, modern headquarters building in Quito and it has another large office building in Guayaquil. Offices and facilities for other agencies are located in various rural and urban cites throughout the country including an office in each provincial capital and cantón, where an Agricultural Service Agency (ASA) office is located to carry out Ministry functions.

Functions

The primary purpose of the Ministry is to assist the agricultural sector in carrying out its basic functions; providing the nation's food supplies at reasonable prices, earning reasonable returns on its resources, contributing to export earnings, protecting the country's natural resources and contributing to the it's economic development (MAG 1985; Espinel). To accomplish this MAG has the responsibility for formulating and implementing agricultural policies. Its activities include providing technical assistance to farmers (extension and training), some inputs, marketing services, storage facilities; information on production and marketing; administering price supports; promoting animal and plant health; licensing imports; conducting agricultural research; implementing agrarian reform and colonization; constructing and operating irrigation, drainage and flood control projects; and promoting agricultural development. MAG, in conjunction with the National Development Bank (BNF) also programs and allocates credit to the sector.

Organization

The MAG consists of the Office of the Minister, four Subsecretariats, a number of adjunct or attached agencies, linkages with other agencies and complete or partial ownership of a number of parastatal and mixed private/public sector enterprises (Figure 11.1; GOE 1986b). The organizational structure of the Ministry is complex with many different and sometimes overlapping units, created at various times in the history of the Ministry and its predecessor organizations to carry out the multiple tasks and activities assigned to it.

The Minister is in charge of operations and policy, serves as a member of the cabinet and is an official representative to other government units including the Monetary Board, National Development Bank, the boards of public and mixed enterprises and development agencies. The Minister's Office consists a Ministerial Council, internal auditor, publicity department, advisors for legal and science matters, a department for economic and international affairs which also houses the Policy Analysis Unit, a unit for coordination of the Ministry's adjunct agencies and the forestry directorate. The Minister is concerned primarily with policy, with most of the day-to-day operations being implemented through the Subsecretariats.

Each subsecretariat is headed by an Under Secretary and each is composed of Directorates which are subdivided into Divisions and/or National Programs. Heads of Directorates and all superior or equivalent units are political appointees, while civil service personnel head the lower units.

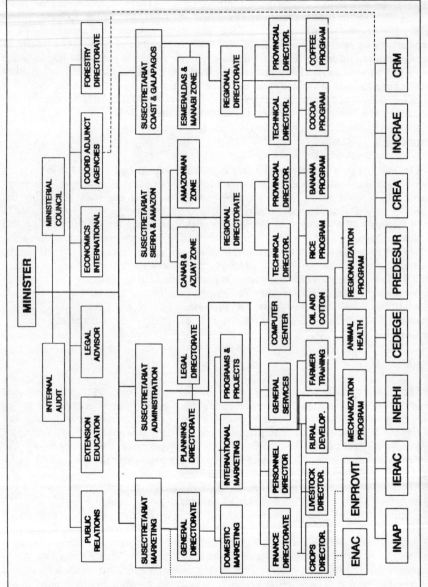

272

Figure 11.1 Organization Chart of the Ministry of Agriculture

The Subsecretariat for Administration handles administrative details through the Directorates of General Services, Finance, Planning, Legal Matters and the Computer Center. It also contains the administrative units of the National Programs for Crops, Livestock, Rural Development, Mechanization and Animal Health plus the Small Farmer (*Campesino*) Training Institute (INCCA) and the National Program for Agrarian Regionalization (PRONAREG).

The Subsecretariat for Marketing was created in 1984 to help solve one of the most persistent problems of the sector, a costly and inefficient marketing system (Chapter 8). This unit was created with a single Directorate but with Divisions for domestic and international marketing. The unit is in charge of the Market News Service which provides daily information on market prices for agricultural products. It also was assigned the task of overseeing two of the Ministry's adjunct agencies, the National Agricultural Storage and Marketing Company (ENAC) and the National Company for Basic Products (ENPROVIT).

The two regional subsecretariats, one for the Sierra and Oriente regions and one for the Coast and Galápagos, also were created in 1984. Zonal subunits were added in 1987 for the Amazon, the Azuay-Cañar area and Manabí-Esmeraldas. The Costa Subsecretariat is located in Guayaquil and has its own administrative unit.[3] The primary purpose of these regional units is to provide technical and other types of assistance to farmers as a means to stimulate and improve agricultural production practices. They are composed of the Technical Directorates and, in the Costa, the national crop programs (bananas, cacao, coffee, rice and cotton, and oil crops). They contain the Provincial Directorates which conduct MAG programs for their areas and which oversee the ASAs. MAG technical assistance efforts are carried out directly by the technical units and national programs, through producer organizations and the provincial agricultural offices that extend into each cantón via the ASAs.

Programs

Ministry programs are as varied as the country's agriculture (MAG 1987a). One of the more important is to provide technical assistance, under the regional subsecretariats, to producers of a wide variety of products. These include the traditional food crops (rice, wheat, barley, soft corn, cassava), grain legumes (beans, peas, lentils), many fruits and vegetables, traditional exports (bananas, coffee, cacao), non-traditional exports (flowers, abaca, melons, asparagus), feed grains (corn, sorghum), native crops (quinua, triticale,[4] oca, melloco) and industrialized crops (soybeans, oilpalm, cotton). Technical assistance also is provided through the rural and regional development programs. Plant and animal sanitation programs carry out activities to control the severe disease and pest problems that are endemic in tropical regions. The ministry has some 613 extension agents distributed among the country's 21 provinces and varying from 72 in Pichincha to 3 in the Galápagos (Jordán p. 241). However, these agents are scattered among the many programs and agencies of the ministry; there is no organized extension service (Chapter 12).

The Division of Rural Development complements and, to a certain extent, duplicates, a similar program in the Ministry of Social Welfare's (MBS) Secretariat for Rural Development (SEDRI). The MAG division works primarily with indigenous communities to conduct training, provide technical assistance, reforestation and soil conservation services, and construct infrastructure such as roads, bridges, water supply facilities, irrigation works, schools, community buildings, health facilities, storage buildings and sanitary facilities. The Training Division provides courses and other training for small and indigenous farmer groups. The Ministry also cooperates with the Military to provide agricultural training to recruits under the Agrarian Conscription Program. A mechanization program provides tractor and other machine services for farmers whose operations are too small for them to acquire their own machinery.

The forestry program is involved with reforestation, timber production and improvement, wood products development, watershed protection and agro-forestry activities that promote development of tree crops. The forestry unit also is in charge of operating the county's 2.8 million hectares of parks and natural areas including the Galápagos National Park. A soil conservation unit conducts a modest program, relative to what is needed, to protect the Nation's natural resources. PRONAREG does soils mapping and related activities to improve utilization of the country's agricultural resources and works with the National Institute of Meteorology and Hydrology (INAMHI) to provide agro-climatic data. Information, planning and policy analysis units provide data, information and analyses to assist Ministry administrators in developing appropriate programs and policies for agriculture.

Adjunct Agencies

Several semi-autonomous agencies charged with specific agricultural or rural development functions are attached to MAG. Each has its own budget and administrative unit. The Ministry is involved because the agencies have important impacts on agriculture and have common goals and objectives. The Minister, or his representative, sits on their Boards of Directors, may appoint or affect the appointment of the agency heads and may have influence through the budgetary process. A unit in the Minister's Office is charged with coordination of activities by the adjunct agencies.

The National Institute of Agricultural Research (INIAP) was founded in 1959 and began operations in 1961 at what is now the Santa Catalina Experiment Station (Dow and Solís; Chapter 12). It has grown to encompass six experiment stations, five research farms and three research centers plus its headquarters in Quito and an office in Guayaquil. Research is carried out on a wide variety of crops and livestock, with supporting research in soils, diseases, nutrition, entomology, weed control, engineering and a limited amount of economics. A very modest extension, outreach and technology transfer program is conducted through publications for producers, field days, farm plots and an on-farm production research program (PIP).

Management of water resources is the function of the Ecuadorian Institute of Water Resources (INERHI), an adjunct agency of MAG created in 1966 (Keller, et al.). The majority of its activities is directed to irrigation, an important function for agriculture due to the existence of arid areas and normal seasonal rainfall patterns with the existence of distinct wet and dry seasons (Chapter 7). Drainage and flood control also are important activities. Irrigation in the highlands, which has been practiced for centuries, is carried out primarily by local, private associations of water users and generally involves small areas and projects. INERHI provides some assistance to the privately run associations. However, its primary activities involve the study, design, construction and operation of public irrigation projects, with the largest located in the Costa region.

Agrarian reform and colonization are functions of the Ecuadorian Institute for Agrarian Reform and Colonization (IERAC) which was created with the passage of Ecuador's first agrarian reform law in 1964. The basic functions of IERAC are to implement the agrarian reform law and to prepare and implement colonization plans for areas on the agricultural frontier, now located mainly in the Oriente although until recently the Northern Costa was still being colonized (Bromley). While land redistribution continues under agrarian reform, a large part of IERAC's current activities is titling land previously distributed.

ENAC and ENPROVIT perform marketing and pricing functions within the agricultural sector. ENAC owns and operates a network of storage elevators, built with Inter-American Development Bank financing in the 1970s and early 1980s and used to store such grains as rice, corn and soybeans. ENAC supports farm prices by buying grain from farmers at official prices, storing it and reselling it after the harvest season is over. ENPROVIT's basic function is to provide food in low income areas at "reasonable" prices (Riley; also Chapter 8). For this function it operates a chain of retail outlets in selected areas, including many rural towns. It sells basic foods plus other products considered to be essential. Both ENAC and ENPROVIT have required large subsidies from the national treasury to cover operating deficits.

Five regional development agencies attached to MAG include: (a) the Commission for the Study of the Guayas River Basin (CEDEGE) whose primary function is to plan and implement development activities in the most important river basin in the country; (b) the Center for Rehabilitation of Manabí (CRM) which promotes and carries out development activities in Manabí Province; (c) the Center for the Economic Recovery of Azuay, Cañar and Morona Santiago (CREA) which has similar functions for those three provinces in Southeastern Ecuador; (d) the Regional Program for the Development of Southern Ecuador (PREDESUR) which covers the provinces of El Oro, Loja and Zamora Chinchipe; and (e) the Institute for the Colonization of the Amazon Region (INCRAE) which has functions similar to colonization activities of IERAC as well as developmental functions.

Public Enterprises

An important public involvement in agriculture is through the ownership, complete or partial, of business enterprises of various types. MAG is associated with businesses that produce, process, import and distribute agricultural inputs as well as operations that produce, buy, store and distribute agricultural outputs. These activities were greatly expanded during the era of military government and high oil revenues.

Examples of wholly owned enterprises are ENAC and ENPROVIT (which were discussed above).[5] Others are the National Semen Company (ENDES) which provides artificial insemination services and the National Fertilizer Factory (FAB), a small factory which makes fertilizer from organic wastes. In general, the state enterprises require subsidies of various types, often including specific budgetary line items.

Mixed enterprises are those in which the public sector owns a portion of the shares of a corporation. The portion can vary from a small percentage of the stock to nearly complete ownership. The largest public investor in mixed companies is the National Finance Corporation (CFN), although the MAG, National Development Bank and other government agencies own shares in many businesses.[6] The government uses the purchase of shares as a way to help finance new companies or as way to save financially troubled enterprises. An advantage of the mixed enterprise approach is that the firm can continue to operate as a private sector enterprise even when the government owns nearly all its stock. Agriculturally related mixed firms are in seeds, fertilizers, tea, palm oil, sugar, milk, food processing, alcoholic beverages, wood products, citrus products and a crop insurance company. The two most important are seed and fertilizer companies, which control a large share of the sales of those two important agricultural inputs (Chapter 8).

Other Public Sector Agencies

In addition to MAG, a large number of other government agencies have important impacts on agriculture. The sector is large, heterogeneous and complex and has a wide variety of soils and climates which, when combined an equatorial and Andean location, makes production of most crops feasible. Since everyone must have food and other agricultural products, the sector affects and is important to all Ecuadorians. To serve this variety of interests and activities involves a similarly complex and extensive set of institutions. Thus, all ministries and most other public sector agencies have some connection with agriculture: providing products, services or information to some part of the sector; receiving its output; regulating its activities or those of the agroindustry and marketing subsectors; or utilizing its resources for related activities.

Other Ministries

Every ministry affects the agricultural sector to a greater or lesser extent. The Ministry of Defense operates a number of large farms and many of its draftees obtain training in carrying out agricultural and rural development activities. The taxing and other economic activities of the Ministry of Finance affect farmers and agricultural exports. An agency of the Ministry of Finance values property for tax and agrarian reform purposes. The Ministry of Health operates clinics in rural areas and oversees a program that requires medical personnel to serve in rural areas. The Ministry of Education and Culture (MEC) operates Ecuador's public schools, including agricultural high schools and provides teachers in rural areas; activities that have greatly reduced illiteracy since 1970. The Ministry of Public Works (MOP) constructs rural roads for which a portion of the oil revenues is earmarked, as well as providing electrical and telephone services through state enterprises. INECEL, MOP's electric utility, has an active program for rural electrification and IETEL is responsible for telephone and other communications services. The Ministry of Labor has farm-related activities, including enforcement of labor laws and minimum wages, regulation of unions and support of worker training.

The Ministry of Industry and Commerce (MICIP) is probably the most important non-MAG agency affecting agriculture. It has many linkages with the sector, several carried out jointly with MAG. Agro-industrial activities come under its purview as does most international trade. Imports of inputs and exports of agricultural products require permits which must be approved by both MAG and MICIP. The importation of food products such as wheat is programmed jointly by the two Ministries. The Grades and Standards Institute (INEN) is part of MICIP. While the use of official grades and standards is not extensive, they are used in agro-industry and are becoming more important for grains and other products traded on the commodities exchange. Fisheries and seafoods functions are handled by a MICIP Subsecretariat located in Guayaquil. Its activities cover farm-produced shrimp as well as commercial fishing.

The Ministry of Government and Police affects agriculture through the National Police, which is charged with enforcing the Prices and Quality Control Law, the basis for consumer price controls. While price controls on many food products were eliminated or relaxed during the Febres Cordero administration, price regulation has received more emphasis under the Borja government and the law has not been repealed. The police also enforce anti-speculation (price gouging) activities which are illegal. The enforcement of these laws may be sporadic and inconsistent but they affect farm prices by causing uncertainty, raising the costs of marketing and holding down consumer prices, causing lower farm level prices.

Other Government Agencies

The Central Bank of Ecuador (BCE) affects credit, interest rates, exchange rates and the money supply (Chapter 9). The Central Bank is a primary indirect source of credit for agriculture through its financing of BNF, CFN, ENAC, ENPROVIT and private bank loans to the sector. A subsidiary organization, the Fund for Development of Marginal Rural Areas (FODERUMA), provides financing for many small farmers and for rural development.

The National Development Council (CONADE), in the office of the Vice President, is in charge of national planning. It makes a four-year plan for each government, which becomes a guide for investment activities, although there is no necessary connection between the plan and what is actually implemented (CONADE). The planning is done with the cooperation of units from other agencies, including MAG.

The National Institute for Statistics and Censuses (INEC) is in charge of national statistics. It conducts censuses including the agricultural census, although the last agricultural census was in 1974. INEC also conducts an annual survey of agricultural production based on an area sample frame, the National Agricultural Statistics System (SEAN). This project is to develop a set of agricultural production data based on procedures that permit a valid statistical evaluation of the information (Chapter 6).

Private Sector Linkages

Agricultural production, marketing and processing functions generally are carried out by the private sector. The several government agencies with responsibilities in those areas interact not only with the individuals and firms involved but with organizations to which the individuals and firms belong. Many of these have been formed to enable the private sector to interact more effectively with the public sector. A relatively large number of agricultural organizations exist. They vary with respect to membership, functions, resources, influence and stability (FIDA; Jordán). Despite the apparent organized nature of the sector, producers tend to be quite independent and there has been little cooperation among organizations that have common interests.

Quasi-Public Organizations

Some agricultural organizations are required by law. These include Agricultural Centers, four Chambers of Agriculture and a federation of the four. The Chambers are, in turn, part of a larger system which include industry and trade and which were created by law, although predecessor organizations had existed. The four agricultural chambers are located in separate geographical areas, the Costa, Northern Sierra, Southern Sierra and Oriente. The Federation is headquartered in Quito and is composed of the Presidents of the four chambers with the chairmanship rotating annually.

Agricultural Centers were created in each cantón with farming interests under the same law that set up the Chambers of Agriculture. Every farmer must be a member of an agricultural center. Membership in a center provides the individual with a farmer identity card which permits access to certain services, the most important being, perhaps, the ability to borrow money from BNF. Although farmers are legally required to join a Center, many do not. Each center elects a delegate to the Chamber of Agriculture in its region and these delegates are the only members of the Chambers.

Comunas are economic and political organizations, recognized by the 1979 Constitution, which must be registered with MAG.[7] They serve as governing agencies for sub-parochial communities (Jordán; FIDA). Cooperatives are used by the GOE to achieve agricultural objectives. Some provide goods and services for their members. Many are non-functioning production cooperatives that were formed primarily for obtaining state-owned land (Chapter 10).

Finally, there are professional organizations or *colegios* in economics, journalism, agriculture, accounting, etc. To obtain employment, particularly in the public sector, one must belong to the appropriate professional organization, which requires a degree from an Ecuadorian university. The primary organization to which this applies in agriculture is the Association of Agronomists (*Colegio de Agrónomos*). While ostensibly assuring competence, this requirement primarily denies employment to non-members.

Private Sector Organizations

Purely private sector organizations encompass a wide variety of types and sizes except that there is no nationwide general farm organization comparable to the American Farm Bureau Federation in the U.S. Despite the lack of a general farm organization most agricultural and agro-industrial interests are represented by one or more organizations.

Ecuador produces a wide array of agricultural products and there are producer organizations for most, with various local, regional and national groups. Other organizations may represent farmers from specific geographical areas, small farmers or indigenous farmers. Producer associations are varied in their activities, some exist for political or social purposes only, while others offer many services including inputs, technical assistance, diagnostic laboratories, research, marketing and training. Processing firms are represented by agro-industrial associations as well as by the Chambers of Industry. Agricultural marketing is probably the most unorganized activity in the food and fiber industry of Ecuador, except as marketing is part of overall agricultural activities and organizations. Small retail operations sell much of the food and these are organized into a large, effective, national organization, the National Federation of Retail Merchants (FENACOMI).

Historically the Indians, subjugated at the time of the Spanish conquest, provided the bulk of the farm labor under the *hacienda* system, a generally exploitative regime. Gradually, however, the recognition of the needs and rights of this group grew and indigenous organizations began to be formed. A 1937 law formally recognized this and the Ecuadorian Federation of Indians (FEI) was formed. It and other organizations have attempted to protect and extend their interests. Rubio Orbe (pp. 109-110) listed such organizations together with a national level coordinating group (see, also, Chapter 10).

Labor unions represent a very limited number of farm workers. These tend to be concentrated in those farm activities where there are plantation and/or industrial types of activities--sugar, oilpalm, bananas, etc. Federations of local unions connect the agricultural labor unions into the national network. Union efforts to improve working conditions have produced results, as in the recent extension of social security to farm workers or, historically, the minimum wage laws, the 13th, 14th and 15th month wage supplements and an extensive set of labor laws.

A number of nonprofit foundations are important in the agricultural sector of Ecuador. They help promote, protect, or develop agriculture, farmers and natural resources. The Nature Foundation (*Fundación Natura*) is active in environmental protection and education, natural resource conservation and reforestation. The Science Foundation (*Fundación Ciencia*) has conducted research in areas such as health and agriculture. The Agricultural Policy Institute (IDEA) conducts agricultural policy analyses. The Foundation for Agricultural Development (FUNDAGRO) is designed to help overcome some of the weaknesses in Ecuador's agricultural research, extension and education programs.

Agriculture in the National Budget

The national budget of Ecuador is managed by the Ministry of Finance and monitored by the Controller General. Government revenues come from direct and indirect taxes and from the sales of products and services by government agencies and enterprises. A large share of the government's revenue is derived from petroleum sales, with nearly one-half typically from taxes on petroleum or sales of petroleum and its derivative products.

About one-fourth of total Government expenditures are for investments in schools, roads, dams, buildings, equipment, etc., while the other three-fourths is used for current expenses including the such government services as education, defense, health, justice, agriculture and economic development (BCE 1987a, pp. 283-284). Servicing the public debt has been taking an increasing share of public revenues, accounting for 23.6 percent of current expenses in 1986.

The Ecuadorian Tax System

The public revenue system of Ecuador depends on a wide variety of petroleum and other taxes, fees and other income sources (Colyer 1988a). Import duties, income taxes and sales taxes are the main sources of non-oil revenue. One of the characteristics of the tax system is the earmarking of significant portions of revenues from many sources for specific uses. This process begins with the Constitution which requires that 30 percent of the national budget be used for education.

The laws and regulations with respect to the distribution of oil revenue are very complex, including earmarking, although the general revenue budget receives substantial amounts, too. Eighteen government entities are entitled to receive oil revenues with the proportions determined by complex formulas that depend on, among other factors, the price of oil (BCE 1987a, Appendix 3). A major earmarking is for the military which, according to the World Bank (1987a), receives over 28 percent of the total. Agriculture receives very little directly but rural road development receives a relatively large share, 5.5 percent.

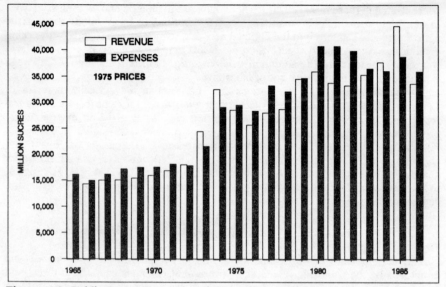

Figure 11.2 Public Sector Revenue and Expenditures (Except Public Corps.)
Source: BCE 1982a, 1987a

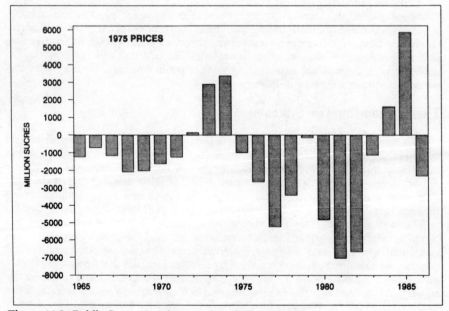

Figure 11.3 Public Sector Surpluses and Deficits, 1975 Prices
Source: BCE 1982a, 1987a.

Trends in Public Revenues and Expenditures

An examination of real (1975 = 100) government revenues and expenditures from 1965 through 1986 indicates that they tended to increase slowly through 1972 but increased sharply in the following years as higher oil revenues became incorporated into the budget (Figure 11.2). Government revenues declined in 1980-1982, rose again from 1983 through 1985 but dropped precipitously in 1986 due to a very sharp decline in oil prices. There were budget deficits in all but five of the 22 years examined (Figure 11.3). The last half of the 1970s and early years of the 1980s had large deficits which were compensated for by borrowing from international sources. Oil revenues had not increased as expected and to carry out its planned programs the government borrowed in anticipation of future earnings.

Debt Management

The external public debt of Ecuador has grown significantly as a consequence of continuous borrowing to cover deficits as well as for investments and other purposes (Table 11.1). The private sector also borrowed extensively from foreign sources in the 1970s and early 1980s. When the economic crisis of 1982-1983 occurred the solvency of these firms was threatened because the debts were dollar denominated. The problem was resolved by "Sucretization" of the debt. The government took over the dollar obligations and allowed the debtor companies to repay the loans in Sucres.[8] Thus, nearly all the current foreign debt of the country is owed by the government.

The proportions of budget deficits financed internally and externally varied considerably from year to year. Of the total, 41.8 percent was financed from external sources. However, about one-half the total amount was in 1986 when petroleum prices dropped precipitously (Table 11.2). The country was able to borrow from a number of foreign sources to help overcome the deficit produced by the drop in oil revenues. A similar situation occurred when the March 1987 earthquake destroyed some 16 miles of the oil pipeline and interrupted exports for several months.

Public Expenditures on Agriculture

Real total public expenditures (current outlays and investments) for agriculture rose during the first years of the oil boom but began to decline after 1974 and reached an oil-era low in 1983 (Figure 11.4). Expenditures increased slightly after 1983 but were only 57 percent of the 1974 peak in 1985. Real expenditures in the 1980s have been considerably less than in the 1970s.

The proportion of total agricultural to total public expenditures declined substantially between 1974 and 1982 (Figure 11.5). Government expenditures continued to rise through 1981 and were substantially higher in 1985 than in 1974, while expenditures on agriculture declined. The total economy of the country grew more rapidly than the agricultural sector during the 1970s and it could be expected that the proportion of expenditures on agriculture also would decline. However, public expenditures on the sector dropped relatively more than the participation of agriculture in the country's economy.

The pattern of public expenditures for agriculture decreased substantially between the oil boom and the post-1982 austerity periods but affected the various MAG agencies differently. The average decline for the Ministry and its adjunct agencies

Table 11.1   Ecuador: Public and Private External Debt (Million of U.S. Dollars)

Year	Public	Private	Total
1975	456.5	56.2	512.7
1976	635.8	57.3	693.1
1977	1,173.8	89.9	1,263.7
1978	2,078.4	496.2	2,574.6
1979	2,847.8	706.2	3,554.1
1980	3,530.3	1,121.5	4,651.8
1981	4,415.9	1,542.3	5,868.2
1982	4,558.6	1,628.5	6,187.1
1983	5,164.8	1,523.8	6,688.5
1984	6,804.0	177.0	6,981.0
1985	7,343.1	96.9	7,440.0
1986	8,241.9	58.1	8,300.0
1987	9,187.0	43.0	9,230.0
1988-Est.	9,454.0	39.0	9,493.0

Source: El Comercio.

Table 11.2   Ecuador: Budget Deficits and Sources of Finance
(Million of Sucres, Current Prices)

Year	Surplus + Deficit -	Amount Financed[a]		Percent External
		Internal	External	
1970	- 1,545.0	1,534.9	11.1	0.7
1971	- 1,733.0	1,641.6	55.8	3.2
1972	- 893.4	-61.1	954.5	100.0
1973	- 227.5	196.0	31.5	13.8
1974	- 21.3	21.3	0.0	0.0
1975	+ 609.4	-802.2	-235.6	NA
1976	- 2,160.4	1,874.7	385.7	17.8
1977	- 4,292.8	3,241.5	1,081.3	25.2
1978	- 3,765.7	3,862.5	-96.8	0.0
1979	- 1,607.3	2,716.4	-1,109.1	0.0
1980	- 4,148.5	2,771.0	1,553.3	37.4
1981	-16,835.8	9,177.3	7,658.5	45.5
1982	-17,866.9	7,878.6	9,988.3	55.9
1983	-14,047.3	16,313.0	-2,265.7	0.0
1984	- 6,784.8	10,843.0	-4,058.2	0.0
1985	+21,970.5	-18,185.8	-3,784.7	NA
1986	-29,641.8	7,073.1	22,451.3	76.1
Totals	105,568.2	61,397.2	44,171.0	41.8

Source: BCE 1982a, 1987a.

[a]Some data adjusted to obtain correct totals. Negative numbers for amounts financed
indicate net repayments.

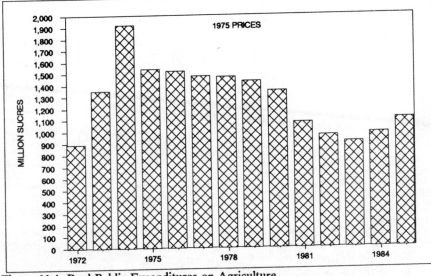

Figure 11.4 Real Public Expenditures on Agriculture
Source: BCE 1973b-1986b.

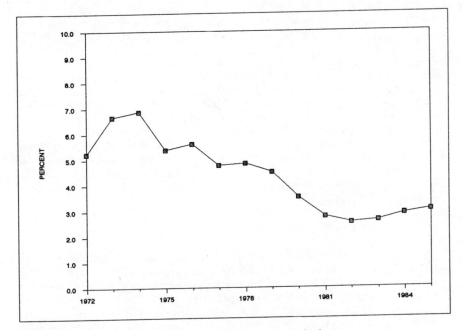

Figure 11.5 Share of Total Public Expenditures on Agriculture
Source: BCE 1973b-1986b

Table 11.3 Average Real Public Expenditures on the Agricultural Sector (1975 Prices)

Unit	Average '73-81	Average '83-86	Percent Change
Ministry	618.8	388.4	-37.23
INIAP	113.9	96.7	-15.11
IERAC	152.5	113.7	-25.45
INERHI	205.2	138.0	-32.73
CEDEGE	76.1	85.9	12.85
CRM	111.8	59.7	-46.62
CREA	72.5	49.8	-31.33
PREDESUR	103.6	100.1	-3.46
INCRAE	14.8	14.4	-2.29
All Units	1436.3	1098.7	-23.50

Source: BCE 1974b-1986b; GOE 1984, 1985, 1986a, 1987, 1988.

combined was 23.5 percent, with considerable variations, from a 12.8 percent increase for CEDEGE to a 46.6 percent decrease for CRM (Table 11.3). Expenditures for INIAP, the research agency fell by 32.7 percent.

Declines in real expenditures of the magnitudes shown in Table 11.3 have very significant impacts on the ability of MAG and its agencies to function effectively. Few of the cuts were made by personnel reductions, although a decline in real wages appears to have occurred as wage increases were kept below the rate of inflation (CORDES; Spurrier). The maintenance of personnel levels means that a significant share of the cuts were in operating funds, reducing MAG's capacity to implement programs.

Expenditures on agriculture by the public sector are relatively low in Ecuador when compared to those of other Latin American countries (Table 11.4). This is based on a comparison of Ecuadorian expenditures in 1980 with those for nine Latin American countries in a study by the International Food Policy Research Institute (IFPRI) reported by Elías. Public expenditures on agriculture per hectare of cropland were substantially lower than for any of the other countries except Argentina and were the lowest per person employed in agriculture. A conclusion of the IFPRI study, based on statistical analyses of 1950-1980 data for the nine countries was that growth in agricultural output was positively related to public expenditures on agriculture (Elías p. 44). Thus, the low level of expenditures in Ecuador appears to have contributed to the slow growth of the sector.

Public Investment in Agriculture

Total real public sector investments (capital expenditures) in the agricultural sector increased during the early years of the oil boom (Figure 11.6). They increased markedly in 1980 and 1981 with the restoration of democratic rule but decreased in 1982 and the subsequent years of economic crisis. However, the share of public expenditures used for investments fluctuated around a downtrend during the years 1965 to 1986 (Colyer 1988a, pp. 48, 70). Relatively large shares of the investments were for infrastructure built by the MOP as well as for schools by the MEC and irrigation through adjunct agencies of MAG.

Table 11.4 Government Expenditures On Agriculture for Selected Latin American
Countries, 1980 (Current Dollars using Official Exchange Rates)

Country	Per Hectare of Cropland	Per Person Employed
Argentina	9[a]	279
Bolivia	181	136
Brazil	169	485
Chile	163	393
Colombia	195	373
Costa Rica	119	143
Ecuador	76[b]	72
Mexico	296	663
Peru	177	137
Venezuela	538	1,004

Sources: Ecuador: calculated from Central Bank and Ministry of Agriculture data;
other countries: Elías.

[a]Includes "cultivated pasture."
[b]Based on acreage cropped. If the "potential cropland is used the expenditures
 decline to US$25 per hectare.

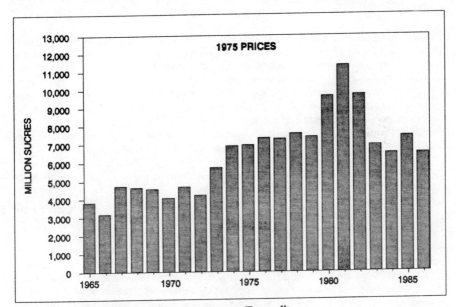

Figure 11.6 Total Public Sector Investment Expenditures
Source: BCE 1973b-1986b.

The proportion of total public investment in the agricultural sector has varied considerably over the years of analysis. During the period 1973-1981 the average proportion of the public sector investment budget going to agriculture, through the

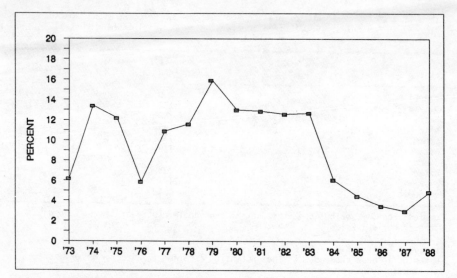

Figure 11.7 Share of Public Sector Investments in Agriculture
Source: BCE 1973b-1986b.

Ministry of Agriculture and its adjunct agencies, averaged about 11.3 percent but varied from 5.9 in 1976 to 15.9 in 1979 (Figure 11.7). Investments in the sector remained at about the same proportion through 1983 but declined sharply in 1984 and have remained below five percent since then. About three-fourths of the agricultural investments are made through the adjunct agencies with the largest proportion being for the irrigation activities of two, INEHRI and CEDEGE. Around three percent of the agricultural investments are made in INIAP, with a similar amount going to the four MAG-owned state enterprises. However, relatively more was invested in ENAC in the 1970s when most of its storage facilities were being constructed.

Foreign Assistance Programs

Prior to the oil era, Ecuador was one of the poorer nations in South America and was the recipient of a wide variety of assistance from the international donor community. With oil revenue and rapid growth in the 1970s there was a slackening in the volume of aid. The benefits of the oil revenues were not evenly distributed and poverty remained as a characteristic of large segments of the population. Thus, many donor programs were continued to assist disadvantaged groups. Other assistance was solicited to help meet the gaps between planned development activities and oil revenues that did not increase as rapidly as projected. The country borrowed extensively from commercial sources to carry out its ambitious consumption and investment activities. This massive indebtedness and its costly servicing combined with a worldwide economic recession, natural disasters and declining oil prices produced a series of economic crises in the country and there has been a resurgence in assistance activities in the 1980s (Colyer 1988b).

Table 11.5 Official Development Assistance to Ecuador (Million Dollars)

DAC Country	1980	1981	1982	1983	1984	1985	1986
Grants:							
Australia	-	-	-	-	-	-	-
Austria	0.2	0.2	0.2	0.1	-	-	-
Belgium	0.6	0.5	0.7	1.1	0.8	0.9	1.5
Canada	-	0.3	0.1	0.7	-	0.3	-
Denmark	0.1	0.1	0.1	0.1	0.1	0.1	-
Finland	-	0.0	-	0.0	0.0	0.0	-
France	2.1	1.7	1.0	1.2	2.5	1.5	3.2
W. Germany	11.1	10.2	9.2	8.3	7.2	7.7	12.7
Ireland	-	-	-	0.0	0.0	0.0	0.0
Italy	0.1	1.3	2.7	2.3	9.5	4.9	4.9
Japan	0.8	1.4	2.3	1.2	0.8	1.8	3.3
Netherlands	1.5	1.7	1.1	1.2	1.4	1.7	2.4
New Zealand	-	-	-	-	-	0.0	0.0
Norway	0.1	0.4	0.0	0.0	0.1	0.0	0.0
Sweden	-	-	0.1	0.1	0.2	0.2	0.2
Switzerland	0.3	0.2	0.6	0.4	0.4	0.3	0.2
United Kingdom	2.0	1.5	1.2	1.0	0.7	0.8	1.2
United States	1.0	2.0	4.0	4.0	8.0	8.0	14.0
Total DAC	19.7	21.5	23.2	21.9	31.8	28.2	43.6
Multilateral	8.4	8.7	6.2	7.0	6.4	5.5	8.3
EEC	1.0	3.9	1.1	6.6	0.3	0.8	0.8
Net Loans:							
Belgium	-	-	-	-	3.5	-	-
Canada	-	-	-	-0.4	-0.2	-0.2	-0.2
Denmark	-	-	-	0.0	0.0	0.0	-0.1
Finland	-	-	-	0.9	-	0.3	-
France	-	-	-	-	-	0.1	1.8
Germany	1.7	3.4	4.8	0.2	0.3	0.9	0.6
Japan	3.8	0.5	-	-0.5	0.4	-0.1	-0.4
Netherlands	-	0.3	0.3	-	-	-	0.0
United Kingdom	0.2	-	-	-0.4	-0.1	0.0	-0.1
United States	-	-	1.0	1.0	4.0	22.0	10.0
Total DAC	5.7	4.2	6.1	0.8	7.9	22.9	11.6
Multilateral	15.7	27.4	14.9	13.1	65.3	53.9	49.0

Source: OECD 1984, 1988.

Foreign Assistance Participants

Economic aid to Ecuador includes assistance from a large number of the array of multilateral, bilateral and private voluntary donor agencies that have evolved since World War II. Net flows of official development grants and loans from Development Assistance Committee (DAC) countries for the years 1980 to 1986 have been substantial (Table 11.5).

In 1986, when the average price of oil declined from US$28.50 to US$12.90 per barrel, net assistance from the international agencies increased by US$445.5 million (BCE 1987a, p. 360). Most of this was in the form of loans from the World Bank, US$127 million; the Inter-American Development Bank (IDB), US$113.3 million; and the Andean Reserve Fund, US$175 million. United Nations agencies contributed over US$16 million in technical assistance distributed among 16 sectors but with the

Table 11.6 Official Development Assistance to Selected Countries

Country	Million Dollars					Dollars	
	1982	1983	1984	1985	Average 1983-85	Per Capita GNP	Assistance
Bolivia	147.4	173.6	171.9	282.1	193.8	410	31.2
Costa Rica	80.3	252.1	217.6	280.1	207.5	1,160	82.0
Ecuador	53.0	63.7	136.2	135.8	97.2	1,220	10.7
El Salvador	223.1	295.0	262.8	345.1	281.5	710	52.0
Guatemala	63.7	75.8	65.4	82.8	71.9	1,120	9.3
Honduras	158.1	191.6	289.6	276.2	228.9	710	54.2
Panama	41.0	47.0	72.1	69.2	57.3	2,100	26.9
Perú	187.9	297.1	310.1	316.4	277.8	990	15.2

Source: OECD 1984, 1988.

majority going to agriculture, health, and transportation and communications (UNDP 1986, 1987, 1988).

The governments of over 20 countries have had official economic assistance programs in Ecuador. A report for 1986 listed nine countries which had provided US$18.8 million in assistance (UNDP 1987, p. viii). The United States provided 41 percent of that total followed by West Germany with 21.1 percent and Italy with 16.8 percent. The report also lists contributions from Belgium, Canada, Sweden, France, Korea, and Chile. In addition the two Chinas, Great Britain, Holland, Japan, Israel and Spain have provided support. Over one-third (US$6.8 million) of the assistance listed by United Nations Development Program was for agriculture (UNDP 1987).

Although assistance to Ecuador increased in the 1980s, the level remained low on a per capita basis when compared to other Latin American countries that also were major recipients of U.S. assistance (Table 11.6). During the period 1982-1985 of seven Central and South American countries only Guatemala received less assistance per capita than Ecuador's average of US$10.70.

A large number and variety of private voluntary organizations (PVOs) operate in Ecuador. The individual programs tend to be small in terms of the amounts of money involved and the efforts generally are directed at the more economically disadvantaged groups. The PVOs operating in Ecuador can be classified into three broad groups. One consists of purely charitable groups such as CARE, the Red Cross, Foster Parents Plan and Save the Children. Another is composed of religious organizations including Catholic Church, several protestant churches and the Mormon Church. Another category is a miscellany of business/labor/foundation associated groups, such as the International Executive Service Corps, Farmer to Farmer Program and American Institute for Free Labor Development.

Numerous activities by academic, scientific and business organizations also provide various forms of technical and financial assistance. Among these are the academic institutions which have contributed to research through faculty and graduate students financed by various means, as, for example, the U.S. Fullbright program which provides grants to U.S. university faculty for research and teaching in Ecuador and for Ecuadorians to go to the United States to study or participate in other academic endeavors. Cooperative efforts with institutions in Ecuador and have helped to strengthen generally weak institutional research capabilities.

Multilateral Assistance Programs

The agricultural sector has been the recipient of a very significant share of the multilateral assistance extended to Ecuador, including many of the larger loans by the development banks (World Bank and IDB). The sector also has benefited from assistance extended to other sectors such as education, health, energy, transportation and communications, aid that spills over to agriculture due to general impacts or from projects implemented in rural areas. In terms of volume of assistance for development, multilateral bank loans dwarf the amounts made by other agencies. Multilateral agencies have financed a wide variety of programs related to agriculture, from strengthening central institutions to direct assistance to individual farmers.

The World Bank has been involved in Ecuador for many years. Through June 30, 1987 the Bank and its associated agency, the International Development Association (IDA), had made Ecuador a total of 46 loans for US$1,149.8 million (World Bank 1987b, p. 160). This total includes three loans for US$159 million approved in the Bank's Fiscal Year 1987. The value of loans in existence on June 30, 1987 was US$884 million of which US$242 million had not been disbursed. The Second Agricultural Credit Project for US$48 million was approved in September 1986. This loan was to increase farm employment, farmers' incomes and agricultural production, especially the production of exportable products.

As a result of the debt crisis in Latin America and the problems faced by many countries, the World Bank has increased its adjustment lending activities vis-à-vis project lending. In Ecuador this took the form of a US$100 million Agricultural Sector Loan primarily for imports of agricultural inputs. The loan was dispensed in two disbursements, about half in 1986 and the remainder in 1987. The second tranche was conditioned on the country making a number of policy adjustments in the agricultural area. Although the GOE did not meet all the conditions for release of the second tranche, it was released because of progress in reforms and problems caused by the drop in oil prices and the March 1987 earthquake.

The IDB, established in 1959, made its first loan to Ecuador in 1961 (IDB p. 71). The total value of the loans made to the country through 1987 was US$2.3 billion with US$817 million (35 percent) going to the agricultural, forestry and fishing sectors. Over half the total loans have been made in the five years, 1983-1987. Of the total, US$1.2 billion had been disbursed by the end of 1987. In 1988, there were loans for 32 projects with a total value of US$1.7 billion, of which 42 percent (US$701 million) had been disbursed (Eguez p. 1). In addition to the loans, technical and other assistance grants of over US$21 million (US$493,000 in 1987) have been provided to Ecuador (IDB p. 74). In 1987 a US$200 million agricultural credit loan was approved by the IDB, as the third stage of the Global Agricultural Credit Program and following loans of US$54 million and US$120 million in 1983 and 1985, respectively. These are channeled through the National Development Bank (BNF) for lending to the farm sector (Chapter 9).

The Daule-Peripa project, located in the Costa area north of Guayaquil, is among the most important financed by IDB in Ecuador, with IDB funding of US$457.2 million. The main purposes are generation of electricity, irrigation, drainage, navigation and flood control. Its reservoir will hold around 6 million cubic meters of water and cover 50,000 hectares when filled. Crops to be irrigated include rice, bananas, corn and soybeans (Chapter 7).

Under an IDB fund to assist low-income groups, a small loan (US$500,000) was

Table 11.7   United Nations Assistance for Ecuadorian Agriculture

United Nations	-- Amount Contributed (dollars) --		
Agency	1985	1986	1987
U.N. Development Program (UNDP)	726,246	758,735	520,235
Food & Agricultural Org. (FAO)	1,232,655	627,806	70,806
Educ., Culture & Sci. (UNESCO)	13,100	12,400	72,300
Atomic Energy Org. (IAEO)	69,510	143,788	491,686
World Food Program (WFP)	2,187,934[a]	3,500,000	3,500,000
U.N. Children's Fund (UNICEF)	276,600	119,000	120,300
Environmental Program (PNUMA)	2,798	--	2,109
Totals	4,508,843	5,162,529	4,777,436

Source: UNDP 1986, 1987, 1988.

[a]The WFP total contribution in 1985 was $3.5 million with the remainder being handled through the Ministry of Health.

made in 1987 to a federation of organizations for low income farmers from Baba and Vinces in Guayas Province to enable them to construct a processing plant for coffee, cacao and rice. Some 2,600 low income farmers belong to the member organizations of the federation. In addition, a grant US$125,000 was made to provide administrative assistance to the company operating the processing plant.

UNDP (1987) reported a total of US$16 million of assistance by several U.N. agencies in 1986, with nearly one third of the total used for agricultural programs. The largest contributions were by the World Food Program (WFP) with US$3.5 million annually during 1986-1987 for food for work programs administered by MAG's Rural Development Division (Table 11.7). The work is carried out primarily in indigenous communities and involves constructing infrastructure such roads, bridges, community buildings and schools.

The U.N.'s Food and Agricultural Organization (FAO) has an extensive program in Ecuador, although its total funding is limited and has been reduced due, in part, to a reduction in U.S. support of U. N. organizations. Its 1987-1988 activities include projects for the management and conservation of soils in the Paute River Basin, monitoring land use in the Amazonian region, food production assistance to 4-F clubs, administrative assistance to BNF, irrigation assistance at the farm level, extension training and integrated rural development. In 1986, the UNDP contributed to integrated rural development projects (US$497,582), for improving the administration of agricultural credit programs (US$105,553) and to conduct small rehabilitation activities (US$150,600), all jointly with FAO. Other FAO programs were for small dairy farm development, soil management in the Guayas River Basin, support for planning in the southern area of the country, training trips and consulting.

The Interamerican Institute for Cooperation on Agriculture (IICA), part of the Organization of American States (OAS) conducts technical assistance programs in Ecuador in cooperation with a variety of institutions (UNDP 1987). Ecuadorian institutions include the MAG, MBS, University of Guayaquil, CREA, FUNDAGRO, CONADE and PETROECUADOR. International agencies include the World Bank, Inter-American Development Bank, Andean Development Corporation (CAF), the Cartagena Accord, U.S. Agency for International Development (USAID) and Canada's International Center for Development Research (ICDR). The Institute supports policy analysis activities (MAG), research and extension, integrated rural development

(SEDRI), animal and crop health programs and marketing of agricultural products. IICA also supports Andean regional activities in animal health and agricultural research with the latter including the international agricultural research centers.

The three Latin American-based international agricultural research centers, the International Potato Center (CIP), International Center for Wheat and Corn (CIMMYT) and International Center for Tropical Agriculture (CIAT) provide research services. They help fill the gap between research needs and what the country can afford. The centers provide new plant varieties, assist INIAP, provide training and help maintain genetic variability. INIAP and CIP have joint projects for controlling potato diseases and for maintaining potato germplasm through in vitro means. There is a cooperative program with CIAT for increasing the production and use of cassava as an ingredient in livestock feed. CIMMYT's activities in Ecuador encompass research on wheat, barley, triticale and corn. Ecuador also cooperates with the International Board for Plant Genetic Resources in the collection and maintenance of germplasm for potatoes, oca, melloco, other Andean root crops, amaranta, quinua and capulí. Research from other international centers also contribute as, for example, rice varieties from the International Rice Research Institute (IRRI).

The Organization of American States (OAS) has funded scholarships and the Intergovernmental Committee on Migration. The latter was provided US$36,500 for training in agricultural production techniques, research on technology and its cultural foundations, pork production in the Otavalo area and rice, corn and cacao processing and marketing in the Vinces and Baba areas of Guayas Province. In 1987 OAS also contributed funds for work on cattle diseases, production of legumes for human consumption, evaluation of marine resources and for scholarships for study in the areas of mechanization, nutrition and the environment.

Bilateral Assistance to Agriculture

Bilateral assistance encompasses assistance from the government of a foreign country to Ecuador. Generally these are government-to-government activities but the aid may go to non-government organizations, as permitted by bilateral agreements. Historically, the U.S. has been the principal provider of bilateral aid for Ecuador but a substantial number of other countries have supplied significant quantities of assistance for the agricultural sector. Some have provided more aid than the United States in given years, especially in the last half of the 1970s and first half of the 1980s.

U.S. Programs[9] The United States has provided assistance to Ecuador's agriculture since World War II when it helped establish the country's first agricultural experiment station. The amounts were small but increased under President Truman's Point Four program and under PL 480 food aid after 1954. Assistance received another boost under President Kennedy's Alliance for Progress in the 1960s when the U.S. assistance program was renamed, becoming the USAID. Programs declined during the seventies after the large increases in oil revenue and the emergence of the reformist military regime. With restoration of democratic rule in 1979 assistance levels increased and the economic crises and natural disasters of the 1980s led to additional assistance. With the election of the market-oriented Febres Cordero government in 1984, resumption of PL 480 food aid provided added funds for agricultural and other activities. Funding levels were maintained after the election of Rodrigo Borja in 1988.

The USAID/Ecuador Mission's 1998 projects for agriculture are varied and

Table 11.8 1988 USAID Agricultural Assistance Programs in Ecuador

Project	Funds: Grant US$1,000	Loan US$1,000	PL 480 S/.1,000
Rural Technology Transfer Systems	5,300	2,600	210,000
Sheep Improvement Subproject			148,000
Integrated Pest Control Subproject			23,500
Dairy Production Improvement			19,000
Cattle Production & Marketing			37,000
Agricultural Sector Reorientation	7,100	1,700	356,000
Land Titling Project	3,300	7,000	
Integrated Rural Development	300		30,000
Promotion of Nontraditional Exports	2,400	8,000	
Agr. Research, Extension & Education	7,000		1,752,000
Wilson Popenoe Foundation (Scholarships)	680		
Coastal Resources Management	650		
Forestry Sector Development	1,600	6,500	
Environmental Education	900		
Promotion of Rural Youth Training	448		15,000
PL 480 Financed Projects:			
Technology Transfer Program			52,000
Agr. Sector Development Promotion			50,000
Agroecological Survey			20,000
Dairy Control & Registration			20,000
Andean Region Cooperative Research			16,000
Rural Water Projects			250,000
Calf Milk Replacer Project			45,000
Credit Institutional Improvement			24,000
Agricultural Commodities Exchange			100,000
Marketing Systems Promotion			13,000
Yuca (cassava) Production			78,500
IDEA Endowment			400,000
FUNDAGRO Endowment			2,000,000
Totals	29,678	19,800	5,708,500

Source: USAID/Ecuador 1988.

substantial (Table 11.8). Major USAID projects include promoting the development and transfer of agricultural technology, agricultural policy analysis, improvements in agricultural information, land titling, forestry sector development, promotion of nontraditional agricultural exports and development and protection of the country's Costa resources. Funding from grants, loans and food aid for the life of all projects extant in 1988 was US$52.9 million. Major projects usually last 3 to 5 years, although they are often extended or renewed. Potential funding for agricultural activities was expanded considerably after 1984 through the use of PL 480, Title I and the Agricultural Adjustment Act, Section 416 funds, both derived from the sale of surplus U.S. agricultural products (Table 11.9). Wheat, nonfat dry milk, vegetable oil and sorghum have been imported and sold, producing large amounts of local funds that are programmed for development activities by a joint GOE/USAID committee. The agreements under which the products are imported provide broad guidelines for the use of the funds. Funds from food aid sales have been used to provide government counterpart funds for several of the USAID-funded agricultural projects, fund a number of smaller projects and make emergency road repairs.

Table 11.9 Monetized Food Aid for Ecuador, 1985-1988

Product	Program	Year	Value: Dollars US$1,000	Sucres Million	Uses Permitted
Wheat	Title I	1985	15,000	1,424.7	Agriculture & Rural Development
Wheat	Title I	1986	5,000	750.0	Agricultural Development
Wheat	Sugar Quota	1986	1,500	185.1	Agricultural Development
Wheat	Section 416	1987	4,350	826.5	Agricultural Development
Wheat	Sugar Quota	1987	2,900	557.0	Agrricultural Development
NFDM	Section 416	1987	1,740	330.6	Agricultue & Dairy Development
Soy Oil	Emerg. Food	1987	4,496	867.7	Earthquake Area Reconstruction
Sorghum	Section 416	1988	5,500	2,750.0	Agrricultural Development

Source: USAID/Ecuador.

Many other smaller projects of both the private and public sectors have been funded besides those under PL 480 programs. These have included grants for environmental education activities, improvements in rural youth training through the establishment of 4-F (4-H) clubs, dairy sanitation and registration, rural water projects, development of a locally produced calf milk replacer, improvement of credit institutions, establishment of an agricultural commodities exchange and cassava production and processing.

The Peace Corps has been in Ecuador since its founding in 1962. It conducts development activities through the use of volunteers who receive a small salary and a small amount of support. The volunteers' activities are in response to requests by Ecuador, with a substantial share in agriculture, forestry and rural development. Over 3,000 volunteers have served in Ecuador with current levels of around 200 per year. Its agricultural and rural development activities include support of 4-F club activities, integrated rural development, agricultural extension for small and low-income farmers, animal production in tropical areas and fish culture. Natural resource activities embrace forestry, reforestation, silviculture, soil conservation, environmental education, and assistance to the National Parks.

Other Countries As noted above, most of the DAC countries have provided assistance to Ecuador, including agricultural programs. Assistance also has been provided by Egypt, Israel, Korea, the Chinas Chile, Brazil and Honduras. Although the levels of assistance have been small, several countries have provided significant amounts for agricultural programs.

Belgium has had recent projects supporting irrigation, forestry, rural development and fishing, with life-of-project funding of over US$5 million. Its irrigation activities have been through INEHRI and were directed to irrigation districts and assistance for small-farm irrigation. Reforestation, agro-forestry and related activities are financed in Chimborazo Province. Rural development activities encompassed a number of small projects to assist communities develop their agricultural, artisan and other activities. These activities also utilized Belgian volunteers to carry out the technical assistance activities.

Canada has several relatively small projects, most in support of agricultural research and some through other agencies. Support of research through INIAP, in 1987, included production and processing of quinua, production and utilization of corn and cassava (yuca) for small farms in Manabí Province, virus-free seed potato multiplication, potato marketing in Latin American and tropical forages for the

Amazonian region. Canada, with IICA, has funded research on crops to substitute for sugar cane, participated in integrated rural development financing and, through Fundación Ciencia, sponsored research on Chame, a fresh-water food fish.

French assistance in Ecuador is conducted through its Office of Overseas Science and Technology Research (ORSTOM). In 1974 it began collaborative effort with PRONAREG to study and map the country's natural resources and to provide a better basis for their use and protection. This highly successful cooperative program, with its emphasis on natural resources, has continued and in 1987-1988 there were agriculturally related activities with life-of-project funding of over US$10 million. France has related agreements with the Ecuadorian Center for Geographic Research (CEDIG), National Polytechnic School, Remote Sensing Center (CLIRSEN), Economic Research Institute (IIE) and Military Geographical Institute (IGM).

The Federal Republic of Germany, primarily through its Agency for Technical Cooperation (GTZ), has provided both grant and loan funds, with the agricultural activities being grant funded. The active German agricultural and forestry projects in 1988 were a forestry development program, the Livestock Development Project (PROFOGAN), a coffee disease and pest control effort and a project for the development and rational use of fuel wood. According to the MAG (1987b) and UNDP listings of assistance projects these have a total life-of-project funding of over US$9 million.

The Italian assistance program has concentrated on agricultural machinery, irrigation and marketing of perishable products. The Mechanization Program of the MAG was provided with US$3 million worth of equipment and technical assistance under a project that ended in 1987. Major activities currently underway or ready to implement are an irrigation project with CEDEGE (US$5.2 million), a development project for Northwestern Esmeraldas Province (US$2 million) and one to determine and solve marketing problems for perishable products in Tungurahua Province.

Japan has been increasing its level of assistance to Ecuador. In 1988 projects included forestry management in Napo Province and forestry development in Bolívar Province. They also are financing the development of activities to produce shrimp larvae.

Switzerland has had a long association with Ecuador and in 1987 had ten active projects with length of life funds of US$4.7 million. The two largest are to support research in fruit production, primarily apples, and reforestation activities (each about US$1.1 million). Others are to improve agricultural implements, to assist small rural cheesemakers, irrigation, food self sufficiency, rural development, the reintroduction of vicuñas to Ecuador and the donation of funds for rice mill for the Union of Campesinos of Vinces and Baba, Los Ríos Province. Although the current cheese project is not large, it is part of a US$12 million effort that started in 1979.

Three other DAC countries, Great Britain, Denmark and Holland, have made recent contributions to agriculture. The Dutch projects reported by MAG are for a study of the lower Guayas River Basin and for the study of oilpalm disease problems. Denmark contributed for equipping an agricultural technical institute. Great Britain has had a long-term research program with INIAP at the Pichilingue Experiment Station to improve cacao varieties with emphasis on disease resistance.

Non-DAC countries contributing to agricultural development activities are Chile, both Chinas, Egypt, Honduras, Korea and Spain. Chile and Egypt have contributed scholarships for the study of agricultural subjects. Honduras is supporting genetic research on bananas and plantains. The Republic of China (Taiwan) provides technical assistance for rice, vegetables, fruits and pork production, including programs for horticultural products in the Galápagos and assistance for food production by indigenous groups in Napo Province. Korea has contributed agricultural machinery for use on small farms and Spain is supporting projects for integrated rural development, forestry, irrigation and the environment. Israel has supported irrigation activities in the Costa but has no current project with the MAG. The Peoples Republic of China (mainland) provides technical assistance for various types of projects, an interest free line of credit for project purposes and equipment for mini-hydroelectric generation projects. Activities by other socialist-block countries have been minor in recent years although some educational activities have continued. The recent changes in Eastern Europe undoubtedly will affect these programs, especially educational programs which promote communism.

Private Voluntary Organizations

The Technical Assistance Clearing House Directory listed 55 PVOs with programs in Ecuador (Boynes). Of that total, 32 were religious organizations, 12 were charitable groups and 11 were in the business/labor/foundation categories. The listing is incomplete and it is not feasible to determine the precise number working in the country. The objectives of the PVOs are to provide relief, promote development and conduct missionary work. Activities include agriculture, nutrition, health, family planning, education, culture, community development and proselytizing. PVO's tend to work with economically disadvantaged groups including indigenous communities and have an agricultural orientation.

One major activity has been food and feeding programs. CARE and Catholic Relief Services (CRS) have been involved with those activities which were initiated in the 1950s. In recent years feeding programs have been criticized as being ineffective from the viewpoint of improving the overall nutritional status of the recipients. They also have been criticized for causing production disincentives. As a consequence several agencies, including CARE in Ecuador, have discontinued feeding programs. CRS, however, has continued its program which receives food from the U.S. PL 480 Title II program, milk from the European Economic Community and support from other sources including the Catholic Church of Ecuador.

The CARE program has evolved into development-oriented activities, viewed as having longer-term impacts that do not create dependencies. This includes agricultural development with programs to promote soil conservation and improved farming techniques in farm communities with limited resources. One project, financed by USAID, is to assist farmers in Chimborazo Province to effectively utilize irrigation facilities that were built under another USAID project. Other CARE projects include production of fruits and vegetables in both the Sierra and Costa regions; soil use, conservation and management in the Sierra; and reforestation, jointly with the Peace Corps, in Cañar Province.

Other PVOs involved in agricultural development include Foster Parents (*Plan Padrinos*) which operates a demonstration farm, works with an integrated rural development project to promote citrus production and helps construct rural infrastructure in Bolívar Province. The International Executive Service Corps has an office in Ecuador and has had a number of projects including some with agricultural interests (Elton). The Farmer to Farmer program has financed U.S. farmer visits to Ecuador to assist with problems and visits by Ecuadorian farmers to the United States. Organizations such as American Cooperative Development International and American

Cooperative League United have provided technical assistance for cooperatives. The American Institute for Free Labor Development, an organization of the AFL-CIO, has a project to assist farm worker organizations in Esmeraldas Province. Several religious organizations provide technical and financial assistance for agricultural development as well as carrying out missionary activities. This has included substantial efforts by several evangelical groups in rural areas.

Donor Assistance Problems

It is common for donor-funded projects in Ecuador to be delayed for lengthy periods of time and for serious problems to develop in implementation that imperil the achievement of project objectives. Some of the apparent delays are due to unrealistically optimistic scheduling in project design, some are due to unforseen and unforeseeable circumstances, others are caused by the nature of the development process or the institutional structure within which the projects must be carried out. Project failure can be caused by poor design, unrealistic objectives or implementation problems.

A major constraint to implementation of many projects is a requirement for counterpart funding by Ecuador. This has been a particularly difficult problem in the last few years because of the severe economic situation, especially if the counterpart funding is for investment or even additional operating funds. Projects for which the counterpart consists of in-kind support such as office space and the assignment existing personnel to work on the project have fewer problems. USAID partially solved the problem by agreeing to accept funds derived from monetized food aid as counterpart for some of its agricultural projects.

Other frequent constraints are the delays in processing the documentation to implement a project. The GOE consists of an extensive bureaucracy which operates under a complex set of rules and procedures. Most jobs have very well defined specifications as to duties and responsibilities. It is often difficult to change a position or transfer an individual employee. Rules dealing with contracting, purchasing and employment can cause undue delays. Implementation may be affected by jurisdictional disputes, organizational jealousies or the failure of key personnel to carry out assignments. The are frequent shifts in leadership positions in many government agencies, due in part to low pay levels, and a new agency head may not be supportive of ongoing efforts in which he had no input. The new leadership may want to revise the procedures or may change personnel. There may be conflicts with counterpart personnel because of pay differences between foreign technical assistance and government employees. Importation of project supplies and equipment can be held up in customs, although the agreements usually call for free imports. At times goods are delayed by inadequate transportation or strikes, they may be damaged due to inadequate handling or poor storage, or may be diverted from their intended uses or "lost" before reaching the project.

Some implementation problems are caused by the donors. The laws, rules and regulations under which they operate also can cause delays, may contribute to project design flaws or cause problems in procurement of project resources. Requirements to obtain project equipment or supplies in the donor country (tied aid) may result in products which are inappropriate or incompatible with existing equipment in Ecuador. Conditions for undertaking a project may be unacheivable or unrealistic, especially if they involve changing laws, regulations or customs. The tendency of the World Bank,

USAID and other donors to promote economic reform as an integral part of their programs has exacerbated the problem. Political requirements of foreign assistance laws, such as the Bumpers Amendment that prohibits assistance that would result in competition for U. S. agricultural exports, can also reduce the utility of assistance programs.

Another problem is a lack of coordination among the various donor agencies. CONADE has the function of coordinating foreign assistance activities but it is not particularly effective and its authority varies from government to government. Furthermore, there is no formal or consistent mechanism for the donor agencies to coordinate or even exchange information on activities, although the UNDP attempts to collect and provide information about assistance activities. As a consequence the GOE may deliberately or unknowingly ask more than one agency to undertake similar activities which can result in unnecessary duplication and a waste of limited development resources. At times two donors may be attempting to accomplish opposing objectives in a similar activity or the same area. For example one may be funding colonization in an area where another is attempting to prevent intrusions that will damage an environmentally sensitive region.

NOTES

1. Previously the President could not succeed himself but could be reelected at a later time. The new provision was probably in reaction to the election of Velasco Ibarra at four different times.

2. This approach gives a somewhat stronger representation for the smaller more rural provinces since they have a representative for each 100,000 of population, whereas larger provinces get an additional deputy only for each additional 300,000 people.

3. This regional separation is due largely to the long existing conflict between the Costa and the Sierra and the desire of each region to have its own units and facilities and be independent of the other. The Costa area is quite different and needs to have specialized programs and local services, but the separation complicates administration where there are common interests or problems that affect both areas.

4. Triticale is not native to the Andean region but is included in this group for purposes of MAG programs.

5. The largest state enterprise is PETROECUADOR, the petroleum corporation, and the Electric Company (INECEL) is the second largest. The state also owns the railroads, two airlines (Tame and Ecuatoriana), the telephone company (IETEL), and several smaller enterprises.

6. CFN, at the end of 1986, owned shares in 50 companies including agroindustrial (9), cement (5), wood and furniture (4), metals (6), chemicals (2 including fertilizer), finance (9), paper (1), fishing (1), industrial parks (3), services (1) and others (4) (CFN).

7. *Comuna* is a Spanish word that can be translated as commune, community or municipality with commune as the more common translation. That word, however, is not an accurate representation of the meaning of comuna as used in the Ecuadorian context for a community of indigenous people where resources may be, but are not necessarily, collectively owned and farmed. Therefore, the Spanish word will be used to maintain the distinction.

8. The government took over the debts at what turned out to be very favorable conditions for the private sector debtors. The debts were converted to Sucre values at official exchange rates which were considerably lower than open market rate, giving the debtors a windfall gain of considerable proportions.

9. The USAID program in Ecuador is relatively small in comparison to those in countries such as Guatemala and Honduras, which had 1988 annual U.S. economic and military assistance obligations of US$181 million and US$255 million, respectively, compared with about US$21 million for Ecuador (USAID p. 23).

REFERENCES

BCE (Central Bank of Ecuador). 1987a and 1982a. *Boletín Anuario, 1982 and 1987*. Vols. 5, 10. Quito: Banco Central.

_____. 1986b-1973b. *Memoria Annual, 1986-1973*. Quito: Banco Central.

Boynes, Wynta, Excc. Ed. 1983. *Nonprofit Organizations in Development Assistance Abroad*. 8th edition. White Plains, NY: UNIPUB.

Bromley, Raymond. 1981. "The Colonization of the Humid Tropical Areas in Ecuador." *Singapore Journal of Tropical Geography* 2:15-26.

CFN (National Finance Corporation). 1986. "Memorandum 5493." Quito: Corporación Financiera Nacional, December 12.

Colyer, Dale. 1988a. "Foreign Assistance Programs for Agriculture." Quito: USAID, Assessment of Ecuador's Agricultural Sector, Working Paper 6-88, September.

_____. 1988b. "Agriculture and the Public Sector." Quito: USAID, Assessment of Ecuador's Agricultural Sector, Working Paper 6-88, September.

CONADE (National Development Council). 1987. *Informe del Presidente de Consejo Nacional de Desarrollo al H. Congreso Nacional*. Quito.

Constitución de la República del Ecuador. 1988. Quito: Ediciones Jurídicas.

CORDES (Corporation for Development Studies). 1987. *Resultados Económicos de 1986 y Perspectivas de 1987*. Quito: Apunte Técnico 9.

Dow, Kamal and Rómulo Solíz. 1984. "Generation and Transfer of Technology." Quito: University of Florida, August (unpublished paper).

Eguez T., Marcello. 1988. "32 Proyectos Con Inversión de 1.674 millones de Dólares Financia el BID". *El Comercio*. Quito: July 25.

El Comercio. 1988. Quito: July 21.

Elías, Victor J. 1985. *Government Expenditures on Agriculture and Agricultural Growth in Latin America*. Washington, D.C.: International Food Policy Research Institute, Research Report 50.

Elton, Wallace W. 1986. *Ten Thousand Strong*. Stamford, CN: International Executive Service Corps.

Espinel, Marcos. 1988. "Exposición del Señor Ministro de Agricultura y Ganadería en el Instituto de Altos Estudios Nacionales." Quito: Unidad de Análisis de Políticas, MAG.

FIDA (International Fund for Agricultural Development). 1988. *Informe de la Misión Especial de Programación a la República del Ecuador*. Quito: Informe No. 0098-EC.

GOE (Government of Ecuador). 1988, 1987, 1986a, 1985, 1984. *Registro Oficial: Presupuesto de Estado*. Quito.

_____. 1986b. *Registro Oficial*. No. 556. Quito: November 4.

Hurtado, Osvaldo. 1985. *Political Power in Ecuador*, Encore Edition. Translated by

Nick D. Mills, Jr. Boulder, CO: Westview Press.

IDB (Inter-American Development Bank). 1988. *Annual Report 1987*. Washington.

Jordán Bucheli, Fausto. 1988. *El Minifundio: Su Evolución en el Ecuador*. Quito: Corporación Editora Nacional.

Kasza, Gregory J. 1981. "Regional Conflict in Ecuador: Quito and Guayaquil." *Inter-American Economic Affairs* 35:2:3-2.

Keller, Jack, et. al. 1982. *Ecuador: Irrigation Sector Review*. Logan, UT: Utah State University, USAID/WMS Report 12.

MAG (Ministry of Agriculture). 1985. *Organización y Objetivos, 1985*. Quito.

_____. 1987a. *Informe de Labores, 1986-1987*. Quito.

_____. 1987b. "Proyectos de Cooperación y Credito Externo." Quito: Asesoría Económica y de Asuntos Internacionales, Junio.

OECD (Organization for Economic Co-operation and Development). 1988, 1984. *Geographical Distribution of Financial Flows to Developing Countries, 1981/83, 1985/87*. París.

Riley, Harold. 1983. *Ecuador Agriculture: An Assessment and Direction for Development - Marketing Study*. Washington, D.C.: World Bank Report No. 4522-EC, Aug. 22.

Rubio Orbe, Gonzalo. 1987. *Los Indios Ecuatorianos*. Quito: Corporación Editora Nacional.

Spurrier, Walter R. 1987. "Unemployment Worsens." *Weekly Analysis* 17:6:(Feb. 16).

Torres, Luis F. 1987. *El Control de la Constitucionalidad en el Ecuador*. Quito: Pontifica Universidad Católica del Ecuador.

UNDP (United Nations Development Program). 1988. *Cooperación para el Desarrollo, Ecuador, Informe 1987*. Quito: United Nations.

_____. 1987, 1986. *Informe Anual de la Asistencia para el Desarrollo, Ecuador 1986, 1985*. Quito: United Nations.

USAID (U.S. Agency for International Development). 1988. *Agency for International Development: Fiscal Year 1989 Summary Tables*. Washington, D.C.

USAID/Ecuador. 1988. "ARDO Programs." Quito: U.S. Agency for International Development.

World Bank. 1987a. "Ecuador: Country Economic Memorandum". Washington, D.C.: Report 6592-EC.

_____. 1987b. *The World Bank Annual Report 1987*. Washington, D.C.

12

THE HUMAN CAPITAL

AND SCIENCE BASE

Morris D. Whitaker

Production of an agricultural surplus is of critical importance to achieving more rapid economic growth in developing countries, especially those with large agricultural sectors. Past models of economic development recognized the importance of the surplus for sustained economic growth but failed to identify the conditions and factors necessary to produce it. They did, however, recognize the need for increases in agricultural productivity in order to increase supply and shift the internal terms of trade against the sector (see Chapter 1).

This chapter treats the human capital and science base for Ecuadorian agriculture as one of the principal sets of inputs necessary for sustained increases in agricultural productivity. Human capital is defined to include the level of general education of rural people and of scientific and technical education. The term "science base" is broadly defined to include agricultural education, research and extension institutions and their sine qua non human capital. It is used throughout this chapter to mean the set of people and associated institutions involved in training agricultural scientists and technicians, and in accessing, adapting, generating and diffusing new and improved technical practices for agriculture. The science base is synonymous with the concept of a research, extension and education (REE) system, which often is used to describe it. General education institutions for rural people contribute directly to improvements in agricultural productivity through improving the literacy and basic skills of farm families and are complementary to the science base.

The following sections review and analyze: the concept of efficient technical change and main sources of increased agricultural productivity; the nature of the problem-- limited agricultural land and low agricultural productivity--and the interrelatedness of the sources of productivity growth; empirical evidence from Ecuador and other countries about the relatively high economic returns from investments in human capital and a science base for agriculture; Ecuador's educational system and human capital formation for agriculture, including general education of rural people and technical and science education; the research system; extension programs; and special efforts to strengthen the REE system. The last section presents conclusions and recommendations.

Efficient Technical Change

The principal challenge for any country attempting to produce a sustained agricultural surplus is to attain an efficient path of technical change (Hayami and Ruttan Chapter 3). Efficient technical change is defined as that which permits the substitution of the abundant for the scarce factor of production, given the original resource endowment. If agricultural land is limited and labor is abundant, as is the case in Ecuador and most developing countries, then efficient innovations will facilitate the substitution of cheap labor for expensive land. In this case, a path of chemical-biological innovations permits modern, technical inputs such as improved seeds and fertilizer to be substituted for scarce land thus increasing its productivity (yields) and the utilization of abundant labor. If land is relatively abundant and labor is in limited supply then innovations must save the scarce labor. A path of mechanical innovations permits machinery and other equipment to be substituted for labor in this case, thus increasing the use of land and raising the productivity of labor. Hayami and Ruttan theorize that market forces induce efficient technical changes by causing farmers, businessmen and public employees to resolve constraints to agricultural growth imposed by limited land or labor.[1] Government interventions in product and factor markets, such as fixed, overvalued exchange rates, direct subsidies to industry, controlled prices and trade barriers discriminate against agriculture and reduce and distort incentives to make investments which relax resource constraints in the sector. Ecuador's macroeconomic policy matrix discriminated heavily against agriculture during the 1970s and, while it has improved in the 1980s, still favors internal growth based on import-substitution industrialization (Chapter 2). The macroeconomic policy matrix thus constrains efficient technical change in agriculture by reducing and distorting the prices of agricultural products and factors relative to their scarcity prices.

It is widely accepted that three principal sets of variables explain most of the differences in agricultural labor productivity between developed and developing countries (Hayami and Ruttan Chapters 5 and 6). These are: (a) capital accumulations internal to agriculture including the original endowment of land and improvements to it (e.g. clearing, leveling and irrigation), livestock and perennial plants; (b) human capital, including general education of farmers and technical and scientific education for a science base; and (c) modern industrial inputs (machinery, fertilizers, improved seeds, etc.) that substitute directly for the limiting factor of production.

These three sets of variables each explained roughly one-fourth of the 10-fold gap in agricultural labor productivity between 21 developed and 22 developing countries in 1980 (Hayami and Ruttan p. 152). Most of the balance was explained by scale economies associated with larger farm size in the developed countries, with a small unexplained residual. These results are a basis for optimism that developing countries such as Ecuador can substantially increase agricultural productivity. Investments in general education for rural people, a science base for agriculture and the provision of modern, industrial inputs can increase productivity by several times, even if population pressure causes decreases in land per worker. Market forces play a critical role in efficiently allocating public and private sector resources among these three broad, interrelated sets of investment targets.

Nature of the Problem

Ecuadorian agriculture is afflicted by two closely related problems. First, all its good agricultural land is in production and exploiting new lands entails relatively high and increasing social and private costs. Second, productivity is low which makes it difficult to absorb abundant labor at higher real wages and to compete internationally. Investments in internal capital accumulations, the science base and human capital and modern, industrial inputs tend to be highly interrelated, with some minimum critical mass needed in each in order to make investments profitable in the others. Limited investments have been made in the science base and rural, primary education. Investments in improvements to the land through irrigation have been substantial but are relatively unproductive because of inadequate investments in the science base.

Limited Agricultural Land

Almost all available agricultural land is in production (Chapter 4). Labor is increasingly abundant relative to land, given Ecuador's burgeoning labor force which is growing at 3.4 percent per year (Chapter 5). An efficient path of technical change focused on chemical-biological innovations will increase the productivity of land and its capacity to support more and more people. Increases in yields provide the basis for increased employment and incomes of those who derive their livelihood from the land. A general path of chemical-biological innovations does not, however, obviate the need for complementary mechanical innovations.

Emphasis on chemical-biological innovations will reduce pressure for agricultural expansion into new-lands areas with their very fragile soils and ecology. Such investments will facilitate the increasingly urgent need for the government to protect fragile lands, reduce soil erosion and environmental degradation and maintain the rich genetic diversity of the flora and fauna found in Ecuador.

Low Agricultural Productivity

Agriculture in Ecuador is characterized by relatively low levels of productivity as measured by yields. Yields are low relative to those achieved by neighboring countries, and also to experimental results in Ecuador (Table 12.1). Ecuador generally has lower yields than the weighted average for 12 other South American countries and is especially deficient in the cereals. For example, Peru's rice yields were over two times greater than those of Ecuador. Yields of milk, eggs and soybeans were above the average but even for these products Ecuador still was substantially below its neighbors with the highest yields. These averages mask some important variations within and among crops (see Chapter 6). Thus, one must be careful not to conclude that low productivity affects all farmers and all crops equally.

Yields, or production per unit of land, are only a partial measure of productivity. An equally important measure is output per worker but data limitations preclude a careful analysis of trends in this important, partial productivity index. Data in Chapter 5 revealed that agricultural GDP per worker was only one-half that of the next lowest sector (services) and was only one-third the national average. These GDP data are consistent with the general perception of low levels of wages and incomes in rural areas and strongly suggest that the productivity of labor in agriculture is relatively low.

Interrelationships among Investment Targets

The three investment targets which increase agricultural productivity--land

Table 12.1   Comparison of Yields Between Ecuador and South America, 1986-1988
             (Weighted Averages)[a]

Crop	Ecuador	South America	Gap with South America (%)	Highest Yield Country in South America			Colombia	Peru
				Country	Yield	Gap		
Wheat	972	1,815	-46.5	Chile	2,878	-66.2	1,740	1,278
Rice, paddy	2,302	2,571	-10.5	Peru	4,809	-52.1	4,697	4,809
Corn	1,369	2,360	-42.0	Chile	7,109	-80.7	1,360	1,962
Barley	889	1,625	-45.3	Chile	3,113	-71.5	1,908	1,170
Soybeans	1,890	1,815	+4.1	Argentina	2,128	-11.2	1,998	1,795
Peanuts	893	1,896	-52.9	Argentina	2,204	-59.5	1,442	1,892
Milk	1,672	1,303	+28.3	Argentina	2,213	-24.5	958	1,236
Eggs	8	7	+11.9	Colombia	14	-40.5	14	6

Source: USDA.

[a]Crop yields in kg/ha/year and yields of livestock products in kg/animal/year.

improvements and other internal capital accumulations, human capital and a science base and modern industrial inputs--are interactive and improvements in one tends to enhance investments in another. For example, investments in general education for rural people enhance the capability of farmers to understand and adopt new technologies, while investments in the science base make literacy and technical education more valuable to farmers and their children. Investments in technical inputs make the science base more viable and profitable, while the availability of modern inputs increases the demand for cost-reducing technologies which utilize the modern inputs. Thus, all of these variables must be addressed at some minimal level if significant progress is to be made in moving toward a science-based agriculture and substantial increases in productivity.

Longer-term investments which augment land area and improve land quality, such as irrigation and drainage projects, explained about 9 percent of the differences in labor productivity between developed and developing countries in the Hayami and Ruttan study (p. 152). Such investments are highly complementary to those in human capital and a science base and modern industrial inputs and are very important given Ecuador's limited agricultural land. Chemical-biological innovations involving high-yielding varieties require timely and adequate applications of water in order to respond optimally to fertilizers. Consequently, irrigation can be an important element of improved packages of technology when land is the limiting factor and there is sufficient investment in the science base and human capital.

The disappointing economic performance of public irrigation projects described in Chapter 7 is at least partially due to limited complementary investments in the science base, especially research, documented below. Relatively large past investments in irrigation infrastructure provide an important basis for potentially large increases in agricultural productivity. To realize the potential benefits of such investments will require, however, major investments in complementary human capital and a science base for the sector and macroeconomic and sectoral policies that will assure efficient technical change and a supply of modern, industrial inputs. Such complementary investments and policy reforms will make irrigation projects much more economically viable by increasing efficiency of water use, yields and net farm income.

Economic Returns to a Science Base

There is a large and growing body of empirical evidence that economic returns to investments in research, extension and associated education programs are relatively high around the world, compared to other social and private investment alternatives. Returns ranged from 20 to 110 percent per year in 34 studies in various developed and developing countries (Evenson, Waggoner and Ruttan). A similar review of 10 studies of returns to agricultural research in South America found returns ranging from 11 to 119 percent (Scobie Table 16).

Ecuador has experienced limited success in its efforts to generate, access and diffuse improved technologies even though average yields still are relatively low. Yields have increased, rapidly in some cases, and technical changes explained an important part of the increases in production for most major crops during the past two decades (Chapter 6). A recent study found a benefit-cost ratio of 2.46 for expenditures on agricultural research in Ecuador between 1971 and 1981 (Posada T. p. 67).

Education and Human Capital Formation

Ecuador's educational system has not made the contribution to agricultural and economic development that is necessary. It is characterized by anachronistic structures and rigidities that are increasingly outmoded and irrelevant to the needs of a modern society and especially to agricultural development. Education in the rural primary schools emphasizes basic literacy, with little emphasis on problem-solving skills or vocational education related to agriculture, home economics or natural resources. Learning is largely by rote and drop-out rates are high. Attrition also is relatively high in the secondary schools where students must select areas of specialization by grade 10 (age 15) and then start over again if they wish to change areas of study. Very few students opt to study agriculture with most enrolled in humanities programs that lead toward the study of law, economics and medicine at the university level. Higher education is in chaos, especially public universities and institutes. Public universities are free, with no entrance exams or standards, and are overcrowded with many marginal students. They also are each administratively autonomous, governed by the students and are highly politicized. Their graduates are poorly trained and consequently are unable to contribute much to economic growth and development.

Structure and Organization

All education in Ecuador is under the jurisdiction of the Ministry of Education and Culture (MEC). MEC is directly responsible for all primary and secondary schools and two-year normal colleges and technical institutes. The universities and polytechnic institutes are each autonomous entities but their budget support is channeled through MEC. The National Council of Agricultural Science Faculties (CONFCA) coordinates the disparate activities of the various faculties of agriculture.

The education system is comprised of four basic components, pre-primary school, primary school, secondary school and higher education (Figure 12.1). Kindergarten is the entrance point in formal education at age five but in practice is not always offered, especially in rural areas. Students enter the first grade at age six and are awarded a certificate for graduating from primary school after successfully completing grade six which qualifies them to enter secondary school.

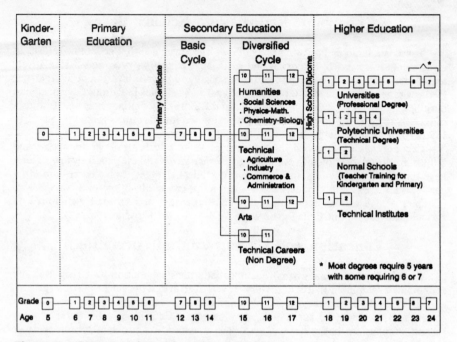

Figure 12.1   Structure of Ecuador's Education System
Source: Prepared by author.

Secondary school is divided into two three-year cycles. The first, or basic cycle (grades 7-9) consists of a general-education curriculum which is required of all students. Students must choose an area of specialization at the beginning of the second three-year cycle (grades 10-12) from: (a) humanities (social sciences, physics-mathematics and chemistry-biology); (b) technical (agriculture, industrial and commercial-administrative); and (c) arts. Within agriculture, students may specialize in agronomy, livestock or food science. There also is a two-year program following the basic cycle which is called "technical careers" which provides non-degree training and is an exit point from formal education. Once students begin an area of special study they can only change to another area by completing the required courses for that area of specialization. Changing the major area of study also requires revalidation, through formal testing, of any required courses that have been previously taken. Students who complete the two three-year cycles are granted a graduation diploma (*Diploma de Bachiller*) which permits them to enter into higher education.

Higher education consists of four kinds of schools: two-year technical institutes, two-year normal schools for training primary school teachers, polytechnic universities, and universities.   The polytechnic universities generally offer four-year technical degrees and the universities offer 5-7 year professional degrees depending on the course of study and the university. Most universities offer fields of study leading to the degree of agricultural engineer (*Ingeniero Agrónomo*).   Attainment of this degree requires five to six years of study, including a thesis and an additional year of practical work in rural areas (*Año Técnico Rural*). Other specialized degrees in agriculture also

Table 12.2 Enrollment and Desertion Rates During Six Years of Primary School for Each First Grade Class of 1980-1981, 1981-1982 and 1982-1983 by Urban and Rural Areas[a]

First Grade Class of:		Enrollment by Grade						
		First	Second	Third	Fourth	Fifth	Sixth	Seventh[b]
1980-81	U[c]	159,391	139,093	134,850	132,897	128,433	123,732	149,898
	R	229,224	162,677	133,257	120,805	101,667	91,482	26,828
1981-82	U	162,650	143,232	138,430	138,343	132,355	126,153	152,242
	R	222,119	161,217	150,019	118,962	105,424	95,778	27,728
1982-83	U	173,255	147,404	142,806	141,252	134,978	131,151	146,291
	R	222,728	164,397	134,870	122,876	107,220	99,832	26,898
		Cumulative Desertion Rates (%)						
1980-81	U	100.0	12.7	15.4	16.6	19.4	22.4	6.0
	R	100.0	29.0	41.9	47.3	55.6	60.1	88.3
1981-82	U	100.0	11.9	14.9	14.9	18.6	22.4	6.4
	R	100.0	27.4	32.5	46.4	52.5	56.9	87.5
1982-83	U	100.0	14.9	17.6	18.5	22.1	24.3	15.6
	R	100.0	26.2	39.4	44.8	51.9	55.2	87.9

Source: Whitaker, Colyer and Alzamora Appendix Table 12.1.

[a] Each row presents the succeeding enrollment of the first grade class for the year indicated. For example, in 1980-1981 there were 229,224 first graders in rural schools. Of these, only 162,677 registered in the second grade (1981-1982) and 133,257 in the third grade (1982-1983) etcetera.
[b] First year of secondary school.
[c] U=Urban and R=Rural.

are offered but no graduate programs at the M.Sc. or Ph.D. level are available.

Primary Education

Primary education appears to have much less value to rural than urban people as revealed by relatively high desertion rates in rural primary schools (Table 12.2). These rates were calculated by following several first-grade classes through the six years of primary school, based on matriculation at each grade.[2] The cumulative drop-out rate was 55.2 percent for rural students who started the first grade during 1982-1983 and began sixth grade during 1987-1988 compared to only a 24.3 percent drop out rate for urban areas for the same period.[3] Approximately one out of two rural primary students still leave school by the start of the sixth grade, compared to only one out of five urban students.

Most of the attrition in rural primary schools occurred during the early grades and primarily during first grade. Of children who started primary school in 1982-1983, 26.2 percent had left school by the beginning of second grade, accounting for almost half the total attrition of 55.2 percent by the beginning of the sixth grade. Another 13.2 percent left by the beginning of third grade and 5.4 percent by fourth grade for a total of 44.8 percent, or over four-fifths of total attrition of 55.2 percent. A similar pattern exists in drop-out rates in urban areas.

The relatively high drop-out rates in rural areas and especially in the early grades is a cause for serious concern. **Rural families apparently place less value on primary education than on their children's labor.** In economic terms, the present value of future family income streams is perceived to be greater with little or no primary schooling for children in about half of rural families. In essence, the costs of going to school (including foregone family income) are perceived by family decision-makers to be greater than the value of any future benefits of primary education. Moreover, these perceptions result in very high attrition in the early grades suggesting that even basic literacy skills are viewed as conferring very little economic or social benefit.

Several interrelated factors help to explain relatively high drop-out rates in rural schools. First, the low value placed on primary schooling is a general indictment of primary rural education. The curriculum is too abstract and remote from problems affecting rural people and does not provide practical skills to solve every-day problems. Facilities and complementary supplies, audio and visual aids and library materials are seriously deficient.

Second, the relatively low levels of investment in a science base for agriculture, documented below, also reduce the value of primary education. There is little incentive to become literate in the absence of sustained opportunities to gain from these skills. If there were continual flows of new technical knowledge being produced by the REE system, incentives to acquire the basic skills necessary to understand, adopt and benefit economically from improved technologies would be greatly enhanced. The benefits from a primary education in rural areas will increase as the science base serving agriculture is improved. Conversely, improvements in primary education will facilitate the adoption of new technologies and enhance opportunities to increase productivity and incomes and thereby make social investments in the science base more profitable.

Third, most rural people are indigenous or mixed blood (*mestizo*) who historically have been exploited, first by the Incas and then by Spanish. These people have been systematically excluded from access to the benefits of economic growth for centuries and continue to bear much of the brunt of discriminatory macroeconomic policies even today. Such an environment of structured isolation from opportunities for economic growth is a contributing factor to the low value placed on education in rural areas.

Secondary Education for Agriculture[4]

Most secondary schools are located in urban areas and educate a high proportion of Ecuador's high school students. For example, during the 1988-1989 school year there were 650,369 students in urban secondary schools or 88 percent of the total, compared to 92,858 in rural secondary schools with only 12 percent of the total (Whitaker, Colyer and Alzamora Appendix Table 12.2). Attrition also is relatively high in rural secondary *Colegios* or high schools (Table 12.3). In rural schools, this rate was 40.9 percent by the ninth grade for students who started the seventh grade in 1983-1984 compared to 30.3 percent for urban schools. The cumulative rate was 74.3 percent by the 12th grade in rural schools compared to 51.5 percent for urban schools. This probably overestimates the desertion rate by rural youth from high school because some go to urban areas to begin the diversified cycle in grade 10, just as they do to begin the basic cycle in grade seven.

As noted above 55.2 percent of rural children who start the first grade drop out by the sixth grade. Assuming another 5-6 percent drop out in the sixth grade, a little more than 40 percent start the three-year basic cycle of secondary school (seventh grade) in either rural or urban high schools. The attrition rates in rural secondary

Table 12.3   Enrollment and Desertion Rates During Six Years of Secondary School for Each Seventh Grade Class of 1980-1981 through 1983-1984 by Urban and Rural Areas[a]

Seventh Grade Class of:		Enrollment by Grade					
		Seventh	Eighth	Ninth	Tenth	Eleventh	Twelfth
1980-81	U[b]	135,368	110,425	99,317	103,117	78,361	64,982
	R	24,225	17,695	14,173	8,612	6,228	5,003
1981-82	U	142,294	114,593	104,187	104,361	81,114	71,073
	R	26,575	20,271	16,175	9,779	7,233	6,441
1982-83	U	148,034	117,791	102,387	104,333	87,127	74,109
	R	28,369	20,076	15,826	9,927	7,620	6,899
1983-84	U	148,995	116,347	103,915	109,278	88,013	72,247
	R	25,658	19,168	15,170	10,572	8,599	6,582
		Cumulative Desertion Rates (%)					
1980-81	U	100.0	18.4	26.6	23.8	42.1	52.0
	R	100.0	27.0	41.5	64.4	74.3	79.3
1981-82	U	100.0	19.5	26.8	26.7	43.0	50.1
	R	100.0	23.7	39.1	63.2	72.8	75.8
1982-83	U	100.0	20.4	30.8	29.5	41.1	49.9
	R	100.0	29.2	44.2	65.0	73.1	75.7
1983-84	U	100.0	21.9	30.3	26.7	40.9	51.5
	R	100.0	25.3	40.9	58.8	66.5	74.3

Source: Whitaker, Colyer and Alzamora Appendix Table 12.2.

[a]Each row presents the succeeding enrollment of the seventh grade class for the year indicated. For example, in 1980-1981 there were 24,225 seventh graders in rural schools. Of these only 17,695 registered in the eighth grade (1981-1982) and 14,173 in the ninth grade (1982-1983) etc.
[b]U=Urban and R=Rural.

schools suggest that roughly 15 percent of rural youth who started school in the first grade begin the second, three year cycle of high school, where specialized study of agriculture may begin. Finally, about 10 percent of those who started rural primary school are enrolled in the last year of high school, so that less than one in ten rural youth graduate from high school. In contrast, about four out of ten urban youth graduate from high schools. For most rural students and a surprisingly high number of urban students, a high school education has less value than alternative uses of their time. The higher drop out rates for youth from rural high schools is explained by the same three reasons as for children from rural primary schools discussed above.

There were 272 high schools offering specialization in agriculture in the diversified cycle during 1988-1989 distributed geographically as follows: Costa, 114; Sierra, 127; and Oriente, 31.[5] Agriculture is not a popular option according to enrollment data. During the five years 1981-1982 through 1985-1986 there were an annual average of 1,956 students registered in agricultural fields in the last year (12th grade) of the diversified cycle in the 272 schools (Table 12.4).

Students specializing in agriculture were only 3.1 percent of total students in the 12th grade. This is very low compared to the relative importance of the sector, which accounts for 16.8 percent of GDP, 55 percent of foreign exchange earnings and 44 percent of employment (see Chapters 3 and 5). The most popular area of study in the diversified cycle is humanities with 65.0 percent of 12th grade students on average

Table 12.4   Enrollment in Last Year of Secondary School, Five Year Annual Average
             by Area, 1981-1982 through 1985-1986

| | Urban | | Rural | | Total | |
Specialization	Number	Share (%)	Number	Share (%)	Number	Share (%)
Humanities	38,721	65.7	2,103	54.3	40,824	65.0
Technical	19,119	32.5	887	22.9	20,006	31.9
Agricultural	1,075	1.8	881	22.8	1,956	3.1
Total	58,915	100.0	3,871	100.0	62,786	100.0

Source: Unpublished data from MEC, Division of Statistics.

during the five-year period. Humanities and other technical areas each had more students enrolled than agriculture even in rural high schools, although agriculture is relatively more popular than in urban high schools.

The low number of students trained in agriculture in high school reflects the relatively poor quality of such training, limited and low-paying employment opportunities and the generally low esteem associated with agricultural training. The faculty that teaches the technical courses in agriculture is dominated (70 percent) by high-school graduates in technical agriculture, often from the same school (Joint Subcommittee p. 52). The lecture method is widely used with little in the way of library materials and visual aids. Laboratory and field experiences tend to be extremely limited. Most high school graduates in agriculture obtain low-paying jobs in agriculture and the degree usually is terminal. Few go on to the universities or technical schools.

There were an average of only 7.2 agricultural students in the 12th grade per agricultural high school--an extremely small number suggesting a very inefficient system. In essence, Ecuador has dissipated its scarce educational resources in too many agricultural high schools and poorly trained teachers.

Higher Education

Higher education for agriculture includes four two-year technical schools and 21 of 22 general and polytechnic universities which offer technical and professional degrees in agricultural fields. The four technical schools provide two years of specialized training to high school graduates in agriculture in specific areas such fruit culture. They suffer from the same deficiencies as the agricultural high schools.

Fifteen universities offered a total of 39 professional degrees in agriculture in 1989, with nine in agronomy, seven in veterinary medicine, six in forestry, five in animal science or livestock management, three in agricultural engineering, two in management of agricultural enterprises and seven in a variety of other specialties (CONUEP; Whitaker, Colyer and Alzamora Table 12.5).[6] Graduates must study from 5-7 years, depending on the university and degree and complete a thesis in order to receive their professional title. They also are required by law to complete one year of professional service in rural areas (Año Técnico Rural). Those who complete only their classes, without doing the thesis are recognized formally as *egresados* but without the title.

The most popular areas of study at the university include medicine, law and economics, while study of agriculture is relatively limited. There were 186,672 students enrolled in Ecuador's universities during 1988 based on preliminary, unpublished data from the National Council of Universities and Polytechnic Schools (CONUEP). These data are not yet available by college or department but the share of agricultural students can be inferred from earlier data. Enrollment in the 30 agricultural degree programs in 1983-1984 was 4,500 and had been growing at about 15 percent per year (Joint Subcommittee p. 55). At that rate, agricultural students would comprise about 4 percent of all university students in 1988. There were 261 graduates or an average of only 8.7 per faculty during 1983-1984 out of 393 egresados (Joint Subcommittee p. 55). The number of graduates may have increased slightly since then but still is very small relative to the number of faculties and the importance of the agricultural sector.

Higher education in agriculture suffers from many of the same problems as technical training in the secondary schools. In 1984 the faculties were comprised mainly of part-time teachers, only 20 percent worked full-time and another 12 percent half-time. Salaries were relatively low and most professors had other employment. The majority of teachers had terminal degrees from Ecuadorian universities with 47 percent being *Ingenieros Agrónomos* and 21 percent veterinarians. Only 18 percent had Master's degrees and only a few had their Ph.D. (Joint Subcommittee pp. 55-56). Consequently, there is substantial inbreeding among the faculties of Ecuador's agricultural universities, with resultant stagnation of knowledge and inherent resistance to new ideas and concepts. The situation has probably worsened since 1984 although more recent data are not available.

Ecuador's agricultural universities are mainly teaching institutions with little involvement in research. The limited research that is done is mainly through thesis work, with some guidance from the major professor.[7] The quality of thesis research varies widely depending on funding support and related guidance from outside entities such as the National Institute of Agricultural Research (INIAP) and foreign technical assistance programs. Library and other research facilities are deficient and linkages to the international network of agricultural science are extremely limited. Resource constraints and poorly trained faculty result in little laboratory or field work. Classroom lectures dominate student-teacher contact and most of the largely urban-raised students graduate with little or no practical experience in agriculture.

While the general assessment is pessimistic, some universities have become more involved in research over the last few years, through research contracts with INIAP, the Foundation for Agricultural Development (FUNDAGRO) and others (Venezian and Moncada pp. 44-45). These institutions are beginning to become a more integral part of the agricultural science network in Ecuador, although their contributions are small.

As a result of the in-bred faculties and very limited research experience most agricultural graduates have little appreciation or understanding of research methods or the scientific process. Consequently, graduates have little to offer to REE institutions without additional training and experience. Most graduates of the agricultural universities find employment in public sector agencies in agriculture, usually in a major urban center, where they live and spend most of their work-time in administrative and bureaucratic functions.

Thus, there is an extremely limited number of university graduates in agriculture and the quality of their training is relatively poor. Universities are not developing the requisite human capital needed to move quickly from a resource-based to a science-based agriculture. Resources for higher education are spread too thin. A more focused effort is needed with substantial upgrading of a few key faculties. Careful attention needs to be given to hiring young, well-trained faculty at the M.Sc. and Ph.D. levels in order to introduce hybrid vigor and break the cycle of inbreeding which assures mediocrity. The higher education system needs to be linked into the international science network for agriculture and more completely integrated into the national REE system, especially in research.

Agricultural Research

Ecuador's agricultural research system has been the subject of many detailed analyses over the last decade (Venezian and Moncada; ISNAR and IICA; Whitaker and Alzamora; USAID; IICA and MAG; Joint Subcommittee; Posada T.; Dow and Solíz; and MAG and USAID). While most of the studies focused broadly on the science base for agriculture, including education and extension, they emphasized research and the role of INIAP. Most studies blurred the distinction between the science base and the research system as one component of the science base; the term "research system" was used synonymously with "science base" or with "REE system."

The conclusions of these studies are quite uniform and consistent. The research system was found to be underfunded, overextended and understaffed, with too few senior scientists and well-trained technicians and with similar constraints in education and extension. The research, education and extension functions operated with little coordination and did not constitute a systematic science base for agriculture. While the above studies are the main sources for most of the conclusions which follow, additional data are provided and analyses made. The research system is described only in general, given the excellent studies that are available.

The Research System

Ecuador's agricultural research system is dominated by INIAP, with very limited involvement of universities and other agencies. It was approved as an autonomous institute in 1959 and began to function in 1961. It lost its autonomy in 1973 when it became an adjunct agency of the Ministry of Agriculture (MAG) during a reorganization. INIAP still has budget and administrative autonomy but the Minister appoints INIAP's Director and serves as president of its Administrative Council (see Chapter 11). It also is subordinate to the policies and strategies of MAG. It has undergone three major reorganizations during the last 10 years.

INIAP has the usual array of executive, advisory and support services which have grown so rapidly that they now comprise most of the staff and offices (ISNAR and IICA pp. 16-25). At the operational level is an office for agricultural research, divided into two directorates, one for the Costa and a second for the Sierra and Oriente. Each regional directorate is further divided into experiment stations and farms.

INIAP has seven experiment stations and nine experimental farms located in the principal agro-ecologic zones of the country (INIAP). The major share of research is carried out in four experiment stations: Santa Catalina, Pichilingue, Boliche and Portoviejo. The experiment stations are organized by programs focused on crops and livestock and by departments focused on disciplines. The programs of each station vary and emphasize the most important crops and livestock in the area where the station is located. The departments are more standardized among stations and include Plant Science, Entomology, Weeds, Soils and Fertilizers, Seed Production and Laboratories. There are substantial differences in departments among stations in terms of their size and quality. The research programs are coordinated closely with production research programs (*Programas de Investigación en Producción--PIPs*) which are carried out on cooperating farms and provide a feedback system from farmers to researchers as well as involving researchers more directly in outreach activities.

Despite the serious problems and constraints discussed below, INIAP has been a relatively productive institution. Through 1988 it generated 105 improved varieties of wheat, barley, oats, rice, potatoes, soft corn, sorghum, hard corn, soybeans, african oil palm, rice, cotton, beans, lentils, cacao, coffee, peanuts, pasture grasses and castor beans (IICA and MAG p. 39). The selection of these improved varieties and multiplication of basic and certified seeds by INIAP is an important basis for increases in production through increased yields of both Sierra and Costa crops during the last two decades (see Chapter 6). INIAP also has developed improved cultural practices for both crops and livestock which have contributed to increased productivity. These research results were reported to farmers through more than 500 seminars and 300 field days and 1,000,000 copies of diverse bulletins and other publications. In 1988 INIAP researchers carried out 1,487 experiments (*ensayos*) in 71 products, an average of 10 per researcher (ISNAR and IICA pp. 21-23).

One reason for its modest successes is its program of identifying and training university students for its research staff. INIAP selects students in their last year from various university faculties and provides them with scholarships as part of the Año Técnico Rural program. The students work at INIAP experiment stations where they learn basic research skills and do their thesis as part of an INIAP research project, under close supervision and guidance of INIAP scientists. The numbers of students trained under this program have ranged from 15-40 per year, depending on the number of positions assigned by MAG (ISNAR and IICA p. 37). INIAP hires the most capable of these graduates into its research staff. In essence, INIAP provides the closest thing there is to post-graduate training in agriculture science in Ecuador. It also has had a fairly good program of advanced training for its staff in various degree and nondegree programs abroad. Unfortunately, INIAP has had major difficulty in retaining its scientists, because of relatively low salaries in the civil service.

Low Levels of Investment in Research

Investments in research declined steadily in real terms at 7.3 percent per year between 1975-1988 and fell to the lowest level in 1988 since 1968 (Figure 12.2). Research expenditures as a share of agricultural GDP also declined steadily after 1975 and were only .17 percent of GDP in 1988 compared to a high of .85 percent in 1975. The decrease was especially rapid after 1985 with real research expenditures (in 1975 prices) averaging only S/.67.2 million during 1985-1988, compared to S/.109.1 million during 1979-1984 and S/.135.4 million during 1973-1978. The rapid erosion of investments in research during 1975-1988 stand in sharp contrast to INIAP's first 14 years. The real level of funding increased in almost every year between 1961-1974 at an annual average rate of 17.4 percent. During the same period research expenditures as a share of GDP also increased steadily to the all-time-high in 1975.

The pattern of rapid decreases in investments in INIAP research during 1975-1988 after substantial growth in the earlier period is exactly the opposite of the experience of most of the developing world. Preliminary data for 52 developing countries showed an average investment in agricultural research of .94 percent of GDP during 1980-1985, up from .69 percent during 1970-1979 (ISNAR and IICA p. 47). Not only did Ecuador reduce investments in research while the rest of the developing world was increasing its investments but it spent substantially less than the average, at only

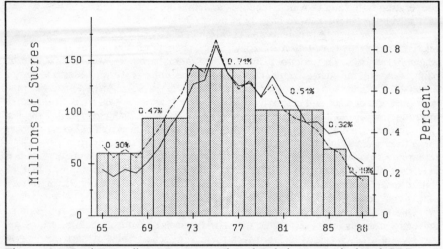

Figure 12.2 Real Expenditures on Research and Relation to Agricultural GDP,
            1965-1988
Source: Whitaker, Colyer and Alzamora Appendix Table 12.3.

.47 percent of agricultural GDP during 1980-1985.

The 1988 level also is much lower than the standard recommended by ISNAR and the World Bank of between 1 and 2 percent of GDP (ISNAR and IICA p.45). For Ecuador to catch up from its 1988 level of .17 percent (S/.865 million in current prices) to the average of .94 percent achieved by the 52 developing countries during 1980-1985 would require an INIAP budget of S/.4,784 million, nearly six times greater than in 1988. This is an increase of roughly US$9.0 million on a base of US$2.0 million (at the 1988 average free market exchange rate of S/.436/US$1). Achieving the mid-range recommended by ISNAR and the World Bank of 1.5 percent of GDP will require nearly a nine-fold increase in INIAP's budget or US$15.5 million more.

Lack of Political Will

A recent article suggests that low fiscal capacity rather than political will is the reason for low expenditures on agricultural research in most developing countries (ISNAR). It argues that the standard of 2 percent of agricultural GDP for agricultural research may not fairly reflect the priority accorded agricultural research by developing countries. It disaggregates the standard into four components (agricultural research expenditures as a share of public expenditures on agriculture, agricultural expenditures in all public expenditures, public expenditures as a share of GDP, and GDP as a share of agricultural GDP). It presents data that show developing countries, on average, are doing almost as well as developed countries in terms of the first two components. These data, along with the assertion that developing countries even borrow to finance agricultural research, are cited as evidence of political will and priority for agricultural research. The problem, according to the article, is the lower fiscal capacity of developing countries (as measured by the share of public expenditures in GDP) and their heavy dependence on agriculture (as measured by GDP as a share of agricultural GDP). The article concludes that the international donor community should help national research systems while countries undertake structural and fiscal reforms.

The argument is not convincing. Political will is measured by how a country chooses to allocate its scarce public funds year after year, rather than the share of GDP expended on the public sector relative to more developed countries. All countries along the development spectrum face a public budget constraint so that priorities (political will) are directly reflected in the way a country chooses to collect and expend public funds. The reality is that most developing countries have engaged in profligate public spending for subsidized industrial sectors, bloated public bureaucracies, uneconomic irrigation works, modern arms and militaries and similar public goods. Concomitantly, the public treasury is used to provide extensive subsidies which are captured mainly by various interest groups constituting the political power base. Most developing countries have followed policies for several decades that have discriminated against agriculture and rural people while subsidizing industry and urban people, who largely control political power (Krueger, Schiff and Valdés). They have depreciated the role of science and human capital in agricultural development which have largely been accorded low priority relative to other investments and expenditures. These have been and continue to be the priorities and political will of many developing countries. Thus, the problem of low investments in agricultural research is not low fiscal capacity per se but lack of political will or priority given the fiscal constraint.

Evidence from Ecuador suggests that there is little political will or priority for agricultural research even based on the disaggregated measures suggested in the ISNAR article. Ecuador spent only 6.6 percent of its public sector budget for agriculture on research compared to 10-11 percent on average for both developed, and developing countries. And it spent only 3 percent of its total budget on agriculture relative to 9-10 percent on average in other developing countries. The conclusion is clear: agriculture is very low priority in the public sector and research is relatively low priority within agriculture. The Ecuadorian government has opted instead to wastefully spend its scarce resources on a variety of other higher-priority but relatively unproductive investments and subsidies (see Chapter 2).

Expending 1 to 2 percent of agricultural GDP on agricultural research is the necessary investment range for building a viable science base for agriculture on the basis of experience in developed and developing countries; as the ISNAR article indicates 2 percent has become the accepted target. Investments in the science base are fundamental to overall economic growth and development. They are one of the two principal foundations for faster economic growth and greater fiscal capacity, rather than a byproduct of them as the ISNAR article implies.[8]

An annual INIAP budget of US$17.5 million is necessary to reach the 1.5 percent target. This could be generated with an endowment of roughly US$175 million at 10 percent yield. While this may appear relatively large, it is only about one-tenth of the amount already committed to new irrigation infrastructure and can be expected to yield much higher social returns. A reallocation of US$175 million to endow Ecuador's agricultural research capacity would greatly increase the returns on the balance of relatively unproductive irrigation investments and significantly enhance international competitiveness and economic growth.

The donor community should continue to help strengthen national science bases for agriculture and on a longer-term basis. But it does not follow that they should do so while governments continue with ineffective, outmoded macroeconomic policies, incur fiscal deficits to sustain large recurring subsidies and make other unproductive investments. Donor support should be conditioned on clear evidence of increased funding and priority for agricultural science from host governments, along with more responsible fiscal policy.

Too-Few Senior Agricultural Scientists

Ecuador has significantly underinvested in senior agricultural scientists (ISNAR and IICA pp. 39-43; Venezian and Moncada pp. 29-30). The number of senior scientists with post-graduate degrees in INIAP is inadequate to produce the level of new technical knowledge needed for rapid, sustained increases in agricultural productivity. The research system had only one Ph.D. and 49 M.Sc. crop scientists on its roster in 1989. It also had 170 other more junior scientists at the undergraduate level, Agrónomos and equivalent (Table 12.5). Several especially deficient areas include natural resources, animal sciences, agricultural economics and rural sociology. Moreover, the ratio of research assistants to all researchers is about .25 compared to a norm of 1.0, so that researchers do not have adequate support (ISNAR and IICA p. 40). Despite these deficiencies, INIAP has contributed to the modest increases in yields noted above, primarily because of its training program for new staff. A freeze on hiring in effect since 1988 has drastically reduced recruitment of promising young researchers.

The "Brain Drain" and Inadequate Salaries

Attracting and maintaining a minimum critical mass of agricultural scientists has been a continuing problem for INIAP and appears to have worsened during the late-1980s (ISNAR and IICA p. 38-39). INIAP lost four out of five Ph.D.s and 18 of 67 M.Sc.s between 1986 and 1989, or one-third of its senior scientists in a three year period (Table 12.5). While numbers of scientists increased gradually during the 1970s and remained relatively constant until 1986, INIAP has been plagued with constant turnover of senior scientists. The principal constraint to attracting and retaining agricultural scientists is the relatively low salaries offered in the civil service system to which INIAP belongs. Salary differentials are especially great for agricultural scientists with postgraduate training and for experienced, proven undergraduates with professional diplomas. The result has been a continuing "brain drain" from INIAP. Ecuador's private sector has attracted the majority of experienced undergraduates and some M.Sc.s who have left the system in the last few years; senior scientists usually have found employment with international agencies in Ecuador or have gone to other countries. While these scientists may continue, in some cases, to make a contribution to agriculture, most are lost to the science base. Given the increasing internationalization of Ecuador's economy, the salary differential likely will widen without remedial action.

Limited International Linkages

A large number of formal agreements with various entities in the international network of agricultural science exist but these have not been institutionalized and the actual linkages are very tenuous and weak. As a result, Ecuador's science base for agriculture tends to work in isolation compared to many other national systems (Posada T.; Joint Subcommittee). There is ample evidence that national research

Table 12.5 Research Staff in INIAP, 1974-1989

Years	Ph.D.	M.Sc.	B.Sc.[a]	Total
1974	5	38	114	157
1975	5	38	115	158
1976	5	38	117	160
1977	5	39	134	178
1978	5	36	147	188
1979	6	51	119	176
1980	4	49	147	200
1981	5	54	117	176
1982	5	55	117	177
1983	5	28	169	202
1984	5	67	163	235
1985	4	67	162	233
1986	5	67	153	225
1987	4	67	160	231
1988	3	58	153	214
1989	1	49	170	220

Source: INIAP, Personnel Office.

[a]Ingeniero Agrónomo and equivalent degrees in other areas, which are roughly the same as a B.Sc. in the U.S. system.

systems substantially increase their productivity as they become fully articulated into other national systems, international and regional research centers and foreign agricultural universities (Hayami and Ruttan; Arndt, Dalrymple and Ruttan). Such linkages eliminate duplication of effort and save scarce resources as the national science base exploits research results from the international agricultural science network. Such results from one country may have the potential of conferring large benefits in other countries but must be accessed and then adapted by the national research system to fit different agroclimatic and ecologic conditions in the new location. The principal constraints to improved and sustained linkages are not enough senior scientists and limited financial resources (Posada T. pp. 28, 31). Ecuador's national science base must improve its capacity to access research results from the international science system, adapt them to the unique socioeconomic, agroclimatic and ecologic conditions of Ecuador and generate requisite new knowledge, if growth in agricultural productivity is to be maximized.

Lack of Focus and Priorities

The science base has diluted its effort and taken on more than it can be expected to do given the mix and size of its staff and its financial resources. For example, research is organized into nine research support programs which interact with eighteen crop and livestock commodity programs and four production systems programs. Several professionals must handle multiple product programs simultaneously and even in varietal improvement, cases have existed of a single researcher attempting to handle more than one crop (Posada T.). The problem has become more difficult with the rapid loss of senior scientists since 1986, as inexperienced junior scientists have had to fill positions for which they are not prepared.

Research programs are spread across a wide variety of crops and livestock but almost exclusively in production activities. Post-harvest handling and storage, processing, marketing and consumption are largely ignored in the design of research and extension programs. The extremely important set of natural resources issues affecting agriculture are not addressed by INIAP at all. They are dealt with on a sporadic and ad hoc basis by private foundations such as *Fundación Natura*, MAG's National Forestry Directorate and in a few university faculties of biology.

Research tends to be confined to research stations and demonstration farms, especially since the PIP program has been reduced because of budget constraints. Results tend to remain "bottled up" on the stations and to be less relevant to farmers and especially to other entrepreneurs in the food system. Ecuador's research system needs to focus on fewer crops and livestock, cover priority problems over the entire range of the food system, strengthen the PIP research effort of on-farm trials and feedback from farmers and more fully integrate and include natural resource, economic and social concerns into research design and recommendations. A recent study by Espinoza and Norton is being utilized by INIAP as a more objective basis for setting research priorities in production agriculture.

Discontinuity of Effort and Short Term Focus

Agricultural research suffers from discontinuity of policies, personnel and leadership. For example, there have been six Directors General of INIAP since 1981. Each new administration of INIAP has resulted in changes in the emphasis, organization, key personnel and allocation of funds (Posada T.). Even though INIAP is an autonomous agency, INIAP's Director must meet political as well as technical criteria and the agency thus has become subject to short-term political pressures. The result is a relatively short-term horizon and a tendency toward centralized planning and management of research, with changes in priorities as the government changes. Agricultural research, however, requires a longer gestation period than the four-year term of any administration. Because research results tend also to be location specific even within a country, a decentralized system is more efficient (Hayami and Ruttan Chapter 12). In South American countries the trend is toward autonomous, decentralized systems, such as Brazil's public research corporation, EMBRAPA.

Technology Transfer

The studies of Ecuador's research system generally have reviewed the status of extension and technology transfer services but in less detail than for research (see especially Venezian and Moncada; ISNAR and IICA; Joint Subcommittee; and MAG and USAID). This is likely due to the reality that extension efforts are much more disparate, with no dominant institution carrying out the extension function, similar to INIAP in the research arena. In fact, Ecuador does not have an national agricultural extension system, per se. There are a large number of public and private sector agencies at the national, regional and local levels that separately and independently provide technology transfer services to a variety of target groups. There is practically no coordination among them. Also, linkages between extension entities and the research system are weak and very tenuous. Consequently, there is no systematic diffusion of improved technologies to Ecuador's farmers, which constitutes another major deficiency in the science base.

Brief History

A significant effort was mounted in the early 1950s to develop an extension service focused on the education of farm families. Prior efforts by the government to assist farmers, dating from 1901, had focused on provision of technical services. The Division of Agricultural Extension was established in 1952 under a bilateral agreement between Ecuador and the U.S, with assistance from the Interamerican Cooperative Agricultural Service (SCIA). In 1954, the Agricultural Extension Service was organized under the auspices of the Ministry of Development and SCIA. The Service was based on the philosophy of farmer education rather than provision of technical services. Extension offices were established throughout the country with home economics and youth (4-F) programs. Extension efforts were focused on increasing productivity and programs were established for bananas, rice, coffee, cocoa, wheat and sheep, among others.

With the establishment of the Alliance for Progress in 1961, U.S. support for SCIA ended and the Agricultural Extension Service became part of the Ministry of Development. In 1964 the Ministry of Development was separated into the Ministry of Industry and MAG, with the Agricultural Extension Service belonging to MAG. In 1968 MAG concentrated all its extension-related programs into the General Board of Agriculture and Livestock Extension. In 1970 MAG, along with its agricultural extension program was recombined with the Ministry of Industry into the Ministry of Production. Then in 1973 agriculture and industry again were separated and reorganized as separate ministries.

The 1973 reorganization had profound impacts on the nature and philosophy of agricultural extension. The Ecuadorian Andean Mission sponsored by the United Nations, which was concerned with rural development, was joined with the agricultural extension program to become the Office of Rural Development in MAG. In this new model of extension, the focus was on technical assistance to groups of small farmers organized in communes, associations or cooperatives and on provision of credit, inputs and other technical services via these organizations.

Current Extension Services

In 1985 the structure of MAG was again modified, with Regional Subsecretariats established for the Costa and the Sierra (see Chapter 11). The primary purpose of the regional subsecretariats was to provide technical assistance to farmers and to improve agricultural productivity in each of the principal regions. Each Regional Subsecretariat was organized into Provincial and Technical Directorates and five National Crop Programs in the Costa Subsecretariat (bananas, coffee, cocoa, rice, corn and soybeans, and cotton and oil crops). Each Provincial Directorate was further divided into Agricultural Service Agencies (ASAs) located in each County (*Cantón*). The Regional Subsecretariats carry out their extension programs via the ASAs.

MAG also has National Programs for Crops, Livestock, Rural Development, Mechanization and Animal Health, plus the Campesino Training Institute and the Regionalization Program. These National Programs directly provide technology transfer services through both producer organizations and the ASAs. Concomitantly, many of the technical personnel from these National Programs are assigned to the Regional Subsecretariats to assist in carrying out their programs of technical assistance.

Other national and regional public agencies, most administratively adjunct to MAG, also are engaged in a wide variety of extension and outreach activities. National level agencies include the Ecuadorian Institute of Water Resources (INERHI), the National Seed Company (EMSEMILLAS), the National Fertilizer Company (FERTISA), the Ecuadorian Institute of Agrarian Reform and Colonization (IERAC), the Subsecretariat of Integrated Rural Development (SEDRI) of the Ministry of Social Welfare and the Fund for Marginal Rural Development (FODERUMA) of the Central Bank. Important regional agencies that carry out technology transfer activities include the Study Commission for the Development of the Guayas River Basin (CEDEGE), the Regional Program for the Development of Southern Ecuador (PREDESUR), the Center for the Rehabilitation of Manabí (CRM) and the Center for the Economic Recovery of Azuay, Cañar and Morona-Santiago (CREA). The magnitude and range of services varies from institution to institution but can be relatively large.

Many other private organizations both at the producer and processor level and among philanthropic and charitable organizations are involved in their own technology transfer efforts and also serve as mechanisms for public sector programs.[9] Principal among these are four regional Chambers of Agriculture (*Camaras de Agricultura*) which are comprised of representatives from Agricultural Centers (*Centros Agrícolas*) in each County.

No System of Agricultural Extension[10]

There is no agricultural extension system in Ecuador but rather a large number of public and private sector entities that engage in technology transfer activities on an ad hoc basis with little or no coordination. As a result, efforts to diffuse improved technologies are inadequate and relatively ineffective. Extension programs are designed and administered independently with no common criteria or sense of priorities in the allocation of resources. Technology transfer programs tend to be disparate and scattered, with overlapping programs and substantial duplication of effort. For example, SEDRI and MAG's National Rural Development Program both focus on integrated rural development projects especially in poorer areas of the Sierra and both rely on support from other MAG agencies such as INERHI, IERAC and INIAP. The commodity approach of MAG leads to specialization at the extension agent level, with the possibility of different agents working with the same farmer. Also INERHI duplicates many services provided by MAG; e.g., the machinery pool belonging to INERHI's Pisque irrigation project is only a few kilometers from that of MAG's National Mechanization Program (PRONAMEC). Many similar examples could be cited. The public sector could play a much more positive role in coordinating and rationalizing public and private efforts into a national extension system. It is constrained by especially serious deficiencies in the organization of pubic extension programs and in its capacity to conceptualize, plan, manage and evaluate a national extension program as one element of a science base for agriculture.

Unclear Extension Philosophy

There is no clear approach to technology transfer, which further limits the effectiveness of the various extension efforts. There was a clear philosophy of farmer education in the 1950s when SCIA provided assistance to Ecuador's extension program. This was altered radically in 1973 when the military government opted to focus on organization of small farmers and provision of subsidized inputs. This model has evolved and there is not a clear approach or philosophy of agricultural extension. Each agency has its own objectives, with little sense of a common philosophy or understanding of who comprises the target groups, or methods to be used.

Inadequate Linkages between Extension and Research

The linkages between the research system (INIAP) and the ad hoc extension entities are tenuous. The large number of independent and uncoordinated extension entities places a major burden on the research system and INIAP. Each entity must rely almost exclusively on INIAP for improved technical information. INIAP maintains agreements with a relatively large number of uncoordinated, independent extension agencies, which further stretches its very limited human and financial resources. Consequently, effective communication between the two functions is constrained and limited. The research that is done tends to stay on the experiment stations, for want of an efficient diffusion system and because of INIAP's tendency to limit on-farm and regional research (Posada T. p. 33). One critical constraint is the general absence of well-trained subject matter specialists in the extension agencies. There is little capacity in the extension agencies to interact professionally with INIAP's researchers in interpreting research results or in providing feedback from farmers to the researchers.

Farmers Isolated from the Science Base

There are very limited and tenuous linkages between the majority of Ecuador's farmers and the science base that is supposed to serve them. The problem is especially serious for resource-poor farmers generally. This reflects, to a large extent, the deficiencies in technology transfer noted above. Extension workers usually are the primary and continuing contact with farmers and the linkage between farmers and researchers. To the extent that linkages between the extension and research functions are weak, researchers are less likely to understand and focus on resolving critical production problems. Scientists and technicians in the research system also need to have direct communication and feedback from farmers in order to direct human and financial resources toward the most urgent problems. The reductions in INIAP's PIP program and regional trials because of resource constraints further isolates researchers from the real world of agriculture. Workers in the science base should feel that the farmers are their clients and establish effective channels of communication to assure that valued customers are well served. In return, they should be rewarded when they make substantial contributions to production agriculture. Unfortunately, such an incentive system does not exist because of institutional constraints and distortions in agricultural prices caused by the macroeconomic policy matrix.

Special Efforts to Address Constraints

There are three significant efforts financed by foreign donors which are addressing various of the constraints set forth above, in addition to on-going programs in research, extension and education. Included are the Program for the Development of Agricultural Technology (PROTECA), the Foundation for Agricultural Development (FUNDAGRO) and the Rural Technology Transfer Project (RTTS).[11]

PROTECA

The Inter-American Development Bank (IDB) made a loan of US$46.3 million matched by US$15.4 million (in Sucres) from the government to finance PROTECA (IDB). This program has four components: technology generation via INIAP, technology transfer through MAG's provincial offices and national crop programs, production of improved seeds through EMSEMILLAS and INIAP and strengthening all of the involved institutions. The project has been under implementation since March 1987, with very little progress after nearly three years of effort. The project suffered from changes in leadership with resultant changes in priority areas and crops and much slower implementation than planned. PROTECA is designed to establish a revitalized system of technology generation and transfer by restructuring from within MAG. It is reported that PROTECA priorities are often different from those of INIAP and of MAG which has further constrained and confounded implementation. The project also appears to suffer from a flaw in design. Most of the budget is allocated to physical capital (infrastructure, vehicles, equipment, etc) when human capital clearly is the greatest constraint in the science base. It now appears unlikely that PROTECA will realize its objectives by 1992 when the project ends, without major redefinition and restructuring, probably with IDB intervention. Moreover, it is unlikely that the project can produce the higher yields and productivity necessary for Ecuador to repay the US$46.3 million it borrowed from IDB without such changes.

FUNDAGRO

The U.S. Agency for International Development (USAID) and the government approved the five-year Research, Extension and Education Project in May 1988 to provide US$9.0 million to FUNDAGRO (USAID). One innovative feature of the project is the establishment of a US$2.0 million endowment for FUNDAGRO which provides for its continuation after grant funds are expended. The purpose of the project is to develop FUNDAGRO's capacity to serve as a catalyst for improving, strengthening and integrating diverse research, education and extension efforts. The project focuses on strengthening existing public and private efforts to develop and deliver improved technologies especially to farmers with small and medium farms.

FUNDAGRO has been relatively successful at assembling a competent staff, organizing itself and attracting outside grants from the Kellogg Foundation, the International Center for Development Research of Canada (ICDR) and the Andean Development Corporation (CAF). It has funded research and extension programs in a few selected commodities (coffee, dairy, cassava and potatoes) with INIAP and other agencies. It has entered into agreements with several important public and private Ecuadorian foreign agencies involved in agricultural science, including INIAP. It also has supported strengthening of several agricultural technical schools and university faculties and has provided scholarships for the Año Técnico Rural program.

An important and innovative feature of FUNDAGRO's programs is its "Research-Extension Linkage Units" (RELU's). Each of its programs has such a unit which seeks to strengthen ties between farmers and researchers by developing a cadre of extension specialists. Its programs link researchers, extension workers and farmers into an integrated, science-based system focused on releasing the constraints farmers face. FUNDAGRO's programs also link the national science base into the international science network serving agriculture, with direct support from international science institutions such as the Interamerican Center for Tropical Agriculture (CIAT) and the International Potato Center (CIP).

One fundamental issue is FUNDAGRO's capability of achieving its primary objective as a catalyst for the science base in the face of INIAP's debilitated state and small and decreasing public investments for agricultural research. FUNDAGRO clearly can help exploit improved technical knowledge from the international science network and the small amount that is produced in Ecuador's universities for a few years. But FUNDAGRO's longer-term success depends on a viable INIAP.

RTTS

USAID and the government also have financed the RTTS project, at a level of US$9.8 million, plus significant levels of local currency. The project helps farmers' associations to directly access new technologies and links them to the international science network and to the national science base, with technical assistance and training from two U.S. universities. The private associations serve as mechanisms for accessing and adapting new technologies and for extending them to their members and to other farmers, with emphasis on reaching groups of smaller farmers, such as cooperatives. There are four subprojects: Sierra dairy, sheep, short-cycle crops, and dual-purpose cattle. The project terminates in August 1990.

Conclusions

Ecuador still relies heavily on its natural resources as the basis for its agricultural growth and is struggling to make the transition to a science-based agriculture. One pervasive problem is the scarcity of human capital and the grossly inadequate and underfunded science base.

Resolution of the constraints and establishment of a viable science base will require major changes in policies and priorities. The most fundamental need is to substantially increase investments in research and senior scientists. Funding for research must be increased by almost nine times in order to reach 1.5 percent of agricultural GDP, the mid-point of the range recommended by ISNAR and the World Bank (ISNAR and IICA p. 45). Concomitantly, the institutional constraints to paying competitive salaries in INIAP and throughout the REE system must be removed to attract and retain a critical mass of senior scientists.

Two important, complementary changes are required. First, the hodge-podge of institutions now involved in technology transfer must be integrated into a streamlined, more efficient extension system with a common philosophy and mechanisms for coordination and development of a cadre of extension specialists. Second, the technical and higher education system must be focused and strengthened, with resources concentrated on fewer technical high schools and university faculties. Special funding should be provided to strengthen the research capability of key agricultural universities and to integrate their faculties into the national research system.

Macroeconomic policies which discriminate against agriculture need to be changed to provide greater incentives for modernizing the sector (Chapter 2). Growth in agricultural productivity is seriously constrained when macroeconomic policies discriminate against agriculture because agricultural profitability and incentives are reduced (Timmer, Falcon and Pearson). Achievement of short-run social objectives through discriminatory macroeconomic policies is inherently antagonistic to a dynamic food policy which attempts to increase rural productivity and incomes while simultaneously reducing urban hunger.

This conundrum is aggravated by the reality of an increasingly interdependent world economy and powerful economic forces that induce painful adjustments in any country whose macroeconomic policies become distorted. Analysts of food policy for the government need to carefully analyze and define the reductions in agricultural productivity caused by various scenarios of food consumption and other subsidies. These trade-offs must be taken into account in the design and implementation of macroeconomic policies if rapid increases in agricultural productivity and growth are to be realized.

Establishing a viable science base for agriculture and complementary macroeconomic policies is critical to more rapid and sustained growth and economic development in Ecuador. A revitalized science base, founded on a strong, productive research system, is the principal mechanism for releasing the constraints to growth imposed by limited supplies of agricultural land and related natural resources. Failure to invest in the REE system and make the transition from a natural-resource-based to a science-based agriculture will doom Ecuador to a much lower path of overall economic growth than is otherwise possible.

NOTES

1. The Hayami-Ruttan synthesis of agricultural development theories hypothesizes that technical changes are endogenous within the agricultural sector and are induced by market forces. See Chapter 1 for a more detailed description of the Hayami-Ruttan induced innovation model and how market forces influence various public and private agents to work independently on improved technologies which can substitute for scarce land or labor.

2. The desertion rate for the sixth grade for rural and urban primary schools can not be clearly determined by comparing 6th and 7th grade enrollment. This is because many rural children attend secondary schools in urban areas after completing the 6th grade, due to lack of rural secondary schools. Comparing enrollments for sixth grade with those for the first year of secondary school (7th grade) would overestimate the desertion rate of rural children and underestimate urban desertion rates.

3. Drop-out rates by sex also were analyzed but there was practically no difference either in rural or urban areas or by grades. It appears that the forces that cause children to leave primary school do not impact the sexes differentially.

4. See Joint Ecuadorian/North Carolina State University Subcommittee, referred to hereafter as the Joint Subcommittee (pp. 50-57) for a more detailed analysis and history of secondary and university education for agriculture in Ecuador.

5. Unpublished data obtained from MEC/Division of Statistics

6. These fifteen universities, plus another six universities also offer four-year technical degrees in 21 majors in the same general areas as the professional degrees.

7. Some professors accept consulting assignments or other employment that may involve research activities; these are usually divorced completely from their academic activities.

8. The second is an outward-oriented, sector-neutral set of macroeconomic and development policies, and abolition of privilege and subsidies through structural reform (see Chapter 2).

9. See Joint Subcommittee (pp. 41-46) and ISNAR and IICA (pp. 77-79) for more detail about private institutions involved in technology transfer in Ecuador.

10. Extension efforts suffer from the same constraints that affect research, especially low salaries, inappropriate mix of scientists and lack of focus. These constraints are not discussed separately for extension.

11. See Chapter 11 for a more complete list and discussion of other foreign-donor projects which address constraints in Ecuador's agricultural science base.

REFERENCES

Arndt, Thomas M., Dana G. Dalrymple and Vernon W. Ruttan. 1977. *Resource Allocation and Productivity in National and International Agricultural Research*. Minneapolis: University of Minnesota Press.

IDB (Inter-American Development Bank). 1986. "Informe de Proyecto PROTECA." Quito: Ministry of Agriculture, August.

CONUEP (National Council of Universities and Polytechnic Schools). 1989. *Guía Académica de las Universidades y Escuelas Politécnicas*. Quito: CONUEP.

Dow, Kamal and Rómulo Soliz. 1984. "Generation and Transfer of Technology." Quito: University of Florida, August (unpublished paper).

Espinoza, Patricio and George Norton. 1989. "Research Priorities in Ecuador." Quito: INIAP and FUNDAGRO.

Evenson, Robert E., P.E. Waggoner and V.W. Ruttan. 1979. "Economic Benefits to Research: An Example from Agriculture." *Science* 205:Sept. 14:1101-1107.

Hayami, Yujiro, and Vernon W. Ruttan. 1985. *Agricultural Development: An International Perspective*. Second Edition. Baltimore: The Johns Hopkins University Press.

IICA and MAG (Interamerican Institute for Agricultural Cooperation and the Ministry of Agriculture). 1988. *I Seminario Nacional Sobre Transferencia de Tecnología Agropecuaria en el Ecuador*. Edited by B. Ramakrishna and A. Cisneros. Quito: IICA, February.

INIAP (National Institute of Agricultural Research). 1989. *INIAP: 30 Años de Investigación*. Quito: INIAP.

ISNAR (International Service for National Agricultural Research). 1990. "Why Are Expenditures on Agricultural Research so Small?" *ISNAR Newsletter* 12:January:2.

ISNAR and IICA (International Service for National Agricultural Research and Interamerican Institute for Agricultural Cooperation). 1989. *Reforzamiento del Instituto Nacional de Investigaciones Agropecuarias: Base para un Sistema Nacional de Investigación Agropecuaria*. The Hague: ISNAR, June.

Joint Subcommittee (Joint Ecuadorian/North Carolina State University Subcommittee). 1987. *Reorientación del Sector Agrícola: Una Estrategia para Acelerar la Aplicación de las Ciencias con el Fin de Aumentar la Productividad en la Agricultura Ecuatoriana*. Quito: USAID, February.

Krueger, Anne O., Maurice Schiff and Alberto Valdés. 1988. "Agricultural Incentives in Developing Countries: Measuring the Effect of Sectoral and Economywide Policies." *The World Bank Economic Review* 2:3:255-71.

MAG and USAID (Ministry of Agriculture and U.S. Agency for International Development). 1979. *Baseline Study of Agricultural Research, Education and Extension in Ecuador.* Quito: MAG/USAID, June (Study made under auspices of the Board for International Food and Agricultural Development).

Posada T., Rafael. 1986. *Ecuador and the CGIAR Centers: A Study of their Collaboration in Agricultural Research.* Washington, D.C.: The World Bank, CGIAR Study Paper Number 11.

Scobie, Grant M. 1986. *Partners in Research: The CGIAR in Latin America.* Washington, D.C.: paper presented to the Executive Directors of BID, Feb. 18.

Timmer, C. Peter, W.P. Falcon and S.R. Pearson. 1983. *Food Policy Analysis.* Baltimore: The Johns Hopkins University Press.

USAID (U.S. Agency for International Development). 1988. *Project Paper: Agricultural Research, Extension and Education.* Quito: USAID, May 12 (FUNDAGRO Project).

USDA (United States Department of Agriculture). 1989. *World Agricultural Trends and Indicators.* Washington, D.C.: Economic Research Service, Statistical Bulletin Number 781, June.

Venezian Leigh, Eduardo and Jesus Moncada de la Fuente. 1989. *Ecuador: Propuesta de un Sistema de Investigación y Transferencia de Tecnología Agropecuaria.* Quito: MAG/USAID, September.

Whitaker, Morris D. and Jaime Alzamora. 1988. "Low Productivity in Ecuadorian Agriculture." Quito: USAID, June 14, Assessment of Ecuador's Agricultural Sector, Working Paper 5-88.

Whitaker, Morris D., Dale Colyer and Jaime Alzamora. 1990. *The Role of Agriculture in Ecuador's Economic Development.* Quito: IDEA (Agricultural Policy Institute).

13

MODERNIZING AGRICULTURE

Morris D. Whitaker

Previous chapters analyzed the role of agriculture in Ecuador's economic development in great detail and from a variety of perspectives. The general conclusion that emerges is that agriculture, a key sector of the economy, has been undervalued and depreciated by past policies. Ecuador has not taken full advantage of opportunities for more rapid and equitable economic development inherent in production agriculture and related economic activities. It has continued to rely mainly on an internally oriented development model long after many developing countries opted for more outward-oriented policies. Economic growth has been based largely on import-substitution industrialization with inherent constraints on the rate of progress. Much of the substantial windfall gains from the petroleum boom were expended on a relatively large, unproductive public sector bureaucracy and a variety of other recurring subsidies. They might have been invested more prudently, especially in human capital and a science base for agriculture and natural resources. The consequence has been a stagnant economy for most of the 1980s, with real Gross Domestic Product (GDP) per capita in 1989 at lower levels than at the beginning of the decade.

It is fully within the realm of possibility for Ecuador to attain more rapid rates of economic growth and development and improve the welfare of its people. The stagnation of the past decade and the continual reduction in per capita GDP can be reversed with agriculture being the pivotal sector for rejuvenating the economy. Greater rates of agricultural and economic growth will require changes in macroeconomic and sectoral policies and corresponding reallocations of public expenditures. The general set of policies and programs needed to induce such improvements is relatively well known and accepted by most development economists. It has been successfully adopted by a variety of developing countries around the world, including Chile, Costa Rica, Paraguay and Bolivia in Latin America. These countries have experienced higher rates of growth after policy reform and some Pacific Rim countries have progressed to the status of newly developed countries in two or three decades.

The focus on agriculture is not an argument for agricultural fundamentalism; the recommendations presented in this Chapter will lead to evenhanded development of all the productive sectors. The emphasis on agriculture derives from its major and growing role in the economy. It also is based on opportunities for growth inherent in a large, relatively untapped international market and the production of tradeables in which production agriculture and related economic activities appear to enjoy a comparative advantage. Both internal and external markets can be exploited as bases for more rapid and equitable economic development especially if agricultural productivity is increased. This latter point is very important, because improvements in efficiency, based on scientific advances, are the primary way that countries will develop and maintain comparative advantages in the emerging world economy.

Mobilizing political support for the policies and programs needed in Ecuador for more rapid growth will be difficult but possible with courageous, futuristic leadership. Most of the interest groups that compose the current political coalition will be exposed to greater economic risk and uncertainty in the short term from modifying policies. The necessary policies and programs will reduce and eliminate subsidies and will cause substantial shifts in relative prices. Changing prices will, in turn, induce reallocations of private investment which will result in decapitalization and losses for those whose investments are sunk.

Resistance to requisite policy changes will be tempered by the prospects of much more rapid rates of economic growth. The period of uncertainty and risk will simultaneously provide great opportunities for higher returns from investments in new, more profitable alternatives. More importantly, the proposed policy changes will permit more rapid expansion of the economy with increases in employment, productivity and income. The economic pie can be much larger in five to ten years than would be possible under the old policy regime and more equitably sliced.

This chapter summarizes, integrates and synthesizes the results of the analyses in previous chapters and presents recommendations for modernizing agriculture as the primary basis for more rapid economic growth and development during the 1990s (see Whitaker, Colyer and Alzamora Chapters 13 and 14 for more detail). The following sections present and discuss: the principal findings of the study which expose commonly held myths about the agricultural sector; several factors that have contributed to agricultural development and which collectively can serve as a foundation for building a more productive, robust agricultural sector; recommendations for resolving the principal constraints to more rapid agricultural growth which build upon the existing foundation; an interpretation of the political economy of subsidies which derive from the principal constraints and constitute a second-level pervasive constraint to agricultural growth and economic development; the issue of the sustainability of high-input agriculture; and a perspective on the emerging scenario of agricultural and economic development during the 1990s and early 2000s in an Ecuador without petroleum exports. The book closes with a call for expeditious actions to avert the disruptive effects of forced economic policy changes.

Myths about Agriculture

This section reviews the principal findings of earlier chapters. The convention employed is to contrast commonly held myths or notions about Ecuadorian agriculture with the results of this study.

Macroeconomic Policies and Incentive Structure

Myth: The macroeconomic and development policies of the past have provided special incentives to agriculture and especially to the small-farm sector and rural people. *Reality*: The structure of incentives inherent in macroeconomic and sectoral policies associated with import-substitution industrialization has subsidized industry and urban dwellers and has discriminated against agriculture, especially against the small-farm sector and rural people, for the last three decades. The negative effect of the macroeconomic policy matrix completely swamped the positive effects of sectoral policies and shifted the internal terms of trade against agriculture, in contravention of market forces. Employment growth has been severely constrained by such policies which have most seriously affected unskilled rural and urban people. Total GDP is likely smaller and the distribution of income more unequal than it would have been with more neutral macroeconomic policies.

The Oil Boom and Petroleum

Myth: The oil boom and the petroleum sector have generally been good for the Ecuadorian economy and have provided substantial additional resources for modernizing the agricultural sector. *Reality*: A large share (79 percent) of the proceeds of the oil boom were expended on salaries for a burgeoning public sector bureaucracy which imposed a major, recurring fiscal burden on the economy. Thus, only 21 percent was left for productive investments from direct oil revenues. The oil boom led to a spending spree of unprecedented proportions as the government went into debt for infrastructure in transportation, communications, utilities, education and health care while private investors imported capital equipment, raw materials and consumer durables on credit. Public and private purchases abroad contributed substantially to the large foreign debt which now is so burdensome. The oil boom shielded the economy for at least a decade from having to address the distortions inherent in import-substitution industrialization by providing a source of funds for subsidies to industry, home goods and urban people. When the boom ended in 1981 and foreign credit dried up the economy was nearly bankrupt, with large foreign debts and little investment from oil revenues in increased productive capacity.

Illegal Substances

Myth: Ecuador has very serious problems with illegal drugs similar to those of its Andean neighbors. *Reality*: While drug related problems do exist, they are not nearly as serious in Ecuador as in Bolivia, Colombia and Peru, due to historical circumstances, fortuitous conditions and active programs to combat drug trafficking. The production and use of coca was and is not a practice among the indigenous communities of Ecuador as it has been for centuries in Bolivia and Peru. Ecuador's location, size and conditions place it in a relatively poor competitive position to be a major processor and dealer in drugs vis-à-vis Colombia where first the production of marijuana and then the processing of cocaine resulted in its dominant position in South America in those illegal activities. Recent Ecuadorian governments have had active policies of combating narcotics and the current government is developing a new law to further strengthen its capacity to fight drug trafficking. Ecuador's relatively small size and the limited areas where drugs can be produced and processed make control relatively easy, although there are areas where such activities can and do take place. The country also has been used for money laundering and for the trans-shipment of drugs and drug-processing materials from and to its neighbors, especially Colombia. There is a potential for serious drug problems in Ecuador but to date they have been relatively minor and manageable.

The Importance of Agriculture

Myth: Petroleum and industry are the most important economic sectors. *Reality*: Agriculture is the most important of any of the economic sectors on the basis of a number of indices. It generated more foreign exchange reserves than petroleum during 1886-1988 and will generate almost as much during 1989. While petroleum is a non-renewable resource which will be exhausted by the early 2000s, agriculture can produce indefinitely under an appropriate policy regimen. The sector increased its relative importance in the 1980s after declining in the 1970s and was tied with industry in 1988 as the most important sector at 16.8 percent of GDP, as farmers responded to an improved macroeconomic policy environment. Agriculture employs more of the labor force than any other sector by a large margin, although labor productivity is very low.

Agricultural Growth

Myth: Agriculture has been relatively stagnant during the 1980s, just as it was in the 1970s. *Reality*: Agriculture grew very rapidly in the 1980s compared to its slow growth in the 1970s. Agricultural GDP grew at an average annual rate of 6.2 percent per year in real terms between 1982-1988 and 8.1 percent between 1984-1988, compared to only 2.5 percent during 1973-1981. Agriculture has led economic development in every year since 1984 with the fastest rates of growth of any of the major economic sectors, except for 1988 when it was in second place behind petroleum (which had an abnormally high growth rate as it recovered from a major pipeline rupture). Agriculture responded to incentives inherent in the structural reforms of 1981 and subsequent macroeconomic policy improvements. The emergence of agriculture as the leading economic sector during the 1980s was part of a major reversal in the structure of economic growth relative to that of the petroleum-boom era of 1973-1981. The industrial sector stagnated during 1982-1988 as import-substitution opportunities were exhausted with growth of only .2 percent per year, after increasing at the very rapid annual average rate of 10.2 percent during 1973-1981.

The Public Sector and Agriculture

Myth: Agriculture receives relatively high levels of government support for operation of public agencies serving the sector and for investments in supporting infrastructure. *Reality*: Public expenditures on agricultural programs have always been relatively low and have declined substantially since the peak reached during the oil boom. Agriculture now receives about 3 percent of total public expenditures and only about 5 percent of public investments in capital and infrastructure, compared to highs of 7 and 16 percent during the oil boom and to an average of over 10 percent in other developing countries. The level of real expenditures on public programs for agriculture was nearly 40 percent less during the 1983-1987 than during 1973-1981, while total government expenditures increased substantially. Agriculture not only receives a much smaller share of government expenditures than its importance would suggest but has been relegated to continually lower priority in the allocation of scarce public funds. Favored sectors include education, the military, transportation and communications, and health with 20, 10, 8 and 6 percent, respectively of total public expenditures. During 1983-1987, service on the public debt accounted for over one-fourth of expenditures.

Agricultural Subsidies

Myth: Subsidies to agriculture benefit mainly resource-poor farmers with small holdings. *Reality*: The greatest share of subsidies to agriculture are captured by well-to-do farmers with large holdings. For example, most of the benefits of subsidized credit and price support programs are captured by larger landowners, who usually are organized into formal associations with substantial political leverage. Subsidies on irrigation water are capitalized into land values and the present value of all future subsides are realized upon sale of the land, in direct proportion to the amount of land owned. Several public agencies and businesses provide services to farmers in competition with the private sector, but at lower-than-market prices. The larger, more influential farmers derive most of the benefit from such subsidies. Public enterprises usually operate at a loss, which contributes directly to fiscal deficits and inflation. Inflation, in turn, is a regressive tax which impacts the poor most heavily and who thus bear most of the burden for the subsidies.

Agriculture and Trade

Myth: Food and other agricultural imports exhaust most of the foreign exchange earned from agricultural exports, primarily bananas, coffee, cacao and shrimp. *Reality*: Agriculture has generated a relatively large trade surplus for decades that now is approaching US$1.0 billion per year. Agricultural exports averaged US$1.2 billion during 1986-1987. Imports of processed food, capital equipment and inputs for agriculture, and raw agricultural products for industrial processing (such as wheat, barley, unrefined vegetable oils and wool) were US$309 million for the same period. After paying for these imports there was an agricultural trade surplus that averaged US$857 million annually during 1986 and 1987. This huge trade surplus covers about three-fourths of the rest of industry's very large import requirements.

Food and Agriculture

Myth: Agriculture is unable to feed the population because production for domestic consumption falls short of meeting demand. *Reality*: Ecuadorian agriculture more than meets the country's food needs through a combination of domestic production and trade. Agriculture produces most of Ecuador's food requirements and generated enough foreign exchange during 1984-1987 to import almost four times the amount of processed food and raw agricultural products that were imported, after paying for all inputs and capital equipment used in agriculture. A corollary of this myth is that Ecuador needs to be self-sufficient and to produce all its food domestically, with increased emphasis on Sierra crops. In fact, Ecuador is completely self-reliant (as opposed to self-sufficient) and enjoys a higher standard of living by trading agricultural products than if it were to attempt to produce all its food needs domestically.

Nutrition and Diet

Myth: There is not enough food available to meet the minimum average dietary requirements of the population. *Reality*: Apparent consumption per capita in 1985 was 117 percent of the minimum standard for energy (calories) and 125 percent for protein. Past studies of apparent consumption that found food deficits utilized minimum requirements that were too high for Ecuador. These requirements were based on too-high body weights and too-pessimistic assumptions about the quality of protein in the diet. While average availability exceeds minimum requirements, many do not have economic access to a nutritious diet. However, malnutrition among children, especially ages six months to three years, appears to be as much a function of poor feeding and health care practices, as a lack of food. The diet shifted over the last three decades from a "rural" diet toward an "urban" diet. Consumers substituted bread and noodles (from imported wheat), rice and animal proteins for traditional soft corn, domestic wheat, barley, potatoes and legumes. These changes were caused by subsidies, increased incomes and rapid urbanization. Even rural people tended to consume a more "urban" diet.

The Small-Farm Sector and Subsistence Agriculture

Myth: Farmers with small holdings, who comprise the majority of rural people, are largely engaged in full-time subsistence farming and have little to do with the market economy or urban areas. *Reality*: Most farmers with small holdings sell the majority of their agricultural production commercially and are part-time farmers who earn most of their family income from non-farm and largely urban sources. Subsistence agriculture does not accurately describe very much of Ecuadorian agriculture in the 1990s. The largest share of family income of small farmers in the Sierra came from off-farm sources according to household surveys in the late-1970s. Moreover, significant amounts came from urban employment and other nonagricultural sources. Most of the production of the farm was sold commercially to satisfy increased demand in the large and rapidly growing urban centers. Although more recent data are not available, farm families continue to be closely tied to urban centers where some members of the family work and return to the farm regularly in a commuting process referred to as circulation. Other members of the family carry agricultural and artisan products for sale in urban centers and act as middlemen for other families. The cost of these permanent, continuing flows between small farms and the urban centers is subsidized substantially by low fuel prices.

The Agricultural Frontier

Myth: Ecuador has abundant agricultural land that remains to be exploited. *Reality*: All the good and marginal agricultural land is now in production. Agricultural land use in the Sierra and Costa exceeded prime cropland by 45 percent and the sum of prime and marginal cropland by 2 percent on average during 1980-1985. Land use has expanded since then into ever more marginal areas. Soil erosion is a major and increasingly serious problem, especially in the Sierra. There are extensive virgin lands in the Oriente and Northwest but they are fragile, covered with tropical forests and generally not suitable for sustained agricultural production. The costs of bringing such land into production will be very high, both privately and socially.

Natural Resources

Myth: There are abundant tropical forests, coastal mangrove swamps, fisheries, water and other natural resources that can undergird Ecuador's economic development for decades. *Reality*: While Ecuador is endowed with abundant natural resources, degradation is occurring at increasingly faster rates, with the high likelihood that some of its most important natural resources will be destroyed or depleted within another 10-15 years. Most Ecuadorians act as if these resources are so abundant that they can be used at current rates indefinitely as the principal basis for economic growth. The facts are, however, that agricultural and economic growth already are being constrained by degraded natural resources, with very serious limitations in clear view.

Sources of Growth in Agricultural Production

Myth: Increases in agricultural production during the 1970s and 1980s have been mainly due to increases in land under cultivation. *Reality*: Increases in yields also have been important in explaining changes in crop production. Most of the principal crops of both the Costa and the Sierra experienced moderate to rapid increases in yields during the last two decades. Increased yields in the Sierra generally helped to sustain production by offsetting the effect of decreases in cultivated area. In the Costa, increases in yields generally were associated with concomitant increases in land area for most crops. The Costa appears to have benefitted from sectoral policies which subsidized new import-substitute crops, while the Sierra generally did not receive such subsidies, except for dairy production.

Agricultural Productivity

Myth: Agricultural productivity is about the same in Ecuador as in neighboring countries in Latin America. *Reality*: Productivity in agriculture is relatively low even in comparison with neighboring countries, despite the modest increases in yields noted above. For example, yields for principal cereal crops are from 11 to 47 percent lower than the average for 12 other South American countries. While soybeans, milk and egg yields are modestly higher than the average for South America, they are from 25 to 60 percent lower than the South American countries with the highest yields. Low productivity is highly correlated with insufficient investments in research and extension, and limited human capital which are primary constraints to greater productivity.

Irrigation and Agriculture

Myth: Public irrigation projects are an efficient way to increase agricultural production and productivity and to help resource-poor farmers. *Reality*: Existing irrigation projects are highly subsidized and very inefficient with a large share of the benefits being captured by large landowners. There is substantial evidence that actual economic returns to most public irrigation projects are much lower than projected in feasibility studies and many are probably negative. Principal problems are very low levels of efficiency in the irrigation systems and in on-farm applications of water and relatively low yields due to the general absence of improved technologies and modern factors of production. The state absorbs 96 percent of the combined capital and operating costs of public irrigation projects at an annual cost of US$22.7 million. Economic benefits of these projects are estimated to be only US$8.4 million so that most of the subsidy is wasted. Public irrigation is very expensive; new projects will cost US$2.2 billion and increase the share of irrigation projects to 20 percent of the foreign debt.

Agricultural Credit

Myth: Subsidized interest rates increase investments in agriculture and help small farmers as intended. *Reality*: Savings and investments are reduced by subsidized interest rates and loans are concentrated among influential borrowers who capture most of the subsidies. Interest rates in Ecuador have not only been subsidized for most of the last three decades, they have been negative in real terms much of the time. Public financial intermediaries have been decapitalized as the real value of loan repayments is much less than the value lent, while borrowers have received large windfall gains. There is substantial excess demand for loans at negative real rates of interest and non-market mechanisms have been used to allocate credit principally to larger farmers. Small farmers receive only a small share of subsidized loans because they lack influence and pay higher transactions costs. Thus, subsidized loans for ágriculture generally are substituted for more expensive credit by influential borrowers without increasing investments, or are diverted to other uses including foreign savings. Savers are unwilling to save at negative real interest rates and seek alternatives to hedge against inflation such as investments in real estate or foreign demand and time deposits. The international capital market provides a very viable alternative for many savers which has led to significant capital flight and a very low savings rate in Ecuador.

Agricultural Research

Myth: Improved technologies for agriculture can be imported easily by the private sector and therefore a strong national research capacity is unnecessary. *Reality*: Improved technologies are location-specific depending on soils, rainfall, temperature, pests and diseases among other variables and require a strong national research system. Technologies brought from other countries almost always must be adapted to the new environment. Moreover, research results tend to be public goods so that private investors usually cannot capture benefits from investments in research. Therefore, a strong, publicly supported research capacity is necessary to access, import and adapt new knowledge generated in other countries and to simultaneously develop improved, in situ technologies.

Controlled Prices

Myth: Support prices for producers and maximum prices for consumers for the few basic food items still being controlled are necessary to increase agricultural production and benefit poor consumers. *Reality*: Increased production and productivity have been constrained and most of the benefits of controlled, low prices have been captured by wealthier consumers and intermediaries. Prices at both the producer and consumer levels have generally been below market levels as measured by border prices in Colombia and Peru. Excess demand at the low prices has resulted in non-market allocation of the products. Only the most influential consumers are able to purchase at the official price, usually through group affiliation. Less-influential, poor consumers receive little benefit from controlled prices. These people either face shortages caused by the illegal exports, pay bribes, accept lower quality products, or purchase at much higher prices on the black market. Farmers have less incentive to invest in agriculture and less is produced than would be at the market price. Incentives to modernize the sector also are reduced and improvements in productivity are constrained. The few cases where producer prices have been above market prices have resulted in excess supply, widely fluctuating market prices and large public purchases to support the price that later have had to be sold at a loss.

Gender and Farming

Myth: Most farmers in Ecuador are men who spend full-time in agricultural pursuits. *Reality*: Feminization of farming, especially of small farms in the Sierra and parts of the Costa, accelerated during the late-1970s and early 1980s as males increasingly worked off the farm. While women sometimes also work off the farm the trend has been for them to operate the farm and engage in complementary marketing and artisan activities while the men work for large farmers or in urban areas in construction or low-skill services. Women usually manage the farm jointly with their husbands, are responsible for day-to-day decisions and provide most of the labor. Most such "feminized" farming is commercial and, along with related activities, generates roughly 20-25 percent of family income. It is on the basis of the source of income that such farmers are described as part-time in the discussion of the small-farm sector above. The economic stagnation of the 1980s has resulted in fewer off-farm jobs and may have forced some males back onto farms, although conclusive data are not available.

Poverty

Myth: Poverty is much more prevalent in urban areas where low-skill migrants are forced to eke out a marginal existence in the informal sector than in rural areas where subsistence needs can be more easily met. *Reality*: The incidence of poverty is greater in rural than in urban areas. It is estimated on the basis of data from the late-1970s that about 25 percent of rural and 20 percent of urban people are in a state of critical poverty (not having enough income to provide minimum dietary requirements). Another 20-30 percent of urban dwellers and 50-60 percent of rural people are in a state of relative poverty (enough family income for basic food but not enough for other basic necessities). The GDP per worker in the low-skill services and construction sectors which are located mainly in urban areas is about twice as high as in agriculture. Also, urban people have access to health, education and other social services not widely available to rural people. These facts help to explain why the indices of absolute and relative poverty are higher in rural than urban areas and why rural to urban migration continues at fairly rapid rates.

Population Growth

Myth: Population growth has slowed to the point where it is not a serious impediment to improved standards of living during the next decade. *Reality*: The population still is projected to grow at the high annual average rate of 2.6 percent between 1990 and 2000 even though the rate has declined from the very high 3.3 percent observed between 1962-1974. There will be nearly 3.2 million people added to the population during the next decade, for a total of almost 14.0 million in the year 2000. The high rate of population growth places special demands on agricultural development. Agriculture must grow faster than the relatively high rates of growth in the population if there is to be an increase in availability of food per capita. Since food is the principal wage good for most people, improvements in their well-being will depend largely on very good performance from the agricultural sector given high population growth. Urban population growth is projected to continue at relatively high rates while rural population will grow much more slowly. The rural population is projected to grow absolutely and will add another 275,000 people by 1995 for a total of 5.1 million. These trends are expected to continue throughout the 1990s.

Migration Patterns

Myth: Migration is primarily from rural to urban areas with little other migratory movement. *Reality*: Migration patterns are very complex and census data also reveal large migration from urban areas to other urban areas, from urban to rural areas and among rural areas. For example, there were over 1.0 million people who reported in the 1982 census that their last migratory movement was from urban areas, with 716,000 moving to other urban areas and 355,000 to rural areas. Nevertheless, the result of these complex migration patterns has been relatively large net rural to urban migration (estimated at about 630,00 between 1974 and 1982). Quito and Guayaquil have absorbed the greatest numbers of migrants and are the principal urban centers of Ecuador. Other secondary cities also have absorbed significant numbers of migrants with county seats in the Costa provinces experiencing the most rapid rates of growth.

Labor Markets

Myth: Labor markets largely are segmented and inefficient in Ecuador with large numbers of workers trapped in low-paying jobs because of structural barriers to mobility. *Reality*: Labor markets linking agriculture and the other economic sectors are relatively efficient, moving large numbers of rural people out of agriculture and into higher paying employment in nonagricultural activities, largely in urban areas. While there is evidence of segmentation in urban labor markets, especially in the public sector and parts of the industrial sector, the stagnant economy and lack of new higher-paying jobs appear to be the major barriers to upward mobility for most of the labor force, along with generally low skill levels and limited investments in human capital.

Bases for Agricultural Growth

This section summarizes several key factors contributing to agricultural development since the mid-1960s. These positive factors constitute the foundation for potentially more rapid agricultural growth and modernization. If this potential is to be realized, however, remedial actions must be taken which build on this foundation and simultaneously address the significant obstacles which constrain progress.

More Favorable Macroeconomic Policy Environment

The macroeconomic policy environment became somewhat more hospitable for agriculture in the 1980s, after three decades of discriminating against the sector and tradeable goods generally and heavily subsidizing industry and home goods in an inward-oriented approach to development. The modest improvements began in 1982 when the Hurtado government was forced to impose austerity measures and structural reforms in response to the international debt crisis. The Febres Cordero government implemented an outward-oriented development model intended to address the more fundamental stagnation of the economy. The country also has had to respond to a series of major exogenous and internal events and factors, including the disastrous El Niño weather of 1983, the fall in petroleum prices during 1986, the rupture of the main petroleum pipeline in 1987 and several large budget deficits.

Although the nature of reforms has varied among and within governments and there have been some reversals, the net result through time has been movement toward more outward-oriented macroeconomic and trade policies and a more equal set of incentives across the economic sectors. Devaluation of the exchange rate, elimination of most taxes on agricultural exports, more responsible monetary and fiscal policy, some movement toward market prices and interest rates and some liberalization of trade policies all have combined to improve incentives for agriculture and tradeable goods generally.

Strong Performance of Agriculture

Agriculture has performed very well over the last three decades even with the constrained and reduced incentive structure. The sector grew slightly more rapidly than population on average even during 1965-1981, the height of the import-substitution period. Then growth rates accelerated with improvements in macroeconomic policies after 1982, and agriculture led economic development among the principal sectors for most of the 1980s while the rest of the economy was relatively stagnant. Agriculture also has generated large trade surpluses and clearly has made Ecuador even more self-reliant in providing for its food and fiber needs. This is reflected in the availability of substantially more food per capita than is needed to meet minimum nutritional requirements.

The relatively strong performance of agriculture in the face of limited incentives bodes well for the future, given the relative importance of the sector in Ecuador's economy. The responsiveness of farmers to improved incentives after 1982 is an especially important index when considering alternatives for more rapid economic growth. Full implementation of outward-oriented and sector-neutral macroeconomic policies which remove subsidies to industry and home goods and restore incentives to agriculture and tradeable goods can be expected to generate large increases in agricultural production and productivity and relatively higher rates of economic growth.

Commercialization of Agriculture

The rapid commercialization of agriculture during the 1970s and continuing into the 1980s is another positive basis for future growth of agriculture. Rapid growth of urban areas and huge windfall gains from petroleum exports along with the agrarian reform, induced substantial structural changes in agriculture. Large *haciendas* shifted rapidly to commercial production of underutilized lands as a basis for avoiding expropriation. The concomitant elimination of shareholder (*huasipungeros*) and similar arrangements along with greatly expanded urban markets and associated economic incentives resulted in most smallholders shifting quickly from subsistence to commercial production.

These shifts augur well for the future development of the sector for two closely related reasons. First, farmers across the spectrum have demonstrated that they are willing to mobilize and shift resources in response to changing economic conditions.

Farmers are economic agents and respond quickly to improved incentives. Second, there now is a fairly long and wide base of experience in dealing with changing economic incentives as most farmers have participated in a market economy for a decade or more. This increasingly sophisticated base of market experience is an important foundation for expecting rapid responses to further improvements in the incentive structure. It also is a basis for expecting complementary social investments in human capital and a science base to generate relatively higher rates of return.

Substantial Improvements to the Land

There have been substantial improvements to the land over the last two decades, especially in irrigation infrastructure, which provide a foundation for much more rapid growth. An estimated one of every five hectares of cropland were under irrigation in 1987. Public projects currently under construction will add another 108,000 hectares for a total of one of four hectares under irrigation by the mid-1990s. Public projects under design or serious study would add nearly 300,000 more irrigated hectares if completed and almost 40 percent of cropland would be under irrigation. Other improvements to the land include flood control, drainage, leveling, fencing, removal of rocks and terracing.

These improvements can make land much more productive but most of the potential has not been realized because of failure to make complementary investments in human capital and a science base for agriculture. Investments in irrigation infrastructure have largely been wasted and the small benefits that have been produced are captured by larger farmers through a highly subsidized water tariff. Nevertheless, past investments in irrigation and other improvements to the land provide a solid foundation for expecting high returns to future investments in the science base.

Emergence of a Science Tradition

Increases in yields explain an important share of the changes in production for most of Ecuador's major crops, which indicates that many farmers already have a substantial base of experience in adopting improved technologies. Increases in yields accounted for much of the increases in production (principally Costa crops) or cushioned decreases in production caused by reductions in land area (mainly Sierra crops) since 1965. The National Institute of Agricultural Research (INIAP) has been a key agency in developing and helping to diffuse new technical knowledge although its capacity and hard-earned prestige are waning quickly because of greatly reduced funding. Farmers have been responsive to opportunities to reduce costs of production inherent in improved techniques of production. These realities demonstrate the beginnings of greater dependency on science as an input to agricultural production and the emergence of a science tradition. The importance of technical change in explaining changes in crop production suggests that past investments in research, education and extension, while modest, have been socially profitable.

Two aspects of improvements in yields are especially germane to future growth of the sector. First, even though they have increased, yields still are relatively low compared to the rest of South America so that substantial increases in productivity are possible with existing and largely proven technologies. The practical implication of this is that Ecuador can substantially increase yields at a relatively low cost. Second, the experience of INIAP in generating improved technologies and Ecuadorian farmers in adopting them is an important part of the foundation, along with past improvements to the land, upon which greater investments in the science base can be built.

Good Natural Resource Base

Ecuador has a good endowment of natural resources, which is a partial basis for future agricultural growth. The Sierra and Costa have 3.1 million hectares of prime cropland (22 percent of their total area), 1.3 million hectares of more marginal cropland and 2.5 million hectares of pasture land, with much more limited amounts of good land in the Orient. Ecuador also has abundant surface water resources that are relatively well distributed throughout the country. The minimum flow of rivers just to the Pacific ocean is sufficient to irrigate twice the total land in crops in 1989. The country has adequate rainfall and moderate temperatures although it is affected by recurring periods of drought and excessive rains. Most of the Oriente and much of the Northwest are covered with virgin tropical forests which contain large quantities of commercial hardwoods and other important species. Such forests cover about one-third of Ecuador. The country also has 1,821 square kilometer (km^2) of mangrove swamps and abundant other coastal resources which support a major fishing industry and shrimp farming.

These natural resources have been the principal basis for past agricultural development and are a partial foundation upon which future growth of agriculture can proceed. Two notes of caution are in order. First, the natural resource base, per se, is much less important than human capital and modern, industrial inputs in explaining differences in agricultural productivity among countries. Even more critically, natural resources are being depleted or destroyed at fairly rapid rates. While the natural resource base may serve as a partial foundation for growth of agriculture, Ecuadorians need to be realistic about its limitations. Substantial complementary investments and policy changes must be made to achieve rapid rates of agricultural development and simultaneously conserve natural resources.

Principal Recommendations

This section sets forth the major recommendations for more rapid agricultural growth and general economic development. While the agricultural sector has progressed, especially during the 1980s, it has been restricted from reaching its potential by an interrelated set of major obstacles. These key constraints must be addressed in concert through an integrated policy matrix which builds on past successes if agriculture is to make its potential contribution to economic growth and development.

An Outward-Oriented Macroeconomic Policy Matrix

One of the two most important recommendations of this study concerns the need to move quickly to a sector-neutral, outward-oriented set of macroeconomic policies. The importance attached to this recommendation is based on the fact that biased macroeconomic policies have swamped the effects of positive policies and programs intended to directly help agriculture. If macroeconomic prices continue to reflect government intervention rather than the actual value of products and factors, resources expended to strengthen agriculture will largely be wasted. Four principal changes are needed: (a) eliminate non-tariff barriers to trade and establish a low uniform tariff that can gradually be phased out; (b) reduce and eliminate the public sector deficit by reducing government waste and inefficiency, increasing public prices and improving the tax system; (c) unfetter capital markets and let interest rates be determined in the market place for financial transactions; and (d) establish a single, unified exchange rate for all foreign trade transactions. Such changes will permit agriculture to compete with the rest of the economy on an equal footing for the first time in decades. They will also improve incentives for domestic production or importation of modern industrial inputs that, along with new technical knowledge generated by the science base, can substitute for limited land and other increasingly scarce natural resources.

A Science Base for Agriculture

Establishment of a viable science base for agriculture is of equal importance to shifting to an outward-oriented macroeconomic policy set as the two principal foundations for future growth of the economy. These two major recommendations are synergistic and more rapid, sustained agricultural and economic development is dependent on both being implemented. Establishment of the science base results in the production of new technical knowledge. The outward-oriented macroeconomic policy matrix provides broad-based incentives for investing in agriculture, including the production or importation of modern, industrial inputs which complement and incorporate new technical knowledge. The new technical knowledge and modern, industrial inputs substitute directly for limited land and natural resources and thus release the constraints to growth imposed by the resource endowment.

There are five principal recommendations for strengthening the science base for agriculture: (a) make INIAP autonomous and greatly increase funding so INIAP can assemble a critical mass of senior agricultural scientists; (b) pay competitive salaries for scientists and technicians in extension services, technical schools and universities; (c) consolidate and streamline the disparate extension services of the Ministry of Agriculture and related public sector entities; (d) strengthen selected technical high schools, technical institutes and universities with special emphasis on expanding university research capacity; and (e) integrate research, extension and education programs into a cohesive, national system with viable linkages back to farmers and forward to the international science network.

Greatly Increased Investments in Human Capital

The stock of human capital must be substantially increased in order to modernize agriculture. There is a pervasive shortage of scientists and technicians throughout agriculture and most rural people suffer from inadequate general education. Lack of human capital is the single greatest problem affecting agricultural growth and is treated separately from the science base to emphasize and highlight its importance.

The principal components of the science base--education, research and extension institutions--all suffer from not having enough well-trained, experienced scientists and technicians. Senior scientists, defined as experienced Ph.D.s or those who have attained equivalent capability, are seriously deficient. Ecuador has relied mainly on its undergraduates with some trained to the M.Sc. level to staff its science base, erroneously believing that such training would be adequate for the country's research needs. While some of these become senior scientists in the full sense of the term, most do not.

The main recommendation for attracting and retaining a critical mass of senior scientists--competitive salaries--already has been made above but merits elaboration because of its importance. As a result of low civil service wages, a significant number of the most promising and capable scientists and technicians leave the science base each year for better jobs. The key to releasing the constraints to growth and productivity imposed by increasingly scarce and degraded land and other natural resources is a minimum critical mass of senior scientists and associated junior scientists and technicians in REE institutions. Higher competitive wages are urgently needed as the primary basis for rapidly augmenting the supply of such human capital. The other recommendations--increased budget support; streamlined, stronger institutions; and improved linkages among elements of the science base--are important complements to competitive salaries in inducing scientists and technicians to make their careers in the REE system.

Improvements in primary and secondary rural education and the science base are needed to increase school retention rates and the value of general education to agriculture. More than half of rural children do not finish primary school and only one in ten complete high school. One recommendation made above--to strengthen selected technical schools and universities--addresses the problem of too many such schools resulting in high costs per student. Another problem appears to be the irrelevance of the curriculum to the needs of rural families. A third problem is that the constraints in the science base combine to reduce the value of general education to rural people. Improvements in the curriculum would provide people with improved skills to more easily interpret and adapt improved technologies. A more productive science base that produced a sustained flow of new, more profitable technical knowledge would make education more valuable to rural people by providing them with the literacy skills needed to access the readily available, improved technologies.

This study did not include a detailed analysis of primary and secondary education; hence no formal recommendations for improving the general education curriculum are made. The general evidence suggests, however, that the curriculum for rural primary school children needs to be substantially modified. In this regard, a much more careful evaluation and analysis of primary and secondary education needs to be done.

A Market-Based, Private Agricultural Economy

Another set of recommendations focuses on the establishment of market pricing for agricultural products and a reduced and modified role for the state. These recommendations are complementary to those made above. Market prices for all agricultural products and factors will induce public sector investments in the science base to be focused on highest priority needs of private producers and consumers. Prices that reflect actual supply and demand conditions will provide incentives to farmers to adopt new technologies that release the most serious constraints to growth and to produce the mix and level of products consistent with consumers' wants. An outward-oriented macroeconomic policy matrix will provide much greater incentives to invest in agriculture, directly complement market pricing and allocation of agricultural products and factors, and make public investments in the science base more profitable.

Three recommendations are made for improving the market economy in agriculture: (a) sell, close or substantially reorganize most public businesses and some agencies serving agriculture; (b) eliminate the few remaining price controls on agricultural products at the consumer level and eliminate or modify those at the producer level; and (c) increase government services in grades, standards and market information. These recommendations, if implemented, will allow the economy to function more efficiently and will assure the highest rates of return possible to public investments in improvements to the land and the science base. They also will result in reduced public expenditures and a modified role for government which will contribute to greater agricultural production and productivity.

Better Management and Conservation of Natural Resources

The two most important recommendations for conserving natural resources already have been made. The establishment and strengthening of a science base for agriculture and shifting to an outward-oriented macroeconomic policy matrix together will permit modern, industrial inputs to be substituted directly for limited land and scarce natural resources and reduce pressure on them. These two recommendations mitigate increased demand (from growing population and higher incomes) for using natural resources in agricultural production by providing a substitute set of more productive inputs.

The recommendations made in this section directly complement these two key recommendations. The complementary recommendations focus on creating and improving incentives for private resource conservation. Three recommendations are made: (a) modify tenurial arrangements and provide greater incentives for private conservation of natural resources; (b) improve the science base for natural resources as a way to increase productivity and better management; and (c) consolidate and strengthen management of natural resources. Ecuador, because of its extensive tropical forests with their unique areas of biological diversity, is at the center of international concern about deforestation. Policy prescriptions usually focus on improved management through the establishment of reserves, buffer zones and better policing as the basis for protecting and conserving renewable natural resources and enforcing public property rights. Improved management, by itself, will fail since it does not address the principal causes of resource degradation--increased demand for natural resources as inputs for agricultural production. It clearly is, however, a necessary complement to the other key elements of a policy set to conserve natural resources.

Reliable Agricultural Data and Analytical Capacity

The data base serving agriculture must be substantially improved and updated and analytical capacity enhanced as another fundamental basis for more rapid agricultural development. Government policies and programs will be no better than the data and analyses which undergird them. Private decisions based on erroneous conceptions will tend to reduce production, productivity and profitability relative to those made with more accurate information. Three principal recommendations are suggested: (a) carry out an agricultural census as quickly as feasible; (b) improve data collection and management; and (c) continue to enhance analytical capacity in agricultural economics for policy studies and data development and management.

Slower Population Growth

Ecuador's population is projected to grow rapidly during the 1990s with a burgeoning labor force and increasing pressure on natural resources and social services. Reducing the rate of population growth will amplify the effects of more rapid economic growth, reduce ecologic stress and lead to greater improvements, on average, in individual well-being. Thus, the recommendations made here are interrelated with and directly complement those made above for fomenting agricultural growth and overall economic development. Reducing the rate of population growth is an important objective of the set of policies needed for more rapid and equitable economic development. Two recommendations are proffered: (a) develop a more specific government policy for reducing the rate of population growth; and (b) provide more focused instrumentation of the policy with greater public financial support for private entities engaged in educational programs and family planning services.

The Political Economy of Subsidies

Ecuador's economy can be divided into two basic sets of people; the poor and all others, described as the affluent for want of a better term. The poor are those with too little income to provide basic food, clothing and shelter. Subsidies usually are justified politically to help the poor but, in fact, the affluent often receive most of the benefits. The poor generally wield little political influence while the affluent dominate the political process and government. Subsidies distort and limit economic development and generally leave the poor relatively worse off.

The affluent comprise interlocking sets of special interest groups, each of which benefits from a public subsidy of some kind. Each of these groups tends to politically support the vested interests of all the others with respect to the subsidy, upon the basis of reciprocity. Principal interest groups include public sector employees, industrialists, transport owners, building contractors, larger farmers organized by commodity groups and by region, the military, labor unions in both the public and private sector and affluent urban dwellers who may also belong to one or more of the other groups.

Each of these groups receives one or more kinds of public subsidies via various mechanisms. Public sector employees and the military receive subsidies in the form of wages and salaries that are, on average, higher than their productivity; in short they receive more than they produce. They also tend to have preferential access to products at low, controlled prices. Industrialists benefit from tariff and non-tariff trade barriers, an overvalued exchange rate which reduces their import costs, tax exonerations, subsidized credit and direct subsidies. Larger farmers reap most of the benefits from subsidized credit, subsidized irrigation water, price supports, directed technical assistance and subsidized machinery pools. Taxi and bus driver-owners receive periodic fare increases, waivers of tariffs and restrictions on importation of vehicles and highly subsidized prices for petroleum derivatives. Building contractors receive subsidized credit and benefit from the overvalued exchange rate for imports of construction materials and equipment. Union members, especially those associated with public sector employment, are subsidized by collective wage increases and other benefits prescribed by an ambitious labor code that on average exceed improvements in their productivity. Various firms borrowed abroad and were caught in the interest rate crisis in 1982 received substantial government subsidies. Their loans with foreign banks were assumed by the government and converted to Sucre balances at a highly overvalued exchange rate and long repayment periods. Finally, the affluent people who live in urban areas tend to receive most of the subsidies to utilities and petroleum derivatives. For example, one study estimated that the wealthiest 10 percent of the population, who were concentrated in Quito and Guayaquil, consumed 90 percent of all energy in Ecuador in 1987. This small segment of the population was the beneficiary of most of the relatively large subsidies to electricity and gasoline, even though such subsidies are justified and maintained on the grounds they benefit primarily the poor (Kublank and Mora).

The poor also benefit directly from many of the same subsidies as the affluent. Subsidies are very important to the poor but they receive relatively much less than the affluent of the total of each class of subsidy. The poor include mainly small farmers with limited resources and the self-employed in the urban informal sector, who together constitute roughly 40 percent of the labor force. The affluent groups which constitute the majority of society usually support the continuation of subsidies. While often nominally antagonistic to each other, they constitute an informal political coalition which maintains the status quo. This is ostensibly done to help the poor but through the coalition the affluent capture most of the subsidies. The poor are not yet a cohesive political force and tend to support the populist proposals of the affluent classes since they also derive direct, albeit relatively small, benefits from public subsidies. This tends to explain, at least in part, the anomaly of how Ecuador, with its very skewed distribution of income, has remained an island of relative calm while its neighbors have been rent by social unrest.

The development of a society dominated by special interest groups which are the principal beneficiaries of large government subsidies has been underway for decades, with a significant boost during the petroleum boom. Such recurring subsidies and the political processes that maintain them have become institutionalized elements of the fabric of Ecuadorian society. Indeed, subsidies for almost all Ecuadorians--affluent and poor--have become a traditional way of life and many have no other experience. The problem appears to be especially serious in the large public sector where there is little correlation between productivity and remuneration. The problem is also serious in agriculture where larger farmers are assured a profit via recurring increases in support prices, combined with subsidized credit and other subsidies sufficient to cover costs and guarantee a return on investment. It is unlikely farmers will want to leave this safe haven and confront the risky and uncertain world of market forces. This helps to understand why the private agricultural sector often gives only lip service to efforts to move toward a market-based economy.

The existence of large and growing public subsidies to a large segment of the population has been and remains a major constraint to economic growth and development. Subsidies introduce distortions into product and factor markets that result in misallocation of resources, less production than is possible and an inappropriate mix of products relative to consumers' preferences. In short, subsidies reduce the rate of economic growth relative to a market-determined rate.

Subsidies also are inflationary since they generate deficits which must be funded from some source. The petroleum boom provided the source for financing subsidies during the 1970s but the government was forced to turn to foreign borrowing and central bank credits (increases in the money supply) during the late-1970s and 1980s. Subsidies have contributed directly to the large fiscal deficits of the 1980s which have been and are financed through internal credits and external borrowing. Consequently, they have been an important cause of the rapid rates of inflation observed in Ecuador during the last decade. Much of the foreign debt of Ecuador can be traced directly to various subsidies captured by affluent, special interest groups. Examples include foreign loans for irrigation infrastructure, generation and transmission of electricity, assumption of private debt by the government, recapitalization of public banks and to cover recurring fiscal deficits. Moreover, the government continues to contract additional external and internal debt, even in the midst of the foreign debt crisis, to benefit special interest groups (e.g. the large multipurpose irrigation projects in the Costa).

Inflation acts as a regressive tax on the poor and especially those with fixed incomes. Thus, resources are being wrested away from the poor via an inflation tax to provide subsidies which benefit mainly the affluent and this has continued for years. While Ecuador is relatively peaceful now, the status quo can not be maintained indefinitely. One critical problem is how to break out of the unproductive and potentially socially disruptive cycle of subsidies mainly for the affluent and get onto a path of more rapid economic growth that will provide broad-based opportunities for increased employment and income. A second closely related problem is to design welfare programs that benefit the poor rather than the affluent and help to close the gap between them. The subsidies inherent in such welfare programs are necessary for more stable, rapid economic growth. Subsidies to the poor can be provided without reducing growth or engendering inflation if appropriate welfare instruments are utilized along with conservative fiscal policy, in a more rapidly growing economy.

A Caveat about High-Input Agriculture

One caveat needs to be raised about whether a science-based, high-input agriculture can be sustained. The principal recommendations of this study have focused on the need to shift from a traditional, natural resource-based to a modern, science-based agriculture as the principal foundation for more rapid economic growth and conservation of natural resources. The degree to which a high-input agriculture is sustainable needs to be carefully considered in developing and disseminating improved technologies. While a science-based agriculture can reduce pressure on natural resources and increase economic growth, important hidden costs emerge in the form of externalities associated with the use of modern, industrial inputs, which must be taken into account socially. The high social costs resulting from intensive use of chemicals, fertilizers and irrigation are cases in point. These hidden costs of high-technology agriculture take the form of pollution and environmental degradation so that the net improvement in natural resource conservation from shifting to a science-based agriculture may be less than expected.

The principal question concerns the economic and environmental sustainability of high-input systems relative to the gamut of less-intensive systems which are less productive but might be more socially and even privately profitable and sustainable because of lower costs. For the immediate future in Ecuador, it appears that a substantial increase in the use of new technical knowledge and modern, industrial inputs will result in higher social returns than more extensive systems given the relatively low levels of agricultural productivity. Moreover, it will generate substantially higher growth rates necessary to fuel more rapid economic development consistent with Ecuador's high rate of population growth. Research programs, however, should be carefully designed to address the question of sustainable agriculture. Public and private entities should clearly consider the range of technological alternatives and the negative externalities associated with modern, high-input agriculture, as they formulate investment plans and public policies for the transition to a science-based agriculture.

Ecuador without Petroleum

The Ecuadorian economy is at a major crossroads with very little time to decide which way to turn.

It will become a net petroleum importer in about 13 years unless significant new reserves are found. Recent exploration has not yielded major new discoveries and future prospects are poor. Almost 80 percent of current production is already from secondary recovery, at increasingly higher costs and the profitability of tertiary recovery is being actively analyzed. Internal demand and clandestine exports are burgeoning at the highly subsidized prices, which could shorten the life of reserves by two or three years. Thus, Ecuador will very likely have to make the transition to an economy without petroleum exports around the year 2000.

Agriculture will play an increasingly important, pivotal role in the economy as petroleum reserves are depleted. Primary agricultural production and processing will constitute about one-third of the post-2000 economy. Agriculturally related activities will permeate the rest of the economy and account for much of the production of the other economic sectors. As much as 50-60 percent of the country's GDP will be derived directly or indirectly from agriculture.

Agriculture today is based largely on exploitation of natural resources and internal capital accumulations. All good and marginal agricultural land is in production, yet demand for food and fiber is increasing rapidly, mainly from relatively high rates of population growth. Soil erosion is rampant and degradation of other natural resources is accelerating to alarming rates, especially tropical forests and coastal resources. Crop and livestock yields are among the lowest in South America. The pressure on natural resources from agriculture will grow more intense as petroleum is used up.

Four principal problems are forcing Ecuador onto this dead-end road to economic stagnation and environmental crisis. First, the science base for agriculture is seriously deficient with only extremely limited capacity to generate and incorporate improved technical knowledge. Second, and closely related to the first, the stock of human capital for agriculture at the scientific, technical and general levels of education is grossly inadequate compared to the needs of the sector. Third, the macroeconomic policy matrix continues to artificially depress the prices of agricultural products and tradeables relative to industrial and other home goods. Fourth, rapid population growth erodes the benefits of the modest economic growth that is realized.

It is especially urgent that the research system be revitalized as quickly as possible if ecologic and economic disaster are to be avoided. This strong conclusion rests on three realities: (a) the research pipeline is nearly empty after continual funding cuts and loss of most of Ecuador's senior agricultural scientists; (b) it will take at least 2-3 years at a minimum to start up the research process again after the decision to do so; and (c) the long gestation period associated with agricultural research will require another 6-8 years for an adequate, sustained flow of improved technologies to be produced. Thus, even under optimal conditions the research system can not be making it maximum contribution to growth and development until close to the year 2000 when petroleum reserves will be nearly exhausted.

If petroleum reserves are depleted before the transition to a science-based agriculture, Ecuador's natural resources will quickly become even more intensively exploited for agricultural production. Agricultural growth will be constrained to relatively low rates for a time by the inelastic supplies of natural resources and will eventually stagnate as natural resources are exhausted. The end result of failing to invest in the science base, human capital, improved macroeconomic policies and slower population growth will be environmental crisis and economic stagnation.

Act Expeditiously

The time for Ecuador to act is now, before a depressed economy and exogenous events force the country to impose the recommendations made above in the midst of economic and political crisis. All the recommendations made in this Chapter-- establishing outward-oriented macroeconomic policies, strengthening the science base for agriculture, augmenting human capital, moderating population growth, eliminating price controls and government interventions in agricultural markets, improving management of natural resources, and upgrading agricultural data and analytical capacity--can be strongly justified as part of an evolving government program to stimulate economic growth, which is the single most important challenge facing Ecuador's economy in 1990.

Several Latin American countries have adopted such policies, some with more foresight and planning and, consequently, less disruption than others. It is instructive to compare the convulsive reactions to such changes in Argentina, Bolivia, Brazil and Venezuela with those in Chile and Costa Rica. The former countries waited until crisis situations made the establishment of outward-oriented macroeconomic and related policy changes inevitable and then paid a high price in terms of major adjustments and shocks to their economies and ensuing social, economic and political chaos. Chile and Costa Rica acted with more foresight and experienced less difficulty in the transition; they now have among the highest growth rates and lowest inflation rates in Latin America. Chile's economy grew in real terms at 10 percent in 1989 with a 21 percent inflation rate; Costa Rica grew at 2.3 percent in real terms with 10 percent inflation (El Comercio).

Ecuador is not yet in a crisis situation and should carefully consider the sad lessons of it neighbors in waiting too long to make urgently needed reforms. The stagnant economy, inflation over 50 percent, low productivity in agriculture, increasing degradation of natural resources and the tendency to expansionary fiscal policy in 1990 are not bases for complacency.

Implementing the recommendations presented in this chapter will require strong leadership, a clear vision of the future and political acumen. Achievement of more rapid, equitable economic growth can only be realized through statesmanlike actions which subjugate short-term, self-serving political agendas to the more fundamental, longer-term needs of the people of Ecuador. Fortunately, a viable democratic system and enlightened leadership have already moved the economy in the direction of the recommended changes, albeit slowly.

Three principles, summarized from those recommended by the former Minister of Finance in New Zealand during 1984-1988, are suggested to guide the process of implementing the recommendations (Douglas). First, the needed reforms should be implemented as a set in a single major initiative. Attempting to reform the economy one step at a time gives special interest groups time to mount counteroffensives to block the losses of their subsidies. A big package of reforms will help assure that losses to any particular group are offset by gains, while a piecemeal approach will result in losses without gains. Second, the reforms should be implemented quickly and carried out at full speed. The recommendations will take several years to implement fully and the benefits will lag behind the costs which will endanger the viability of the reforms. Third and finally, the reforms should all be focused on giving economic power back to individuals. Governments of every persuasion have found that sick economies do not respond to regulation or ideological commands as the events in Eastern Europe and Russia during 1989 and 1990 so clearly demonstrate.

As Douglas points out, "The abolition of privilege is the essence of structural reform." The substance of the recommendations in this study is the abolition of privilege and the exaltation of individual economic choice as the basis for a more prosperous, egalitarian Ecuadorian society.

REFERENCES

Douglas, Roger. 1990. "The Politics of Successful Structural Reform." *The Wall Street Journal*. New York: January 17.

El Comercio. 1990. "Contradictorios Resultados en los Países de la Región." Quito: January 23:A-7.

Kublank, P. and D. Mora. 1987. *El Sistema Energético del Ecuador*. Quito: ILDES.

NAME INDEX

350

SUBJECT INDEX

abandoned cropland 82, 84, 96, 97
advanced technologies 4
AFL-CIO 296
Africa 36, 85, 222, 224
agrarian 2, 18, 74, 79, 101, 102, 106, 129, 154, 155, 159, 251, 257-259, 261, 271, 273, 274, 275, 276, 320, 337
agrarian reform 79, 154, 155, 159, 251, 257-259, 261, 271, 274-276, 320, 337
· agrarian reform law 274, 275
agricultural census 247, 277, 342
agricultural centers 259, 277, 278, 320
agricultural chemicals 88, 99, 152
agricultural commodities 6, 11-13, 22, 30, 35, 38, 88, 198, 203, 212, 217, 218, 220, 292, 293
agricultural commodities exchange 30, 203, 292, 293
agricultural credit 16, 102, 225, 226, 233, 240-243, 245, 289, 290, 334
agricultural development 4, 5, 7-11, 15-21, 26, 27, 33-35, 67, 68, 76, 78, 79, 83, 153, 161, 185, 187, 188, 220, 225, 252, 258, 263-265, 271, 279, 293-296, 298, 305, 311, 315, 321, 324-326, 328, 335, 336, 339, 342
agricultural economics 18, 20, 159, 220, 224, 245, 316, 342
agricultural economists 8, 101
agricultural education 156, 301
agricultural employment 114, 116, 123, 127, 153
agricultural exports 12, 20-24, 27, 34, 35, 37, 48-51, 53, 54, 56, 66, 210, 211, 233, 276, 292, 297, 331, 337
agricultural extension 18, 210, 293, 318-321
agricultural frontier 16, 78, 80-84, 87, 88, 96, 136, 275, 332
agricultural graduates 311
agricultural growth 8, 9, 12, 15, 16, 21, 22, 28, 103, 116, 117, 298, 302, 323, 328, 330, 336, 339, 340, 343, 346
agricultural imports 51-53, 69, 331
agricultural inputs 11, 31, 52, 53, 87, 96, 151, 218, 233, 275, 276, 289

agricultural investments 239, 242, 286
agricultural labor 121, 127, 248, 252, 279, 302
agricultural land 73, 80-84, 92, 97, 128, 136, 146, 155, 156, 162, 241, 301-304, 324, 332, 346
agricultural loans 22, 225, 232, 240, 242
agricultural marketing 16, 40, 193, 196, 197, 199, 220, 250, 278
agricultural organizations 255, 277
agricultural prices 6, 321
agricultural pricing policies 12, 19
agricultural productivity 3, 7-9, 68, 74, 88, 125, 188, 233, 240, 255, 263, 301-304, 316, 317, 319, 323, 324, 328, 333, 339, 345
agricultural products 3, 6, 7, 11, 13, 17, 21, 25, 30, 35, 40, 49, 51, 131, 150, 151, 186, 193, 198, 225, 227, 231-234, 273, 276, 278, 291, 292, 302, 331, 341, 342, 346
agricultural research 8, 9, 14, 18-20, 28, 88, 96, 151, 159, 166, 207, 210, 219, 259, 271, 274, 279, 291, 293, 305, 311-315, 318, 323, 325, 326, 334, 338, 346
agricultural science 10, 156, 305, 311, 316, 317, 322, 325
agricultural scientists 301, 316, 340, 346
agricultural sector 5-7, 10-12, 21, 22, 25, 34-37, 43, 48, 55, 66, 67, 71, 97, 122, 127, 131, 159, 193, 212, 214, 219, 220, 222, 225, 226, 228, 229, 231-234, 236, 239, 240, 242, 243, 248, 267, 268, 270, 271, 275, 276, 279, 281, 284, 285, 289, 291, 292, 298, 311, 324, 326, 328, 329, 336, 339, 344
agricultural sector loan 233, 289
Agricultural Sector Reorientation Project 219, 220, 222
agricultural stagnation 26
agricultural statistics 134, 147, 159, 218, 219, 277
agricultural students 310, 311
agricultural subsidies 331
agricultural surplus 2, 3, 5-7, 10, 17, 19, 301, 302

352